Dionysus, Christ, and the Death of God

STUDIES IN VIOLENCE, MIMESIS, AND CULTURE

SERIES EDITOR

William A. Johnsen

The Studies in Violence, Mimesis, and Culture Series examines issues related to the nexus of violence and religion in the genesis and maintenance of culture. It furthers the agenda of the Colloquium on Violence and Religion, an international association that draws inspiration from René Girard's mimetic hypothesis on the relationship between violence and religion, elaborated in a stunning series of books he has written over the last forty years. Readers interested in this area of research can also look to the association's journal, *Contagion: Journal of Violence, Mimesis, and Culture.*

Dionysus, Christ, and the Death of God

VOLUME 1

The Great Mediations of the Classical World

Giuseppe Fornari

Michigan State University Press · *East Lansing*

♾ The paper used in this publication meets the minimum requirements
of ANSI/NISO Z39.48-1992 (R 1997) (Permanence of Paper).

Michigan State University Press
East Lansing, Michigan 48823-5245

LIBRARY OF CONGRESS CATALOGING-IN-PUBLICATION DATA
Names: Fornari, Giuseppe, 1956– author.
Title: Dionysus, Christ, and the death of God : / Giuseppe Fornari.
Description: East Lansing : Michigan State University Press, 2020.
Series: Studies in violence, mimesis, and culture | Includes bibliographical references and index. | Contents: Volume I: The great mediations of the classical world — Volume II: Christianity and modernity.
Identifiers: LCCN 2019030311 | ISBN 978-1-61186-356-7 (v. 1 ; paperback) | ISBN 978-1-61186-357-4 (v. 2 ; paperback)
Subjects: LCSH: Sacrifice. | Christianity and other religions—Greek. | Christianity and other religions—Roman. | Christianity and other religions—Judaism. | Sacrifice—Christianity.
Classification: LCC BL570 .F67 2020 | DDC 200.94—dc23
LC record available at https://lccn.loc.gov/2019030311

Book design by Charlie Sharp, Sharp Des!gns, East Lansing, MI
Cover design by David Drummond, Salamander Design, www.salamanderhill.com.
Cover art: Detail of *Isle of the Dead* (1880), by Arnold Böcklin (1827–1901), oil on canvas, 110.9 cm × 156.4 cm, from Wikimedia Commons.

green press INITIATIVE

Michigan State University Press is a member of the Green Press Initiative and is committed to developing and encouraging ecologically responsible publishing practices. For more information about the Green Press Initiative and the use of recycled paper in book publishing, please visit *www.greenpressinitiative.org.*

Visit Michigan State University Press at *www.msupress.org*

Contents

PREFACE

The Black Sun of Europe

1. The Bloody Magic of Mediation

A literary reference may prove an effective introduction to the themes of the present work, related to ancient Greece in a comparison with Western culture passing by way of Christianity, the watershed both dividing and uniting them. What I have in mind is the salient scene in Thomas Mann's great novel *The Magic Mountain* first published in 1924 and possibly his masterpiece in some respects, certainly his most ambitious work from a historical and philosophical point of view.[1] But in the first place, if we are to interpret the novel properly and glean what is useful for introducing the themes of my work, we must understand the title. The mountain in question is magic but not by way of metaphor in a simply psychoanalytical and impressionistic sense, but in the fullest and most disturbing sense of the word. The novel recounts the powerful, overwhelming experience of "magic" that has influenced the whole of Western culture and if, on the one hand, it involves the soul of European

I want to express all my gratitude to Keith Buck, who translated much of these two volumes from Italian, and to Kenneth Quandt, whose help in editing and improving my book stylistically and conceptually has proved to be priceless.

man subjectively, on the other hand its roots penetrate deeply into a powerful, objective past that is still far from dead. The novel's flowing narrative is intended to put this in the form of an allegory, but a credible and concrete one, without purely aesthetic or psychological effects. Critics recognize the significance of the episode that I have in mind, the scene of Hans Castorp's dream, even if the reasons for it escape them. The editor of the latest Italian edition of *The Magic Mountain* defines it as "one of the most controversial passages in all of Thomas Mann's works," and also as "the vital heart" of the novel,[2] but when he tries to pin down its significance he resorts to a psychoanalytical kind of explanation that really explains nothing of the background to the event, nor seriously considers the historical symbolism woven into the scene. Certainly, Sigmund Freud's ideas are relevant but for reasons that are not exactly psychoanalytical. If this were not the case, the story would lack the power to take us straight to the heart of the themes of this inquiry.

Hans Castorp is staying in a Swiss sanatorium, symbolizing Europe on the eve of the First World War. He loses his way in a blizzard while skiing and takes shelter behind a mountain hut but, dazed by the wind and cold, falls unconscious. He has a vision, or rather a rapid series of visions, fitting into each other in a carefully calculated crescendo. At their very core is ancient Greece, with the associations that Greek civilization could evoke when the novel was written, but what leads up to this point cannot be reduced to any known scheme, except superficially and misleadingly. Mann is never a writer to be deciphered instantly; he wants the reader to accompany Hans Castorp, passing through the various interpretative layers that come between ourselves and the vision of Hellas. As a symbolic and narrative device, the dream is indebted to Freud and psychoanalysis, but the historical references are not allowed to be submerged into the indistinctiveness of the psyche. On the contrary, the dream shows how the psyche itself is created by history and history's hermeneutic and cultural stratification, of which an obscure but traceable nucleus does exist. Freud in *Totem and Taboo* was the first to attempt to identify this obscure originary point, following in the footsteps of Friedrich Nietzsche, another writer with whom Mann was quite familiar.[3] In this way the dream formula is strangely helpful in gradually defining common ground for hero, author, and readers.

Initially, in his dream, Castorp has a vision of a green parkland, a memory of "his birthplace" in north Germany that he has not seen for years, banished in self-exile to the magic, ambiguous world of the sanatorium. The familiar landscape forms a "magic whole" reminding him of the performance of "a world-famous Italian tenor, whose throat poured forth a glorious stream to touch human hearts with its powerful, god-given art" (Mann here indulges in recollecting a performance by Enrico Caruso).

The mounting splendor of this singing is finally overwhelming; the scene changes, transfigured into an enchanting sunlit Mediterranean landscape, full of woods, bays, and islands, and populated by figures that seemed to him like "children of the sun and sea": youths playing with horses and practicing with bow and arrow, girls making music and dancing, lovers walking affectionately along the shore.

> "How truly delightful!—Hans Castorp thought with sheer rapture—They convey a sense of joy that bowls me over! How handsome and healthy and intelligent and happy they are! Yes, they are not only well-made physically . . . they are thoroughly intelligent and lovable as well. That is what excites and captivates me: the spirit and wisdom, I might almost say, that presides over their nature and makes them live and stay together like this!" By that he meant the affability and polite consideration, equally distributed among all of them, apparent in their dealings with one another, and the easy deference, hiding behind a smile, they showed each other, that was almost imperceptible and yet constant and quite evident thanks to the profound understanding and idea that united them and was incarnated [*eingefleischten*] in them; also the dignity and, indeed, austerity, resolved however in cheerfulness, that governed all they did or did not do, acting as an ineffable spiritual influence, serious in character but alien to sullenness of any kind and devout in a sensible way . . . though not entirely unceremonial [*ohne alles Zeremoniell*].[4]

Here there is a double symbolic shift, from Germany to Italy and from Italy to the classical world. At the heart of the romantic German landscape, as its historical and spiritual necessity, a growing need develops to complete itself with the radiant harmony of the south, which in the German tradition has Italian connotations. These are first recalled by the sublime singing of Enrico Caruso and then develop spontaneously through what Italy signifies and through its very geography: the long peninsula leading down to the civilization of Rome and finally to the Greek world, as Johann Wolfgang Goethe, Mann's supreme point of reference, recorded in his *Italienische Reise*. And so the romantic natural world of the north, pervaded by the irresistible call of the Mediterranean, gives way to a vision of the classical world as reinterpreted by German classicism and more recently by the late romantic culture closer to Mann himself. This sophisticated procedure allows Mann to depict and reexamine the image of the classical and Hellenic world created by German culture and by European culture as a whole: over the centuries, the idealization of ancient Greece had embodied all that European intellectuals could imagine by way of the indeterminately desirable, a real paradise lost regarded with nostalgia by generations of artists, thinkers, and writers. However, Castorp's reverie has still to undergo its last and most dramatic shift. Mann would like to go on believing in Goethe's dream of Hellas but now knows that behind the harmony something else lies concealed (and, besides, he knows full well that even with Goethe things are none too reassuring in Hellas). The catastrophe of the First World War left Mann bitterly disillusioned, and his Hellas, derived from the neoclassical and romantic traditions with touches of the *Jugendstil*, betrays the tormented awareness irresistibly drawing him, and his readers along with him, toward another, different Greece, Nietzsche's archaic Dionysian Greece. This had already occupied a central place in *Death in Venice*, published in 1912, where Aschenbach's Dionysian nightmare is the prelude to his imminent death and prefigures what was soon to happen in Europe.[5] As in the novella, the oneiric reevocation in *The Magic Mountain* is much more than just a classicistic reassessment of vexatious modern matters having their origin in libidinous impulses or political disasters; the dream has something "magical" about it, in a collective, archaeological sense, that can explain the impulses and the disasters and intimates a remedy that is to be feared as much as desired. In the behavior of the "children of the sun," Castorp observes "the easy deference, hiding behind a smile" and a sensible devoutness, even if "not entirely unceremonial." He notes their "profound understanding" of each other and the "idea that united them and was incarnated in them," but the prevailing tenor, the foundation, underlying this incarnate (*eingefleischten*) union appears ambivalent to him. An invisible rift runs through it leaving these inhabitants of the south not entirely carefree and spontaneous. This passage is so extremely delicate that it requires more detailed comment. My use of the image of the "foundation" (the German *Grund*, which we meet later with the meaning of "motive") is justified but not sufficient in itself since it evokes in terms of space a factor all human beings depend on, a factor lying under the reality that derives from it. But there is also the question of explaining the phenomena resulting from the foundation and what it is about them that renders their "foundation" secretly visible, a question we must answer in order to gain access to what it is that has been founded. Indeed, what exactly are we to understand by "foundation"? Adopting the spontaneously phenomenological method of Mann's text, I want now to anticipate a key theoretical question discussed in the introduction, a question that my inquiry will set out to articulate properly so as to rectify and remove past and future misunderstandings.

The spatial, architectural metaphor of the foundation is fundamentally correct provided it is not absolutized but confined to its effective scope, which is to make possible and support the entire arch of a culture, of a whole world that finds its real strength and substance in the visible. The nature of Hans Castorp's dream, appearing as an apparition, confirms this. The second architectural image of the arch suggests the real nature and function of the foundation; to found, certainly, but so as to develop and unite, connecting terms that would otherwise remain unrelated, unable to form a whole, powerless to interact and build thereby the very structure of a culture. This necessity and this function correspond to what I mean by *mediation*, that is to say, the intangible connective element acting as a *medium* capable of linking men to the world, and to the divine sphere that made the world possible in ancient times. As a consequence, this world-facilitating medium is able to unite human beings and make them exist, in fact, at the very moment that they unite. Mann's text brings out this problem in all its incalculable necessity and urgency, since nothing is more vital and fragile than the mediations from which men derive. In the nature of things, these mediations must originally have been religious in character, since human beings cannot mediate themselves and be born spontaneously by themselves.

All that we know of mankind's cultural history suggests this, with further support from an internal, genetically phenomenological analysis of the way in which human cultures take shape and develop. If mediation is in fact what functions as medium, as an intermediate means or "go-between," it is also, and above all, the supreme point of reference, for which I use the term "mediatory," what offers men a common direction precisely because it is above them, transcends them.[6] Such a powerful, productive arrangement, with nothing like it in the animal kingdom, could not have been produced by simple accidental changes, nor by a mere accumulation of circumstances. Instead, a crystallization must have occurred; a new collective experience, a dynamic force created by some event, or rather some series of events, must have finally condensed into a new significant organizing state, into the very beginnings of man and culture. What we are investigating takes us toward the origins not just of the European crisis that Thomas Mann writes about but still more toward the origins of human culture itself. That the two are closely linked is proved by the fact that the philosophical tradition to which I will be referring—a line of thought running from Nietzsche to Freud, Émile Durkheim, Georges Bataille, and René Girard—takes shape and develops in close relationship to the European crisis. Indeed, it is the most valuable legacy of that crisis, substantial, irreplaceable, and offered to all other cultures by European culture at its best. In Castorp's vision, Mann is drawing our attention to the central place of mediation in the lives of the "children of the sun" and the terrible difficulty of making it work; the cost exacted is high, but it is known and at the same time concealed. It is this concealment that justifies the foundation metaphor, this dovetailing together of the immense organization of the world with the transcendent mediation that re-presents it—that is, makes its cause apparent. This crucial displacement and articulation implies a price to be paid proportionate to its value, as Castorp is not slow to grasp.

In his dream vision Castorp reaches a degree of sympathy bordering on complicity with what he sees; he comments on a mother suckling her child, a smiling stately figure that "passersby greeted in a particular way that summed up everything about which the general behavior of those men and women was so eloquently silent." In his overexcited enthusiasm, Castorp begins to wonder "anxiously if it was right for him to look, if as an intruder . . . he might not be guilty of a real crime by being there and spying on such radiant, highly civilized happiness."[7] This association of superior, ideal happiness and accusations against an intruder just for "being there and spying" is most eloquent and corresponds to a theme found in mythologies throughout the world: the intruder who spies and so must be punished, as we shall see in Euripides's *Bacchae*. There is something far from idyllic underlying this scene, and it now emerges. The enthusiastic and anxious visitor notices a "handsome boy" below him; their eyes meet and then he gazes at a point beyond Castorp, and takes on "a serious expression, frozen, inexpressive and unfathomable, a deadly impenetrable look." Filled with deep foreboding, Castorp turns to look in the same direction; he sees the columns of an ancient sacred edifice and realizes that he is standing on its steps. As if answering a call, he turns and heads toward the inside and finds himself facing another row of pillars.

> Passing through these, he now came to a massive temple, greenish-grey through the ravages of time, with a steep flight of steps at its base and a broad pediment resting on the capitals of sturdy almost squat columns tapering toward the top, with grooved round blocks jutting out sideways here and there. Using his hands to help him and sighing deeply because of his increasing sense of oppression, Hans Castorp clambered up the high steps and reached the forest of columns of the atrium. It was vast and dense; he walked around inside as among the trunks of the beech trees by the shore of the pale sea, deliberately avoiding the central part [*die Mitte*], and trying to move further away from it. But his wanderings kept bringing him back until he again found himself where the columns divided, in front of a marble sculpture of two female figures on a plinth, apparently a mother and daughter: the elder, more venerable woman had an expression of gentle divinity, but her eyelids were lowered sorrowfully over empty, pupil-less eyes. She was seated, clad in a tunic with many pleats and a robe, with a veil covering the wavy hair of her matronly head. The younger woman, standing beside her and held close in a maternal embrace, had a round, virginal face, her arms and hands swathed and hidden in the folds of the robe.
>
> For obscure reasons [*aus dunklen Gründen*], as he contemplated these statues his heart felt heavier still, weighed down by a sense of anxiety and foreboding. He hardly dared to go around the two figures and pass through the double row of columns behind them, and yet felt compelled to do so. The metal door to the inner temple then came into sight; it stood open before him, and the petrifying sight that met his eyes caused his knees to buckle beneath him. Inside there, between flaming braziers, two half-naked women, grey and disheveled, with pendulous hags' breasts and dugs as long as a finger, were intent on a heinous task. They were tearing apart

> the body of a small child over a basin, tearing it apart with their hands in savage silence—Hans Castorp could make out fine tufts of fair hair smeared with blood—and they devoured the pieces, the delicate bones cracking between their teeth while the blood dripped from their revolting lips. Hans Castorp froze in horror. He wanted to cover his eyes with his hands and could not. He wanted to run away and could not. But in the meantime the women, occupied with their loathsome business, had seen him and shook their bloody fists, directing insults at him, unvoiced but with extremely vulgar, obscene epithets, and in the very dialect of the town where he was born [*Heimat*].[8]

Thanks to this final, brilliant touch the circle closes, because the two hags intent on ritually ripping apart and devouring the baby reveal the mediatory foundation hidden not only from the Greece of Dionysus as reinterpreted by Nietzsche but also from German and European culture until Mann penetrated its many layers to arrive at this terrible bloody center. We can now understand the extremely serious underlying meaning of the joyful harmony that sent Hans Castorp into ecstasies, as well as the ritual background that allowed the mother to suckle her child so tenderly, a touching sight that nonetheless made Castorp feel like a sacrilegious intruder, with a sense of guilt to expiate. The fact is that someone has to die for these idyllic scenes to continue. The mirror-like correspondence between the baby at its mother's breast and the baby savagely torn to pieces and eaten highlights the logic of substitution underpinning a complete system of rules and exchanges. The "profound understanding" and "idea" uniting the children of the sun and incarnate in them, becoming "flesh of their flesh" (*eingefleischten*), as it might be rendered in a different translation, is quite literally the raw flesh of a human being devoured in the inner sanctum of the temple, that is to say, in the innermost, most sacred part of the community. This victim is the displaced articulation that enables collective mediation to crystallize, he is the dark spot that allows the sun of all the others to shine, and in the final analysis he is the sun itself, hidden and at the same time secretly indicated as to its real nature by the brightness of the ritual flames that it feeds. There is nothing natural about the harmony of the children of the sun; on the contrary, it is the final result of a long collective effort, whose secret ferocity is an answer to a pressing need, the need to avoid an evident, very grave danger.

To understand what that danger is, it is enough to make the harmonious equestrian contests and archery training only slightly more intense, and the idyllic scene is at once transformed into a competitive situation, liable to degenerate into extreme violence. Rivalry and violent conflict can spring from simply wanting or doing the same things, whether in play or earnest: we see it happening again and again, in ancient Greece, just as in Greek tragic theater, and it also happens here in *The Magic Mountain*, where the elegant discussions about philosophy, education, and worldly matters become tough ideological combat, deadly dueling, leading up to the apocalyptic climax of the First World War.

We need therefore to understand the forces and critical thresholds that give rise to cultural mediations, and it is here that René Girard's mimetic theory proves indispensable in helping us to grasp aspects that might otherwise pass unnoticed beneath the novel's intellectual paraphernalia and Wagnerian proportions, though Mann shows himself to be fully aware of the dynamics and dangers. These aspects consist in the role of imitation or mimesis in human life. As Girard sees it, mimesis brings the human beings to converge on the same goals and objects, but this very easily turns to strife, to fierce conflict, quick to spread within a group through similar, intensified imitation of the violence. Though this role is evident, it is problematic, as will be made clear later in this preface and in the theoretical discussion in the introduction. For the moment we should note that Mann's imaginative creation contains something over and above Girard's theory, according to which reciprocal imitation in human relations is destined to become closer and closer until it degenerates into rivalry and violence, and finally becomes the persecution on a collective scale of some scapegoat who has to be killed, sacrificed, and so discharges the violence of the many on the single victim. If it is true to say that Girard develops Freud's ideas as set out in *Totem and Taboo* and reworked in *The Magic Mountain*, it is even truer that we would be wrong to consider Mann's scene reductively as a mere illustration, whether illuminating or imperfect, of a preestablished theoretical scheme. Over against Girard's theoretical objectivism, which will come in for careful analysis in the course of the present study, can be set a more psychological, subjective type of interpretation such as we find given by the editor of the Italian edition of *Der Zauberberg* where Castorp's dream is seen to represent a psychoanalytical exploration of the character's sexuality and body. These two symmetrical, conflicting readings differ greatly in the degree of their theoretical commitment and explanatory power, and yet both, in their different and complementary ways, prevent us from entering the real dimension of the ideas expressed in this remarkable novel. We will start by taking a critical look at the second type of interpretation, where the erudition only carries us still further from the truly fruitful direction.

The profound reflection to be found in *The Magic Mountain* is not concerned with the specious workings of collective or individual psyches, or with some indeterminate sexual unconscious of no real interest to us, but with the mediations from which German and European culture derive. Thomas Mann, following Nietzsche's lead, traces the earliest source of these mediations to Greece but, through Greece, what comes horrifically to light is the originary source of the mediations of all human cultures. There is motive enough for this conclusion in the power that it brings out throughout the narrative; to deny the cognitive commitment that I attribute to the novel would be to impoverish it disastrously. It is not hard to realize that only daring exploration and representation of that kind could match the huge scale of the historical tragedy; and Mann had, in fact, already begun to have his forebodings before the actual outbreak of war. There is nothing psychologistic about his investigations, and we should not be misled by the dream form of the narrative, since it is this symbolic mode that not only makes it possible to represent a revelation that cannot come by the same route as our waking rationalizations but also highlights the aspect of community showing how we are all equally complicit and involved. Castorp himself says as much when he wakes up and tries to make sense of the disturbing vision that has just come to an end:

> "It seemed just a dream to me" he murmured deliriously to himself. "A fascinating dream all the time and I made everything up myself. . . . The leafy parkland, the pleasant humidity and the rest, the lovely things and the horrible things as well, almost as if I knew it all beforehand. But how can you know things of that kind and imagine them for yourself, how can you make yourself happy and distressed in this way? And where does the beautiful bay with the islands come from? Or the temple complex indicated by the glance of that attractive lad who was there on his own account? I could almost say that we do not dream with our own spirits, we dream in an

> anonymous and collective way, though in our own particular fashion. Perhaps the great spirit of which you are only a tiny part dreams through you, in your particular way, dreaming of things it has always secretly dreamed of . . . its youth, its hopes, its happiness, peace . . . and its banquet of blood. I am lying here next to my column and I still have the real vestiges of my dream in my body, the freezing horror of the banquet of blood and the deep joy before, joy at the happiness and the devout morality of those pure human beings."[9]

These words need to be weighed most carefully, regarding both content and implications, or we will misrepresent the text and the author's intentions and, more seriously, underplay the dramatic importance and urgency of the themes that we are being asked to consider, themes that go far beyond any authorial or textual gloss. The dream's anonymous, collective dimension does not refer to a Jungian-type collective unconscious since Mann is not dealing with atemporal archetypes but with very real events, both in the remote past and in the imminent future awaiting Hans Castorp and Germany together with Europe. Little time is to elapse before this revelation becomes worldwide, "globalized" as we say today, unthinkingly. The anonymous collective aspect simply means that all human beings derive from what is revealed in Castorp's dream, in a similar way to what had already emerged in Nietzsche's text about the death of God where he declares that all mankind shares in that ancestral collective murder. In highly tormented vivid colors Nietzsche imagines the condition of a "super-mankind" burdened by its knowledge of having murdered God, who sends the Earth spinning out of orbit to wander through the cosmic darkness. Castorp, on the other hand, tries to move in the opposite direction, acknowledging his deep-down derivation from the bloody dream, the reality relived in his vision, and unwilling to detach himself from the life that it made, and makes, possible. And with that we come back to the other extreme represented by Girard's more anthropological position that, if applied as an interpretive key, oversimplifies the scene in a way that is as enlightening as it is partial. Though Mann's explorations bear out Girard to a certain extent, the substance of what he has to say cannot be neatly pigeonholed, since it is not deduced from a theory but is the living experience of something alive, of a reality possessing life and desiring it with all its might. If we are to recover this essential dimension, we must recover an entire cultural landscape, of which Girard's theory is a simplified offshoot, valuable in enabling us to recognize a huge problem so far largely ignored but damaging if transformed into a definitive theoretical formulation that blinds us to the process that produced it and through which its further development should be pursued. Mann's position is dramatic and meaningful in a different way: here we have a great writer taking the traumatic events of the Great War as the starting point for reflection on Nietzsche's announcement of the murder of God, in the light of Freud's further developments in *Totem and Taboo*. Mann oscillates between the vital need to kill and transfigure God positively and, following the revelation of that event and process, the destruction that might ensue in the devastated modern world. I shall come back later to Mann's complex and contradictory movement; it is extremely problematic and at the same time determined as necessary, since the alternative is the destruction predicted by Nietzsche, clearly symbolized by the cosmic dislocation of the Earth.

There are in fact references to Freud, and though blinkered in Mann's version, they are such as to go far beyond their psychologistic surface and draw on the fourth essay in *Totem and Taboo* where Freud is at his most daring and forward-looking, formulating the major discovery in anthropological thinking, and not only anthropological, made in the twentieth century. This was the discovery that human culture originated in an event of savage violence: the killing of the primordial Father at the hands of his sons, united against him, who then immediately dismembered and devoured him. This discovery also gave the original impulse to Girard's theory. Mann's use of the hypothesis extends beyond anything that Freud, for a start, could have imagined. Guided by his insight and making free use of representation, Mann seizes its full potential. He avoids lapsing into psychologism, for the good reason that all psychology springs from this originary event, and he also avoids the dangers of overly abstract theorizing. Unconditioned by Freud's scientific and systematic concerns, Mann starts from Nietzsche's reflections on the Greece of Dionysus and tragic drama, which were the background to Freud's investigations as well. He sets them out again in historical terms, not in an archaeological sense but as a real living datum to which we can relate. And that is the second reason why we should see Mann's intention and the resulting text as a lucid, conscious investigation of the bloody origins of European culture and of all human cultures.

The sacrifice evoked by Mann and the context in which he sets it are definitely not the fruit of his imagination or the result of some sort of literary cut-and-paste. Castorp's vision reproduces the symbolic ritual structure of the Eleusinian Mysteries, very freely as regards details but with surprising scientific accuracy as to their significance. In the course of this study we will be examining the Mysteries and will substantially confirm Mann's penetrating insight.[10] The temple complex described in the novel corresponds to the plan of the *Telesterion*, the large religious edifice at Eleusis, characterized by a veritable forest of columns and by housing the small archaic shrine of the *Anaktoron*. As my reconstruction will show, it was there, inside the *Anaktoron*, that the Orphic account of Dionysus was reevoked and reenacted presumably through animal sacrifice, with Dionysus devoured by the Titans and restored to life by Zeus. The marble statuary is even more clearly recognizable; from all that we know about the rites and myths associated with Eleusis, the two women can be safely identified as Demeter and Persephone. Without anticipating the subject of the second chapter at this point, I must just point out the remarkable extent to which Mann's investigations and my own agree. The sacrifice described in *The Magic Mountain* is the Dionysian rite par excellence, the *omophagia* (from Greek ὠμός, raw), the devouring of a raw victim, that is, to be precise, a living victim. This was the climax at the heart of the *sparagmos*, the dismembering, which meant the dismembering of a human victim in the most archaic versions of the rite. In our case, the victim is Dionysus who was torn to pieces by the Titans while still a child. In Mann's text their place is taken by the two hags, who are female like the bacchantes and look like the Erinyes as described by Aeschylus. The violence is thus concentrated, sparing the children of the sun from direct contamination and allowing the mothers to suckle their babies or, to be more precise, the surviving babies. What he took from Nietzsche, assisted by Freud's hypothesis in *Totem and Taboo*, enabled Mann to understand something that Girard was to express more explicitly decades later, that is, that what counts in the founding process of cultural mediations is not the father figure as such, nor a son who takes his place, but the victim, any victim that will serve the purpose. In Mann's scene this victim is a newborn babe, in line with the myth of Dionysus, but it is quite evident that it could be anyone at all—Castorp himself for example, if he were accused of intruding, of *mala curiositas*.

There is, then, a single inquiry running from Nietzsche through Freud to Mann and beyond. Although means and end results vary greatly, this continuing inquiry provides us with the most profound and powerful subtext for grasping the meaning and importance of the extraordinary scene developed in *The Magic Mountain*. The same hermeneutic line led to Girard's illuminating simplifications and, through them, to the present book about ancient Greece and Christianity. The present inquiry is too vast and ambitious to be easily understood or welcomed, obliged as it is to draw on more specialized studies that it must, in the nature of things, both go beyond and infringe upon; and it is not likely to be looked on kindly by the specialists who lend it their involuntary services. Which explains why a comparable undertaking by a great writer almost a century ago, though successful, has never received due recognition from the many scholars who have studied the works of Thomas Mann, while it is practically banned by disciplines that ought to be giving it extreme attention (which means attention to things extreme)—history and philology for a start and especially the metadiscipline of philosophy. More than from any other discipline, a response should come from philosophy, and sooner or later must come if philosophy is to save itself from inanity and extinction.

We will return now to the consequences of Mann's inquiry, as expressed through Castorp's thoughts and in the concluding pages of *The Magic Mountain*. These turn out to be vitally important for our correct understanding of European and world history in the nineteenth century, which may sound paradoxical since we are dealing with a work of literature. However, beyond any distinction to be made between literary and scientific genres, every distinction between culture and the real world falls away where culture is instrumental, as it should be and as it is in its finest achievements, in gaining real knowledge about man and the world. Castorp's final choice is not to shun what the vision of the children of the sun has shown him, in the sense that "homo sum, humani nihil a me alienum puto" (I am a man and deem nothing human to be foreign to me), to quote Terence in the spirit of Castorp's motto *placet experiri* (It is pleasant to experiment). Here, Mann's awareness of the Dionysian *omophagia* keeps his argument safe from the temptations of humanism, to which he was always nostalgically prone, understandably in view of the inhumanity that doomed him to disappointment. However, the point is that only inhumanity could lead to humanity. And that experience is not buried in time; it is a structure arising again and again, and ever more visibly in fact. Here Mann has to deal with a very dense historical and conceptual crux, in an attempt to establish the point of resolution between the savage development of life and its destruction.

Meanwhile, Castorp's words show Mann to be fully aware of the value of the omophagic ritual as mediation for the entire community of the children of the sun. When Castorp awakes, he feels as if he is still lying beside the temple column and senses at once the necessary link between "the freezing horror of the banquet of blood" and his "joy at the happiness and the devout morality of those pure human beings." Indeed, he affirms his right to be there next to the column "and dream such things," and goes so far as to declare somewhat solemnly: "I know all about mankind. I have known its flesh and blood" (Ich weiß alles vom Menschen. Ich habe sein Fleische und Blut erkannt).[11] This statement is the first in an impressive series that provides a further commentary on the dream scene, and the attempt to ascribe it to the character's sentimental and sexual history can only impoverish it disastrously since what is at issue here is the very definition of "life's unruly son [*Sorgenkind*], man."[12] The references made to other characters in the novel—to Madame Chauchat, the Russian with whom Castorp has a love affair, and the rivals, Naphta and Settembrini, who compete to be his mentor—show that something very different is at stake; in comparison, individual characters shrink to the status of occasions and symbols serving to express, though inadequately and partially, the experience of a truth that takes possession of Castorp and appears to us as universal.

The significance of the "banquet of blood" as the mediatory event that allows the entire community of the creatures of the sun to exist is conveyed with consummate rhetorical skill. It is left up to the reader to draw the final inference, in the knowledge that it is by no means automatic:

> Now, at the foot of my column, the view I take is not so bad. . . . My dream represented the human condition, mankind's affable, sensible, respectful community behind which, in the temple, the horrific banquets take place. Maybe those cheerful creatures were so polite and charming to each other precisely because they had that horror secretly in prospect? The conclusion they would draw from it would be really refined and loving![13]

The column that Castorp is reluctant to leave (a few lines further on he makes the point again: "This is what I see from my column") represents the realistic view of sacrifice, deriving from Nietzsche and Freud. Castorp is no longer prepared to forego this view since it provides him with the only correct perspective on experience, his own and that of mankind as a whole, not just Greece, Germany, and Europe. However, those remain the main points of reference in the gigantic parable of *The Magic Mountain*, to whose complications and coimplications we must shortly return. The last sentence in the above quotation ("The conclusion . . . refined and loving") sounds doubly ironic, on one level because it appears simply ironic and, on a second level, because it is not, since, in the new, clear perception of character and author, the "conclusion" drawn by the children of the sun is, in effect, "refined and loving." The immediate consequence following this is Castorp's firm, resolutive decision: "In the depths of my soul I desire to be on their side." Choosing to side with the radiant creatures is all one with Castorp's opting for life as opposed to death that, in the novel, signals his waking to awareness. The life for which he opts is something more than *amor vitae*: it is the sudden irruption of love as the single real substance of life.

> Love opposes death, love alone, not reason, is stronger than death. Love alone, not reason, prompts good thoughts. Form, too, is only made of love and goodness: form and morality of a community that is affably judicious and in fine condition among men . . . with the unspoken prospect of the banquet of blood. . . . *In the name of goodness and love, man must not allow death to dominate his thoughts*. And with that I wake up . . . Because that completes my dream and I have reached the objective.[14]

Waking from the dream does not mean coming back to reality as opposed to the oneiric sphere; on the contrary, it means realizing in life what Castorp had understood in the liminal, revelatory experience of the dream vision that had given voice to the fully accepted beauty of life and its foundational horror, normally destined to remain unspoken and passed over in silence. However, that is no longer possible at the historical and cognitive height now reached by Mann, who still has at the back of his mind the mountain walks during which Nietzsche had his revelation of Zarathustra. Though the comparison is highly pertinent, it nonetheless displays all its ambiguity when we remember that Nietzsche's vision of Zarathustra was a real doubles experience, clearly very much like the hallucinatory experiences of doubling that afflicted him from adolescence onward and plunged his mind into delirium between 1888 and 1889, at the time of his final crisis in Turin.[15] Mann wants to reach a stable new settlement, but stable in a very different way: a Goethe-like serenity interwoven beneath the surface with a profound experience of the opposites. However, under the dramatic pressure of what had happened between 1914 and 1918, his narrative inspiration carried him further, thrusting his hero toward the final abyss of the Great War, the shattering of old Europe's humanistic dreams, spreading the banquet of blood worldwide. Nietzsche and Mann's Faust no longer finds a Gretchen to save him, nor can he expect to see the miraculous vision at the end of Goethe's *Faust, Part Two* that unfolds the mystery of the Virgin, of the love that sacrifices everything so that the mystery of redemption may take place.[16] In the sinister recesses of European history during the first half of the twentieth century, Mann is far indeed from those perspectives, but he remains nostalgic for them, with an ethical quality not to be found in Nietzsche. To throw more light on this complicated situation, we can find help in the further layers of interpretation that have accreted around the question that Mann lived and set before us. These bring us back to Girard's perspective, in itself conflicting with Mann's vision, and to a further perspective worked out by myself in conversation with Girard by which I sought to vindicate Mann while overcoming his ambiguities.

2. *Kultur* and *Zivilisation*: An Unresolved Dilemma

Girard makes the victim the decisive criterion for evaluating and judging history, human history as a whole as well as European history, basing his claim for the truth of the victim on a source outside history, namely biblical revelation, the "foundation" of the Jewish and Christian religions. According to Girard, this revelation hinges essentially on an awareness of the victim, the scapegoat essential to the existence of human communities, finally fully revealed and demystified by Christ's crucifixion.[17] In this perspective the whole of European history appears as marked by the acceptance or refusal of this awareness, while the ideologies that have caused so much bloodshed throughout history are characterized by their attempt to return to the ancient forms of scapegoat persecution and sacrifice definitively exposed to be false by the Christian revelation. For Girard, too, Nietzsche plays an exceptional role in this affair: although he was too perceptive, and too humiliated in his personal life, not to see the scapegoat, Nietzsche's deliberate reaction was to insanely extol violence and sacrifice, epitomized in his eyes by the pagan figure of Dionysus. At the same time, he inveighed furiously against Christianity since it reminded him of the total refusal to persecute scapegoats personified and symbolized in the crucifixion of Christ. And this brings us to the theme that was the starting point for my own research, Nietzsche's opposition of Dionysus to Christ, outlined in a fragment written in the spring of 1888 and considered by Girard to be the major discovery of nineteenth-century religious philosophy.[18]

With reference to the Dionysian cycle that inspired Euripides's *Bacchae*, Girard underlines the fact that Dionysus is, first of all, the savage god who incites an entire group to victimize in the most primitive way, that is, by mob lynching and dismemberment. For Girard, Dionysus is himself the victim, first murdered and then divinized, the sacralized projection of collective violence that ends up confirming the rightness of what the group has done. Girard highlights how Nietzsche's fragment contrasts Christ's message and testimony to the savage cult: Christ suffers the same fate as all victims of the Dionysian type, but in his case the victim is shown to be innocent and his death condemns the violence of his executioners. Nietzsche's great discovery, in Girard's view, consists in having detected that the opposition between Dionysus and Christ is radical and profound precisely where their histories are similar, in fact identical: what changes is the interpretation, the viewpoint adopted. For Girard, this means that what was previously an inextricable muddle as to the roles of executioner and victim, is, for the first time, made perfectly clear and resolved through Christ's Passion, since Christ appears to be and declares himself to be what he really is: the innocent victim of mob fury unjustly turned against him. In this way, Christ's message serves to prevent us, not from committing acts of violence entirely of our own making, but from transforming the violence into unanimous sacrifices that can transfigure victims into no less violent divinities. To underline Nietzsche's originality here, Girard refers to his use of contemporary ethnographic research, which was uncovering myths and sacrificial rites analogous to Christ's Passion in many parts of the world. Nietzsche used this material but rejected out of hand the ethnologists' superficial deduction that placed Christianity on a par with primitive religions. However, despite his brilliant inspiration Nietzsche fails to follow it out but instead sticks to the ideal of pagan restoration Girard attributes to him for choosing to confuse once again the difference that he had perceived by making it the single exception, as unique as it is pathological, to the healthy necessary rule of Dionysian sacrifice.

My original interpretation of the scene in *The Magic Mountain* was influenced by this illuminating contrast brought out by Girard. However, the light thrown on the subject comes at a price, an excessive reduction and a conflictual tone hardly compatible with understanding the historical and textual data taken as a whole. If we are to avoid making the data say what they do not say, and to allow them to say what they do in fact say, then we need an approach more attentive to the phenomena. The circumstance that Nietzsche's speculations about ancient Greece are central to his philosophy, and also reverberate throughout the scene in *The Magic Mountain*, allowed me to neatly combine two questions: the question of the difference between Dionysus and Christ, and the question of the difference between ancient Greece, which exemplifies the sacrificial and pagan past closest to us in cultural terms, and our own cultural identity which has been deeply influenced by Christianity and the Bible. Nietzsche's razor-sharp interpretive option made possible this cross-comparison, but at the same time, its very complexity made increasingly clear to me that the option could not be simply categorized as nostalgia for sacrifice according to Girard.

The reason for this simplification on Girard's part deserves some further comment in order to make clear the implications and complications of the comparison with Greece prompted by the scene in *The Magic Mountain* that also gave the initial impulse to my own research. In Girard's view, once the decisive difference of Christ versus Dionysus is introduced, there is no reason to pay any further attention to Dionysus—that is, to classical culture as a whole but especially to Greek culture, which Dionysus epitomizes in terms of sacrifice. Consequently, Girard openly attacks the prestigious, privileged position enjoyed by Greek civilization for hundreds and hundreds of years, as being now finally unmasked dependent on the bloodiest of sacrifices. For Girard, all that counts is the truth of Christ crucified; as a cognitive and moral weapon this is all that is needed to settle every question and understand what is really important. In his none too indulgent view, enthusiasm for Greece is only an ill-disguised enthusiasm for the successful persecution of transfigured and concealed victims, which necessarily turns to hatred of the Gospel truth since it instead reveals "with what tears and with what blood" Hellas, apparently so bright and beautiful, is stained.[19] Girard's reply to Nietzsche thus follows the line of the de-Hellenization polemic, originally Protestant, which consists in rejecting any conceptual interpolation of a Greek origin in the correct perception of the biblical and Christian message. Instead, this perception should be based entirely on faith in God, and not on abstract dualisms and metaphysical conceptualizing derived from Plato and Aristotle. However, the analogy is appropriate only up to a certain point. While de-Hellenization originates in a historically stratified and complex problem of interpretation, and attempts to clarify it according to its own criteria, Girard's thinking takes practically the opposite direction: starting out from what is clear, definitive, and in itself strictly rational, it brushes aside everything that fails to fit in, in the belief that any authentic experience of religious faith can only coincide ultimately with the truth of the victim. In rejecting, or tending to reject, all hermeneutical intermediation and retroaction, Girard's thinking approaches Nietzsche's to no small degree: the fervent champions of Dionysus and Christ are more alike than they might care to admit. Having said this, though, we should also recognize that Nietzsche's ideas and writings spare no opportunity to prove his opponent right, attacking Christianity headlong with, here and there, a prediction of the most frightful human sacrifices. Richard Wagner, who was also a significant figure for Thomas Mann, plays a distinctive, strategic role in this dispute, no less important for having largely gone unnoticed. Nietzsche idolized and hated Wagner but was certainly deeply indebted to him for identifying Dionysian Greece as the historical, symbolic model for a colossal re-founding of the entire European world, in which the old religions would be replaced by a sacrificial musical theater, envisioned in a more polemical and destructive means by Nietzsche and a more spiritual and conciliatory way by Wagner. In his maturity Nietzsche became more and more anti-Wagnerian and countered the Christian influence in Wagner with the authentic Dionysian spirit, while for his part the anti-Nietzschean Girard opposes the Christian Wagner to the Dionysian Greece of the philosopher of the will to power.

There is no need to go further into these historical and conceptual intricacies now, since they will adequately be treated by my inquiry as a whole. However, there is one point about Nietzsche's relationship to Wagner that I have already noted in my previous inquiries, namely, that Nietzsche's entire design hinges symbolically on ancient Greece and was made possible by Wagner's choice to adopt the ritual theatricality of Dionysus as a consciously modern venture, aiming to revive ancient theatrical and sacrificial experiences in new and different forms. The spirit of this endeavor was thoroughly modern precisely because it reached down to its most ancient roots, a spirit something Nietzsche was never to abandon. Indeed, he went further and replaced Wagner's metareligious theater with a theatrically tinged suprareligion, a one-man show starring the superman, the supraman, until the final curtain rang down on his reason. Greece is, then, the symbolic laboratory for creating and developing these fascinating and dangerous alchemies to achieve what had appeared in ancient Hellas still to be youthful and inchoate. And that is how Nietzsche sees Hellas in *The Birth of Tragedy*, Hellenizing enthusiastically but not yet discerning the radical nature of his modern reappraisal, because encumbered by its dependence on Wagner. Undoubtedly, the visceral polemic against his rejected but ever-present model had a powerfully heuristic function and led Nietzsche to discover, in the para-religious staging of the death of the gods (*Götterdämmerung*), the death of God that was to be announced on the stages of the world, though temporarily without an audience.

The "founding" scene in *The Magic Mountain* has been for me the ideal test for gradually bringing these enormous questions into focus, as well as the related and no less enormous difficulties of interpreting them. What had at first appeared to be a particularly well-chosen exemplum for a spectacular opening illustration turned out in time to inspire and guide a wider process of historical and philosophical clarification. The interpretation of the scene that instantly occurred to me was, in itself, forceful and immediate, which is not to say that it was wrong but that it was still too closely bound to the unilateral thinking behind it. Thomas Mann now knows the dark origin of the bright mediations of the children of the sun, and knows that the same origin is shared by the German society from which Castorp comes. This is indicated in the text by the "very dialect of the town where he was born" spoken by the hags in their voiceless, obscene whisperings against Castorp, the hateful intruder who has just discovered their sacrificial secret. Here, then, is the perception that concealment is necessary to sacrifice if it is to perform its mediatory action—the concealment to which Girard refers—and that some unspecified historical force is removing sacrifice from this functional, corroborative concealment. Identification of this force with the Christic revealing of the crucified victim meets internal and external criteria of consistency and shows Girard, and Nietzsche before him, to be at least partly right in setting Christ in opposition to Dionysus. The impulse given by Christianity finally obscures the sacrificial sun of German and European society, and man's violence due to its constant need for fresh victims to sacrifice becomes visible, as Hans Castorp discovers to his cost when he is drawn together with everyone else into the slaughter of the "universal feast [*Weltfest*] of death."[20]

At this point in my earlier research into these themes I thought it possible to start at once with the laser-sharp contrast between Dionysus and Christ. In the face of the dramatic fact that the old barriers no longer withstand, Mann responds in a way analogous to Nietzsche and, in the case of sacrifice, appears actually to refuse to recognize the difference between the perpetrator and the victim of violence. When Castorp regains consciousness, he asks himself the right question about the connection that must exist between the bright and beautiful world of the radiant creatures and the hidden horror of the omophagic banquet, but he makes a significant shift immediately after when he sets the infant omophagy on a par, *side by side*, with the carefully controlled joy of its beneficiaries. Even if we recognize that Mann says not a word in defense of the cannibalistic murder of an innocent baby, he nevertheless gives the clear impression of wanting to relieve the situation and cloud the issue through the ambiguity of irony ("The conclusion . . . refined and loving"). Irony, in its ability to convey the opposite meaning to what it appears to say, seemed to me to reveal a kinship and analogy with sacrifice, which has to appear to be the opposite to what it really is. My further response at the time, not ineffective as a transitional interpretive step, was that the reader is eager to forget the horrific vision and more than willing to collaborate with the author and his strange irony, perhaps by meditating on the insoluble mysteries of human existence. This sleight of hand, I thought, made it possible for the choice that had already been made to be openly stated. Castorp declares total solidarity with the children of the sun, feeling deep down within him that their reasons for living are his own, reasons without which neither of them could live as they have always. And therefore Castorp, I concluded, like so many of his fellow Europeans, wanted to be a child of the sun, to return to an existence no longer torn apart but that could only be achieved at the cost of tearing someone else apart. The weak point in my inference was that I overlooked another possibility, namely that the author's strategy might be subtler and more structured: to allow the reader to draw whatever generic, complicit conclusion while he himself had a different continuation for the narrative in mind. But let us take things in order. The signs of Mann's complicity in sacrifice are certainly not lacking, just as they are not lacking in the culture that inspired him, but they bring up a need different from the dilemma between sacrifice and antisacrifice that Girard has in mind.

As a key to interpret this situation I used a distinction rife in German and European culture at Mann's time, a distinction he himself explicitly and repeatedly makes clear. This is the distinction between *Kultur*, in the strict sense of what appertains to a particular ethnic group or nation, and *Zivilisation* in a universal sense, the civilization that is increasingly bringing the world's highly diverse cultures to share the same common features, what nowadays goes by the name of globalization, a term thoughtlessly overworked by the media. Mann takes as his starting point the fact that violence is necessary to *Kultur* since it can only guarantee its internal unity and cohesion by concentrating the violence latent in human communities in sacrifice. This need for violence conflicts with civilization (*Zivilisation*), that is, with the gradual refining of society and its laws, and the progress of democracy and human rights, all seen as endangering the survival of the social structure, as a destructive and undifferentiated demagogy that seeks to revoke humankind's dependence on the very historical mediations that have enabled it to exist.

Mann bases his argument on a conceptual dichotomy borrowed from the German philosophy of the period, and from Nietzsche and Oswald Spengler in particular. When I brought this dichotomy into play, I realized that Girard's criterion was too simple and peremptory to be applied to a question of such complexity and that it could only lead to condemning sacrificial *Kultur* and endorsing the universalism of *Zivilisation*. The problem is that civilization considered on its own is the debased, distorted image of an antipersecutory need that is in itself perfectly understandable. The most recent and revealing version of this debasement is the ideological terrorism of the "politically correct" or, in politics itself, the deafening rhetoric touting the absolute value of "human rights" and "democracy" and seeking to impose them at all costs. The real point, which Girard can help us to understand but not to resolve, is not to choose between two political or historical tendencies, which were essentially of little interest to him, but rather to understand the distinction between persecutor and persecuted, between slaughterer and victim. This distinction enables us to establish our relative distance, near or far, from an invisible laser beam cutting in two our every thought and action (and therefore all our historical, political, and theoretical groupings as well). We see it exemplified in the apologue or *mašal* of the Judgment of Solomon where two women claim to be the mother of a child but only one, the real mother, is prepared to sacrifice her motherhood and finally her own life to save the child from being cut in two. The distinction, not mediatable in any other way, contains the precious element of truth that substantiates and underpins Girard's extremism; *tertium non datur*, there can be no middle course where the choice is the life or death of a child. And it has to be said that Mann's sacrificial scene shows us the Judgment of Solomon turned upside down, with no divinely wise king to test the two mothers who are now transformed into cannibalistic monsters, united in devouring the child. Other scenes like the Judgment of Solomon will come within the scope of our inquiry. For the moment we should note how Mann is so dazzled by the historical reality of *Kultur* and the hypocrisy of the prevailing *Zivilisation* that he fails to make this distinction clear or, rather, fails to do so *immediately*. His main concern is not to settle and define but to experience from within and to understand with no exclusions. We will make a brief biographical and intellectual survey of part of Mann's life, which will perforce be structured by the journey I took in coming to understand it. Mann makes an extremely significant observation in *Reflections of a Non-Political Man*, written only a few years earlier and charged with the emotional urgency of the First World War, the event that was to bring *The Magic Mountain* to a close:

> Culture [*Kultur*] does not exclude "bloody savagery" [*"blutige Wildheit"*], whereas civilization [*Zivilisation*] mitigates the savagery, enlightens superstition, and discourages passion. Culture binds, civilization brings

> dissolution [*Kultur ist Bindung, Zivilisation Auflösung*]. It is obvious from immediate experience. Who is going to stop me from seeing things this way, if this is the way I see them?[21]

Kultur must bind at all costs, which not only does not exclude bloody savagery, but actually demands it. In the face of such explicit statements, never explicitly denied by Mann, I practically closed off my analysis just by documenting the writer's complicity, along with most of European culture, in the violence of the children of the sun. The question posed in the last sentence only strengthens this conclusion since it unintentionally conveys a gnawing vexation, a taboo that Mann projects outside himself and attributes to the hated supporters of *Zivilisation* (the French writer Romain Rolland, and above all his brother-rival Heinrich Mann) but really comes from within his own consciousness. Not for nothing this taboo was to prove powerfully effective in Mann's hostility to Nazism, his choice of exile rather than compromise with a more brutal and vulgar, more standardized and less aristocratic version of that same *blutige Wildheit*. The inconsistency here seemed a good thing to me, as evidence of the writer's good faith. In exile in America, Mann decided to openly reinstate the law of the God of Abraham, Isaac, and Jacob, the "God so strangely sublime [*wunderlich hehren*]"[22] who speaks to us in the Judgment of Solomon and whom Nietzsche had tried to banish, perhaps in despair that any divine wisdom could prevent his dismemberment.

This is true in part, but it is a part by no means partial if we think of the person concerned, an innocent child, whose right not to be carved up, divided, and torn to pieces, as in the cannibalistic banquet in Castorp's dream, is at last recognized today after enormous effort and much conflict (and after all, the idea itself of "right" is also "strangely sublime," and has little to do with current political caricatures). But does this conclude the argument once and for all, as Girard believes, or has it only just begun? Is it a closure or an opening? The choice lies with whoever wants to consider these questions along with me, but it seems obvious to me that the only real alternative is the second. Everything points to it, and corroboration comes from a more complete and comprehensive analysis of Mann's efforts to find a response to the terrible history of Germany and Europe. They are evidence of how heavily collective and historical mediations weigh on human existence in all its aspects, and how terribly difficult it is to define and apply them to understand

and possibly influence the destiny of communities and peoples. The problem has yet to be solved and is far from being fully answered by Girard's idea of sacrificial foundation, nor is it adequately explained by his theory about the central place of imitation in collective and individual human life, as I shall make clear in the introduction. Meanwhile it is essential to understand that by not acknowledging the hard work and apprehensions of those who have long meditated on these questions, we also fail to acknowledge the contribution of past periods and individuals. This substantially means to obliterate history, and that is something we must reject. It would be time to recognize that the entire world to which we belong, expression of the victorious side in the last European war, reveals its true face in the claim to represent the only possible Good, and in a particularly insidious manner seeing how cleverly it is disguised. And might not the victors' arrogance, suffered for three-quarters of a century now (though all the upheavals make it seem more like a thousand years), express and constitute the more subtly violent civilizing process opposed by Thomas Mann? The picture, then, is both stimulating and complex but in a different, far more controversial way.

There could be no excuse for ignoring a whole dramatic period in European philosophy, involving major thinkers and writers and especially notable for its reflections on the mediations decisive for human civilization. At the present time we are far indeed from giving our own response to this question, seeing that the only version admitted, or even admissible we should add, is the systematic denial of any mediation whatever in the name of an indifferentiation that is only the more destructive the less concerned it is to recognize what it destroys, a tendency that Girard's radicalism ultimately, albeit unintentionally, endorses. As a consequence of this ideological arrogance, we live surrounded by the terrorism of the "politically correct," of a violent invasive form of democracy that comes to be the opposite of what it claims to be. And the plain and simple proof of this is the reception that greets such criticism today: either total indifference or, worse still, violent partisan misunderstanding, often the prelude to those lynchings by the media or by due process of law that we have come to regard with indifference nowadays, so long as we are not the victims.

The problem that vexed Thomas Mann was the need for shared mediation in setting up and maintaining cultures (*Kulturen*). He sensed that this shared constructive bond had to be sacrificial, since it was sacrifice alone that enabled the children of the sun to create harmonious relationships and to evolve an aesthetic and ethical dimension. By that time the global character of the phenomena, especially at the economic level, had already grown much more than we might suppose in our superficial way, and in the face of its advance, there was a growing perception of a serious crisis in the ancestral mechanism that had preserved human culture and made possible its finest achievements over the millennia. In Italy, years before Mann, the same concern was felt by Gabriele D'Annunzio, a writer consigned to the limbo of aestheticism by the well-intentioned detractors of Italian culture, and unfairly insulted by Mann himself in his *Reflections*.[23] Girard's response to this serious problem manages to be both highly pertinent, in more clearly stressing the debt owed by cultures to sacrifice, and terribly curt, maintaining that there is no further need for sacrifice following Christ's revelation of the victim, to which the only alternative is immediate destruction. In other words, space no longer exists to reflect on the problem or to find margins for maneuvering, understanding, and choosing. A singular short-circuit where, to assert such a scheme, much weight is inevitably given to the ever-active forces of destruction rather than to forces that would defend the space of human life. Thomas Mann's ideas, on the other hand, aim to move precisely in that latter direction, as an unbiased reading of his text must confirm. It cost Mann a great deal of effort to reach a conclusion, so great in fact that he places the strongest emphasis on it, speaking through the character of Castorp:

> Now I have it [*Nun habe ich es*]. My dream has made it absolutely clear, so clear I shall always know it. Yes, I am enraptured and excited by it. My heart beats strongly and it knows why. The reason it beats is not only physical, like the fingernails on a corpse continuing to grow; it beats humanly and the cause is my inner happiness. It is a philter, this realization from my dream.[24]

This realization is the real magic "philter" that gives the character a sense of protection like a talisman, good magic this time, a spell that keeps him safe because it is based on knowledge, on awareness that includes ancient magic and reveals its deeply human meaning, yawning wide over the greater mystery of man's provenance, the stuff of which he is made. We can recognize two aspects to Castorp's realization (which is also Mann's since author, narrator, and character coincide here). The first is, without doubt, an inadequate perception of the subtle yet sharp distinction between slaughterer and victim, ultimately between Dionysus and Christ. This explains certain opaque, ambiguous areas on account of which Mann never comes to renounce the dangerous, unbalanced formulae of the *Reflections of a Non-political Man* where he even declares his support for the "bloody savagery" required to maintain *Kultur*. Nonetheless, there is more to it than that. In the first place, these pages in *The Magic Mountain* are the result of profound rethinking in the aftermath of the *Reflections*. Mann realizes that a loving attitude and experience of love must be an integral part of his idea of *Kultur*. We might define this love as "universal" except for the fact that Mann's investigations lead him to understand that love of men is never love of mankind in the abstract but love of human beings with a real, historical existence, love of their lives and culture. It is *Zivilisation* that proceeds in terms of the universal love of mankind, an axiomatic abstract definition that showed its true face during the Terror in revolutionary France, that is to say, during the first great affirmation of the principles of universal civilization. The theory of the victim can itself fall victim to this rational principle if we assume that it provides the definitive, categorial answer to the question of man, and consequently use it as a weapon to destroy every culture in history, and ultimately human history itself. On the other hand, though Mann's love for the children of the sun is ambivalent and unresolved, there can be noticed in it a certain acceptance of their dependence on sacrifice, something that Castorp recognizes in himself as well.

To tell the truth, Castorp's inner sensations of rapture and warmth might be the effect of applying Freud's ideas more psychoanalytically, more psychologistically. This part of the vision might lend itself most readily to being interpreted in physical and sexual terms except that any psychologistic reading is confuted by the contextual framework for these words, the epoch-making drama that they anticipate and express. Through Castorp, Mann loves these strange creatures of the sun for what they are, for the men that they are, which cannot exactly be said for the more peremptory categorizations of the modern theory of the victim. Typically, *Zivilisation* excludes what is the secret of every human experience, of every experience in life and history, namely, that taking part in violence can be, and really is, the true way to achieve the most authentic awareness of violence and overcome it in the most authentic manner. Proof that this is, in fact, the deep meaning of Castorp's realization comes in the novel's final pages where the narrator comments on the catastrophe engulfing Castorp together with Germany, Europe, the entire world. We are in the thick of fighting in the Great War:

> All these young men in the flower of their youth with their knapsacks and bayonets, their mud-spattered capes and boots! Very different scenes might come to mind if we imagined them in a fine humanistic spirit, in a kind of dream. We might imagine them as they lead horses stamping and splashing through the waters of a bay, while they walk along the shore with their sweethearts, lips close to the ear of a tender bride, or happily draw their bows together and exchange friendly advice. Instead, here they are: killed by gunfire, face down in the mud. That they went gladly, albeit terrified beyond belief and inexpressibly homesick, is quite another matter, shameful and at the same time sublime; in any case, it ought not to be a reason for bringing them to this carnage.[25]

The vision of the children of the sun returns for the last time, and in a way that could hardly be more enlightening. As long as it is caught up in its beautiful appearances, Castorp's vision remains the fruit of his humanistic imagination, but behind it, and before it, too, since we are all now within the depths of the temple, there is the bloody banquet of a foundational omophagy, no longer called by that name, replaced now by the "universal feast of death." As Mann knew from personal experience, those glad festivities had begun in the feverish, suicidal atmosphere of summer 1914. He describes that gladness in measured terms as "shameful" and "sublime," shameful as to the consequences and the failure to be aware of them, and sublime in giving tragic expression to what is humanly finest and most cherished: the attachment to one's history and existence, to *Heimat*, home and homeland. This is confirmed by the fact that the same identical sentiment, censured and pointed out as odious in the defeated, is celebrated and vaunted to the skies in the victors. Italian culture, to which I belong, with its experience of both victory and defeat, ought to have been ideally placed to grasp this; instead, it tried to tag on blindly behind the victors of the last world war, while the victors themselves, intent only on power, remained completely oblivious to all the toadying. Finally, and punctually, as its importance demands, comes the writer's condemnation: never should their gladness have been the motive for leading these creatures of the sun to be slaughtered. The significance of the connection here and the condemnation can be grasped from rereading another passage, if we give it due attention and respect. Castorp has apparently been hit by enemy shellfire, but that is not the case, not just yet:

> He falls. No, he has thrown himself facedown because the howling of a hound is coming closer, a huge shell bursts, a filthy sugar-loaf rising from the depths of the earth. He lies with his face in the cool mud, legs apart, feet turned out, and heels to the ground. The product of brutalized science [*verwilderten Wissenschaft*], carrying the worst charge it is possible to imagine, hurtles across and thuds into the ground thirty paces away from him, like the devil in person, and explodes underground with mad, terrifying violence, raising a fountain into the air as high as a house, a fountain of earth, fire, iron, lead, and shreds of human flesh. Because two of them were lying right there . . . two friends who, in their extreme danger, threw themselves down next to each other; now, mixed up together, annihilated.[26]

With an effort the writer manages to rein in the emotion behind these words; they are restrained and perhaps lack the force of contemporary writings more fully inspired and more desperate or, if you will, less desperate in clinging to the traditional humanistic heritage. Nevertheless, these words are appropriate to conclude the evolution of Mann's ideas from the *Reflections* to the individual and mass enchantment of *The Magic Mountain*, whose ambivalence shows us the destiny of contemporary European man, fated to prefigure the destiny of global man. Not a very enviable role, but it needs to be recognized. Indeed, the old Europe ought to be the first to recognize it and restore greater respect for its culture and history, which cannot be evaluated according to the victors' uncomprehending parameters.

This does not mean we are now on the side of *Kultur*, after essentially supporting *Zivilisation* so far, albeit with significant qualifications. What the contemporary world lacks is a perception of the tension between these two extremes, a tension that becomes an appalling caricature as soon as their true extent and importance are lost, as is now the case. This same lack of perception has made globalization a subterranean process that depletes and destroys cultures. If *Kultur* is indispensable in defining man and what is proper to him, *Zivilisation* is indispensable to single cultures in overcoming the limitations of their violence. *Kultur*'s real content can no longer subsist without *Zivilisation*'s power of contamination and exchange; however, for the polar tension between the two to reveal its full potential, we need to throw off the ideological blanket that currently stops us from thinking or even seeing and brings us to doubly deny the light of the sun, as a metaphor for what is evident, and as a symbol for an ancient history illegitimately removed from sight.

Only this type of approach can make the difference between Dionysus and Christ, which is also a reciprocal relationship, useful to us; and show it to be a strangely relational and reciprocal difference, with Christ's revealed singularity not only including the reasons for the phases that preceded it but, still more, recognizing in them the historical and cultural conditions that made it possible. This observation encapsulates the sense of my reappraisal of the religious and tragic knowledge that flourished in classical Greece and its comparison with the Christian message. With the right stimulus, Christ's message shows profound interaction with that knowledge and its themes and allows us to see a cognitive and moral goal toward the achievement of which we should direct our intellectual and spiritual resources, otherwise doomed to bankruptcy: the attainment of humanity through a complete, shared recovery of human history, nothing disdained, nothing excluded.

With that goal in mind, in order to work out the theoretical lines for our inquiry we need to recover the philosophical tradition to which Mann and the thinkers already mentioned belong, besides others that it is right presently to discuss. Thus I shall come to define the historical and theoretical approach I think is essential if we are to avoid schematic contrasts in dealing with these themes: the mediatory or ecstatic-objectual conception.

GNOSIOLOGICAL INTRODUCTION

A Disregarded Philosophical Tradition

> 125. *The madman*. Have you heard of that madman who lighted a lantern at the bright sunshine of the morning, ran to the market, and began ceaselessly screaming: "I seek God! I seek God!"?
>
> —Friedrich Nietzsche, *The Gay Science*

1. Nietzsche's Death of God

The inspiration behind the scene in *The Magic Mountain* was aphorism 125 in Nietzsche's *The Gay Science*, an aphorism marking the start of a tradition of thinking about man's origin that I regard as the most daring and forward-looking legacy of European culture at the turn of the twentieth century, and seminal not because it offers a theory of human origin but because it intercepts and registers human origin overpoweringly and prophetically. We must now take a closer look at the assumptions and implications of the aphorism, and then pursue a further investigation and reflection on all that this will bring to light.

The most remarkable aspect of aphorism 125, and the least noted in spite of being present in *The Magic Mountain* as well, is the manner in which the death of God, understood as the killing of God, affects the person who proclaims it: not in pedantic, academic terms as a mere hypothesis but with the full impact of a sudden revelation, of *absolute certainty*. This is not the fruit of a fevered imagination; Nietzsche's madman is not concocting an ingenious scene for his listeners, the sarcastic, anonymous market crowd who are only too ready to sneer at his professed desire to seek God. On the contrary, it is his listeners who are dominated by the most presumptuous fancies, imagining that they have no need of God since for them there is no origin to be sought, no mystery of existence to be fathomed. The crowd consisting of "many who did not believe in God" shows that it already interprets the death of God as simply the nonexistence of God.[1] It is as if Nietzsche's text foresaw its ironical, misleading popularity as the founding text of modern atheism, a success hailed by a dull, monotonous chorus with dissenting voices few and far between: Sigmund Freud indirectly, Thomas Mann in his novel, Georges Bataille in terms of life experience, and finally René Girard more theoretically, though all the voices were dominated, with varying emphases, by an analogous certainty: that what is involved here is an act of collective violence that was the start of everything and that we are destined to rediscover it as our definite legacy to future ages.

Nietzsche's prescience is not some inexplicable gift of prophecy but comes from the fact that he is well acquainted with the crowd of unbelievers in the marketplace: his madman was, and in some respects still is, one of them. The death of God made banal as pallid, intellectualized atheism is the version that Nietzsche would most readily believe and, in fact, it reappears in *The Gay Science* and in *Thus Spake Zarathustra*. However, in his isolation, no longer sustained by the *idola theatri* of a success that he longed for but never enjoyed, he is neither willing nor able to be so conformist: another revelation comes to him. He travels alone on this road to Damascus,[2] and it is not the God killed and resurrected in the person of Christ who speaks to him through the silence but the nameless divinity killed in the dim and distant past that has yet to rise again, to be reborn, Nietzsche hopes, as *Dionysus redivivus*, the Eternal Return. He proclaimed the death of God but discovers no new interpretation of God, nor states the definitive intellectual truth about God. On the contrary, he is reached by the truth of an Event (*Ereigniss*, as he writes[3]) from which we all derive, and our lives too in its huge wake—too great to be noticed as a rule. This immense appeal for complicity encapsulates ideas about the origin of man and culture that twentieth-century philosophy and human sciences were to develop.

Nietzsche's madman silences the atheists in the marketplace with the following apostrophe: "Where has God gone?—he cried—I will tell you! *We have killed him* [*Wir haben ihn getödtet*]—you and I! We are all [*Wir alle*] his murderers!"[4] That nails them at once with the ring of a truth that, once spoken, speaks for itself even if it is not immediately understood, and his listeners will do all they can to falsify it. The pronominal "we are all" indicates not just solidarity among all human beings in committing this murder but even more our dependence on that murder in order to come to exist as humans; otherwise the phrase would be a piece of empty hyperbole, overexcited rhetoric. There is here an anticipation of twentieth-century concepts explaining the origin of mankind from the killing of a victim transformed into a god.

The fact is that Nietzsche's text—and the same is true of the *Bacchae* as we shall see when we analyze its theological background—does not speak flatly of a divinity as existent or nonexistent but rather of a historical process underlying divinity, a theogonic, divinizing process that is at the same time an anthropogonic, humanizing event. This is the very dawn, the stage where nonexistence produces existence and vice versa. God exists for the same reasons that man exists, and the revelation that man's existence derives from a killing, that is, from the cruelest act to qualify for nonexistence, casts a sinister shadow over mankind, evoked by Nietzsche's aphorism in terms of a cosmic wrenching away of the Earth from its Sun. To discover God's nonexistence/existence is equivalent to discovering man's existence/nonexistence. Far from marking a new era entirely entrusted to mankind, a *regnum hominis* free of illusions, the announcement of the killing of God shows itself to be the killing of mankind since man's historical existence derives from that *other* theogonic, divine killing. If the divine spring runs dry, the spring of humanity also dries up disastrously. Nietzsche could see only one alternative: to seize Promethean-like the divine secret of existence/nonexistence, the secret of the divinization from which humanization, hominization derives. This explains the epoch-making question marking the culmination of the entire aphorism: "Shouldn't we also become gods [*zu Göttes werden*]?"[5]

Like the Greek god Dionysus, humankind will have to divinize itself. However, in the extreme terms reached by Nietzsche through applying them to himself in the first instance, this divinization would prove to be the most revealing but least propitious outcome. Since divinization presupposes that the divinized victim has been killed, humankind's self-divinization could only amount to its sacrifice.[6] And only in that way could the painful, thrilling spectacle of man the god-maker revealed to himself be brought to an end, while awaiting its triumphant repetition in the Eternal Return, a Return of the Identical whose cosmic significance is also apparent seeing that its realization appears as irremediably historical, and thus irreversible, definitive. Nietzsche's own fate bears this out, finally consumed with the truth of the death of God in Dionysian madness. And this theme shows us the authentic background to what Mann was attempting to do in the scene of Castorp's dream, that is, to defend mankind, and the vital power of love sustaining our existence, *from* and *within* the most appalling revelation. And so he moves in the opposite direction from Nietzsche's scorching meteor.

Nietzsche's daring formulation, based on the sharp contraposition of an apparent reality and a substantial and concealed truth, did not suddenly arise from nowhere but belongs to the deepest stream of German philosophy. An important precedent of his inquiry was the Copernican revolution proclaimed by Immanuel Kant in his *Kritik der reinen Vernunft* (*Critique of Pure Reason*—first edition, 1781; second edition, 1787), a few years before the French Revolution. According to Kant, human knowledge does not depend on an objective external world, as traditional metaphysics and common sense maintain, but as it appears to our forms a priori and transcendental, that is, preceding the experience and yet inseparable from it. We know only the phenomenon (German *Phänomenon*, from the Greek φαινόμενον) or appearance (*Erscheinung*), which is distinguished from the noumenon (German *Noumenon*, from the Greek νοούμενον) or thing-in-itself (*Ding an sich*), the absolute reality we can think of without being capable of knowing it. The crucial point of Kant's thought is that what we human beings take for objective reality is the transcendental appearance made possible by the logical organization of our mind: this means that human knowledge is potentially a historical and cultural process, not simply a natural one. Truth is no longer an *adaequatio rei et intellectus* (congruence between reality and intellect), as was believed in antiquity and the Middle Ages, but the result of the human *intellectus* defining its own phenomenal and conditional *res*. Nevertheless, and precisely because of this, the noumenal and unconditional *res*, the *Ding an sich*, remains the final and necessary horizon of thinking and, from a moral and religious standpoint, reveals itself to be the hidden source of Kantian knowledge.

Subsequently Arthur Schopenhauer, a post-Kantian philosopher who was to be greatly influential on Richard Wagner and Nietzsche, sought to discover what the noumenon is for human beings and concluded that they have it within themselves as will-to-live, that is, the universal principle of life incarnated in each being, which is also an unending source of sorrow and misfortune from which they must detach themselves in order to reach the negative salvation of *noluntas* (the nonwill). Under the spell of Schopenhauer's metaphysics and Wagner's art representing the noumenal world of German mythology, Nietzsche began exploring the noumenon and discovered that it corresponds to the mystery of human origin taken as a historical event. Already in the *Die Geburt der Tragödie* (*The Birth of Tragedy*, 1872) the dichotomy between phenomenon and noumenon, appearance and absolute reality, becomes the opposition between on the one hand the Apollonian principle, linked to the "beautiful appearance" (*schöne Schein*)[7] of art and civilization, that is, to the appearance of the *principium individuationis* (the principle of individual existence), and on the other the Dionysian principle, expressing "the intimate profundity [*Grunde*] of man" and characterized by "the horror" and "the ecstatic rapture" (*wonnevolle Verzückung*) accompanying "the violation of the *principium individuationis*,"[8] clearly an aesthetic description of human sacrifice given that the human being is the individual being par excellence. According to the historical-philosophical reconstruction of *The Birth of Tragedy*, this opposition, which in preclassical Greece was complementary, became conflictual through the Socratic-Platonic and then Christian fight against Dionysiac reality, and finally evolved into the splitting between *Zivilisation* and *Kultur*.

In nineteenth-century Europe, and with particular intensity in Germany, we notice an authentic short-circuit between the old metaphysical reality and the human being left to his bare condition as natural and historical *Ding an sich*. In the same period, the natural sciences began to freely explore all the phenomenal aspects of reality, including the human world and history. It was only a question of time before German and European culture discovered a new historical and human *res*, no less absolute in its value than the previous world of metaphysics, but much more unpredictable and fragile since it derives from wholly immanent, terrestrial forces.

Starting from these premises, Nietzsche shows himself to be fully part of a whole series of insights and discoveries where philosophy, science, art, and literature appear in an unexpected dissonant harmony, if we know how to recognize the common theme, the overall keynote: the disquieting and yet irresistible exploration of the human noumenon that science was proving to be through and through a phenomenon open to rational inquiry like anything else. As background to aphorism 125, besides Kant and Schopenhauer, we need to place not only Wagner's idea of musical theater as a theogonic and anthropogonic event developed through the noumenal legacy of German mythology, not only the preceding Hegelian and post-Hegelian idea of history's completion, but also the first scientific theory to offer a rational explanation of human origin as an animal species, Charles Darwin's theory expounded in *The Descent of Man* in 1871, just one year before Nietzsche's *The Birth of Tragedy*. Following the same rationalistic approach Freud wrote *Totem und Tabu* (*Totem and Taboo*—1912–13), the first major attempt to delineate human origin within a more fully organized framework. So we must now venture into a maze of theoretical argument, far removed from the artistic evocations of Mann and Nietzsche, in order to identify the heuristic tools necessary to develop their hidden potential.

2. Freud and Durkheim

There can be no doubt that Freud intended to continue and complete Darwin's scientific work by demystifying religion, showing it to be the outcome of man's parental and psychic relationships that were being brought to light by the new discipline of psychoanalysis. However, the real credit for not ignoring the human facts (in the sense of Latin *facta* and Greek πράγματα: things done, actions) in their specific, irreducible meaning belongs to the old positivism (not to its present counterpart, based on ultraspecialized division rather than on ontological reality). Some years before Freud, in *Les règles de la méthode sociologique* (*The Rules of the Sociological Method*—1894–95), Émile Durkheim gave his definition of sociology as the science that studies social facts on a par with *choses*, with "things" plain and simple: "social phenomena are things [*choses*] and must be treated as things"; he added: "Actually, a thing is everything that is given [*donné*], everything that offers itself or rather imposes itself to observation."[9] The latter statement brings out the unmistakable, independent meaning of social phenomena as facts with a collective significance that exerted a peculiar compelling force over the individual members of society, a force external to the individual but permitting the individual to exist and form an idea of himself or herself.[10] In saying this, Durkheim goes further than he intended and, to a certain extent, anticipates the phenomenological method developed by Edmund Husserl some years later, dissolving from within the Kantian dualism of appearance and noumenon in the sole phenomenon understood as manifestation, that is, as correlation between an object manifesting itself and a subject moving toward the object in its intentionality. Unlike Husserl, Durkheim points out the irreducible character of social and historical phenomena, irreducible according to the rules of observation of natural science. A similar reflection, though quite independent of Durkheim's positivistic premises, led to my own phenomenological-historical method, which provides the basis for my analyses,[11] and whose aim is to realize Husserl's intention "to go back to the 'things themselves'" (auf die "Sachen selbst" zurückgehen),[12] taking these "things themselves", however, as human *facta*, as historical and cultural *pragmata* or *erga*, present both outside and inside ourselves.

Freud lacks Durkheim's and Husserl's sophisticated methodological vision, but his demystifying reductionist design, aiming to explain psychic and anthropological facts, goes beyond Darwin's naturalism, which was limited to treating man as a zoological species. In *Totem and Taboo*, Freud does not tackle the question of the meaning of human culture as such, but he does address the problem of the meaning of the origin of the human being. He admits implicitly that there is to be found in the human being a wide spectrum of representation and behavior, a radical value, with no real parallel in the animal kingdom. The great divide between nature and culture is still missing. That was to be outlined in Claude Lévi-Strauss, not by chance a product of the Durkheimian school of sociology. Meanwhile, the difference emerges only gradually, through the facts, the *pragmata*, the *facta*, that psychoanalytical inquiry accumulates and interrelates until they finally condense into an explanation.

This explanatory condensation happens in the fourth essay of *Totem and Taboo*, after Freud had read William Robertson Smith's *Lectures on the*

Religion of the Semites with its conjecture that the totemic meal was the earliest form of sacrifice practiced by the Semitic peoples.[13] In this sacrifice the animal victim was devoured live in order to feed directly on the flesh and blood and thus create kinship between the members of the group, a bond felt to be physically magical in character. The rite of omophagy that we saw in Thomas Mann reappears here, in the form of an ethnographic and anthropological hypothesis, first inspired by the celebrated description of a camel sacrifice found in a fifth-century *Life of St. Nilus*.[14] For several reasons, Robertson Smith regards this as the very earliest form of sacrifice: the elementary nature and force with which elements, material and symbolic at one and the same time, blend in a strictly unanimous, collective mode; the fact that the totemic meal clearly precedes interpretations of sacrifice in terms of giving, with their assumption of the notion of ownership, introduced later; and that the role of fire in the camel sacrifice is either absent or derivative, only applying to human victims whose flesh was burned and not devoured. (This is correct, but Robertson Smith is wrong to conclude that human sacrifice came later than animal sacrifice.)

Freud now had at his disposal all the elements needed to work out his hypothesis for the origin of mankind. The totem concept actually plays a secondary, instrumental role,[15] since it substantially indicates a collective center of attraction around which, in my terms of mediation, a group converges. In the new territory mapped out by Freud, the term "totem" is equivalent to the killed, divinized victim. There is, however, a further element that contributes by way of premise to Freud's development of the scene.

In James Jaspar Atkinson's essay "Primal Law," published in 1903, the Darwinian horde is described as dominated by rivalry between the dominant male and younger brothers excluded from the females and ready to unite to kill their father.[16] Although he is almost completely forgotten today, Atkinson provides the missing link between Freud's hypothesis and Darwin's scenario of the horde. Most perceptively he stresses and develops two observations made by Darwin regarding sexual rivalry between male oxen and male wild horses, two males had been seen to form an alliance against a dominant rival. Atkinson extends this observation with some of his own.[17] At the very origin of the human species, in his view, there was a scenario of collective violence with the young males opposing the dominant father,[18] but the maternal love of the females for their sons corrected this violent disposition, thus enabling father and sons to live together. The primal law of avoidance between males and females of the same horde was the consequence of this.

In an important note to the fourth essay in *Totem and Taboo* Freud stresses Atkinson's generalization that "the conditions of the primal horde as imagined by Darwin are clearly observable in herds of wild oxen and horses and regularly lead to the killing of the leader of the herd."[19] Freud also acknowledges Atkinson's idea of the killing of the father of the horde and the remedy afforded by maternal love. Freud raises no immediate objections to Atkinson's theory, but at the same time he will not let himself be persuaded by it, which indicates how deeply he had reflected on the matter while lacking a clear explanatory framework. In fact, the females of the horde are not the remedy for disputes between the males but their cause, and it would take a different factor to restore social cooperation. The nature of the problem of the group's life is dramatic and simple, and the relevant factor must have something to do with its extreme manifestation, violence, and therefore with the climactic outcome of that violence, the collective killing. The generic role of this central step is entirely absent in Atkinson and was suggested to Freud by Robertson Smith, though Freud is unable to overcome the difficulty that the killing of the father, rather than putting an end to the problems, sparks off hostility among the brothers. In spite of these snags, which were all the stronger because of his reluctance to define culture thematically, Freud was not to be put off the right track, leading from the world of biological drives dominated by instinctual determinism to the world of symbolic relationships where the variables of evaluation and choice are introduced, albeit within the libidinal structure of human beings.

Freud was far from harmoniously resolving this complex alchemy of motives and suggestions, but if he had been more scrupulously, pedantically scientific, it would never have achieved expression as a conclusive theory. Here, then, is the scenario of the origin as Freud formulated it, with the young brothers banished by the primeval father:

> One day [*Eines Tages*] the banished brothers united, struck down the father and devoured him, putting an end to the paternal horde. United they dared to do and succeeded in doing what would have been impossible singly. . . . Their progenitor was certainly the model [*Vorbild*] envied and feared by each member of the band of brothers. Now, in the act of

> devouring, they achieved complete identification [*Identifizierung*] with the father, each appropriating a part of his strength. The totemic meal, perhaps the first real feast [*das erst Fest*] of mankind, would serve to repeat [*Wiederholung*] and commemorate this memorable and criminal act [*Tat*], the start [*Anfang*] of many things, such as social organization, moral sanctions, and religion.[20]

The scene thus sees "the start [*Anfang*] of many things" that were without this significance in the biological state (social organization, for example) or did not even exist (moral sanctions and religion). It can therefore be described as the first explanation of man's origin as a cultural being, though the concept of culture is not thematized as such but emerges by itself due to the unwittingly phenomenological method followed by Freud, with its old-fashioned positivistic respect for the facts (*pragmata*, *facta*). Moreover, this origin is not the final result of an indefinite series of minor changes and adaptations of the sort Darwin and Atkinson postulated in naturalistic terms, but resides in a specific, traumatic event buried in the mists of time and yet present in the deep structure of the human being; and although the event is natural in origin, it turns out to be intrinsically historical. In other words, the human being does not simply have an origin remote in time and unverifiable in principle. The human being *is* that origin, an origin verifiable in the light of the psychoanalytical method. If it is true to say that psychoanalysis conditions and limits Freud, causing him to distort his originary scene, the converse is equally true and valid, that analysis of the psyche turns into anthropological observation to confirm the truth of the scene.

The reciprocal nature of this explanation not only led to the most glaring non sequiturs in Freud's theory but also provided nearly all his followers, as well as many of his critics, with a pretext for converting the hypothesis of *Totem and Taboo* into a mere psychoanalytical fancy, a symbolic scene that never happened—in other words, into a myth. And that is how Lévi-Strauss unhesitatingly defines Freud's hypothesis, implicitly seizing on Freud's own definition in *Massenpsychologie und Ich-Analyse* (*Mass Psychology and Analysis of the Ego*—1922[21]): a "scientific myth of the father of the primal horde" (wissenschaftlichen Mythus vom Vater der Urhorde).[22] This is extremely ambiguous as a definition because Lévi-Strauss understands it in a twofold sense: as nonscientific myth when taken to be real, and as symbolic and therefore scientific myth when taken to be unreal. Freud, on the contrary, leaves the question open as to whether or not his *Mythus* is unfounded, but since he is referring to the constructive myth of the hero (the father) in which the subject can identify and achieve self-fulfillment, the process must be presumed to be real. At the end of *Totem and Taboo* he had already considered the possibility of a purely imaginary and symbolic scenario but had dismissed the idea at once, arguing convincingly that it was impossible to distinguish imagination from action at the most remote stages of human history, and putting the seal to his final pronouncement with a famous line from Johann Wolfgang Goethe's *Faust*: "In the beginning was the deed" (Im Anfang war die Tat).[23]

We can grasp the real significance and scope of Freud's contribution if we realize that neither the totem nor even the psychoanalytical father were strictly necessary to what he was trying to do, as I shall explain later. Meanwhile it should be noted that his theory had no immediate effect for several decades, though he himself remained fully convinced of its validity throughout his career and referred to it on several occasions, making some remarkable insights, right up to his last work, *Moses the Man and Monotheism* (1938).[24] However, we shall not understand the developments of Freud's idea unless we take into account the other major innovation in anthropology and philosophy that preceded and accompanied his work. This was Durkheim's sociology, and we would do wrong to restrict it to the field of sociology as currently understood.

Durkheim's work is based on the study of social facts, understood as the collective realization of actions and representations, totalizing because they involve an entire society. Religion provides the most ancient and widespread example of this, as Durkheim ascertained in his major work *Les formes élémentaires de la vie religieuse* (*The Elementary Forms of Religious Life*—1912), published shortly before Freud completed *Totem and Taboo*. According to Durkheim, religion shows us authentic manifestations of collective thinking, implying a decision shared by everyone, the more binding the less consciously it is presented. This totalizing and "performative" approach brings Durkheim to a new and decisive reform of Kantian philosophy, a second

Copernican revolution, that amounted to tracing back the real a priori of the human mind in collective religious representations.

These representations correspond to "the ideas that philosophers, beginning with Aristotle, have called the categories of understanding [*entendement*]: the notions of time, space, gender, number, cause, substance, personality, etc. They correspond to the most universal properties of things."[25] Unlike the infinite number of particular and complex ideas, absent in some ages and societies, the general "categories of understanding" possess something irreducible and show themselves to be widespread in all periods and cultures:

> These fundamental notions seem to us as almost inseparable from the normal functioning of the intellect. They are, as it were, the skeleton of thought [*Elles sont comme l'ossature de l'intelligence*]. Now, when we analyze primitive religious beliefs methodically, we naturally find the principal categories among them. They are born in and from religion; they are a product of religious thought.[26]

This means that religion is the originary source of human knowledge, not simply as a previous and archaic stage of culture, but as an organic and rational view of the totality of world that is always potentially present and active in our thoughts and actions. Such a powerful representation, having little to do with what we usually mean by religion, cannot arise from single individuals but only from the community taken as a whole: "religion is an eminently social thing [*chose*]."[27] A particularly effective demonstration of this statement is given at the end of *The Elementary Forms*:

> There is no individual experience, no matter how broad or prolonged, that could make us even suspect the existence of a whole genus embracing the universality of beings. . . . This notion of the *whole*, which lies at the basis of the classifications I have cited, cannot come to us from the individual himself, who is only a part of the whole and never comes in contact with more than an infinitesimal part of reality. And yet there is perhaps no more fundamental category. Since the role of the categories is to encompass all the other concepts, the category par excellence would indeed seem to be the very concept of *totality*.[28]

As this universal notion transcends its more individual and empirical manifestations, and at the same time is at the root of their possibility of existing and becoming an object of knowledge, they are transcendental in a fashion very close to Kant but are completely social and collective, that is, religious. Religion is nothing but the first self-representation of human societies, the creative tool with which they manage to define and understand themselves. The principle according to which everything comes from the totalizing representations of religion taken as a collective phenomenon appears to be and to some extent actually is a typically positivistic and reductionist conclusion, but Durkheim's theory surprisingly shows itself to be richer than that, if we consider it is no less true the opposite way, that is, that it is possible for everything, for every collective fact and knowledge, to go back to religious representations.[29] Many critics of Durkheim's *The Elementary Forms* were puzzled by the strange ambiguity of his idea of religion, which seems to oscillate between a metaphysical role and positivistic dismissal.[30] Nevertheless, this very ambiguity gives religion fresh recognition and vitality, which a more conventional approach would be unable to achieve. Not by chance Durkheim's last and unfinished project was a search for a new form of immanent and moral religion, made possible by the unavoidable and creative tension between collective rules and individual freedom.[31] Going beyond Durkheim's program, we can philosophically conclude that at the beginning of the twentieth century the dizzy oscillation between existence and nonexistence dominating the aphorism of the death of God intensifies beneath the rational and revelatory mask of Durkheimian sociology.

Apart from the philosophical implications of Durkheim's discovery of the strange and unclassifiable equivalence between religion and society, totally ignored by philosophers as well as sociologists themselves, we should remember that, to a certain degree, it prepares the search for an event capable of explaining how this collective decision arose together with its representational and cognitive consequences. Undoubtedly the scenario in *Totem and Taboo* furnishes a first draft of such an explanation, though the difficulties were so great that unsurprisingly the connection remained idle for a long time and Durkheim himself explicitly outlawed the idea of explaining the rise of human society as a whole.[32] Nevertheless, Durkheim's society already potentially contained and indeed *was* this refused and noumenal origin, temporarily frozen in the rational totality of its representations.

The work of Claude Lévi-Strauss, founder of anthropological structuralism, has particular relevance in this context for his developments following on Durkheim and for the Cartesian clarity with which he delineates the inner, irreducible features of human culture. We shall have the occasion to compare his contribution to that of Bataille, who, starting from similar premises, reached completely different conclusions and—so to speak—began defrosting the social totality of Durkheim.

3. Lévi-Strauss and Bataille

Significantly, there are important critical comments about *Totem and Taboo* at the end of Lévi-Strauss's most complete and representative work, *Les structures élémentaires de la parenté* (*The Elementary Structures of Kinship*—first edition, 1947), whose title and self-definition as sociological are both inspired by Durkheim.[33] Lévi-Strauss's main objection to Freud is that a universal structure such as exogamy, with its sophisticated rules for exchanges and crosses between human groups, cannot derive from a single event but is inherent in human beings as such.[34] For Lévi-Strauss, as I have already noted, the answer given in *Totem and Taboo* is a myth, at one and the same time too daring and too timid because it does not identify a real event but a scenario that every culture projects outside itself, the main purpose being for it not to happen. According to Lévi-Strauss, Freud correctly identifies the central nexus between the taboo on incest and the organization of exogamy but makes the mistake of taking the symbolic imagery of cultures literally instead of as a mythical, ritual dramatization that reproduces social life in an inverted form in order to ensure its regular performance in the real world. For Lévi-Strauss, this amounts to a failure to focus on the specific character of human cultures; and the theoretical dividing line that he would uphold against *Totem and Taboo* is the need to distinguish between culture and nature. Culture organizes in discontinuous, meaningful ways what appears in continuous, meaningless ways in nature; culture makes recognizable and regulated what remains forever confused and without rules in nature. This is not an absolute opposition but an interlinked, organic relationship made possible by cultural differentiation. Lévi-Strauss thus puts a fresh gloss on Durkheim's principle according to which society, taken strictly as *fact*, shows itself to be something unique and irreducible.

The most interesting feature of Lévi-Strauss's reaction to Freud, though he subsequently played it down, is to be found in *The Elementary Structures of Kinship* where he identifies the point of transition and transformation from nature to culture in the rules instituting marriage and the family. This is the amazing moment when diachronic factors linked to the continuing transformation of reality, and as such coming from nature, stand in equilibrium with synchronic factors that express what is specific to culture, that is, its power to develop and preserve human life and institutions. Matrimony is essentially reciprocal exchange organized through time according to fixed rules, introducing and maintaining reciprocity in the biological and instinctual sphere, the very sphere where differences and quarrels could most easily arise. It is, in short, the originary institution where culture becomes reality while in its greatest jeopardy:

> Marriage . . . is the necessary condition for reciprocity to come about, but at the same time it always jeopardizes the existence of reciprocity. . . . However, if we want society to continue, we must run the risk: to safeguard the social perpetuity of alliances [*alliance*] we have to compromise with the inevitability of filiation and, in short, with the biological infrastructure of man. But the social recognition of marriage (and, that is, the transformation of a sexual encounter based on promiscuity into a contract, a ceremony, and a sacrament) is always a stressful venture; and we can understand why society attempts to protect itself against the risks by continually, almost maniacally, putting its stamp on marriage.[35]

The laws of linguistics inspire Lévi-Strauss's idea of a structure for cultures that is both genetic and logically defined, and in analogy with those laws the accent falls on the deep organization of the *langue*, which makes a human language what it is in respect to the ever-changing *parole*, the language of individual speakers. And this leads to postulating the nature of a danger, already interpretive and symbolic, that is a real danger, more than anything else, to the extent that it is always potentially present. Lévi-Strauss comes short of absurdly asserting that the danger of conflict and destruction latent in sexual exchanges never materializes, but he does argue that it cannot be the normal outcome compatible with culture. Where there is pure violence, there is no longer culture, and therefore where there is culture, there can be no pure violence. Culture is the signifier-defense against chaos and as such makes it possible to represent the objects of nature, once again in perfect analogy with language. As Lévi-Strauss explains, quoting Ernst Cassirer: "Language . . . is itself a mediator in the formation of objects,"[36] which means that society's rules of transformation and exchange allow the world to exist, enable it to be experienced and represented as a set of objects having meaning.

Lévi-Strauss's contribution allowed the questions raised by Freud to be reformulated more thoroughly, but the price paid was their immediate and definitive closure since the structuralist approach is inevitably biased toward already constituted cultures, unable ultimately to conceive any different genesis from what those cultures themselves conceive. Just as he had criticized Freud, a similar but inverse criticism can be leveled at Lévi-Strauss for taking the symbolic formulation of cultures too literally and not giving due weight to the dramatic reality that shaped them. The strict distinction between nature and culture serves above all else to discern the latter without enabling us to really understand the transition from one to the other. Quite evidently, while Lévi-Strauss rightly considers reciprocity to be central to marriage and society, he is unable to answer the question of its origin. The highly organized and wisely asymmetrical reciprocity of exogamic rules cannot be the result of an instinct precisely because it overcomes and controls instinct. Nor can it be self-generated, since the contract defining this reciprocity is its result, not a contrived preliminary.

There remains only one alternative: ritualized reciprocity, with its linguistic ability to mediate and define the object, results from a nonritualized reciprocity, an exchange of blows capable of destroying the two duelists or of altering their relative status. Freud's hypothesis may raise its head again, even if it has been shown to be inadequate. With Bataille we come to a further attempt to understand the problem.

In *L'Érotisme* (*Eroticism,* 1957) and, even more perceptively, in the posthumous *L'Histoire de l'Érotisme* (*The History of Eroticism*), Bataille sets out from Lévi-Strauss's distinction between nature and culture, and accepts the consequent view of matrimony as an exchange between the two dimensions that makes social exchange possible. However, he objects that this view fails to recognize the real drama that introduced matrimony and the violent opposition that never ceases to fuel it. The opposition of nature to culture appears abstract to Bataille; on the contrary, he relates the radical nature of the transition to a real struggle fought out between the animal dimension and the dimension that was to become man. In *L'Histoire de l'Érotisme* he writes: "the transition from animal to man implies not only their formal states but the drama in which they were opposed."[37] Without fully grasping the consequences of this reversal in approach, Bataille inconsistently endorses Lévi-Strauss when he dismisses the originary scene in *Totem and Taboo* as fanciful myth, only significant because it never happened.[38] But the universal nature of the incest taboo implies a very different eventuality: "It seems to me difficult to imagine that a sanction such as this prohibition could impose itself so powerfully—and universally—unless it concerned generative violence [*la violence génésique*]."[39] This bears the general sense of Freud's argument, though Bataille is not fully aware of where it leads: "At the origin there was necessarily a set of consistent vicissitudes, if not a brief drama; we shall never be able to say what happened, but we know that the outcome amounted to a decision on which there could be no going back."[40] It is typical of Bataille to start from his own experience and record with great acuteness the phenomenological and historical effects of causes that he is unable to identify consistently; once identified, however, they would even allow him to draw on the abstract categories of nature and culture as well without falling foul of the scientific formalism that he criticizes in Lévi-Strauss. Anyway, his reconstruction of human origin gives us "different movements coinciding,"[41] where "the totality of the possible" is displayed every time,[42] conflating together various moments and aspects since Bataille is incapable of a more organic arrangement.

Matrimony turns out to be not so much the point of balance between nature and culture, through regulation of sex, as it is the cultural colonization of animal sexuality, subjected by matrimony to the social criteria of productivity and usefulness—that is to say, of economics and labor. Therefore, the point of balance lies elsewhere, and it is a dynamic, tensional balance with marriage at one extreme, normative and reassuring, and, at the other extreme, eroticism, that is, the sexuality of biological origin normally prohibited in man, from which culture must defend itself although it cannot exist without it, on a par with death and what represents death. (The parallel here is invalidated by residual naturalism and becomes valid only in relation to sacrifice as an institution.) Sexuality is the natural dimension in a human being that arouses horror and disgust in culture, but to completely renounce it would mean to deny man's very existence: the problem is that marriage domesticates and destroys this animal dimension and, by prohibiting it, risks extinguishing its vital source. Thus, far from being the suture knitting together nature and culture, matrimony confirms their antithesis and suggests the need for an equal and opposite compensatory movement to reaffirm the validity of the norm, once one has had the experience of transgressing it. Eroticism is the transgression of the matrimonial and social order permitted by ancient and archaic cultures at appropriate moments, in the form of exceptional rites and orgies, metabolized by human desire as a polarity between the norm and its violation, whose purpose was to confirm the norm, not to destroy it. Eroticism cannot exist without being dangerous for those who live it, and in the field of the psychology of desire, it expresses what sacrifice once fulfilled in the field of religion and symbol.

Bataille's analysis of the erotic dimension demonstrates a more general cultural law: the rational organization of society and the economy, centered on work and the accumulation of wealth, can only endure if the wealth produced and accumulated is from time to time dissipated and destroyed by consumption, totally expended with nothing in return. The originally ritual version of this is to be found in many archaic cultures in the form of the potlatch: a competition in gift-giving that usually ended with the death of the loser. Both eroticism and total expenditure are evidence of human derivation from sacrificial and religious structures that have become for modern man the existential experience of *chance*, living moment by moment in the knowledge that life is only irreversible expense (*dépense*) and ecstatic sacrifice getting nothing back. Bataille takes up Nietzsche's experience of the death of God but more forcefully, going beyond its sinisterly destructive implications and following a singular course in which life and thought intertwine in a sort of anthropological phenomenology applied to himself. He makes it clear that the annihilation in the background of the killing of God is the ritual and symbolic sphere from which human cultures derived mediations qualified to define the world, the object. However, Bataille has nothing to say about the creative and objectual potential of sacrifice; its aspect as a destroyer of culture is what principally emerges rather than its intended aim to construct and stabilize. Lévi-Strauss, on the other hand, puts the whole accent on the end purpose.

This brings us back to the theoretical problem already indicated. Although Bataille directs his efforts toward achieving a unified theory of culture and religion, they could never have been brought to a successful conclusion, conditioned as he was by a twofold origin; the two institutive moments of work and consumption, marriage and eroticism, life and death, security and sacrifice remain opposites in a constitutive dichotomy and do not refer to a single generative process. Thus the human species appears to have hominized itself through work, adopted from the Hegelian and Marxist tradition, and achieves real hominization only later, in the destructive and therefore boundless experience of sacrificial destruction, the only experience in which human beings can assert their independence from the utilitarian logic of survival and their irreducible supremacy in respect to their normal pursuits.[43] It is clear from this that Bataille was aiming at a new philosophical definition of the human condition rather than a consistent theory, for which he showed the need but to which he failed to acquire the necessary means. As a result of this fertile and unresolved aporia, his great contribution to the enigma of human origin has been systematically undervalued. And so we come to Girard's conception, already met as counterpoint to the conceptions of Nietzsche and Freud in our initial analysis of *The Magic Mountain*.

4. Girard's Mimetic Theory

A more consistent vision of man's origin is given by Girard's mimetic theory, although what it gains in terms of consistent explanation comes at the price of simplifications and exclusions, with repercussions for the theory as a whole. One of the many similarities between Girard and Freud is that both come to formulate their concepts most completely in stages and consider each stage to be a natural development of the previous one without taking account of their differences and inconsistencies as well. As a result, their discoveries are important but partial and we have to evaluate them in a context wider than their authors envisaged. To the extent that Girard's basic ideas can be useful in developing this inquiry, I will summarize them in the order of their discovery and definition.[44]

The first stage consisted in exploring what he defines as mimetic or triangular desire in *Mensonge romantique et vérité romanesque* (literally: *Romantic Lies and Fictional Truth*—1961) The human being on its own is incapable of understanding what it desires: for this, a fellow human being is indispensable, one who can act as model and mediator between the first human being and the object of desire by indicating a desirable goal for the model's follower to try to attain through imitation or mimesis. Girard therefore introduces the idea of mediation but identifies it with the desiring or mimetic process since it depends on a model who becomes the focal point of the process. Girard's mediation leads ever more easily to a situation where imitator and model converge on the same object until there is *double mediation* in which both act as models for one another, an imitative symmetry synonymous with reciprocal rivalry making each contender the monstrous double of the other. In *Mensonge romantique*, great writers of modern literature, particularly Miguel De Cervantes, Stendhal, Gustave Flaubert, Marcel Proust, and Fyodor Dostoevsky, show us the mimetic truth of desire, concealed by the romantic lie that attributes it to the will of the desiring subject alone, and document its gradual emergence in European society as the checks and hierarchical distinctions of the ancien régime that had prevented more direct rivalry slowly fall into decay. The modern experience of mimetic desire begins to develop in the world of *Don Quixote*, still dominated by old social orders originating in medieval times, but it answers criteria of *external mediation*, that is, neutral and distant mediation, so the madness of desire affects the hero, but the rest of society remains untouched. The great nineteenth- and twentieth-century novelists, however, illustrate the transition from the old external mediations to the *internal mediation* of double mediation, with model and imitator indistinguishable, and they also show us the only way out of this infernal scenario: fictional conversion, the coming to awareness of the destructive nature of desire. In Dostoevsky, who was the most daring and futuristic explorer of the modern inferno of desire, this becomes manifestly a religious, Christian conversion.

In this way, in *Mensonge romantique*, as in the following essay on Dostoevsky,[45] Girard finds a simple, intuitive explanation for human violence, sparked off for the same reasons that bring human beings to live together, and he applies it to a no less simplified but equally powerful vision of human relationships and Christianity's response to their fundamental inadequacy. Years later the theme returns in *A Theater of Envy: William Shakespeare* (1991),[46] where mimetic theory and its subsequent developments are recapitulated with the help of the works of the greatest English dramatist. The positive aspects of Girard's analyses bring with them certain defects, since the one-sided nature of his approach tends to impoverish and schematize the rich nuances and implications present in the writers under consideration; it is especially noticeable in his treatment of an ironic, metanarrative writer like Cervantes,[47] and of Flaubert, whose truly spiritual dimension is ignored, while moreover he attributes to Shakespeare a final farewell to the stage that is more Girardian than Shakespearean. Anyway, it is significant that his literary analyses focus on the noumenal core of mimetic desire, which proves to be the real hidden cause of human phenomena. This explanatory attitude led him to pursue his researches beyond the literary field into anthropology in a way not wholly unlike Bataille though Girard is far less explosive, less like Nietzsche, and closer to the rationalism of Lévi-Strauss.

La violence et le sacré (*Violence and the Sacred*—1972), Girard's first book of anthropology, starts by observing that ancient cultures had a strange perception of the enormous danger presented by mimetic desire and its degeneration into violence. This is evidenced by the superficially inexplicable and irrational taboos prohibiting anything at all that might arouse mimetic desire or even evoke it by association—above all, the terrifying doubles symbol, the target for a wide range of prohibitions and ritual limitations, as in the disturbing case of a twin birth. Girard perceives a consistent logic running through the huge mass of apparently contradictory data gathered by ethnographers at the turn of the twentieth century. This is the logic of mimetic violence and of the only defense against it available to archaic communities: the mechanism of the single victim. Mimetic competition between human beings can indeed spread like wildfire within a social group and plunge it into an appallingly destructive situation: the *mimetic differences crisis* or doubles crisis, where the rivals are transformed into the doubles of one another and multiply. Salvation comes through setting off an analogous imitative mechanism that brings all the rivals to converge on a single victim, chosen arbitrarily, so that they seize on a residual differentiation and avoid being engulfed in reciprocal slaughter. The victim functions as mimetic attractor drawing the collective violence to be discharged on itself, and peace is miraculously restored. Here we have the essential mechanism of the *sacred*: the harmful violence within the group concentrated on and expelled through the victim, and utterly transformed into a force for good. Hence, the paradoxical features of the sacred: a divine force on which the group depends and a saving power as long as it is remote and outside the group, but becoming mysteriously impure and destructive once again when it comes close and enters within the group. The sacred is simply violence expelled and divinized, a notion that finally provides a unified explanation for all archaic religion.

The ideas of Girard outlined in *Violence and the Sacred* come to gravitate and condense around two central themes, a theoretical and historical comparison with Greek tragedy and his criticisms of Freud and Lévi-Strauss. The first of these will be dealt with in the First Part, but it is worth mentioning the latter two now, both to understand Girard's peculiar place in the theoretical tradition being presented here and to introduce my own views on mediation and the object.

In *Violence and the Sacred* Girard recognizes *Totem and Taboo* as the forerunner to his own program and condemns the conspiracy to consign Freud's book to "ridicule, indifference and oblivion,"[48] above all on the part of followers of psychoanalysis who elsewhere feign veneration for their master. If we are to grasp the real genius in *Totem and Taboo* we must strip away the psychoanalytical apparatus; it misled Freud in the first place and kept him from the full truth of the scapegoat victim; he came close but remained bound to the psychoanalytical myth of the father combined none too happily with the Darwinian notion of the horde. After outlining the scene of the murder of the *Urvater*, and without solving any problems since the sons are left still facing the reasons for their conflict, Freud describes a second origin scene in which the parricide sons show themselves to be equal as brothers in dealing with the insoluble task of sharing out the females. With Freud the undifferentiated mimetic crisis comes *afterward* when it should really come *before*, but he lacks the courage to acknowledge such subversion. To do so would mean overturning and destroying the entire edifice of psychoanalysis founded on the precedence and universality of the Oedipus complex. Instead, what ought to emerge clearly is the truth of mimetic desire leading to the doubles conflict, resolved by the scapegoat victim attracting the unanimous violence of the rivals united against it.

Girard's answer to Lévi-Strauss is more gradual and circumspect in approach, partly because of structuralism's direct influence on the anthropological development of mimetic theory, and it recognizes Lévi-Strauss's definition of the institution of the family as derived from exogamic relationships and not from the family regarded as a separate entity in a naturalistic way. For Girard, however, the basis of those relationships is not the positively reciprocal nature of exogamic exchange, whose destructive dangers would be essentially symbolic, but the precedence of the endogamic taboo, being all one with the terrifying reality of the outbreak of the doubles crisis: "we need to think of the family as deriving from the taboo and not of the taboo as deriving from the family."[49] By giving prominence to the positive reciprocity of family relationships functioning normally, and to that alone, Lévi-Strauss's structuralism recognizes the structure at a static level but fails to see its innate dynamism, and so remains "confined in the structure, a prisoner of the synchronic, incapable of seeing change as violence and terror of violence."[50]

An interesting aspect of *Violence and the Sacred* is Girard's stated intention "to bring about a 'return to Freud,' but without abandoning the structuralist perspective,"[51] thus securing his place in the tradition that I have described, though failing to fully recognize its various threads and connections, as his treatment of Bataille goes to show. Girard allows that *L'Érotisme* sets out the dramatic problem of sexual taboos quite explicitly but takes care to add at once that it only occasionally overcomes "the decadent aestheticism [*esthétisme décadent*] of which it is the extreme expression."[52] This is really unjust since *L'Érotisme*, with rationalism of a sort Lévi-Strauss at his best might envy, tackles the enigma of the contrast between animals and men head on, and so proves itself to be a great anthropological text, not the second-rate literary product that Girard would have us take it to be. The polemical edge typical of Girard has to be valued for its heuristic function within the historical context, but for that very reason it should be seen for what it is, namely, the sign of definite limits. Mimetic theory developed within the regime of these blind spots, and they prevented it from fully recognizing the contribution made by the authors that it attacked.

In a similar way, the dismissal of Freudian psychoanalysis is founded on real arguments but fails to register the fact that the role of the libido in the scene of origin in *Totem and Taboo* is to remind us of the importance—not to be underestimated—of the object in triggering the crisis and resolving it.

Girard is similarly justified in writing off the Oedipus complex but fails to realize that the father-figure in Freud is linked to the essential question of identification, whereas the identification process itself cannot be entirely reduced to the generic mimesis that satisfies him. The anthropological phase of mimetic theory confirms the objectual exclusion that characterized it from the start, and now becomes an axiomatic theorem. As a result, the cultural significance is completely flattened, reduced to its violent, sacrificial genesis. Freud is criticized for not seeing that "in terms of signification there is nothing that does not stem from the murder itself,"[53] but expressed in that way Girard confuses the consistency of a completely genetic explanation with a total reductionism in which *the explicatio* destroys the *explicandum* since, as far as he is concerned, culture has no independent dimension once its origin in the murder has been ascertained. No wonder, then, that he should adopt Lévi-Strauss's schematism in dismissing *Totem and Taboo*, and while he rejects Lévi-Strauss's description of it as myth, he repeats the charge that Freud refers to the killing of the primeval father as a unique and unrelated event.[54] There is no truth in this since the killing of the father is repeated, anyway, in the periodic totem sacrifice and in other later forms of human sacrifice, something that Freud unhesitatingly recognized.

The problem resurfaces in Girard's penetrating but dismissive criticism of Lévi-Strauss, which is very little inclined to recognize the cultural phenomena highlighted through the efforts of structuralism. Thus he can ignore the detail of Lévi-Strauss's attempt to connect the synchronic and diachronic planes, in *The Elementary Structures of Kinship*, by seeing the institution of matrimony as the delicate, vitally strategic transition from nature to culture. The fact that this was not successful, and was based on a rationalistic distancing from the reality of the crises against which archaic societies had to defend themselves, in no way detracts from its function both as preamble and crowning achievement to Lévi-Strauss's work, even if the initial impulse became lost in the arrogant, antihistorical scientism of his later years.[55] Apart from the historical inaccuracies in Girard's criticism, excusable in view of his pressing theoretical needs, it has to be said that he takes no notice of what really interested Lévi-Strauss—that is, the irreducibly specific character of human culture, acknowledged by Lévi-Strauss thanks to Durkheim's positivistic and inadvertently prephenomenological methodology. Girard's solution, on the contrary, only confirms his destruction of the culturally specific in what ought to explain culture. In his words, "positive exchange is only the reverse of prohibition,"[56] but in this way matrimonial and social reciprocity, with its capacity for making the world livable and practicable, is transformed into a simple reversal and parody of an omnipresent negativeness. And again, "the game of violence . . . plays the leading role *in every respect*, even in respect to logic and significations" (Le jeu de la violence . . . joue le premier rôle sous tous les rapports, même celui de la logique et de significations),[57] but such a postulate makes it impossible to assign an independent role to the sphere of "logic and significations," which is tantamount to the sphere of culture as a whole, including the science which Girard is always referring to.

These drastic limitations, however, enabled Girard to bring his theory to its fullest formulation in *Des choses cachées depuis la fondation du monde* (*Things Hidden since the Foundation of the World*—1978). Given the sheer scale of the undertaking it is easy to understand the price that had to be paid in simplification and digression. While that has to be said in all fairness, it contradicts Girard's frequently repeated claim to have reached the definitive explanation. The opposite is true: the success of a theory is to be gauged not only by the difficulties that it resolves but by the prospects that it opens up or, to put it another way, in the words of Walter Benjamin, the truth is not what solves mystery but what does justice to it,[58] bringing together in a tensional unity noumenal ideas and phenomenal representations.[59] Having in mind this sense of free philosophical inquiry, open to both scientific knowledge and its metaphysical horizon, I decided to title this introductory chapter after Benjamin's *Erkenntniskritische Vorrede* ("Gnosiological Introduction"; literally: "Foreword in terms of a theory of knowledge") in his *Ursprung des deutschen Trauerspiels* (*The Origin of German Tragic Drama*).

Two new elements make their appearance in *Things Hidden*: (1) a theory of hominization, the most organic development from Freud's ideas in *Totem and Taboo*; (2) the inclusion of the Judeo-Christian revelation in Girard's anthropology, the vision present in his writings in the 1960s now developed in a historical-anthropological key, which helped me introduce the theme of Greek culture into this study as the major term of historical comparison with Christianity. I shall concentrate mostly on the passage concerning hominization, needed to outline my mediatory theory of the origin of culture, and shall mention only briefly Girard's interpretation of the Judeo-Christian legacy, which is fertile in heuristic terms but presents internal difficulties and must be considered later.

In regard to hominization Girard adopts Darwin's evolutionary vision en bloc without more careful thematization and assumes that internal mimetic behavior in a certain species of primate increased, making ineffectual the hierarchical organization that enables gregarious mammals to live together and cooperate. The ensuing mimetic crisis led to strengthening a mechanism widely documented in the animal kingdom—the alliance of two contenders against a third—but this time it took the form of the mimetic alliance of all against one.[60] There followed an *infracultural phase* where there was gradual growth in mimetism in the prehuman animal, that is, in its cognitive capacities and intraspecific contentiousness, with periodic mimetic crises and outbursts of spontaneous collective violence. A real state of culture was only reached when the protohuman communities learned how to repeat the crises and their victimary solution artificially and under control, and so created the very first human institution in the shape of sacrifice, coincident with the birth of religion and symbolism.

In this manner, the theory of the sacred and sacrifice first outlined in *Violence and the Sacred* is expounded and explained historically as fully as the underlying premises permit. *Appropriative mimesis,* the result of imitative convergence on the same objects, becomes *rival mimesis* in the relationships of rivalry that trigger the mimetic crisis; and this mimesis between doubles tends to converge on the bearer of any residual difference, no matter what, through the mechanism of single victimage. Girard draws on the concept of transfer to describe what happens, a concept gleaned from his readings in ethnography[61] and made universally known by psychoanalysis, where it takes a quite different meaning: when all the members of the group converge on the victim, a *transfer of aggressivity* occurs and the victim is seen as a monster responsible for the violence devastating the community. Then, as soon as the victim is expelled and killed, there is a *reconciliation transfer*: the victim is considered responsible, no less miraculously, for the peace suddenly descended on the group and becomes its saving divinity.[62] The sequence of the double transfer taught the first human communities the twofold, symmetrical logic of antimimetic prohibition which protects the community, and ritual mimetism which imitates what is normally prohibited.

The force of sacred taboos and the projection of the victim outward in accordance with the expulsive character of the sacred caused the community to expand into the surrounding world in search of fresh victims, and thus transformed sacrifice into actual exploration of the world through *substitution*. Evidence of this is provided by hunting and the subsequent domestication of animals. Animals were assimilated to the founding victim until it was learned how to keep them close to the community so as to superimpose them as exactly as possible on the original internal victim; this extension of sacrifice enabled the domestication of species best fitted to cohabit with humans. Girard's most striking example of substitution comes from James George Frazer and Arthur Maurice Hocart especially, but there is also a precise precedent for it in Bataille.[63] This is the example of sacred monarchy where for some reason the execution of the human victim is delayed, making it impossible to perform the sacrifice according to the prescribed ritual so that the victim remains, paradoxically, a god not dead but alive. At that point, he is deemed to have a radically different status and becomes the object of general fear and veneration.[64] A substitute victim is sacrificed in place of the living god, but it is characteristic of sacred monarchy for the divine monarch to be sacrificed later, at the expiry of his mandate, which may not run for very long. Substitution only becomes the rule when monarchy is well established as an institution, even though the king is never quite removed from the position of sacrificial victim.

However, Girard most notably applies his theory in relation to myth and Christianity, two major themes that were to run through his work from then on, beginning with *Le bouc émissaire* (*The Scapegoat*—1982). Myths, for Girard, are nothing but the interpretation available to archaic communities for the overwhelming experience of unanimous violence against the single victim that enabled them to survive their internal mimetic crises. Everything is projected outside in the unanimously shared perception of dangers coming from the sacred in the form of divine visitors from outside or natural catastrophes, which are nothing other than the transfiguration of the collective crisis. Peace returns when the visitor from outside is sent away or someone dies and the impending disaster is averted. It always follows the same pattern of salvation for all through individual sacrifice (*at-one-ment*), a pattern interpreted by the archaic communities, according to the only view available to them, as the omnipotent victim against whom there is an imperative need to defend themselves but who, once killed, becomes beneficent. The real causal relationships are inverted and transfigured; however, this world turned upside down sends out precious signals, and we can fully recover the reality by isolating them from the confused mass of fantastic matter in which they are immersed and turning them right side up again. And so we discover that the victim gifted with menacing and magical powers against whom the community defended itself by making him fly from cliff tops (Tikopia myth of Tikarau) or return to the bottom of the lake from which he came (Ojibwe myth) turns out to be none other than a human victim thrown into a ravine or drowned.[65]

The myth always presents the hero as committing undifferentiating crimes to which society has to respond by expelling him, followed by his transfiguration into a beneficent divine being. The best-known example from myth, and the one to which Girard gives much attention, is Oedipus, guilty of parricide and incest and therefore banished from Thebes. He is really to be interpreted as a typical example of a sacred monarch accused of the two most serious differentiating crimes in the ancient world and sent away for that reason. The crimes, recounted in Sophocle's *Oedipus Rex*, are so serious that a divine prestige as a superhuman hero accompanies him into exile, and to this second portion of his story Sophocles devoted a second tragedy, *Oedipus at Colonus*. But to take these mythical actions literally as Freud does with his Oedipus complex, where all men become guilty of the crimes ascribed to the son of Laius, is to remain ensnared in mythology and lapse into a second-rate mythology. Lévi-Strauss does much the same thing in interpreting myth according to the structuralist scheme of the savage mind, where order is introduced through a single subtraction from nature's undifferentiated continuum that enables the differentiated organization of culture.

The connecting link between the ancient, archaic world entirely subject to myth, even where myth is held up to question as in Greek tragedy, and our own world, which has become mysteriously capable of deciphering myth, is provided by persecution texts. These are historical and legal documents typical of medieval and early modern times that record cases of persecution, especially of witches and Jews accused of undifferentiating crimes such as commerce with the devil or of causing plagues or other scourges.[66] The first transfer is still active in these texts, with the guilty party demonized and judged to deserve the most horrific punishment, but the second transfer shows itself to be no longer active, so the victims do not finally undergo divine transfiguration. What we have here are half myths, which makes it easier to recognize the genesis and workings of real myths. According to Girard this special class of texts, characteristic of modern Europe, owes its existence to a cultural influence that has profoundly shaped our world, the religious legacy of the Bible, that is, of Judaism and Christianity, systematically seen by Girard for what they have in common and not for what divides them.

Where the Bible has influenced cultures, it has acted as an antimythic force; for the first time in history it stood up for victims against their persecutors and taught a view diametrically opposed to the view of all mythologies worldwide. This is eloquently borne out by biblical texts such as Psalms, where the voice of the persecuted is often to be heard calling on God against the lynchers; or in the book of Job—the subject of Girard's *La route antique des hommes pervers* (*The Ancient Way of the Wicked*—1985)—where the hero is abandoned and persecuted by everyone as a result of the misfortunes that afflict him; or again, in the episode of the Judgment of Solomon, where the king's command to cut the disputed child in two, a typical sacrificial solution, is really a ruse to identify the real mother, who chooses to sacrifice herself in order to save her child; and in Genesis, in the story of Joseph, where we find a sort of anti-Oedipus accused of crimes comparable to the Theban king's but whose innocence is claimed all along, right up to the moving reconciliation with his brothers who had wanted to eliminate him.

But the place where this antimythical logic really triumphs with overwhelming clarity is in the Gospel texts. Jesus appears as the vanquisher of sacrifice and its controlling, persecutory logic: "I will have mercy and not sacrifice" (Mt 9:13 and 12:7). He came to announce "things which have been kept secret from the foundation of the world" (according to Mt 13:35 and taken by Girard as the title for his book of 1978), and to bring mankind the alternative message of the love and forgiveness of the God of Israel whom he called Father. Christ was particularly vehement in attacking the false, exterior ritualism of the scribes and Pharisees. These took great care to appear righteous in what they did whereas they depended on persecutory mechanisms that they did not recognize and so renewed under the deceptive semblance of justice.[67] For Girard, the hypocrisy of scribes and Pharisees is representative of the way in which every human cultural order works, completely dominated by the persecutions lying unseen at its foundation. He defines this culpably ignorant and passive dependence as *persecutory misrecognition* or *unconscious*, Girard's unwitting translation in anthropological and religious terms of the Kantian noumenon. According to him, Christ's marvelous power to disentangle and openly reveal the human noumenon is encapsulated in two great Gospel teachings concerning the *skandalon* and Satan.

The *skandalon* is the stumbling block, not the insipid "occasion of sin," as it is often banally translated, but the perverse mechanism through which we constantly fall by the wayside along the path that should take us to the object of our desire, only to discover that the block causing us to stumble is the adversary who bars our access, and whom we consequently come to hate. However, the entire mechanism is set in motion by our mimetic dependence toward the enemy who, before becoming our enemy, is the model on whom we depend. Thus the *skandalon* is the mechanism of mimetic desire and the resulting rivalry. The figure of Satan only illustrates the collective consequences of this scandal on a universal scale, namely, the mechanism of the persecution of victims around whom the collective scandal condenses, and of the sacrifice that sanctions their persecution, thereby guaranteeing the religious and cultural organization of human communities. For this reason, Satan means "the accuser" in Hebrew, and the Gospel of John defines the devil as "murderer from the beginning" (8:44).

Christ's daring, subversive teaching soon brought him to the malevolent attention of the "powers of this world" who decided to apply their eternal logic of persecution and sacrifice to the importunate prophet. And so Christ was fated to suffer crucifixion, but with his great lucidity he clearly foresaw the outcome of his mission, with all the scandals crowding on his head. On the eve of the Crucifixion, in fact, he predicted that the infernal power of the scandals and Satan would infect all the disciples, starting with Judas, and even Peter who protested his love and faith. That is what happened, and it is vividly illustrated in the episode of Peter's denial of Christ.[68] Nevertheless, it is precisely then, when totally forsaken and dying an appalling death, that Jesus is silently victorious because this is the proof of the truth of his teaching. His resurrection the third day later no longer corresponds to the ignorant divinization by his persecutors because this time the miracle linked to the victim disappoints their expectations; it occurs not for the sake of revenge (if it were so, it would confirm their expectations) but to manifest the whole truth, the truth of the victim hidden since the foundation of the world. Only the true God, a God completely independent of men's violence, could bring about and vouch for such a revelation.

This is the basis for Girard's explanation of the West's uniqueness in demystifying persecution texts, and ultimately myths themselves, and in rejecting sacrifice, thereby introducing a bold, dynamic mentality that led the countries of Europe to break free from the ancient bonds of the sacred, develop the scientific revolution, defend the victims of violent persecution, recognize the rights of the poor and oppressed, and influence cultures throughout the world until they, too, are finally forced to drop their previous dependence on sacrifice and the sacred. This emancipation heralded great advances and great dangers as well since, in a world demythicized by Christianity, humankind stands alone with its responsibilities. It is now up to human beings to decide whether to create the Kingdom announced by Christ or bring about the destruction described in the apocalyptic passages in the Gospels and Revelation, the last book in the Christian Bible. In either case there would be an *apokalypsis* in the sense of a final revelation that could be the end of the world if humankind is unwilling to bow to the truth from which it derives. This apocalyptic strain in Girard's thinking is accentuated in later works, which are also affected by the extremism of his initial position.[69] From the theoretical viewpoint they add little to what Girard had already said in his writings in the 1970s.

In *Things Hidden* Girard undoubtedly applies his mimetic theory of the sacred and sacrifice to surprising effect, throwing an unexpected, unifying light on a huge variety of cultural institutions and historical phenomena; just for a moment we seem to glimpse the possibility of a single, all-embracing explanation for mankind and culture. This heuristic, explicative élan casts a luster over the whole book, though it must be said that the scale of the task and the variety of controversial argument and counterargument that gradually becomes necessary, make the exposition less than straightforward and lucid. The difficulty is apparent in the earlier parts of the book concerned with hominization and the origin of culture where the shifts in argument here and there are most engaging but just as confusing as to the actual stages in development of the processes described. And again, in the parts concerning the Judeo-Christian revelation, where our interest is most aroused, once the effect created by a skillfully selective vision has worn off and more considered reflection sets in, we remain equally uncertain as to their accuracy and completeness. But the major doubts arise over the reliability of the singular fusion between what claims to be scientific research and religious revelation, unhesitatingly embraced by Girard, giving no place for philosophical or historical mediation. Nor should we forget that the work was originally to be presented in the style of *Violence and the Sacred* and not as a book-length interview. However, since the undertaking was so complex and ambitious the dialogical format was decided upon following Girard's encounter with Jean-Michel Oughourlian.[70] At the time it made sense from the publishing viewpoint, though now, decades later, its compromissary character is fatally obvious. Girard was wrong, therefore, to consider this book as a sort of definitive incunabulum, apart from a few points of detail needing clarification. The optical illusion of a "definitive theory" has had its repercussions on the debate that should have taken place and has turned out to be largely a confrontation between detractors and supporters equally biased one way or the other. To introduce my mediatory theory, I now want to provide a sample of the critical discussion that the importance of Girard's ideas demands and that the rest of my study aims to illustrate. I shall try to show that we need to refer to the *entire* philosophical tradition here presented in order to obtain needed hints for a more advanced theory.

5. The Insufficiency of Imitation and the Need for Mediation

The roots of Girard's ideas about anthropology lie in Lévi-Strauss's structural anthropology and are evident in his use of the concept of difference, in the method applied to reading myths, and in his espousing Lévi-Strauss's aim to achieve a synthesis between the synchronic and diachronic aspects of culture. None of this is surprising when we remember the influence of structuralism in France, and in many other countries, in the 1960s. And there can be no doubt that, compared to Lévi-Strauss, Girard made great strides forward; he showed the idea of the sacrificial rite as marginal to be untenable, rejecting Lévi-Strauss's reproach to sacrifice for wanting to return the differentiation irreversibly introduced by myth back to the undifferentiated state and, moreover, for wanting to do so because of the anxious state of a thought that from time to time ceases to believe in itself.[71] Certainly, the problem is not this influence per se, but rather the failure to place that influence in its widest theoretical context while overlooking the philosophical background to many concepts and issues, though, for that matter, Lévi-Strauss was the first to ignore it on account of his scientistic contempt for philosophy. Also out of his lack of a wider philosophical frame Girard's reliance on using Freud remained polemical because of the debate about psychoanalysis then raging in France and unjustly excluded an original thinker like Georges Bataille for belonging to neither side. The main difficulty is that Girard adopts the Lévi-Straussian ideas where they come closest to the concept developed in his earlier works of literary criticism, including their drastic reduction of desire to the all-absorbing action of a model that becomes an obstacle and a rival, extinguishing every relationship to the object originally designated and desired. This noumenal negativism is the essential mark of Girard's thinking and is to be found in his critical reassessment of structuralism.

Its effect is apparent in the substantially anobjectual view of mimetism presented in *Violence and the Sacred*, where desire is able to assert itself by being completely detached from the object. Girard comments on the situation following the killing of the Freudian *Urvater*: "Desire no longer has any preferred object" (Le desire n'a plus d'objet privilegié),[72] omitting to add that in the Freudian scenario mating remains the "preferred object" and the primary cause of conflict. The formula of *Violence and the Sacred* has no time to linger over such nuances and hurries on to annihilate every objectual function: "Rivalry has a thousand pretexts because it has only one object after all, supreme violence [*la violence souveraine*],"[73] which is as much as to say, the destruction of every possible object. This means that "to admit the infinite character of violent mimesis" is to give up completely "the objectual anchorage [*ancrage objectal*] of desire."[74] Consequently, only the new logic of sacralized prohibition can assert itself within the group: "Wherever violence has broken out, prohibition arises" (Partout où la violence a flambé l'interdit s'élève).[75] Explaining culture as due to the "infinite character of violent mimesis" concentrated in the scapegoat victim leads, for Girard, to the most radical of reductions. This emerges from the passage that I commented on earlier: "in terms of signification there is nothing that does not stem from the murder itself." We can agree with this statement as far as the *genesis* of cultural significance is concerned, but it cannot embrace in toto the new symbolic and semantic dimension of culture. It would be like saying that a logical or mathematical operation is just as worthless since it is founded on ritual murder, an absurd statement in itself since human culture has the power to open up and multiply representational and interpretive horizons that break down the barriers of instinctual closure and give access to an independent and potentially infinite cognitive dimension. In order to explain culture Girard not only destroys every objectual aspect,[76] but actually denies that human culture in itself can be an object. Proceeding in this fashion he fails to meet Durkheim's unintentionally prephenomenological thesis, a method endorsed by Freud, all things considered, and taken to rationalistic extremes by Lévi-Strauss. Girard confines himself to turning these extremes upside down in disputatious fashion and ends by destroying the initial terms of the problem.

In *Things Hidden* this approach influences the overall structure of the theory of hominization, where the "infinite character of violent mimesis" assumes the role, in an inverted form, played by culture's formal rules for barter and exchange in structuralism, rules that sweep away all the "false objectual priorities" (fausses priorités objectales).[77] The difference is that, while for Lévi-Strauss the cultural structure remains intangible in its synchronic self-sufficiency, for Girard the violence sacralized and expelled through the victim turns into a humanly unreachable cultural noumenon, a black hole taking in and swallowing everything unless a proper, respectful distance is observed. Over against Lévi-Strauss's excessively rationalistic synchronia, Girard sets an equal and opposite excess in the shape of a monstrous and terrifying diachronia that crushes everything within itself. The first real transfer, or prototransfer, in Girard is the prohibition itself, because fear alone is obviously not enough, something that Freud had not grasped in the second scene of the fatherless brothers:

> If the members of the group were simply afraid of each other, they would have again ended up killing each other [*s'entre-tuer*]. In a certain sense the past violence has to be incarnated in the reconciliatory victim; there is already a need for a kind of collective transfer [*une espéce de transfert collectif*] that can arouse fear of this victim's return in force to take revenge, and unite the will of the whole group to prevent this terrifying experience.[78]

The transfer of aggressivity can be activated, then, only because it is concentrated on the victim and incarnates the "terrifying experience" of the crisis in the victim. The meaning of "a kind of collective transfer" is not limited to the intermediate step between animality and culture but alludes to a real intermediate transfer situated halfway between the transfers of aggressivity and reconciliation, inclining ultimately toward the former. This sort of multiplying of transfers turns out to be rather obscure, offering no explanation as to how cultures could be constituted in positive terms. Human culture cannot be terrified animality defending itself against terrifying symbolism but must be a wholly new situation containing within itself its defining criteria as well as the power to reappraise the biological sphere and confer meaning on it. However, all this escapes Girard's negativism and results in a mechanical juxtaposition or rather a dazzling overall picture that is more convincing than Freud's but on closer inspection hardly less problematic.

To point up the contrast, Girard's explanation forgoes content that has to be brought back in later to a certain extent in order to supply material for his reconstructions, but it is done surreptitiously and uncontrolled. The main theoretical difficulty created in this manner regards the concept of object, previously eliminated from the definition of mimetic desire, and now returning in uncontrolled, naturalistic forms. The object comes to be both the instinctual object of the animal condition and the result of the new symbolic perception, while the transition from one to the other is never made explicit, let alone explained. The difficulty reappears whenever Girard tries to describe the scene of origin in greater detail:

> It seems to me that the victimary mechanism, in its most elementary form, is to be seen as a marvelous machine [*une prodigieuse machine*] for arousing a new type of attention, the first noninstinctual attention. At a certain level of frenzy, mimetic polarization starts to center on the single victim. Having satisfied itself on this victim, the violence necessarily ceases, and the din is replaced by silence. This maximum contrast between fury and calm, excitement and tranquility, creates the most favorable circumstances for arousing this new attention. Since the victim is the victim of all members of the community, all eyes are fixed on the victim at this instant. As a consequence, beyond the purely instinctual object, the food and sex object, or the dominant congener, there is the corpse of the collective victim, and it is this corpse that constitutes the primary object for the new type of attention.[79]

The role of first noninstinctual object is assigned to the dead body of the victim. As Girard states a few pages before this: "At the moment when the violence stops and peace is established, the community's attention is fixed on this victim it has just killed; in short, it discovers the first corpse."[80] A completely new object takes the place of the previous instinctual objects: the corpse of the victim perceived as such. However, because he conceded too little before, Girard has suddenly to concede too much. In fact, it is not clear how, and by virtue of what causal factor, it could be possible to perceive the cadaverous object. The unanimity of the perception and the contrast between the states of crisis and peace appear insufficient; these comments by themselves remain on a sociological and psychological level or come within the naturalistic psychology of the Freudian horde, from which Girard sought to distance himself. There are two possibilities: either the dead body of the victim is gifted with a prodigious power to hypnotize the community, in which case the force capable of conferring that power should be at the center of discussion, or the prodigious power is projected onto the corpse by the group, and in that case the victimary object remains in itself an object indistinguishable from the previous instinctual objects and it becomes necessary to explain the factor able to discern it and show it in a new light.[81] In either case an element is lacking, an element that acts as a *medium*, a means of mediation making it possible not only to establish a connection, previously nonexistent, between subject and object but more importantly to fix the moment of their birth as inseparable cultural polarities. Girard fails to focus the concept and suddenly changes the status of the object from biological to symbolic; as a result, we pass from a practically total objectual negation to a fully formed cultural object, a total improbability at the inchoate stage of things Girard is attempting to reconstruct. The improbability is illustrated by the immediately following reference to the cultural institution of the tomb, as if to the basis of culture:

> It is always as a *tomb* that culture develops. The tomb is none other than the first human monument erected around the expiatory victim, the primal cradle of meanings [*significations*], their most elementary and fundamental place of origin. There is no culture without the tomb, no tomb without culture. The tomb is at most the first and sole cultural symbol.[82]

But the grave is an extremely complex cultural institution and implies a high degree of representational and symbolic development. If we accept the victim as "transcendental significant" (signifient transcendental) of humankind[83]—a definition that I accept but one that needs to be clarified and examined further—then the burial of the victim cannot be "the primal cradle of meanings" because the grave is in itself an extraordinary metasacrificial and potentially metalinguistic invention, and therefore presupposes sacrifice and language.

The cultural advantage of the grave really consists in offering a symbolic sign substitute for the victim, far more durable and ever available for the community and its rites.[84] The cultural and cultual acquisition of such an institution is obvious, as well as the increase in security for communities that could draw on such a resource to manipulate and develop their symbolic, expressive, and cognitive capabilities. The tomb's metasacrificial and metalinguistic potential generated the power, characteristic of the human mind, to duplicate the levels of symbolic and logical representation, and triggered abstract thinking as *we* understand it (the italics will be explained in a moment). What Girard asserts is not entirely unfounded but errs from the theoretical and historical viewpoint, as the archeological evidence shows. The first documented tombs, discovered in Palestine, date from about 100,000 years ago,[85] whereas the first human species identified as such, and already assuredly possessing cultural characteristics, date back over 2.5 million years ago.[86] The topic deserves further reflection as it gives important clues for a more satisfactory and updated view on the process of hominization.

Burial is a cultural attribute of our species *Homo sapiens* (to which the earlier italicized pronoun referred) and of *Homo neanderthalensis*, the species that competed with *H. sapiens* for tens of thousands of years but evidently failed to exploit the enormous potential of the invention of burial in an entirely symbolic and exosomatic direction. Actually, the role of the Neanderthal man cannot be underrated, as spectacularly shown by the recent discovery of paintings attributed to him and much earlier than the oldest comparable works of art made by *H. sapiens*.[87] We have only a few tantalizing fragments of a very long and largely unknown evolutionary history, previously begun with *Homo heidelbergensis* from which both *H. neanderthalensis* and *H. sapiens* stemmed, and probably having to do also with the mutual contacts between the two latter species until the genetic absorption of Neanderthal by *H. sapiens* through patrilineal descent.[88] Anyway, what appears to be really new in our species is its massive mental/cultural development, perhaps also related to a greater demographic dynamism, and the halting of big somatic changes that occurred at a certain point, huge evolutionary and metaevolutionary steps that could be connected with the development of funeral burials. Not by chance—this is my conjecture—some tens of thousands of years after acquiring tomb burial, *H. sapiens* produced its most sensational cultural manifestations with systematic and increasing forms of artistic expression while, once this symbolic and metarepresentational capacity was fixed once and for all, the macroevolutionary features of the species became more or less definitively fixed and there was explosive cultural evolution.[89] Girard's intuition about the tomb is not entirely wide of the mark but suffers from glaring cultural and chronological confusion attributable to a deficient vision of how culture really functions.

Going back to the problem of the definition of the object, we must by now recognize the centrality of this question to our thinking on the subject, and the impossibility of postulating either a nonexistent continuity between the biological and the cultural or an equally contrived discontinuity. The object of the origin could not be a simple biological object nor could it be an object already formed and perceivable as such because a new *function* arises in correspondence with it, a capacity to construct the future perception of symbolic objects starting from a unanimous experience that brings in their potential, opens the way for them, creating a new threshold that we can call the threshold of *objectuality*, of the faculty to recognize real objects distinct now from the animal on the way to hominization and its biological horizon. This, however, makes only more pressing the need to define and understand the causal factor permitting such a portentous transformation. Girard's notion of transfer goes in the right direction but remains rigid and mechanical, since it refers to a simple shift from the community to the victim, without considering the most relational and inward meaning present in the psychoanalytic transfer. Thus it proves to be heavily inadequate, blocked by the artificial prominence Girard gives to prohibition (to the prohibition transfer, we might say) and his failure to define the cultural threshold to access the objectual dimension. And so I come to the question of mediation. Cesáreo Bandera, one of the more intelligent and attentive scholars following Girard in the development of mimetic theory, produced a few years ago a study that seems to me the perfect introduction to this topic.

In this study, *A Refuge of Lies*, Bandera sums up his perplexity regarding Girard's depiction of the scene of origin in these words:

> If the exponential increase in animal mimetism, if human "hypermimetism" is a purely natural, biological phenomenon leading automatically, in a totally unconscious way, to the victimage mechanism, or rather, since the word "victim" is inappropriate at this point, to the violent convergence of all against one, which suddenly brings a cessation of violence to the group, then at that point the purely natural biological process has reached its goal. It ends as soon as violence stops, except for its tendency, common to all life processes, to repeat itself in similar circumstances. Nature, pure biology, has nothing more to do or to say. The group, the horde, has survived for the moment. And we are still, at this point, dealing with an animal group that has randomly stumbled on a collectively generated mechanism of survival—an evolutionary improvement perhaps, but still an automatic mechanism for the temporary cessation of intraspecific violence, that it is all.
>
> In principle, this mechanism can be repeated indefinitely without altering anything fundamental about its animal character. Adding hundreds of thousands or millions of years . . . in principle does not change anything. Animals can continue to be animals forever.[90]

The argument is revealing but it does not show, as Bandera believes, the inadequacy in principle of all attempts to explain the rise of culture starting from conditions of the evolutionary process that we can conjecture or reconstruct; what it shows is the inadequacy of Girard's attempted formulation, expressed as it is in quite insufficient negationist terms and based on a concept as generic and indeterminate as imitation or mimesis. The difficulty lies not so much in the question itself but in the way Girard has framed it from the very beginning. Not realizing this, Bandera comes to a quite disarming conclusion, one consistent with the assumption that Girard's scene is the *only* way to deal with the problem of human origin; he concludes that only a supernatural revelation, such as may be postulated through an act of religious faith, can provide an interpretive framework adequate to explain the transition. And so we come to the unresolved crux between scientism and revelationism that is the aporia that underlies Girard's thinking:

> Faith, not natural science, tells us that such a revelation occurred before the violent crisis (even if it was, conceivably, only for an extremely short period). Faith also tells us that it was actually the violent crisis and its victimizing resolution that clouded everything, spoiling man's relation to nature, and distorting his vision of the world out there. It is indeed faith, Judeo-Christian faith, that tells us that it was the world out there, full of trees and all kinds of animals, inhabited by the spirit of God, that became the first symbol, the first meaningful being-there in the eyes of man.[91]

This is closely argued but misleading, and it bankrupts Girard's project since if we assume that the prehuman animal enjoyed even for an instant this inexplicable revelation that had flashed the world onto its mind as "the first symbol, the first meaningful being-there" we must give up all idea of a rational explanation that is not only valid philosophically and scientifically but also compatible, because established quite independently, with a theological and religious vision of human origin. At this point Girard's idea of a scientific theory eventually coinciding with religious faith, that is, with the "Judeo-Christian faith," implodes on itself and turns into the destruction of scientific consistency in the name of an act of faith scarcely compatible with any criteria of probability and rational demonstrability. Bandera's observations present us with a whole series of improbabilities, from the "extremely short period" of revelation in virtue of which the prehuman animal conceived the world as possessing meaning, shooting ahead like a rocket compared to the achievements of lengthy cultural evolution; and finally, as a consequence of the Fall, of the original sin of collective violence, this suddenly culturalized animal fell into the sinful state of persecutory unconsciousness, thus combining Bandera's argument once and for all with Girard's theory, regarded as the only valid theory, and conserving, moreover, its weakest aspect, its cultural negativism. The cure appears worse than the disease.

Above all, Bandera fails to consider that there is no advantage in reducing the time span of the presumed revelation down from the hundreds of thousands or millions of years passively endorsed by Girard, in hopes that an enormous time span might obscure an objective difficult for the arguing.

The aporia remains the same whether spread over millions of years or concentrated in a split second: the only difference, more apparent than real, is that in the first case the solution is fallaciously scientific and in the second fallaciously religious and faith-based. But, just as the theory of evolution by itself cannot demonstrate the truth of Girard's scene, no advantage accrues to the "Judeo-Christian faith" from such a supposition, and it ends up appearing even more incredible than our contemporary scientism would have us believe. Consistent in a different way with the Christian (and I think I may safely say, Jewish) tradition is the principle, not of the rational demonstrability of revelation but of its compatibility with rationality.

The first thing to do to avoid falling into Bandera's revealing impasse is to forgo giving the concept of imitation or mimesis the central role, as simplistically maintained by Girard, who considers this to be intuitively self-evident, just as he does the concepts of desire and transfer. In that way I will be able to retrieve important aspects of other theories that form the disregarded tradition to which I am here referring.

One circumstance that also emerges incidentally from Bandera's comments is that imitation is absolutized as the only possible approach for description, and explanation can add nothing more than it contains, namely the imitative or gregarious behavior that we share with many evolved animals, particularly with many superior mammals and above all with the primates, our ancestors and fellow members of the same biological group. This emerges clearly from the work of two authors worth reexamining at this point since they unintentionally anticipate certain themes of crucial importance for my perspective.

6. Anticipations in Durkheim and Freud

The first is Durkheim who, in an important note to *Les règles de la méthode sociologique*, criticizes Gabriele Tarde for recognizing imitation as the genetic factor giving rise to all social phenomena. Durkheim objects that the explanation simply fails to explain the *explicandum*:

> It appears quite clear [*bien résulter*] that imitation not only does not always express what is essential and characteristic in the social fact but actually

> never expresses it. No doubt every social fact is imitated and . . . tends to spread [*se généraliser*], but this is because it is social, that is to say, binding. Its power to spread is not the cause but the consequence of its sociological character. If social facts alone produced this effect, imitation might serve, if not to express them, at least to define them. But an individual state that spreads [*fait ricochet*] does not cease to be individual for that reason. Moreover, we might ask ourselves if "imitation" is the most appropriate word to describe propagation due to a coercive influence. Using this single term confuses very different phenomena that ought to be kept distinct.[92]

What characterizes "social facts" is their "coercive influence" affecting individuals through the mere fact of existing and shaping every aspect of their lives, to such a degree that an individual independent of society is inconceivable. This coercive influence spreads through imitation, which, for Durkheim, consists essentially in the response of each individual to a collective stimulus that is to be explained in itself and responds to distinct, more original characteristics. Durkheim refuses Tarde's positivistic idea of imitation, against which he will never stop being polemical,[93] and it is true that Girard's further criticism that Tarde ignores mimetic violence and the victimary solution, the two devastating phenomena on which Girard insists, makes his own mimesis appear to be a far more complete phenomenon, suitable to rank as a universal explanatory principle. However, this is not so. Imitation remains imitation and nothing else, as Bandera rightly states, whereas the victimary process has its own unmistakable features as does, above all, the resulting new collective configuration, a state of peaceful unanimity around the victim, which all the evidence suggests is not the flat social reconciliation imagined by Girard but a new state radically and qualitatively different. And that state, with its internal dynamic and huge potential, is the real factor for explaining culture, while imitation is the necessary but insufficient prerequisite for what takes place in the scene of origin, besides being its behavioral and social consequence once the origin has been realized.

Durkheim is unaware of the genetic processes leading from animal imitation to human society, but he registers, as it were, the point of departure—the generic imitation indispensable for social life—and the point of arrival: the coercive, constructive force that governs society's operations as a whole. And from this he draws the scientifically correct conclusion that they are two clearly distinct phenomena and that only the coercive/constructive factor introduces what is essential in human societies, going beyond imitation's simple action/reaction mechanism, which in itself does not rise above the horizontal behavioral plane of individual members of society (this is why Durkheim speaks of an "individual state"). It is true that in certain cases imitation becomes collective and actually unanimous, but then the resulting situation is completely different precisely because it is connected. The frighteningly specific phenomenon of the *mass* came to obsess the writer and essayist Elias Canetti, given its capacity to do things that no single individual would ever do alone,[94] even *des actes d'atrocité*, as Durkheim perceptively observes,[95] though he refrains from examining them more closely.

It would be unfair to criticize Durkheim for a lack of perception without bothering to understand what he wanted to say. When he writes of a coercive force marking out social facts, what he has in mind is not just the mass but something else besides, a phenomenon not exceptional in itself but important exactly for being unexceptional, since it evinces the powerful silent factor on which the existence of every human society depends, an invisible, ubiquitous constraint enabling the members of a society to live together, to collaborate, and, by complying with it, even to become free, creating their own small but significant area of action and choice. This powerful phenomenon corresponds to what I mean by *mediation*, with the difference that my mediation also includes the critical moment of genesis, and does so without any reductionistic impoverishment since collective mediations fulfill their purpose, their internal raison d'être under normal stable working conditions, creating and defining human reality and the world, which correspond to what I mean by *object* and the *objectual dimension*. Understood in this way, mediation shows itself to possess a distinct and independent meaning in respect to imitation, but to establish the concept firmly it seems appropriate to go back to Freud since he was also drawn to the distinctive phenomenon of the crowd or mass and, in trying to explain it, had to decide between imitation and other factors emerging from his analyses.

Freud deals with the subject in *Mass Psychology and Analysis of the Ego*, written after the catastrophe of the Great War and the appalling phenomena of organized mass violence associated with it,[96] and that were also cause for some of Thomas Mann's reflections. Freud mentions Tarde's imitation in passing and devotes much more attention to a series of closely related notions, such as Gustave Le Bon's suggestibility (chap. 2), William McDougall's group mind and the emotional contagion that binds it together (chap. 3), and Wilfred Trotter's gregariousness (chap. 9). Freud allows some truth to these reconstructions but remains dissatisfied with their partial, descriptive character, feeling the need to identify "another source" (eine andere Quelle) that can explain all aspects of the mass phenomenon: primarily the need for a leader and the ability of the mass to organize itself in stable hierarchies endowed with a tradition, such as the ecclesiastical and the military.[97] Freud differs little from Durkheim in seeing the mass as possessing a creative, stabilizing potential fundamental for society; by comparison, the ephemeral mass, the crowd, dominated by irrational impulses that can quickly turn to violence, is an unstable transient phenomenon and deceptive if considered in isolation since it tends to lead scholars to favor defensive, negative evaluations that prevent proper understanding (as Girard shows). Unlike Durkheim, however, Freud is well aware of the scenario of collective violence, first formulated in *Totem and Taboo* and repeated in *Mass Psychology*; his cautionary remark thus takes on special interest because it helps us to see that Girard's evaluation of the social fact was too reductive, even if it was a reaction to centuries of overoptimistic, superficial judgments that had cast a shadow over thinking about history and society, bringing discredit on all attempts to reach a more realistic vision.

I will leave aside Freud's strenuous efforts to square mass phenomena with psychoanalytic theory and look briefly at the partial or potential significance of some of his insights. His attitude toward the often-invoked factor of suggestibility or suggestion is one of basic scientific dissatisfaction: he refuses "to accept that suggestion, that ought to explain [*erklärte*] everything, should in its turn be excused from explanation [*Erklärung*],"[98] and this reaction could and should be our own when we think of a partly overlapping concept like imitation. The statement to start from is: "the mass is held together by some power [*Macht*],"[99] which is to be explained in itself, and is referred by Freud to the libido. This can unite human beings through a reciprocal bond of an amorous-sexual type, founded however on the distancing of the libidinal object that is transferred, shifted onto a common object, the supreme leader (*Oberhaupt*, *Führer*); the mass-individuals (*Massenindividuen*) organize themselves around this figure, making them mutually inaccessible, that is, accessible on strict conditions shared by all, with everyone obeying him as a consequence. Freud recognizes in this singular, elementary phenomenon the manifestation of a drive that is certainly libidinal but at first undifferentiated and connected to the emotional needs of the psyche, the libido of the ego leading to identification (*Identifizierung*) with a model for the ego, normally the father, that in this way becomes part of the ego's ideal.

This distinction goes beyond Freud's definition of narcissism, not simply because the drive at the basis of identification is not fully spent in self-desire, correctly targeted by Girard as illusory, but also because, on the contrary, it impels the ego to seek models with which to identify. Nor can Freud's identification be reduced to imitation as Girard understands it because it is not a generic, ubiquitous phenomenon shared with animals and only differentiated in human beings by its intensity, but a specifically human force hinging on the role of the model identified with, and it is itself directed toward defining and attaining the object, either directly or indirectly. Freud is straitjacketed by a psychologism that intercepts the phenomena that allow us to overcome it if we take the psychoanalytic mosaic to pieces, its figures fragmented as in a cubist painting, and reassemble it to make a more intelligible picture, in which other pieces not used by Freud can also find their place. And undoubtedly Girard's work of dismantling is useful here, provided we are prepared to ignore once again his more consistent but too partial image, an image that might be compared to a surrealist painting, seductive and easy to understand at the cost of overall intelligibility. This procedure may require twice the effort, but the reward is more than double and potentially exponential, opening the way to greater clarity about theory and to a new threshold in explanatory insight.

Only at first glance are Freud's analyses psycho-analyses, and proof of their potential comes from the impetus that they acquire as soon as they are brought into contact with the scene in *Totem and Taboo*. At the individual level, Freud established that "identification is the most ancient, originary form of emotional bonding [*Gefühlsbindung*]";[100] but if we remain at the level of subjective psychic history, as nearly all commentators do, we would have to transform the references to *Totem and Taboo* into the symbolic, imaginary projection of a solipsistic and ultimately unreal psychic drama, such as we find theorized in Lacan's structuralist Freudism. However much he may waver, finally presenting his future readers and followers with the ambiguous formula of the "scientific myth," Freud essentially moves in the opposite direction since he realizes that the strict pertinence of falling in love and hypnosis to mass identification, and the ways in which they differ from it (love's absorption in its object and the provisional, imaginary character of hypnosis), point toward a more ancient condition at a phylogenetic, not ontogenetic, level where exceptionally powerful collective identification must have occurred. This is why Trotter's gregariousness (*Herdentrieb*) is inadequate, describing the effect of this unprecedented aggregating force without penetrating to the cause: "from this drive [*Trieb*] no path [*Weg*] leads toward the need for a god [*Gottesbedürfnis*]."[101] Only such a divine figure could silence the "originary envy" (ursprünglichen Neid) that would divide the members of the community and establish new aggregating relational modes.[102] The conclusion is quite clear despite the implicit complications that still remain: "Social sentiment depends therefore on reversing an initially hostile sentiment and turning it into a bond [*Bindung*] of a positive kind having the characteristics of identification."[103] Man is therefore not a *Herdentier*, a gregarious animal, a banal social animal, but a *Hordentier*, an animal coming from the primeval horde, the *Urhorde*, that was the site of the creation and crystallization of the salient features of his whole history. The further, phylogenetic corollary is that "mass psychology is the oldest [*älteste*] form of human psychology,"[104] a destabilizing deduction, typical of Freud at his best, that takes us back beyond psychology of any kind whatever, essentially because it takes us to its very source.

The fact, then, that the leader of Freud's primeval mass was originally the father is in itself misleading and irrelevant, once we have put the accent on the identifying function of this divine father. In *Mass Psychology* the emphasis falls increasingly on the "divinization process" (Vergötten wurde) of the primeval father,[105] who is described in terms of Nietzsche's superman, situated in a distant past rather than an indeterminate future and restored to the present by psychoanalytical archaeology, in a temporal, cognitive concentration going beyond what Freud intended and reminiscent of Nietzsche's scenario announcing the death of God. If, on the one hand, as Girard writes, "it is the horde that incarcerates the collective murder within the paternal significance [*signification*],"[106] on the other hand this same horde, understood in its genetic signification, renders the father superfluous. In the expressions *Urhorde* and *Urvater*, the accent is on the *Ur-*.

Thanks to Durkheim and Freud, the strengths and limitations of Girard's ideas are now apparent, and that allows me to outline some of the essential points of my mediatory theory. I shall only touch on these, however, not because the time is not yet ripe to evaluate my inquiry into history but because I want the reasons for my approach and its consequences to emerge from the historical phenomena in the course of the inquiry itself. In this way I shall be able to trace back to my earlier commentary on Thomas Mann and the Dionysian scene in *The Magic Mountain*.

7. Mediatory or Ecstatic-Objectual Theory

In a transitional chapter in *Mass Psychology* Freud sets out a series of questions that are only apparently of secondary interest. After asking himself whether the leader of the mass might not be replaced by an idea or an abstract entity (*ein Abstraktum*),[107] he adds the following comment:

> The leader [*Führer*] or the guiding idea [*führende Idee*] could also evolve negatively; hatred of a certain person or institution could have a unifying effect and lead to emotional bonds [*Gefühlsbindungen*] on a par with positive attachment.[108]

There is a potential connection with Girard's scenario here with the victim in place of Freud's *Führer* and with the advantage that Girard's hypothesis has no need to assume arbitrarily that the psyche, father, leader, or guiding idea already exists: from this angle Freud's wavering between the ambivalent aspects of hate and positive attachment appears as superfluous rather than simply confusing, and everything is traced back to a single mechanism, to a universal, pliable factor such as mimesis. Nevertheless, Freud's vaguely explorative, wavering formulation has the advantage of conserving a greater quantity of data and stimulating hints: its cubist-like fragmentation of the psyche maintains more real and spatial coordinates compared to Girard's overselective surreality. The ambivalence between hate and positive attachment becomes less irritatingly generic if we place the accent on the need in every case for *Gefühlsbindungen* to constitute the mass, that is, for malleable transformative bonds whose value is not simply ambivalent but twofold, both destructive or creative according to how they are directed; and although Freud offers no explanation here, it is this creativeness that justifies introducing the *führende Idee* as a possible substitute for the *Führer*. Other systemic reflections, left aside so far, might find their proper place here.

Freud's ambivalent bonds (*Bindungen*) anticipate to some extent Bateson's double binds,[109] paradoxical causal structures that face a subject in front of two unavoidable and contradictory alternatives, bringing about an undecidable situation from which this subject (animal or human) will emerge either with serious damage to its faculties, in the case of a failed solution, or with cognitive empowerment when the solution is successful. Bateson's double bind, used by Girard only in negative terms for describing his rivalry,[110] is much clearer compared to Freud's ambivalence and, together with a systemic and complex approach, provides a useful epistemological and logical framework for the phenomena we are going to study. However, systemic or complex approaches can prove their pertinence only by acknowledging the highest complexity, that of the human cultural systems studied in their inner laws of existence and functioning.[111] As Durkheim wrote, this opens up to science "a new world that surpasses all the others in complexity [*dépasse tous les autres en complexité*],"[112] and we should explore and know such a world by means of a phenomenological-historical approach aiming to grasp the specific value of human culture, and its destructive/creative double bonds or double binds open to new feedbacks with external things transformed into meaningful objects. To this end all the theoretical contributions explained here must be made to interact, gaining a more organic and elastic view that is much more than the sum of its parts.

As regards the originary scene, we are in a position to reconstruct the most likely and logical sequence of a state of a double-binding internal crisis leading to a victimary solution, which was Freud's imperfect conjecture, more clearly delineated by Girard, at the cost of postulating the improbable situation of a terrifying total prohibition that might paralyze the hypermimetic animals and force them to make immediate, anxious attempts at sacred engineering in order to fend off the divinized violence. Freud's identification continually lapses into the realm of the psychological, which it ought to be establishing, and is insufficient to interpret the need for a leader to polarize the group's positive bonds, charged with an emotional force, at first manifested negatively, which now needs to be re-created in a positive way. This need for a leader ought, instead, to be related to my broader, more comprehensive idea of mediation and its constitutive link to an object that is to be understood as free of Freud's libidinal restrictions. Having shown us the shortcomings of Girard's theoretical model, the notion of the object suggests a more credible reconstruction of the genesis of culture.

At first, as Girard rightly insists, we must hypothesize a state of crisis but not one that entails, as he imagines, the absolute annihilation of the instinctual object. A much more likely situation would be a repeated experience of crisis, a series of crises that caused confusion in the relationships of dominance typical of prehuman animals and set at risk the fulfillment of the instinctual object that according to Freud is primarily mating, though not exclusively libidinal since Freud himself is the first to insist on the need for an affective tie as no less important. Moreover, the sexual object is only the most sensational instance of all the instinctual objects characterizing the life of prehuman animals. I call this crisis, originating in the conflict to gain a biological object no longer controlled by relationships of dominance and collectively threatening its attainment, an *objectual crisis* (while if the emphasis is on mediation as it is taking shape or on the crisis in mediations that are already historically constituted, I speak of *mediatory crisis*). In the large majority of cases, the crisis arose from sexual motives and began with the male members of the group but rapidly came to involve all its members, on account of the growth in mimetic ability of the infrahuman animal: without this sexual gravitation we could not understand the universality of the incest prohibition, conceivably only starting from internal conflicts forging to exogamy, though not in Girard's style since the whole process is triggered by the need to reach a safer object. Once the crisis had been resolved by singling out the victim (when this worked, obviously), the instinctual object turned out to be, far from destroyed, simply *returned*, with the new critical thresholds for spontaneous collective control introduced by the objectual crisis, influenced and shaped by the unprecedented experience of the collective violence resolving the crisis. So there is a double-binding sequence, *object-crisis-object*, with each sequence producing a biological object no longer the same as before since it is charged with the traumatic episode that makes it once more attainable, while the altered conditions gradually make it a center of attention that can no longer be entirely reduced to the sphere of instinct.

This infracultural process of destabilization and reconstitution of the biological object was in the first instance sexual, but not exclusively so, and it must have influenced the evolution of the infrahuman animal, modifying its somatic makeup and increasing the sexual differentiation/complementarity to give greater stability to the male–female bond, as Darwin understood.[113] Without a more complete and satisfactory grasp of this infracultural stage, which Girard correctly postulated but did not describe, we shall understand very little of the subsequent introduction of culture.

To arrive at the origins of culture we need to be thinking of crises of increasing seriousness as what was at stake grew in value and came to occupy a presymbolic, presignifying position. In all probability the first crises did not follow the convulsive pattern of the lynchings for which we have historical and ethnographic evidence but resembled the sporadic outbreaks of collective violence encountered in chimpanzees and other mammals.[114] These episodes then became more frequent, changing in time from occasional incidents to regular occurrences. We may imagine the crises intensifying, either gradually or even with increasing speed, until a crisis arose that was virulent enough to lead some groups to extinction but which other groups overcame thanks to a correspondingly powerful victimary solution. This reconstruction fits in with Robertson Smith's hypothesis, with which Freud agreed, that the totemic meal is the most archaic sacrifice of all.

Omophagy, exemplified in the Dionysian cults and evoked by Thomas Mann, could be the very earliest symbolic form of collective violence, humankind's real scene of origin. Here we have an overwhelming experience that presumes no cultural tools and is performed quite literally with teeth and fingernails. This appears to be the absolute starting-point for symbolism, not separable from a dismembering of animal origin but at the same time having protosymbolic value that is assumed at once by all those taking part in the dismemberment. Moreover, such protosacrifice implies that collective action has now become magically and sacrally effective, at a powerful and elementary level where there is absolutely no distinction between sacrality and magic, and where the role of any recognizable divinity is quite superfluous. Divinity is not the unlikely result of a projection by those taking part in the collective action, as Freud and Girard still rationalistically postulate, but *the action itself* (Goethe's *Im Anfang war die Tat*), the living experience of a divine force taking possession and entering all of them to become part of their bodies in a physical-symbolic way that contrasts completely with the distancing strategy for the sacred imagined by Girard. When we come to analyze Greek Dionysian theology we shall find that what is essential about Dionysus, as Euripides represents him, coincides with the bloody deed perpetrated by his followers.

The experience of the object in that act is an experience no longer animal and not distinct from the experience that makes the object attainable. It must be conceived as *ecstasy* in the literal sense of the Greek ἔκ-στασις, that is, being "outside oneself" according to the settled sense suggested by the Greek verb *histemi*.[115] We have here a kind of ecstatic, collective proto-object containing the potential for all future developments and leading to the gradual signification of instinctual things, now understood as real objects, that is, as things endowed with a meaning—nay more: objects that are now the source of meaning because they stand before the community (they are literally *ob-jecta*:[116] compare German *Gegen-stände*) and make conceivable a stably organized world, though elementary.

With his conjectured contemplation of the dead body, Girard is in too much of a hurry to immediately thing-ize the first noninstinctual perception by seizing on what seems to be the most pertinent object, the victim. But by doing so he fails to address the central problem of defining the object and establishing its cultural origin; the biological, precultural object is confused with the culturally qualified object, and the object ends up actually being expelled from the real cultural phase, destroyed by the competing mimetic desires in their reciprocal rivalries and in the expulsive logic of prohibitions and the sacred. However, the real phenomenological, genetic, and historical nature of culture and of the cultural constitution of the human being is another thing altogether and shows us a meaningful system structurally directed toward an object that is no longer instinctual with the aim of achieving that object stably; in a word, its orientation is objectual as I have defined the term. Girard mistakes the pathology of rivalry and violent crisis for the physiology of human cultural systems, even though it is true that human physiology could only have become organized in response to extremely serious internal pathologies that threatened (as they continue to threaten) the survival of an animal so complicated as to win through only in extremis after exposing its entire endowment, at first biological and then cultural, to the crisis. More than any other philosopher, Bataille grasped the extreme, ecstatic nature of human being, so extreme and open to ecstasy that it transcends nature itself from which it nevertheless comes.

The ecstatic Event that is the source of every object and is itself Object, not in the static sense of an already defined reality but dynamically as an *objectual function* that can transform things into objects (*obiecta*), invents and colonizes the world. It is therefore what acts as a mediatory force between the group and symbolically connotated reality, the protomediation that serves both as intermediary and supreme model although it is still indeterminate and perceived on the level of a divinizing and sacral experience.[117] For this reason, I define my theory as *mediatory* or, with regard to the genesis of culture, *ecstatic-objectual*. My theory does not accept at all the mechanical functioning of Girard's transfer and if anything it is closer to Freud's identifying transference, though without any psychology involved; and, needless to say, it rejects Girard's artificial distinction between the two transfers since it concerns a single indivisible process, a single genetic act of group reorganization at the expense of a victim cast out of the group so that it may reenter in transfigured, creative forms that become the real purpose of the whole process. But it is the very idea of a transfer that must be rejected, since it depends on a positivistic idea of imaginary or even hallucinatory experience, whereas we have to understand how it was possible to discover a new dimension of meaning that becomes a perception of the whole world.[118] No hallucination can produce culture, otherwise science itself would be a sort of bad dream. The ecstatic-objectual mediation is not a dreamlike projection, but the new source of the community's objectualizing energy and a new level of reality, definable neither as imaginary nor simply objective, but rather *imaginalis*,[119] that is, existing in an unprecedented relationship between a detached external object and a collective subject that to some extent corresponds to Husserl's correlation but in a radically historical and genetic fashion. This mediatory and mediating process is a new symbolic reality, open to possibly endless future symbolic developments through which it remains intact and actually invigorated, representing the true lifeblood of every culture and every human being.

Omophagy is not necessarily the only way envisaged by my version of hominization; to work effectively it only requires the omophagic scene to be the most incisive and influential event in the life of prehuman communities, remaining so impressed on the group's memory that it became repeatable in ritual and, to the extent that the protohuman animal will develop its expressive and linguistic capacities, an enigmatic fact (*factum*, πρᾶγμα) to be remembered and explained in myth. Only a particularly violent event of great intensity as an experience would appear adequate to leave a mark on memory and behavior so permanent as to bring about collective repetition, imitation by the group itself, thus giving rise to the first real sacrifice. In my theoretical formulation, I should point out, the role of imitation is still important, not as the definitive explanation precluding all further thoughts on the subject but as a general, instrumental factor that acquires direction and becomes fruitful only when the mediatory and ecstatic-objectual event crystallizes. It cannot therefore be confused with mimetic desire, which, as real desire, belongs to a very much later stage in history and, as a mimesis of animal origin, belongs to antecedent events that were in themselves necessary but not sufficient. To round off this chapter and demonstrate the potential of my approach I want now to give a brief outline of how the various stages in hominization can be reconstructed starting from my idea of mediation and taking into account recent scientific research.

8. Hunting, Fire, and Burial

In principle, ecstatic-objectual mediation can adequately explain all stages of the hominization process, which is to be understood not as a series of successive stages but as so many attempts to resolve the paradox of a prehuman animal cohabiting and interacting with a symbolic being destined to become modern man over a very long period of time, the absolute predominance of *H. sapiens* being of relatively recent date only. The long infracultural stage, recognizable in *Australopithecus*, forebear of the *Homo* genus, was followed by a first hominizing stage linked to species that were capable of working stone with some plan in mind, and probably endowed with language: *Homo habilis*, the first species with stable cultural attributes of which traces remain, and *Homo rudolfensis*, another possible species that appeared at the same time or a little later.[120] We might hypothetically assign the omophagic origin of culture to those early species, but it goes without saying that, as far as such remote ages are concerned, we lack a huge amount of data and wait for further discoveries that will affect the present picture.[121] One element does clearly emerge from a detailed analysis of Bed I at Olduvai Gorge in Tanzania, the oldest known site relating to early hominids (namely *H. habilis*)[122] that is associated with both faunal remains and stone tools, the taphonomic analysis suggests that these first hominids were active hunters without the passive scavenging attributed to them in previous reconstructions.[123] This is a tiny but highly significant item of information, because group hunting making use of stone tools implies complex coordination and a long process of learning involving some forms of articulate language and corresponding cognitive capacities, together with collective transmission of acquired knowledge. A mere process adaptive to environmental conditions is no doubt necessary but not sufficient to explain such a sophisticated organization which shows itself to be both exosomatic in the creation of a long-term cultural lore, and endosomatic, primarily in the increase of brain size and the creation of new specialized brain areas. There had to be a powerful generative source capable of causing and nurturing such massive changes, a source very close to the hominids and within the group, and sacrifice appears the best candidate.

Other finds could provide further clues, like the use of red ochre,[124] a universal symbol for dried human blood in archaic cultures, whereas the circle of stones recognized in Olduvai Bed I, which I myself had once seen as a possible symbolic reproduction of a circle around the victim, cannot be credited with significance since it is probably the accidental result of depositional events.[125] Nevertheless, something of my previous reasoning about the Olduvai find remains valid, for the same scientist who dismantled the old hypothesis of an intentional stone circle writes that the site "acted as a 'central place' to which hominids repeatedly brought surplus food. This behavior was probably triggered by intentional foodsharing."[126] Thus there was a spatial organization around "a 'central place'" of essential value to the whole group: from a strictly scientific viewpoint, this would seem related only to hunting and eating animal food, but a wider analysis suggests that the activity of "intentional foodsharing" must have had a symbolic meaning as well, considering that the act of intentionally sharing meat had important religious connotations in the archaic and ancient world, as we shall see in Greek civilization. Even though the available data will not support a protoreligious significance of such a place, such a significance gives a perfect rationale for this central and shared (sharing) organization of the collective space.

A second highly important stage, richer in fascinating data, was reached with *Homo erectus*, the first species to go out of Africa, colonizing Asia and creating thereby a differentiation that many scholars today recognize as two distinct species: *H. ergaster* for Africa and *H. erectus* for Asia. *H. ergaster/H. erectus* was responsible for the second great leap in human evolution, the use of fire; not for nothing did the ancient Greeks in their myth of Prometheus, the Titan who helped humanity "by stealing the far-beaconing flare of untiring fire,"[127] fix this at the origins of human history. The passive domestication of fire might have taken place already 1.5 million years ago,[128] and is not to be explained away by functionalistic pseudo-explanations about prehistoric man recognizing the usefulness of combustion.

It makes no sense to imagine that innovations and discoveries can be explained in terms of subsequent advantages deriving from them that for the most part were inconceivable at the time of their inception. In the case of fire especially, it is of little use to imagine that prehistoric man found it natural to come near a natural (actually mysterious) phenomenon that certainly terrified him as much as it normally terrifies all other animals. Certainly, some animal species developed adaptive attitudes toward fire, such as "opportunistic fire-margin hunting or scavenging,"[129] but these behaviors appear to be occasional and limited, while we need to explain why humans have been attracted by fire as such, to the point of changing their habits and modifying their physical characteristics.[130] A more consistent explanation is that if human beings managed at some time to curb this impulse to flee, it was because fire started to become an *ob-jectum*, a *Gegen-stand* now conceivable in itself, as an entity endowed with meaning because it was an ecstatic source of perception and cognition. We can imagine a sacrifice performed with fire and sacralizing fire, but there is no need to postulate a specific sacrifice performed in the manner of Girard's theory, in a still mechanical and exterior way. It would have been enough if one or more members of a community died in a fire, their death then being assimilated to the death of a sacrificial victim and leading to their sacralization and sacralization of the flames that killed them. Ecstatic-objectual mediation is not a predetermined mechanism but a flexible creative function interacting with the community and the surrounding world in a great variety of different ways, and it is not exhausted by a single process. Whatever may have happened in detail, fire became the community's divine and mediatory force; it was domesticated and kept within the community, again according to dynamics that conflict with Girard's idea of expulsion, since fire became a permanent and central acquisition in the life of the community: at this point the unlimited positive spin-off from this extraordinary new resource became apparent, and it was all seen as a gift of its divine mediation. Needless to say, even if the direct cause of the discovery of fire was not sacrifice by burning, such sacrifice must have gone hand in hand with the use of fire in order to ensure its safekeeping. We begin to grasp the divine status of fire if we think about the most impressive source of fire on earth, volcanic activity, a real kratophany (manifestation of divinity through a superhuman power) that is always an object of worship and sacrificial interpretations in both ritual and myth in all the archaic cultures acquainted with this devastating phenomenon.

Another possible clue to the mediatory origin of this discovery might come from the fact that ignition, the active domestication of fire, appears have been discovered several hundreds of thousands of years later.[131] Leaving aside the important question of a precise chronological reconstruction, humanity was in any case left for quite a long period with complicated and unsafe techniques for conserving the "untiring fire," but the objective difficulty of finding an effective procedure for lighting was not so great after all if we think of the highly developed activity of dressing stone.[132] The simplest explanation of this slowness could be that any manipulative technique of fire went against its sacred and divine character, so that it was only after a long period of time that human beings became self-confident enough to handle this superior and godlike force on which the whole community depended for its survival. We might even imagine the moment when the active domestication of the god-fire was performed as a kind of prehistoric and impersonal (prepersonal) version of the Christian Eucharist, where the son of God dies and is born again bringing light to humanity. That really could be the igneous version of what Nietzsche, evoking in aphorism 125 the ancient symbols of light and celestial bodies, would call the death/birth of God. A further sign of the numinous sacredness of fire is the incredible persistence into historical times of very old rites for conserving a perennial hearth. Such a persistence was possible only thanks to the capacity of teaching and transmitting the knowledge related to fire through a language even more complex than that necessary to learn hunting and stone dressing, and directly points to the sacred and cognitive function of myth.

I have considered the example of fire at some length, not just because it is objectively important but also because it seems to illustrate my theoretical approach very clearly. Enough has already been said about the third decisive stage of *H. sapiens*, linked to the discovery of burial, for its theoretical aspect to be understood. A big jump in time is involved here given that between *H. erectus/ergaster* and *H. sapiens* we have, as already said, the still little-known history of *Homo heidelbergensis*, who gave origin to *H. neanderthalensis* and *H. sapiens* and began colonizing Europe, and we shall examine below a spectacular image coming from the Neanderthal man and capable of shedding a limited, but powerful, beam of light on this largely unknown history. For now I want to focus on the momentous step of the invention of funeral rites for it provides us with further invaluable clues about our own species and the cultural heritage possibly shared with *H. neanderthalensis* since this species also practiced some forms of burial, though apparently in less systematic fashion. It must be added that the earliest known burials involved only a tiny fraction of the population, may even have been animal burials, and in some cases reveal marks or possible traces of violence, all elements that are perfectly well explained if we start from the hypothesis that prehistoric burial practices derived from sacrificial rites. However, the tendency toward a common treatment applied to a restricted section of animals and human beings highlights the fact that things are more complex than an evocative scenario of established and defined funeral rites. Besides, there is a wide range of treatments of corpses/carcasses in the oldest known finds, not only inhumation of the whole body or inhumation incorporating mutilations like beheading, but also exposition and funerary cannibalism.[133] We can perceive a selective and classifying attitude according to criteria that in general elude us, apart from a few clues detectable with the help of the sacrificial hypothesis. In any case, the elasticity of my mediatory approach in its structural and explorative connection with the object should be appreciated, since in itself it allows for a wide variety of possible solutions depending on the circumstances and the environment. The particular power I assign to inhumation is not in contradiction with other ritual solutions and could probably have interacted with them, with a tendency both to prevail and intertwine, as the archaeological evidence confirms.

Historically, grave burial rites are intertwined with funeral cannibalism, which must be a very ancient practice, and with fire applied to the dead bodies because their sacrificial potential was felt to be too dangerous and called for such radical measures as cooking and incineration. Always a decisive factor in eating, burial, and incineration was the need to neutralize the dead through sacred taboos and to make them beneficent by establishing the correct formula for sacred commerce with them, a new reassuring formula for possessing and being close to them. If funeral cannibalism, closely linked to omophagic sacrifice and useful as a reliable source of supplementary protein, can be deemed the earliest way of dealing with dead bodies, incineration would seem to have come at a later stage but before the discovery of burial, though in actual fact the contrary appears to be the case. Incineration conserves the character of nonperformed burial and implies a capacity to represent the dead as independent beings with whom a proper, stable relationship is to be created, which relates to its prior stabilization as representation and symbol through burial. Nevertheless, this is now our established way of distinguishing and classifying such ritual objects, and we may easily imagine more fluid situations interacting with the experiences of a human group, like those just described relating to environmental fire.

Another important point has to do with our use of the category of "religion," normally excluded in today's scientific research without any serious discussion,[134] and vice versa utilized in a loose way by the theoretical approaches explained in this chapter, apart from the more rigorous case of Durkheim. My idea of ecstatic mediation fills this lacuna nicely, considering that it requires only an initial division between a kind of collective protoself and the surrounding world newly perceived as an external and superior object, where "religion" is the simplest and most intuitive label for such an extraordinary experience. Thus we have to rule out our complex idea of religion as a set of cults and beliefs concerning defined divinities. It must be emphasized again that a belief in divine figures with recognizable personalities, far from going back to the beginnings of culture as Freud and Girard affirm, has to be connected to the decisive stage of burial abstraction. However, all those who were specialists in charge of the sacred and sacrifice must have had a personalizing function linked to sacrifice; such figures as witches, sorcerers, shamans, guardians of fire (usually old women), or in more developed societies sacred monarchs and priests, were substitute victims, provisionally and permanently. In all these cases the determining factor is once again the power of the sacred to mediate and objectualize, investing certain figures with a precise role made possible by their close association with sacrifice. A member of the group could be invested with the sacred's mediatory power in a variety of unexpected ways, not necessarily substitutive in the sense of a nonperformed sacrifice: once sacrifice is vigorous as a cultural and objectual engine, it can produce variations on the slightest provocation and by reason of any symbolic proximity where, at a particular moment, the substitution became a mental substitution as well.

A further conjecture might shed light on this crucial passage, which is related both to *H. sapiens* and its relationship with the Neanderthal man. An essential role might have been played by the shaman, the ecstatic figure capable of reliving manifold and extreme forms of sacrifice, beginning with dismemberment.[135] A more recent hypothesis, held by David Lewis-Williams and other scientists, explains prehistoric art as a kind of stenographic record of shamanistic collective experiences and considers the shaman to be a decisive figure in *H. sapiens*' hominization and the development of his incredible mental powers.[136] This idea could have much wider implications if we interpret in a similar way the oldest complex painting recently discovered in La Pasiega (Spain), dating back to more than 64,800 years and attributed to *H. neanderthalensis*.[137] It is an articulated red ochre image representing, on the left side, a "scalariform motif" as it has been called,[138] a kind of three-rung ladder with two partially depicted animals at the top and bottom and a large ribbon-like constellation of regular spots over it; and on the right side a human figure with ornithomorphic features dancing and presumably experiencing a vision, perhaps evoked by the symmetrical and inverted body that completes his figure. Analogies with less ancient evidence related to shamanistic rites are impressive[139] and suggest a similar explanation but much earlier than so far supposed, that is, the ecstatic experience of another dimension whose ritual performance is represented in the anthropo-ornithomorphic figure while the ladder and the ribbon-like formation might describe the stages and final result of a ritual ascent. Also notable is the chiastic scheme of the two symmetric and inverted parts of the animals, probably a cervid and a swine, that are the representational results of sacrificial and hunting practices of dismemberment, and the dynamic system of compositional weights and counterweights of the anthropo-ornithomorphic dancer, apparently coming from the empty space in the middle of the ladder: there is a figurative rhythm possibly connected to a musical part of the performance, and expressing in any case a very complex mental life. If my reading is correct, the role of shaman might have been previously influential for the cultural/mental evolution of *H. neanderthalensis* as well,[140] though an accessory hypothesis would be that this role became particularly systematic and intense in *H. sapiens* up to the point of reaching an entirely cultural evolution. The greater number of artistic finds dating since roughly forty thousand years ago suggests an increasing frequency of such artifacts and a more intense social and psychic life in our own species, which substantially stops its somatic evolution in the same period.

Leaving aside the richer landscape deriving from the recent discoveries and to be studied and discussed in much more depth, it must be added that the shamanistic theory is extremely fascinating, but alas it is still conceived in the positivistic terms of hallucinatory experience, whereas this transition should be interpreted as the discovery of a new objectual dimension of reality, that is, of reality understood as object and world. My idea of ecstatic-objectual mediation provides a more consistent explanation of the shamanistic cult and its possible relationship with our speciation. The shaman was a real incarnated mediation, endowed with all the magic and sacramental means for reinstating and reinvigorating an objectual sphere constantly on the verge of crisis. And sacrifice provides the engine for such a spectacular process. The shaman was the human and divine go-between thanks to whom *H. sapiens*, already symbolically and logically prepared by the ritual doubling of the grave, acquired the power to mentalize sacrifice, and in this way developed more individualized figures of sacred mediators needed for the salvation of the community.

There remains a question to be dealt with before taking up my inquiries into ancient Greece and Christianity, namely, Why to start from ancient Greece? What are the reasons that make it advisable or necessary in the light of the theoretical and genetic arguments set out above? One answer has already been provided by the scene in *The Magic Mountain*, but something more should be added. Greece is the perfect example of a great culture situated halfway between the archaic world from which it came and to which it remained bound by a thousand ties, and our world, profoundly shaped by Greek and Roman civilization but at the same time separated from it by the even more profound influence of Judaism and, especially, Christianity. Greece thus provides the perfect testing ground to examine and verify the great compendium of culture represented by the philosophical tradition reviewed and hopefully carried forward in these introductory pages.

It will also be interesting to see whether the Judeo-Christian tradition—and Christianity in particular, since it represents that tradition in its most theologically daring and historically influential form—really did perform the demystifying and revelatory role ascribed to it by Girard and previously attributed to it by Nietzsche though in hostile, inverted terms. From their diametrically opposed viewpoints both encourage us to make a full-scale comparison of ancient paganism and Christianity, a subject too vast in itself to be dealt with in this already overextended chapter. I would just add that the comparison contains much truth, the fundamental truth of Western civilization, but not only in the conflicting and polemical terms imagined by Nietzsche and Girard, who both subscribe to a logic of rivalry expressed by the historical opposition between *Kultur* and *Zivilisation*. At a deeper level, we shall find a common lore and very similar problems for discovering universal mediations capable of taking shape at different levels and conquering new realms of reality. This is proved by the fact that the hostility or indifference shown at present toward the Christian tradition is matched by growing marginalization of the Greek and Roman tradition that is its indelible background (not to mention the decline of cultures, like the Italian, entirely founded on balanced dialogue between Christian and classical elements). We shall put these claims to the test, step by step, as we explore the texts, topics, and authors in the course of this study.

I propose to start by going back to the ritual situation evoked by Thomas Mann: the sacrifice of the child Dionysus. It takes us straight to the heart of the ancient Greek world of myth and ritual, and to the problems of method, theory, and history implicit in studying it.

VOLUME I

The Great Mediations of the Classical World

Mystery Cults and Tragedy

Though they make procession for Dionysus
and chanted hymns to the shameful parts
this is the greatest shame:
the same are Hades and Dionysus
for whom they rave and make bacchanals.

—Heraclitus of Ephesus

Lady, who are these others in the moon's vat
Sleepdrunk, their limbs at odds?
In this light the blood is black.
Tell me my name.

—Sylvia Plath, *Maenad*

1.

The Labyrinth of Mythology

1. The Place of Myth in the History of the West

Myths are an invaluable resource for studying ancient civilizations, and even more so for the clues they provide to previous human history, the infinite prehistory that saw the birth and development of humankind and left little more than mute, fragmentary traces. Classical mythology, to which we must now turn, has obviously come down to us in the form of written texts—those that survive of course—but there must have been oral transmission over an extremely long period of time. Such a tenacious transmission can only be explained with the great importance attached to what had to be faithfully transmitted and appears not to be separable, therefore, from the divine and performative power of rite and its strong tendency to remain inalterable. In their oldest detectable forms myths appear to be one and the same with rites, though their goal was to narrate and make intelligible the enigmatic event itself represented by ritual and the mysterious external reality that the ritual allowed practitioners to control and stabilize. These different functions stress an asymmetry between the two halves of this mediatory unity, a unity never perfectly symmetrical and uniform because it arises from the collective experience of crisis and the subsequent solution of sacrifice, which first had to be done and then had to be told, so as to recover and expand the objectual need from which it arose. The representation and knowledge of the world stemmed from the process of destruction and rebirth of the sacrificed object made necessary by the objectual crisis, and this asymmetrical and reconstructive movement gave mythology its typical cognitive momentum, widely studied by Claude Lévi-Strauss, so that we can safely say that myth was the very first science of humanity, by far older than philosophy (a good explanation for the bias against sacrifice and philosophy of that scholar). In parallel with myth, we must add the fascinating case of the various arts (dance, music, painting, sculpture), having the very same ritual origin but using different expressive means: actually, they were the rite itself reproducing itself, as in the Neanderthal picture where we perceive, together with the visual-symbolic reproduction of a shamanistic performance, a dance and perhaps a musical part of the represented ceremony.

In historical times, as the relationship with ritual became looser, mythology acquired an increasing autonomy and evolved into its manifold derived forms, such as literature; sciences like mathematics, astronomy, and medicine; genealogical tales about the kings; law; etc.—all of them forms that were controlled by a powerful sacerdotal caste in the Near East civilizations but became detached from their religious matrix in ancient Greece (particularly regarding philosophy and science) and Rome (above all regarding the juridical and political field), while other postmythical forms such as literature and historiography were equally shared by both civilizations. In the classical world mythology remained vital, alongside its many derivations by now specialized and independent, and became a flexible all-purpose instrument, offering an almost unlimited range of combinations that could transmit both ancient and revised material of every type. Its focus was politics and propaganda in centralized Rome, where mythology remained more institutional and ritual in character, while in polycentric Greece, split up into numerous local traditions and open to a diversity of cultural influences, it was more varied and sapiential.

However, this first description, which is roughly based on what we saw in the introduction and anticipates what we shall see in the following chapters, can only be the beginning of our inquiry from a methodological and theoretical viewpoint. How do we reach and define the object of all the myths and at the same time establish a sound explanation of their origin?

Are there some recognizable laws or regularities that lie behind them? In order to give a satisfactory answer, we should avoid applying to mythology too abstract and indiscriminate a method but start from mythology itself, as required by an authentic phenomenological-historical approach.

These marvelous and terrifying "stories" (μῦθοι in Greek, *fabulae* in Latin) are so stratified and various that their overall interpretation presents a problem, not only because of their enigmatic appearance, infinite kaleidoscopic mutations and diversity of derivative forms and versions, but also for an intrinsic reason that on closer scrutiny reveals itself to be the key for solving the riddle they present. Mythology creates so many interpretive difficulties because it possessed the characteristics of interpretation *ab origine* and has always been interpretation throughout its never-ending history. Moreover, since that hermeneuticity is structural and relates to an active desire to communicate or to dodge communicating, what appears to be a further hermeneutic complication in fact allows us to trace the history of the interpretations of myth and to establish with certainty that an internal key to interpretation has existed all along , not unlike the keys familiar to us for the simple reason that they are dealing with the same need, the same problem.

Such an approach does not underrate the presence of breaks and interruptions. Indeed it assumes their existence since wherever there has been a desire to communicate something to someone there has always been a complementary need to deny it to someone else. Mythology is a set of stories told in favor of someone and against someone else. While, on the one hand, their transmission followed the chain logic of repetition and inherited tradition, on the other they went through many alternations based on the logic of ousting and hostility. Thus there were various epochs of mythology that reflected and gave support to corresponding mediations and supplanted others, and they bring us effortlessly to the time when the break with the past was more marked, and we shall need to pay particular attention to these turning points in mythology if we are to understand it properly and insert our own interpretive position into the picture we are trying to reconstruct.

In order to catch the shift from the ancient approach toward mythology to our own, we must make a short excursus into what we shall deal with at greater length in the Intermezzo and the second volume. I am referring to the Christian affirmation of the Eucharist, the only bloodless sacrifice, which ushered in the beginning of our era, for the first time interrupting the immemorial continuity of sacrificial rites, an almost invisible event that was destined to have far-reaching repercussions on the Western reading of mythology as well.

This interruption in ritual is unparalleled in antiquity outside the extraordinary religious melting-pot of Middle Judaism;[1] not by chance, the only comparable break occurs in 70 AD[2] after the Romans destroyed Jerusalem and the Temple when the Judaic sacrificial cult suffered a serious and irreversible crisis. This is not the place to go into the details of those complicated cult changes; for our present purposes we need only note that the Christian concentration and revision of sacrifice in the Eucharist certainly predates the fateful destruction of the Temple, whereas it was only with the second Judaic war and the total destruction of the Jewish capital in 135 AD that the interruption in the Jerusalem cult became final and complete. However, it must be added that the great cultic change of the Eucharist, concentrating the previous sacrificial rites in the very person of Jesus, was prepared by the concentration of sacrifice in the Jerusalem Temple, together with its highly controversial status according to the contrasting views of several Jewish sects: the best-known example is the community of Qumran, which boycotted the sacrificial service of the Temple and replaced it with "their entire liturgical and ethical practice" while waiting for the final battle against the forces of evil.[3] A strong eschatological attitude was inseparable from these daring ritual innovations, usually following a kind of interim logic, but it remains undeniable that the Qumran community never rejected the sacrificial practice, which was indeed destined to continue and to be renewed in the Last Judgment,[4] whereas it was the sacrificial metamorphosis of the Eucharist, in which sacrifice is transformed and overturned from within into an act of love, that was to become newly influential and historically irreversible. As a matter of fact, the reversal of sacrifice liturgically practiced by the followers of Jesus constituted an authentic silent revolution in ancient culture and would hardly have come about without deep roots in their master's teaching, fully part in its turn of the animated religious debate in Middle Judaism.[5]

The reconfiguration of sacrifice in Christianity is underrated by many interpreters today, but its real scale and central importance can be gauged from the fact that it threatened the survival of the new religion in connection with the highly sensitive question of the rites celebrated in honor of the Roman emperors. We shall deal with all this later, as far as possible, but in the present chapter, a related, and equally unnoticed , phenomenon brought about by Christianity ought to be mentioned, namely the radical interruption in transmitting the myths of the Greco-Roman world, long firmly entrusted to universalist processes of syncretistic coexistence but now suddenly exposed to complete, radical denial. Many aspects of the Christian rejection show it to be the typical reaction of one cult asserting its own rites and myths in the face of surrounding cults accused of impotence, falsehood, and wickedness; what is new is the connection with the central event of Christ's Passion, an event both ritual and mythical (told in *mythoi*) but first of all a fact, a concretely historical and documented *factum*, imbued with the biblical sense of history and with the rationally verifiable historicity previously established by Greek historians, which had influenced the composition of the historical books of the Old Testament. It is hard to determine this cultural influence because of denominational and confessional interests that have an inherent tendency to exclude it, and we shall come back to it. Nonetheless we are in a position to appreciate that the Christian interpretation of myth presents a highly original combination of factors, and while these component parts went unperceived by Christians themselves, they would condition successive ages and with the passage of time bring about a profoundly different approach to mythology as a whole.

The Christian revolution in mythology occurred in two major phases, needing about a thousand years to achieve its full potential. The first phase was Christianity's antipagan reaction itself, undoubtedly rejecting classical mythology in order to assert its own mythical-narrative world, but in doing so it introduced a more exacting criterion for admission, a new objectual threshold suitable for certifying certain myths as permitted, separating them from those that were unacceptable, now ignominiously branded as *mythoi* or *fabulae*. According to validation and control criteria that were to become the basis of subsequent methods, acceptance was given to all sacred stories strictly subordinate to and serving the absolute mediation of Christ. The second phase is represented by Christianity's critical reaction to the colorful miracle-filled mythography of the Middle Ages; it recognized the affinity to earlier mythologies and at the same time rediscovered the classical origins of its own rational standards for validation and control. A direct result of this was the rediscovery of ancient mythology by the humanists, beginning with Christian revision and reappraisal as seen at its most exalted level in Dante's

Divine Comedy, then followed by Giovanni Boccaccio's *Genealogia deorum*, and finally culminating in the Renaissance emulation of classical style.

From then on, the study of mythography in the West became increasingly independent. The Christian mentality induced a dual movement of rejection and recovery that became intermingled in a sort of self-reflection at the very dawn of the modern age when the wide-reaching geographical discoveries made European humanism aware of the immense variety of mythologies widely extant in space even more than in time. The coexistence of different mythological systems gradually entered Western European consciousness, disturbing the traditional scheme whereby the better mediatory and religious alternative over time came out on top and this led to unprecedented interactions and retroactions, but always starting from the humanist reappraisal of classical mythology in late medieval and early modern times. This all brought about great changes in hermeneutics that were to interact increasingly with the validation and control criteria of modern science. The forerunner of these changes in the early eighteenth century was Giambattista Vico's philosophy according to which human history follows providential cyclical laws of development starting from more primitive and vigorous stages, dominated by the "very bodily fantasy" (corpolentissima fantasia) of mythology,[6] and ending up in a more decadent phase from which a new fruitful cycle is destined to arise. His revolution actually consisted not so much in opposing his historicist vision against Cartesian rationalism as in demonstrating the latter's inadequacy and the need to surpass it with a superior rationality that was conscious of its own history.

That was the stated aim, but it remained very far indeed from being really achieved. No interaction took place between all these changes and contributions, in a willing, conciliatory spirit of cooperation; instead, what followed was a fierce logic of antagonism and opposition, typically human in itself but made worse by the modern crisis in traditional mediations and the fact that the mediations put forward to replace them were being used up at an ever faster rate. The humanist criteria and Vico's cycles were thus respectively opposed and ignored, though they still combined indirectly, stealthily so to speak, with both the scientific Enlightenment in its advance and the anti-Enlightenment reaction of romanticism and idealism that came after, but without a reconciliation between the two sides of the mythological contention, between rejection or acceptance.

As a result, after the birth of modern ethnography in the eighteenth century,[7] and the interest shown by Vico and the romantics in peoples as leading actors in a collective mythopoeia, rationalism returned in a new guise as positivism. This was by no means a monolithic block but included, in varying degrees, problems of comprehension that had arisen before, only now they were placed under the reassuring aegis of factual science (and how far positivism really was from being monolithic becomes obvious once we realize it could never have come into existence without the checks carried out much earlier by the church to test conformity with positive religion, that is, religion revealed and founded on fact). Positivism saw the need for a strictly scientific ethnology based on the vast amounts of ethnological data made generally available through European exploration and colonization. This scientific and cultural activity, albeit unpalatable to many nowadays, produced results of incalculable worth, as mentioned in the previous chapter, and led to the last major changes in the modern study of mythology. And that brings us to the themes of this chapter and of this first volume in general, where the dissociation between rejection and acceptance proved to be extremely fruitful.

Positivist ethnology brought classical studies to interact powerfully with knowledge of the great heritage of myths possessed by peoples at that time classed as "primitive." The more progressive scholars began to debunk the conventional, celebratory images—ancient no less than modern—of Greek and Roman mythology; they recognized a much earlier element in them, which endorsed Vico's view of primitive humanity but in an unexpected and traumatic way. For the first time, infinitely more archaic interpretations began to make their appearance among the partial, projective interpretations of Greco-Roman mythology, revealing the luminous classical world as home to ferocious religious practices and savage customs, where human life was a variable completely subordinate to the precise, effective performance of the rite. The price paid for classical harmony turned out to have been both high and well hidden. And yet, despite knowing this, the European world continued to take Greco-Roman civilization as its role model for culture and education. It was indeed a further reason to study it, not, however, with a view to elevate it to an eternal objectual sphere but to grasp and investigate the changeable, transitory nature of all cultural orders. A subtly anticlassical mentality came to disturb the *hortus conclusus* of the old humanism, and bolder spirits ventured to taste of the forbidden fruit of the tree of knowledge of Good and Evil, fruit prohibited not by the God of the Bible this time but by the classical gods and heroes who had very good reason to cloak themselves in the splendid but mysterious apparel of an inscrutable mythology. Not by accident, Protestant Germany at the same time saw a formidable movement develop with a new scientific and philological approach to the study of the formation and significance of Old and New Testament texts, with particular reference to the enigmatic figure of the historical Jesus, which we shall be looking at in the Intermezzo and second volume of this book. But now we will pause to consider the *felix culpa* of the demythologizing of the ancient world.

The episode in *The Magic Mountain* mentioned earlier sums up this fall from the classical Eden, and its nostalgic evocation, in excellent fashion, and clearly has reference to the previous century's revolution in hermeneutics that was now irreversible. Friedrich Nietzsche's philosophy provides the most spectacular testimony to that revolution, accompanied by the more systematic and sober research of his friend Erwin Rohde and preceded by Johann Jakob Bachofen's investigation of matriarchy. This semiclandestine distribution of the forbidden fruits of knowledge could only benefit the historical study of antiquity, with a comparative approach that revealed a face never seen before, especially of ancient Greece whose civilization had been the cradle of philosophy and science and was the most studied and acclaimed. It all came about with an irresistible logic having historical necessity on its side, and in spite of the opposition and incomprehension of the more traditional philologists, such as the young Ulrich Von Wilamowitz-Möllendorf who, not without some good arguments but also polemically misunderstanding the reasons of Nietzsche's *Zukunftsphilologie* (ironically, the philology of the future), fiercely attacked *The Birth of Tragedy*.[8] Proof of the enduring validity of the new approach advocated by Nietzsche is to be found in the studies of James George Frazer and the Cambridge school of ritualists, with their enviable knowledge of the ancient world and their prephenomenological positivism which excluded none of the facts, and also in the work of the school of Émile Durkheim in France which influenced studies in England as well,[9] not to mention similar developments in research in Germany and Italy, unjustly ignored today.

But coming back to our methodological and theoretical concerns, what scientific justification is there for all these studies of classical antiquity and ethnology to turn to mythology in their quest for information about epochs and cultures otherwise lost in an impenetrable fog? The interpretive question we started from is restated with greater awareness in the complexity of its method and retroactions. The legacy of Greek rationalism, rediscovered in the West during the late Middle Ages and Renaissance, does not fail to raise its objections, with modern science, but an essential remark is that these very objections revive and carry further a conflict with mythical-religious knowledge that can be documented at its earliest in classical Greece, for example in the criticisms voiced by Hecateus of Miletus, Xenophones, and Heraclitus.[10] This first polemic against traditional mythology, developed inside a cultural world in our eyes a little less mythological, exhibits to us an interpretive conflict that has arisen *within myth itself*. A more phenomenological and internal viewpoint is thus required, capable of establishing a hermeneutic relationship with us taking in view one origin through all the conflicting viewpoints here considered. We can already sense that science and philosophy are simply the result of such conflicts and give expression to new metamyths that have been shaped and defined by pitting themselves against their predecessors, much older myths now felt to be inadequate in respect to the new cognitive and objectual achievements. In the modern age, with the growing rebellion against traditional religious and political mediations, this conflictual relationship could only intensify and deepen; historically, the Protestant Reformation provides the clearest example of a successful revolt of this kind.

All modern civilization was established by rejecting en bloc myth and everything it represented, that is to say, the prestigious institutions of the past and above all the church since the Reformation no longer understood the historical reasons for its existence. The Protestants took stories that had been regarded as true for hundreds of years and were the keystone of all historical verification, stripped them down to their essential scriptural nucleus—the first of the nuclei that would eventually constitute modern Bible studies—and in practice rejected all the medieval developments, condemning them as demonic mythical error. After the Protestant revolt against the perverse *fabulae* of the church of Rome, the Age of the Enlightenment with its appeal to reason discredited myth still further and consigned all mythology to the black night of superstition and the irrational. The fact that positivism in the nineteenth century retrieved this collection of stories confirms the metamythic fertility of all these reactions, even if the positivists paid the price of having to surround this mountain of information with a *cordon sanitaire* of skepticism and detachment. By way of compromise they agreed that archaic and classical mythology could be studied scientifically as long as they themselves and the general public were assured it was being done in the name of positive science, farsightedly prepared to examine all these beliefs because confident that it no longer had any mythological and religious illusions. Moreover, they could not have carried out that work without forcefully excluding the religious factor that had blocked or held back independent rational investigation in modern Europe following the bloodshed in religious wars of the sixteenth and seventeenth centuries.

This age of scientific inquiry was resoundingly successful in spite of the serious aforementioned limitations, which were necessary in themselves though they in turn came to hinder further progress in research. The best work of the period produced results to some degree definitive, demonstrating that myth has cognitive value since, as long as it has life, it rests on a solid basis of generative anthropological structures, such as are most accurately illustrated by Durkheim's social and religious categories. In that way it was gradually recognized that myths are not *fabulae* that change and vary at will, except in those periods when they have lost their vitality; on the contrary, they are tenacious configurations capable of enduring for thousands of years, because they are the self-interpretations of entire communities and the explanations they had to rely on to realize and represent their cults effectively—in a word, to survive. This also showed that fully vital myths formed an indivisible unit with the rites they explained and commented on.[11] However, it took some time for the idea to prevail that the rite precedes its accompanying myth, as can be seen from the fluctuating views of scholars in the late nineteenth and early twentieth centuries, and from the disparagement of sacrifice by Lévi-Strauss, with his characteristic scientistic animosity.

The extreme conservatism of myths derives from their genetic-structural linkage to the performative effectiveness of rites, so that they are able to transmit to a fully historical epoch symbols, themes, and behavior coming from the earliest prehistoric times. Their enormous heuristic potential also comes from this, since their interaction and compactness allows us to recover very ancient material and make credible reconstructions even analyzing single features where the larger whole has been lost but the inner logic is still traceable once we look at those features in the light of other mythical-ritual data and circumstantial evidence provided by history and archaeology. I am here anticipating my method for interpreting myths because I want to emphasize its close relationship to the great age of anthropology at the turn of the twentieth century when a similar approach was initiated in various forms, a resumption of a hermeneutic tradition going back to the Romantic period and beyond, to Vico and earlier scholarship ever since the Renaissance. For the most part those predecessors went unnoticed or met opposition, but now we see them clearly for what they were, which may indicate that a new phase in understanding myth is beginning, poised to overcome the misunderstandings systemic to modernity. The workings of myth can best be illustrated by a concrete example, and the following fits in well with the observations made at the end of the introduction and with what follows here.

The mythology of fire provides impressive proof of the power of conservation and transmission contained in the myth-rites that have come down to us. Frazer argues convincingly for their division into two large groups: an earlier group belonging to the phase of passive domestication when man learned to use fire but not how to light it and a second group linked to active domestication when fire-lighting techniques were acquired.[12] Today we know that passive domestication was the achievement of *Homo ergaster/erectus* and might date from about 1.5 million years ago, which means we may fairly conclude that myths and rites involving a sacred fire that must never be allowed to go out, such as the flame kept alight by the Vestals in ancient Rome, go back through myriad intermediate passages to this far-off period of prehistory. The Roman cult of Vesta puts us in mind of the likely role of prehistoric women in keeping the fire alive while men were hunting, but its most striking analogy with prehistory is sacrificial. Any Vestal found guilty of causing the flame of Vesta (*Hestia* in Greek) to go out, and thus putting the future of the Eternal City in jeopardy, was condemned to scourging, a harsh punishment closely connected to the death penalty by being buried alive to which a Vestal was sentenced if she was found guilty of having lost her virginity (*incestum*).[13] This latter rite, often performed in case of plague or military plight, has always to do with the life of Rome seriously impaired by the supposed guilt of the convicted priestess and, therefore, with the hearth of Vesta, symbolically identified with the Vestal's body.[14] The clear relationship between these sacrificial penalties and a divine fire deeply linked to women and endowed with a collective meaning makes it easier to imagine, in a less differentiated and sophisticated society, the real ending of an Australian myth in which an old woman is blamed for a fire going out, when the community's very survival depended on it, and is expelled in the wilderness.[15] Vico's "very bodily fantasy" of myth finds its explanation in the bodily destiny of a sacrificed victim at its roots.

With this we come to Girard and his use of mythology. More than anyone else, he sought to show how myths derive, systematically and covertly in his opinion, from real stories of collective violence perpetrated on victims. His explanation appears well suited to the archaic story of the Australian myth, whereas it appears to be no doubt pertinent but less at ease with the complex procedure of the Roman punitive rite, a skillful mixture of magical beliefs, subtle liturgical and juridical distinctions, and surprising inversions like the mourning over the condemned Vestal while she is being taken to her grave as if she was already dead: what is at stake is an objectual meaning compromised by the alleged crime of the victim, and this must be much more than a sheer cover-up of the real collective crime, given that it implies a whole cultural world to be studied on its own if we want to understand it, as emphasized in this case also by the lack of a corresponding myth, substituted for by the postmythical records of ancient historiography. A similar objection, though within a simpler cultural frame, can be made regarding the aboriginal myth as well. In Girard's work the cognitive and archaeological recovery of mythology is found singularly combined with rationalistic diffidence regarding it. In a certain sense that singularity indicates a conflictual synthesis of the two principal modern tendencies concerning myth, the one mistrusting it as essentially unreliable and false and the other attaching a great importance to it as historical source; the compresence of these two contradictory factors, together with Girard's characteristic extremism, is another sign that we are not far from finally achieving a less divided view of myth and its central significance in human cultural processes.

We will take our cue from the contribution made by Girard's researches to the present inquiry, with their suggestion at the time of the right point of attack to begin to scale the rugged, deceptive heights of Greek *mythos*, which Thomas Mann presents for us in a delightful modern narrative version. We shall thus be able to appreciate how modern investigations had the way prepared for them by the Christian cancellation and reformulation of myth, while they have an even older debt to Greece for the development of *logos* within the *mythos*.

2. Curetes/Titans

It is not without significance that the Curetes myth, related to the birth of a divine child and the Cretan origin of Greek civilization, attracted Girard's attention in *The Scapegoat* and led him at once to show its clear relationship to that myth in which the baby Dionysus is killed by the Titans.[16] Like Nietzsche and Thomas Mann before him, Girard sensed the importance of this Greek myth of origin, having to do with the birth of mankind as we shall see, and his more strictly anthropological understanding of the real nature of Dionysus enabled him to recognize the presence of a more general mythical scheme that is simplified in the Curetes myth. According to his analysis both versions tell the same story of the killing of a helpless infant by a group of adults, but differ in their development and disguise, and that provides the essential starting-point. And it is indeed merely a start , since this only opens a broader question involving the mediatory and cognitive value of mythology. Besides, this mythologem has connections extending far beyond the Curetes-Titans comparison considered by Girard, which lead back to the ritual and mythical configuration of the labyrinth, the most detailed and varied *mythos* in the Greek world, whose ramifications we shall trace down to the Christian Middle Ages, a course of inquiry that will give us an occasion to read deeply into the civilization that produced it.

Moreover, this course will provide an adequate framework in which to discuss and finalize the method to be adopted for interpreting the archaic and ancient mythological material, our main source and not infrequently our only source, for reconstructing the long cultural and religious history from which the material comes, by no means a simple endeavor as the short interpretive history of myth just outlined has shown. We must avoid both mechanically combining the various methods available and arbitrarily choosing one of them with the pretense of exclusive validity. I have no hesitation in stating that some methods are better than others, but the problem now is to demonstrate such a statement, and this implies the risk I am speaking about.

The proper way out is "to go back to the 'things themselves,'" as Edmund Husserl said,[17] avoiding any prejudicial interpretation, for the very reason that myth is already an interpretation in itself and therefore provides the principal support for our hermeneutic enterprise. Thus I have no intention of defining mythology at the start , apart from its generic description as a set of stories (μῦθοι, *fabulae*) relating to the sacral and divine world, since I want the outstanding features of myth and its countless derivations to emerge phenomenologically, and not in a way decided a priori, from the theoretical and historical observations that I shall be making here. We will assemble the phenomenological data of the Curetic/Titanic myth and the wider mythologem of the labyrinth and incorporate them in a genetic and historical comparison that will be capable of detecting the different interpretive layers that will take us to the very heart of mythology, to its originary interpretation of the origin. Unbiased observation makes it evident at once that not all the data are one and the same, in the first place because human cultures are not uniform in themselves, as Lévi-Strauss rightly emphasized. Instead, they are a complex symbolic organization where some parts are more important than others, but this is due to the fact that, contrary to what Lévi-Strauss holds, they convey hints about their very genesis. This latter point was part of Girard's contribution in reading myths, and it will serve our purposes, too, as long as we disregard his passive and reductionist view of mythology.

The most complete account of the Curetes myth is recorded in the third book of Strabo's *Geography*, concerning the island of Crete and its traditions. The author is describing the Cretan orgiastic rites and gods, and this introduces the myth of the birth of Zeus, threatened by his father Cronus who devours all his sons at birth to conserve his power. The story is set in a cave on the slopes of the highest mountain on Crete, Mount Ida:

> On Crete orgiastic rites accompanied not only the cults of these gods but also characterized the cult [*hiera*] of Zeus, for which the officiants are similar to the Satyrs in Dionysian rites. The Cretans call these officiants Curetes, young men who typically perform dance movements armed from head to foot, and tell through them the myth of the birth of Zeus, where Cronus is shown as being in the habit of devouring his newborn sons [*tekna*], and Rhea tries her best to dissimulate her labor pains, withdrawing to give birth to her last child in order to save him and asking the Curetes

> for help. Using kettledrums [*tympanon*] and other such sound makers and performing a dance in armor and hullabaloo, the Curetes surrounded the goddess with the purpose of frightening Cronus and absconding the baby without him noticing. The tradition also says that they afterward raised the child, taking the same precautions.[18]

Strabo dwells on the collective figure of the Curetes with a degree of attention that we may already define as ethnographic, and in a spirit of an encyclopedic and rationalistic curiosity influenced by the Aristotelian school and characteristic of the Hellenistic and Roman periods.[19] It is important to note that his method, derived in particular from the rational method of Theophrastus and Stoic philosophy, is already fully comparative and concerned with classifying the many myths he sets out according to their resemblance and difference. Strabo is perfectly aware that mythology is a system of endless transformations and wants to organize the multifarious whole, using them as a means to learn the history and customs of the country he is studying. The tone is descriptive and sober, no longer with any meaningful religious connotation but fully conscious of the central role of religion in ancient societies.

In this way we are provided historical and anthropological information that is lacking in the more vivid and religiously engaged account of Zeus's birth in Hesiod's *Theogony*, which can be usefully compared to Strabo's, especially as Hesiod in turn uses very old Minoan mythical material.[20] In the *Theogony* Rhea, "surrendering to Kronos, bore resplendent children," but he "swallowed them, as each / reached its mother's knees from her holy [*hieres*] womb."[21] The mother, "when she was about to give birth to Zeus, father of gods and men, / . . . begged her dear parents, Earth and starry [*asteroenta*] Heaven, / to devise a plan [*metin*] so that she could bear / her child in secrecy."[22] Rhea is advised to go to Crete, where she manages to cheat Cronus in a more substitutive way, swaddling a large stone as a baby and handing it to the monstrous father, who "puts it away in his belly" and is defined by the poet as "the brute" (*schetlios*).[23] The monstrosity of the father is implicitly stressed by the incestuous character of this primordial copulation among gods, still awaiting a more differentiated world of which the grown-up Zeus, "father of gods and men," will be the mediator. Interestingly, the Curetes are absent and their place is taken by the ruse of the stone wrapped as a baby, a more archaic detail transformed by Hesiod into a symbolic motif in his narrative,[24] which has a recognizable precedent in the Hittite myth of Kumarbi.[25] In this myth, Kumarbi, the cupbearer of the great god Anu, fights against him and swallows his genitals and semen; Anu tells Kumarbi that he is going to be pregnant with several gods destined to be born from several orifices of his body. So Kumarbi tries to get rid of one of his offspring by devouring him but is cheated into trying to eat a stone; and finally, probably in another myth, he is replaced by one of his sons, a storm-god.[26] There must be a combination here between ancient cults based on homosexual coupling/sacrifice and the sacrifice of a baby that was later substituted by a sacred stone, where the link might be the symbolic equivalence of the phallus to a newly born child clearly present in Dionysiac mythology.[27] Also interesting is Kumarbi's male pregnancy followed by a birth from several parts of his body such as the head, a motif present in the mythology of Zeus and Dionysus.[28] In Strabo the collective figure of the Curetes appears more specialized, rationalized, and humanly recognizable but is nevertheless ritual since his description of the Cretan cults is precise and circumstantial. Therefore, the two Greek accounts we are analyzing interpret their mythical-ritual materials at different historical levels—closer to the archaic divine mediations in Hesiod and more scientifically detached in Strabo—but nevertheless both are grounded on interpretations already active in the myths they use, whose main aim is to explain and support the necessity of an orderly world with its proper divisions and laws.

In both Strabo and Hesiod the symbolic atmosphere is of a tale twice originary: in space on account of its setting on the island of Crete from where Greek culture knew it derived historically, and in time through evoking the reign of *Kronos*, the archaic divinity who preceded the light-bearing reign of Zeus, recalling the primitive and ferocious mediations that historical Greece was proud to have left behind. Herodotus's historiography, with its unquenchable curiosity about the great civilizations that overshadowed Greece for a long time, culminates in the epic tale of the two Persian wars and represents this constitutive attitude of Hellenic mentality at its best, an attitude destined to become an archetype of the Western world. We find this same awareness of the meaning of Hellenic civilization in a tragedy like *The Persians* by Aeschylus, and later in the so-called *archaiologia* by Thucydides, one of the peaks of Greek rationalism. In this historical premise to his *Peloponnesian War*, the historian freely uses both mythology and the Homeric poems to reconstruct the formation of Hellas starting from a condition of weakness and the scattering of its manifold tribes.[29] Thus we attain a view of a very rich cultural landscape, which began with the various stages internal to the mythic narratives, and then evolved as literature, historiography, and philosophy, and is now in a position to retroact on the modern interpretations of myth if only we hold together this whole historical and cultural process. While taking some details from Hesiod, we shall be mainly concerned with Strabo's version, since it is more explicit about the collective role of the Curetes and has been used by a modern comparative scholar like Girard, but we must always bear in mind the larger background I have just outlined.

In the *mythoi* reported and interpreted by Strabo and Hesiod, which we must compare and combine together, what strikes the reader at once, since it is what the texts *want to*, is the warped, exaggeratedly monstrous nature of the father. Not content with getting rid of his sons, he must devour them greedily, as underlined by Hesiod's Cronus who swallows them as soon as they "reached [their] mother's knees from her holy womb." We get the impression that the myth is trying to show us *too much*. Freud's primeval father comes to mind as he tries to hold off the rebellious horde of his sons, even if it seems more likely that a distortion of that kind originated with the sons, keen to inflate the father's power to monstrous proportions because he has the females of the horde that the sons would also very much like to possess. In itself, the parallel between the ancient myth and Freud's scenario is not inappropriate, especially as regards their content—the recurrent theme of conflict between the generations—tempting the interpreter to be guided by the kinship roles, by their "differences" to use a category much-favored by Lévi-Strauss, considered inescapable by him, while Girard would demystify it in his anobjectual way. However, if we follow psychoanalytical or structuralist logic and cling to kinship roles in order to make sense of the myth, we end up being foolishly trapped: as yet there are no rival-sons, for as soon as they appear they are swallowed, and the father is not so much a father as a gigantic stomach equal to the sum of the sons devoured. Essentially, this is undifferentiation, with the residual kinship differences revealing themselves as, above all else, a cover-up, which is not to say that they are without any value, since the myth means to show us their negation in somber hues. Postponing for the moment the question of the family and sexual object, it is worth noting here that the parallel with Freud and the conflicting interpretations of Lévi-Strauss and Girard stimulate an important reflection.

The relationship between Freud's scene of origin and mythology is in some ways recursive and evasive, as is confirmed by his own definition of it as a "scientific myth" and the opportunity given his critics to demolish it. In *Totem and Taboo* Freud, like the myth, still assumes the father-sons relationship to be exclusive, taking literally what is, at least in part, being held back or disguised and leads to an inversion of cause and effect typical of myth. Unable to make a fuller reconstruction, which would imply that the answer had already been found and the conflict resolved before starting, Freud's explanation has to begin from where it happens to find itself, projecting *before* what only came to exist *after* but what because of its enormous importance appears to be the originary reality. Nevertheless, it would be quite wrong, as well as ungenerous, to brand Freud's text as "mythical" in a depreciative sense. First of all, the text begins to *deconstruct* the anthropological material in the right direction, though the difficulties show that it needs to be continued and made more consistent; and besides, it shares a similar need for explanation with the Curetes myth, but at a much more differentiated level of cognitive assurance, of cultural autonomy. The birth of Zeus presents us with an explicitly mythic *construction*, namely an attempt to *remedy*, rather than to explain, a serious problem threatening the community, one that clearly has something to do with the undifferentiation symbolized by Cronus. However, it is not a question of myth and science in total opposition, as Girard thinks, nor of Lévi-Strauss's linguistic-formal assimilation of the two; it is, instead, a matter of two distinct but connected levels of rational stabilization: in the Curetes myth the need for explanation comes *after* the need to be saved from the collective crisis, while in Freud's modern scientific myth the need for explanation comes *before* but keeps distant whatever threatens its theoretical and practical coordinates, what presents a threat to the setting-up of the new psychoanalytical science. Myth is a science that is still unstable and in need of practical confirmation, of ritual acts that will establish and strengthen it; science is a stabilized myth that has put all immediate conflict behind though the possibility of such conflict has never entirely vanished and must be kept at a distance. This signifies, then, that there exists some form of continuity as well with Girard's work of explanation and finally with my present interpretation in terms of objectual mediation. But let us return to our analysis.

In the *mythos* recorded by Strabo, we encounter a collective character, the Curetes, who unexpectedly come to incarnate sons made absent by an undifferentiator father. The Curetes must save the last remaining son, the last objectual, human chance that might save the community from the monstrous crisis about to engulf it. But a telling detail shows us that the problem really lies within the symbolic group of Cretan warriors and not outside it: Cronus appears so stupid that the infernal din raised by the Curetes obtains the result of frightening him without any further suspicion on his part. What is really happening becomes clear when we consider the other detail to which Girard draws our attention: the Curetes are warriors and therefore *armed*. But what are their weapons for? If we had not been told that they want to save the child's life, their frenzied gyrations would give us every reason to fear the worst. The percussion instruments mentioned by Strabo (τύμπανα, kettledrums or tambourines) are hardly reassuring since, as Strabo says earlier, they are associated with mystery and orgiastic rites of an omophagic nature. It is time to apply my *comparative method for myth and ritual*, taking Frazer's comparative method as starting point but avoiding its naturalistic and positivistic ingenuousness, and to compare other myths where we can well expect to uncover corresponding ritual behavior. In one such myth Zeus strikes the Curetes with a thunderbolt to punish a crime which bears a curious resemblance to their good deed here, when they spirited away Epaphus, son of Io and Zeus, at Hera's instigation. We are told that "because Hera hated this son and persecuted him, she gave him to the Curetes to hide. *They hid him so well that Io could not find him again*."[30] The Curetes are clearly specialists here, which suggests actual ritual specialization, and even if the myth goes on to say that Epaphus was found, significantly in the far Phoenician city of Byblos, his mother's failure to find him has sinister overtones, even more so if we consider the resemblance of this myth to that of Isis in search of the dismembered body of Osiris.[31]

But who are the Curetes more exactly? With their collective figure, the mythical-ritual associations begin to multiply. They are demons born of the Earth (*gegeneis*), metalworkers and thus makers of weapons, obviously linked to the sacral corporation of blacksmiths. They assist Rhea or a mother goddess and have similar functions and characteristics to the Corybantes, Idaean

Dactyls, Telchines, Cabeiri, and so on.[32] These Cretan warriors, with their dances and activities associated with the earth and the world underground, are closely involved with the events and symbolism of the Cretan labyrinth. This appears actually to be a cave with numerous tunnels where initiations took place and metals were extracted and worked.[33] At the same time, as stressed by a scholar closely acquainted with Thomas Mann, Karl Kerényi, it was a spiraling dance, the labyrinthine dance, performed around a central point: a god or a youth to be initiated.[34] Thus the scene described in the Curetes myth is like a palimpsest of several rituals, especially as the cave on Mount Ida was one of the most important cult sites on Crete. In short, the Curetes are really a collective labyrinth, represented as a group and as a place or, more precisely, as an event occurring in a place and within a group. The archaic labyrinth therefore was a dance connected with a sacred space and consecrated to a certain place where the group could coordinate and form around a center, quite evidently sacrificial.

According to Kerényi, the labyrinth dance was performed with a rope to keep the dancers together. This rope is the thread that Ariadne gave to Theseus to keep him from losing his way in the labyrinthine edifice of the Minotaur, and in a revealing, secondary version of the myth, it is the rope with which she hangs herself on discovering her abandonment. Plutarch tells how Theseus comes to Delos after abandoning Ariadne (which is equivalent to sacrificing her) with the freed Athenian youths and joins them in a dance, *choreia*, imitating the windings of the labyrinth and the evolutions needed to find the way out: this is the dance of the cranes (*geranos*) because as the performers dance around the sacrificial altar they identify with crane-birds, a metamorphosis typical of many ritual dances.[35]

This dance has undoubtedly prehistoric origins, as is suggested by the shaman-like identification with wild animals, dating back to the rituals of Paleolithic hunting societies of *Homo sapiens* and to the Neanderthal's rite witnessed in the painting of La Pasiega, where the shamanistic identification is with a bird ready to fly. Other archaeological finds provide us with more specific evidence. In the proto-Neolithic site of Göbleki Tepe in Anatolia (ninth millennium BC) have been discovered bas-reliefs representing cranes with human legs, evidently shamanistic dancers metamorphosed into these animals;[36] and in the Neolithic city of Çatal Höyük (sixth millennium) have been found crane plumes used for the same purpose.[37] Therefore, leaving aside the still largely unknown cultural history shared by *H. sapiens* and Neanderthal, Minoan civilization derived this dance from a very long cultual tradition coming from Anatolia and adapted it to a mythical-ritual whole strictly connected to the labyrinth and its characters. Ariadne corresponds to an ancient Cretan goddess, also called the "Lady of the Labyrinth,"[38] and must herself have been crane-like in appearance, since cranes are among her most frequent manifestations and attributes. In such a disguise, as Kerényi rightly understands,[39] she is to be associated with the sacrificial flight theme, implying that the victim was thrown into a ravine or underground chasm. Ariadne's death by hanging evokes another sort of "cultual flight" (kultische Fluge),[40] well documented in the cult of Artemis and in various Greek myths. After having clearly detected the prehistoric origins of the crane dance, Kerényi convincingly shows its relationship with death and the afterlife.[41]

All these sacrificial and funereal associations are a reminder that the labyrinth is often identified with tombs and the hereafter. The labyrinth-cave where the victim met his death easily becomes the tomb where the dead victim's body or what remained of it was buried. Thus we can go back in time to a fundamental ritual and cognitive transition without which *Homo sapiens* could not have evolved as far as the logical-mental conformation that makes these remarks and reconstructions possible: the invention, up to a point shared with Neanderthal, of tomb burial, a ritual certainly accompanied by myths and one that in itself, performatively, sets up a distinction between the victim and its enduring sign, the basis of *H. sapiens*' huge symbolic development. The earliest known burials are found in caves, which were not dwellings and thus clearly connote sacred places.[42] It has never occurred to archaeologists and paleontologists that these burials might be the result of human sacrifice. However, the hypothesis of ritual mediations centered around human sacrifice makes perfectly intelligible the following circumstances: the small number of individuals involved, which is an established fact; a high proportion of children with skeletal signs of disease and trauma in one of the oldest known burial sites, the Qafzeh cave;[43] and, in general, few but significant signs of violence on the buried bodies. In a later prehistoric triple burial in Moravia, to which I shall return at the end of the chapter, there are obvious signs of ritual sacrifice, recognized as such by expert opinion.[44]

These findings thus confirm the great antiquity and wide diffusion of mythical and ritual material relating to the labyrinth and the afterlife, providing valuable information for interpreting the Curetes' dance and the musical instruments played, the flutes and drums that were effective means for reaching states of shaman-like possession and trance that are typical of these collective gods and of the sacred associations they inspired, such as the Corybantic groups.[45] The question now is about the identity and nature of all these collective mythical characters.

3. Collective Transformations

These Curetes, interchangeable with so many other doubles of collective figures in myth,[46] are the narrative, performative symbol of a capacity for disguise and duplication that Girard links to the rival doubles of his mimetic crisis, but we should not overlook the representational and cognitive value of the symbol since without this power of duplication the abstractive mental capacity of *H. sapiens* would not exist nor, as a consequence, the present discourse that allows us to discuss it. More than a group of doubles, the Curetes are primarily a duplicating function around which the community begins to represent itself through projecting the myth, directed outward, in a sacral and divine dimension, which, at a certain stage in differentiation, it will be possible to turn inward, so as to make the community itself more representable. In ancient Greece this step occurs with the development of the representations of the *polis*, when the community of the gods is infused into civic institutions opening up symbolic spaces for the community to give a shared account of itself, as happens variously in tragedy, historiography, and philosophy. This corresponds to a transition found in countless different forms, in mythologies worldwide; one example, close to ancient Greece in terms of history and geography and of special interest as it is more archaic, is the Sumerian Anunnaki (or Anunnaku). The Anunnaki are the gods of the underworld (called in this role also "the seven judges"), who appear to be very close to the demons that chase and kill the lover of Inanna Dumuzi[47] and at the same time are identified with all the gods in their decisional and creative activities. It would be a mistake to regard as real only the first mythological function of these demons/gods, since the second function shows its structuring capacity, without which the civilizations of Mesopotamia would never have developed. This is not a matter of underestimating the violent processes underlying mediation but assigns a precise role to them, giving them real weight, not just in response to our mythical (in modern language "ideological") need to reassure ourselves by removing violence from ourselves under a theoretical guise.

Sons that unite against their father, and brothers, especially twins, that become rivals are all symbols of the rivalry that flares up among men, symbols of multiplication involving any number from two upward. At the same time, the fact that such happenings are retold and interpreted in a *mythos*, that is, in a story, implicitly tells us that a symbolic space has been created, a starting point for the unrepresentable to become representation, for the inconceivable to be transformed into a conception of the world and into a collective institution that vouches for that conception. Their character as a duplicating function, linked to violence and arms on the one hand and to the generational father-son succession on the other, helps us to understand the role of the Curetes in initiation rites, namely in the sacrificial metamorphosis through which a youth suffered symbolic sacrifice to become wholly integrated with the initiating group. The real or potential danger of the Curetes, indicated by the details that they are metalworkers as well as warriors and that they are really beating leather shields transformed into drums,[48] is their genetic link to violence and capacity to master it and trigger a new symbolic cycle by reenacting the crisis that would threaten to bring about its very destruction. These elements are enough to support our comparative scrutiny, but the story of the Titans confirms it, by exposing the ritual background to the Curetes myth, where it is transformed and revitalized, and also by making clear the connection with the labyrinth mythologem.

I will start analysis of the Titans *mythos* with Girard's description, where the nature and the scope of his ideas about the myth are expressed in the simplest terms:

> To draw the child Dionysus into their circle, the Titans dangle certain trinkets [*des espèces de hochets*] before him. Seduced by these twinkling objects, the child steps forward and the circle closes round him. All the Titans together murder Dionysus, then cook and devour him. Zeus, the father of Dionysus, strikes the Titans with thunderbolts and brings his son back to life.[49]

Girard's exposition of the Titanic myth omits or misunderstands several important elements—the backstory of the ambush; the meaning of the "trinkets," that were not *des espèces de hochets* but objects of ritual import; the most archaic conclusion of the story[50]—and yet it has the merit of reaching at once the essential point. While child murder is averted in the Curetes version, here, it is not. Monstrousness is directly present in the group, since it carries out a lynching, though kept hidden behind a mask multiplied and projected outside monstrously and symbolically, the mask of a collective doubles divinity. This second myth is clearer than the first in every way, and Girard is absolutely right to compare the two since, once the comparison is made, it appears intuitively obvious. The circling dance round the child takes on its real meaning as a deadly tightening spiral. Where the Curetes' benevolence was suspiciously disguised as aggression, here there is violence camouflaged as benevolence, which is altogether more convincing. The act of cannibalism itself appears much more realistic with a whole group united against its victim, in place of just one solitary ravenous ogre.

However, once again, the comparison should lead to a wider discussion of myth capable of bringing together its genetic aspects, linked to the processes to overcome internal violence, as well as the representational, cognitive aspects. Girard, following in the footsteps of scholars such as William Robertson Smith, Frazer, Arthur Maurice Hocart, Freud, Adolf Ellegard Jensen (and in more moderate doses, Kerényi), essentially clarified the diachronic and historical genesis of mythology from situations of crisis, while Lévi-Strauss, in the wake of the Durkheim school, made an equally important in-depth study of the symbolic meaning of mythology that has to be investigated according to its formal, internal (synchronic) logic. What is missing is the real factor joining the two together, and I believe that my idea of mediation supplies it. Mediation as I understand it embodies the very genesis that comes to condense and organize around a meaningful center capable of making the world representable and accessible, establishing new thresholds for reproduction and retroaction; at a certain point, these then become capable of seeing themselves through the process that we call thinking or science, a process in which myth, historically, has an integral part and one in which—it must be stressed—all the cultural forms deriving from myth, such as the figurative arts, literature, historiography, and philosophy, also form an integral part. The key to understanding my approach to explanation and interpretation is provided by the concept of *reversibility* and *retroaction*. But let us proceed step by step, starting from an approach closely connected with my own and yet profoundly different: Girard's approach, whose conclusions are diametrically opposed to what I hope to demonstrate.

In Girard's opinion, this transition from the Titanic to the Curetes version made by a single mythic scheme, originating in real acts of ritual infanticide, exemplifies a universal law:

> When we observe the disappearance of the collective murder in the transition from the Titan myth to the Curetes myth, we understand that this kind of transformation can occur only in one direction. . . . The collective murder can certainly vanish from mythology, indeed it always does, but once it has disappeared, obviously it cannot reappear; it will not show up again after the cards have been reshuffled [*de quelque pure combinatoire*], armed to the teeth like Minerva issuing from the head of Jove. Once a myth has passed from the Titan form . . . to the Curetes form, a return to the previous form never takes place; it is inconceivable. In other words, mythology has a *history*.[51]

Girard's reading of the myth provides us powerful gain in knowledge but it hardens into a univocal and finally deterministic criterion of historical evolution, excluding from the start what is culture's specific acquisition, its capacity for independent, potential retroaction. In this way we should postulate not only the irreversible nature of victimary concealment but also its uniqueness as explanation: mythical formations having their roots exclusively in persecutory processes. Any creative dimension of the double-binding critical situations of human groups is excluded or simply not considered, while the historical and anthropological evidence points in the opposite direction: at a certain moment, myths form, and postmythic texts that are very much involved with them become capable of perceiving the ritual and social conditions at their origin, something we shall find copiously documented in Greek tragedy. And the same evidence shows that countless myths existed earlier still whose genesis can be reconstructed and is found to consist in the objectual interpretation of natural events linked to the community's history or location, which would be impossible if they were exclusively dependent on their explanatory causes and devoid of any autonomy. On account of their reliable antiquity and universal ubiquity, myths about nature provide the most immediate cues for reflection on their capacity for representing and knowing the object of external reality.

In this connection we can cite the multitude of myths concerning astronomy, studied in a fascinating book by Giorgio Diaz De Santillana and Hertha Von Dechend, *Hamlet's Mill*.[52] These cosmic-religious stories are usually explained simply as the result of natural observations, though they must really refer to powerful ritual experiences that endowed celestial bodies and phenomena with divine meaning. Actually, we are closer to the origin of what we today call science, initially one and the same with the magical *and* experiential capacity to deal with a nature that was sacred and superhuman in itself.[53] The cognitive value of these stories is undeniable since, as a cultural whole, they led to the astounding capacity to observe and calculate the movements of the celestial bodies found in all ancient civilizations. Myths that recall natural catastrophes are especially intriguing, such as the Sumerian and Babylonian accounts of a great flood, the source of the biblical Flood, and the myths of the Native American Klamath tribe living in what is now Oregon. In these tribal myths, the memory of the collapse of the volcanic caldera of Mount Mazama, thereby creating the present-day Crater Lake, is handed down as the killing of the sun by a divine trickster or as a fight between divine beings: in a case like this, a date can actually be given to the mythologem since the event occurred seven thousand years ago.[54]

However, remaining within the historical and cultural area of this inquiry, we can instance the Greeks' mythical interpretations of Etna: in *Prometheus Bound* Aeschylus takes Hesiod's *Theogony* as his basis for an account of Zeus destroying with a thunderbolt the monster Typhon, or Typhaeus (son of Gaia like the Titans, and analogous to the Curetes), and burying him beneath the mountain, where Hephaestus, the god of fire, keeps watch over him. This is an etiological explanation for the terrible destructive power of the Sicilian volcano, in the wake of Pindar, who first had the idea of transferring the Hesiodean myth of Typhon from Greece to Sicily, where he went to the court of the tyrant of Syracuse, writing by the way the oldest known Western description of a volcanic eruption witnessed at the foot of Etna:[55] "from its gorges holiest [*hagnotatai*] springs erupt / of tremendous fire,"[56] with a religious vocabulary still echoing the sacred origin of all that pertained to the phenomena of fire. Accompanying these mythical dramatizations, there are the interpretations of Etna and other volcanoes in the neighborhood of Sicily as the entrance to the menacing, chthonic kingdom of the dead, a tradition alive into the Middle Ages.[57] This gave rise to an ancient legend about Empedocles that met with enormous favor right down to the time of Friedrich Hölderlin and Nietzsche according to which Empedocles threw himself into Etna to demonstrate his power to descend into Hades and be reborn, a tradition linked to the interpretation of the wise man as an initiatic and shamanistic figure.[58] At the same time, the cognitive aspects of the Empedoclean legend are expounded by the doxographic tradition according to which Empedocles was capable of explaining the rocks and cliffs on the terrestrial surface as being "formed by the action of the fire present in the depth [*en bathei*] of the Earth" after having been "pulled by its flame."[59]

There is no need for detailed analysis to show in all this evidence related to nature the explorative function of myth and mythical perception, spectacularly detected in the more stratified, sophisticated classical world: Pindar and Aeschylus witness the literary developments of the *mythos*, Empedocles shows the sapiential and soteriological developments to be linked to Orphism and Pythagoreanism, while its etiological aims are pursued in the naturalistic rationalizations of traditional mythology at the turn of the fourth century BC, as documented at the beginning of Plato's *Phaedrus*.[60] In these cases, as in others that I could name, the interpretive, cognitive role of mythology is strikingly clear, with no *direct* origin in collective persecution processes. This does not alter the fact that they are part of a world mediated by sacrifice and conditioned by fear of the violent crises spontaneously created by natural disasters but do so exactly by using means with a certain degree of autonomy to represent and explain the real world.

Originally there was nothing innocuous about these myths, as can be seen from the frequent interjection of symbols and events of a sacrificial and lynching type. On the other hand, there was not even a bloody factor that subjected the entire content to itself. The above examples of volcanoes, especially the legend of Empedocles throwing himself into Etna to show the power of his sacred knowledge to defy and defeat death, give us a further level of sapiential reading, deriving from the mythical-ritual dimension. If we were to apply Girard's method mechanically to this, it would mean conjecturing that Empedocles, or some substitute for him, was *really* thrown into the crater of the volcano. Apart from any considerations of detail, since the story of Empedocles's death is undoubtedly a symbolic legend, there is no need for such strict literalness, for that would exclude the heuristic, interactive flexibility illustrated by the proliferation of mythology in various directions without any particular effort. Certainly volcanic sacrifices existed, and presumably had something to do also with the ancient interpretation of the Oregon eruption; they are at the root of the initiatory and sacrificial stories surrounding Empedocles and are further indicated by the evidence of ritual and oracular activity on Etna and other volcanoes in the area.[61] But there is no need to automatically assume the presence of human sacrifice where what is going on, as is clearly the case in ancient Greece, is merely a creative use of narrative and symbolic structures, mythical-ritual in origin, certainly, but reshaped to fit in with the new sapiential mediations characteristic of Greek culture.

In order to explain the absence of evident sacrificial solutions in less archaic myths, Girard resorts to his principle of the persecutory unconscious or misrecognition, stratifying in the course of time to cover up and alter the more archaic, bloodier versions, concealing ever more deeply and irremediably the originary collective violence and its more recent sacrificial derivatives. It becomes patently obvious that Girard's ideas cannot explain the creative developments of myth, but it would nevertheless be wrong to dismiss the idea that myth derived from collective violence and sacrifice, an idea previously supported by scholars who contributed in large part to the human sciences in the last centuries. A relevant and even massive misrecognition in myth is in itself undeniable.

It is evident that archaic cultures are largely unaware of the violent price of their mediations, though this is not the whole story that Girard takes it to be. A more scientific analogy would be the blind spot of Heinz Von Foerster, the point of discontinuity in the visual field caused by the entry of the optic nerve and compensated by our brain on the basis of the surrounding items of information.[62] This analogy is at least free from the condescension or blame so irritating in Freud or Girard, but it has to be strongly enhanced and developed. Historical and cultural perceptions are much more articulated and complex, not only because our eyes check the visual field with their continuous movements, but moreover because the human blind spots contain the possibility of feedback (i.e., to retroact on this constitutive lack up to the point of acquiring new knowledge). As seen in the introduction, the modern philosophy of knowledge has provided us with a surprising illustration of this universal tendency: the Kantian *Phänomenon/Erscheinung*, with its impossibility to know the noumenon, has been actually the premise to reach the Husserlian phenomenon capable of dissolving into itself the old noumenon, but this in turn becomes the premise to discover that the previous impossibility was not imaginary, since it corresponds to the real costs of human mediations, to the bleeding blind spots necessary to the constitution of our own visual fields. In other words, we have the possibility to retroact upon the very limits of our condition, and this possibility comes to the fore at some points of our cultural development, in different forms and degrees, until we become aware that the limits themselves are the condition of our awareness, of our knowledge. This amounts to say that myth, after being aroused by sacrifice, contains in itself the potential to know it, transcending itself because it is born from transcendence, that is, from the ecstatic experience of a transcending Object source of meaning and knowledge. We become able to debunk myth thanks to myth, through the infinite developments that form its history, and from which our knowledge derives.

These reflections allow us to exploit all the explanatory capacity of the modern demystifying theories of myth, among which Girard's method holds an important place, to overcome their intransitive reductionism after recognizing its historical necessity, and to link it up to the mediatory processes that all modern thinking tends to distort, deny, and reject. We shall therefore see that Girard's corollary of the irreversible nature of mythic evolution is not compatible with the existing documentation and take that as our cue to find a more comprehensive method for interpreting myths and rites, and then develop and expound it in the rest of the inquiry.

If we return now to the Curetes/Titans sequence, we immediately find a variant of the Titan *mythos* not mentioned by Girard since it does not chime in with the direct line of development as he sees it. This is the bloodiest version in which the Titans cannot wait to boil Dionysus but devour him immediately, in the omophagic rite that we find in Thomas Mann, and in the end are punished by Zeus. It sounds like the most archaic version of all, and it is the inner motor driving the entire mythical-ritual pattern, the horrific core of the Dionysian in Nietzsche and the Greek myth of origin par excellence, given that humanity was molded from the ashes of the Titans by Zeus.

Here we have the ritual palimpsest of the Curetes myth in its first "writing," to borrow Jacques Derrida's much-abused image, and yet the provenance of the version as we know it is not so remote but goes back to Orphism, about which we shall have much to say in the next chapter. As a religious movement Orphism cannot be traced further back than the sixth century BC with any certainty, which by no means excludes a more archaic stage begun in the eighth century through the Eleusinian Mysteries,[63] but what we should pay attention to is that more ancient variants of the omophagic myth undoubtedly existed—as the ritual forms documented by the myth go back into prehistory, and besides there are plenty of myths in many ancient cultures in which the origin of the world occurs from the dismemberment of a primordial being—and that Orphism chose to base its explanation of the origin of humankind on one of these omophagic *mythoi*. There was therefore a cognitive retroaction by the myth upon itself, whatever value one might then choose to place on the significance and import of the Orphic phenomenon; whereas Girard's attempt to trace the Orphic myth to some biblical influence is completely ad hoc and takes no account both of the real redaction history of the Bible and of the myriad links binding the Orphic concept to the civilization in which it unquestionably arose.[64]

I shall be dealing with the questions of comparison raised by Orphism in the Intermezzo. Meanwhile we now have the means to complete this chapter's exploration by finishing our analysis of the labyrinth mythologem in which the Titan/Curetes myth has its place. For a series of reasons this represents the best introduction to Greek civilization, expressing, in ways that may be defined as prehistoriographic, the historical influence of Crete and the Mediterranean that led to the birth of Classical Greece; but more than this, the mythologem embraces impressive layers of ritual that can be traced back to distant prehistoric times and brings us into direct contact with the Hellenic world's most shocking sacrificial cult, the cult of Dionysus from which we have never really strayed.

4. The Labyrinth Mythologem

The theme of the labyrinth has fascinated men in every age, an ambivalent fascination systematically linked to violence and death. So much more surprising, then, is it that nobody has yet seriously investigated why it should have persisted over thousands of years and always exerted such attraction/repulsion, including the present-day scholars concerned with the subject. The following reaction is quite symptomatic and comes from the beginning of Giorgio Colli's *La sapienza greca*, an innovative collection of ancient Greek texts that proved most helpful to me in preparing the first edition of this work:

> This harsh [*aspro*] myth remains obscure, elusive in its primitive features, the Labyrinth is so seductive as a symbol that overimaginative [*ispirata dalla fantasia*] interpretation is inevitable, the primitive action of the myth has been forgotten, and we possess no relevant texts old enough to hazard a reconstruction. The general lines can be made out and suggest in the crudest fashion the theme of Dionysus's contradiction. Perhaps they are the most pertinent—if only indicatively—in foreshadowing the god's profound significance.[65]

Colli was a classicist deeply influenced by Nietzsche—and was coeditor of the most reliable German edition of his *Werke*—but forcefully took Nietzsche's thought back to its juvenile Schopenhauerian inspiration, with the result that he never reached the full import of Nietzsche's most important later insights on ancient Greece and Dionysus. As a classicist, he is too perceptive not to see that the figure of Dionysus leads to Crete and the labyrinth myth, but he shrinks from the appeal of this association, although everything in his able study so clearly points to it: "the Labyrinth is so seductive as a symbol that an overimaginative [*ispirata dalla fantasia*] interpretation is inevitable." He does not take into account that the "very bodily fantasy" (corpolentissima fantasia) of the primitive peoples according to Vico exhibits a sacrificial origin as soon as it is revisited through Nietzschean eyes. Colli is reluctant to recognize that the labyrinthine symbol is seductive precisely because it is *not* inspired by what is meant by imagination or fantasy in the passage quoted. Imagination, as something entirely subjective and unreal, is seductive only to our psychologistic imaginings, which assume a subject preexists the factors from which it derives and itself has no origin. In the end, however, nothing is less seductive than such imagination suspended in a bodiless void. For we do have an origin, we *are* our origin, and what we find most seductive and disturbing is precisely what relates to this origin, and it speaks to us since it is the historical, "bodily" phenomenon from which we come and out of which we are made. A different meaning of fantasy or imagination takes shape, related not to a still nonexisting subject but to the "imaginal," *imaginalis* experience capable of giving shape to a new object starting from tearing apart what previously was the biological object.

In his perceptive and disappointing passage, Colli jumps to the conclusion that "the primitive action of the myth has been forgotten," unwilling to see that the action is not at all obscure and elusive, as he declares, and by no means forgotten, since it is none other than the "harsh" myth of the Dionysian omophagy standing at the very center of Nietzsche's conception and fate. The author fails to see the contradiction in what follows, when he admits: "The general lines can be made out and suggest in the crudest fashion the theme of Dionysus's contradiction." How could anything at all be made out—and what's more "in the crudest fashion"—if the original myth is so obscure, elusive, and forgotten? What is "Dionysus's contradiction"? Something metaphysical, something seductive in the romantic sense from which Arthur Schopenhauer was not so distant, or is it not rather something so tremendous and concrete that we recoil from it in alarm? Is not this "the god's profound significance"? And what text is older than ourselves and our violent history? Such then is Colli's tortuous attempt to return to Dionysus while blind to the Dionysian and Nietzschean truth before his eyes. Through the force of his novelist's imagination, of his *imaginalis* exploration, Thomas Mann definitely makes us see much more. Nothing is more real than imagination when it is used well, essentially because it originates in the ecstatic-objectual mediations that it can recover when it is isolated from all the contingent factors that normally obscure it. The obscurity is not in the "harsh myth" of the labyrinth but in the shroud of darkness cast around it by our fears.

The Cretan maze is the place of the originary omophagy, from which there is no escaping since it represents in itself the violent undifferentiation, the objectual crisis of the frenzied mob that finally finds its object, its *objectum*, in the victim on whom they all hurl themselves. At the same time and for the same reason, the labyrinth symbolizes the originary theophany, the manifestation of the sacred and divine that appears as a center of bright light, as splendor that must be worshiped. The labyrinth is also a matter of learning how to escape, how to save yourself from it or rather how to use it as a means to salvation. Theseus saves himself from the Minotaur because he learns to follow the plan of the maze, which means that he will have its secret in his keeping and be transformed into a humanized Minotaur enabling others to save themselves from the inextricable building waiting for its human victims. The Cretan mythologem holds further surprises in store for us, but for the moment this chapter will probe its layers of ritual and sacrifice. These all clearly show the necessity of unveiling the mystery of the mythologem, ridding it of the literary and erudite incrustations that prevent us from penetrating to the bloody truth at the origin of ritual and sacrifice, and to the somber salvation nourishing the rational tranquility of that truth. Only the labyrinth can save from the labyrinth, and this confirms the real nature of the knowledge that teaches us how to pass through it and enables us to recognize it as palimpsest.

The convulsive movements of the mob, the consequences and transformations of which are to be seen in the labyrinthine mythology, are reproduced ritually by frenzied dancing, later becoming the complex choreography of the labyrinth with its spiraling gyrations.[66] At a more recent stage in prehistory, the labyrinth must have taken on the specific features of a sacred place where a dance of a commemorative, initiatory kind was performed. In the case of Crete, this place was originally a cave where sacrificial rites and, in certain cases, burials were performed. What we are witnessing here, therefore, is the inculturalization of *Homo sapiens*, accompanied as if in a counterpoint by the kindred cultural process of Neanderthal, and the presence of burial and the arts of music and dance suggest the inculturalization is well under way. From being part of ritual performance, those arts would become sophisticated artistic forms of expression. Other symbols add further details of this phase of the Cretan mythologem. Ancient sources describe the cave on Mount Ida as overflowing with honey,[67] "the innocent [*amemphei*] poison of the bees," as Pindar defines it,[68] closely related to ambrosia and ichor, the nectar and the blood of the gods. Once we possess the key of sacrificial interpretation, we can see that these are all transparent metaphors for the blood of the victim and its powers of sacramental transitivity, once its transitive genesis has been accepted.[69] In one version of the birth of Zeus, the child god is nurtured by bees, an animal transformation of the Curetes/Titans, which as a swarm recalls the frenzied mob of lynchers, coordinated and directed toward one end by its sacrificial *obiectum*, now inverted to become its initiatory objective. In another version, certain individuals want to enter the cave, but after seeing the blood from the god's birth, they are chased away by bees as big as men.[70] The various elements combining here need no special comment except for the theme, found in only one account, of the doubling of the group of participants: the Curetes are metamorphosed as bee-men, while the intruders with their *mala curiositas* correspond to the wicked Titans.

As we pause now to consider the recurrent metaphors of light that form an integral part of the Cretan mythologem, we must certainly not overlook their twofold aspect but must both recognize their bloody genesis and grasping their religious, initiatory, and cognitive value precisely in that, and thus comprehend both the historical price paid and the real substance. Without the *imaginalis* light of the divine from which the light of consciousness comes human beings could know nothing, and yet this light is the result of a historic drama, of a radical traumatic break that forced the prehuman animal to see something that it would otherwise never have seen. For human beings this light is none other than mediation with its intermedial capacity to illuminate objects, to light the world: only a supreme trauma could have pushed them so far. In this way, an immensely long prehistory, our most real history, is made visible.

The cave on Mount Ida, overflowing with honey-blood, shines at night with supernatural light, the light of the sacralized and mediatory victim, casting its light on thousands and thousands of years that would otherwise have remained buried in darkness, guiding us along obscurely winding ways, past the symbolization of *Homo sapiens/neanderthalensis*, through *Homo heidelbergensis*, and back to *Homo ergaster/erectus* and its contribution to hominization. The divine light, in fact, goes back to the fire of victimary sacrifice and undoubtedly belongs to a certain phase in the development of the labyrinthine rite. The victim of the labyrinth could be burned alive, as the myth of Talus would suggest: this Cretan warrior and man of brass would make himself red-hot and clasp intruders in a deadly embrace. Frazer does not confine his interpretation to this mythical and ritual material all by itself but links it, with good comparative arguments though perhaps too literally, to infant sacrifices made to Baal by the neighboring Phoenicians, with whom Crete was in close contact as suggested by the myth of Epaphus.[71]

The metaphor of the sun, used so perceptively by Thomas Mann to indicate the sacrificial victim, reveals its inner origin and its ability to give signification to the world but takes us back to a stage even more remote than the domestication of fire, to a less visible stage that made things visible starting from the mediation of a killed victim, the imaginal visibility that enabled noninstinctual attention to be shown toward the splendor of the flame, its divinization. This divine visibility is the source of energy for all the light symbolism of the labyrinth, and the Cretan female theonyms, inextricably bound up with labyrinth rituals, suggest as much, whereas the idea of ritual combustion, the positivist explanation, is ingenious but not sufficient. Another Cretan name for Ariadne was *Ari-dela*, the Most Bright,[72] and the name of her daughter, Pasiphae, has a similar meaning, the Resplendent One. In themselves these names become divine attributes. In the *Hymn to the Curetes* found on a Cretan inscription (third century BC), Zeus is defined as lord of all that is *ganos*, that is, both wet and bright,[73] a perfect synthesis of the two aspects recognizable in labyrinth mythology, fire and blood; and he himself is called Curete,[74] sealing in the child become king of the gods both the transfigured victim and the objectual result to which all aspire. And so we come back to the Curetes/Titan mythical complex from which we started.

Possessing these elements now, we may safely conclude that the Orphic myth of the Titans shows the sacrifice underlying the labyrinth myth at its most archaic stage. The more frequent version, with the divine child being cooked, implies the invention of fire and specific rules for dividing the food and so belongs to a later stage. The Curetes myth corresponds to the evolution of the ritual in the form of a dance performed in a sacred cave. The successive phases are distinct, from omophagy to anthropophagy with the flesh being cooked, and then to child sacrifices burned inside a bronze bull-like statue, corresponding in Frazer's view to the Minotaur and the taurine statues of Baal.[75] In the Curetes story the objectual disorientation of the labyrinth is distanced and concentrated in the living labyrinth of Cronus, whose stomach finally contains all his sons. Cronus incarnates the victim perceived as a menacing destroyer, on whom the community projects responsibility for the crisis, on a par with Typhon, that unparented double buried beneath a volcano. On the other hand, Zeus, who finally defeats his father with the help of other monstrous incarnations of the crisis, such as the Hecatoncheiri or Hundred-handed, represents the saving, mediatory aspect of the transfigured victim. He is the residual human object defended by the Curetes; and thanks to this difference Cronus's swallowed sons are able to see the light of day again. From the cannibalistic rites evoked by the Titans myth we come to rites of initiation in the Curetes myth.

The various elements in the Cretan mythologem go through countless reciprocal transformations and present us with a scenario of combinations; the transfiguring concealment is certainly a decisive aspect of this, but it is part of a sequence and, seen within the overall process producing it, it can restore details not maintained by any single version and interpret them so as to make them indirectly eloquent. Cronus in person is one of the Titans, like them a son of Uranus and Gaia, of Heaven and Earth. The Curetes therefore turn out to be revised and corrected second-generation Titans engaged in defending the victim from an old associate of theirs, who is the last Titan to survive into the new version of the myth and comes supercharged with all the violence of the others. The structural identity of Titans with Curetes is corroborated by the Epaphus myth, where the Curetes suffer an identical fate at the hands of Zeus, and receives further confirmation from the sources, which confront us with a wealth of texts and symbols of inestimable worth and power for interpretation and knowledge. Strabo notes various links between the Curetes and the Dionysian sphere as well as a tradition that the Titans offered the Curetes-Corybantes to Rhea as armed servants.[76] He reports other authors as saying that these were also Cronus's children. The historian Istrus (third century BC) tells us that the Curetes sacrificed children to Cronus.[77] There is an iconographic source, now in Bologna: a late ancient Greek ivory pyxis representing the Curetes in the act of stabbing the child Dionysus who is seated on a throne looking into a mirror. It is a ceremony of enthronement in which the throne regains its ancient function as a sacrificial stone.[78]

Clearly there is plenty of evidence; however, the particular difficulty here is not to amass the evidence but to make it stand up as proof, starting from specific premises that, the moment they are disputed or ignored, take the phenomenological ground away on which the proof was to stand. The danger is that we find ourselves in the situation of the Aristotelian who simply refused to look through Galileo's telescope: sheer prejudice, barring the way to all knowledge and science, and yet at the same time something that might incline us to look into the laws of optics to find out how the instruments actually work. To check the significance of the analyses carried out so far and preview the comparative background for their development, we can transfer them to another eon of civilization, to the Middle Ages and Dante where, filtered through the mediation of Christianity, there is a quite surprising linkage with the Cretan mythologem. The comparative method for interpreting myths and rites put forward here has constantly drawn strength from the strong cord running between modern times and remote prehistory, and if ancient Greece represents an essential intermediate stage in this, Christianity stands as its symmetrical equivalent and is closer to ourselves, the two of them forming, as it were, the two focal points of the immense elliptical orbit that we must travel. Let us see then if medieval Christianity can offer any elements to make our attempt to bridge the gap between ourselves and the archaic and ancient labyrinth safer and less reckless by supplying us with a direct illustration of the transition from ancient mythology to Christianity.

5. From Prehistory to the Middle Ages

The motif of the labyrinth runs all through Dante's *Inferno*, to the extent that the inferno as a whole might be thought of as an immense labyrinth in which the damned, guilty of rejecting God's love, are held prisoner. The real torments of hell begin in the second circle, and there at the start sits Minos, the Cretan king who had the labyrinth built. The mythical labyrinth monster is given an ingenious new twist by Dante: a long tail coiling around his body, used to point each damned soul to its destined circle. At the start of the seventh circle, the circle of the violent, we find the Minotaur, "Crete's infamy" (l'infamia di Cretì).[79] Here, perhaps, the features of the classical beast are magnificently inverted: a human head set on the body of a bull. In the narrative, Dante and Virgil only just manage to escape the Minotaur's wrath. At first sight, there is nothing very surprising in Dante's recourse to the labyrinth story: it was well known in the Middle Ages and often reproduced in cathedrals with Theseus taken to symbolize Christ. In fact, Dante's Virgil refers to Theseus in addressing the Minotaur. What is remarkable, however, is Dante's confident linking of the labyrinth to the theme of the afterlife and to human violence, the real and truly infernal driving-force throughout the first part of the *Divine Comedy*. Canto XIV, still in the circle of the violent, has even more specific ties to the mythical material we have been reviewing.

First comes the unprecedented verbal violence of Capaneus, who was eventually punished by Jove's thunderbolt like the Giants he mentions (and like the Titans, who are often confused with them). And then this highly pertinent evocation:

> A mountain stands there that once was gay
> with waters and leafy branches, called Ida:
> now it is deserted. And like something forbidden [*cosa vieta*]
> Rhea once chose it as a safe cradle [*cuna fida*]
> for her little son and, to hide him better
> whenever he cried, had them raise a mighty din therein [*vi facea far grida*].[80]

After our mythological journey among the collective figures of Greek mythology, it is quite extraordinary that Dante should refer to the Curetes myth immediately after another myth and figure that are perfect parallels to the Titans. Dante combines these mythic elements of Greek origin by using his Latin sources,[81] but he perfectly understands their etiological connotation and inserts them in the Christian view of human history as derived from original sin, to which the contrast between the past fertility of the mountain and its present state of abandon alludes. With profound religious and anthropological insight, he intuited the link between them, highly relevant to the theme of the canto itself: the violence that distances man from God. Obviously Dante could not see that the Curetes are the mythical-ritual transformation of the Titans. Besides, as a man of his age, he remained suspended between rejecting St. Augustine's "false and lying" (falsi e bugiardi) gods of antiquity and accepting ancient myth as a prefiguration of the Christian religion.[82] In Dante we find the two extremes between which Christianity has always moved in relation to the classical world, extremes which modernity was unwittingly to inherit as regards mythology: total opposition or reorganized adoption, irreconcilable conflict or excessive harmonization. It would all seem to derive from preconceived theological views, and all regarded as equally outmoded by our modern consciousness, but the opposite is true, given that modernity did not perceive the medieval roots of its own awareness and increasing wavering on myth, destined to become the antagonism between *Kultur* and *Zivilisation* in the nineteenth century. It was precisely in its religious oscillation, where what was stated at either extreme immediately appeared to be contradictory, that Christianity found its way to relate to the culture of the ancient world and what it represented.

Dante sensed that the irreducible opposition between Dionysus and Christ brought fresh clarity to things, a possible starting-point to set up a new nonoppositional relationship, and this basic intuition opens up a broader horizon of understanding but one that is never defined once and for all, since it is destined to reappear throughout history at increasing levels of definition. It can be seen in the thoroughgoing study of the opposition carried out by Nietzsche in the nineteenth century, on the side of Dionysus and *Kultur*, and by Girard in the twentieth century, on the side of Christ and *Zivilisation*. This oscillation is illuminative because it has never been definitively concluded at a historical level, and my thesis is that it expresses the interpretive space opened up by Christian mediation, a space carrying forward a tendency already present in the ancient world where it was less keenly perspicuous since it still fell short of the separation that total opposition was to make possible.

Dante not only realized that this mythic material was the oldest available to him but understood that the cave on Mount Ida represented an origin as old as humanity itself. In fact, the lines quoted introduce one of the most singular symbols in the *Divine Comedy*, the Old Man (*Veglio*) of Crete, a large statue standing in the cave of the Curetes, made out of metal and other materials. This symbol is inspired by the statue seen in a dream in Daniel 2:31–45, where its different parts indicate the various heathen empires finally superseded by the eschatological triumph of Israel's God. With originality, Dante blends the biblical allegory and the mythic symbolism coming from Crete in one organic and highly imaginal view.[83] The *Veglio* represents the *vetus homo*, old humanity in its fallen state of sin that Christ has made new, but still in an inverted manner, given that we are in the midst of hell and the old man with his tears from which flow the infernal rivers provides the explanation of hell's complex hydro-punitive network. At the same time, the statue alludes to the history of the empire in transferring the imperial eagle (the *translatio imperii*) from Troy to Rome, toward which the *Veglio*'s head is turned, with all the ambiguity of the hoped-for harmony between church and empire and of their ferocious strife. Thus the statue evokes a very serious state of corruption and Dante's hope to save contemporary Christendom through his epic poem by expressing the mediation of Christ in its real capacity to join heaven and earth, human history and divine revelation, and pagan antiquity with the salvation destined for humankind.

These theological and conceptual coordinates seem almost as remote from us as the mythic and magic universe of archaic Greece, but show themselves to be much closer as soon as we perceive the specific meaning of Western (Latin) Christianity, once it underwent the shock of the collapse of the Roman Empire. St. Augustine's *De civitate Dei* provided a spiritual answer to this huge mediatory crisis, opposing the invisible *civitas Dei* to the external *civitas diaboli*, but this very scheme betrays an anxiety about human salvation that was destined to become the unmistakable mark of western Europe.[84] The same anxiety was felt by Dante, who wanted to provide a final solution, even though his grandiose project would turn out to be a complete failure, historically.

In spite of that, the very excess of the Western eschatological tradition, tormented by the idea of achieving its saving mediation, conceals in itself an unseen historicity and is the premise of our historical sensibility. With the complete disparagement of human nature in its fallen state, distanced from God—a contemptuous attitude promoted by St. Augustine in particular—the notion of original sin itself came to be an irreversible drama within the very heart of man as a cultural, historical being. Dante recognizes this theological and metaphysical reflection, as well as the centuries-old inconclusive debate that it set off, but he already begins to move its conclusions in the direction of a historical, religious origin traceable through the symbols and myths that define it. The origin exists and is a means for interpreting the history that begins there.

Through this comparison with a medieval Christian writer another aspect becomes immediately clear after a lapse of many centuries, namely that Christianity is not a sort of antimyth to demolish previous myths with its definitive truth but is, in turn, a mythical system examining closely the core of knowledge and objectual acquisition contained in the ancient myths, a system that is developed by always casting ahead with the goal of mediation toward new horizons, new awareness. It is precisely because Christianity shares in mythology that it brings fresh factors to its understanding, which tend toward increasing historicization and humanization. This tendency is particularly characteristic of Latin Christianity, with the restlessness and moral and historical anxieties distinctive of its religious vision which, after the fall of the Western Roman Empire, was a vision no longer endorsed in itself by enduring political institutions.

This preamble enables us to grasp the motifs of discontinuity and continuity in Dante, medieval poet and thinker, that separate him from and connect him with the distant past that he sets out to explore, placing him more or less halfway (in one of the two focal points of our historical ellipse) between the knowledge of the ancients, which moves within the parameters of myth, and modern knowledge, which proudly believes it has put all myth behind it, and blindly forgets the several layers in the interpretive history of mythology (i.e., cancels the myth as interpretative endeavor). This complementary imbalance between ancient and modern shows a wealth of context in the ancient that the modern's greater awareness is in danger of losing at any moment, lapsing into ideology—second-rate mythology—inferior in itself because intransitive and closed off from exchange, which is the very soul of cultural mediations. In this context, Christianity, chiefly Western Christianity, plays an irreplaceable role of historical and hermeneutic intermediation.

Dante's understanding already inclines in the direction of our own, incompletely in regard to the data available to him and yet that incompleteness is compensated by a sense of assurance unknown to us with our wealth of documentation and methodological subtleties. The myth holds an Ariadne's thread to guide us, but it is within the labyrinth of myth that we must look for it. And the Ariadne thread does not fail to help us even in a decisive moment of the whole *Divine Comedy*. In canto XXVI of *Purgatorio* the purging souls are about to pass through the final purification taking them to paradise and perform movements of joy reproducing those of the old crane-dance to symbolize their escape from the labyrinth of perdition under the guidance of Theseus-Christ, as represented on the floor of Chartres cathedral.[85] From the prehistory of Göbleki Tepe and Çatal Höyük we find ourselves in the core of Western civilization, and this is due to the symbolic and cognitive power of myth, capable of crossing many millennia, ceaselessly adapting to ever new shapes and needs.

We shall have other occasions to call on Dante to point the way through the infernal labyrinth of sacrificial rites and myths, and to find our way out, guaranteed to us by the figure of Virgil, the symbol of natural human knowledge, the only possible prerequisite for access to divine revelation, which consists, ultimately, in more thorough humanization. We have far to go, and the violent implications of the labyrinth myth tell us that the way will not be easy. But therein lies its necessity, its potential significance for salvation. We must pause now, though our journey has just begun, to consider an internal detail of the mythologem that can be understood without lapsing into naturalism as long as we keep it inside its strictly collective framework; this detail is the persisting linkage to the sphere of the family and sexual generation.

It is interesting that all Dante's scholars, in commenting on canto XIV of *Inferno*, devote their efforts to the impressive allegory of the *Veglio* and pay little attention to the previous image of Rhea choosing Mount Ida "like something forbidden [*cosa vieta*]" in order to get "a safe cradle" for her baby, although this preparatory scene offers us a revealing and intentional contrast. In Dante the ancient Cretan myth becomes the potential reversal of a diabolical contiguity between violence and sexual desire to which Jupiter's mother reacts with employing "something forbidden," that is, by going to a forbidden place that remains the only hope for salvation in the abyss of objectual destruction. There is little doubt that this is for Dante a hidden pagan prophecy about the coming of the Christian Redeemer, represented in canto VI of *Purgatorio* as the ancient king of the gods crucified on earth for saving humanity (*o sommo Giove / che fosti in terra per noi crucifisso*).[86] The crucifixion of Jupiter/Christ fulfils the scene on Mount Ida and illustrates the final way out of the maze and its sacrificial couplings: the divine child who knowingly accepts becoming a "cosa vieta" and being sacrificed so as to solve the human knot of violence from within.

In the ancient myths things are more uncertain and complicated than in the *Comedy* but the objectual hope for salvation is not different from Dante's and his comparative symbolism emphasizes revealing analogies to them. The Cretan myths are always characterized by a recognizable family pattern and at the center of the labyrinth we always find a child born out of irregular sexual relations. For the community these represent the overturning of procreation as protected by the order of the family, on which the community relies for stability and permanence. The irregularity of a son conceived in violation of the rules governing the institution of the family is counterbalanced by his death as an evil monster at the hands of his beneficent double (the Minotaur killed at the hands of Theseus), by his unjust murder being followed by divine rebirth (Dionysus devoured by the Titans and given a new life, reborn from his father, Zeus), and by his being protected as a divine infant whose killing is transfigured and configured in the form of an initiation ceremony (Zeus saved by the Curetes). Through these strands of evolution, we are able to make out, in the middle of the collective labyrinth, a mythical-ritual updating of the mystery of generation with its dangers and its vital importance for the life of the community, reminding us that the first object in real terms for human beings is represented by their fellow human beings with whom they have dealings, in particular those dangerous and necessary dealings that are human sexual relations.

All the character-types in the age-old drama of copulation, with its dangerous yet essential outcome for society's objectual existence, are to be found variously overlaid in the winding ways of the labyrinth, and they are constantly evoked in a state of affairs still lacking the reassuring mediations that the mythical-ritual machinery takes on the task to confirm. In the Cretan mythologem, along with the collective divinity, we repeatedly see a female divinity who has the features of a mother goddess, a goddess of love, or a virgin goddess: sexual characteristics that are all cross-referential from the point of view of the sacred. The male god may appear as a divine child of the mother goddess, or as her *paredros*, that is, as a lover and companion subordinate to her, or as the father to her children with the full status of husband.

These two types, male and female, combine variously with one another and with the collective divinity (who, in turn, may be male or female) and correspond to a leitmotiv of the labyrinth mythologem, indicated affirmatively or negatively by the generative function of the mother goddess Rhea, by the failed matrimonial ambitions of Ariadne, and by the married Pasiphae's perverse mating with a divine bull that gave birth to the Minotaur: the motif of the *hieros gamos*, the sacred wedding, perfectly recognizable in our myths that tell of the copulation of a female divinity with Cronus or Zeus, where complete success could only be assured by the sacrifice of the participants, or of one of them, often the weakest and last on the scene, the troublesome newborn baby who in order to be accepted by society had to go through the bloody mediation of sacrifice or else find an acceptable substitute. The mythic material suggests that the sacred coupling took place inside the labyrinth and that the divine child born as a result was sacrificed to the mother goddess. This is what Hera's fury in the Titans myth indicates. However, as Ariadne's story shows, death could be the mother's fate as well. The *paredros* of the goddess is killed in many other myths; for example, in the myth of Venus and Adonis, deriving from the story of Dumuzi/Tammuz and Inanna/Ishtar found on Cyprus and throughout the Near East. Some of the prehistoric tombs referred to earlier contain the remains of children or fetuses, pregnant women, or women with a child. In the Moravian triple burial, resulting in all likelihood from a human group sacrifice, two men and a young pregnant woman are buried in positions with clear sexual significance and red ochre covers the woman's genital zone, which is covered by the hand of the man on her left.[87] This area of research is likely to produce further revelations. It was no accident that Dante placed Minos at the start of the circle concerned with desire in one of its most frequent and powerful manifestations, sexual desire. This desire has to be understood neither as the automatic manifestation of an already-formed libidinal instinct, nor as the simple consequence of indeterminate mimesis, but rather as the cultural interaction of collective mediations on the individual's somatic and biological constitution, with the aim of reliably perpetuating the human object in its renewal from generation to generation.

We shall now examine a single mythical-ritual whole, where the labyrinth theme will serve very well as a key: the Eleusinian Mysteries and the Orphic movement that, in my opinion, were closely linked. These in turn will then provide us with a key to the whole of Greek civilization.

2.

Orphism and the Eleusinian Mysteries

1. Comparative Incomprehension

The Greeks themselves thought of Orphism and the Eleusinian Mysteries as among the most significant manifestations of their religious life, if not the most important, and we have already seen Orphism's role in the development of Greek thinking about myth. However, there remains much controversy as to their interpretation. This cannot simply be due to the fragmentary and circumstantial nature of the evidence, which applies equally to many events and phenomena in antiquity, but instead results from religious or antireligious bias in collating the fragments, from individual prejudice leading to tendentious interpretations and even to denying that any sense is to be made of the material. The real difficulty may lie in the very fact that Orphism and the Mysteries are the most profound religious expression of a civilization of crucial importance to ourselves both historically and symbolically, and the contradictory, confused state of research on the subject would appear to confirm it. The failure to perceive the religious and historical importance of the transition from Dionysus to Christ, which applies to practically all those studying the subject, inevitably has repercussions on the analysis of cults centering on Dionysus, as we shall see.

Between the end of the nineteenth century and the beginning of the twentieth, Orphism and the Mysteries came to be seen as precursors of Christianity. Christ was regarded as a particularly successful variant on the theme of the god who dies and is born again, a central figure in the various mystery cults found throughout the ancient world. This is the position taken by James George Frazer and many other scholars engaged in the vast cognitive undertaking of comparing religions, which proved a failure because it could not provide a consistent explanation for similar myths and rituals recurring all over the world. But the underlying reason for the failure of comparativism may be seen in its confusion of the standard sacrificial religions of the ancient world and Christianity, thereby violating the basic principle of positivism, respect for observable data, a principle that these scholars generally followed and at its best even proved to be prephenomenological.

Their confusion took hold widely and remains the dominant view among countless cultured people as well as the public at large, but it does not alter the fact that it was a serious rebuff, scientifically speaking, deep enough to still condition researchers unconsciously. Our indifference and mental sluggishness easily blind us to the difference between the brutal violence of archaic sacrifice and the real meaning of Christ's Passion, because that difference lies precisely at the point where they resemble each other most closely. Nonetheless, objectively and objectually, such blindness remains an error. And it is patently obvious that if the difference is ignored, no transition is even possible, no mediation in the sense of a communicating intermediate measure and of a symbolic cultural model capable of recognizing in itself the history that made it experienceable: the entire Christian dialectic interpreting history and religions is rendered pointless before it is conceived. Without troubling about matters of belief, this is deplorable from a purely historical and cultural viewpoint.

Frazer, Durkheim, and Freud were not so very wide of the mark in their attempts to give a unified explanation for religion, but they were bound to fall short basically because *one* of the phenomena, the Judeo-Christian tradition, on which their theory ultimately depended, would not entirely fit in with the others; on the contrary, it silently interacted with them, though through the conditioning of a dramatic, conflictual logic of historical and religious opposition. Nietzsche's position can be seen as a farsighted but desperate attempt to correct the mistaken position of comparativism, rejecting its positivist leveling-down and praising Dionysus anew in its place. This turnaround had the merit of relaunching the whole question, but the effect on Nietzsche personally was so terrifying that nobody dared openly follow him.

While a Joseph De Maistre or an Alessandro Manzoni, with their strongly cognitive view of Christianity, would have diagnosed the causes of these failures at once, even without being aware of all their potentialities or premises, these very same causes have proved too embarrassing, too *revealing*, to be admitted, and the strategies applied to the question, which is the subject of the present chapter, have been modified. On the one hand, the importance and scope of Orphism and the Eleusinian Mysteries have been played down almost to the point of denial and on the other, in an attempt to pursue Nietzsche's interpretation but in a diluted form, Orphism has been seen as a sort of alternative religion to Christianity. At the same time, the Orphic references to crude violence at the origin of mankind have been attenuated in two ways: by turning either to a Schopenhauerian metaphysics, as in Colli, or to the ahistorical paraphernalia of Jungian collective archetypes, as in Kerényi, who glorifies the cult of Dionysus as the worship of *zoe*, corresponding to "the experience of *infinite life* [*unendlichen Lebens*]" distinguished from *bios*, the "finite life" of the single individuals.[1] Kerényi's distinction is evocative and pertinent but tends to minimize or even justify the sacrifice of the individuals to the divine force from which they come, turning it into a humanist idol after the style of the vision in *The Magic Mountain* but lacking the illuminating ambiguity Mann gives in that scene.

Leaving aside the fact that already in antiquity the Dionysian cult was substantially a drama, such sophistical, diversionary efforts to tip the balance in favor of Dionysus, when confronted with the plain documentary evidence, turn out to be an even greater failure than the attempts of the comparativists. Who could *openly* propose a return to the god of a cult where human sacrifice is an essential component? What we see here, once again, is the confutation of Nietzsche's endeavor, no less theoretically than de facto, but without the ecstatic illuminations of the reckless eulogist of Dionysus who, unlike his mediocre, trendy commentators, did not back out and paid the price for it. Then why not—we might ask ourselves somewhat ingenuously—try the one avenue as yet unexplored, that is, to thematize phenomenologically the content ascribable to the teachings and figure of Christ, taking its hermeneutical potential seriously? And why should we deny ourselves a dialogue with those voices that in Greece were looking for religious and sapiential mediations closer to human reality, though without finding a definition nearly as stable?

However, to avoid precisely this, contemporary scholars have an implicit twofold objective, and they seem prepared to go to any lengths to achieve it. They refuse to recognize not only comparativism's defeat in confusing paganism and Christianity but also the failure of attempts to restore Dionysianism. Certain French structuralist scholars, led by Marcel Detienne and Jean-Pierre Vernant, have tried in vain to seize the high ground, vaunting their "culinary theory" whereby the only thing that matters in sacrifice is the ritual preparation of the flesh, not the spilling of blood.[2] Likewise, they protest that a single concept of sacrifice valid for all cultures is an arbitrary idea coming from the Christian tradition: as if to die under the obsidian blade of an Aztec priest, to be torn to shreds by a crazed Dionysian mob, buried alive like the Vestals, throated, impaled, flayed, beheaded, stoned as substitute victims in all the civilizations of the ancient world, no one excluded, were all quite different and strictly not comparable—as if they were not quite simply what common sense tells us. But the resources of formalistic differentialism are infinite. Even allowing that some of these examples could be considered as sacrifice, can cannibalism or the death penalty be fairly described as such? Certainly, these scholars' contribution to classical studies should not be underestimated, but they contrive to do something here that never even occurred to Galileo's academic colleague who refused to look into the new instrument to gaze at the sky: they deny the very existence of telescopes. The final goal is openly declared by Detienne in his introductory essay of *La cuisine du sacrifice en pays grec*:

> Today . . . it is important to say that the notion of sacrifice is indeed a category of the thought of yesterday, conceived of as arbitrarily as totemism . . . both because it gathers into one artificial type elements taken from here and there in the symbolic fabric of societies and because it reveals the surprising power of annexation that Christianity [*l'étonnant empire que le christianisme englobant*] still subtly exercises on the thought of these historians and sociologists who were convinced they were inventing a new science.[3]

The polemical thrust is directed to Frazer and Durkheim, but also to Girard whom Detienne mentions in the last long endnote.[4] Sacrifice would therefore be an invention of imperialistic and all-embracing Christianity, a reasoning that dusts off in an inverted way the old argument of the *furta Graecorum* with which the first Christian apologists explained the resemblances between Christianity and the pagan rituals and myths.[5] It is not too surprising that the formalistic differentialism turns out to be a glaring indifferentiation blurring cultures and history in the imaginary perfection of its synchronic classifications. Should we suppose that the Vedic reflection on sacrifice or the central role of human immolations in the Meso-American civilizations were the result of Christian influence? Far from discarding sacrifice as "a category of the thought of yesterday," it is this frivolous declaration itself that is to be put in that category which reveals decades later that refusing sacrifice amounts to a refusal of applying rationality to human history.

In this respect, the evolution, or one could say involution, of Walter Burkert's ideas is pertinent. One of the greatest authorities on Greek religion, his fundamental study, *Homo Necans*, still shows the favorable influence of the great age of positivistic ethnology in the Germanic world. The theory he expounds there, that sacrifice derived from the animal behavior of hunting, is unacceptable as a hypothesis because animal behavior and instinct alone cannot explain the birth of culture, though at least it had the merit of admitting the reality of sacrifice; it was, moreover, an anthropologically unidealized explanation. Burkert subsequently acknowledged quite frankly that there were limitations to his hypothesis,[6] but rather than attending to these he gradually shifted the accent in his research toward a kind of skeptical biologically based differentialism, which has appreciably reduced its value. His attitude toward the Dionysian *sparagmos* is particularly revealing. Where *Homo Necans* conveyed a sense of its enormous importance, he later comes to define it as an "exaggerated, paranoic variant" of the sacrificial meal and as "the most bizarre Dionysian myth."[7] There can be little progress in understanding Greek religion when an essential component is dismissed as a bizarre pathological anomaly, though by what standard of normality we are not told.

Moreover, this censorship regarding Dionysus is basically the same as we have already encountered several times in respect to the concept of the origin, the postmodern attempt—brilliantly formulated by Michel Foucault and developed not without wit by his follower Giorgio Agamben—to eliminate once and for all the anthropological noumenon discovered by modern philosophy by alleging it to be paradoxical and illusory,[8] an attempt that reveals much more than what these philosophers supposed once we come to understand the human paradox genetically in terms of my theory of mediation. Swept along on this intellectual wave but not suspecting its true potential, Burkert states quite flatly that "the concept of 'origin' is mythical thinking, applying the tale of birth or creation to the constant flux of reality,"[9] unconsciously using the concept of origin to explain its mythical origin. The objection is superfluous besides, and there is no worth in pointing out, however true it is, that the idea of origin must be applied from a nonreductionistic viewpoint, that is, phenomenological *and* explanatory, as the present study sets out to show in a systematic fashion. The real objection—to the more naive argument of Burkert as to the more acute reasonings of Foucault and Agamben as well—is that the origin is a myth just because myth *is* the origin, and that the result of such refusal cannot be but a surreptitious and regressive mythology which is unaware and devoid of the cognitive object pursued by the old mythology. And finally, the concept of origin cannot be excluded in any genuinely scientific research. Exclusion only occurs when the origin is obscurely sensed as dangerous, which is proof, however negative, of the reality of *this* origin and could hardly be more significant. Burkert's strategy of evasion is really only a more sophisticated version of the old confusion between sacrificial religions and Christianity and ends by devolving into a more nuanced version of the *furta Graecorum* argument. He sees the Passion as an exceptional repetition of pagan sacrifice, while the god who dies and is born again in the Mysteries is viewed as a partial overlap of a Christian interpretation.[10] The concept of origin is only used to quash any reading capable of clarifying the "continuous flux of reality," in a vague kind of perspectivism derived from Nietzsche that in applying its apparent painstaking accuracy dismisses a correct historical perception. Unlike Nietzsche, and without the ideological haughtiness of Detienne, Burkert reduces Christianity and pagan rites to the status of mere cultural influences that mutually cancel each other out. Misunderstanding Dionysus and misunderstanding Christ merge in the end and become one.

By way of introduction to Orphism and Eleusis, I propose to analyze an important papyrus from the third century BC, found at Gurob in Egypt. Although the left half of the text is almost completely missing, the papyrus not only contains many elements of myth but reveals an essential aspect of

Dionysianism in the Mysteries: its character as a complex system of ritual transformations that initiates effectively had to relive. We shall find it useful to consider it alongside an Orphic tablet that is close to it in several respects.

2. The Gurob Papyrus

We will begin at once with the papyrus fragment, published by Josiah Gilbart Smyly in 1921 and here reconstructed thanks to the readings by Colli and West.[11] As Smyly says, the text "was written in prose, but there seem to be many fragments of verse embedded in it,"[12] whereby I follow a compromise between the overall reproduction of the papyrus lines and a different division suggesting the insertion of more liturgical and poetical parts:[13]

. . . so that he may find [*heurei*]
. . . gather <the pieces of raw flesh> [*homa*][14]
. . . through the initiation [*dia ten teleten*]
<mutilated>[15] myself, expiated the fathers' pains [*poinas pateron*]
. . . save me, great Brimo
. . . and Demeter and Rhea
. . . and armed Curetes
. . . . .
. . . so that we may make fine offerings [*hiera*][16]
. . . the ram and the goat [*tragos*]
. . . countless gifts
. . . and near the pasture by the river
<taking the testicles> of the goat [*tragou*]
. . . that he eats the other flesh,
but the uninitiated are not to be present
. . . consecrated to be burned up [*aneire<menon>*][17]
. . . prayer . . .
I call upon <Protogo>nus[18] and Eubuleus
. . . I invoke the wide . . .
. . . you, parched with thirst
. . . of Demeter and Pallas for us
. . . O Eubuleus Irichipegus,

save me . . . <Hurler of Light>ning [*<Asterop>eta*][19]!
. . . Phanes: ONLY ONE DIONYSUS,[20] tokens [*symbola*]
. . . GOD IN THE WOMB
. . . I have drunk cold [*psychron*] . . . ass herdsman [*boukolos*]
. . . formula [*synthema*]: ABOVE BELOW [*ano kato*] . . .
. . . and what you were allowed to squander
. . . throwing into the basket [*eis ton kalathon embalin*]
. . . spinning top [*konos*], bull-roarer [*rhombos*], astragali
. . . mirror [*esoptros*]

This papyrus text seems so hopelessly fragmented as to defy any interpretation beyond isolated details. However, through taking more comprehensive information as a whole, the mediatory theory and its corollary, the unified method for interpreting myth and ritual, enable us to identify a consistent unified system of representation.[21] Among the text's more recognizable elements, we can start by looking at its manifestly ritual nature.

The words are addressed by a priest to a believer (ll. 19 and 27,)[22] initiating him into a mystery cult, with appropriate invocations and ceremonial explanations. Presumably, the believer responds by reciting the initiation formulas.[23]

The verb *heurisko*, I find, has a specific meaning in the context, alluding to the soul's salvation, directly evoked here by the repeated invocation "save me" (ll. 5 and 22). The expression "so that he finds" refers to salvation that can only come after much searching, expressed by the parching thirst of l. 19. This sacrificial thirst (originally for blood), traditionally attributed to the dead, is transformed into an eschatological symbol, into a heartbroken plea for conclusive soterial mediation. The same verb, in the same context, is used on some Orphic tablets placed in tombs as a last sacrament and safe conduct into the next world. It is interesting to compare the papyrus with the following example (from Pharsalus, fourth century BC):[24]

You will find [*heureseis*] a spring on the right of the houses of Hades
and a straight white cypress next to it:
do not even approach that spring closely.
And further on you will find [*heureseis*] the cold [*psychron*] water that
flows

from the marsh of Mnemosyne: and the guardians standing over it,
who will ask you why you have come there.
But tell them the whole Truth [*aletheien*].
Say to them: I am the son [*pais*] of Earth and starry [*asteroentos*] Heaven;
my name is Asterios. I am parched with thirst: let me
drink at the spring.

The most striking features of this text, which corresponds to the papyrus in several ways, are the symbolism of the two springs, the reference to telling the complete Truth (ἀλήθεια), and the cosmic formulas of ll. 8–9 with their play on the words ἀστερόεντος/Ἀστέριος (full of stars/Asterios), to be also connected to Zeus Ἀστεροπετά (Hurler of Lightning) in l. 22 of the papyrus. Comparison reveals that the believer in the latter text has drunk the cold water of Mnemosyne (l. 25), while the believer in the tablet, by doing the same, expects to attain the long-sought-after salvation. There appear to be even more significant links with the sacrificial mediations evoked by the labyrinth and its transformation into a symbol of the afterlife. We are in the dark, unstable, discontinuous region typical of the Greek afterlife, similar to the Egyptian, and still more characteristic of the Mesopotamians' next world, which is dominated by an anguished uncertainty far less frequently found in Egyptian civilization given its great confidence in the laws of the cosmos, represented by the Nile and the monarchic rule of the Pharaohs that was its mediatory and objectual mainstay. In the fragile, spectral netherworld depicted on the tablet, where, however, faith persists in a *logos* answering to a mediation that can only be defined as magical-rational, the dead are able to find their way by obeying the tablet's peremptory injunction not to drink the water of the first spring and not to set off spontaneously in the first direction that presents itself. This is a motif that will be developed in fables and folktales: immediacy as the worst enemy, as literally consisting in a superficial or arrogant refusal of mediation, and consequently making it impossible to access the saving object, the Object tout court.

The divine guardians alone are the mediators holding the secrets of this sacred space, occupying much the same position as the priests in labyrinth ceremonies must have done; and here the analogies to Egyptian eschatology, with its faith in the magic effectiveness of appropriate formulas, start to become more numerous. The guardians subjected the dead to a real examination, for which they needed to show themselves prepared by using the ritual expressions found in the text. In fact, the tablet, just as it was not a simple aide-mémoire, was also not properly an eschatological vademecum or personal talisman, since it had to speak on behalf of the deceased, to guarantee that the conditions laid down by the judges of the otherworld had been met. The atmosphere and eschatological structure are very close to the Egyptian *Book of the Dead*, which was also put into tombs as a token for entering the next world, where the dead person had similarly to find his way in a shifting, treacherous environment and be cross-examined by the gods beyond . The dead Egyptian has to identify with Osiris, the Egyptian god of dismemberment whom all the Greeks considered to be related to Dionysus, a view that falls on deaf ears nowadays because the comparative method has been discredited. And yet the similarities between Osiris and Dionysus are so significant and the links between Egypt and Crete are so well documented that pure coincidence here would be far more amazing than cultural contact, already the norm in the prehistoric world. Naturally, this does not mean there were no differences; rather it points to the existence in Egypt and throughout the Near East of cults where a god was variously dismembered and then reborn to ensure life and fertility, just like Dionysus.

The process of salvation linked to the soterial mediation of Dionysus, with whom the dead had to identify, is represented on the tablet in the form of a dramatized sketch. Though the god is not directly named, we shall be able to recognize his presence and make sense of the papyrus if we first look at Orphism in general, since its central point was salvation through Dionysus.

3. A Digression on Orphism

Orphism was a secret religious movement going back at least to preclassical or even archaic Greece, as can already be deduced indirectly from the antiquity that the Greeks always attributed to the Orphic traditions and, more directly, from the archaic nature of much of the relevant evidence.[25] A few general remarks can serve to strengthen these initial inferences. Tradition has it that Onomacritus founded an Orphic sect at Athens toward the end of the sixth century BC; he compiled a collection of material attributed to Orpheus and, according to the sources, evidently preexisting; he also had the epics attributed to Homer written down.[26] The Orphic writings in question are the *hieroi logoi*, the sacred discourses, not to be confused with Holy Scripture as we understand it or with treatises of a sapiential or philosophical kind, but they undoubtedly contained instructions for performing rites supported by explanations of a mythical sort.[27] We shall return to them later. During the same period the mystic-philosophical movement of Pythagoreanism started in the south of Italy.[28] Since its ideals for this life and its vision of the afterlife have close points of contact with Orphism, it seems reasonable to assume that both Pythagoreanism and Orphism stemmed from a common tradition based on Orpheus, which led directly to the Orphic sect of Onomacritus and strongly influenced the Pythagorean school. In any case, Orphism undoubtedly predates Pythagoreanism.[29] The evidence as a whole makes it possible to link the wandering "sacred wise men" of eighth-century Greece to what were later called *Orpheotelestai*, that is, the initiators to the Orphic Mysteries, charlatan-like magicians who would seem to have been the epigones of a much older model.[30]

The beginnings of Orphism are unclear but clearly appear to merge with the cult of Dionysus. In one direction, the religious phenomenon points toward the proto-Dionysian cults on Crete; in the other, to a shamanistic influence from the north.[31] However, we can assert that the Cretan religion represents the central core of Orphism. Indeed, Cretan civilization and its cultural intercourse with Egypt and the Near East are essential to our understanding of how Greek civilization and religion arose. Given the cultural ties and the existence throughout the eastern Mediterranean of a common cult centered on gods of dismemberment, it seems plausible that contemporary traditions of knowledge would have existed that sought to explain such bloody rites, and that those traditions would have been somehow interconnected and mutually influential. However, all this requires verification. If we look further afield, we can find the dismemberment theme in the Indian Vedic tradition, which was later to acquire a metaphysical aspect with the *Upanishads*. The theme appears variously transfigured and explained, in the persons of Purusha, the primeval man, and Prajapati, Hinduism's sacrificial god par excellence. Indian metaphysics was to develop from the Vedic ritual prescriptions against a background of dismemberment myths and rituals in a way that closely parallels the Greek speculative interpretations, where

Orphism, with its *hieroi logoi* and Dionysian omophagy, was used, first by the pre-Socratics, then by Plato, and finally by the Neoplatonists. Comparativism in its heyday made a start on exploring these relationships; they certainly deserve serious reconsideration, and we shall return to them later.

Meanwhile, we can reasonably assume that Onomacritus's *hieroi logoi* organized and built on religious traditions from Crete, influenced directly or indirectly by the religious knowledge of neighboring civilizations in Egypt, the Near East, and Mesopotamia. The fundamental aim of Orphism's doctrine of myth and ritual was salvation through an eschatological vision based on metempsychosis—again, a notable point of contact with Indian religion. The movement drew its inspiration from the figure of Orpheus, who, according to Jane Ellen Harrison, might really have existed as a religious reformer.[32] In any case, he was a victim or rather a series of victims linked to a sacred or priestly role, though we should avoid making the correspondence too literal. The features of this figure are too indefinite and legendary to allow any concrete historical identification; besides, Orphism is not in the least concerned with it. Orpheus is not at all recognizable as an individual but rather as a set of powers that find expression in a series of anecdotes. He is a wise man, magician, and prophet, but above all, he is the singer of Apollo. His singing has power to charm the forces of the next world, but he is destined to be torn to pieces by the Dionysian women of Thrace. This fate shows how closely Orpheus is related to Dionysus and the Cretan rites of the Curetes and Titans. Apollo and Dionysus are brother gods who both preside over the phenomena of hallucination and ecstatic possession and show their sacrificial identity in Orpheus,[33] whose Apollonian features and Dionysian fate refer to two different levels of interpretation, perhaps representing different but complementary historical influences: there is one Orpheus, public and exoteric, with links to the north and Apollo, and another esoteric, secret Orpheus linked to Dionysus and Crete. What is decisive about Orpheus is a certain kind of sacral mediation that came into his repertoire through the combination of shamanic rituals from northern Asia with bloody group sacrifices typical of Mediterranean cults, whose novelty lay in addressing the individual follower and his or her desire for salvation and so going beyond the purely collective character of *polis* cults.

The Dionysian *mythos* of Orpheus introduces here the central myth and rite of Orphism and its eschatology: the σπαραγμός or διασπαραγμός culminating in omophagy, the devouring of the infant Dionysus by the Titans,[34] evoked in the ritual precept of l. 2 of the papyrus in West's reconstruction: "gather the pieces of raw flesh [*homa*]." In the Orphic account, following the death of Dionysus, Zeus struck the Titans with a thunderbolt (to which allusion is made at l. 22) and mankind was born from their ashes, endowed with magical powers not only because of their supernatural origin but also for a reason we will see in a moment:[35] there is evidence that the crime was attributed to the Titans by Orphism—by Onomacritus to be exact—making an alteration to the earlier conjectural myth of Zagreus, the Cretan divinity associated or identified with Dionysus. That this ancestral crime gave rise to mankind's Titanic nature, that is, the inclination to evil and violence, is the anthropological cornerstone of Orphism's etiological myth. Violence condemns man to the "wheel of rebirth" (*kyklos tes geneseos*), a cycle of painful violent reincarnations,[36] which corresponds to "the fathers' pains" referred to in l. 4.[37] However, since the Titans devoured Dionysus, man possesses a divine Dionysian part that the follower of his sect has to externalize.[38] This is the keystone of the Orphic message of salvation and the real explanation of the magical power attributed to the Titanic ashes. The presence of the omophagy myth can be deduced from this central passage even when, as normally happens, there are only allusive hints. The divine part left by Dionysus is the soul imprisoned in the body (σῶμα), that is, its tomb (σήμά),[39] just as the child god found an unnatural tomb within the bodies of the Titans.

The Orphics, then, placed omophagic dismemberment at the origin of the present race of men. Before then, in the Golden and Silver Ages, there had been races unacquainted with violence. We are still in the area of mythic motifs concerning collective gods responsible for lynching, and precisely for that reason, whether considered to be evil or benign, they performed a mediatory role. This detail of moral qualification had a very different significance in periods when responsibility was mostly collective and objective, and connected to states and actions preexisting any individual intention whatever. The evil mediation of the Titans served to trigger the saving mediation of the child Dionysus. But if we invert the end purpose of the Orphic *mythos* by putting the accent on the typology of the Titanic event, a remarkable anthropological intuition emerges, still more remarkable if related to the scene of origin presented in the introduction where omophagy is conjectured as humankind's first rite. Apart from the possible significance and limitations of this Orphic belief, it is quite evident that it was the ancient Greeks' greatest and most terrible mythical-religious insight, as Thomas Mann, taking his lead from Nietzsche, clearly understood. Orphism's collective murder is mankind's generative misdeed, even though presented in the form of a myth, and the believer had to relive the misdeed as ritual purification. As another tablet puts it, the Orphic must first suffer Dionysus's passion (*pathein to pathema*) in order to be happy (the used formula is *chaire*, "rejoice") in the afterlife.[40] Ritual repetition of the Titanic murder prepared the soul for liberation. According to several accounts, the participants masked their faces with chalk or white powder to symbolize the ashes in the myth.[41] White is a symbolic color of great antiquity and derives from the victim's whitened bones, all that was finally left after tearing the body to pieces. Through the death mask, evoking the magical power of mankind's originary stuff, the Orphic identified first with the Titans and then with Dionysus himself, the god who dies and is born again. A parallel dynamic is to be observed in Egypt where the believer was transformed into Osiris after death.

In Orphism Dionysus is the exclusive mediator of salvation, in a strictly prepersonal way and expressed as a whole, not by what he has done but by what he has undergone: he is the risen god, Dionysus *digonos* (twice-born) in the usual version of the myth and *trigonos* in the more complex tradition evolved in Orphism. Here, Dionysus is conceived by a goddess, generally taken to be Semele upon being struck by a thunderbolt from Zeus.[42] Then, at seven months the fetus is taken out of the mother's womb and sewn by the father, Zeus, into his own thigh. After this comes his second birth (with the Kumarbi motif of a delivery from a male body), his Titanic death, and his resurrection, in effect his third and final birth. The first stage in this oddly composite myth contains the victimary theme in the shape of the *hieros gamos*, the sacred coupling where the sexual act becomes sacrifice: Zeus kills Semele by his union with her. This account, together with other myths and the evidence from the prehistoric burials mentioned earlier, supports the idea that ritual killing of pregnant women and mothers with infants took place in ancient times. The seven-month-old fetus discovered in a prehistoric burial in France becomes highly significant in the light of this myth:[43] premature birth may well have been what Girard calls a victimary sign, both for mother and child. Some prehistoric images show the mother goddess in the act of giving birth, while another widely dispersed prehistoric image represents her as a toad. Marija Gimbutas records a convincing interpretation of this toad image as representing a fetus only a few months old, while other animal images such as the hedgehog might represent the womb.[44] She notes that the fetus-toad resemblance must have been observed by Upper-Paleolithic and Neolithic people but leaves the question of how they came to do so undiscussed. For this to have had such a decisive impact on symbolism, it must have been repeatedly observed and of great religious importance. Such circumstances are most logically explained by sacrifice, in sacrificial dismembering both ante- and postmortem, probably rounded off by acts of cannibalism in cases where burial was not envisaged.

Orphic eschatology simply took over the sacrificial symbols of prehistory and developed them to represent salvation for the initiate. This is described in the last part of the Orphic tablet but first we must look at the course laid down for the dead to follow. The first spring, Lethe—Forgetting, Oblivion—has to be avoided, while the second offers refreshing ice-cold water, which we find in Egypt symbolizing the saving mediation of Osiris.[45] Here it flows from the marsh of Mnemosyne, Memory. It is fascinating to notice how this ancient symbolism is found again in Dante's *Purgatorio*, in the earthly paradise, where the poet bathes in the waters of *Letè* in order to forget his sins and then in the stream called *Eunoè* to prepare him to "ascend to the stars."[46] Of course, the kind of salvation Dante has in view as he crosses these rivers is entirely moral, very different from the Orphic. And unlike Dante's *Letè*, the Orphic spring of Λήθη (from *lanthano*, I hide, I conceal) contains something that must be avoided at all costs, in the strict sense of a sacred destructive force ("do not even approach that spring closely"). It is therefore the sacral polarity of *a-letheia*, which can only become salvation by excluding, and preserving in itself, the objectual destruction threatened by *lethe*.

Aletheia is the negation of concealment, corresponding to what Martin Heidegger translates as "revealment" or "dis-veiling" (*Unverborgenheit*, literally "unconcealment"). With his ingenious translation Heidegger has real insight into the tensional and polar structure that was the secret of Greek ontology, and the mark of its sacral origin, but fails to recognize its nature as logical-religious mediation capable of granting once and for all the object, as in Parmenides, whereas the modern philosopher impoverishes its magical-productive power by transforming it in a concealment of the object. The

Heideggerian reading of the concealing of *lethe*, to some extent, corresponds to Girard's mis-knowing and, to a lesser extent, to Freud's unconscious, though that remains in itself psychologistic. Its real modern precedent, passing back through Husserl's phenomenon, is Immanuel Kant's noumenon, the abyss of the unknowable that in Heidegger becomes the *Grund*, the foundation manifesting itself as *Abgrund* ("Abyss"), the bottomless ground out of which the unconditional of man's freedom becomes visible.[47] All this is pertinent to the same extent that it is not yet sufficient, and we catch the point if we develop in a radical way the historical import of Kant's distinction between phenomenon and noumenon.[48] Once established that it is ontologically and experientially inaccessible, the *Grund* now appearing to be the *Abgrund*, the *Noumenon* getting out of the *Phänomenon*, unpredictably becomes the supreme source of new horizons, of a knowledge both ancient and new. We recognize this potentiality if we reconnect it to the homologous ancient concealments that were ritual, mythographic, cognitive, and whose purpose was to enable the objectual sphere to be dis-veiled, to manifest a light that could not exist without a shadow zone, a blind spot enabling its field of vision to take shape. Moreover, the concealing of *lethe* is not an originary process to which it is always necessary to return, as in Heidegger, nor an irretrievable loss whose only alternative is an absolute revelation as in Girard, but a historical and cultural process that, at a certain point, becomes capable of interacting with and throwing light upon its origin. This is what Orphic wisdom starts to do, in terms that are still mythically ahistorical. After examining the concealment hiding behind Orphism's dis-veiling, we shall be able to go back to its salvation sequence without being conditioned by it, and recover at one and the same time the phenomenal data of the Orphic concept and a nonreductionist explanation of them.

Souls that have not known the dis-veiling Truth of Dionysus must drink at Oblivion's spring to forget their previous lives and return in another incarnation to a new life of sorrows, while souls purified by Dionysian Knowledge drink at the spring of Memory, which gives them access to the final initiation releasing them from the wheel of rebirths. In Orphic eschatology, purified initiates experience salvation-deification, usually imagined as an ascent into heaven, while those not yet purified return to a cycle of expiatory incarnations, an alternative double that is found in Indian metempsychosis as well. The same doctrine, varying in detail, is to be found in Pindar, Empedocles,

Herodotus, and Plato. The souls of the uninitiated were ineligible for purification and doomed to eternal punishment, often imagined as being stuck in a swamp of mud or having to fill a bottomless pot with water.[49] This threefold eschatological scheme (salvation / middle sphere of expiation / eternal punishment) has analogies to traditional Christian eschatology, as we shall see when we come to examine it.

The initiate had to perform appropriate acts and purifications (*katharmoi*) and could then declare himself to be pure. The process is recorded in various tablets, and it is what the soul repeatedly tells Osiris in the Egyptian *Book of the Dead*. In our tablet, as in several others, final salvation is represented by transforming the formula of hierogamy into a cosmic event: "I am the son of Earth and starry Heaven." When the deceased reaches the heart of the labyrinth-afterlife, he or she symbolically reenacts the divine coupling and, through the lightnings of Zeus *Asteropeta*, becomes Asterios, the Starry One, the divine child born of the god of Heaven and the goddess of Earth, like the Titans but in a purified form. Asterios, star-victim, sun-victim, is one of the Minotaur's names,[50] and it is Dionysus himself who dies at the center of the labyrinth and rises again to free the Orphic initiate from the labyrinth of reincarnations once and for all.[51]

With these elements relating to Orphism, we can now return for a moment to the analysis of the Gurob papyrus, before embarking on a lengthy parenthesis dealing with Eleusis, the other dominant ritual referred to in the papyrus.

We can now make better sense of the expression in l.3 of the papyrus, "through the initiation" (*dia ten teleten*), and appreciate its particular soteriological and cognitive tension, the initiatory mediation that is strictly magical-ritual in character. The rest of the passage illustrates this process of salvation-initiation: the *hiera* in l. 8 were sacred objects carried in procession to Eleusis in a basket and displayed by the hierophant (the one who shows the sacred objects); the *symbola* in l. 23 refer to the real or verbal tokens that served to identify the initiate; in l. 26 *synthema* indicates the formula pronounced to enter the final phase of initiation. This is followed by the list of items in the last three lines, clearly symbolic but this symbolism corresponds to recovered objectuality, to a mediation that has already achieved its purpose or is about to achieve it. The ban on the uninitiated in l. 14 has particular significance because it refers to the *arrheton*, the unrepeatable content of the Mysteries, which could only be experienced after long preparations. With all these specific references, there can be no doubt that the papyrus alludes to the Eleusinian Mysteries or some mystery ceremonies directly connected with them.[52]

If we are to understand the text adequately, we need to throw more light on the Mysteries, which, as the papyrus strongly suggests, had close ties with Orphism.[53] Obviously one might speak of Hellenistic syncretism in this connection, as has been done in the past, and it can certainly not be ruled out. Nonetheless, the way in which Orphism and Eleusis are combined symbolically in the papyrus is so profound and structural that it is already valid proof of the link, only further confirmed by a broad range of evidence. We will now assemble this all together as an organic, understandable whole. Then, having got over the hermeneutic difficulties posed by the Eleusinian Mysteries, we can get over those of the Gurob text as well and move on to use it as our guide toward a more satisfactory understanding of one of the most obscure phenomena of Hellenic religion.

4. The Eleusinian Mysteries

The Eleusinian cult can be traced back to the Mycenean period but only grew to considerable importance under Pisistratus when a proper *Telesterion* (hall of initiation) was built, a many-columned sacred edifice where the Greater Mysteries took place.[54] At its center stood the *Anaktoron*, a rectangular construction open to the sky containing an unhewn rock,[55] according to a scheme that we will find again in the Jerusalem Temple. Thomas Mann had the *Telesterion* in mind when he created his temple with its "forest of columns" in *The Magic Mountain*, while the inner sanctum where the episode's central revelation occurs is, of course, the *Anaktoron*. As also suggested by the fact that the great *Telesterion* was built at the same time as Onomacritus founded the Orphic school, there was an essential connection between Eleusis and Orphism. This is often denied or minimized in spite of the wealth of evidence for it;[56] their doctrinal and ritual affinities are especially revealing. The following reconstruction of the Mysteries, in outline, shows us the same sequence of veiling/dis-veiling found in Orphism though they are very different in their spectacular and collective presentation, which indicates a more ancient ritual origin.

The basic idea at Eleusis was a gradual epiphany of the divine, progressing in three stages: first initiation into the Lesser Mysteries of Agra in February;[57] then into the Greater Mysteries in September after the procession bearing the *hiera*, the sacred objects, from Athens to Eleusis; and finally, a year later, access to the top grade, the *epopteia*. In this way, the *mystes*, the initiate denied free access to knowledge (a word connected with μύω, I close the apertures of eyes or mouth) became the *epoptes*, the one who can see (ἐποpᾶν or ἐφopᾶν) or has seen. The different degrees might be distinguished by the veil with which the *mystai* probably had to cover themselves during forbidden parts of the rite,[58] whereas only the *epoptai* had access to the *a-letheia*. This ultimate dis-veiled truth had but one name, Dionysus, the god of many names and many forms, whose identity was kept a close secret but was gradually revealed to the initiate, leading up to the *mysterium tremendum* and *fascinans* of the god's birth, violent death, and final resurrection.[59] In this supreme initiation it was the believer who died and was reborn through the god, thereby achieving in life the destiny of godhood after death promised by Orphism. The initiate, mediated by Dionysus, enters a sort of permanent, irreversible objectual state of which Orphism appears to be a further development, internalized and personalized to a greater degree than in the Eleusinian cult, where the features of a collective labyrinth initiation are combined with the more evolved features of a soteriological religion in itself performative, in the sense of not being tied to a particular body of doctrine but being effective since it is really experienced.

The presence of Dionysus at Eleusis, often superficially denied, is in fact contextually undeniable on the basis of important textual evidence, of which we shall examine possibly the most striking item, and certain indications recognizable in the rite itself.[60] The Dionysian representations at Eleusis form a consistent whole, with only one central element missing: the god is never explicitly named, his identity being veiled by the ἄρρητον (the ineffable, what is not to be spoken). To see this wholeness, we need only interpret the Eleusinian liturgy as the skillfully orchestrated system of symbolic mediations that, in effect, it was.

The first part of the Great Mysteries makes reference to the abduction of Persephone-Core by Hades or Aidoneus and to her mother Demeter's desperate search for her. There are some exact correspondences to the Mesopotamian myth of Inanna (Ishtar) who descends into the underworld and then finds a substitute victim in Dumuzi (Tammuz).[61] Demeter and Persephone performed an introductory role in the central mystery at Eleusis: the otherwise enigmatic marble statues of a mother and daughter described by Thomas Mann refer to this. The *mythos* of Persephone and Hades is not a straightforward fertility myth as Frazer believed. The descent into the realm of the dead (*kathodos*, the way down) recalls analogous descents made by Orpheus, Dionysus, and Heracles, and is followed by Persephone's return (*anodos*, the way up). This double movement with Hades at its center represents the sacrificial rite of *hieros gamos*, such as we find in the Sumerian myth of the descent of Inanna. It will be useful to pause for a moment to consider the myth since it documents the workings of funerary mediations in Mesopotamia and the relative originality of the initiatory eschatology of the Greeks. Inanna, the queen of heaven, wants to descend into the underworld where—as she later explains—Gugalanna, "the great bull of heaven" and the husband of her sister, Ereshkigal, the queen of the afterlife, has gone. At each of the seven gates to the underworld an official icily interrogates Inanna and, one by one, her clothes and ornaments, endowed with magical powers, are taken from her until she finally comes before the queen of the dead naked and helpless:

> The Anunnaki, the seven judges,
> dispensed justice in her presence.
> Ereshkigal looked at Inanna with her gaze: a gaze of death!
> She spoke words to her: words from an irate heart!
> She threw against her a cry: a cry of condemnation!
> The woman, so ill-treated, was changed into a corpse,
> and the corpse was hung up on a peg.[62]

This marvelous but terrible scene practically speaks for itself: indeed, a myth seldom tells us so much as here in the guise of a funeral mediation, exorcising the terror of death by killing a divine figure thought capable of being born again after this fearful descent into the underworld, a figure that must originally have been a female incarnation of Inanna. However, the stratifications are much more complex. Behind Inanna there is another female victim corresponding to Ereshkigal, only subsequently joined by her husband, who has the same taurine attribute as the male god of the labyrinth and is previously described. What we are able to retrace from the Inanna myth-rite leads to the assumption of an earlier sacrifice where the victim may have been a priestess incarnating Ereshkigal, followed by a more institutionalized funeral sacrifice where the female victim is a goddess who joins her husband, that is to say, a queen compelled to join her royal consort who has gone before her into the next world. We have still not completely unraveled the skein of this Sumerian myth-rite: although Gugalanna is Ereshkigal's husband, the fact that the two female figures are sisters makes them doubles of each other, with a typical overlapping of roles between priestess and queen. The detail that Gugalanna takes no part in events, remaining aloof like a sort of *deus otiosus* and being at one point described as having "been killed,"[63] allows us to recognize three possible layers in this fleeting figure: the more ancient as a prehistoric victim of a hierogamous rite probably together with his partner; then in historical times as a substitute victim for Ereshkigal; the more recent as the monarch who can no longer be sacrificed, substituted as victim by other males or couples and accompanied into the hereafter by his consort after dying a natural death. The Inanna myth combines ancient human sacrifices linked to the institution of monarchy and, preceding it, with sacrifices accompanying the monarch's burial. The final version corresponds to this last stage and could correspond to the ritual descent of the queen into the tomb after the burial of the king, with a dramatic progression that multiplies the underworld thresholds to be crossed and isolates the pitiful figure of Inanna, finally divested of all her divine robes and insignia.

The myth contains a bitter reflection on death that has a more literary equivalent in the Gilgamesh epic in the scene of Enkidu's death and the hero's subsequent search for the plant of immortality. It is true that the Inanna's myth concludes with her rise from the dead ("Inanna arose"[64]), but its continuation is highly telling. Her resurrection is conditional, and in order not to go back to the netherworld, she has to choose a substitutive male victim: after having refused some candidates from her retinue, the final choice falls on the shepherd Dumuzi, against whom we find the very same trial scene as before, with Inanna now on the seat of the condemning judge.[65] It is typical of Mesopotamian civilization that there is no real objectual redemption that might revive the world of the living in the world of the dead: above all else, what counts is the process of ritual distancing through substitution that enables the world of the living to exist and not be swept away. This distrustful imbalance is also found in ancient Judaism and its idea of *sheol*, which initially indicated an insuperable limit to the power of the archaic Yahweh, and it was only during the Persian domination, under the probable influence of Zoroastrianism, that Middle Judaism developed the idea of the resurrection of the dead in an eschatological and apocalyptic key.[66] In Greece these same elements developed and took shape following a logic of greater vitality: dramatization is still there, and actually undergoes impressive developments unknown to the civilizations of the Near East, but the Greek version reflects the myriad features peculiar to the Hellenic world, its curiosity, its concentration on civic life, and its passion for *zoe* in all its aspects, as Kerényi quite rightly recognizes even if he omits to recognize the cost. It is starting from such constitutive elements that the mediations change.

In Greek myth we find the doubling of the female figure in Demeter and Persephone is also present, but the initiative is taken by the male god, Hades. To visualize the scene from which both these myths ultimately derive, we need to picture the actors in the sacrificial hierogamy surrounded by the Curetes/Titans in their original role as Anunnaki with their "eye of death," so eloquently illustrated (and inverted in signifying celebration or prayer) by the huge wide-open eyes of Sumerian sculpture; and at the same time we should add the mobility and vivacity of the Greek spirit, promptly reworking these ritual forms in theatrical form, turning them into entertaining drama, and taking the drama out of their tragic core. We find the motif of the descent, analogous to the Sumerian myth, concentrated into sudden or marvelous happenings. The descent into the realm of the dead meant exactly the same in Greek mythology, where allusions to people being swallowed up by the ground or engulfed by water are frequent. In an Eleusinian myth, a swineherd, Eubuleus, sees his pigs similarly engulfed by the ground. Eubuleus is one of the names of Hades; the pig is a symbol of Persephone-Demeter that goes back to prehistoric times.[67] The sacred springs figure prominently on the Orphic tablet because victims were drowned in their waters or—to put it better—they were interpreted symbolically on account of such places: *lethe* corresponds to the spring where the victim vanishes; *aletheia*, the negation of death, of *lethe*, corresponds to the return of the victim as object mediator, truth mediator, an acquisition for salvation that always retains its polar dependence on that hidden face of death. Persephone's abduction by Hades corresponds to rituals in which a girl was sacrificed as a sign of marriage to the chthonic god. This was commemorated at Eleusis by the sacrifice of a pig. It is now clear why Demeter suffers so greatly and despairs. A dying girl was often said to have celebrated her marriage to Hades, an image Euripides applies to Iphigenia when she is about to be sacrificed.[68] This is why Persephone, like Ereshkigal, is the goddess of the afterlife, though with the more reassuring connotation of her seasonal return, connected to the world of fertility so dear to Frazer not because it fits his explanation but because it is the fecund consequence, the ever vital spin-off, of her return. The frequency of these female victims also makes it possible to clear up a common misunderstanding. The interpretations of the numerous images of goddesses going back to the Upper Paleolithic derive not so much from matriarchal regimes, with women enjoying real power, as from women transformed into mediators for the entire community: at first, the mother goddess with attributes ranging from fertility to control over the world of the dead, and then her double-daughter (or sister, as in the case of Inanna). The inclusion of these figures and motifs in the Eleusinian Mysteries confirms the vivacity of Greek culture, steeped in death and rebirth, never forgetting the twofold background influences coming from the Near East and from the prehistoric past.

In the last part of the Eleusinian rite, the abduction revealed its real nature, in association with the *hiera* in the basket, as *hieros gamos* between a male deity (Heaven) and a female deity (Earth), between Zeus and Persephone.[69] This is an animal coupling of the archaic type, such as we find repeatedly in Orphic literature, and must have been reevoked in one form or another at Eleusis as well: Zeus in the guise of a serpent joins with his daughter, Persephone, also serpentlike, just as he had fathered her in an identical incestuous union with his sister Demeter.[70] The prehistoric goddess was often represented as anguine, while the serpent was a natural symbol of the male phallus, and images have been found that show the two attributes quite clearly combined. The Lady of the Cretan Labyrinth, besides her appearance as a bird, also had the serpent as a recurrent attribute: the serpent's sinuous body with its coils readily suggests the labyrinth. The symbol of two serpents intertwined, the caduceus, is found throughout the Near East. In Orphism it represents the weaving of the world, Persephone's peplum, from which all beings were born. From this labyrinthine union in the rite, from this *coniunctio oppositorum*, the true face of the god Dionysus finally emerged, the divine child, Zeus's double, destined to die to appease Demeter and to ensure a divine mediation that was finally stabilized. This union between a hierophant and a priestess was probably only symbolic at Eleusis, but implies its actual performance in some older phase of the rite. Whatever the fact of the matter, it brings us to the third, decisive stage of the rite, the stage that can ensure mediation between the worlds of the living and the dead thanks to Dionysus, twice on the verge of death or dead, and thrice born and reborn again.

At this point, a ram may have been sacrificed—killed, flayed, and finally burned—as Burkert fairly surmises without, however, pursuing the idea.[71] The goat was Dionysus's typical incarnation in Greece; however, a ram might well have provided an esoteric substitute since it was part of Dionysian iconography and its presence at Eleusis is indisputable. Prehistoric iconography shows the sacrifice of rams and bulls to the serpent-bird goddess.[72] The strong ties linking Orphism to Eleusis lead to the conclusion that the sacrifice was a reenactment of Dionysus's murder by the Titans, the initiates identifying with him in the ritual .[73] They relived Dionysus's passion (πάθημα) in full and then through a final identification with the god-victim purified themselves and were reborn. In the flames rising from the sacrificial fire in the *Anaktoron*, Asterios was reborn, the Cretan Minotaur, the starry child of the Orphic tablet with whom the dead identified. The myth of Demophoon-Triptolemus burned over a fire by Demeter, replicating burnt sacrifices in the labyrinth, refers to this and is among the first exoteric anticipations of Dionysus's fate. The bull sacrificed at the end of the rite referred to this final, saving revelation.[74] The crowning experience at Eleusis was *ellampsis*, the enlightenment that came as culmination of the *epopteia*.[75] From plurality steeped in terror and death the devotee emerged with an illuminating, unified experience, with a pledge of lasting objectual possession.

The details of the Eleusinian liturgy are difficult to establish, but it consisted in part of pantomime, dance, and symbolism.[76] In essence, however, it was a δρώμενον (from *dran*, "do" in a sacral context = Lat. *factum*), that is to say, a great ritual action that had to be beheld, made up of doings (*dromena*, its constituent acts) and showings (*deiknymena*) and utterances (*legomena*).[77] This process of intermedial and mediating presentation, largely participatory and ecstatic, ended with a series of φάσματα, apparitions, whose imaginal meaning could only be fully grasped after adequate doctrinal and ritual preparation. As I have already said, we should beware of intellectualizing these *phasmata*, not because they are incompatible with intellectual development, of which Greek philosophy offers a thousand examples, but because it would underrate their precedence as experience, their primal intermedial and *imaginalis* character, very bodily in its performative and magical strength. Eventually the *dromena* had to be done and, in a sacral sense, that could mean only one thing: sacrifice (*sacrum* or *sacra facere*). By all accounts, these apparitions were an unforgettable experience; Plutarch writes reliably of "terrible things" (*deina*),[78] which would be better translated as "terrible and amazing things" to give an idea of the ambivalence of the adjective *deinos*, to be met again later in the *Bacchae*. There must have been sacrifice, and that could only have meant the Titanic sacrifice, an inexhaustible source of inspiration for Greek drama and philosophy, but we must presume its nonmediable originary nature because it is the source itself of mediation. Besides, the centrality of the Titanic event at Eleusis is not so much a question of circumstantial conjecture as might be supposed.

We have the direct testimony of Clement of Alexandria who, being a Christian, had every reason to reveal the Mysteries and may even have been an initiate. His *Protrepticus*, on which I shall have occasion to comment further, was written to persuade educated pagans to embrace the new religion and might well contain all the essential information about Eleusis, though scholars rarely give serious consideration to the relevant passage either because they assume a priori that Eleusis has nothing to do with Dionysus or because they share the customary ideological distrust of Christian sources. In the second chapter of the *Protrepticus*, Clement puts the following disarming question to the reader: "What would you say if I were to expound the Mysteries to you?" and immediately makes reference to the bacchantes consuming raw flesh.[79] After a competent survey of the Eleusinian Mysteries and other mystery cults, he sums up as follows:

> Such are the mysteries of the atheists [*atheon*]! I am right to call them atheists who, not having known the true God, venerate a child torn to pieces [*diaspomenon*] by the Titans and a female in sorrow [*penthoun*], and parts of his body [*moria*] that are truly innominable [*arrheta*] out of shame [*hyp'aischynes*] and awesome [*sebousin*] for being too shameful [*anaischyntos*].[80]

In spite of his critical tone, Clement is very precise about the details, as the terminology used underlines, up to use the notion of *sebas*, what is wonderful and potentially dangerous and shameful at the same time, and imposes a passive experience on the beholder.[81] He refers to the basket of "sacred things," clearly connected to the sexual sphere (as he has said earlier) and so to hierogamy; and then reference is made to Demeter's search and to the climax of the rite. Chronological order is inverted in order to begin with the most important revelation. The phrase "venerate a child torn to pieces by the Titans" explicitly attacks Dionysus's central position at Eleusis, and since Clement's intention is to speak of the rites actually performed there, he can only be referring to a real rite and not simply to a religious belief. In the last century the Italian scholar Dario Sabbatucci remarked that even where the secrecy of Eleusis is known to have been breached, nothing objectively extraordinary has ever come to light.[82] The simple explanation for this is that sacrifice in itself was nothing extraordinary: animal sacrifice was routine business for the ancients, to the point of mere formality at times. What was extraordinary was the revelatory significance, in the ambiguous sense of *aletheia*, that sacrifice came to have in the carefully prepared ritual procedure. Understanding was intuitive and could not be directly rationalized. It was indescribable, indeed ineffable, and corresponds to a particular stage in historical-cultural development. The ancient Greeks had no word to indicate the origin as a historical, human event: it could only be a divine event for them, as in religious and initiatory wisdom, or a cosmic event, as it came to be theorized by philosophical wisdom. And what tragic wisdom was to reveal about the historical origin would consist, above all, in an illuminating oscillation between those two extremes, though it could not find direct expression and had to resort to the manifold guises of the stage and the polysemic texts of Greek tragedy. Besides, what emotional impact could a description of the Titanic sacrifice in animal form have had on noninitiates who, as such, had no precise idea of its real importance?

Clement's reaction itself contains the seeds of misunderstanding: scandalized by the violence in Orphism and the Mysteries, he comes to reject their profound anthropological insights; or rather, he rejects the sacral mediations held to depend entirely on the uncontrolled violence. This is not unlike Plato in some ways; moreover, a clear Platonizing tendency in early Christianity led to idealizing and minimizing man's violent genesis. Nevertheless, even though its most radical significance is not approached, Clement has a sure intuition of the violent origin that modern scholars might well envy. He praises ancient writers, such as Euhemerus, who argued for the human origin of the gods, unhesitatingly identifies ichor as putrefied human blood (II, 36, 3), and links the cult of the pagan gods to human sacrifice, dismissing their temples as really nothing but sepulchers (II, 4, 3). These are intuitions that can finally be developed by a modern inquiry, free at last from any direct religious conditioning and concerned only to explain the phenomena.

Thus we may reasonably conclude that the *a-letheia*, the dis-veiling of the Eleusinian *dromenon*, the bodily and *imaginalis* climax of its soterial mediation, was the Titanic event. According to Hippolytus, another Christian writer, the *visio beatifica* of the ear of corn reaped in silence also occurred at the final stage of the rite.[83] And it was only through the *a-letheia* that the *visio beatifica* could effectively synthesize the fruit of the *hieros gamos*, that is, the divine child who died and was reborn. It seems he was first castrated: there is a documented association of cut corn and castrated victims, probably going back to Neolithic sacrifices and found in the Dumuzi cult as well.[84]

We now possess the materials and links needed to decipher the most important part of the Gurob papyrus that concerns the consequences and purposes of the sacrifice and of the hierogamy so strikingly and revealingly superimposed on that sacrifice.

5. Sacrificial Hierogamies

It is at once clear from the information just presented about Eleusis, and wholly consistent with what we learned in looking at the labyrinth, that the sexual objects hidden in the basket refer to a divine coupling with a sacrificial background, to a divine mediation, both symbolic and physical, that stimulated all the somatic and psychic elements of those involved. But before we look at the symbols in detail, we must try to grasp the papyrus's symbolic organization as a whole.

The same intermedial and mediatory process is to be observed both in Orphism and at Eleusis: a movement back from the apparent multiplicity of the divine to the saving unity of its origin, the god killed and reborn. This pattern also provides the key to the structure of the Gurob text, which proves itself to be a condensed Orphic-Eleusinian *dromenon*. Let us look at the arguments that make this a legitimate conclusion. Lines 5–7 already seem to retrace the divine genealogy through the goddess's various incarnations: Brimo (the Terrible), an Eleusinian name for Persephone,[85] her mother Demeter, and finally her mother Rhea with her armed followers, the Curetes. Then, after a lacuna, the sacred objects, *hiera*, in l. 8 allude to the imminent sacrifice of the animals mentioned in l. 9. The gifts (l. 10) and offerings are to be linked to the *symbola* in l. 23: the sacred objects displayed and sacrificed there indicate the priest's role, while the *symbola* here express primarily the initiate's search for salvation, concretized objectually through things said, done, and brought there. The saving mediation is only to be found when the two components of the rite, the *dromena* of the priest and the *dromena* of the believer, are successfully united. This reconstruction takes account of the parts missing from the text and succeeds in restoring its deep meaning, in a kind of crescendo turning on ritual sacrifice and its signs, both hidden and revealed.

The ram and the goat, τράγος, are animal manifestations of Dionysus, which the papyrus seems to regard as interchangeable, as they were at Eleusis. After the mention of pasture and river, both symbols of the next world,[86] we come in l. 12 to the ritual act at the culmination of the sacrifice: the castration of the god incarnated in the *tragos* by removing the animal's testicles, normally done at the moment of slaughter, an act that came within the sphere of the *arrheton*.[87] This ritual castration was probably performed at Eleusis; if not, it was certainly done symbolically, using beans, which were held to represent the testicles, especially of the dead. In the Pythagorean tradition, they were also associated with human flesh, sperm, the womb, and children's heads, while to eat beans was considered an act of cannibalism.[88] This is virtually a complete catalog of the symbolism of the *hieros gamos* and of the earliest anthropophagous rites and is especially significant in the light of the close links between Pythagoreanism and Orphism. As far as we can ascertain from what survives of the papyrus, the text is constructed to lead toward that same convergence of hierogamy and ritual sacrifice that we saw at Eleusis and in the labyrinth mythologem, indirectly surviving until Dante's *Divine Comedy*. We should, therefore, analyze more closely the ties between bloody rituals and erotic rituals that are scattered throughout the most ancient cults and perpetuated by the Greek cults that reinterpreted them. Sexuality is the most direct and experiential version of the human object around which all cultural mediations turn; by examining sexuality's relationship to them and the conditions under which it might be taken up and developed, we gain an exceptional perspective for understanding our own formative history.

As Lévi-Strauss demonstrates in *The Elementary Structures of Kinship*, nothing is more cultural *and* natural than sex, but we would be wrong to deduce, as he does, that this is the point at which nature meets culture through the rules for exogamic mating. Sex is, rather, a point of insoluble conflict, of unprecedented tension that defines us as cultural beings, and at this juncture Georges Bataille's analysis of eroticism comes to our aid. However, the bridging element of mediation is also lacking in Bataille, the element that can make the sexual and human object steadily attainable, after the experience of its inaccessibility through taboos. Before the sexual object divides, introducing conflict both external and internal, it is actually a dramatic point of convergence. Freud understood this but remained conditioned by the naturalism of the libido. Girard distances himself from Freud's naturalism and sees the convergence but removes all traces of its objectual anchorage in human mimetism and fails to note the independent emergence of mediation. All these authors provide us with essential tools whose value can be recognized only by lifting them out of their rigid theoretical contexts and setting them in motion without an agenda so that they can connect and clash dynamically, and thereby become revelatory.

The association of sex with sacrifice and violence is universal in archaic and ancient cultures, and is at once evoked when we remember how often women were abducted and raped, and were considered to be the supreme exchange commodity, often unavailable in the sophisticated, formalized manner of exogamic exchange so dear to Lévi-Strauss. However, in these societies the erotic object looms large and takes a thousand forms, shaping their imaginations and their taboos, and conditioning and finalizing their rituals, as shown by the ubiquity of genital symbolism in the most ancient artistic finds of *Homo sapiens*. And more than any other object, the genitalia excite desire, provoking mimetic convergence that turns into conflict and finally lynching, according to what we learn from Freud and Girard, with their opposing, complementary lines of thought. This object of collective attraction brings about its own destruction, but at the same time it is evidence of an objectual gravitation in even the wildest mimetic behavior which permits it to transcend itself when conditions are right, and to crystallize into experiences of collective mediation able to reorganize and relaunch their objective direction, and thus to make an objectual acquisition of it.

For these reasons, and with these potentials, the most archaic lynchings began with or focused upon the victim's genitals. Similar behavior, at a rudimentary level, is to be seen among animals where the necessity of mating is by far the major cause of intraspecific conflict and ethologic ritualization:[89] cases of group violence have been observed among chimpanzees in which the genital region was one of the most frequent targets for attack.[90] This precultural origin is not definitively surpassed by culture; rather, it is revised and given new meaning each time. It arises from the human psychophysical complexion to shape and orient it every time according to the directions prescribed by the social environment, in a process that can never be acquired or finished since it is the fundamental datum of humanity, always present as its task and goal, and not as a completed history incapable of generating other meanings. The individual and collective attraction toward the genital region, and toward all associated parts of the body, persists in every age and latitude, and always presents the same drama of attraction and repulsion, the same attention to preservation, and the same destructive violence. In medieval times, images of the devil were struck about the head and genitals with an apotropaic purpose, as can be seen in numerous paintings where the scars of these magical-type treatments are clearly visible. It would be superficial to interpret them in the clichéd terms of Christianity's sex phobia, not so much because the phobia did not exist and had no importance in theological thinking, but because the attitude evidences the centrality of a problem essentially linked to mankind's cultural condition, as the mythic history of humanity with its stain of original sin shows. Christendom sought to understand the problem as a historical and moral datum, and no longer as cosmologically natural.

Predictably, the frequency and violence of these ritualizations increases as soon as we return to the ancient world. The *pharmakoi*, the scapegoats of ancient Athens, were beaten about the genitals as they passed through the streets, to take all the city's troubles on themselves before going on to meet their death by stoning.[91] There are also a great many correspondences with hierogamies of myth. For example, Cronus castrates Uranus and throws the genitals into the sea, and Aphrodite is subsequently born from the sperm that leaks out. This reminds us that sperm, too, seems to have been regarded as sacred when it came from a victim or priest, a status corroborated by its intimate association with honey as a sacrificial symbol. The *soma*, a sacred beverage that features in much of the Vedic liturgy, is identified both with honey as a supernatural food and with the sperm from which ambrosia is derived.[92] The Sanskrit word for this sperm indicates light as well. Honey's erotic-sacrificial significance is apparent from a Sumerian song celebrating hierogamy and concerning the "honey-man," the divine royal lover, describing the parts of his body as made of honey, almost cannibalistically.[93] Orion, the hunter who became a constellation after his death, was a strong presence in Cretan mythology and was generated from the seed of the gods put into a bull-hide wineskin. This same wineskin was used for preparing a fermented drink, hydromel, and was also the leather bag that Zeus's severed member was put into after his fight with Typhon, in another mythical variant derived from the Hittite story of Kumarbi. According to an Orphic myth, Zeus castrated Cronus when he was drunk on honey.[94] The relationship between hierogamy and castration is well illustrated by a Phrygian mystery myth reported by Clement, where Zeus, having committed incest with his mother, feigns self-castration and throws the genitals of a ram into the goddess's lap.[95] Even more striking, and also from Phrygia, was the practice of ritual castration by the priesthood of Cybele, confirming the sacrificial role of the ancient mother goddess. Like Rhea, Cybele had her following of Corybantes or Curetes her priests identified with.[96] At the height of their orgiastic furor for the goddess, these Corybantes/Curetes would wound themselves in various parts of the body and finally castrate themselves in a gesture that represents their bloody coupling with the goddess, yielding the genital object as a token of definitive consecration, of coitus made eternal by this irreversible sacrifice. This rite brings to mind the typical image of Ephesian Artemis, her body covered in bulls' scrotums—and not in breasts, as was once thought.[97] Finally, in this review, we might mention another myth similar to the one concerning Semele in its ritual origin and symbolism: the myth of Dionysus fathered by a thunderbolt from Zeus and represented as a phallus.[98]

All this leads to three main conclusions: (1) the sacred objects in the basket refer to the god's genitals, especially the phallus as is widely documented in Dionysianism; there were also phallic processions in his honor, and among his attributes numbered *orthos*, erect, and *enorches*, testiculate;

(2) the castration derives from the earliest lynchings and so from the primitive rite of *sparagmos* and *omophagia*; and (3) one stage or variant of the *hieros gamos* rite might have comprised the castration and killing of the male partner, possibly at the moment of orgasm. This last conjecture is not essential to our analysis, but the crude realism of the divine sperm and its clear interchangeability with other sacrificial symbols make it credible; besides, as Bataille stresses, orgasm and death are still associated psychologically. The main point lies in the contradictory and double-binding fact that sexual acts and bodily parts become an object in themselves and at the same time are despoiled of the objectual meaning the rite has the charge to put into crisis and then restore: someone had to pay for solving the paradox, either physically or in the reenactment of ritual, and ultimately even anobjectual sexual performances could achieve the same purpose. The mythical evidence coming both from cultures related to Greece and the Dionysiac-Orphic texts suggests faked-hierogamic rites centered on masturbation.[99] But the ritual enactment of the sacrificial loss of the object implies a previous execution of real sacrifices, and the prehistoric art, that is, the figurative reflex of a ritual, gives us a spectacular piece of evidence. A Paleolithic carved scene found in the Addaura cave (near Palermo, Sicily) is impressive in this regard: two ithyphallic figures with their bodies arched back and their heads covered are surrounded by several masked men, among whom two dominant figures appear as shamans leading a ritual. The unnatural posture of the two arched-back men is due to a cord that is strangling them, provoking their sexual excitement. It is not a homosexual coupling, because the two are clearly separated, but a ritual intercourse, perhaps with the Mother Earth, and its climax evidently was the death of the two male partners through self-strangulation.[100]

These are distasteful interpretations, especially in our age of sexual liberation so-called; but if we are to avoid both naturalistic myth-making and antiscientific demonizing, we cannot omit the easily made connection between eroticism and violence of a sort, its inherent brutality to a certain point, itself ritualized and accompanied by objectual reassurances, in a double-bind conflict between aggressive attitudes and displays of affection, and between loss and maintenance of the human object, which betrays the struggle underlying this ever-uncertain mastery born of long practice. It is not just a question of the dangers implicit in eroticism and its diametrical opposition to the sphere of work and matrimony about which Bataille writes, thus defining itself as necessary, complementary transgression of rules that it thereby confirms. Bataille's analyses hit the mark regarding the anthropological and social significance of human sexuality and its expression of the problem of human origin through the unresolvable tension that constitutes our sexuality. He fails, however, to focus upon the genetic reasons for this mutual dependence, the need for orgiastic transgression that lurks within human institutions and the quest for an identity, as such latently objectual, to which even the most risqué libertinism conforms. The diametrical opposition of the orgiastic to the socially useful remains exterior, but it is internal to each of its opposing extremes. This goes back to the long prehistory in which, through sexuality, human somatic structure and psychophysical composition took shape in collective experiences of premediation and ecstatic-objectual mediation for which a sexualized victim was pivotal. Thus sacrificial mediation was most frequently triggered by sexuality and had its repercussions there, not so much because the sexual libido was the cause, as Freud would have it, but because its goal is to attain the object, and for the human adult from a psychophysical relational viewpoint that object is the sexual object in the first instance. Admittedly, the history of eroticism is steeped in violence, but it has constructive and affective value, which should not be overlooked if our aim is to understand eroticism scientifically: eroticism needs to be overthrown for tenderness and the protection given by the family to be possible, and that could not come about if the more savage erotic manifestations did not contain a premise that blindly called for it.

If we consider a typically orgiastic manifestation, such as male homosexuality, which is also unequivocally present in Dionysianism,[101] we will likely notice its complementary character in respect to heterosexuality where family objectuality is the end purpose. In the ancient world, this made it not only compatible with the normal male role in society but actually necessary in situations where sex was expected to be displayed violently or to be an exercise in desire, admissible since it was anobjectual and therefore harmless. Male homoerotism is bound up with the fact that the male has to make his conquest of the object, and is able to do so through mediations (of learning, competing, and authorizing) that come from fellow males, who can take the place of the object if for some reason they catalyze its mediatory flow. The reason in question was often the nonavailability of women in societies with strict rules governing access to them, a matter discussed by Freud in *Totem and Taboo*. These dynamics of objective mediation developed sacrally and institutionally in rites where there was possession of or by a male double, for the purpose of initiation (as with ephebes) or sacrifice (as with prisoners of war). Because of its structural relationship to the search for the object, ritualized male homosexuality is an essentially transient and public institution, proof of its clear preeminence over female homosexuality and perhaps of greater antiquity. In ancient Greece, the place of female homosexuality was, instead, within the withdrawn, derivative dimension of the gynaeceum, the domestic sphere of the *oikos* (house) reserved for women where the sexual family object is present and possessed, and thus can only be reversed ritually through connivance and secrecy. In the cruel, vital game of sex, men and women have constantly shaped and mirrored their social roles, in a complementary fashion always stabilized by an underlying symmetry, the ever-present threat of reversal.

Returning now to hierogamy and its sacrificial implications, the Sumerian myth of Inanna enables us to understand that in protohistorical times the standard victim was a woman, a priestess representing the goddess (Ereshkigal in the first instance), presumably preceded by a hierogamous sacrifice where a couple was ritually killed (this should correspond to the phantomlike figure of "the great bull of heaven," Gugalanna). This priestess then became too powerful and a man alone became the victim, considering that the myths where the male is hunted down and killed by the Anunnaki outnumber the rest and are therefore subsequent (here we have Dumuzi as substitute victim for Inanna), dating back to the fourth millennium BC.[102] This man might have been a king, and subsequently was the substitute for one, as in the Babylonian Sacaea festival analyzed by Frazer, where the Mesopotamian kings had also become too powerful to be sacrificed. In the Sacaea ceremonial the hierogamic aspect is no longer so visible, but is recognizable from the detail that the temporary king, a prisoner condemned to death, could enjoy the king's concubines during his short reign of five days, probably the straightest way to become like the monarch.[103] The Assyrian rite of a substitute royal couple, settled for a few days on the throne when a lunar eclipse occurred, attests a more institutional and hierogamous solution to the same problem, surveilled by the king's most trusted minister and surrounded by a close circumspection.[104]

However performed, the hierogamic-sacrificial substitution had not to be too visible and only its objectual results could be exhibited in such a way as to make the king appear to die and be reborn several times. He was the Lord of sexuality and death, the dominator of fecundity and war, a divine being both mortal and beyond the condition of common mortals, again as brilliantly caught by Bataille: "The sovereign is the one who *is*, as if death did not exist [*est celui qui* est, *comme si la mort n'était pas*]. But he is also the one who does not die, since he dies only to be born again."[105]

We are now ready to complete the symbolic analysis of the Gurob papyrus by focusing on the very meaning of the word σύμβολον, a term that is very rich in ritual and cognitive implications.

6. The Symbolic Organization of the Papyrus

These bloody aspects of pagan sexuality, understandably provoking a strong reaction from the early Christians similar to the previous reaction of Judaism, show us the real meaning of the *hiera*, the gifts, and the *symbola* in the Gurob papyrus, taking us back to the origin of man's symbolic dimension in collective mediations that could steer group violence and reverse it to make it a source of signification for everyone. The first *symbolon* (from *sym-ballein*) was the victim-god assaulted by all the members of the community at the same time. The general sense of the Greek verb is to join together separate parts, but in the *Iliad* it specifically designates the clash of arms as enemies join in battle, an act of violence halfway between the armed dancing of the Curetes and the archaic Titanic lynching.[106] Put together the two meanings of *symballein*—of group hostility and joining together—and we have all the members of a group united against a single objective, the victim. The *symbolon* of the original lynching is the real object of the *dromenon*, the secret of its power of symbolic articulation, its mediatory force as an event capable of reviving the origin.

Following a metonymic procedure, a part standing for the whole as in the choice of the victim, the papyrus now presents the derived *symbolon* of the victim-god as the part of the body from which violent symbolization started. The ritual castration referred to in l. 4, if the reading is correct—"I mutilated myself"—is self-mutilation to be understood here as symbolic,[107] whereas in l. 12 the goat is really castrated. This *symbolon* is referred to in l. 13 ("that he eats the other flesh"), alluding to the ritual sharing out of the flesh except for the "divine portions" reserved for the god and the priest,[108] in this case the testicles that are kept as a token to vouchsafe the god's resurrection. The expression used in l. 15, "consecrated to be burnt up," refers, in West's reading, to the animal sacrifice directly evoked in l. 2. Having completed the sacrificial rite, we are now in a position to understand the further manifestations of the Orphic god, indicating the success of his mediation as ensured by the rite.

In l. 17 the conjectural name Protogonus, the first born, indicates Phanes —the one who appears—the male-female deity of Orphism who was born from the Cosmic Egg, a prehistoric sacred image widely documented in the cosmogonies of many different cultures.[109] Elements of androgyny are a feature of prehistoric religious images as well as being characteristic of various Mediterranean and Mesopotamian gods of dismemberment, and they incarnate in one figure the two elements of the hierogamy seen as complementary and diametrically opposed attributes of divine mediation, as inseparable elements of an originary totality.[110] The mention of Phanes, who presided over the mythical race of men in the Golden Age, evokes Orphic cosmology which would become more complex later with Neoplatonism; the core doctrine, however, must have gone back to the *hieroi logoi* of Onomacritus.[111] One of the earliest attempts to rationalize ritual and myth at a cosmic level, it led eventually to true philosophy, as suggested by the still archaic but already conceptualized version recorded by Damascius and other sources. At first, Water joins with Matter to create Earth; further generations of triads follow before Phanes, also called Metis (wisdom, shrewdness); then come Hesiod's generations of the gods with Uranus and Cronus, and finally Zeus who swallows Phanes-Metis as the last event in this cosmogony, with the Titanic omophagy and rebirth of Dionysus.

The ternary pattern of hierogamy also appears in Orphic cosmology and corresponds to the words of the dead person on the tablet ("I am the son of Earth and starry Heaven"). More than a process of natural procreation, these words suggest the development of the basic objectual scheme of the human family that becomes the generating scheme for the entire universe. This is not because of anthropomorphism, so promptly produced by superficial modern interpreters as a label to downgrade what they cannot understand, but because it is the first cell generating every objectual dimension of human life. But the succession of cosmic triangles could not go on without its hitches, as Girard's mimetic triangle reminds us with its ever-present danger of collapsing into competition for possession and rivalry. The ensuing crisis can be resolved, according to Girard, by the central sequence of his mimetic cycle (selection, sacrifice, and adoration of the victim). However, the normal and physiological outcome of this decisive sequence is not the negative homeostasis of cultural systems as Girard understands them, subject as they are to prohibitions and the stress of preventing further crises, but the good triangle where the model is the victim-god who indicates what is to be desired and prohibits what might provoke a bad triangle of rivalry. Anyway, it is not a question of wasting time in making pointless distinctions between a good and a bad mimesis, but of outlining only one force, namely mediation, that manifests itself while reaching its goal, and is beyond any mimesis as represents its very objectual source and orientation.

It is possible to do so because the cultural processes are the crystallized result of a collective experience of mediation where the mediator, long before being a personalized victim, is a prepersonal victim, an object-victim, an event-victim that enables members of the group to direct certain impulses of biological origin toward recognizable, legitimatized objects, impulses that could be called desire as long as there is no confusion with the more psychological and individual version that we normally have in mind when we use the term. Even if the entire ritual cycle can be described, on Girard's premises, as a triad of triads, since the three stages of the victimary resolution form a bridge between two triangular situations, one destroying and the other saving, the overall sense of the process is nevertheless different, and consists of a new cycle of reciprocal construction, a circular movement that makes life and meaning possible. And here once again we see the need to unite Girard's rigid explanatory logic with Lévi-Strauss's phenomenological sensitivity, starting from the powerful insight of the central moment of ecstatic experience that Nietzsche and Bataille enable us to understand; but it is my idea of mediation that can join together all these passages, fully recognizing the indispensable contribution made by these thinkers. This concretely recognizable ritual scansion can explain the universality of ternary symbolism and why it often multiplied to nine; moreover, it gives us a better idea of how man might have progressed from ritual and myth to more abstract explanatory schemes. Also clearer, possibly, is the mythical-ritual, and, if you will, protophilosophical character of the procedures followed in Orphism and at Eleusis. Only by imitating Dionysus *trigonos* and passing through the three phases of initiation could the believer become *trisolbios*, thrice blest.[112] Three and multiples of three do indeed express the rhythm of the mediations that have become objectual and initiate a saving circular motion with the world, an enlivening, meaningful reversibility. And each time the world is reborn and emerges victorious from the crisis that threatened it, finally confirmed, amazingly, by that same crisis.

After all these explanations and digressions that have opened important windows on sacral and social mediations in Greek and Mediterranean cultures, we are ready to offer some remarks about the final manifestation of the god in the papyrus. After Protogonus (l. 17) we find Eubuleus, another name for Hades as we have seen. Heraclitus tells us he was secretly identified with Dionysus as well.[113] The two aspects come together in l. 21 in the formula Eubuleus Irichipegus, since Ἠρικεπαῖος (or Ἠρικαπαῖος) is one of the names of Phanes who is actually mentioned later. The invocation to Zeus as "Hurler of Lightning" (l. 22), with reference both to the first birth of Dionysus from Semele's womb and the final punishment of the Titans, prepares the final saving invocation to "ONLY ONE DIONYSUS." Through a multiplicity of names and forms, we have finally reached the unity of the divine principle, meaningful even leaving aside interpretations of a monotheistic type or rather henotheistic, that is relating to a supreme god whose oneness consists in dominating others. This divine unity corresponds to the unity of the victim and its mediation that predominates and unifies within a precise cultural context. And so we might do better to talk of henolatry, that is, of a cult centering on one god though not exclusively as in the stage before yahwehist monotheism, whereas monolatry implies exclusivity.

The revelation is preceded in l. 20 by a reference to Pallas Athena, Dionysus's sister who, as Clement reminds us, managed to steal her brother's still-beating heart out from under the eyes of the Titans.[114] This was sometimes reenacted ritually on animals being sacrificed.[115] Besides throwing a macabre light on ancient Greek infanticide rites, it tells us that the divine part of the Titanic sacrifice was the heart, carried from Athens in the mystic basket (*cista mystica*) named in l. 28 (*kalathos*). The heart, thrown into the basket with a verb having the same root as *symballein* (*em-balin*), is the most emotional organ in the *sparagmos*; it might also indicate the other focal point of the lynching, Dionysus's phallus,[116] which has to be present as part of the hierogamy. It was his penis, Clement would have us understand, that was carried to Eleusis, probably together with other sexual symbols, and it was this bloody *pars pro toto*, this sacrificial metonymy, that, after guaranteeing the god's final birth from the phallus or *as* a phallus,[117] guaranteed the resurrection of the believer's divine Dionysian part, as in the final reaping-castration of the Eleusinian vision. Symbolically, the basket is like the leather bag that contained the phallus or divine sperm. In some accounts Demeter, who has just been named in the text, reassembles the god's body; Isis does the same for Osiris.[118] The papyrus refers here to the typical and relatively less archaic version of the Orphic myth, where the Titans cut Dionysus's body up into seven parts with a knife, then boil and roast it, but are stopped from eating it by Zeus who intervenes to punish them, "attracted by the aroma" as Clement specifies.[119] The number seven refers to Dionysus's premature birth at seven months, which also motivated the interval of seven months between the Lesser and Greater Mysteries.[120]

The *symbola* are the keystone of the remaining text. They refer primarily to the formulas and sacred expressions recited by the initiate, to which ll. 23–26 make direct reference: "GOD IN THE WOMB" alludes to Baubo, the Eleusinian woman who pleased Demeter by lifting her skirt to reveal the hidden features of the child Iacchus, an anticipation of the hierogamy;[121] the cold water of Mnemosyne (" . . . I have drunk cold . . ."); and the ass, a phallic incarnation of Dionysus leading herds of followers, the flocks of maenads ("ass herdsman").[122] The formula (*synthema*) sums up all the others: ἄνω κάτω, "ABOVE BELOW" (l. 26). A common expression in Greek, on a par with the English "upside down," it takes on a technical meaning in this sapiential context; *ano kato* alludes to Persephone's *anodos* and *kathodos* to designate the hierogamy as a cosmic union of upper and lower, of Heaven and Earth. This union, which as we shall see made possible a ritually controlled communication between the reign of the dead and that of the alive also in the Temple at Jerusalem, took place at Eleusis and was a reenactment of the originary *coniunctio oppositorum*, the atonement made possible by the union of sacrificers and sacrificed in the very act of sacrifice, in order to reach not an abstract *coincidentia oppositorum*, but a *complexio oppositorum* capable of maintaining both of them in a living and tensional unity.[123] Through the opening in the roof of the *Anaktoron*, Heaven was united to Earth represented by the rock below, and finally thanks to Zeus's lightnings, the god was born, making possible the at-one-ment to which the most recapitulatory formula of l. 23 in the papyrus refers: "ONLY ONE DIONYSUS." The throne standing near the *Anaktoron* undoubtedly belonged to this lord (*anax*). Later we shall see how Euripides used the *ano kato* formula in the *Bacchae*.[124]

Although the expression in l. 26 of the papyrus is incomplete, it seems likely to me to be a key term in the initiation formula. With the *symbolon* concept we can distinguish the various strata of sacrifice in all these proceedings: the first *symbolon* is the god attacked by everyone in the frenzy of the *sparagmos*; his *disiecta membra* are, next, his *symbola* and must be reunited starting with the first part dismembered;[125] and the final *symbola* are the different parts of the rite that have to reproduce this same process. To dismember the god again is literally to re-member him. This victimary re-membrance is linked to the principal meaning of the word *symbolon*, the two parts of an astragalus or some such object that was split in two to provide a means of identity for strangers, who could check whether the two halves tallied.[126] The astragalus is a sheep or goat's knuckle-bone, used by the Greeks as dice in various games of chance: in sacrificial terms it denotes the random choice of the victim. The objects listed at the end and thrown into the basket, among them the astragali, are all connected with the priest's *hiera* and the initiate's *symbola*. Their symbolic union here expresses the *aletheia* of supreme knowledge, corresponding to the mediation eventually obtained. The soteriology, the *hieros gamos*, and the cosmogony, along with their relative *dromena*, are all *symbola*, whose parts need uniting in a single origin, in a single atonement that maintains its components in the ritual *complexio oppositorum*.

But there are still other facets to these Orphic *symbola*. The objects named at the end of the papyrus ("spinning top, bull-roarer, astragali . . . mirror") are Dionysus's toys,[127] dangled in front of the divine child by the Titans to lure him into the murderous labyrinth-circle. The mirror stands out among these toys. The same mirror is to be seen on the Bologna pyxis, where Dionysus sits looking at his image in the mirror as he is about to be killed by the Curetes/Titans. With this mirror, the text as we have it breaks off, as if to indicate the *symbolon* of the initiate's supreme vision and of the victimary process it is based on. We shall need then to analyze those summarizing symbols in order to complete our survey of Orphism.

First, however, it is essential to extend our discourse to tragedy, the manifestation of knowledge that went further than Orphism and Eleusis because it used their themes creatively. Only the mirror of tragedy can adequately introduce us to the mirror of Dionysus, to the most burning themes of the culture that secretly recognized itself in Dionysus. Our most effective route is the longest one, the path of the tragic writer who ventured along it farthest of all, Euripides.

3.

In the Heart of the Labyrinth

Euripides's *Cretans* and Its Philosophical Meaning

1. The Ritual Structure of Crete

Many of the themes we have touched on, such as the Dionysian cults, Orphism, the labyrinth, and hierogamy, are found together in Euripides's *Cretans*. The tragedy is set on the island of Crete itself, where those themes most probably originated, and though what remains are fragments, they are rich and vivid enough to make it worthwhile to look at the text as a whole, using my mediatory and comparative method.[1] With this approach the text is placed in a strange relationship where it seems to keep at a distance and yet be close to us, a relationship that we shall have occasion to investigate.[2] Further support for our analysis will come from comparison with Euripides's *Hippolytus* which was written some years later, though an earlier lost version predated the *Cretans* by several years.[3] Both are stories of tragic passion: *Hippolytus* is about Phaedra, daughter of Pasiphae and Minos, king of Crete, while the *Cretans* tells of Pasiphae's disastrous passion for a white bull sent by Poseidon from the sea as a mark of her consort's regal status. Because Minos omits to sacrifice the bull as he should have done, Poseidon inflicts the terrible passion on Pasiphae as punishment. Minos's ritual omission has repercussions on all involved and leads to an extremely serious mediatory crisis that threatens the objectual stability of the community. There are indirect references here, filtered through the layers of the myth and rite, to a bull-god cult typical not only of Crete but of a wide area of the Mediterranean and Near East. Clearly, however, in Euripides's tragedy, the cult is no longer functioning; the result is the birth of the Minotaur, Asterios of the Orphic tablet, the son of Zeus's lightning, the divine child in his aspect as monster. The story, the *fabula*, of the *Cretans* finds its logical conclusion in the themes of the labyrinth and Daedalus, its cunning artificer.

But to what rite is the tragedy referring, always presuming that we can put the question in such specific terms? The answer is to be found in an important fragment of the parodos (πάροδος), the introductory speech of the chorus. But the text presents problems that give difficulties to scholars, so that the validity of its relation to Greek religion has often, and quite wrongly, been denied. The chorus consists of initiates to Idaean Zeus, and is therefore equivalent to the Curetes:[4]

> Child of the Phoenician woman of Tyre, son of Europa
> and mighty Zeus, O lord
> of Crete of the hundred cities,
> I came here leaving behind the truly divine temples,
> well covered with great beams of native wood
> hewn by the Chalybes' axes,
> and with cypress joined together by the ritual bull glue [*taurodetoi kollei kratheis*][5]
> in accurate joints [*harmous*];
> and leading a holy life [*hagnon bion*], since
> I became an initiate [*mystes*] of Idaean Zeus,
> and having celebrated the thunder [*brontas*][6] of Zagreus the night wanderer [*nyktipolou*]
> and the feasts [*daitas*] of raw flesh [*omophagous*]
> and raising on high the torches [*daidas*] for the Mountain Mother,
> sanctified [*hosiotheis*], of the Curetes
> I had the name of Bacchus.
> And wearing pure-white clothes I flee
> the birth of mortals, and without approaching

the urn of the dead, I take care not to eat
food in which there has been life [*empsychon*].

The person addressed is Minos, son of Zeus and Europa. Zeus abducted Europa and carried her over the sea to Crete where he mated with her in the shape of a bull. Hierogamy with a bull is present as a leitmotiv from the outset and eventually comes to involve all the characters in the tragedy.

The temples "well covered with great beams" are a metaphor for the community's ritual supports, constantly needing to be renewed by repeated sacrifice, and now set at risk by Minos's failure to sacrifice the bull. The Chalybes armed with axes for cutting the roof beams are a reminder of the pervasive collective presence, the collective figure of the Curetes. But there are other noteworthy details: the roof of the temple, besides being of cypress—a tree associated with death in the Orphic tablet—is held together with "ritual bull glue." Jane Ellen Harrison suggests this might be bull's blood mixed with mortar;[7] in any case, the ritual connotation is obvious. By specifying this constructive, ritual detail derived from bull sacrifice, the text forcefully underlines the gravity of Minos's liturgical omission, which threatens to tear apart the social fabric held together through the taurine rite, clearly alluded to by the detail of *harmous*, "in accurate joints." The joints are coming apart; the temple might collapse at any moment. This signifies the interruption of the sacrificial procedure of the *symbola* with unforeseeable consequences. In short, the ritual and symbolic references contained in the fragment are as circumstantial and penetrating as any modern anthropologist could desire. The survey already made in the previous chapter convinces us that Euripides knew what he was doing in his choice of subject and its development in this tragedy.

The whole fragment is dominated by the strange lifestyle of the initiates on Ida, described as ἁγνός (l. 9). This adjective is the poetical equivalent to ἅγιος and is used by the tragedians to express a state of consecration, of ritual purity set apart from the normal conditions of life. Semantically *hagnos/hagios* expresses what is to be feared because it belongs to the sphere of the sacred (corresponding to the Latin *sanctus*), and to *agos*, meaning both guilt and expiatory sacrifice.[8] A whole range of meanings and terms unfolds before us with one common denominator: all are related to the sacred (*hieros*) through sacrifice, the sacred act par excellence, indicated by the neuter plural *ta hiera* designating the victims as well (as with the Latin *sacra*).[9]

Without this system of ritual mediation that called for skill and calculation in its management, violence would have brought down the fragile edifice of culture. There can be no mistaking the real nature of the holy life on Ida: the saintliness of the figures mediating the sacred, seeking to concentrate it objectually through killing the sacrificial victim, is identical to the saintliness of the maenads in the *Bacchae* who tear Pentheus to pieces. Through Girard's theory of the expelled, divinized sacred we can grasp the bloody genesis of this transition but not its inner workings or significance, which require us to consider another essential aspect neglected by Girard: the objectual mediation that dealings with the sacred make possible thereby making human existence possible. Whoever leads a "holy life" (*hagnon bion*) eventually becomes *hosiotheis*, "sanctified," purified (l. 14), an expression that introduces the essential nuance conveyed by *hosios*: that which the gods permit to men on the strength of the sacrifice performed.[10] All these cultic and mythic elements, so skillfully brought together in the text, describe the *Orphikos bios*, the consecrated life of the Orphics. Euripides wants us to feel its appeal and power, but at the same time we are not to nurture any illusions. His aim is not to carry out a modern type of demystification, implying there is some sort of alternative, but to show the cost and effectiveness of the sacred mediations that gave rise to the Greek world.

The *Hippolytus* contains a succinct description of a similar lifestyle with direct reference to the Orphics. At this point in the tragedy, after Phaedra has hanged herself and left a letter accusing Hippolytus, Theseus attacks Hippolytus, his son, and his ascetic habits in particular:

> Now, go boast and fool others with your diet of greens
> and cereals, make Orpheus your master
> and play Bacchus in your mystic garb, with all those smoke-filled books [*bakcheue pollon grammaton . . . kapnous*]:
> you have been caught red-handed. I cry out to everyone to keep away
> from people like you, out to catch their prey
> with holy words [*semnois logoisin*] when what they are scheming is all contemptible [*aischra mechanomenoi*].[11]

The same vegetarian diet for purification is followed by the Idaean initiates; references to the hunting of Zagreus have become accusations against the deceitful Hippolytus, himself a hunter devoted to Artemis. Hippolytus emerges from Theseus's words as what we would now call a hypocrite, and a very strange figure: a vegetarian hunter who kills his prey and then boasts innocence of their blood, and similarly tries to capture new converts by means of "smoke-filled books."[12] There is wordplay here alluding to the vagueness and inconsistency of these writings. Theseus is talking about the *hieroi logoi* of Orphism, but the circumstance that the Derveni papyrus was in fact a chance survivor of its owner's funeral pyre has prompted the idea that Euripides is also alluding to the burning of these manuscripts in funeral ceremonies where the deceased was cremated along with texts intended to magically ensure his salvation in the next world.[13] This conjecture is perfectly sound and confirms the technical accuracy of the allusion. The references to Orphism are therefore deliberate, and the fact that Hippolytus has the same lifestyle as the holy men on Mount Ida leads to the conclusion that Euripides already wanted Orphism to figure in the *Cretans*, with a sophisticated reconstruction of its Cretan roots.

Hippolytus shows further development and insight. Zagreus the hunter and the Idaean initiates merge in the single figure of Theseus's son, trampled to death beneath the hooves of his own horses when they take fright at the sight of a monstrous bull rising from the sea. The sacrificial genesis of the character is made plain by his horrific destiny, a fusion of the Idaean bacchantes' feasts of raw flesh with the theme of the divine bull, bringer of misfortunes. Even if he is innocent of Theseus's charges, it is not the end of the connotations as to the character of Hippolytus. Once again, however, the Oedipal line suggested by the myth is a red herring: the crucial factor is not his innocence of his father's charges but the illusory nature of his vaunted purity. The horses that kill him coincide symbolically with Hippolytus, the name itself obviously deriving from the animal. He may be a proud follower of Artemis, but his purity is flawed by violence, making him no more innocent in the end than any of the other characters. It is as if this Orphic hunter is destroyed by the revelation of his real mythical nature, in which bull and horse are interchangeable. Both the *Cretans* and the *Hippolytus* show the ineffectiveness and the real sacrificial origin of Orphism. Since it is far from being the usual business of literature in the usual meaning of the word to do so, it would seem appropriate at this point to ask in what sense it is "literature," a pregnant question when set in relation to our previous remarks about myth. In fact, all the evidence points to literature having originated in the *mythos* that accompanied rites, explaining them by narrating them. What we need to understand is the way this was done and its cognitive implications.

Greek tragedy is evidence for seeing literature as the development and transformation of myth. Just as the *mythos*, the story, is itself potentially literature, so literature continues the story in forms varying according to how this new literary *mythos* reacts with the old sacral narratives from which it comes. Literature as a continuation may connive at the victimary blind spot necessary for the formation of the *mythos* but may also adopt a critical view, questioning the representations deriving from myth as the ties binding myth to ritual begin to loosen. The unified method for interpreting ritual and myth assumes an original unity, beginning to break up and subdivide into dramatic and literary symbolism: otherwise the spheres of literature and drama could not have become organized or have even existed. Greek tragedy, placed in the historical phase when the breaking-up occurs, utilizes it and asks questions about it. This is myth-ritual asking questions about its own origins and nature, seeking to know itself, even if doing so presents a threat to its integrity and inner coherence. The double bind of human representation, that is what it represents because it is not what it represents and not what it represents because it is what it represents, is transformed into paradoxical but necessary questions about the theatrical space opened up by this "not," this negativeness transformed into acting and theater, allowing the negative side of existence to be represented and retroacting on the blind spot from which its history began. These spectacular double binds at the origin of the spectacle of tragedy will accompany us throughout our analysis of this great expression of Greek civilization. The true nature of Euripides's achievement in the *Cretans* emerges once we grasp that the radical nature of the inquiry into the cults represented and evoked on stage tends to coincide with the investigation into tragedy that does the representing and evoking. This becomes clear if we take the religious reconstruction of the fragment seriously, with anthropological and historical realism, since Euripides has put together its major elements quite deliberately.

Idaean Zeus is the Cretan male divinity, coinciding with the archaic form of a god of dismemberment destined to become Dionysus, who either replaces him or merges with him. One of his names is typically Orphic: Zagreus, the great hunter who takes his prey alive.[14] He is defined as *nyktipolos*, night wanderer, indicating the nocturnal nature of the Cretan and Dionysian rites; similar darkness covered the Eleusinian initiations. The maenads (μαινάδες from μαίνομαι, to rage, be furious), Dionysian women possessed by the god in orgies, also wander about the mountains at night. This is the *oreibasia* (mountain roaming)[15] in the wild realm of the sacred, not yet filtered by the community's mediations or metabolized by its devices for representation and control, a ritual reproducing the objectual crisis relived by the bacchantes who give themselves up to total possession by the god. Divine mediation can only be reestablished providing the same conditions of crisis and annihilation that originated it are experienced in full, and therein lies the essential characteristic of the cult of Dionysus: its coverage from top to bottom of the entire sacrificial spectrum capable of bringing the god back to life through the experience of killing and devouring him. At the climax of possession—the state of *ekstasis*, complete self-abandon[16]—the *sparagmos* erupted, culminating in omophagy in its earliest form. Quite clearly, the lifestyle (*biotas*) of Zagreus "the night wanderer" is an indispensable ingredient in the *Orphikos bios*.

The most serious mistake, at this point, would be to imagine Euripides as doing archaeology for the sake of the narrative, with a retrospective glance at exotic lifestyles and strange behavior to entertain the Athenian public and guarantee success. Without doubt the practical needs of the theater played their part but only as the first level of a far more complex exploration of the vast cognitive repercussions of this theatrical archaeology that, to the attentive spectator, appears as an archaeology of the theater. Beneath the surface, the inquiry into the Dionysian cults traced back to their Cretan origins is also an inquiry into the structural ties binding Dionysus and the genre of tragedy. The omophagic feasts come to represent not only the origins of Orphism but also of the tragedy representing those feasts and Orphism.[17] Something very singular is taking place in the text, because Euripides, in his fertile no-man's-land between the old ritual *mythos* and the new literary *mythos*, in the double bind of a representation that represents itself and stakes its all, is prepared to stake and risk everything that he can, and even undermine the very existence of his art.

Our descriptive categories are decidedly inadequate to define such a singular figure, too close to the sacred mediations that he evokes to be considered modern and at the same time far too aware to fulfill the ambiguously sacral role implicit in the stories as staged. This is a continuation of the work of his great predecessors, but Euripides takes the double bind of tragic theater to the level of representation of itself that could not be taken further without breaking the rules of the genre. The search for knowledge recognizable in Euripides had already been undertaken by Aeschylus and Sophocles, but they appear more deeply involved in the sacrificial dynamics of the mediations that they put on the stage, with a cognitive retroaction less free, less daring, because hopeful of regaining the power of the mediations. When Aeschylus puts on stage the mechanisms of the reflected duplication of violence, he shows himself to be the herald of the new ideal of justice in the Athenian *polis*, and the prophet of the advent of divine mediation in the city and its institutions. Sophocles takes deconstruction a step further but not to the point of demystifying the divine; what especially comes to the crisis point in his tragedies is the relationship of gods to men. The involvement with violence, whether active or passive, condemns men never to reach the divine. In Aeschylus we meet the new collective objectuality of the *polis* that overcomes the objectual inadequacy of previous mediations, not rejected but incorporated at a higher level. In Sophocles the divine and political object is never cancelled out but becomes unattainable, indicating that there is no solution to the mediatory crisis afflicting classical Greece, and Athens in particular.

In origin, this Greek view of divine mediation has nothing in common with what was to be Christian religious mediation. The divine superiority to humankind is charged with the violence that it overcomes and takes into itself, violence that can be released at any moment as soon as the conditions regulating its stability cease to operate, a lapse into violence always potentially present that acts automatically, in accord with laws expressing the essence of the god, not his personal will. The convergence here with the theology of the *Brahmana* analyzed by Sylvain Lévi is structural and denotes a very ancient magical-religious stratum preserved by both civilizations in their respect for ritual conservatism,[18] though in Greece it quickly became unstable due to the absence of a prestigious, integrated sacerdotal caste. The Greek tragedians increasingly concern themselves with the conflict between this archaic divine automatism and the new ethical awareness of individual responsibility, a conflict that Aeschylus attempts to resolve in his *Eumenides*, with its themes of justice and the sacred; for Sophocles the conflict is mysteriously insurmountable as expressed in *Oedipus Rex*, and even the extreme mediatory effort of *Oedipus at Colonus* fails to really resolve it. Euripides starts from a profound rethinking of traditional religion and the Mysteries, still looking for a positive way to define the divine, as emerges from his first surviving work, the *Alcestis* (438 BC), which I shall be discussing in the conclusion. But in the course of his explorations of religion, including the *Hippolytus* among his mature works, the most archaic divine mediations are retrieved in full, in such a way as to expose the now unacceptable cruelty and the irremediable break with the objectual sphere that harsh treatment once restored: thus we have both Aphrodite's savage cruelty in driving Phaedra mad in order to punish Hippolytus, and Artemis's insensitivity, her sole concern being to avoid contamination by the dying Hippolytus. The objectual fracture already present in Sophocles is confirmed and widened, with developments that begin to undermine the superiority of the gods, who once possessed the power and the responsibility of healing the rift. The affinity or identity between human and divine behavior, previously guaranteeing the convergence of the two orders and making them functionally and symbolically recognizable, is now transformed into a horrifying, revelatory superimposition, into mediations incapable of any mediating because they are assigned to destroying an unrecognized and teleologically unrelated human object.

The divine mediatory duplication no longer works in Euripides, not so much because it reveals what is human, something that was already happening and served a fundamental purpose of sacral mediations, but because it is revealed in an unrelated way, left to itself, divested of the capacity for transition that would enable it to reach fulfillment and salvation, intramundane or eschatological. The divine double has to save, being a double that makes contact and completely fulfills its mission as a magic double made effective by the rite; on the other hand, where it recedes into the background and declines, it remains a double that duplicates and no more, destroying what it should save and emptying it of objectual meaning. This phase corresponds to the theological crisis to be observed in Euripides, and if, on the one hand, this achievement crowns the work of Aeschylus and Sophocles, on the other, with the tragic art destined to quickly decline, he appears almost unique, marking a sort of intellectual borderline, in the sense of a boundary that none were to cross after him.

This characterization of Euripides might be continued in terms of converging opposites: a tragedian too close to sacral mediations to fit squarely with our idea of a professional man of letters and too insightful to be confined to the religious mediations about which he writes. Inevitably, his art aroused Nietzsche's antagonism: it was too demystifying to suit his purposes. *The Birth of Tragedy* doggedly accumulates a whole catalog of the most-abused commonplaces about Euripides in order to dismiss him, which only goes to show how far Nietzsche's judgment could be clouded by a consuming desire for neosacrificial palingenesis and a belligerent return to an unlikely neo-Dionysian mediation. In fact, Nietzsche in person was to relive the double bind sounded out by Euripides thousands of years before, with the macroscopic difference of an aggravation and self-confidence made possible by Christianity's historicizing. In Nietzsche there is a return to a space of oscillation between a divine mediation that duplicates because it saves and a mediation that fails to save because it simply duplicates, but with an additional variable that makes him see Euripides in a dual guise: as forerunner of a loathed unveiling and as hidden director of the doubles, still able to manipulate their masks. How, in short, could Nietzsche fail to detest his own involuntary double *ante litteram*?

Returning now to the parodos of the *Cretans*, we will plot the associations and connections with the sacrificial mediations as they unwind and combine through the text. There is some striking etymological play on the words δαῖτας (from *daiomai*, I tear, I divide), indicating the feast in the sense of dividing up pieces of flesh (with Dionysus *Isodaites*, the sharer in equal parts, presiding over it), and δᾷδας (from *daio*, I burn), the torches that lit the maenads' rites and key moments in the Mystery ceremonies. Thus, in the juxtaposition of the two words, the entire evolution of sacrifice according to the Titanic myths is powerfully condensed, from the anthropophagic tearing apart of the raw flesh to the cooked flesh, symbolized here by fire;[19] however, the concentration destabilizes since it contracts all these phases into a sort of symbolic acceleration that corresponds to the loss of effectiveness of their ritual solutions. We shall meet the most complete version of this representational and textual solution in the *Bacchae*.

The Mountain Mother is the prehistoric goddess of the erotic-sacrificial cult, both wife and mother to Zeus-Dionysus. Her companions, the Curetes, with whom initiates identified, are named in l. 14.[20] According to the latest reading, the expression used here makes the transition, ritually and explicitly, from the protectors of the child Zeus to the Dionysian identity of the Titan myth. Eventually, however, the axes of the Chalybes had to fall on somebody in order to roof "the truly divine temples" and ensure their mediatory protection. The pure-white garb of l. 16 refers to this bloody purification, making possible objectual control of the impurity that would otherwise overwhelm society. White is the color of the bull-Zeus and Poseidon's bull, of the cypress on the Orphic tablet, and, earlier, of the Titans' chalk.[21] The alternation of the extremes of black (night) and white expresses the entire spectrum that the community must be able to cover, following the relevant rules, the appropriate rituals, capable of reconciling and coordinating, at different times and in different places, states in themselves completely contrary. The purification concluding the fragment gives release from the cycle of rebirths and requires a vegetarian diet (ll. 16–19), which is the same as Hippolytus's. We pass from one extreme to the other of the "holy life," from the paroxysmal violence of the *sparagmos* and omophagy to asceticism. This transition codifies the character of Hippolytus and is finally deconstructed in the epilogue of his eponymous tragedy, becoming his destruction. The theatrical duplication attests to the ineffectiveness of the mythical-ritual duplication, breaking up into a series of unrelated events what mediations once made into a single complex as mysterious as it was necessary. The result is an explanatory *reductio ad unum* that in reality divides, frustrating the unification of the rite and evidencing its failure. Pure and impure have only one source, and the vaunted chastity of the bacchantes in Euripides's tragedy is all one with their savagery, but it is precisely this that separates their ingredients, on a par with Heraclitus's *kykeon*, the sacred beverage at Eleusis that separated out if it was not shaken.[22] The ancient unity is shown up as an *aequivocatio*, translated into an unbearable homonym. As Phaedra declares in *Hippolytus*:

> If we knew the right moment [*kairos*],
> two things would not be called by the same name [*grammata*].[23]

Καιρός is what is right and lawful, in the sense primarily of *decus*, the social decency that is Phaedra's obsession and that she was to preserve by her suicide; but this social, family *decus* refers in turn to another *kairos*, the sacrificial *kairos* that required two things to be "called by the same name," thereby making subsequent distinctions possible. The duality in the awareness acquired throws the *aequivocatio* of the ancient unity back in its face, but it is precisely this differentiation with its desire to be intransitive that now expresses the irreversible nature of the process, unable to continue to draw on the *kairos* that it needs.

Euripides shows himself to be aware of the essential point of Orphism's soterial mediation, namely, that it is necessary to pass through the Titanic violence in order to be free of it, but he also realizes that this is impossible, an illusion, both too archaizing and too conscious. Without doubt, Orphism made increasing efforts to spiritualize the movement, while holding firmly to the central role of the Titanic rite, and inevitably, the rites were increasingly interpreted symbolically, as the Gurob papyrus proves. It seems to me highly probable that Onomacritus was working toward this, and Pythagoras, too, in his mystic-philosophical activity. Compared to these various spiritualizing efforts, which were evidently unable to establish themselves as effective sacral and sapiential mediations in the turbulent and culturally sophisticated milieu of the Hellenic world, Euripides takes Orphism back to its roots in Dionysus and Crete, to show its relevance and inadequacies as a religion, which in reality turns out to be part of the problem and not its solution. The critical detachment from Orphism, already documented in the *Alcestis*, is taken further by thoroughly dissecting the origin of its myths and rituals. Let us now look at the beginning of the plot of the *Cretans* starting from these premises.

2. Monsters and Wise Men in Crete

Although only a few brief scenes of the *Cretans* remain, they are highly charged emotionally. The dominant theme of the tragedy is monstrosity, a monstrous act that traditional sacral mediations are no longer able to interpret and control; this is clear from the very start in the surviving exchanges of the initial dialogue, found in fragmentary form in a papyrus. Character *A*, ignorant of the details of what has happened, asks another character, *B*, for information; *B* knows something but is not fully informed since he ascribes the newborn monster to its human parents. Previously I adopted the old reading, identifying the two speakers as Minos and the Nurse, but the Nurse ought to be better informed about the circumstances of the Queen's mating with the bull, and *A*'s third-person reference to the parents precludes identifying the character as Minos. The following text is the result of my checking photographs of the papyrus and comparing old and new readings, taking into account hermeneutic factors previously ignored but essential for reconstructing the wider context about which the text speaks:[24]

> *B* . . . I heard . . .
> *A* <Then tell me how> it happened.
> *B* <Don't be> in a hurry <for painful news.>
> *A* May it turn out <for the best!> We need <to implore> the gods.
> *B* <Don't be well disposed> toward someone who launched an attack like that.
> *A* <I'm completely in the dark>, I want <to know> from you.[25]. . .
> *A* It's a mixture of bull and man, of double nature [*diplei physei*].
> *B* So I have heard: but <what is the beast's body like>?[26]
> *A* Firm over its breast [*sternois*][27] it <carries> a <taurine> head.
> *A* Can you say then whether it has four feet or two?
> *B* <Of dou>ble [*diplous*][28] nature, and all shaggy with its black <hide>.
> *A* Besides that, have you any other <horrors to tell me>?
> *B* <It has a bull's face>; but without a tail.[29]
> *A* . . . have you ever heard its voice?
> *B* <I heard it lowing, like an ox> grazing.[30]
> *A* Have you given it milk from its mother or from a heifer?
> *B* The parents feed it not . . .
> *A* . . . of anger[31] . . .
> *B* <For others, perhaps it is lawful to do [*dran*] that>,[32] not for the parents.

The Minotaur in its double nature, uniting and multiplying the alternatives of being four-footed or two-footed, is the living incarnation of an objectual crisis, which unites and confuses what is by nature distinct; it is the inexhaustible root-source of paradoxes, frustrating *A*'s generic religious compassion and having as its logical consequence the partial or erroneous information of the two characters. The taurine child is the living expression of the double nature of Minos, descendent of the bull and bull-king, a sort of mythical résumé of the king's history. From a symbolic viewpoint, Minos is the father of the Minotaur, as the beast's name suggests and as *B*'s misunderstanding emphasizes, factually wrong but allusively correct and perfectly understood by the audience. This amounts to saying that Minos is responsible for the crisis breaking out on Crete and already prepares the way for later developments. The king must avoid becoming confused with his monstrous son, in order not to return to the original victimary role of kings, which they might re-adopt at any time if things took a turn for the worse. In fact, the myth relates that once every nine years Minos descends into the cave on Mount Ida to receive instructions from his father, Zeus. As Frazer fully appreciated, this is a transfiguration of a sacrificial test the Cretan sacred king had to undergo,[33] and Frazer himself connects the "octennial" ceremony of Minos to a sacred marriage "in the form of bull and cow."[34] Leaving aside the interesting astronomical associations of Frazer's reconstruction, this amounts to identifying a substitute victim in the taurine infant, although the substitution would entail overcoming insuperable difficulties, overcoming a double bind even more confusing than the double bind, human and animal, of the little Minotaur. If Minos chose to acknowledge paternity of Pasiphae's child he could no longer kill him, and the monstrosity, remaining in the family and in the kingdom, would therefore affect him; if he did not acknowledge paternity he could kill the child but would have to reveal his wife's unnatural act, repudiate her, and put her to death as well, destroying his family as a consequence, and so the monstrousness of such ruthless behavior would fall on his own head just the same.

Besides, the double bind is shared by both parents, as subsequently transpires in the tragedy, dividing and uniting them for the same reasons. The Minotaur would demand a necessary and impossible sacrifice. *A*'s final words seem to refer to the urgent need to placate the *ira deorum*, while *B*'s underline the impossibility of doing this starting from the family as defined and accepted, morally and ethically, in Greece. In any event, the Cretan king's family is doomed to remain monstrous, almost suggesting a group sacrifice that might go to the root of the problem by reviving the most ancient glories of the labyrinth hierogamies. But the living symbol of the Minotaur holds further refinements in store for us.

The unrealistic sturdiness of his limbs is underlined by the head "firm over its breast," and also by Raffaele Cantarella's previous conjecture *harmois* ("steady on its limbs") recalling, with potentially inverted meaning, the "accurate joints" (*harmous*) of the Idaean temples. This ingenious reconstruction may be improbable by text-critical standards, but that hardly detracts from the effectiveness of the semantic correspondence. The two joinings refer to and exclude each other in turn: the stability of the temples, the group's sacrificial *harmonia*, can only be ensured by unjoining what has been firmly and unnaturally joined in the Minotaur. According to Heraclitus, this ἁρμονία has to remain "not manifest" and is "stronger" (κρείττων), better, than the "manifest" one: *harmonie aphanes phaneres kreitton*.[35] The word "stronger" (*kreitton*) is not used metaphorically here but has the sense of making the best use of consciously directed strength, corresponding, in the ontological and cosmic field, to the mediatory and objectual force of Fire that, according to Heraclitus, is "intelligent" (*phronimon*) and suggests by itself the best sacrifice, that made with fire.[36] Up to a certain point, Greek philosophy was moving in the same direction as tragedy, with implications and developments tending in any event toward a mediatory healing of the rift that would overcome the objectual crisis brought to the stage by tragedy by logical-cognitive means. But tragedy, unlike philosophy, was not seeking to transform sacrifice on a cosmic scale; it represents sacrifice, it "does" it cognitively. The last line of the dialogue on the Minotaur refers to this sacrificial logic, displayed and at the same time concealed, with the verb δρᾶν, "to do/make" in the sense of *sacra* or *sacrum facere*. This *sacrum* is unable to be powerfully cosmic as in the case of philosophy; its impotence to settle and resolve the knots in the plot is a constant, and typical of Euripides.

The problem, as *B* says, is that the sacred action ought to be performed in a *lawful* way, that is, as prescribed by ritual. His comment comes just before the entry of Minos who, as the parodos has already revealed, consults the sons of Ida; however, the fact that the plot has yet to unfold tells us that the sacrificial experts leading their "holy life" have not come up with a solution. Tragic duplication only repeats and confirms the proliferating duplication of the entire *fabula*. The sons of Ida belong to a mountain sphere incapable of interacting with the uncontrolled sphere of the sea, and their impotent wisdom reproduces this rift in the Orphic factions, failing to deliver their promised salvation, and in the chorus that confines itself to circumstantial comments on the circumstances of the action, as is regularly the case in Euripides. Circumstantial but by no means innocuous. We might fairly suspect that the Idaean initiates, having from their first words stressed the victimary signs of foreign origin and monstrous birth ("Child of the Phoenician woman of Tyre etc."), are about to politely toss the ball back into the king's court. Myth becoming literature retroacts on its historical and religious premises: its *harmonia* cannot be reestablished in the preestablished harmony of art where literature is an end in itself, and in that way it sends us a message, a higher form of knowledge.

The only solution for the time being is to put the Minotaur at the center of the labyrinth, apparently, in both tragedy and myth, built for that purpose by Daedalus. The labyrinth takes the construction imagery of the first temples a step further and becomes part of a conscious plan; built to a rational design and meant to contain the spreading monstrousness, it really connives at it as well. The figure of Daedalus, as far as we can infer, develops the sapiential motif already evinced in the proto-Orphic sons of Ida and, by reason of his mythical connotations, comes to represent wisdom in its various aspects, and even evokes tragic wisdom itself.

Although the scenes where Daedalus appears have unfortunately been almost entirely lost, the traditional mythic material yields useful information when seen in the context of the play. Daedalus is an artificer full of cunning (*metis*), a sculptor of lifelike statues (*daidala*), and skilled at joining wood with glue (*kollei*).[37] He is therefore an expert in the *harmonia* to be made with wood from the temples of Ida, and an archaic forebear of Heraclitus, the theoretician of harmony in the *kosmos*. As an expert craftsman, familiar with wood and glue, he knows how to create *charis*, the beauty that captivates, harmony in an aesthetic sense. During the fifth century BC, the sacrificial procedure of the *symbola-harmoi* became both a work of art and a cosmic image. Originally meaning an ornament, *kosmos* came to signify universal order, a semantic evolution epitomizing the enormous expansion of the objectual range of Greek culture from embellishments originating in ritual to philosophical and scientific observation of the natural world. We do not know if Euripides actually exploited this nuance of meaning, but given his philosophical interests, he must have been perfectly aware of it. In any case, as a recognizable feature in the Athenian cultural background of the time it would add to the connotations of the character. Another fifth-century Greek wise man, the philosopher Empedocles from Sicily, makes the same connection in explaining the birth of living things, whose bones are "joined by the glue of Harmony" (*Harmonies kolleisin arerota*),[38] a Harmony it would be wrong to interpret in antisacrificial terms because of its connection with *Eros*, since in reality it comes substantially from the regular sequence of Love and Hate, the two universal principles re-membering and dismembering all beings, according to the cosmic transformation of a law that, in Euripides's tragedy, still has a ritual and largely archaeological value.

At first glance Daedalus's *metis* might appear to be secular and metaritual; however, structural ties with ritual are actually maintained, as the labyrinth mythologem goes to show. The *Iliad* speaks of Daedalus clearing a space where Ariadne, herself the daughter of Minos and Pasiphae, might dance (χορός).[39] In the traditional version of the myth, undoubtedly the version followed by Euripides, Daedalus has become the architect of a real building, a petrification of the labyrinth reminding us that architecture originated in ritual: in the tomb. Initially the tomb must have conferred a prearchitectural meaning on caves chosen for burial in prehistory; then it became a proto-Neolithic sanctuary linked to the cult of ancestors but not to a still nonexistent city like at Göbleki Tepe; transformed with the agricultural revolution into an altar to the god-victim and throne for the king-victim, it gave origin to temple and royal palace respectively, its symbolic expansion, and spatial organization; the city then took shape and grew around these mediatory places as a public and universal place going in contrast with the limit and defensive organization of the village.[40]

However, one further aspect to this illustrates the mentalizing of the metasymbol and metalanguage of the tomb, deemed in my reconstruction to be the secret of the shamanistic and representational achievements of both Neanderthal and *Homo sapiens*, yet destined in our species to become not only an expanding and universalistic attitude toward the external world but also a specializing mentalization that was gradually more sophisticated as civilizations developed through history up to the point of internalizing the previous shamanistic phase, transforming its visionary experiences into complex thinking operations linked to the ritual and mythical activities of priests. Daedalus illustrates the unmistakably Hellenic phase of this evolution by now independent from a sacerdotal status: although still mediated through the typifying processes of myth, he begins to emerge as an individualized and professionally specialized wise man. There must have been an invisible model, *a mental labyrinth*, clear in the mind of this architect-choreographer, the sole possessor of the blueprint, before he began to build the ritually stratified space of the labyrinth, little by little to become the labyrinth par excellence.

Daedalus, the labyrinth-man, ends by being imprisoned with his son, Icarus, in the labyrinth of his own devising. He finally manages to escape but at the price of sacrificing his son, yet another incarnation of the divine child that must have been interestingly developed by Euripides. A fragment, once ascribed to the *Cretans* but now thought to belong to the *Bellerophon*, provides some idea at least of how the figure of Icarus might have been treated in the *Cretans*: "And if I then should fall into the damp abyss [*bathos*] of the sea? / How will I be able to get out, winged as I am?"[41] We should note how Euripides transforms the traditional story: it becomes, on the one hand, a cosmic play of contrasts (sea/sky, high/low) and, on the other, a psychological motif retroacting on the *mythos* and humanizing it, as we shall see more patently with Pasiphae. But whatever we make of these details, we can draw more general conclusions about the episode of Daedalus's flight with Icarus from the traditional myth. To make good their escape, Daedalus attaches to Icarus and himself animal transformations of the god-victim, as was done in the crane dance, but the end result is a typically Euripidean tragedy within the tragedy. With artificial monstrosity and fearless manipulation of the doubles, through the most terrible of sacrificial substitutions, wisdom barely manages to save itself. The fact is that the substitution conceals the sacrifice of the wise artificer himself.

Icarus is clearly a double of Daedalus: his wings of wax are melted by the sun, the incandescent symbol of the center of the labyrinth, and he plunges beneath the waves, a ritual substitute for the mob overwhelming the victim. We already know about labyrinthine depths in connection with wetness, and we shall encounter the theme again in the *Bacchae*. Another myth, evidently predating the Icarus myth for its less psychological import, concerns Daedalus and Perdix ("partridge"), his nephew, rival as inventor, and a further mythical double of himself;[42] out of jealousy, Daedalus causes Perdix to fall to his death from the Acropolis. The ambiguity between ritual and metaritual of Daedalus's *metis* or cunning has the ambivalence of the Orphic practices though transposed to a knowledge-based setting. Since Daedalus is the mythical creator of the *choros*, the further question arises of the author's relationship to his *choros* and the system of characters that turns on it, not to mention the wider chorus, the audience. Knowledge can represent itself on stage but cannot save itself, let alone save others: it is a mediation whose objectuality ends at the representational level of its own fiction, making fiction of all that it touches.

Before addressing such questions, we need to get closer to the heart of the action. The salient moment is to be found in another fragment: Pasiphae, the principal female character, appears for an instant powerfully projected in a theatrical space that looks like an emanation of the labyrinth. This is the best occasion for observing a still partial, unaccomplished transition from the mythical-ritual dimension to the dimension of psychology and desire.

3. The Minotaur's Mother

A few lines suffice to evoke what must have been one of Euripides's most extraordinary female creations, bringing together the persecution of Hippolytus with Phaedra's insane desire. The fragment comes at the climax of the conflict between husband and wife, when Minos has evidently decided to cast Pasiphae in the role of sacrificial victim. Although her fate is sealed and she knows it, she makes the following passionate defense.[43] This is the opening sequence of her speech, her *rhesis*:

> *Pasiphae (to Minos)* Even by denying, I could never convince you:
> now it is indeed clear how things stand.
> If I had offered my body to a man
> deriving some furtive sexual pleasure [*Kyprin*],
> certainly I would have appeared rightly lustful.
> But now—since I went mad [*emenamen*] because a god assailed me—
> I suffer; and it is an unwilled misfortune,
> completely inexplicable. Why ever, indeed,
> as I looked at that bull, was my heart struck with an indecent obsession
> [*nosoi*]?
> Was he perhaps handsome to look at on account of his clothes
> or his tawny mane? Or did a dark light
> shine in his eyes, and a beard darken his face?

It was certainly not the attractive body of a bridegroom!
And so, to mate with him,
I got inside . . . the hide of the moving heifer.
And not even to make the groom . . .
of sons. Why then did I go mad because of his obsession [*emainomen nosoi*]?
It was his demon [*daimon*] that filled me with misfortune as well
and, above all, it was him . . .
because he did not sacrifice to the sea-god, as he had
promised to do, the bull that appeared [*phasma*] to him.
Therefore, Poseidon turned against you,
to do justice; and went for me like that.
And now you cry out and call the gods to witness,
you, who did this and put me to shame?
I, who gave birth to it blamelessly [*kouden aitia*],
concealed the fatal blow of the god [*daimonos*],
While you, evil monster, really thinking to display
fine and honorable things for your consort
proclaimed it to all, as if you had nothing to do with it.

The heroine of the myth herself speaks to us and makes her confession, through the two labyrinths of an age-old myth and a text reduced to a few fragments, reconstructed, besides, by the unsure hand of philology. Pasiphae, that is, "she who shines for all,"[44] the queenly daughter of the Sun, still fills the stage with light and moves us with this personal account of the more revolting aspects of what befell her. The representational retroaction of tragedy on the *mythos* starts to become psychology or rather, on the contrary, it is the *mythos* being acted on stage that is transformed into psychology, thus bringing character and audience face to face with an irreducible dimension, where the old *mythos* is now found incomprehensible and the incomprehensibility is used in self-defense as an *argumentum ad absurdum*. A similar movement occurs in Aeschylus's *Prometheus Unbound* in regard to theology, and in Sophocles's two plays about Oedipus regarding the relationship between blame attributed to *genos* and individual responsibility. This development of myth as reflected through tragedy enters into human phenomena that are now attributed to eroticism and desire.

In this last case, the most frequent mistake in interpretation, and the easiest to make, is to assume that the sphere of sex or desire is originary, a mistake made in different ways by Freud, Bataille, and Girard. Freud interprets his libido naturalistically and gives it as unvaryingly valid in all times with the disastrous result that the Oedipus complex is projected back in time even as far as the prehuman animal. Bataille interprets eroticism more profoundly as a cultural ritualization that makes what is normally prohibited supremely desirable and finds relief from time to time in the transgressive subversion of ritual orgies. Sexuality with Bataille is still unvarying, however; culture finds it ready for use and just fits it into its games of prohibition/transgression, so much so that homosexuality is glossed over by Bataille as a mere eccentricity. In both Freud and Bataille, at different levels, there prevails a naturalistic dependence that prevents them from bringing the phenomena of desire into historical focus. Girard is more drastic and sees imitation as the sole source giving direction to mimetic desire, which originates in the objectual uprooting of the crisis and becomes potentially capable of making any object desirable. Mimetic rivalry is the fatal consequence, and the destruction of an object that has finally become a matter of indifference. However, this clearer focus is achieved at the expense of being able to take account of reality, and at the expense of the human tendency to construct and define it: the decisive objectual aspect is neglected while imitation assumes a disproportionate role that its generic, ubiquitous nature prevents it from fulfilling, eventually becoming ahistorical and unvarying, not wholly unlike Freud's libido.

As a consequence, Girard's theoretical model also assumes the presence of mimetic desire in all ages and cultures, to the point of projecting an elementary form of it onto the scene of origin, but applying this generic model to the more remote periods in time diminishes its historical verisimilitude. The concept of objectual mediation, on the contrary, enables us to identify the structures that originate the direction and realization of what we might call the sphere of desire. In doing so, however, we must beware of making it a kind of essence, by recognizing its real nature as a set of impulses of biological origin given form and significance by the mediations shaping them, and never forgetting the objectual gravitation that makes sexuality the first affective, relational object for adult humans. Human sexuality has always existed (or we would not be here to talk about it) and has survived the crossfire of taboos and transgressive eroticism, but in its most archaic phases it was indistinguishable from the mediatory, sacral forces on which the community depended. Euripides's tragedy attests to a phase when sexual desire began to be psychologized and individualized, but complete personalization was impossible because the sacral and suprapersonal were so powerfully involved. In the seventh century BC, the poet Sappho describes the experience of her love affairs as if the presiding divinities of love (Aphrodite and Eros) were responsible, which is what makes her amorous confessions, no matter how personal or fictional they really were, so shocking; this is not the surprise appearance of subjectivity like our own, using religious metaphors, but the development of a subjectivity starting from the divine mediations that the poet sensed as its personalizing source.[45] In Euripides's Pasiphae, this subjectivity originating in rite and myth turns like a raging lion against the now incomprehensible and alien mediations. Sexual desire, previously mediated by ritual, becomes impossible and so absolves the queen of Crete from all blame (*aitia*) and personal responsibility. What was willingly done by Sappho, through the conventions of a new literary genre, becomes an act of rebellion with Pasiphae, and the resulting form of desire has enjoyed huge literary success precisely because it is not subjective, not desire in a psychological sense.

For over two thousand years Pasiphae has fascinated poets and playwrights and become synonymous with lust at its most appalling: from Ovid to Dante, who defined her as "she who imbeasted herself in the imbeasted timbers" (colei che s'imbestiò nelle 'mbestiate schegge),[46] from Jean Racine's *Phaedra* in the seventeenth century to Gabriele D'Annunzio's version in the twentieth, not to mention the more perverse erotic games of our contemporaries. The starting point is always Pasiphae's desire and her daughter's incestuous passion for the man-horse Hippolytus, categorized in terms of current morality but shown to have a far more ancient genealogy that depersonalizes it and reveals it as a prime element in anthropology, a mythical-ritual palimpsest. And the same could be done with desire in its contemporary form if it were viewed through the right optic. While modern men and women want at all costs to see their desire even in the most distant past, and so prevent themselves from understanding either one or the other, the right thing to do is to use the remote past as the mediatory, genetic premise of desire. Euripides gives us the chance to observe something that looks like our idea of desire *in statu nascendi*, a strange combination of ritual planning and personal drives, their elements now visible and potentially in a position to be disassembled.

Erotic desire degrades Pasiphae like an all-powerful demon, because originally it *was* an all-powerful, insatiable demon, a δαίμων, as she says twice. But Greek rationalization deprives the myth of the rite's divine metamorphosis, transforming it into a para-ritual scenario, with Pasiphae climbing inside a dummy heifer covered with hide to deceive the bull into mounting her, a stratagem devised by the indefatigable Daedalus and put together with his sacrificial glue. Thus an ancient ritual is made visible through beginning interpretation from one of its derivatives, unbridled sexual desire, with technological rationality serving its ends. For centuries, Euripides has been wrongly classed as psychological when he is really revealing the mediatory and religious foundation of what was already becoming psychology for the ancient Greeks, and has become so for ourselves. Pasiphae indicates a ritual state, the basis of our psychology but not yet psychology properly speaking. This is the state of the sacrificial rite of hierogamy, evoked indirectly in *Hippolytus* when the chorus illustrates the power of Aphrodite. Ancient iconography shows Pasiphae convulsed in ritual possession exactly like the maenads, but the stylization is tediously prepsychologistic, so to speak, since antiquity attempted to defend itself from what was genuinely embarrassing about the myth of the bull lover. If it had only been a mysterious classical-type perversion, no one would have thought any more about it. But Pasiphae's desire is not to be mythologized: it is the prehistory of desire which has its origin in the ritual mediations recounted in mythology. Dante sensed this anthropological undercurrent and so placed the Minotaur at the entrance to the circle of the violent in his *Inferno*, describing Pasiphae's son as "Crete's infamy . . . / conceived in the fake cow."[47] Violence is the direct consequence of what Pasiphae does and suffers, a violence stigmatized by Christianity in condemning not only pagan idolatry but the drives transmitted through it. However, substituting the *daimon* of sex with the demonization of sex was the preliminary to desacralizing and humanizing sex, turning it into an object of human responsibility. Pasiphae's monstrous mating, as her *rhesis* in the tragedy implies but leaves us to intuit, takes us back to what happened in the labyrinth.

From the fact that Daedalus connives at Pasiphae's copulation with the animal we can deduce that the taurine hierogamy took place at the center of the labyrinth. Union of the *symbola-harmoi* has become union of the flesh, as evoked at Eleusis. In the finally decentralized version of the myth of Ariadne, where an island replaces the center of the labyrinth, her suicide corresponds to the ancient sacrifice of the female component, and the manner of it, by hanging, to an early phase or variation of the Mesopotamian hierogamy. The Minotaur, according to Frazer a bronze statue used for sacrificing children, represents a more recent version or a variant of the rite typically involving the sacrifice of the divine child. Besides, prehistoric finds have shown or suggested that a sacrifice of the woman or of the child were not mutually exclusive. The woman inside the cow suggests a form of human copulation under a disguise of animal skins, though mating with the animal-god may literally have occurred; Herodotus, for example, speaks of an Egyptian hierogamy where a woman copulated with a goat in public,[48] and a most sensational case is the Indian horse sacrifice where a ritual bride was mated with the animal's phallus after it had been killed.[49] Returning to the question of ritual disguise, we may conclude that the *daidalon*, the lifelike artificial image, originated in the simulacra and disguises created by using the skin of the dead victim. An example of this occurred during the Athenian *Bouphonia* in which the skin of a sacrificed bull was used to simulate the live animal. The Aztec human sacrifice was a particularly bloody variant of this type of rite, with an air of even greater antiquity about it: immediately after the sacrifice, the priest put on the dead victim's skin or had a statue draped with it.

We have now reached the bleeding heart of the labyrinth. To pursue our analysis of the tragedy of the labyrinth, we need to reproduce and intensify the oscillations that will at least allow us to explore its twists and turns, aiming at a unifying point for an overall view of the labyrinth of tragedy, a point, naturally, from which we can make our exit. By keeping to the formula just reached we can move far from the center without forgetting its location and nature; the formula to follow is the monstrous tangle of a bloody coupling, two serpents intertwined in the Eleusinian knot, and intertwining bodies and limbs bearing a sinister resemblance to tangled intestines. We may appear to put the labyrinth behind us as we continue our analysis, but in fact, since we remain in the sphere of tragedy, we remain within the labyrinth.

A completely new situation is made possible by the tragedy: Pasiphae, the main female character, like her husband before her, intervenes actively in the myth, in the destructive/constructive double bind that brought her into being and now opens out as theatrical, verbal space. The crimes that she tries to excuse reflect the double bind of mythical accusations, as recognized by Girard, crimes from which there was no escape for the victim and firmly considered by the persecutors to have been really committed. However, this is not the exclusively passive, complicit process that Girard imagines. Through the tragedy's double bind, the victim begins to ask herself about the process in which she is involved: an individual character begins to emerge presenting the mythic story in a partially psychological guise. The more questions she asks herself about the myth the more inexplicable it appears, and the fact that it is inexplicable becomes the very means to attempt to free herself from the myth: an extraordinary process, though it may seem like a trapped animal struggling in a snare, where the harder it pulls at the rope the tighter the knot becomes, the double bind that set the entire representation in motion. Her passion for the bull is not denied, its physical reality forcibly conveyed in the rapid sequence of questions, but she denies responsibility, invoking divine causality as the source of all notions of desire and will. Every psychology was a theology in origin. *Kypris*, Aphrodite, the goddess invoked by Sappho and punishing the hero in *Hippolytus*, is erotic desire; Pasiphae is struck by this uncontrollable, and therefore divine, force; Phaedra, too, but in an even more abhorrent way. Pasiphae would appear to be damned by the absurd, vile nature of her actions, but they actually demonstrate her moral purity: she claims to have been possessed by a demonic obsession, by a divine disease (*nosoi*). In this way, by asking questions about herself, Pasiphae regains knowledge of divine possession, indicated here by the verb *mainesthai*, but she is unable to see the entire process of which ritual possession was a part, transforms it into a scandalous affair to be hushed up, and attributes all the religious, social, and moral misconduct to her husband. What happened to her remains inexplicable, creating a need for explanation that is not satisfied; so we must add it to what we require for reconstructing a more comprehensive historical and hermeneutic sequence.

Pasiphae might well echo these words of Phaedra's nurse:

> For what shines on earth
> we conserve a love without hope,
> both through inexperience of another life,

and through ignorance of the netherworld:
we are content with empty fables [*mythois*].[50]

Such questioning empties out the myth, even if nothing replaces it. And two thousand years later, those "empty fables" become Macbeth's more emotionally charged but analogous "tale told by an idiot, full of sound and fury, signifying nothing."[51] With William Shakespeare, the myth—the fable, the tale—transformed into theatrical space becomes nihilism, the anguished contemplation of nothingness. If the experience of a different life for the living, and a different life for the dead, is missing, then nothing can save us from the empty fable of myth, nothing can make us see that such a fable, though deceptive, is not so empty since it is filled, and indeed created, by the collective dynamics that give rise to the mythic function; this is the sound and fury that signifies nothingness in real terms, that is, death for those who suffer them, as in the case of Macbeth. By itself the comparison cannot fill the intervening centuries from Pasiphae's day to our own, but reconstruction becomes possible once we see that the *mythos* begins to read itself through the words of the heroine, a painful act of self-separation, necessarily in the form of emptying out and unresolved conflict. Prisoner of her own myth, trapped in an inescapable deceptive, savage fable, Pasiphae is compelled to countercharge Minos with the same accusations as in the myth; in that way she confirms the sacrificial logic at the origin of her own story. The truth is revealed in a final gesture at the climax of her speech:

You then have ruined me, since you are to blame [*'xamartia*],
I suffer [*nosoumen*] because of you. So, if you want to kill me
in the sea, kill me: you are really an expert
in acts of murder and slaughter!
And then, if you long to feed on my raw flesh [*omositou*],
do so: don't forget your feasts.
But, free and quite blameless
I shall die, to pay for the guilt that is yours.[52]

The queen makes a final attempt to turn against Minos the charge that already holds her prisoner, and this makes the final image deeply moving, an image of freedom and innocence joined to death accepted with pride, not with resignation. As Pasiphae struggles helplessly, the trap closes around her with neat symmetry: mating with the bull from the sea corresponds to dying in the sea, though it could be said that she was deprived of this spectacular death, apparently being buried alive in the royal palace together with the Nurse. But her real revenge is typically Greek, that is, cognitive in nature, and it is a response to the Cretan king's undignified revelations. The description of the mechanism about to be triggered produces the final revelation that exposes the real nature of the temples held together with ritual bull glue, of the labyrinthine architecture, and of the sea drowning the victim. Minos, with his substitution strategy, is an Orphic adept; the omophagic feasts are none other than cannibalistic killings. This is a bold move on the part of Euripides, but must not be confused with demystification of the modern kind, as I shall make clear in the following chapter. We should not overlook the dual valence of this procedure: setting the story in a mythical past and on an island at the edge of the classical Greek world makes revelation possible but at the same time confines it to a remote, sacral dimension suffused with the prestigious, horrific atmosphere of the traditional mythologem.

At all events, it must have had a remarkable effect on the public, especially on the more informed and cultured spectators. Euripides subtly reveals the hypocrisy of the Orphic rites and shows up the complicity of Daedalus's knowledge as well. For anyone looking for reality beneath the embellishments of myth and a setting far removed from us in space and time, the only reality is a sordid game of hide-and-seek where the least able and least fortunate player becomes the victim. The Coryphaeus tries to steer the situation back to the official viewpoint, namely, a sudden calamity coming from outside and willed by the gods, but his words carry no weight because the divine superstructure is revealed as a parody of what is wrong among mortals, and the final consequence of admitting that would be suffered by whoever held the highest position among men. The sarcasm and anger of Minos's reaction is due to that, not to any matrimonial crisis, as a modern audience might imagine in its desire to find a psychological thread in this tangled skein that has nothing psychological in its origin:

Coryphaeus It's clear to everybody that this is a case
of bad luck . . . don't let anger get the better of you, my lord.
Minos How sharp her tongue is! . . . she cries out!

(*to the guards*) Hurry, hurry: she must be put under armed guard.
Seize this wicked woman, so she may have the death she deserves,
she and her accomplice [*xynergon*]: into the palace [*domaton*] lead them . . . ,
where they may see heaven's vault no more.

Coryphaeus Wait, my lord: the matter calls for reflection:
a ruthless man . . . is not wise in his decisions.

Minos It is already decided that the sentence [*diken*] shall not be deferred.[53]

The conclusion of the argument is ruthless, in the spirit of *dike*—that is, of justice in the form of controlled revenge, basically, where revenge is not simply unbridled rivalry but a ritualized institution to regulate rivalry and give it a legal basis. A major divinity for the Orphics, *Dike* transposed the human need for revenge onto the plane of rewards and punishments in the next world; and in ancient mythology Minos himself becomes the ruler and judge of the kingdom of the dead, a role he retains in Dante's *Inferno*. However, in Euripides these institutional and religious aspects of Minos lose their power to mediate and compensate, fall away, and are replaced by full-blown, patent retaliation.[54] The woman condemned with Pasiphae is the Nurse, who must have been her accomplice, analogous to the Nurse and Phaedra in the *Hippolytus*.[55] The two women are dragged into the palace, now symbolically equivalent to the labyrinth, a sacrificial space that no longer leads to the light of salvation but to endless night, to a ghastly, slow death of being buried alive.

Labyrinth symbolism appears in another fragment that is controversial since it comes from a satire on Euripides, *The Frogs* by Aristophanes. In my opinion we can give it provisional acceptance when we consider that an Athenian playwright writing about the labyrinth could hardly omit some reference to Euripides's best-known play on the subject. In this fragment Icarus is calling on the Cretan sons of Ida to free him; the building where he is held prisoner is certainly the labyrinth, described in very similar terms to Minos's palace:[56]

Icarus Come then, Cretan sons of Ida,
take up your bows, hurry,
come quickly to surround [*kykloumenoi*] the palace.

And the virgin [*pais*] Dictynna, the fair Artemis
may she search the whole mansion [*domon*] with her hounds.
And you Hecate, daughter of Zeus, raising
in your hands the two splendid torches,
light our way.

The identification of the chorus with the Cretan community now becomes explicit, just as the labyrinth openly reacquires the scenarios of collective violence that, transformed into art and architecture through ritualization, originally gave birth to it. The hounds symbolize the savage mob and also appear in the *Bacchae*. Artemis, originally an ancient Cretan deity, is another double of the Mountain Mother and of Pasiphae herself. Her Cretan name, Dictynna, comes from *diktyon* meaning a hunting net; the same metaphor underlies the Orphic image of Persephone's peplum and the labyrinth's tangled snakes and intestines. Hecate, goddess of the underworld, is often portrayed as a hound or accompanied by hounds; her double torches well represent the mediatory crisis now spreading throughout the island and cast a symbolic, sinister light of knowledge and death. If we put together the Cretans encircling the labyrinth and Icarus drowning "into the damp abyss of the sea," we have at once the original scenario that produced these symbols: the victim overwhelmed by mob fury. A new type of stimulus to knowledge takes hold of characters and chorus, and finally the audience, who could recognize themselves in the action on stage.

We should not be misled by the apparent mildness of the Coryphaeus's words ("a ruthless man . . . is not wise in his decisions"). The ambiguous role of the chorus in tragedy, so splendidly intuited by Freud at the end of *Totem and Taboo*, is really the ambiguous role played by myth in tragedy, and by the collective violence from which myth derives. Just as tragedy cannot free itself from the myth that feeds it, so it cannot do without the chorus from which it originated. Knowledge in tragedy cannot be separated from complicity, from being part of the same plan that triggers knowledge, and the *choros*, both in the text and on stage, is the function where this generative, destabilizing double bind finds expression in speeches whose poetic beauty compensates for the inability of the *choros* to respond to the drama that it accompanies and expounds. The inherent ambivalence of the chorus becomes the ambivalence of the audience as it watches and listens; and it is ours, too, as we read the tragic *mythos* and recognize ourselves in the nihilism of Phaedra, Pasiphae, and Macbeth. In the end, however, we approve of their deaths as the consequence of their fatal misdeeds. What alternatives or ways of escape could there be for such paradigms of the libido for sex and power? Questions of the kind usually remain unformulated, ritually silenced by the derivative mediation of an untouchable literary tradition, a substitute for the ritual mediations in which ancient tragedy had its place. It is not a matter of demystifying ancient or modern literary games but of understanding the representational activity that calls for our comment and concerns us.

The ambiguity hidden within so many of our literary and theatrical enthusiasms is to be seen in the behavior of the chorus in *Hippolytus* when the queen hangs herself to save her honor. Compromised by the Nurse, who has disclosed her illicit love affair to her stepson, she accuses him of trapping and raping her. At this crucial moment, the chorus of women divides and one group asks the other:

> Friends, what shall we do? Shouldn't we enter the palace
> and release the queen from the noose strangling her?

The hesitation of these bystanders amounts to an answer in itself since, in such situations, immediate action is quite obviously essential if a human life is to be saved. So when the answer comes, we are already prepared for it. Nonetheless, it is spine-chilling:

> What for? Aren't they with the young maids?
> Doing too much doesn't make for a safe life.[57]

Before we jump to conclusions, we need to take into account the cultural context, that is, the drama of Greek womanhood as prisoner of the female condition, confined to the home, to οἶκος, and duty-bound to safeguard its honor and serve its reproductive ends. Female mediation in the ancient world had the task of safeguarding the reproductive, sexual object within the closed intimacy of family and home, while male mediation guaranteed its possession in public. Phaedra and Hippolytus failed to carry out their complementary roles: she broke the reproductive and endogamic rules by falling in love with her husband's son, and Hippolytus refused his reproductive role quite violently, as emerges from the tirade in vv. 618–24, not so much aimed at women as at the division of tasks between men and women designed to maintain and perpetuate human society. The tirade proves secretly fatal because Phaedra listens unseen and realizes that her case is hopeless.[58] As a last resort to silence the scandal and restore her compromised honor, she chooses suicide and accuses her lover of attempted rape, an attitude fully shared by the chorus of women though not to be openly expressed since female suicide was deplored as threatening the existence of the *oikos* and removing the object necessary prerequisite to male objectual mediation.

As in many other cases, the chorus acts as intermediary between the demands of the theater and those of society; alien to our modern morality that disapproves of suicide and still more of not acting to save people from suicide, it not only fixes a difference but collates the two, outlining subtler forms of continuity. Author and chorus differ greatly in their viewpoints, but at the same time they are not entirely separate, so knowledge is transmitted to the audience in this twofold form.

In the last dialogue between Minos and the Coryphaeus in the *Cretans*, the decisive piece of advice is conveyed more indirectly by a subtly substitutive allusion. Since the entire tragedy turns on the interruption in sacrificial mediations caused by Minos, to invite him not to sacrifice Pasiphae is equivalent to saying he should sacrifice himself, as many other characters in Euripides do. The ruthless man is not simply the man who sacrifices but the man who sacrifices in an ineffectual, nonlawful way. The refusal of the chorus to support the king's plans for substitution is given final expression here. Minos, the potential scapegoat unwilling to sacrifice himself in his taurine version, is unable to close the circle with a substitute scapegoat. On the other hand, the implicit rituals of the chorus produce nothing, being now too weak and too visible to achieve effective results as in ancient times. Like a senator in Tacitus, Minos should change his own sentence to suicide, but suicide cannot replace an act that is effective only when mediated and willed by the gods. Tragic representation renders ineffectual the sacrifice from which it arose, just when it needs to draw strength from it. And that tension can give us further information about the characteristics of the tragic sphere and the double binds that open and close it, as well as about the coordinates to be followed to construct and define the area of our inquiry.

The paradoxical logic that we are exploring opens the way for some fundamental theoretical, methodological, and historical explaining, with the tragic theater as its object; and it is by no means a passive object since it triggers the explanations and makes their further development possible. Tragedy thus appears to us in spontaneous dialogue with philosophical knowledge, at a time before an ancient controversy and subsequent specialization contrived to separate them. If we follow the way back, avoiding the many detours and ambiguities, and reverse the misleading signposts, we obtain a surprising new arrangement; a completely different picture emerges, though made up of elements that we thought we knew, a picture that will help us rethink and refashion the main theme running through our comparison of antiquity and Christianity.

4. Tragic Impersonality and Its Philosophical Background

We have seen how the conflict between Minos and Pasiphae erupts at the visible center of the tragedy. Each casts in the other's face the unresolved violence of the mediations on which they depend, or rather the noncredibility of those mediations, obeying a partial logic that both threatens and confirms the overall framework of the myth. Both are condemned to self-fulfillment and self-rejection. When Pasiphae speaks out against her husband's persecution of her, the poignancy of her words should not make us overlook, in turn, the persecutory tenor of their defensive tactic. Both characters clearly recognize violence when it is outside them but refuse to see it within themselves, placing the onus entirely on the other person. The mirrorlike symmetry in their battle of words becomes substantial in their persons, although accompanied by differing degrees of knowledge. Euripides does not confuse the positions of Pasiphae and Minos, but recognizes them as reciprocally dependent, belonging to the same universe of words and deeds, a universe that finally closes on them like a trap. The different levels of truth—the subjective plane of the individual characters in the tragic *fabula* and the objective plane of the play as a whole—are deployed according to a sophisticated strategy that is far from excluding moral distinctions, attempting to fit them within a larger system.

So we now have the textual and interpretive principle that we need to understand the art of the tragedians, and especially of Euripides since his was the most audacious. According to this principle, which it seems right to call *tragic impersonality*, the author as a basic function of the text is not identifiable with any of the characters, and no one character holds in itself the entire truth of the *fabula*: the representation's cognitive and performative action transcends its single parts, and even the author's frequent sympathetic or ideological statements are constantly concealed by the intrinsic logic of the representation. However, this constitutive law of the Greek drama is never organized once and for all, never reassuringly reliable to any extent. And even if I speak of an overall action transcending the single parts, it must be said that impersonality in Greek drama is a horizontal, distributive transcendence, a systemic law that dominates the story, though it never resolves into internal homeostasis, so that surrounding the law there is always an obscurely menacing environment, *another* unknown, destructive transcendence that ends by blindly prevailing. In logical-cognitive terms, typically modern but with recognizable precedents in the ancient sacral and ontological sphere, we could say that tragic impersonality is a transcendentality that never takes effect fully and has repercussions on the parties that it should subsume, bringing them out into the open and at the same time endangering them, even to the point of destruction.

This impersonality is the organizing, distributive force that enables Greek drama to *impersonate* its characters, in the twofold ambiguous sense of putting a mask (in Latin *persona*) on them and giving them credibility as centers of decision, action, and ultimately passion. The tragic stage is the place where the impersonality of fate, of the divine, of the *kosmos* is transformed into characters, and where these fragile creations, which so fascinate and enthrall us since they are made of the same stuff as ourselves, are brought to their ruin, causing the personality and the person of each to revert to the forces of impersonation and personification that now depersonify and depersonalize them, making them regress to the prepersonal reality at their origin that inexorably swallows them up. Tragic impersonality therefore shows itself to be much more than just a principle of theater. It is a cosmic, sacral, and ontological principle to which, however, there is no answer or remedy because, in the final analysis, it corresponds to the obscure background from which arises, and ultimately sinks back, every possible mediation and objectual dimension, and every subjectivity desperately clinging to the one or the other.

It is possible to make out a moment of emergence and condensation to which tragic impersonality can be traced back in what we might call philosophical impersonality: a moment when factors that later developments were to differentiate until they opposed one another still come together and vitally combine. The law of tragic impersonality is to be found indirectly expressed right at the very beginning of Greek philosophy, if the most extensive fragment of Anaximander is read in this light. In this enigmatic text all beings (ὄντα) draw their birth from the place to which their ruin is heading "according to Necessity [*kata to chreon*]; in fact, they do justice [*diken*] to one another, and take revenge [*tisin*] for their injustice [*adikias*], according to Time's order [*kata ten tou chronou taxin*]."[59] The last word of the fragment, τάξιν, conveys the idea of an imperative provision and translates as order or system, but is also an order, a command. The text is describing a distributive, revolving law according to which all the *onta* are arranged around a center of origin and destination, meaning generation and death. The conclusion seems bitter, though we must not forget that doing reciprocal "justice" means the restoration of an effective "order" allowing the beings, the *onta*, to exist. Thus, it is also a law of life, not only of death.

Anaximander is actively elaborating, in a cosmic-ontological way, the same themes the tragic reflection was going to develop some decades later. The closest preamble to his philosophy comes from a source very close to tragedy, the Orphic wisdom, evoked by the notion of an originary ἀδικία counterbalanced by the penalty of *Dike*. Anaximander's *adikia* becomes more recognizable if we admit a connection with the Titanic guilt, that is, the Orphic myth of the child Dionysus devoured by the Titans and his murderers then punished by Zeus.[60] Both *Dike* and *Chronos* (overlapped with the god *Kronos*) are Orphic divinities, and their presence in the fragment, together with the retributive vision of the destiny of the *onta*, cannot be a sheer coincidence. The Titanic *mythos* and ritual is transformed by Anaximander into a law of the *kosmos* explaining the life and death of every single being in a universal and impersonal way, as coming from and going back to the Divine (*to theion*), the *apeiron*, the Boundless, that is "ungenerated and imperishable" (*ageneton kai aphtharton*), and "free from death and destruction" (*athanaton . . . kai anolethron*).[61] This religious-sapiential reading, thoroughly developed, actually makes sense of the mysterious and apparently sinister atmosphere of the main fragment, to be connected to the self-confident environment of the *polis* of the sixth century.[62] Anaximander's dramatic description of the birth and ruin of all the *onta* finds its saving solution, rational and mystical at the same time. It is a wonderful and unexplored scenario, nevertheless objectually unaccomplished, for it does not actually explain the real dramas and perplexities of human existence, a question destined to find in Athens unforeseeable answers that will ultimately prove to be a lack of answer.

Tragic knowledge takes up Anaximander's idea, still imbued with a strong sense of an all-encompassing totality, and breaks down its organic form and structure, causing its stratified components to emerge in the dramatic events of tragedy. These components start becoming visible in the crisis that urges them on until it tears them apart in the second half of the fifth century, reaching its climax in the Peloponnesian War and its aftermath, to a certain extent anticipating the disappearance of mediations that characterizes the modern outlook. We can now understand better the part played in the *Cretans* by the community, and by the sacrificial mediations that it needs; the Orphic initiation, formerly an initiatory model of the workings of the *kosmos* and the *polis*, is degraded to a clique of ineffectual performers of the most appalling sacrifice, the sacrifice that originated tragic impersonality itself, the distribution of theatrical parts that turns out to be the sharing out of body parts, dismembered and devoured. In tragedy the coordinates, which in Anaximander lay in a pervasive and distributive transcendence at a cosmic and impersonally theological level, do not manage to reorganize themselves nor to find a different configuration.

The peculiar difficulty facing the art of tragedy is the impossibility of distributing these theatrical and sacrificial parts to produce a new order, a new transcendence in the *polis*, such as Aeschylus had attempted in the *Oresteia* trilogy, performed in 458 BC.[63] In this way the tragedian is caught up in the coordinates that his knowledge was initially supposed to unravel: like Sophocles, he manifests his desire to attain an order that is both a divine command and a social and moral order, and his despair of ever achieving it; and then, like Euripides, he comes to thematize this failure and, in an incredible variety of experiments, orchestrates all possible attempts at a solution but in the end sadly realizes that he lacks the power to find one.

A clear expression of the paradoxical structure of Greek tragedy is to be found in the vibrant, challenging environment of the sophistic intellectual world, later charged by Plato with corrupting Greek culture with its idea of *logos* detached from the axiologically oriented mediations of the *kosmos*. Gorgias, the brilliant sophist from Sicily whose teaching was a great success in Athens, states that tragedy's "marvelous show for the eyes and ears [*thaumaston akroama kai theama*], with its stories and passions [*tois mythois kai tois pathesin*]," is all "a deception in which the deceiver is more right [*dikaioteros*] than the nondeceiver, and the deceived is wiser [*sophoteros*] than the nondeceived."[64] In this extremely elegant enigma Gorgias plays on the gnosiological and ethical nuances of *dikaios*, crossing them over and turning them around. More than anything else, the enigma describes the position of the tragedian. Through his wonderful theatrical fiction, he demonstrates more truthful and therefore more ethical justice compared to anyone who knows nothing of the secrets of that fiction; and those who are deceived and believe in his fiction show greater wisdom than the undeceived. At the same time, the enigma corresponds to the situations found in tragedy, where the deceiver appears ethically right, and so appears to be right in the sense of conforming to the ways of the world, and the deceived shows superiority in *sophia*, the knowledge enabling us to live thanks to deceptions shared by the majority of people, while the knowledge of the deceiver who deceives in the theatrical way, because he is not deceived, remains powerless. We may therefore conclude that Gorgias sees a principle of reversal at work in tragedy whereby what is false (= wrong) appears to be true (= right) and what is true ultimately appears false, making the author both the director and the victim of what is seen on stage. The writer of tragedy cannot transcend the representational game because, after dominating it at first, he is dominated by it and thus part of a tragic circularity that, for Gorgias, is the very substance of human existence, a view close to the pessimism of Euripides in his maturity.

This perniciously skeptical, bitter philosophy prompted a reaction from Plato. In his view, it had helped to throw Hellenic civilization into a state of objectual confusion responsible for the fifth-century crisis and the death sentence passed on Socrates, that is, on the philosopher who had indicated the only way out of the crisis: the cognitive and moral conversion of the individual soul toward a superior reality. In Plato's response sophistry is blamed together with tragedy, and his forceful disassociation from the two provides the occasion for a keenly perceptive description of the position of the poet. The passage occurs in the *Laws*, and though the assumptions and implications remain much underrated, it contains the most advanced thinking to come from philosophy in the middle of the fourth century concerning the tragic knowledge of the previous century. Here, the Athenian who speaks for Plato in the *Laws* imagines that he is addressing the lawgiver for a new model of *politeia* being worked out in this dialogue and explains why very strict limits (but not a total ban) should be set on poetry:

> There is an ancient myth [*palaios mythos*], O Lawmaker [*nomotheta*], often told by us and approved by others, according to which the poet, when he sits on the Muse's tripod, is no longer in himself [*emphron*] but like a fountain at once lets forth what flows into him and, since his art consists in imitation [*mimeseos*], by putting characters [*anthropous*] on stage that contradict each other, he must necessarily say things that often conflict with what he thinks, and cannot tell whether this or that is true among the things said.[65]

Although Plato is speaking about poets in general, the reference to the performative representation of conflicting characters—literally of men (ἀνθρώπους)—tells us that he is thinking of tragic poets in particular, whom the Greeks felt to be the continuators of Homeric poetry. These, then, are the main target for his criticism and censure, toning down what had already been said in the *Republic*. The παλαιός μῦθος corresponds to ancient traditions regarding the divine origin of poetry; these traditions were centered on Athens, suggesting an allusion to Orphism that had written down both its own sacred discourses (*hieroi logoi*) and the Homeric epics in Athens. It is not Plato's intention to reject the poetic *mythos* wholesale but to subordinate it to the cognitive mediation of his philosophy. What poetry lacks is the rational, veritative criterion governing all Plato's thinking. The poet gives himself up to conflicting representations that take over his mind (*phren*) and prevent him from mastering the *logos* that ought to become *logismos*, that is, the rational capacity for argument. His inability to exercise control condemns him to wavering between extremes of indecision, an oscillation essentially dis-educative and corruptive that is transmitted to the public. This has to be opposed by the lawgiver's criterion of consistency and organic unity, and it is fascinating to see how Plato feels the need to use the example of burial to illustrate this difference between poetry and lawmaking: between the two extremes of a flamboyant mausoleum and a mean grave there is a happy "medium" (*metrion*), the choice of a dignified unostentatious tomb.[66]

Now in his old age, Plato is probably thinking of his own burial as well, and his curious choice of a funereal example may have been prompted by association with Orphism, as well as with the woeful aspects of tragedy (with which he evidently felt some affinity), but following on what has already been said about the role of burial in establishing human thinking, we should not let the mediatory significance of this passage escape us. The tomb in fact symbolizes the intransitive acceptance of death becoming an intermedial means of transformation, the metasymbolic and metalinguistic place that turns this irremediable step into a source of commemoration and life (or, in more Platonic terms, of recollection); in a word, this is sacrifice becoming the rule for *imaginalis* and life-giving exchange through death and beyond it. What is new about Plato, as with Socrates before him, is that the collective, religious tradition is not sufficient; there is need for an inner reason for what is the "medium," and philosophy provides it, as the Athenian imagines telling his lawgiver: "But you should not argue as you just did in talking about a medium [*metrion*], you should discuss what this medium is and to what precise extent: otherwise don't think the discourse [*logon*] can ever become law" (*Laws* 719e). Plato's rejection of the tragic impersonality, and the sophistic knowledge that recklessly accorded with it, hinges on the mediation of the *logismos*, the ontological-rational basis of *logos* traced back to its suprasensible origin thanks to sacrifice in its performative and ritual aspects (716d). His project is to join together the awareness of the human being aroused in the Socratic revolution and the pre-Socratics' powerful sense of a cosmic-divine mediation coming from the totality of Being. Plato's motives reveal what has changed in respect to the previous century and provide our best guide for a close examination of this structuring and destructuring principle of tragedy, along with what has emerged from modern research.

The poet is not to be condemned because his art is imitative, since Plato considers μίμησις to be a law derived ontologically from reality as a whole. According to this law, sensible reality derives from the ontologically supreme principles of the Ideas, answering to a criterion of descendent isomorphism to which the ascendant isomorphism of the real *logos*, the philosophical *logismos*, must correspond. The problem with poetry, as with the *logos* of the sophists, is that *mimesis* breaks away from its axiologically subordinate position and becomes an uncontrollable force, a permanent objectual crisis that destructures the congruity between men and Ideas that forms the basis of the Platonic community, the *politeia*. Not to be discounted as an influence on poetic *mimesis* is the Muse, that is, the sacral mediation from which poetic inspiration flows, and Plato takes it very seriously. But the Muse's influence proves to be detached from the rational framework of knowledge, wandering at will and deadly dangerous, and so must be carefully controlled to bring artistic *mimesis* back to its proper mediations, the ontological-spiritual mediations that also enable the relationship with the divine to be interpreted correctly. By the time of Aristotle, living in an age dominated by the universalist mediation of the kingdom of Macedonia, this dramatic vertical tension has disappeared, and in his *Poetics* the art of tragedy can once again enter the domain of philosophical rationality, though no longer vitally rooted in the context of the *polis* that had fostered it. Plato, on the other hand, is still close to fifth-century tragic theater and, like Gorgias, taps into its living source, a performative principle that he nonetheless felt to be a threat. But we need only invert his words of evaluation to retrieve tragedy's power to reproduce, its capacity for plastic and distributive identification, and its destabilizing speculative potential.

Anyway, this journey around the ancient reflection *of* and *on* tragedy starting from the *Cretans* raises another complementary question: How and how much did modern culture take notice of it and interact with it? This introduces a wider frame of problems, bringing us from ancient Greece to our own historical and cognitive position to the point of touching the very raison d'être of the present work, always with the principle of tragic impersonality as our bright red thread.

5. Tragedy and/or Revelation?

Among the modern interpreters who have come closest to the originary force of Greek tragedy, Girard occupies an important place after Nietzsche, who was too seriously infected by it to be objective, and Richard Wagner, whose main interest was its application to staging drama. In the case of Girard, mimesis provides a slippery ground for comparison with ancient Greece, and actually his analyses stop short, blocked by a concept of imitation that is too modern and indeterminate, defining it as a universal force detached from the object and confused with mediation. On this account, Plato is seen as rejecting *mimesis*, which is not the case since he always refers to correct ontological *mimesis* with the Ideas. It is also interesting that Girard ends by expressing a limitative opinion not so very different from Plato's, though for symmetrically opposite reasons, deeming the tragic writer to be carried away by the mimetic content of a sacrificial crisis that he records with insight but has no power to control. Consequently, in *Violence and the Sacred*, when Girard speaks of "tragic inspiration," he underestimates the tragic author's achievement in being able to recognize the mediatory force of sacrifice and interact with it on a representational and cognitive level.[67] For Girard, this "inspiration" is no longer the response to a mediation regarded as inadequate, as it was for Plato, and has become the recognition of concealing forces, without admitting their creative potential; as a result, the Greek tragedian no less than his modern critic is cast into a sort of objectual void, too much like the situation today for the comparison to be completely credible textually and historically.

Girard is aware of the anthropological exploration of the tragedians, especially Euripides, and follows them in the right direction, but he fails to realize the extent to which his own research gains active support from Greek tragedy, where the mediatory function of sacrifice is actually better understood than by himself, and he ends by mistaking the knowledge of violence displayed by the texts for plain and simple complicity with violence.

Of course, the difficulty noted does exist. Tragedy confirms the enigma of Gorgias, the fears of Plato, and Girard's diffidence to a certain extent by adding to the danger of complete or partial misunderstanding of what is intended, thereby casting not a little doubt on what is intended by tragedy as a whole. The tragic text reveals and conceals, accuses and excuses, which leaves open questions as to the scope and significance of the author's function which ought to control it but is really unable to perform a function in some way transcendental, in an ancient and not Kantian sense, including in itself the transcendent dimension of mediation. Tragic impersonality is a system of knowledge and, at the same time, a system misrepresenting knowledge, in which the ambiguities of the chorus and the investigation of the *mythos* embodied in the characters can only take us back in the most problematic fashion to the invisible hub around which everything turns, and which interested Gorgias and Plato: in a word, the author, whose prestigious and elusive role closely resembles the role of Daedalus, stage designer of the *choros*.

In order to understand this situation better, we need to start from the datum closest to the modern world and so easier for us to verify: its distinctive logical organization/disorganization, already pointed out by Plato, in a context where social mediations inspiring tragic poetry were weakening, a decline that has reached a vanishing point in our time. So we may as well start with a clear-cut differentiation in the modern style that will allow us to grasp what has happened in the interval and the extent of the hiatus dividing us from the universe of the Greek tragedians. In his book on Shakespeare Girard distinguishes, on a textual level, between the presence of the victim as a consciously developed element, that is, as *theme*, and as a structuring, founding component of the text itself, that is, as *structure*.[68] For Girard, the stories of Dionysus and Christ provide the two extremes for comparison in this regard, identical stories but with totally different meanings. They show the same persecutory event, in the full light of the Passion, where the innocent victim is completely thematized, and in the distorting perspective of myth, where the victim provides its unperceived genetic structure. This logical distinction enables Girard to reach an absolute content, lacking any intermediate means of approach or comprehension, since such content coincides with revelation tout court. The distinction between victim as theme and victim as structure is therefore absolute; if we blur or gradate it even slightly, we fall into complicity with violence, the tragic definition of human culture. The representational and moral clarity gained in this way introduces a criterion for interpretation that simplifies and orientates but at the cost of blurring the whole outline, leaving everything not covered by its unqualified formula vague and indistinct.

Girard's distinction makes us think about the problem more consciously but is unable to settle the matter once and for all. The development of my inquiry, stimulated by the chiaroscuro of his ideas against the background of Nietzsche's contrasting chiaroscuro, deals with Girard's terms of comparison on two distinct but connected levels. On the first level, by checking historical documentation we can establish whether the contrast was so radical, and we already possess enough evidence to maintain, as we are now seeing in ancient Greece, that every culture reaches a certain perception of the victims as required by its mediations, though admittedly the criteria and degree of insight vary greatly and envisage some form of involvement and dependence. However, this apparently confusing multiplicity ends by posing the question in its true entity and takes us to another order of reflection that, for one thing, has to assimilate the historical acquisition that perception and knowledge of the victim as the tragic price paid for human cultures actually exists, with the Judeo-Christian or, more simply, biblical tradition being particularly favored in this respect, in spite of fluctuations and inconsistencies making it necessary to distinguish between the pure principle and the various ways in which it has been understood, or more often misunderstood. There is no singular privilege in that, no exemption from a universal rule of violence and persecution. It is possible to demonstrate that it was Greek tragedy that influenced the Jewish perception of sorrow and misfortune, as held by Simone Weil, though such influence has become so penetrating thanks to the prophetic pathos that paved its way and remains the primary inspiration of biblical thinking.[69]

This means that the Judeo-Christian tradition makes no claim to exclusive rights to this knowledge, as if it were a given attribute or possession; on the contrary, the knowledge found here in a varying, conditioned form is also present in other traditions and cultures, but in the Bible tradition it ends by appearing as a qualifying element of divine mediation. I shall refer then to the Judeo-Christian tradition or, more specifically, to the "revelation of Christ" (or the Christic or Christian revelation according to the emphasis required) to indicate the presence of that knowledge in a historical and phenomenal sense. This is not meant by way of an apologia, since any such intention would conflict with my phenomenological, genetic approach and be hardly consistent with the phenomena we are speaking about. To speak of "Christ's revelation" with the meaning given here has no religious or confessional value since the historical Christ never thought of this kind of interpretation, conceived in modern terms of genesis and genealogy, and similarly much of the Christian tradition has never thought in this way. On the one hand, the expression is a symbol and *mythos* or rather a story bringing certain truths into history according to the criteria accessible to religious mediations at the time when it took shape and in subsequent periods; on the other hand, it transmits a potentially universal principle of objectual recognition, to be noted as an emerging phenomenon and criterion for interpreting history.

These remarks reflect the three successive stages in the development of my own research: the contrast *between* Dionysus and Christ was the theme of the first stage, seeking to comprehend the significance and import of their opposition; the second consisted in understanding the transition *from* Dionysus *to* Christ and the necessity of bringing Christ's revelation to interact with the previous economy of sacrifice to rescue it through a mediation able to assimilate sacrifice and apply its logic from within; the third stage, the subject of the present study, aims to illustrate how these two principles, these two historical and religious symbols, coexist and interact. For this reason the book is simply devoted to the sacrificial mediations that have had reference to Dionysus *and* Christ, symbolic and religious, opposing and mutually connected, which is not to say that they are equal in status but comparable, with a reciprocal relationship, a reciprocal involvement whose result has been the possibility to recognize who bears the cost of human mediations, who sinks to the darkness of objectual destruction in order to make the others see the light of objectuality and life. We may reach in this way the truth of the victim, interpreted not in the sense of a category or theory, not as a symmetrical reversal to which to appeal, but as a human reality that, once discovered, becomes indelible and undeniable, revealing in turn to be a retroacting and unlimited source of mediation. We are before what we may call the noumenal ground (*Grund*) of human knowledge and history, and yet not in the intransitive manner supposed by Girard, but in the full transparency of the human and historical phenomenon. This suggests by itself the errors we have to avoid and the inquiry we have to pursue.

There is no need to make special claims or argue for the victim as a truth to oppose against the appearances of the existing world. The Jewish and Christian apocalyptic tradition favors the language of a revelation overthrowing its wicked enemies, but this is a symbolism answering historical and expository needs we shall encounter in the Intermezzo and second volume, and is not to be taken literally. The victim as a mediatory and veritative function at the root of human cultures does not require claims and polemics, for any intent of retort betrays it and vitiates its mediatory potential, degrading its *res*, its reality, to a thing stripped of any objectual meaning. Once manifested, the victim does not destroy phenomena; on the contrary it confirms and realizes them. We have only to let it speak for itself and act *alongside* all the other themes demanding our attention: it silently asserts itself. The coordinates provided by Girard come close to a solution but go no further than to overturn Nietzsche's contrary position; they remain too spare and schematic with too much of the combative spirit of the apologist to delineate the process fully as it really is. Anyway, in the textual dimension that draws all the attention of the victimary structuralist Girard, it is worth observing that there can exist, and do exist, a thousand intermediate degrees between theme and structure, the intermediate dimension, that is to say intermedial and intermediary, where tragedy acts and is defined. We begin to leave behind us any modern rift between noumenon and phenomenon, between founding and founded, between referent and language, to gain access to the mediatory, intermediate signification, to the Platonic *metrion* for arguing, which allows us to tear to pieces every destructive antithesis, every irreducible, intransitive dilemma.

We may realize the necessity and the extent of such passage, first, looking closer for a moment where to detect the historical origin of tragic impersonality, and then coming back to define a different and more satisfactory approach. When set properly in motion, the terms themselves of Girard's contrast prove the utility of the concept of the double bind, namely for description rather than explanation. As a relational, causal system it is not synonymous with rivalry, as Girard believes, but is capable of becoming creative if successfully transformed into a tool and resource. Bateson pointed this out but failed to recognize the historical and cultural value the human double binds had acquired. Tragedy provides the perfect example of the double-binding and double-bound condition of humanity that, at a certain stage in its cultural development, succeeds in describing sacrifice as well; but this is only thanks to abilities derived from sacrifice itself. Thus all humankind's efforts to free itself from sacrifice only confirm its logic and tighten the knot binding humankind, the knot of its origin, a situation corresponding closely to tragedy's double-binding system, which appears to open up paths to knowledge only to close them off again, to give voice to its characters and then silence them once and for all, and to infuse life into them the better to make them die.

There could be a logical, and not only logical, alternative to the paradox of the double bind, an alternative to the contradictory knot generating the narrative, requiring and at the same time excluding what it narrates. If there were a more comprehensive representational system that solved and explained the problems posed by what is represented, then there would be complete *transcendence* of the lesser set and the creation of a new horizon of knowledge, of a new language to penetrate beyond the "empty fables" of the *mythos* and their insoluble dilemmas. This is the cognitive and moral need expressed by Girard's contraposition, and no doubt the lack of such a language to transcend the doubles of desire and violence is described in the *Hippolytus*.

However, this is not completely the case with the principle of authorial impersonality, since it realizes in the most spectacular manner the contradiction of the double bind between representation and represented: as Gorgias understood, the author now takes his place in a higher cognitive system, sufficient to expose the terms of the paradox though not to explain them. The double bind of the characters is not resolved but taken to its consequences, with the mediations of the chorus affording scant and deceptive consolation. The transitive force of tragedy, its undecidable character, extend horizontally and come to involve the public by way of the *choros*; however, the traces of its history are apparent, providing the link between the impersonality of the ancients and the individualism of modern man, between the double-binding dependence of the former and the latter's need for freedom, doomed to remain a pious hope as long as it is kept in the dark about bonds of which it thinks itself free and independent. The mediatory function of the *choros* is a constant presence hanging over Greek drama, though it becomes increasingly ineffective as the genre evolves, and it is precisely through the *choros* that the historical and social genesis of tragic impersonality is made clear to us, its birth in the community, the real suprapersonal and impersonal source that brings up from within it the individuals that compose it and makes them reenter when their existence ends. We should not overlook the part played by the Cretan community in the labyrinthine wanderings of the main characters. Though hardly sketched in, it is decisive, with the chorus as its ambiguous spokesman, a part not yet developed by Euripides to the extreme degree or the inner depletion reached in the works of his late maturity but recognizable once we sense the pivotal, collective value of sacrifice as an institution.

We get therefore a twofold passage. Our reconstruction demonstrates the necessity for the Middle Ages and modernity to go beyond such a paralyzing and finally defeating state of things as antiquity was incapable by itself of overcoming. Judaism and Christianity, as Girard points out, brought an alternative need onto the scene of history, the need to transcend the tragedies of humanity and solve them definitively thanks to a divine revelation. But the intermediate shades excluded from Girard's formulation are inadvertently made visible by the absolute chiaroscuro on which he insists; the very dryness of that formulation, when considered carefully, suggests a vision that is inclusive and nuanced in a different way. With this in mind, we need to examine the defining extremes of chiaroscuro very thoroughly, starting with the strictly theological terms of the problem since they will help to complete the last step in this lengthy discussion, as recursive and winding as the labyrinth that occasioned it.

The shared transcending, the objectual, incarnate transcendence intended by Christianity, could not have dropped down from above onto totally passive men and women, prisoners of the human condition. The reason why Christianity's message of incarnate transcending had such a massive impact on the ancient world was because it reflected a tendency and a need, recognizable in this world and more widely in human experience as such, hidden away like nuggets of gold in the stony gangue of historical and cultural processes. In respect to the sacrificial mediations of the Greco-Roman civilization, the mediation of Christianity introduced a crucial new element, but it would be a theological error, as well as a historical and philosophical one, to interpret it with a miraculous, uncontextual criterion. The fact is that Christianity, preceded and accompanied by Judaism, made it possible to perceive a new threshold of retroaction in regard to humanity's mediatory conditions, a threshold that could not even have reached formulation had it not responded to an intrinsic feature of human cultures.

When I first came to write on this subject, to approach the logical double-binding structure of tragedy and define the difference from Christianity, I adopted a hierarchical-type view similar to Alfred North Whitehead and Bertrand Russell's theory of logical types and to Alfred Tarski's theory of metalanguage, combined with a transcendental view of knowledge borrowed from Immanuel Kant.[70] But this was intended to be no more than an initial, approximate description, still depending on the modern necessity for logical-conceptual, gnosiological, and methodological clarification in order to gain access to its object. But once the object enters into a preselected method, confirming its relevance, it interacts with that method's distinctions, modifying and extending them correspondingly. In this way, starting from the very premises of a systemic approach, it becomes clear what is historically peculiar to the human cultural systems, capable as they are of bringing to the highest point of intensity processes and interactions already existing at the biological level, up to the threshold of self-retroaction that is their most spectacular feature, both specific *and* universal. It is thanks to this paradoxical feature if the human systems have, indeed, managed to involve the whole natural world, a retroacting capacity that reached its peak in the cognitive results obtained by our own species.

The logic of cultural systems is actually far more sophisticated and not restricted merely to organizing different symbolic and logical levels, which is only a prerequisite in human cultures for the capacity to retroact that offers possibilities for *all* the symbolically distinct levels to interact and combine. Circularity or transitivity is the salient, and resilient, element in every culture, contrasting or distinguishing, usually in order to put back into circulation, to seek new forms of communication and exchange, of hybridization and reconfiguration, in a sort of continuing dynamic and reversible distribution of the transcendental factor, going far beyond resilience meant as sheer resistance and success in solving problems. This fundamental aspect was understood by Lévi-Strauss with his idea of exchange as the basic structuring permutation in exogamic organization and cultural differentiation, but as Bataille rightly objects, he made a formal process of it, ignoring the dramatic historical reality that created and shaped it. Girard, pursuing his aim to simplify and explain, reacted to this sophisticated, abstract rationalization, but his response was too rigid and made cultures too strictly dependent on the drama at their origin, not recognizing the autonomy of symbolic forms always directed toward an object nor their cognitive and consciential feedback loop on the processes that generated them . The truth is that circularity, potential at least and never entirely silent, is the fundamental law of human intelligence, as it is of culture which allowed it to organize and develop.

And so we come to the most difficult interaction of all.[71] Indeed, it would prove impossible before crossing the qualitatively distinct threshold of the interaction and retroaction with our own origin, with the factors from which human mediations derive. The transcendental configuration of knowledge, which Kant traced back to the knowing subject and Durkheim to collective categories, proves capable of looking at itself and its own history, setting all its constituent parts in motion again, leaving behind not only Kantian idealism and the barrier erected between phenomenon and noumenon but also Durkheim's social holism and its inability to explain the collective factor. Once the human being has explained himself and opened out, he is in a position to look at nature, on the one hand, and at transcendence on the other, recognizing their circularity and reciprocal involvement in the transparency of the historical phenomenon, devoid now of the destructiveness of the tragic circle and of its impersonality, making and breaking the individual. If hominization can be said to consist in the prehuman animal making an ecstatic departure from itself and becoming capable of objectual and symbolic focalization, precluded in the biological sphere precisely because the prerequisites for it are to be found there but still unrealized, we can now say that another real threshold in the conquest of awareness has been reached: the attainment of self-knowledge as species and genus, the knowledge of one's own history, the acquisition of what I call *historicity*. Like the first, this second threshold consists not in a single sudden definitive breakthrough but in a series of small steps along the path of human progress that are still far from coming to an end; indeed the present study forms an integral part of the series, albeit minimal. This remark is meant to place our reflections about tragedy, and the knowledge that it transmits, within a wider context in which the Judeo-Christian tradition plays a part, not as a counterrevelation but as a surprising, potentially inclusive development, though initially it had to adopt an oppositional stance, indispensable for acquiring a new symbolic and cultural threshold.

We now have the means to pursue our inquiry into that distinctive form of performative thought, of staged philosophy, that is Greek tragedy. It now takes its place in a larger movement that, far from reducing its importance, only increases it, because this is mankind's path to self-knowledge.

The representational universe of tragedy can supply further details about the growing level of consciousness reached by classical Greece regarding its own origin and, indirectly, human origin itself. The wealth and range of its themes makes the loss of the *Cretans* particularly regrettable, but fortunately another tragedy, the *Bacchae*, a veritable *summa* of the mediatory and sacrificial inquiry carried out by Greek culture in the fifth century, has survived almost complete. It is obvious from the text, as we shall see in the following chapters, that Euripides's main objective, beyond Orphism and Eleusis, was Dionysus himself, that is, the mediatory source of tragic art, confirming Plato's fears and potentially defeating their defensive strategy. Here, the tragic double bind reaches its furthest point and concludes a cycle but in so doing it opens up new horizons.

4.

Sacrificial and Erotic Metamorphoses in the *Bacchae*

1. Omophagic Ecstasy

Of one thing we can be certain: if Greek tragic wisdom came to reflect deeply on the violent sacrificial mediations of its own world, then it was not by way of a purely intellectual exercise or an accident of some isolated creative genius. Tragedy was able to reach new representational and cognitive thresholds relating to these matters because it experienced the rapid succession of mediatory and objectual crises that afflicted and shaped Greek civilization in the sixth and fifth centuries BC. Already at the end of the sixth century, development of the *polis* moved swiftly ahead, especially in Athens, where new social classes arose tied to the urban environment and antagonistic to the old aristocratic landowning classes.[1] The early part of the fifth century saw war with Persia in two great waves, which brought Greece to discover itself and the strength of its politico-military organization. This was in spite of internal divisions and rivalries that were also the spur of its creativity (more or less like the Italy of the Middle Ages and the Renaissance) but remained politically unresolved by the twofold victory over the Persian Empire because the ensuing Athenian hegemony did not lead to unification of the multifaceted galaxy of Greek city-states. And in the final decades of the fifth century, war between the opposing blocks of Athens and Sparta was a catastrophe for Greece; all dreams of a Mediterranean hegemony came to an end, and in the *polis*, the beating heart of Greek civilization, an irreversible crisis set in. Plato's attempts to react to the slow decline proved of no avail, and in the second half of the fourth century Macedonia became the new dominant power, marking the start of the Hellenistic period.

Athenian tragedy develops alongside this extraordinary series of crises, which were either brilliantly overcome or, if not overcome, brilliantly reworked artistically and intellectually. Tragedy develops rich and varied ideas about violence and possible remedies for it—I say this not to endorse political interpretations of tragedy that completely ignore the centrality of religious mediations in the ancient world, and are therefore anachronistic, but to illustrate the extremely close relationship of tragedy to the contemporary situation. Certainly, the situation needed to be tackled with the weapons of the Greek *logos*, but it had to be done within the civic organism that was the inspiration, target, and platform for the *logos*. Suffice it to say that the world of tragedy is a world of marvelous acquisitions and illumination, bought at a high price, however, in the thick of fierce fighting with no holds barred. This is especially true of Euripides, the tragedian who pushed furthest with these investigations and concluded in utter disillusionment, during the disastrous Peloponnesian War. This is apparent in his last, presumably uncompleted, work *Iphigenia in Aulis* and in the *Bacchae*, his masterpiece, which he wrote shortly before and which we shall now consider.

The *Bacchae* recounts the most typical story in the Dionysian cycle, how Pentheus, king of Thebes, attempts to oppose the cult of Dionysus, who appears in the city as a Stranger from Asia, and is subsequently cruelly punished. The leitmotiv here and in the analogous tale of Lycurgus is the struggle between Dionysus and a hero connected to him but opposing him and suffering fatal defeat; in other words, a conflict between Dionysus and an anti-Dionysus. We shall meet the same pattern again when we come to consider the origins of tragedy. Not by chance, a work attributed to Thespis, regarded by the Greeks as the father of tragedy, is called *Pentheus*, while the same title is sometimes given to the *Bacchae* in the manuscript tradition.[2] Aeschylus, too, turned to the subject in two lost cycles about Lycurgus and about Dionysus at Thebes, the latter also comprising a *Pentheus*.[3] The theme thus takes us back to the birth of the tragic genre, as we shall see, but it is already clear from the context that the interest toward the Dionysian Theban cycle is stimulated by the particular character of the Athenian environment, culturally vibrant and suffering from continual growing pains, making it a means to represent and interpret what is happening at the time, contemporary events helping to create that environment itself and becoming more pressing and finally dramatic in the last three decades of the fifth century.

This circumstance, which should be seen as supplemental to the basic inspiration for Euripides's whole career and not detracting from it, is part of the reason why his Dionysian play is deeply innovative, making use of the emblematic, warning *mythos* of the Theban anti-Dionysus defeated by the god. The originality lies not so much in the material, actually derived from careful study of the tradition and the works of his predecessors, as in the radical, organic nature of its treatment. The solemn, archaizing style of the text only serves to underline its critical stance toward the mythical and religious archetypes under scrutiny,[4] as a revised version of a remote, obscure tale aiming to make people think about an imminent future story involving not just Athens but all Hellas. It is a distant view, corresponding to the late date of composition of the *Bacchae*, burdened with historical and personal disappointments if we think of the scant success Euripides enjoyed in Athens during his lifetime,[5] and easier to understand when we remember the real and symbolic distance from Athens to the court of the Macedonian king Archelaus, where it was written and in all likelihood staged.[6] Euripides was there by invitation, and the Dionysian motif clearly refers to Macedonia. Probably there is also a symbolic allusion to the new historical energy that Euripides sensed in semibarbaric Macedonia, fresh and vigorous in contrast to the ruin of civilized Greece, its human and moral resources shamefully squandered in the conflict between Athens and Sparta.[7] There is an undoubted air of prophesy in this allusive work of a clever courtier, not conflicting in any way with an entirely text-based reading as the defeat facing Athens since it is precisely the relentless advance of Thracian and Asian Dionysus that evidences the collapse of the proudest *polis* of all and the fatal failure of any appropriate transcendental and objectual mediation to save it. Divine mediation as experienced in Greece and Athens is a total failure, and if it postpones mediations to the future, it is because a new historical cycle can make a fresh start compared to the fifth-century *polis*. The originality of Euripides's approach to Dionysus and his skill at representation on several levels are also indirectly confirmed by the sensation created when the work was given a posthumous, prize-winning performance in Athens, with the audience evidently recognizing the drama of their city in the drama on stage, and by the fact that it was widely performed down to the Christian era, gradually consigning rival works to oblivion.

For these reasons the *Bacchae* is the best place to verify the ongoing sapiential inquiry that I attribute to its author. Viewed in this perspective, the tragedy appears as a milestone, a boundary stone, and a gravestone marking the close of a historical cycle, the failure of an era, and it sets itself in a destabilizing relationship with its own genre. If tragedy represents the double binds of culture and its mediations, the *Bacchae* is an attempt to get beyond them. This effort, unsurpassed in antiquity, produced new cognitive double binds that we must endeavor to follow if our interpretation is not to fall short of its original aim. The history of the challenge to Dionysus is also in part the history of not very successful efforts to decipher it, which has usually meant making it acceptable by domesticating it. But there is very little to domesticate in this tragedy, if we only have ears to hear. The only way to take up the challenge is to do what Euripides must have done: to submit to the awful fascination of Dionysianism, and tell it as it is.

We will start by examining a passage from the parodos, unequaled in the ancient world for the number of mythical-ritual references to Dionysus.[8] For convenience, I have split it in two. By now we are familiar with the subject and the atmosphere of the first section, but it seems much more agitated than anything we have seen so far:[9]

> O secret dwelling of the Curetes
> divine caves of Crete
> that witnessed the birth of Zeus,
> there, in the caves the Corybantes with their triple-crested helms
> [*trikorythes*]
> found for me
> this circle of tightly stretched skin [*byrsotonon kykloma*]
> and mingled its sound

> with the feverish Bacchanal and the sweet breathings of Phrygian
> flutes [*aulon*];
> then they placed it in the hands of mother Rhea
> to accompany the bacchantes' cries with its obsessive rhythm;
> from the Great Mother it passed then
> to the Satyrs seized by delirium [*mainomenoi*],
> entered the giddy dances [*choreumata*]
> of the trieteric feasts [*trieteridon*]
> that throw Dionysus into ecstasy [*chairei*].

This sequence concludes the central hymn of the parodos and repeats the myth as we have it from Strabo. The explanation regarding the musical instruments used by collective divinities is, in fact, to be found soon after the passage quoted in the first chapter.[10] Here once again is the Idaean labyrinth-cave, Cretan Zeus, Rhea (the Great Mother), and Dionysus with the now-familiar, noisy retinue of male characters, augmented by the bacchantes. Thus we have the following sequence, divided in pairings formed by a divinity and its collective paredri: Curetes—Zeus | Corybantes—Rhea (—bacchantes) | Satyrs—Dionysus. The perfect symmetry of the male divine mediators (collective and individual) in the first and last pairings seems to be altered by the presence of Rhea, accompanied by her male helpers but with the female group of bacchantes following in her wake. We shall consider how this complicates the scheme later.

Meanwhile, it should be noted that we have here a complete mythical history of the drum, the orgiastic instrument par excellence, used to induce ecstasy in the paroxysm of the rites. The Corybantes-Curetes are characterized by their triple-crested helms (τρικόρυθες), derived from ancient rituals, and noted here with ethnological accuracy.[11] The ternary symbolism is reinforced by the trieteric feasts in l. 133, held in alternate years at Delphi in honor of Dionysus. The Corybantes invented the drum, complementing its deafening sound with the hypnotically beguiling notes of the Phrygian flute,[12] recalling the flutes that used to accompany animals on their way to sacrifice. Together the instruments create an obsessive, penetrating, overpowering musical background to the bacchantes' rhythmic shouting and singing. In the explosive uproar of orgiastic music, all the community's taboos fall away one by one, drawing nearer and nearer to the confusion of a violent crisis, and no less perilous for being reproduced by the rite since to perform the savage ritual at once poses the distressing question of its success, of its power to restore a threatened world temporarily destroyed. The impression given by the text, and underlined by music to match in stage performances, is not, however, of any likely and expected ritual compensation. The Dionysian ecstasy is relived to its very climax, with no real guarantee of returning to the previous state of things.

With heads rolling, hair flying wildly, foaming mouths, and eyes upturned in god-possession,[13] the maenads abandon themselves in the wild circling dance of the *choreumata* (l. 132),[14] the swirling trance in which sacrifice finally becomes possible. The second section concerns the sacrifice. Here we no longer have the indeterminate atmosphere of myth, nor the complex narrative and metamythological strategy of the *Cretans*. Euripides's art now deals with the ritual aspect of the story directly. In the *Cretans* and the *Hippolytus* it was filtered through character and events to a greater degree. In the parodos of the *Cretans*, for example, the cult elements, although extremely dense, were evoked by the chorus in a descriptive, almost ethnographic tone. In the corresponding part of the *Bacchae*, the ritual content becomes incandescent, interrupting the objectual illusion of the characters' self-justifications, for an instant at least. We realize that Euripides, in this work of his late maturity, is going for broke. It is not a simple description, but a synthesis of what the Dionysian rite actually was in its essence,[15] with a typically Greek procedure of hierarchical exchange between concept and experience where the first dominates and the last word is left to the comprehension of the spectators.

Helped along by the ritual instruments, the orgy rises to its dark climax:

He is sweet [*edys*] on the mountains, when among the frenzied
ranks [*thiason*]
he falls to the ground
in a faint under the skin of the sacred
fawn, craving
the blood of the slaughtered goat, the ecstasy of flesh devoured alive
[*omophagon charin*],
flinging himself over the mountains of Phrygia and Lydia,
he, our Guide, the Roarer [*Bromios*]—euoi!
Milk flows over the ground, wine flows and the nectar of bees.[16]

Without exaggeration, this is the first time in classical literature that nothing is held back in describing the culminating phase of a ritual crisis. This is achieved thanks to the covering symbolism of theatrical representation and the pressure applied by a great tragic writer capable of pushing to the limits of what can be represented, to the threshold where all representation ends because that is its point of departure. There never will be a comparable boldness and clarity in the biblical texts either, absorbed as they are by the necessity to censure similarly bloody sacrificial rites that were well known in the eastern Mediterranean and to find an alternative theological mediation.

Dionysus becomes supremely sweet when the desire for blood becomes devouring, total. This is Dionysus "supremely terrible [*deinotatos*] and sweet [*epiotatos*] for men,"[17] where we should not forget the sacral ambivalence of δεινός, the *tremendum* that is *fascinans*,[18] the prodigious that contains the marvelous and horrific, just as the pulsations of the beating heart consist of systole and diastole, pulsations, however, coming strangely closer, with singular, lethal literalness. What does Dionysus's fearful sweetness consist of? The answer is not an explanation, but an action. Beneath the skin of his most innocent and helpless animal manifestation, the god falls to the ground in the hypnotic trance of ritual possession, thirsting for fresh blood and craving living flesh. But it is he who falls victim and is about to be torn to pieces.[19] This is the ὠμοφάγος χάρις, the ecstasy of devouring the still-living flesh of the victim, the indescribable moment when maximum violence and maximum freedom coincide. Sweeter than milk or honey, and more intoxicating than wine, the blood spills over the ground and covers everything. All the liquid metaphors of Dionysianism reassume their real nature here. This is the epiphany of Dionysus *Anthroporrhaistes*, the mansmasher,[20] of Dionysus *Omadios* or *Omestes*, the devourer of living flesh, who coincides with Dionysus *Bakchos*, the god of orgies, and Dionysus *Lysios*, the Releaser and Liberator.[21]

These references to the most savage Dionysian cults were not just literary images or erudite citations, as we can well appreciate from the celebrated episode in Plutarch describing the sacrificing of three young Persian noblemen to Dionysus *Omestes* just before the battle of Salamis.[22] Themistocles ordered them to be sacrificed at the suggestion of his soothsayer and under considerable pressure from most of his forces. Admittedly the version given by Plutarch is controversial, since it contradicts the most reliable accounts of the battle on several points (he, or rather his source, maintains that the three prisoners were taken in an attack on the island of Sphacteria, an attack that actually took place at the end of the sea battle), and so the story may be mere propaganda against Themistocles. However, considering the vividly realistic detail and the likelihood the Greeks would retaliate for a similar act committed by Persians on a Hellenic prisoner sacrificed because of his beauty,[23] it could be based in fact but made more dramatic by turning the three Persian prisoners into noblemen captured in battle, a typical case of rhetorical *amplificatio*.[24] For us, the most interesting aspect of the story is the fact that it was in any case considered plausible as a historical or propagandistic account. In the ancient world, human sacrifice before, during, and after battles was a routine wartime measure, essentially because warfare itself was interpreted as an immense human sacrifice, with victory going to whoever performed it with most bravery and ingenuity, and in the manner most pleasing to the gods. This savage, religiously mediated violence provides the constant background to Greek and classical history, and Dionysus becomes its representative par excellence though certainly not the only presiding divinity.

The human sacrifice to Dionysus *Omestes* described by Plutarch is evidence—at least insofar as it was perceived in ancient Greece as possible and closely linked to religious meaning of warfare—that Euripides's tragedy is not a literary myth but exists in the dimension of contemporary history, revealing, through myth, the originary nature of the sacral and political mediations desperately needed by Greece. In those years, with the Peloponnesian War drawing slowly to its tragic close, anyone in the audience in Macedonia or especially in Athens who cared to remember the survivals of sacrifice in classical Greece and in bordering areas might make an instructive comparison with the ruthless slaughter still going on, so memorably chronicled by Thucydides. Dionysus in the *Bacchae* embodies the recourse to violence without which no ancient society could have founded and maintained its mediations. You needed to take great care to protect yourself against it precisely when you needed to resort to it, like a dangerous vaccine. The double bind of Dionysus is the originary double bind of all sacral and divine mediations, the paradox of the god who is hunter and hunted, devourer and devoured, slaughterer and slaughtered.[25] This is the Dionysus *emphanes*—manifest—of l. 22, the *daimon* that reveals itself to mortals, the double face of the Orphic Phanes.

Nothing can stop this violent revelation on the Euripidean stage, no more than it can be stopped on the stage of history and politics.

The history and ritual structure of this violent unveiling was anticipated in the parodos; we now come to its climax in the narrative. The ritual core of the *Bacchae* will allow us to understand better the Greek mentality that inspires its formulation without which we could not grasp the real meaning of the way followed by Euripides.

2. The Dis-veiling of Sacrifice

Pentheus, who comes from dragon stock, is the anti-Dionysus and aims to rid the city of the Dionysian frenzy. He imagines himself to be immune to it, unaware that he is really the man of suffering (Πενθεύς = πένθος, torment)[26] in whose fate the power and true nature of the god will be manifested when he himself is fatally infected with the Dionysian fever. He finally suffers the *sparagmos* on Mount Cythaeron, screaming out in vain to the very end as he is torn to pieces by his mother, Agave, and the other Theban bacchantes blinded by the god.[27] What remains of his body, after the gore-stained bacchantes have finished playing a bloody ballgame with it, is scattered far and wide over the wooded slopes. His mother then impales his head on her thyrsus and carries it aloft in triumph. As the chorus repeats in its third stasimon, the third time it interrupts the story with a standing song:

> What is knowledge [*to sophon*]? What gift
> more beautiful from the gods to mortals
> than to grasp in your hands
> the heads [*koryphas*] of the enemy?
> Beauty [*ho ti kalon*] is ever a friend.[28]

This bestial elation must have grated sorely on civilized Athenian ears, and the slightly less refined ears of the Macedonian court eager to hear the latest and best from the capital of Attica. Grasping the enemy's head in your hands would call to mind another not infrequent act when the hands held the enemy's severed head; the lines are even more striking when we consider the transition made from dismissing knowledge as useless to praising beauty, the "gift . . . from the gods" and "a friend" because it comes from the Dionysian bliss of triumphing over the enemy.

The anthropological and ritual conclusion to be drawn from this dense mesh of descriptions, associations, and allusions is perfectly clear. The real Dionysian sacrifice is human, its crowning moment in the most complete and archaic version being the *omophagia* of the still-living human body, a cannibalistic act of identification, becoming one with the god-victim through eating him. Omophagy, anthropophagy, and theophagy were originally simply synonymous.

Representation of the rite is so horrible that Euripides would seem to shrink from the last step of sheer savage cannibalism. But that alone is the original assumption underlying the *sparagmos* in the *Bacchae*, as is clear from the most archaic version of the Titanic myth. Only by eating the god can one become completely *entheos*—deified, possessed by the god.[29] After recounting the myth of Dionysus's dismemberment, Firmicus Maternus tells how the Cretans commemorated Dionysus's death at the hands of the Titans and appeased the divine wrath by going off into the forest, every other year, amid much noise and shouting, to tear a living bull to pieces with their teeth.[30] The bull as an incarnation of the god appears several times in tragedy: Cretan Zeus, the Minotaur, Dionysus *tauros* and *taurophagos*, bull and bull-eater, slaughtered and adored in the metaphorical labyrinth of the forest.

Euripides is understandably reticent over the horrifying details of cannibalism, in order not to violate the decorum of tragedy, but his anthropological deconstruction does not shirk such a crucial aspect, already illustrated in the surviving fragments of the *Cretans*. If we are to decipher the message, we need to get under the skin of the text to identify and penetrate a refined authorial strategy; Euripides scatters verbal clues here and there to create a second level of meaning, invisible yet always present, interacting with the first with differing degrees of revelation, corresponding to the differing degrees of perception in the audience. We can find countless clues scattered throughout the text that disclose the originary nature of the rite, once we possess the means to decode them. Pentheus's role as *symbolon* is underlined in several places by the use of the verb *ballo*, with its compound forms and derivatives.[31] Metaphors from hunting and trapping, with their patent sacrificial connotation, recur throughout. But when Dionysus, in l. 848, tells the chorus that Pentheus is about to fall into his fatal trap, he actually uses the expression *es bolon*, "ensnared," where *bolos* means a hunting net but also refers to the captured prey, the *symbolon* of lynching.[32] Just prior to this, in the fast-moving ambiguous dialogue where the victim starts to fall for the god's trickery we find the verb *balein* in l. 830, meaning to wear a bacchic garment but also to perform the act of killing while wearing one. In l. 837 *symballo* is a covert allusion to the imminent lynching.[33]

When the slaughter begins, Agave wrenches off her son's shoulder; ὦμος in l. 1127, clearly a pun on ὠμός, the raw quivering flesh of ὠμοφαγία.[34] In l. 1184, Pentheus's mother, carrying his head in triumph and still delirious, urges the chorus to join a banquet ("join the banquet [*thoinas*] therefore"), and in l. 1242 she invites her father, Cadmus, to celebrate the victory in identical terms, using an expression that Cadmus repeats with tragic irony in l. 1247. The word, *dais*, is not new to us but its pertinence to sacrifice is revealed here as never before, for *dais* is the division of the pieces of flesh, the *symbola* of the victim that are to be devoured. The chorus's invocation (ll. 1017–19) and Agave's identification of her victim as a lion cub (l. 1174) and calf (l. 1185) are also Euripides's reminders of the primitive theriomorphic version of the story. According to this, Pentheus was turned into a bull and devoured by the maenads transformed into panthers; in the tragedy, they describe themselves as the "swift hounds of the Fury [*Lyssas*]" (l. 977). This completes the bull hallucinations previously suffered by the king, the most terrible of all occurring when he sees two suns and two Thebeses, and brings out the archaic Cretan aspect of his adversary:

> you look like a bull showing me the way,
> with on top [*krati*] two horns [*kerata*] that you have grown.
> Were you already a beast before? Because now you are a bull.

The "top" (*kara*, meaning both "head" and "summit," perhaps with further wordplay on *kratos*, "power" and "victory") is to become Mount Cithaeron where the doubles evoked will close in on him once more, in the shape of bacchantes. This might be hinted at by the word *keras*, which, besides meaning "horn" means "top," and also describes a military deployment: and it is two ranks of Theban and Asian bacchantes who drag Pentheus away, along with Dionysus, to meet his fate on the top of the mountain. Euripides, through the metamorphic, polysemic bull image and a whole galaxy of associated symbols, makes us understand all there is to understand. In the *sparagmos*, originally omophagic in the Cretan feast, the Stranger coming from Asia is fully revealed as Dionysus Zagreus, the hunter of human prey, alluded to in l. 1192 by the most elegant wordplay: "Our sovereign is a hunter, indeed" (*ho gar anax agreus*), with *x-agreus* similarly reproduced both in live performance and in the *scriptio continua* of the classical texts.

The analysis of ritual made by Euripides's tragedy might be thought virtually complete, considering the limits of what could be represented in the theater and culture of the time. However, this is only the starting point for further analyses much broader in scope that the tragedy invites us to make providing we have adequate conceptual tools. The interpretive challenge has hardly begun. In the meantime, there is the question of who performs the rite, below and beyond the mythic *fabula* used in the tragedy. This is the way for us to grasp the connotation latent in the title *Bacchae* and the question posed by it. The question was expressed explicitly in a modern form by Sylvia Plath in lines that form the epigraph to the first volume of my study, but if the authentic meaning is to become clear, we must bear in mind the continuity and discontinuity with their implicit ancient sense. This takes us back to the scheme of collective and individual exchanges concealed in the parodos, and before that to the question of how to interpret Euripides's procedure in creating this dense mesh of information, allusions, and transformations.

The conceptual category appropriate to describe what Euripides does would seem to be demystification, but the term is far too modern and assumes the presence of a mystification to be stripped away in order to expose a more authentic and oppressed reality. Such a pathos for covered over authenticity and oppressed truth is nonexistent in ancient Greece; truth plays a fundamental role but it is as *aletheia*, truth manifested in virtue of itself, not as the result of any demystifying efforts. In Plato, too, whose philosophy has his personal seeking after truth as its hidden mainspring, the quest consists in achieving the right conditions for truth to manifest itself, in supporting and following the ontological structure of reality to arrive at its principle, without any human intervention as such to make it manifest. Consequently, Euripides as well is not to be demystified by some effort to remove the veil or mask hiding the truth; rather, the aim must be to reach a view structured on several levels, where the most hidden and dangerous levels continue to coexist with the more visible levels, closer to the surface. The veils and masks are shaken and even emptied out but not removed, either materially or metaphorically, since there is no independent reality to be brought to the surface, no truth existing entirely apart from its appearances and counter to them. The concealing veil is neither destroyed nor demolished by *aletheia*, which is not to say that things necessarily add up, but that even where they do not, as in the case of Euripides, the addition or subtraction occurs within a whole that is unquestioned since it is the totality of things, of *physis*, of *kosmos*, and remains such whether comprehensible or not. So, keeping to the etymology of the word, we can speak of unveiling, dis-veiling, or even of revelation but we must always bear in mind that the veil remains and returns again, as Martin Heidegger rightly understood, though he extrapolated *aletheia* from its structurally sacral context and imagined it in opposition to *orthotes*, the abstract and formal correctness that in his terms never existed in ancient philosophy.[35]

The dis-veiling triggered by Euripides thus involves the rite and the figures traditionally connected to its performance but remains within these coordinates, no less present for being subverted. This in no way diminishes the sensational nature of what the text shows and implies; it simply restores historical credibility to it and recognition as a brilliant courageous act performed not in the void of a nonexistent Greekness but in the pervasive atmosphere and the reality of its mediations.

We can now begin to answer the question as to the identity of these maenads with their savage bloody rites and the exact nature of their relationship to Dionysus and the other mythical figures encountered so far. This will allow us to take a fresh look at a whole series of historical and interpretive stereotypes that seem to be substantiated by the *fabula* if taken literally, and will help us to understand Euripides's cognitive aims. We shall need, on the one hand, to overcome humanistic culture's embarrassed conspiracy of silence and, on the other, to ignore the morbid sensationalism of so many modern reassessments. The fact that the victim is a man subjected to violence at the hands of a group of women easily takes on sexual connotations that may be present, and often are, in any sacrificial rite and in any lynching; however, the point is to see the significance of this fact and the part played by the sexual object and gender identity, starting from the Greek context and not from ahistorical modernizations. For this, the system of carefully orchestrated symbolic transformations of which the tragic text consists must be analyzed at a more inclusive level.

We will therefore return to the musical instruments in the first part of the passage: the kettledrum (κύκλωμα) is created by the Curetes/Corybantes for the chorus of bacchantes; however, in l. 59, Dionysus, personally inviting the maenads in his train to use drums (*tympana*), ascribes their invention to Rhea and himself. It is not only the Curetes, then, but also the gods personally who put the orgiastic percussion instruments into the maenads' hands. The question naturally comes to mind as to why there is such insistence and emphasis here, preceding and paving the way for the revelation of the omophagy.

In ll. 513–14 Pentheus seems to notice the chorus of the bacchantes for the first time, when he says he will stop it "from playing these dark obsessive drums [*byrses*],"[36] an incidental reminder of the loss of the music accompanying the tragedy, which strikingly underscored the ritual content. Pentheus vainly attempts to halt the Dionysian orgy by imprisoning Dionysus and the bacchantes. The challenge to the god is coming to a climax. Dionysus has just foretold Pentheus's imminent downfall, referring to his *nomen-omen* (*Pentheus* = *penthos*), just as Tiresias had done earlier.[37] The obsessive, shamanistic drumming of the bacchantes sounds a constant counterpoint and ominously underlines the impending disaster. The sacrificial circle is about to close around the young Theban king, the circle first adumbrated in the word *kykloma*, a kettledrum, and now clearly denoted by the maenads' *kyklos*, encircling the fir tree that Pentheus has scrambled up and cannot escape from.[38]

Thus the Corybantes' drum anticipates the basic spatial arrangement of the play, a ritual circle wheeling around the victim and spiraling in on him; the same pattern is found with the Curetes, the Titans, and the labyrinthine dance called *choros*. If we consider the semantic associations for a moment, we note further interesting shades of meaning related to musical instruments: *tympanon* also means a wheel of torture; in Homer, *aulos*, a flute, may indicate a part of the helmet or a spurt of blood; *byrsa*, a drum, can mean both the tanned hide of the dead animal and its living skin. The corybantic kettledrum is also concrete proof of the transition from the Curetes to the bacchantes: the drum with its tightly stretched skin is, as we have seen, none other than the Curetes' archaic hide shield transformed. Change the sex of the Curetes and acknowledge the sacrificial aim at the origin of their protective initiatory rite, and we have the maenads dancing around Pentheus in the frenzied circular movement of the *choros* or *choreuma*. One image helps to interpret the other.

This again poses the problem, encountered more than once already, of how we are to understand the role of identity and the sexual object in this tragedy. Often it is approached by adopting the stereotype of male/female opposition,[39] but Greek tragedy happens to be more subtle and profound in this area than modern, or if you prefer postmodern, commonplaces.

3. The Erotic Destabilizing of the Object

Euripides's Dionysian drama taken as a whole shows itself as a lethal system of transformations, disguises, and misrepresentations that make sense in dramatic and cognitive terms. There is systemic and systematic destabilizing of roles and genders, with the reversing of the sexes as the most obvious example of these allusive theatrical reversals. Persuaded by Dionysus to follow him onto Cithaeron, Pentheus allows himself to be dressed in the ritual clothes worn by the Dionysian female followers of Bacchus, correctly explained as being a feature of many initiation ceremonies transferred to the stage. In those rites of admission to the group, male youths were required to undergo a female metamorphosis, experiencing for the last time the humiliation of their exclusion from the coveted male role, excluded not as women but as inferior, homosexual males. Frequently the ceremonies had homosexual implications with the initiate passively sodomized, as occurred in Athens in the institution of ephebeia and in some mystery cults. Ephebeia was obviously important for education and identity, the ephebe learning from his lover how to become an adult, but in the case of initiation the initiate experienced in dramatic form what it was to be a "non man" and took it upon himself to attain the goal of full male status once and for all.[40]

In Euripides's tragedy, however, the opposite process is at play: the youthful, energetic king of Thebes definitively demeans his own masculinity, a foretoken of the appalling fate soon to befall him. The sexual aspects are simply signs that tell us his downward slide into catastrophe has begun and have none of the pseudo-psychological significance so promptly discerned by today's pansexualism. A further reversal takes place within this firmly rooted modern misunderstanding and closes symmetrically on an unexpected analogy relating to Pentheus. In Euripides's tragedy the failing of the sexual object indicates that the objectual conditions that make it possible to talk in terms of character psychology are being lost; while the failing of the objectual conditions of the human world today causes us to recognize everywhere symptoms and signs of sexual behavior that is losing or has lost its humanizing significance. The provisional conclusion, which we shall need to come back to, is that the public today finds itself in a similar situation to Pentheus after his blinding, in a historical no less than hermeneutic darkness.

Several hints of a homoerotic nature come to the surface as the play unfolds, preluding the grotesque disguise that is to seal Pentheus's fate. Particularly significant is the passage in the second episode describing the Stranger dragged in chains by the guards. Pentheus finds his appearance strangely attractive:

> you are not at all ugly [*ouk amorphos*] in looks [*to . . . soma*], stranger,
> to women—of course—and that's why you're in Thebes;
> and you have curly tresses [*plokamos*], not a bit like a wrestler,
> descending your cheeks and charged with desire [*pothou pleos*]
> and your skin is purposely white,
> not the result of the sun's rays, but of shade,
> to captivate [*theromenos*] Aphrodite with comeliness.

The piece begins with a double negative in the litotes οὐκ ἄμορφος—literally, not without the form, *morphe*, which yields beauty—a double negative intended to soften the eulogy that obviously ends as an affirmation, all the stronger for this reference to formlessness, to the destruction of form that the action is rapidly coming to. Pentheus finally contradicts the attenuating nuance by specifying, unnecessarily, that the compliment holds good only for women, and so implicitly admits to having a feminine viewpoint himself. A reversal in desire and perception appears in these words, the more serious for being expressed by the young warrior king who represents primarily the men of the city. What follows is undermined by the pervasive demon of reversal, of the negative that becomes an affirmative. Pentheus intends his description to be ironic when he remarks that Dionysus's long hair looks very different from the shaven heads of athletes and soldiers exercising in the gym, but he only manages to note the loveliness of the kiss curls, perfect for arousing desire in adult males, which is what happened in the Athenian ephebeia where an adolescent awaiting full entry into civic manhood as athlete and soldier was taken as his lover by a mature man. In contrast to their suntanned menfolk, women in antiquity, leading lives mostly confined to the four walls of the home, the *oikos*, typically had a pale complexion, and that completes the feminization of Dionysus. The climax comes with the "Aphrodite" of l. 459, where Pentheus repeats a charge already made that the Stranger is trying to get into "Aphrodite's graces" (l. 236), but in doing so adopts the dangerous perspective of someone who has suddenly become the recipient of those attentions. As in the *Cretans*, the *nomen divinum* indicates erotic pleasure and the divine power that can capture it, while the emphasis on hunting is sufficient in itself to connote the sex of the person performing the action, and in this case of the person describing it, the king and commander who opposes the Stranger's wanton behavior, incapable of the self-control that ought to characterize a respectable, adult male citizen of the *polis*. The superimposition of the figure of Pentheus on the preceding figure of Hippolytus, marked by a disastrously hypervirile one-sidedness, starts a register of hunting-hunted reversibility found here and there throughout the tragedy.

Everything could be said to confirm the reassuring inequality in the roles of the soft ephebic Stranger and the energetic, masculine monarch of Thebes, but the disparity is only resolved in the riskiest kind of intimacy that demolishes the appearance and destroys the illusory substance of the dominant party simply by giving voice to his male desire. And here another reversal comes into play, this time more ontological than verbal. The fact is that Pentheus's youth contrasts with the showy confidence of his language, and the contrast is the more embarrassing when we remember that there is a god behind the Stranger, compared to whom, Heraclitus tells us, a man is "like a child before an adult."[41] The asymmetry that seemed at first to favor Pentheus is about to settle to the final advantage of his adversary, beginning with the physical description that was supposed to prove his inferiority. The Stranger's ephebic appearance is actually in full agreement with traditions about Dionysus and warrants his divine nature, whereas the real physical and psychological condition of the young king tacitly denies him the role he has the audacity to attribute to himself. As a result, his verbal ephebization of

Dionysus simply brings into play the Heraclitean asymmetry between man and god, between mortal and immortal. This mysteriously reversible difference—as Heraclitus himself reminds us in another of his sayings: "Immortal mortals, mortal immortals"[42]—is nonetheless in its very nature asymmetrical and could not but dominate the rest of the story. The man/god duality in the *Bacchae*, and in the Greek world generally, is tortuous and strewn with pitfalls, as we shall have an opportunity to verify when we analyze the figure of Dionysus as well as the play's conclusion, but Pentheus's error lies not so much in ignoring the complexity of this relationship as in ignoring its very existence.

Not only the difference between man and god but also the symmetric and asymmetric tension maintaining their extremes is brought out into the open in the fourth episode, shortly after the hallucinatory epiphany of Dionysus in the form of a bull. Pentheus is now dressed as a woman, and Dionysus acts as a kind of master of ceremonies, arranging his curls and headband, the ritual ribbon worn by bacchantes:

Pentheus How do I look [*phainomai*]? Don't I look [*stasin*]
like Ino or Agave, my mother?
Dionysus I really do seem to see them, seeing you,
but these curls [*plokamos*] are out of place,
not how I arranged them for you under the headband.
Pentheus When I was inside, shaking my head backward and forward
in jubilant abandon, I put them out of place.
Dionysus We'll set them right for you, seeing we're here
to serve you; but keep your head [*kara*] straight.
Pentheus Here, you fix it [*kosmei*]: we are in your hands [*anakeimestha*].

As we come closer to the catastrophe, the tragic double meanings become more frequent: the verbs of vision (*verba videndi*) prepare the way for the imminent revelation of Pentheus's fate, about to be laid bare in the pitiless light of the sun. The term *stasis* corresponds to the visual and theatrical position Pentheus now occupies, but is also associated, semantically as well, with strives in the human communities where some of the *poleis* convulsed by the Peloponnesian War were in a state of civil war, corresponding to the Dionysian crisis overwhelming the Theban *polis*. In his delirium

Pentheus imagines he embodies his aunt Ino and his mother Agave; and their position and role in this scene preannounces the part they will play in initiating his *sparagmos*. On Cithaeron the enemy of Dionysus will have his curly hair fixed for the last time; the head that the god tells him to keep straight will be cut off by Agave, impaled on her thyrsus, and carried aloft in triumph; the *pluralis maiestatis* employed by Dionysus (ll. 932-33), and echoed by Pentheus at l. 934, expresses well the growing closeness of the two characters and also evokes the ambivalence of Dionysus's double identity as god and Stranger,[43] but it also hints at the collective violence that will be done by the bacchantes when possessed by the god, with whom they come to coincide at the climax of the rite. The verb *kosmeo* connects with the adjective *kosmos*, "ornate, beautiful" used in l. 857, again with reference to Pentheus, while *anakeimai*—a verb used by Agave herself at the very end of the tragedy—also means to be consecrated to a divinity, clearly an allusion to the sacrificial fate awaiting the victim dressed for sacrifice.[44] The way the sex reversal that had emerged in the previous encounter with Dionysus is carried out in the course of the drama shows therefore that the erotic aspects are subordinate to, anticipate, and signal their outcome as sacrifice. However, that is not by any means the end of the question of the erotic object, as an ingenuously material approach might conclude, but restates it more specifically, focusing on why it recurs so insistently, so obsessively. The question of the part played by sexuality in the drama breaks down into two subquestions: one regarding the secondary role of the sexual theme compared to the principal theme of sacrifice, and the other the reason for sexuality being nonetheless so pervasive.

Starting with the first of these subquestions, it is clear that Euripides deliberately includes homoerotic nuances in the text to allude to a more general disastrous tendency, already fully active in the god's miraculous release of the bacchantes that comes just before the passage about the captivating "curly tresses." Our attention is being drawn to the devastating progress of the objectual crisis that is destined to overturn every social and sexual role, and so it is this crisis that is the keystone, the direct message. What matters is not so much the individual objects—religious, cultural, political, human, or sexual—that the play shows to be disintegrating, as the fact that one by one they are beginning to totter and take on a completely opposite meaning and purpose, until they finally collapse.

Girard's concept of mimetic crisis already provides a valid analytical and descriptive tool, ensuring that we understand correctly this organizing and disorganizing function governing the text and recognize its outstanding anthropological realism. However, there is the typical difficulty that Girard's mimetic crisis is limited to the negative aspect of the nondifferentiation caused by rivalrous imitation, without including the positive reverse aspect, the objectual dimension that is the principal goal of collective religious mediations and should be restored by its ritualized subversion and final atoning sacrifice. The object is the center of gravity of the microcosm of culture, and everything must revolve around it so that its power to generate meanings can function. In the end the Girardian analysis itself, with its excessive negativism, unwittingly bears witness to this fact since it clashes with the real development of the dramatic text, and that suggests the answer to the second subquestion regarding the indirect message of the sexual theme.

Girard is right to observe that the mimetic crisis in the *Bacchae* does not fulfill its ritual purpose, showing itself to be an authentic sacrificial crisis, in the precise meaning of a crisis in sacrifice itself, no longer functioning as it should. This has immediate consequences for our argument. Although his interpretation does not enter into overly Freudian complications, the logical deduction to be drawn from it is that the sexual aspect is just as instrumental as the other aspects since everything collapses into mimetic nondifferentiation and reveals itself as a pretext for violence to take root and rule supreme in the community. At this point however in Girard's reconstruction an asymmetry creeps in, since if the sacrificial crisis opens the way for the tragic representation, the latter tries to call a halt in order not to be destroyed by it. To demonstrate his proposition, Girard has to interrupt the whole analysis and settle for one part of it, attributing the violent reconstitution that has failed to materialize in the course of the tragedy to its close, and failing to see that the sacrificial epilogue of the *Bacchae* falls dramatically short of its conclusive ritual target, namely the reconstitution of the body social, analogous to the *compositio membrorum* (re-membrance) of Pentheus's savagely mutilated body. But the corpse of the young king—recomposed in an incredible scene, lost unfortunately, save for a few papyrus fragments and some lines preserved in a cento dating from the Byzantine era, the *Christus patiens*—remains a macabre mass of fragments; and the final announcement made by Dionysus corresponds to this devastated state when he calls for the dispersal of the city's *disiecta membra* (scattered limbs), starting with its founder, Cadmus. Thus the sacrificial concealment is not realized, as we shall see later, and the situation described by the god envisions a community bereft of any objectual foothold, without any center of gravity that might allow it to reunite.

In short, Girard's negativism is finally obliged to play down the seriousness of the crisis it initially emphasized and see it as the standard fulfillment of an anobjectual scheme of concealment that admits no exceptions. What escapes this axiomatic procedure is the fact that the crisis in the *Bacchae* is so serious precisely because the objects it endangers and destroys are *not* a mere pretext, and that to distort and reverse them reintroduces *e contrario* the central value they possessed in normal life. Objectual destruction, far from denying the object's centrality, implies and evinces it, and in Euripides's drama we are brought to relive the terrible experience of its destruction.

This annihilation of gender and sexual identities descends like an avalanche, engulfing sector after sector of Theban society, and comes to a climax in the degradation of the male role, its objectual representative by definition. Not because the life of the *polis* was sexualized, according to the stereotypes of today's ill-digested Freudianism, but precisely because it did not have to be, since male citizens were required to free themselves from the natural needs that women could not escape, subjected as they were to the demands of family life and child-raising.[45] And, in fact, in the *Republic*, when Plato decides to abolish the family and entrust the education and choice of infants entirely to his *politeia*, he automatically gives women equal rights with men. In the ancient world this potential equality was in no way conceived as a value, as we find it in Judaism and still more in Christianity, but rather as a natural equivalence that was normally denied, giving rise to a hierarchy that was even more natural, being based on obvious laws and limitations that only the boldly speculative Plato sought to change, who subsequently felt the need for the "second constitution of the State [*deuteros an polis oikeisthai*] after the best" outlined in the *Laws* that envisions a return to the more realistic picture of the traditional male/female hierarchy.[46]

Once reconstructed, the mediatory context of antiquity disproves modern tendentious interpretations, and it is precisely this that restores the true significance to the breakdown in the male and female roles in the *Bacchae*. A powerful crescendo begins building up when the women possessed by Dionysus are taken away from their female tasks and domestic chores, and already the destabilizing germ of male-female switching is instilled by the parodos, reaching a peak in the description of the god-possessed maenads' defeat of the male forces, which endangers the survival of everyone; to the masculinization of the women there corresponds a symmetrical, inverse movement in the dominating male's admiration of his ephebic prisoner, since he is eventually to become his prey, dressed as a woman; this latent feminization is fully realized in the degrading scene in which the king of Thebes appears in women's clothing shortly to be the victim of the bacchantes' virilized violence. The sexual mediations that Greek society as a whole depended on are completely overturned. Euripides proceeds in an infinitely subtler and more realistic fashion than his modern critics give him credit for; it consists, not in making sex a pretext, but in showing the drama, the tragedy, of making sex a pretext, causing the sexual and gender objectuality that human life depends on to collapse. This perspective is the only one that allows us to make sense of events as they rapidly follow one another, and reconstruct their terrifying course without being misled by single features or sequences.

This detracts not at all from the final sacrificial outcome but, on the contrary, lends it substance and meaning, certifying the objectual failure in the destruction of both. This convergence becomes blindingly obvious when Pentheus is led onto Cithaeron dressed as a woman and immediately takes care to stay hidden because he is afraid the bacchantes will laugh at him: role and sex reversal lays a person open to collective hostility and what may precede or substitute for it—derision, the social and objectual destruction of the enemy through ridicule. However, this point shows yet again the importance of the themes of eros and the body. If sex reversal becomes an instrument of persecution as soon as it is organized and set center stage, this is exactly because that is not the purpose of sexual gender counterfeited in that manner, nor of the initiatory type of ritual inversion. The phenomenological-historical conclusion, which is also strictly textual, is that the sacrifice exceeds the sexual object without eliminating it: indeed it sets it center stage once more. The two subquestions thus finally come together in a single overall answer, and the writer who more than any other provides the means for us to understand this is Georges Bataille.

The *Bacchae* partly corroborates Bataille's concept of eroticism as orgiastic transgression that confirms the collective need for prohibitions just in their breach while keeping the element of danger under control. The danger is controlled but not unreal. Otherwise the ritual transgression would lose its essential character and therefore its potency, which means there must always be a risk of destruction, of a final definitive violation. And in fact Euripides's tragedy shows what happens when orgiastic transgression gets out of control, but already, on its own, it also invalidates any Bataille-type interpretation leading to psychoanalytic-type results, since the bacchantes' cult, on closer inspection, loses its erotic connotation and shows itself for what it is: the transgression of blood sacrifice no longer contained by the rite, frighteningly overflowing and sweeping everyone away. Bataille knows this very well, but by omitting to give it all the necessary emphasis he leaves the door open to pansexualist misunderstandings: eroticism bears a structural relationship to sacrifice and to the crisis that paves the way for it and makes it necessary. The main drawback, however, is that in Bataille's conception that relationship remains unfocused, not so much in its potentially destructive aspects, which are to a certain degree destructive in any case, since Bataille never forgets there is no sacrifice that does not include total destruction in some form, albeit symbolic. Rather, what really escapes his attention is that both sacrifice and eroticism refer to a human reality that is always threatened or denied, and thus to some extent destroyed, but whose cultural endowment enables it always to revive and restore itself objectually. Bataille's analysis stops at sacrifice as the furthest extreme of eroticism, its point of no return, and in so doing he slips back into the Freudian, or pseudo-Freudian error, which he tries to shake off but can never entirely escape. What is missing is the center of gravity and meaning provided by the mediatory object, mediating and mediated, and never more central than when endangered.

Thus we have acquired the means needed to achieve an overall perspective, and suited to the content that ancient tragedy sets before us. Euripides's drama does much more than just show us the continual collective disorganizing and reorganizing of sexuality and its exchanges with sacrifice; it reproduces the dialectic underlying both in the spectacular, sinister contraction of the action, where the verbal and symbolic transgression makes plain its ritual nature deriving from the rite at its origin, breaking forever the finely spun web of compensations that govern sexual rites. We are getting closer to the pulsating core of the tragedy that will also yield precious information about the working of human sexuality that not by chance provides the occasion for the drama.

Eroticism appears in the *Bacchae* as the sign of a delegitimized, subtracted objectuality, as a textual function reflecting the upheaval in the play, and that could not happen if it had Freudian-type objective centrality or, in the symmetrical and opposite case, if it was anobjectual pretext of the Girardian type; Bataille, on the other hand, introduces the right degree of tension to grasp the particular position of eroticism as long as we never forget it gravitates about an object no matter how close or unattainable, or rather an object that matters because it is close at hand *and* unattainable. Just as human sexuality is not a natural object independent of mediations, so it is not their source either; it is simply the most intense objectual motivation of human beings, their most important intermedial function, both bodily and *imaginalis*, and it is precisely that function as effective objectualizing medium that breaks down in the *Bacchae*. That is why, as Pentheus gradually, spectacularly loses all his mediatory influence, his female disguise appears to be such a fitting allusion to the narrative and symbolic organization of the entire drama. We must now look at the overall metamorphic structure, where the aspect of sex and gender is a mask precisely because it is not supposed to be only a mask. The objectual emptying-out of the male and female roles foreshadows the objectual destruction they are tragically instrumental in bringing about.

4. Metamorphosis of a Body Torn to Pieces

We have seen how Pentheus's gradual, degrading feminization corresponds to the symmetrical, reverse metamorphosis through which the women are transformed into men, and take their place dysfunctionally. The twofold correspondence would appear limited through the asymmetry that concentrates the devirilizing process in Pentheus alone and leaves Dionysus's effeminate looks in the limbo of mythic data concerned with the difference between men and gods, between mortals and immortals. But as I have already hinted, it is not at all like that in fact, as we shall see in the following chapters. And as if that were not enough, the asymmetry of Pentheus being the only one affected by female metamorphosis falls apart upon closer reflection. The parodos actually shows the entire male population of Thebes to be threatened by collective feminization and speaks of weapons of war, the typical virile attribute, being transformed into drums and thyrsi by magic, seen against a background of continually shifting processions of men and women. It is the start of indiscriminate reciprocity, and if, on one hand, it disproves Lévi-Strauss's good reciprocity it does not coincide even with Girard's purely negative reciprocity, not because the result is not destructive—it is, more than Girard would care to admit—but because within the destructiveness itself there are cognitive developments that the text casts into our attention. It is well worth looking more closely at the passage.

The metaphorical collective circularity between men and women in the *Bacchae* is expressed indirectly and throughout, fully exploiting the signifying matrix of the mythic material being reworked. Many of the metaphorical procedures are based on reversal, typical of the way in which myth proceeds, the initial situation reappearing as a subsequent or final image: the objectual crisis arising within the community is projected onto the victim who thus becomes its cause, while the group's objectual realities that the myth of origin ought to explain have already been assumed in one way or another by the mythical explanation. This is why structuralism, in order to remain consistent in its formal reading, has to get rid of the time factor and take refuge in a synchronic interpretation, which unconsciously takes on the self-referential character of the text being interpreted and of the community that produced it. Tragedy, on the contrary, proceeds by a kind of antistructuralism, isolating the structural elements to the point of destructuring them, until they merge, in a way that is covertly revealing, with the representational elements that have remained intact. Tragic oscillation sets all the representations of the myth into motion again, at the same time seeming to confirm them. With the virtuosity of a great artist at the very limits of his art, Euripides exploits all the hidden resources of the representational and sacral system in which he operates. As a result of his strategy, the secretly real metaphors move toward the metaphorical realities until they reach their fated union in the *symbolon*. The initiation become slaughter reveals itself to be slaughter that will become initiation. The real ritual sequence is established at the moment of the *sparagmos*, when the metaphorical laughter is transformed and becomes a no longer metaphorical tearing to pieces. When Pentheus removes his disguise in a desperate attempt to be recognized by his mother, it is just as if the whole chorus of bacchantes, played by male actors, had unmasked. A little close scrutiny of the text enables us to reach back from the derived metaphors to the reality that produced them.

The conclusion at this point, as we try to trace Euripides's development of the *Bacchae*, is that violence was perpetrated by men. This should not be taken to mean there was no female violence but merely underlines the fact that their superior physical strength and dominant social role made men the prime movers in acts of ritual violence and lynchings, the victims being women, the weak, and the defeated, such as the aged, children, and prisoners of war. The question of gender mediations comes up once again: these are not to be conceived according to modern distinctions and contrasts but according to the mutually reinforcing, complementary nature of the male and female roles in view of the objectual goals set for them by collective mediations. Thus male violence was fully endorsed and supported by the female element in obedience to the mediations on which they all depended. (Hecuba, for example, wants to eat the liver of Achilles after he has killed Hector.[47]) What is happening here is very different from the superficial gender war to which events in the *Bacchae* are so often reduced: it is the subversion and turning upside down of the complementary objectual nature of the sexes, the women act like men, the men like women, both destroying what they are required to guarantee and safeguard. This corresponds to role-swapping rituals that must be of great antiquity and conveys to us the orgiastic dimension of eroticism analyzed by Bataille. The difference now is that completion of the ritual circuit is no longer assured: the object is not reestablished after its stability and continuity have been broken.

The aim must be not so much to expose the violence and scabrous sexuality concealed beneath the deceptive appearance of the myth as to highlight the entire structure supporting its objectual closure. This need to compromise and subvert sexual and role differentiation that brought reassurance to normal life was at the same time ritual but nowadays is para-ritual and playful, persisting still in contemporary transgressive eroticism. Therefore, any act of exposure, in its apparent claim to truth, makes one extreme of an oscillation unilateral and definitive, while the objectual, publicly revealed part of the oscillation—the so to speak teleological component—remains most important. The reassuring facade presented by a prestigious public figure or exemplary family man caught misbehaving and breaking the rules of matrimonial and sexual ethics is not in itself any less true than what lies hidden behind it; indeed, from the point of view of the offender himself the facade is the only truth, completely unconcerned with the surreptitious affairs on which it is based. A criterion exists for assessing whether the circuit guaranteed in this way serves its objective, that is, remains objectual, or vice versa compromises and destroys the objective, and fails to achieve its end. And that criterion is precisely an achievement or destruction open to verification, and not some moral thesis classed as absolute.

In the same way, in the *Bacchae*, we must uncover the network of stratified violence and sacrificial exchange underpinning the representation, not to demystify it ourselves or put the author in the fascinating but scarcely real position of absolute demystifier but to bring out the radical nature of an ancestral circuit and the seriousness of the situation that arises when it is prevented from working and there is no final compensation. Meanwhile, we now see how we can interpret the internal organization of the first sequence of the parodos, with the maenads skillfully inserted in the genealogy. The female presence of Rhea, occupying a symmetrical, central place in the scheme, has split the collective god into two symmetrical, complementary aspects, male and female, situated at two different stages in the evolution of the myth. The two sequences already prefigure the main points of the story: the mythical and ritual metamorphoses of the crisis-stricken community, and the final outcome resulting in an "ecstasy of flesh devoured alive." The entire representational system in the *Bacchae* is based on the unsuccessful objectual restoration of this bloody exchange of parts, on the absence of the ritual reversibility that had made it possible to overcome the sacrificial drama with its irreversible nature that was nevertheless circumscribed and redeeming.

The tragedy also touches on the vast sphere of the female in mythology and, in the light of a sacrificial analysis, it appears far from delicately feminine; in fact, it reflects a collapsed objectual complementarity where the woman was regarded as the weaker, more delicate part, not simply because she was submissive but because she was the intimate vital guarantee of its attainment and possession. When myth and ritual deal with women in the Greek world, the specter of an abnormal or permanent reversal of functions is frequently projected in a dimension remote in space and time. The story of Pasiphae and the labyrinth or the myth of the Amazons, female warriors denied the use of their bodies and doomed to a savage denial of female objectuality, are exemplary paradoxes, enough in themselves to confirm the reassuring norms of sexual behavior and family life. However, inserted in the new cognitive reversibility of tragedy, this operation ceases to be unrelated and remote, a mere symbol and projection, but comes dangerously close; what was impossible before, except for monsters and gods, now become psychological and moral possibilities that open the way to destabilizing and contaminating interpretations. What disturbed an audience in ancient times was not to find the Muses, Nymphs, and Graces revealed as savage and persecutory figures, blood-thirsty lemures and hordes of cannibals—after all, this was already known and no discovery in itself—but the fact that those monstrous metamorphoses did not remain on stage within the *mythos* but crossed over into the audience and were transformed into a cognitive infection. We will start with the maenads and their ritual, the reality fueling the Euripidean *fabula*.

The maenads were at the center of the Dionysian trieteric festival mentioned in l. 133 and held at Delphi. Like the Cretan bull-slaughtering, it followed a ternary pattern: the year of the god's death followed the first year of his rebirth; following the *symbola* of his dismemberment, carried to Delphi by Athena or Apollo in the mystic cist, came their conclusive recomposition in the *symbolon*. During the trieteric cycle the Dionysian women of Delphi, the Thyads,[48] climbed the wild slopes of Mount Parnassus while possessed by the god, exactly as the Theban women did on Mount Cithaeron. These celebrations started in *Daidaphorios*, the month of the torches (the δᾶιδας of the *Cretans*) at the start of winter, when nocturnal rites were lit by thyrsi-torches and Dionysus leapt triumphantly in their midst over the rocks of Delphi, as Tiresias tells Pentheus.[49]

Whenever Apollo, the complementary god at Delphi and Dionysus's brother, appears, the train of Bacchic women becomes the nine Muses, daughters of Mnemosyne and Zeus or, in a more specifically Orphic tradition, of Heaven and Earth, like the Titans.[50] The Muses are the ecstatic goddesses of poetic and sapiential inspiration. In their most archaic form they induced a violent trance, identical to that of the maenads.[51] The Muses who pick up Orpheus's remains are the same maenads who tore him to pieces. Euripides's text communicates this by a covert reference, placing the name of Orpheus between Nysa, "the cradle of wild beasts," and the Delphic peaks, on the one hand, and the Pieria, seat of the Muses and now of Dionysus, on the other (ll. 556 ff.). The Muses educated Dionysus, as did the Curetes and the Nymphs, female counterparts of the Satyrs. The Nymphs, in particular, who dwell on Cithaeron in the *Bacchae* and had blood sacrifices made to them, could cause ritual possession, madness, and actual death.[52] The number three, with its multiple nine, recurs throughout this mythology. Among the Muses, three are divinities of *Charis*, of aesthetic and sensual attraction. However, these Charites are not the harmonious Graces of Raphael and Antonio Canova but divinities of ecstatic and shamanistic possession, and they could turn into the Erinyes with snakes for hair like the Gorgons, the black hounds of Vengeance that castrated, dismembered, and impaled their victims, and danced in a circle around Orestes calling him sacrificial flesh; or they might become the long-toothed Keres sucking the blood of the dead and dying.[53] The Charites continue their metamorphoses as Gorgons, Sirens, and Harpies, always in the same sacrificial *trimurti*. In every case, they are the Moirae, the merciless goddesses who hand out the sacrificial parts (*moirai*), determine life and death, and preside over Dionysus's birth in the *Bacchae* (ll. 99 ff.). The maenads—who entwine snakes in their hair (ll. 101–4), give themselves the name of bitches,[54] and designate Pentheus as a son of the Gorgons (l. 990)—appear divided into three groups, headed by Cadmus's three daughters (ll. 680–82), the real Moirae for Pentheus. The Charites' career continues, and they become the three goddesses of the Judgment of Paris,[55] a typical double-binding situation for, whatever choice (*krisis*) is made, the result is catastrophic. There is no escaping the sacrificial *trimurti*, just as there is no escape for Pentheus pinned down by Agave, Ino, and Autonoë. In Aeschylus, ritual appeasement must be made before the black *charis* goddesses can become the white Eumenides, who protect Justice, that is, the judicial and civil mediation of the *polis* that he desired. The black/white polarity, customary in the old sacral transformations, is in turn transformed into an objectual stabilization, hopefully definitive. However, once begun, this shift from the tragic to the civic stage showed no sign of stopping; now, with Euripides, it presented a disastrous leap into the past, into the archaic sphere attempting to refashion it and create a new stable synthesis. The white color, symbolizing in Aeschylus the reestablishment of a divine and collective order, becomes in Euripides an announcement of death, in the clear color of the maenads' and Dionysus's skin.[56] This white halo rebounds on Pentheus as a contagious and blinding feminization and as the final disguise as maenad accomplishing his fatal attraction to the effeminate Dionysus.

The *omophagos charis* shows us the Charites in their true colors, already hinted at by the chorus in the first stasimon of the tragedy. Having first called down punishment on Pentheus for accusing Dionysus of licentiously favoring the *charitas Aphrodites,* the chorus turns its attention to Aphrodite herself, to the Muses, the Charites, and Desire (*Pothos*),[57] the mythical incarnation of erotic desire. It is this desire that ambiguously infects Pentheus when he sees the captured Dionysus. His punishment is symbolized by the vine, the grace of Dionysus, *Dionysou charis* (l. 535), that is, wine as a metaphor for the paroxysmal ecstasy and the resulting blood-letting.

The ruinous circularity of these dramatic motifs, before being further explored, does not cease raising questions on its bonds, and double binds, with us as modern spectators and interlocutors. We have avoided the trap of psychologistic anachronism in reading the sexual features of the story, and now we must avoid a similar danger in interpreting its generative core, as we already did in discussing the strongest sacrificial reading of the tragedy in the twentieth century, that of Girard. The purpose is not to draw dividing lines between us and Euripides's masterpiece, but to detect differences so as to discern better connections, the common denominator communicating across to us. It is the same communication that in Bataille describes the common sacrificial ground of human beings, the wound making them feel what they share is on the verge of destruction. Yet along this communicating path we find, before Bataille and Girard, another interpreter to whom both are indebted.

Euripides's text does not simply deconstruct this traditional mythical material but sets it in motion, transmitting its movement down to our own day, presenting us with a fresh image of Greek civilization, less conventional, more daring and interesting than our previous idea. In modern times Nietzsche has come close to this image, following those indirect, contradictory routes that have made Greek civilization such a crux for us, as regards both its spirit and its interpretation. Just how profound Nietzsche's influence has been can be gauged from the exemplary nature of his errors. They constitute a sort of unintentional counterpoint to events in the *Bacchae,* so it is worth considering this aspect for a moment in order to focus our own position regarding Euripides's masterpiece.

In returning to the Greece of Dionysus, Nietzsche was seeking a definitive divine mediation, not in the sense of an acquired ontological status—in accordance with Heidegger's metaphysical interpretation—but as a modern-day repossessing of ancient religious mediations, transformed by permanent objectual reversibility into an anobjectual, impermanent flux, the true face of the Eternal Return in all its crazy destructiveness. In ancient Greece, modern man is fated to see either an absolute, perfect objectuality, detached from the dramatic process that ensured its attainment, or vice versa an empty drama, unrelated and objectless, lacking the objectual purpose that gave it its human quality, its soul. For this reason, what prevails in Nietzsche is the deceptive register of his demystification of Socratic rationalism, an attempt to cover up tragedy's originary Dionysian profundity. This antihistorical unmasking at once overbalances into unmasking Christianity with its false morality and the detested herd, felt by Nietzsche as a constant threat, obsessed as he was by the nightmare of being engulfed by that most typical of modern objectual negations, mediocrity, the indifferent lyncher of all it finds different. This is why Hellas as Nietzsche imagines it is described half the time with stunning anthropological insights and the other half with kitsch idealization à la Biedermeier, the two linked together by clearly pathological statements. The objectual purpose of the ancient Dionysian destruction remains a dead letter just as there is little perception of its true consistency and entity. Even when his evocation of Dionysus "devourer of men" is most convincing, the god's collective aspect remains muted, lurking in the background, ready to spring at the throat of the angry, defenseless philosopher. Nietzsche is a modern Pentheus who, instead of opposing Dionysus, tries to ingratiate himself to the god hoping to acquire his secret. Nevertheless, he is ultimately torn to pieces, in the postritual and psychiatric forms proper to the contemporary world. Nietzsche's problem is to have demystified not too much but too little, not to have demystified the modern prejudice for demystification, in this rashly ignoring the warnings coming down to him from Euripides. It would be difficult to find a more pertinent warning, a warning more *deinos* in a modern way, about how we should proceed in our inquiry, than by supporting and commenting on the inquiry already made by the text under investigation.

Having surveyed the mythological and ritual themes investigated by Euripides, and the right way to approach them, I will now try to establish more precisely the degree to which the text is aware of their significance as cultural mediation. The previously mentioned speech of Tiresias will serve this purpose, taking its realistically bloody metaphor of wine as our guiding motif. We have seen the various transformations of the myth; time now to take a closer look at the moment of birth.

5.

The *Hieros Gamos* of Wet and Dry

1. Hierogamous Games

We have seen the revealing interlacement between sacrificial themes and sexual themes, where the former stress the mediatory source of the community and the latter recall its objectual ends, which the dramatic plot has the charge to exhibit in their essential role and anguishing insufficiency. This erotic-sacrificial intermingling, where the erotic component emphasizes the sacrificial component but the latter emphasizes the heavy implications of the destruction of the former, is active in the most crucial passages of the *Cretans* and *Hippolytus*, and reaches its highest subtlety in the *Bacchae*.

One of the fundamental symbolic and religious themes in the *Bacchae*, and one that brings us even closer to what we saw when discussing labyrinth mythology and the Orphic papyrus, is the *hieros gamos*, the union between Heaven and Earth, above and below, evoked at Eleusis as at-one-ment of the many ritual *symbola* in a single sacrificial and saving experience. It will enable us to have a wider understanding of what Euripides thought about the mythical-ritual mediations of his civilization, views that were the fruit of his knowledge, reflection, and intuition. We must avoid the trap of attributing too much awareness to Euripides, after the manner of the all-seeing superintellectuals served up to us by our pseudo-cultural media; instead, we need to think of intelligent, creative research that, while it understands much, manages to support and exploit even what escapes it and, in any case, actively interacts with what it understands and knows, within mediations understood to be both necessary and inadequate. By situating himself at the vital nerve centers of the matter being narrated, in its double-binding, exponentially productive paradoxes, this scientist-tragedian obtains an organic symbolic and historical context which in turn makes the rules for itself and for whoever is its willing instrument, and is then available to any interpreter who wishes to repeat the operation.

In the first episode, Tiresias's closely argued speech to dissuade Pentheus from opposing the new god (ll. 274–97) is particularly indicative of the presence in the *Bacchae* of ideas about hierogamy and its sacrificial, mediatory value. The speech deals with the mutual relationship between "the goddess Demeter—or Earth" (ll. 275–76) and "the son of Semele" (l. 278), respectively representing "the dry things" (l. 277) and "the juice of the grape" (l. 280). It is therefore a sort of hierogamy, but with allegorical and naturalistic-agricultural connotations that do not appear to fit well in the dramatic unfolding of the story. The passage is so puzzling that a preliminary discussion of the problem of interpreting it seems the best way for finding a satisfactory explanation. Usually it is taken to be a rationalization of myth influenced by the contemporary sophists active in Athens, and more specifically by Prodicus's naturalistic theory of religion, according to which the gods are the divinization of beneficial natural forces.[1] The connection is unquestionable, but the critics confine themselves to noticing it without any further discussion of it, not realizing they are implicitly confusing the viewpoint of the character, the ideas he conveys, and the viewpoint of the author—all of which aspects are connected, of course, but for this very reason must be distinguished. And yet, a few lines above Tiresias himself makes a peremptory declaration to Cadmus that should have been a warning for modern commentators:

> We don't play at being wise [*sophizomestha*] on the gods [*daimosin*].
> The fatherland traditions, for a long time handed down
> no reasoning [*logos*] will be able to subvert,
> not even the wisdom [*to sophon*] of the highest wits.[2]

The verb *sophizomai* has given place to various interpretations and conjectures,[3] though the denotations attributed to it do not vary widely. My own suggestion is that it also contains an allusion to the contemporary sophists, a group still free from the negative reputation they would later accrue in Plato (indeed, σοφιστής originally meant "wise man"), but that it already stresses the vanity of a *logos* and wisdom (τὸ σοφόν) unable to grasp the real meaning and purpose of a shameless sacrificial and ecstatic cult like Dionysus's. The ironic result of the modern debate is that the critics see an exclusive reference to the fifth-century sophistic movement when they should not, and exclude it when they should include it. There are no doubt problems in Tiresias's words, because his position is in itself inconsistent, mixing up an apparently strong defense of tradition and an updated intellectual awareness, as we shall see. Nevertheless, this contrast could not be more pertinent, for it describes with precision what is at stake, that is, the difficult or impossible relation between "the fatherland traditions" advocated by Tiresias and a philosophical thought well known to Euripides, as witnessed by the information that he was a disciple of Prodicus and also Anaxagoras. Even if Euripides shared to some degree that philosophical background, he developed an original reflection on it that remained unperceived for millennia and waiting only for a different historical-philosophical setting to be noticed.

In order to follow Euripides's view in its subtlety and profundity, we must avoid a misunderstanding quite common on religious topics, which according to a modern mentality stresses too greatly a superficial dilemma between the existence or nonexistence of god(s). For the ancients there was no linear existence opposed to a linear nonexistence. They knew that the Divine—*to theion*—is never a mere existence or nonexistence, an abstract attribute by which to establish its presence or the absence through an intellectual procedure, but the divine *res* itself, the *pragmaton* or *dromenon* (i.e. the event, the action, the passion) that is located at the root of divinity, and includes both existence and nonexistence, imbued with their reciprocity and their theological, ontological, dialectical compresence. This is the remote premise that will come back to the fore in Nietzsche's aphorism 125, after Kant's gnosiological revolution, which demonstrates that the existence of God cannot be deduced from the idea of God, because for the human mind existence is the result of experience, not a logical attribute. Kant's argument consists in showing that God is no longer an object of experience for an already defined human rational subject, but it does not exclude, indeed it even secretly implies, the far more ancient outlook of a divine experience making a human subject possible, that is, bringing it into existence. Thanks to the Kantian division between phenomenon and noumenon, it was Nietzsche who discovered the remote, forgotten power of that outlook to generate the human precisely because it is nonhuman. Prodicus and Euripides share an ancient version of an awareness that is similar but developed in the sense of man's relationship either with *physis*, in the case of Prodicus, or the gods, in the case of Euripides, both aspects conflated in the textual operation of the first episode of the *Bacchae*. We can ascertain this if we go into the details of Tiresias's *rhesis* on Demeter and Dionysus.

A historical reconstruction that postulates a strange blend of religious and philosophical considerations in Tiresias's speech could sound aprioristic but finds solid corroboration from the documental data. The fourth-century Derveni papyrus has a very similar mix of themes drawn from Orphic-Mystery wisdom and philosophy, not as a form of eclecticism, as normally held,[4] but for the very good reason that they both had the same problem of attaining objectual salvation by means of mediations other than the traditional ones: these were magical-ritual in the case of Orphism and logical-performative for philosophy. And if that holds true for the fourth century BC, there is even more reason why it should be true for Euripides in the previous century, granting him, of course, greater awareness and interpretive refinement.

In addition, then, to connections with contemporary philosophy, there are in Tiresias's *rhesis* highly competent and precise references to religion, which give us a further level of reading, already arguable in a general way and independently documented. It would therefore be a mistake simply to juxtapose the more conceptual with the ritual elements and jump to the conclusion that the character is contradictory in himself. It is certainly right to talk of contradiction here, providing we look closely at its constituent terms, but before we can understand those terms we must put aside all conventional ideas about rationalism in the ancient world and the religious factor in confrontation with it. Euripides's intention in his depiction of Tiresias is not simply to show the clash between sophistic rationalism and the religious tradition; that conflict is there but not in the ideological, rancorous manner of our modern mentality, so proud to be independent, as it supposes, of mediations that it no longer understands. Tiresias's philosophical awareness is a failure not so much because he cannot or will not understand but because he understands too much. His understanding, therefore, is not the understanding of our rationalistic schemes but of mythical-ritual wisdom as it begins to self-reflect within the theatrical space of tragedy. From being a ritual vision deduced from mythography it turns into a more cosmically abstract reflection of a protophilosophical character. However, Euripides's aim is not to show us philosophical thinking *in statu nascendi* but a middle course, unable to be either one thing or the other. His Tiresias is not advocating a new approach to reality that may bring about profound changes in religious knowledge—as is the case with Anaximander, Xenophanes, Heraclitus, and Parmenides—but he resorts to it in order to legitimize traditional theological forms, to set the acquisitions of the philosophical *logos* side by side with the magical-ritual beliefs and practices of received religion, but no longer with the Orphic archaisms on which the author of the Derveni papyrus was to rely.

The character as Euripides depicts him attempts to resolve or rather cover up the paradoxical situation of blindness and knowledge brought about by events by ingeniously intertwining rationalization and supine acceptance of the tradition, which is, however, doomed to failure by itself. Euripides's strategy is, then, infinitely subtler than might be the case if we did not question the categories that we use to approach it. Some further remarks will suffice to prove this starting from the very text of the *Bacchae*.

Tiresias's speech is substantially a commentary developing what Dionysus, in the prologue, and the chorus, in its parodos (ll. 87–104), have said about the god's origin. Here are the superb words uttered by Dionysus in the first five lines of the prologue:

> In the Theban land I did come. It's me, Zeus's son,
> Dionysus, who saw the light in the lightning
> from Cadmus's daughter Semele:
> once my form [*morphen*] from divine became mortal,
> I arrived at the source of Dirce, at the surge of Ismenus.[5]

Heaven and Earth couple together in order to give his indefinable birth to the god Theban and yet foreigner, a birth celebrated in the supervening fire of the thunderbolt by which his mother was killed. Dionysus is the son of the "Hurler of Lightning" of the Gurob papyrus. Once his "form from divine became mortal"—a hint of disturbing theological profundity that only Christianity will have continued and made human—the aqueous element seems to bless the event and quench its flames. It is pure illusion, as we already saw and still have to see: the water of terrestrial sources would give the impression of extinguishing the igneous element of Mother Earth (Semele was an archaic telluric divinity),[6] but it is its liquid instability to secretly dominate, destined to rapidly submerge the hated city. This hierogamy not promising anything good is evoked again by the chorus in the parodos, which dwells on the god's dual birth, firstly from his mother struck by Zeus's lightning and then from his father's thigh, without any hint at refreshing waters. Dionysus is later called *dithyrambos* (l. 526), which in folk etymology means born twice, since his third birth, the last act in the Dionysian theogony, should be represented in the unfolding drama.

In the wake of these strong textual connections with the incipit of tragedy, with this fateful *incipit tragoedia*, Tiresias has the delusion that he can solve its ambiguity by showing to the real interlocutor of the incipit that its theogony forged by lightning and in vain tempered by water actually is an Eleusinian hierogamy between male and female gods, between Earth and Heaven. If the argument itself is quite clear in its religious features and philosophical implications, its communicative strategy, as is usual in tragedy, does not limit itself to a purely verbal procedure, since it involves the very substance of the character. We should never overlook the emblematic nature of tragedy's dramatis personae, the tragic characters hidden by the mask condensing in one feature and expression their temper and destiny. This is particularly true for a drama such as the *Bacchae*, probably dominated by the contrast between the smiling face of Dionysus and the sorrowful face of Pentheus, the man of suffering, of *penthos* (a theme perhaps later developed in the topos of Democritus laughing and Heraclitus crying).

We ignore the details of Tiresias's dress and mask, but the public was perfectly acquainted with his mythical-narrative aura, to which his very appearance alluded, in all likelihood. The very figure of the Theban soothsayer was living testimony to the argument he is putting forward. He is not simply the bearer of knowledge, of a *logos* to be passed on and no more, since his own person is the consequence of what he is about to recount. So we must first analyze the mythical connotations of Tiresias himself as an indispensable preamble to understanding what he says.

All that the soothsayer is he owes to the hierogamy: his destiny, his professional attributes (his attributes tout court), and his skill in dealing with the divine. All the same, the hierogamy has gone over him like a steamroller and transformed him into what might be called its diachronic personification. Tiresias was, in fact, changed into a woman for having disturbed the sacred copulation of two snakes, and only regained his male identity after an interval of seven years by doing the same thing again.[7] One particularly elegant version of the myth has him kill the female snake on the first occasion and the male on the second, thus creating a direct correspondence between the sex assigned to the killer and the sex of the killed. (Tiresias becomes a woman after eliminating the female and a man again after killing the male.)[8] The marked substitution symbolism of this correspondence suggests both religious rites in which the priest wore a disguise, subsequently evolving into the figure of the soothsayer/voyeur, and initiation rites based on disguise and sexual reversal, as happens to Pentheus at the end of the tragedy. But there is more besides this.

We already have enough information to see that these transformations and reversals refer back to a sacred hierogamy that came into the Hellenic world from Crete and the civilizations of the Near East, Mesopotamia in particular. A glance over the various strata of a ritual evolution that must have been particularly rich and diverse, given its antiquity, makes it clear, as I have already pointed out, that the earliest victim was a woman in those cases where the female part remains largely indeterminate and in the background, while the male victim, represented by Tiresias, is closer and recognizable. The seven-year period is a vestige of the ritual cycle terminating with the sacrifice. The sacrificial-erotic significance of the bisexual soothsayer, as well as the shorter time-lapse from the sacrifice in which he has the part of the male, is reflected in the disability that falls to his lot, his blindness. This can be connected to castration, as Freud would have it in the case of Oedipus,[9] though the reasons for the mythical-ritual association are not the same as the psychoanalytical reasons, and a less a priori, more contextual explanation is possible, correcting Freud while showing he is partially right.

The punishment of blinding consists, in fact, in eliminating the body part that mostly corresponds to sexual desire in cognitive terms. In the case of Tiresias, this happens as voyeurism, a very old cause of rivalry among males that could end either in the killing of the voyeur or his involvement as sexual partner, or in a combination between the two extremes. The blinding of the mythic voyeur, guilty of a *mala curiositas* that will be Pentheus's at the close of the *Bacchae*, appears to be the trace of other mutilations that could be inflicted on the male partner in another double organ far more indispensable for procreation. This might give the oldest explanation of the sexual inversion, linked to a symbolic emasculation, going back to the physical emasculation of a collective violence that starts from there. The lynching is the internal thrust of all this erotic and hierogamic symbolism, imbued with erotic attraction not because it follows an already formed libido, but because it gathers the combinatory fragments of a sexual object destabilized and become a sign of crisis. All we have seen so far on hierogamy and its relationship with the most archaic sacrificial rites finds further confirmation in the mythologem of Tiresias.

In a more etiological version of the myth, his characteristic victimary and divine affliction is explained as imposed on him because he chanced to see Athena bathing naked when he was out with his hounds in the mountains. This is clearly a transposition of a myth mentioned several times in the tragedy, the myth of Actaeon, a cousin of Pentheus, who was lynched by a pack of hounds;[10] the absence of the hounds from the Tiresias myth corresponds to the deletion of a collective function. On the other hand, the best-known etiological explanation of Tiresias's blindness sees him called on to settle a dispute between Zeus and Hera as to who enjoys greater pleasure, man or woman. When he replies that the woman has the lion's share (nine tenths!), Hera punishes him with blindness. This seems to be a rationalized version of the snake coupling; the snakelike partners of the Orphic-Eleusinian tradition and labyrinth symbolism take on their typically Olympian form, with the sacrificial symbolism of their story concentrated in the outsider who both observes and projects the story, the seer/voyeur who has seen too much and must see no more.

It is possible to see Tiresias as victim in a way that would not have entirely displeased Lévi-Strauss, apart from the sacrificial realism, of course: the male part is only one tenth, and so corresponds to the superfluous part that has to be expelled, while the more ancient victim, the woman, with her nine tenths, effectively corresponds to the group where order is restored through expelling the excess part. This collective significance is perfectly recognizable in the role played by Hera as eternal initiator, acting with complete impunity and with no blame attached, in the myth recounted by Tiresias in Euripides, in the myth of Tiresias itself, and in that recounted by him to Pentheus in the second part of his etiological speech—besides the Titanic myth remaining in the background. Moreover, the detail that this part coincides with the male orgasm not only evokes the sinister forms observed in the strata of the hierogamic sacrifice but also further confirms the presence of the castration theme because it suggests some evolution of the ritual leading, at a certain point, to the symbolic elimination of the body part concerned with mating, a sacred emasculation blinding male virility, surrendering it to the female and divine side once and for all, as in the Cybele rites.

Tiresias, then, is a real summa of *hieros gamos* symbolism, which more than qualifies him to present the relationship between Demeter and Dionysus in that respect. We have now to analyze the disquieting implications of his *rhesis* to Pentheus.

2. Blood Wedding

The mythological history of the seer blinded and changed in his sex—the real infratext of his speech—not only makes it superfluous for him to describe the sexual union of the two hierogamous divinities in direct terms, but actually indicates the necessity of not giving an account *apertis verbis*; by staying within the ambit of the *arrheton*, the punishment represented graphically in his own *mythos* can be avoided. It is time to read and comment on the text of Tiresias's speech, divided in two for the sake of convenience. The first sequence is deceitfully descriptive:

> There are actually two
> first things among men, my boy: the goddess Demeter—
> or Earth, if you want to call her that;
> she's the one who nourishes mortals [*brotous*] with the dry things;
> and the one who came balancing her [*antipalon*], the son of Semele,

who found and brought to men
the wet juice of the grape [*botruos*], which deadens the pains
of suffering mortals [*brotous*] when they get drunk with the vine liquor,
and gives them sleep, oblivion [*lethen*] from their everyday evils:
and there is no other drug [*pharmakon*] for pain.
This is one born [*gegos*] a god, poured out as a libation [*spendetai*] to the gods:
it is thanks to him that men possess their riches.

The erotic nature of the relationship between Dionysus and Demeter is evoked by skillful allusion, in a way that immediately translates its significance into mediatory terms. Their male and female functions complete each other and interpenetrate fully and creatively. These two divine principles are the "two first things among men," the cornerstones of the objectual world of life and culture. The life of men does not derive from them separately but from their creative, ritually controlled union. Nevertheless, all this implies an internal opposition that has been overcome, contained, in the double meaning of the word that has yet to be explained. The attainment of the cultural object can be only the result of a process that obtains it because shortly before it has jeopardized every natural object, making a break in continuity that the rite and myth serve to evoke and compensate.

When Tiresias states that Demeter nourishes men "with dry things" (i.e., cereals), he chooses an image that is specific as to quality and, at the same time, generic as to concept. From the viewpoint of a conventional interpretation of the thinking of the sophists and of Prodicus in particular, this detail appears to be naturalistic or philosophical depending upon to the criteria followed by the interpreters, but it really has a precise ritual meaning, probably not so far from the ideas of Prodicus himself though going beyond his attempt at a rational explanation. Dry defines itself by contrast to its opposite extreme: the wet juice of the grape. As wine it makes one drunk, drowsy, and oblivious, which symbolizes the nighttime release from daytime bonds on which being awake depends, that is to say, the deliberate organization of culture and exemption from critical factors that threaten the community, which it must learn to exploit in order to confirm its threshold of objectual definition and arrange a return to healthy normality. The text makes us understand all this by alluding to the literal and symbolic complementarity of male and female mediations.

Dry represents what is different from Wet but, for that very reason, has need of it, just as the female womb needs the male seed to become fertile; while Wet is the violent, possessive, and primarily male impulse and needs Dry to contain and define it. What the passage describes enigmatically, through the theme of sacrificial hierogamy, is a marriage rite in the broadest sense of the term. The cereals, associated with the image of the Dry, are the sign of a highly developed, protective culture with an imperative need to defend itself from the Wet while making use of it. Probably, the cereals are specified as dry to preempt thoughts arising of the alcoholic drinks made from them (like beer, well known since the Neolithic); nevertheless, they are a latent presence in the cereals, just as factors of dissolution and crisis remain latent in culture as a whole. If we want to remain in the mediated, objectual space of culture, then soberly dry nourishment must not be confused with dangerously intoxicating drinks that can induce trancelike states. Therefore, l. 278 expresses such a tensional passage, where Dionysus first appears in opposition to Demeter and just because of this is shown to be complementary to her.

The importance of alcohol, drugs, and hallucinogens in the history of orgiastic cults can hardly be exaggerated. The honey; the pomegranate, apple, and fig trees; the ivy, and grape vines present in Dionysianism provided for fermented liquors, and even when not especially for that supplied substances used in ritual.[11] Through the sacrificial rite, this circumstance converges and becomes one with the process of objectual and symbolic appropriation starting from the body and liquids of the mediatory victim, transformed magically by association into the sacramental *medium* of the victim's power to save:[12] the climactic liquid is blood, but we must think also of a sexual fluid like the male seed closely linked to the phallic aspect of Dionysian cults.[13] The expanded religious and ritual background of Tiresias's speech offers an opportunity to examine the sapiential references, providing further details to confirm my symbolic reading of the text and were probably borne in mind by Euripides as he composed the speech. The red thread is provided for us by the ritual liquids and beverages.

Certainly, it is the association with the orgiastic cults and bloody sacrifices of Dionysianism that makes Heraclitus condemn the predominance of the wet element in the human soul with extreme harshness. This emerges clearly from fragments of his where drunkenness is a symbol of addiction to foolishness and the pleasures of the flesh, and with particular force from one of his most incisive criticisms of religion:

> In vain they purify themselves
> with blood
> contaminating themselves
> as if someone, immersed in mud,
> were to wash with mud.[14]

For Heraclitus this triumph of the principle and experience of the Wet, of the liquid state, is equivalent to the most obtuse, distressing denial of the *logos*, denying, as it were, the mediatory and intermedial force that holds the entire universe together and enables men to remain connected to it and in turn connect with each other on a cognitive and moral level. The expression "with blood" can be joined grammatically to both "they purify themselves" and "contaminating themselves": with the first phrase it expresses the illusory expectation of the participants in these rites, and with the second it describes the real consequences of their foolish behavior. This ambiguous syntax is the sign of a noxious ritual ambiguity and reproduces a slithering effect, like the bloody mud in which the sacrificers sink and wallow in their ignorance that all things derive from Fire, ignorant, too, of the need to assimilate to its purifying, generative principle in order to comply with the law of the *kosmos* and become immortal by drying out one's soul, in accord with the cosmic-sapiential transformation of Orphic soteriology that is set out in the philosophy of Heraclitus.

Euripides is well aware of this critique and can be said to subscribe to its demystifying thesis since he has Tiresias admit implicitly that religious knowledge is inane; but he goes further than Heraclitus and investigates the underlying liturgical logic governing the marriage of Wet and Dry. On the other hand, Heraclitus would certainly not have excluded sacrifice or its symbolic and physical equivalents from his cosmic vision, since they can be traced back to the tensional structure of the *kosmos*, in which the Wet, understood as a religious form of blood-letting, is also seen to be necessary, exemplified by the "slaughtered by Ares" (*areiphatous*),[15] those who sacrifice their lives gloriously for their city and are rightly venerated by gods and men because they foster and confirm the axiological and ontological hierarchy of the entire universe. In Tiresias's speech, however, Euripides goes beyond Heraclitus's cosmic-soteriological arrangement; on the one hand, he returns to the most archaic roots of the mythical-ritual complementarity of Wet and Dry, and on the other, he deconstructs its philosophic-sapiential developments, represented most recently by the sophists.

To realize the full dramatic significance and the possible objective extent of the ritual infratext of *Bacchae* 274–85, we should remember, on my conjecture of omophagy as protohumanity's most archaic sacrifice, that the first sacrificial drink could have been the blood of the victim devoured alive. This blood was perceived physically and magically, and was even drunk by the liter, until the bodies of those caught up in the ecstatic frenzy of the rite were literally drenched in blood. And there is no lack of better-documented parallels in the classical world. We can gain some idea of the solid fact of this bloody ritual liquidity that Heraclitus and Euripides had in mind from the initiation to the cult of the Great Mother, Cybele. In this ritual the throat of a sacrificial bull was slit over a ditch, and about ten gallons of blood rained down on the initiate standing below. When he eventually climbed back out, completely covered in blood, he was worshipped as a god.[16] This is the usual symbolism of hierogamy. The bull represents the sacrificed god, and from the womb of the Earth previously fertilized by the blood, the initiate is born into a new life in the form of the divine child. We can understand how such overwhelming experiences led to an intense sense of the sacrificed victim's regenerative power and capacity to be reborn as a plant or animal, its power to reconstitute the objectual sphere of life in the ways displayed in the rite and explained by the myth. Any and every kind of being could arise from the blood, the flesh, and the divine sperm, and this symbolism must have been gradually enriched, alongside the prehistoric advent of gardening, husbandry, and agriculture.

Indeed, it is fair to assume that gardening, the first rudimentary form of cultivating wild plants, arose from magical-associative symbolic processes of this type, linked to the sacred value of vegetables growing in a place of ritual killing; these associations were then triggered, or intensified where they already existed, with the introduction of burial, suggesting analogies between the interment of bodies and planting seed in the ground, an ancient metaphor to be met again in the Gospel of John. I have no ambitions to establish a precise sequence here—it eludes us anyway and is not strictly necessary for my argument—but rather would make a claim for a mediatory center of signification that makes this signification conceivable one way or another, a center that must have interacted with previous methods of gathering and coordinated them in relation to the religious life of the group.[17] The combination of the mediatory character of the victim, corporeal and sexual objectuality, and the discovery that plants possess intermedial and objectual powers becomes particularly close in the mythical-ritual developments of agriculture following on the so-called Neolithic revolution, with an extremely intense retroaction on funerary symbolism. In Great Britain, prehistoric burials have been found where the ground has been ploughed over, with implications of a sexual nature as well that derive in any case from the symbolism of the bodies of victims sacrificed to this end, a fact corroborated by the frequent sacrifices of women and children in Britain's Neolithic culture.[18] The frequent human sacrifices linked to agricultural cycles, recorded by Frazer and memorably described by Cesare Pavese in his *Dialogues with Leucò*,[19] completely subvert Frazer's own naturalistic theories since, as he has the honesty to admit, they predate agriculture and were performed quite independently of vegetation cycles.

This does not mean that the objects made recognizable by sacrificial mediation were secondary or instrumental; on the contrary, it is their specific significance that conveys to us their importance and value and evidences the power to destroy and create, the power of life and death, of the divine mediator who established these objects and bestowed them on humankind. The agrarian and naturalistic aspects of the cult of Dionysus in plant (*dendrites*)[20] or animal form are a clue to the god's long mediatory history, and we can appreciate its full historic-religious import if those aspects are never severed from the sacrificial dynamism that produced them. And wine itself is proof of this: apparently associated with Dionysus from Mycenaean times, it is the symbol of blood and intoxication par excellence, to the point that crushing the grapes was popularly associated with dismemberment of the god.[21] Nothing remains of the harmless, conventional image of a god of drunken revelry, crowned with a wreath of vine leaves, swaying tipsily from side to side. Once again, as with the maenads, Euripides's text provides invaluable clues to the real archaic image of the god who was their leader.

The effects of Dionysus's wine are said to be uniquely beneficial in ll. 279–85 of Tiresias's speech, but this is because their benefit is steeped in drama, the result of confrontation and conflict, with human beings fighting among themselves and against the ever-apparent limits of human existence. That is why the images used to describe these beneficial effects are systematically ambiguous and never wholly reassure,[22] with a semantic density that reaches the heights of symbolic virtuosity. Wine is a painkiller and this is the work of Dionysus *Lyaios* (from the Greek verb λύω, I melt, I dissolve), but the Greek verb also indicates the real act of destroying (compare the English "dissolve"), whence the modern translation "painkiller". Wine brings sleep and oblivion (*lethe*), terms that describe the effects of drugs often mixed with the wine but are also metaphors for death. Such metaphors are by no means out of place here when we remember the real danger of poisoning represented by such potions as well as their possible associations with sacrifice, if not as ritual, at least as metaphor and metonym. Oblivion (*lethe*) thus becomes an allusion to the death of the sacrificial victim, to his physical and symbolic concealment in the tomb, to his mythical-ritual developments, and lastly to the danger always threatening the hard-won objectual sphere: we should not forget that Lethe is the Orphic spring of the forgetting that leads back to the cycle of Titanic violence. In ll. 277, 279, and 280, there is a pun on *brotous* (accusative plural), the mortals, and *botruos* (genitive singular), a bunch of grapes: one word is an anagram of the other, and they are arranged symmetrically, at line ends, with *botruos* in the middle (a play on words so visual as to be directed at those in the audience who might read the text of the tragedy afterward). The word βροτός, meaning a man destined to die, is equivalent to βρότος, blood. The juice of the grapes— βότρυς—audibly (and graphically) symbolizes their equivalence by its central position and their opening toward and closing after it. Immediately before this, in l. 261, Pentheus attacks the pleasure of the grape (*ganos botruos*) that reigns over the Dionysian feasts (*en daiti*); and we already know that γάνος is the *terminus technicus* for the wet glistening of blood in the Cretan caves. This is the hidden reason for wine being the only remedy, the one medicine for life's troubles, as Tiresias adds (l. 283). The term for medicine here is *pharmakon* and is of great significance since the masculine form, *pharmakos*, indicated the scapegoat in the Athenian Thargelia festival.

In view of the very close connection between the two words it is worth recalling this well-known yet controversial ritual, found in various versions throughout the Greek world and idealized or minimized by generations of scholars. Here, too, we find eloquent traces of hierogamy. In Athens, where it was celebrated each year but also in the event of some calamity requiring it, two persons who were deformed in some way or repulsive to look at were led through the streets of the city, each wearing a string of figs around his neck, one with white figs to represent the women, the other with black figs for the men. As they made their way along, they were beaten about the genitals with fig-tree branches and squills until, finally, they were driven out of the city and usually stoned to death, at least up to the classical age, in all likelihood.[23] It is worth remarking that these wretched outcasts were maintained at the state's expense: the *polis* obviously needed to have a fresh supply of victims ready to hand. The striking of the genitals, the bulbous figs, and the bulbs of squills suggest the scrotum and sex organs in general, while the act of striking the genitals reproduces hierogamic-sacrificial symbolism in ritual form and is a distant memory of dismemberments that began with the genitalia. The fig tree is particularly rich in symbolism, a concrete embodiment of several Dionysian symbols: the phalluses placed in the mystic basket (*cista mystica*) were made of fig wood; the leaves of the tree were called *thria* on account of their shape, referring to the three parts of the male genitals.[24] The central symbolic role of the fig tree in the *pharmakoi* ceremony led Frazer and others at the time to think of ancient fertility rituals associated with caprification, that is, the process for fertilizing male and female fig trees.[25] Indeed, from the context in which these traces of agrarian rites have been found we may safely assume that there were human representatives of the male and female trees as performers in these arboreal-sacrificial couplings and that they met an unhappy end, which is also suggested by the systematic nature of sexual symbolism associated with the plant. The strings of figs also refer to the polarizations of the sacral mediations which are evoked by the black/white pairing: whoever put on the necklace of figs was automatically fated to run through the whole spectrum of sacral mediations, until its oscillation finally ceased, in the completion of the fig-tree torture. The expulsion of the *pharmakoi*, the scapegoats, is *katharsis*, the purging of impurities, the signal that the objectual equilibrium on which the social world depended had been restored.

The notions of φαρμακός and φάρμακον are interchangeable, as Girard rightly insists, though failing to keep in mind the sinister figure of the φάρμακος, the poisoner, the sorcerer or witch. The *pharmakos-pharmakon* is poison and at the same time its antidote, the sacred that brings sickness and health, death and peace; it is—in modern words—the capacity to metabolize and completely transform the crisis into the regenerative drama of a mediation that brings salvation. This is why Dionysus is "poured out" (*spendetai*, l. 284) to the other gods, an expression that has an impressive correspondence with the *soma*, both a sacred beverage and a god in Hindu mythology.[26] A solid version of this same thought is expressed by Brutus in Shakespeare's *Julius Caesar*, corresponding so exactly, in fact, that it is as if Shakespeare had the very line from the *Bacchae* in mind: "Let's carve him as a dish fit for the gods."[27] Just as the image of carving, of deliberate cutting, is intended to suggest the idea of a sacrificial sharing-out, of a collective mediation to be restored on the basis of Caesar's dead body that would avoid a vulgar dismemberment, so the image of the Dionysus-wine being carefully poured out is meant to give the idea of fully achieved divine peacemaking. With tragic irony Shakespeare shows us the failure of the pseudo-ritual procedure wished by Brutus ("Let's be sacrificers, but not butchers, Caius"[28]), while Euripides's character still hopes to make it work, even though the tragic irony of events will prevent it.

The same thought will be developed by Georg Büchner who, in his drama *Dantons Tod*, makes Saint-Just pronounce the following sentence, referring to the next arrest of Danton and ingeniously translating Shakespeare: "We must bury his great body with decency, as priests, not as murderers [*wie Priester, nicht wie Mörder*]. We cannot tear it to pieces [*zerstükken*], it has to go down in the grave with all its members [*Glieder*]."[29] Saint-Just enigmatically alludes to the helpers and allies who represent Danton's political strength and have to die with him, but one understands that this is a more political translation of the same thought expressed by Shakespeare: the complete dismemberment is brought to dry perfection by the ancient image of burial, though this return to mother earth leaves the severed head of the guillotined visible on the surface and the Wet of blood floods on the scaffold of Revolution.

Ancient Greece still ignores these spectacular as well as dramatic developments. The blood poured out both from the Elizabethan conspirators and the French revolutionaries will provide a modern gloss to the evangelic verse:

"His blood be on us and on our children!" (Mt 27:25). In Euripides's drama the danger is not different, but still filtered through the scenic representation, not yet displayed on the stage of history. The Dionysiac world Tiresias is trying at any cost to restore shows us a more orderly way to deal with the problem: in order to keep the cultural space dry, unstained by blood, the liquid *symbolon* of the victim, the glistening wet *ganos*, must flow according to certain rules into the appropriate ritual containers capable of transforming its corporeal medium into life-bringing, fecundating liquid.

The expression "born [as] a god" (γεγώς from *gignesthai*, to become) underlines the fact that it is this that makes Dionysus a god, it is the generative nucleus of Dionysian theology. We are watching the reversal and completion of line 4: "my form from divine [*ek theou*] became mortal [*brotesian*]." After having become mortal from his being immortal—through his form, his μορφή—Dionysus from mortal becomes immortal: it is the theological and dramaturgic translation of Heraclitus's saying: "Immortals mortals, mortals immortals" (*athanatoi thnetoi, thnetoi athanatoi*).[30] But this time the context makes us understand, if we will, what is the internal engine of this *morphe* transforming from divine into human and from human into divine. It is a real morphogenesis of both human and divine, that is, the Hellenic version—blatantly misunderstood—of what two thousand years later will be the death of God. The powerful definition "born [as] a god" is by no means a purely literary image, since it expresses a knowledge both anthropological and theological, literally *theogonic* and *anthropogonic*. The union of Dionysus with human culture completes the ritual mediation leading to his birth as a god. If his blood was not poured into the ritual chalice, mortals could not live or ensure that the blood circulated all through their bodies and all through their society.

There is a certain difficulty about this analogy with the circulation of the blood that needs to be understood. Throughout antiquity, and up to the seventeenth century, there was ignorance as to how the blood really circulated in the body—surprising, if we think of what was achieved by medical science in the ancient world. However, the lacuna ceases to surprise if we remember the religious and ritual implications of any exploration in the medical field. A further reflection of this is the secondary role of anatomy in Greco-Roman medicine,[31] usually more concerned with animals and gods than with human beings. Greek and ancient culture was far too busy controlling and channeling the flow of blood—as evidenced in the philosophy of Heraclitus—to make it a subject of scientific study, so strong were its connotations and implications.

The pharmacological, prepharmaceutical theme dominates the entire *rhesis* addressed by Tiresias to the person who is about to become its passive hero. Toward the very end of the soothsayer's lengthy speech, Euripides has him confirm the double power of the *pharmakos-pharmakon* in a concise, effective phrase: "You are painfully mad [*mainei*]: no *pharmakon* / can cure your insanity but some *pharmakon* caused [*noseis*] it" (ll. 326–27). The verbs are revealing: *mainesthai*, used to denote the madness of Pasiphae and the maenads, and *nosein*, to fall ill or go mad, which almost seems to allude to Dionysus, a real *Dios nosos*, a madness sent by Zeus, with Zeus as its victim.[32] Pentheus is unwilling to recognize ritual remedies, and so the contamination of the objectual and mediatory crisis gradually swallows him up. The only solution is for him to become the *pharmakos*. In one way or the other the hierogamy speech will have its fulfillment. These words make such an impression on the Theban king that he refuses, horrified, to be touched by Cadmus. In this scene, as previously in the *Cretans*, accusations of sacrilege fly on both sides, corresponding to the fatal malfunctioning of the sacral mediations that ought to prevent this from happening.

Wine is a strategic theme, symbolically and ritually, and sees continual development all through the *Bacchae*. In the first stasimon the chorus makes reference to the banquets where wine flows and brings oblivion;[33] in the second, addressing the city of Thebes, the chorus swears by the "ecstasy [*charin*] in the shape of grapes [*botruode*] of Dionysus's vine."[34] When Dionysus destroys Pentheus's palace to escape from imprisonment there, he tells the king he has been freed by "the One who created for mortals [*brotois*] the grape-laden vine [*polybrotyn*]," punning once more on *botrys-brotos* but with the prefix *poly-* adding a highly pertinent collective nuance.[35] These passages can easily be misinterpreted as generic references to the most familiar and obvious aspect of Dionysianism, but they are in truth specific promises of bloody revenge.

Soon afterward we have our first hint of the final *sparagmos* when a breathless messenger arrives to report seeing the maenads in three groups running wild over Mount Cithaeron: neither "intoxicated with cups of wine and the loud music of flutes, / nor hunting Aphrodite in lonely places" (ll. 687–88), which contradicts what Pentheus had alleged. As the decisive action draws nearer, ritual instruments and concealing symbolism become superfluous—or rather, they become real—and Pentheus's interpretation of the Dionysian cult in sexual terms collapses. It might be said to be a quasi-psychoanalytical interpretation, not so very different from contemporary sexually based psychologism, eliminating what truth there is in Freud's theories in its attempt to exorcize the danger, on which depends the attainment of every human object starting with the sexual, by declaring the danger to be physiological and ubiquitous.

Pentheus's charges are strictly false; however, they reveal their truth when decoded symbolically. The maenads are effectively drunk but not with wine. The metaphor of wine, following a process already seen creatively in Heraclitus, becomes reality since the ritual medium is able to guarantee it, just as it can compromise or destroy it. This is what gives the maenads power not only to suckle wild beasts but to cause water, wine, milk, and honey to spring from the ground and from thyrsi. The Wet principle triumphs, gushing from the earth, from the female principle itself that had to preside over the Dry. All this is a consequence of blood's originating wetness. Blood dominates the end of the first account of the messenger: the blood of slaughtered cattle and, we may fairly assume, the blood of the children kidnapped in l. 754; and the blood licked by the serpents coiled round the maenads, a monstrous kind of suckling. Employing the basic metaphor, the messenger concludes: "without wine there is neither Aphrodite / nor any other pleasure for men" (ll. 773–74). Just as all pleasure is mediated by blood, so all control of pleasure is founded on the ritual control of blood. Following the messenger's words, Pentheus, increasingly under the spell of mediatory forces that he does not recognize, allows himself to be persuaded by Dionysus to follow him onto Cithaeron. From now on wine will not be needed: like the Cybelean ditch of initiation, the stage is verbally awash with the glistening blackness of blood.

We now must comment on the second part of Tiresias's *rhesis*, which though it appears a typical postmythical rationalization in fact contains the most spectacular allusions.

3. The Viscera of Lynching

The second part of Tiresias's speech (from l. 286) is even more interesting, if that is possible, since it takes us, in its usual allusive, concealing style, into the very penetralia of the sacrificial mediation, toward the originary nucleus of the mediatory hierogamy that enables culture to be born and live:

> And do you laugh at him just because he was sewn
> into Zeus's thigh [*meroi*]? Let me tell you the real story.
> After Zeus had rescued him from the lightning's fire,
> he took the divine child to Olympus,
> but Hera wanted to cast [*ekbalein*] him down from the sky.
> So Zeus devised a trick really worthy of a god.
> He broke off a part [*meros*] of the Heaven [*aitheros*] surrounding the Earth
> and gave it as hostage [*homeron*], abandoning it as Dionysus
> to Hera's rage; and in time
> the mortals [*brotoi*] said he was nourished in Zeus's thigh [*meroi*],
> changing the names around and inventing a tale [*logon*],
> because the god had once been hostage [*homereuse*] to the goddess Hera.[36]

This second sequence is even harder to decipher according to the usual interpretive criteria, so much so that past commentators have even wanted to delete these lines as incomprehensible, whereas they are undoubtedly authentic. Historical and religious unawareness easily results in bad philology, *pace* the holders of philological objectivity. Everything becomes clear and recognizable once we abandon the well-worn paths and take up the mediatory, sacrificial trail first blazed by Euripides. The passage encapsulates a brief history of sacrifice and its symbolic evolution. First, the allusion to Hera's anger is a direct reference to the mythology concerning Tiresias, as well as to the Titanic myth. Second, death by fire, represented by Semele struck dead by the lightning of Zeus's thunderbolt and related to the anthropophagic cookery of the Titans, is followed by death through casting the victim into space (the verb used is *ek-ballo*), where there is no longer any contact with the magically impure power of the *pharmakos*. At a later stage in the myth's evolution, to placate the fury of Hera, who comes to symbolize collective hatred generally, Zeus breaks off a part (μέρος) of the ether (i.e., the male principle of Heaven) for her to hold hostage (ὅμηρος).[37]

The mythographic image appears even more appropriate if we remember that philosophical theories of sexual reproduction, such as Aristotle's, linked it to the male's active role in gathering together the airy, intermedial element originating in the skies above and identified with *pneuma* or ether (so that we can speak also of a pneumatic dimension).[38] Tiresias's etiological account, however, presents us with a ritual context that is less cosmic and more sublunary, where the male's active role in generation is gained at the price of suffering the most savage sort of passivity. Here we have a clearer explanation of the myth of Tiresias and its dominant theme, castration and sexual reversal. *Meros* is the sacrificial part of the victim cut up and shared out, as the Moirai have already reminded us. The invention said to be "really worthy of a god" is sacrifice and the processes initiated by it, the processes of signification and of metaphoric and metonymic substitution. The hostage to Hera's fury is the *pars pro toto* for the group, first becoming the *symbolon* and then *pars pro toto* for the *symbolon* itself, the divine part, often the phallus, that was then transformed in the subsequent symbolic substitutions, the last of them being the tenth part of pleasure allocated to the male orgasm. The authentic sense of the apparently absurd birth from Zeus's thigh (μηρός) now becomes clear and helps to explain the Kumarbi motif of male pregnancy and delivery of divine children from various parts of the body after swallowing the genitals and sperm of a god: it is really a symbolic survivor of a very ancient act that we have met several times already, the dismemberment of the god-victim starting with the genitals. The Greek capacity of detecting and strengthening the inner rational structure of myth has an outstanding confirmation in the Hittite mythologem developed in Hesiod's *Theogony* and in other derived or connected myths such as the birth of Dionysus and Athena from different parts of Zeus's body. In fact, the shift from phallus to thigh, caused by their proximity,[39] finds a further version in the myth of Athena's birth from Zeus's head, one of Kumarbi's divine deliveries rationalized by Greek mythology in the birth of the goddess of wisdom, an expression of the superior Olympic order planned by the king of the gods. At the same time, the myth of Athena's birth keeps remembering the symbolic interchangeableness of the upper part of male genitals with the upper part of the body. Both the thigh (together with the close part of knee) and the head are the seat of male seed in the mythology and archaic theories on the body of Greek and other civilizations.[40]

Such symbolism, coming from previous cultural stages and Eastern influences, is likewise to be found in other cultures taking us even further East. There are particularly close correspondences to Vedic mythology and ritual. We find an analogous interchangeability between head and phallus in the horse sacrifice, given that the animal was suffocated (an act comparable to beheading) and that the king's chief queen had to take its phallus in order to mime a hierogamy.[41] The close link between the sexual male organ and thigh is widespread in the Indian mythology, to the point that a hymn of *Rig Veda* defines the phallus as "a boneless thigh,"[42] a symbolic and bodily correspondence that could not but involve the ceremonial and divine drink of the gods, the *soma*: the god that personifies this ritual beverage is born, in one of its many versions, from the thigh of the supreme god of heaven, Indra. The equivalence of *soma* and the divine sperm, its relationship with the sacred marriage of the king,[43] as well as its power of sacrificial intoxication support my interpretation. The convergence of Greek and Indian mythology no doubt indicates a distant time when both original peoples shared common rites and myths in the so-called Indo-European stage,[44] whereas the Hittite mythologem shows us a more complex example of less remote cultural influences starting from forgotten similarities.[45]

The myth of birth from a thigh subverts the ritual wedding scenario just outlined by Tiresias, since it covertly describes the most ancient form of hierogamy, the union of the group with its victim that generated the world. Thus we have the most radical explanation for Tiresias's castration-blindness, already encountered in the etiological myth concerning his disability. Like Shakespeare's Brutus and Büchner's revolutionaries, when faced with the impossible task of making butchery appear as ritual division or a triumphant burial, though it is more dramatic and visible in their case, Tiresias's attempt at persuasion defeats itself and starts to expose a little too much of the inner workings of the rite and of his own myth: to function properly, they need the drowsiness induced by wine and sleep, which he invokes in vain. The sense of Zeus's invocation to the god *dithyrambos*, later made by the chorus, is the originating hierogamy, the bare-handed collective sacrifice, the original lynching: "Come, twice born, enter my / male [*arsena*] womb [*nedyn*]" (ll. 526–27). The term νηδύς, the lower part of the abdomen, could hardly be clearer, and the term *arsen* or *arrhen* expresses the physical and generative aspect of masculinity, as its several derivations stress, including *arsenoma*, the male seed. Birth from Zeus's thigh represents the god's rising to new life from the lynching, recalled here by the symbolic double ("twice born") and the revelatory, hidden *symbolon* with which the lynching began. Zeus and Dionysus, like Indra and *soma*, were initially one figure, a single victim torn to pieces, beginning with his private parts and the liquid gushing out from them.

The explanation given by Tiresias appears to be no more than pseudo-rational punning, but the blind seer is really using precise, pertinent terms rooted in myth and anthropology, and his words are fulfilled in the course of the tragedy, secretly clarifying and obliquely revealing not only the Dionysian cult but also the Orphic procedure by *symbola*. The last line of the quote would seem to mark a sophistic explanation but, once we get the right clue, it exhibits on the contrary a much deeper etiology, a historical origin that is really an extraordinary result of Greek rationality. In fact, the "*tale*" (*logos*), the "fable" invented by men—that is, the original accusation blaming the victim—was to become the *logos* of reason and, in the tragedy, the "empty fable" of Pentheus and Dionysus. The interchangeable nature of *mythos* and *logos*, as the interchangeable sex of Tiresias, tells us that the hostage to which the seer refers is really the dismembered victim whose metamorphosis guaranteed the objectual world of culture and was used by the Orphics for their salvation. The μέρος-ὅμηρος-μηρός series continues in the last line, where the verb *homereuein*, to be hostage to, means primarily being united and agreed, that is, unanimous against the victim, in this case against Dionysus-Zeus. The semantic associations could continue: *homeros* is also a token, linking it to *symbolon* in the sense of a passport and evokes, lastly, the typical victimary figure of the blind man who became the poet par excellence for the Greeks and is personified in the tragedy by Tiresias.

The etymological associations and alliterative sound play continue relentlessly and clearly show that the ritual mechanism anatomized in this way cannot possibly function as before. Immediately after the passage analyzed, Tiresias adds that Dionysus has a "part" (*moira*) in Ares, that is to say, he is an inevitable element in the divine mediation of war, as the subsequent image of Dionysian panic routing an entire army shows, a sadly topical image at the time of the Peloponnesian War. It all depends on knowing how to use the right part of Dionysus,[46] the *mania*, the ecstatic, murderous madness, when it turns into *mantike*, the prophetic art, analogous to what happens in the episode in Plutarch describing the sacrifice made by Themistocles where the soothsayer's prophetic skill interprets and channels the Dionysian pressure coming from the Athenian army. Cadmus in his turn reminds his nephew of the fate, *moros*, of his other nephew, Actaeon,[47] the son of Autonoë, who had already been named and whose fate was to be torn to pieces by his own hounds, *omositoi*, devourers of living flesh, a fate indirectly evoked shortly before in the mythical associations of Tiresias. Actaeon's sacrificial *moros* becomes *moria*, contagious madness, the madness of which Pentheus accuses Cadmus when he refuses to be touched, and of which he himself is accused by Tiresias in l. 369: "Pentheus is really mad [*moros*] and talks like a madman [*mora*]."

Pentheus's reply to Cadmus is so severe because it is already charged with the sacrificial implications of what the seer has said: the metonymy of *pars pro toto* is about to descend on the Theban king, and consequently has to be defused by destroying its sapiential basis, its institutional credibility. When Pentheus gives the order to destroy the place where Tiresias prophesizes, he tells them to turn it upside down, already unwittingly using his opponent's technical terms. In l. 349 he uses the expression *ano kato* (above below), which takes on new resonance from the identical liturgical formula in the papyrus. "Above below" is the formula of the collective hierogamy and objectual crisis; Pentheus imagines that he can defy it but has to submit to it in the end. The two characters not only mirror each other but also become increasingly ineffective, drawing the threat of collective catastrophe ever nearer. The religious impotence of Tiresias is followed by Pentheus's political madness, in exactly the same way that the impotence of traditional cults and of the Greek ruling class brought on the disastrous Peloponnesian War, imitating the collective frenzy of the Athenian democracy. The expression "above below," with its social and liturgical connotations, is used by the chorus in l. 602 to threaten the subversive action of divine punishment—preceded in l. 601 by the term *anax* (ἄναξ/ἄνω κάτω) designating the god born in the *Anaktoron*—and is later twice used by the messenger in ll. 741 and 753 to describe the wild fury of the bacchantes in their first dress rehearsal for the *sparagmos*. And so, passing from a refusal induced by threats and by their actual carrying-out, we witness the gradual approach of the sacrificial convergence. In the epilogue, this closing-in on the chosen scapegoat represents the final fulfillment of Tiresias's hierogamy, with nothing left out, not even the arboreal symbolism that I mentioned in regard to the mediated, nonnaturalistic origins of agriculture.

The whole scene leading up to the *sparagmos* is dominated by the opposite extremes of above and below, Heaven and Earth (ll. 1063–85), summed up in a single gesture of Dionysus when he bends the highest branch of the fir tree-thyrsus in a semicircle down to the ground so that Pentheus can climb up. But when Pentheus is outlined against the sky (*aither*) at the top of the tree, one word predominates, *ano*, above; twice placed emphatically at line-ends, it makes Pentheus's role as victim chillingly clear. Confirmation that Euripides did not himself invent the detail of the tree comes from Frazer where he discusses the cult of Adonis-Attis transformed into a pine tree.[48] Various dismemberment rites have the victim hung from a tree before being torn to pieces, which explains why the Greek god of the *sparagmos* is also visualized as a tree. What is now taking place is the *anodos/kathodos* of the hierogamy, the third birth of Dionysus *dithyrambos*, and the metonymy comes to coincide with the metaphor: a part of Heaven is detached and sacrificed to Earth, to the ground where Pentheus will fall to be torn to pieces, to go down to Hades. Tiresias's prophecy is being fulfilled to the letter. After the orgiastic uproar, when the echoes of persecutory laughter die away, we find ourselves at the center of the labyrinth, as silent as the very center of an explosion.

The entire tragedy is a sort of cognitive *hieros gamos*, a Mysteries initiation into the secrets of sacrificial mediation, carried out with such precision by Euripides that it deserves to be called scientific, but this science differs from ours and for that reason has prepared the way for it. What we have here is a completely new display of metaritual and metamythological knowledge, conducting an indirect but constant critique of the initiatory knowledge of Orphism and Eleusis, and taking the double bind of myth and ritual, from which Euripides's own dramatic art originates, to its extreme consequences in terms of what can be represented or evoked. This will be our thread of Ariadne, our guide toward the final revelation, showing us the way through the labyrinth, obedient to its twists and turns, lying hidden in the words and events on stage and in the paradoxes that bring life and death to the characters, and accompanying their oscillatory motion, according to the principle of authorial impersonality already applied to the *Cretans*. Our next step in interpreting the *Bacchae*, and the knowledge concealed within, can only be to examine the character system, with its bearing on a theme already developed by Euripides in the *Hippolytus* and other tragedies, a theme explicitly presented at the beginning of the *Bacchae* by the seer who should be its best exponent: the nature of this knowledge itself.

6.

Sapiential Reflections in the *Bacchae*

1. Textual and Metatextual Knowledge

A general conclusion about Euripides's sources is at once evident: the fragments of the *Cretans* compared with the *Hippolytus*, and the text of the *Bacchae* even more, reveal thorough competence in Orphism, the Eleusinian Mysteries, and the more savage Dionysian rites underlying them. This knowledge on the part of Euripides is not a form of religious syncretism uncommitted to its content, nor an imaginative literary exercise, nor least of all skepticism of a sophistical or rationalistic kind. On the contrary, the scale, daring, and profundity on several levels of the symbolic representation in the tragedies denote a competent, consciously critical, and sustained effort based on hard thinking about the sapiential content of the Orphic and Mysteries tradition. The *Bacchae* is the culmination of this reflection, by which I do not mean that the double bind embedded in the themes and texts, which confers and takes away the meaning that is their life, has been completely explored (there is no modern demystification, which could, in the first place, claim a monopoly on exploring) but that it is probed and exploited with such skill that real knowledge comes to reflect on what is still obscure. And this strange knowledge regarding contradictory and cogent situations which we can refer to the modern concept of the double bind could not ignore the double bond binding its own knowledge. Once again, when talking about the double bind, the point of my analysis is not to put passive reliance on an all-embracing concept that passes description off as explanation—the one basic explanation from my standpoint is the mediation all the way back at the sacrificial event—but to utilize an analytical tool accurate enough to identify a working structure, an organizational and disorganizational matrix given its objectual direction or misdirection by a unique historical situation. In that systemic and retroacting though unresolved sense, the attribute of knowledge becomes the immaterial center of the *Bacchae*; around it the characters revolve and act, or think that they act, while its cognitive and operative superiority is guaranteed by *sophia* and the prestige associated with it in Greece. To understand the tragedy's sapiential message, we need to analyze this knowledge in its various conflicting appearances throughout the drama.

Nonetheless, this step cannot be made using a ready-to-hand descriptive, cataloguing criterion since in the first place it assumes some understanding or at least intuition of the knowledge or wisdom recognizable in the work as a whole and, naturally, in the writer who put it all together. Secondly, for those of us studying the tragedy with the indispensable tools of culture and history, the subject implies our clear awareness of the various hermeneutical wisdoms that have variously attempted over the centuries, in the long exegetical history of the *Bacchae*, to comment on and penetrate the mystery of this masterpiece. This means to say that we only come close to the knowledge at work in the *Bacchae* if we grasp how it is stratified, both inside and outside the text, multiplied and refracted, which evinces its centrality and structure, the creative paradox that reaffirms itself whether it is understood or is misunderstood and eliminated—while keeping in mind that the comprehension this permits is only partial since the work of interpretation is often a question of making adjustments, of deviating or retracing one's steps, at times enabling a solution to be perceived and reached precisely because these attempts initially denied it.

We will start by evaluating the author's knowledge, situated at the margin and at the center of the labyrinthine plot, like a silent Daedalus imprisoned in his maze of words and silences. We shall fail to understand the work fully if we simply identify Euripides with one or other of the characters. If we want the tragedy to speak to us, we must comply with its structure and bear in mind the principle of authorial impersonality, not some abstract and obvious principle but a gradual, hard-won achievement in the development of Greek theater. Naturally, there are oscillations, due not only to the author's unsettled, ambiguous position and the constant pressure on him to please the public but also to his attempts, opportunistic in character, to resolve the tragic text's typical tension in order to achieve a certain effect or advantage; it was, besides, always open to the author to reassert the paradoxical structure that made those attempts possible. What we call art is the unstable result of interaction between collective mediation factors and an individual response alert to them and expressing them. On the one hand, it recognizes and confirms them; on the other, it takes them by surprise and, at a certain level of artistic achievement, such as was reached in sophisticated Athenian circles, even opposes them.

This is the case with Athenian tragedy, so much so that we can characterize it as a distinct theatrical and dramatic mediation that was to reappear in different forms in modern times when the theater was reborn as an independent art, under the protection of Italian and European dynasties, rather than under the more conditioning auspices of a civic community and its religious and political mediations (a position of privilege anticipated in some small measure by Euripides, writing the *Bacchae* for the Macedonian court). In Greek tragic mediation the double-binding relationship of stimulus and blackmail between author and audience is already clearly recognizable, a relationship that the author must, at one and the same time, cultivate (to be a success) and challenge (to stimulate his own interest as well as others'). In this situation of mediatory and actual dependence, *captatio benevolentiae* can come to prevail, especially if it is a question of who comes out on top in the tragedy competitions. Sophocles and, still more, Aeschylus show considerable compromise with public taste, though they manage it quite wonderfully, maintaining a delicate balance between their cognitive inquiries and socially accepted values. This fragile trade-off reaches a breaking point in Euripides, as his lack of success in winning prizes reveals as well as the fact that he ended his days outside classical Greece; nevertheless, tragic impersonality in Greek theater reaches its maximum possible development in his work, that is, the instability governing and finally destroying the system is given its fullest expression.

Certainly, his work reveals occasional unevenness, due—we may suppose—to the difficulties of artistic expression, but the masterpieces of his maturity possess a representational and cognitive power unequaled for two thousand years, until Shakespearean tragedy replicates and develops it further. With Euripides, the power of tragic representation is finally displayed, the power of its intolerable and necessary paradox, as far as it was possible in Greece or, rather, *in limine*, on its cultural frontier marking the future. Adopting this principle of tragic impersonality—that is, of the distinctive artistic and cognitive features of tragic mediation as it was possible in Greece—we can make a rapid and instructive survey of the critical history of his masterpiece.

Failure to recognize the double-binding principle of tragic impersonality at work in the *Bacchae* has precipitated an unresolvable schism among the interpreters of the play. The one camp, Nietzsche among them, has held that Euripides recanted his previous criticism of traditional religion and made amends with the *Bacchae*, in which impiety is punished, as a sort of palinode; the other camp has held it was written to show the absurdity of traditional religion by exalting the figure of Pentheus. More recent commentary continues to be stalled in this opposition, with the refinement of taking sides with the bacchantes as representatives of one or another oppressed group, as for instance the populations of the third world or women as unjustly dominated by men.[1] For centuries, we may say, most commentators in their opposition to each other have unwittingly perpetuated in their interpretations the same double binds that bind the characters of the drama, which in turn has perpetuated their own cognitive blindness, of which they are both the victims and the perpetrators: there could not be a stronger proof for the interpretation I shall here put forward. And it should be added that the first interpretation to begin breaking down this barrier of false antinomies, showing them to coexist within a more complex, more oscillatory system, was set out by Girard in *Violence and the Sacred*.

But even here, in his determination to establish an anthropological truth too long denied, Girard fails to recognize the profundity of Euripides's attempts regarding the tragic doubles, and recognizes the tragic double bind but not Euripides's skill in manipulating it, his creative handling of it. Girard sees him as siding with the chorus in an attempt to resolve the doubles represented and is convinced that the voice of Euripides can surely be recognized expressing his ideas in the first stasimon, with its call to adopt the wisdom and faith of humble folk.[2] This does not mean that Euripides's personal position is foreign to this appeal, but not to differ polemically from the action on stage: there is no reason to hastily dismiss an attitude that has definite cognitive and moral value, and I shall come back to this point at the end of this whole study. Modern commentators, besides underrating the importance and implications of what the tragic text has to say, overlook its destructuring and constructive complexity, its ability to take apart the different levels running through the text and refashion them into a single symbolic web. Only exceptionally are Euripides's ideas filtered through the chorus—as we shall see in the *Alcestis*—or through other characters; and when it does occur, it follows much more organic and externalized rules of style and structure, in accordance with a system that had to be self-sufficient in order to work, or rather had to bow to laws that Euripides had no right to touch, whether to support or reject them. And just as the mythical-ritual logic on which tragedy drew asserted its autonomy only by realizing its heteronomy relative to the divine forces from which it derived, so only by showing himself as hetero-directed by this same logic could Euripides control it and gain independence, all the more penetrating for its being inconspicuous. If he had tried supinely to take sides with the chorus, as Girard states, Girard's own interpretation would not have been possible,[3] or rather, it would not have been supported by many sequences in Euripides, which in fact it is, while other important sequences remain the unmolested preserve of the text, unperceived by this theorist of rivalry and sacrifice as they fail to meet his expectations.

In *Violence and the Sacred* Girard has the means to explain the tragedy of the *Bacchae*, at least in part, but not to explain why he has to refer to it at such great length. The tragic inspiration that he so acutely recognizes in the play should at least weaken to some degree in passages where, as he sees it, Euripides is attempting sacrificial reconciliation. However, the first stasimon, which should make plain his ideological stance, is no less "inspired" than the others. Indeed, it is perfectly successful in communicating to the reader-spectator the illusion of the chorus as a character capable of finding a solution that subsequent events, as they unfold, will destroy. Faced with the alarming and contaminating scale of doubles proliferating in the text, Girard's sifting analysis must find some solid basis and defining distinctions, must endeavor to pin down what Euripides leaves wide open with a disorientating effect, and attributes to him a desire for a sacrificial rearrangement that the conclusion of the tragedy substantially refutes. On the other hand, if Girard had not resorted to simplifications of this textual and theoretical kind, he could never have isolated the difference between Dionysus and Christ, the pivotal point of his thinking that takes Nietzsche's distinction and turns it upside down, most illuminatingly but also most inadequately because overconditioned by the objectual negation that inspired the comparison, and holding too closely to an apologetic design, compelled as such to deny independent existence to the history that it wants to explain. For these reasons the image of Euripides presented in *Violence and the Sacred* is incisive but one-sided and incomplete: if Euripides were just as Girard describes him, Nietzsche would never have damned the author of the *Bacchae* as he did. The theorist of the victim and the theorist of the superman, from their opposing fronts, attempt in the end to block the oscillation, the reversibility, that Euripides, on the contrary, fosters; and both end by attributing to him the same sacrificial recantation, one approving of it, the other rejecting it. This outcome is an eloquent sign of what must be done to free the analysis and restore the context needed for it to proceed without becoming enmeshed in modern interpretive schemes that reveal their usefulness only when seen within the historical period to which they belong.

We now possess sufficient pointers to decipher the role of *sophia* in the tragedy, with the various levels it comes to occupy as it is played by the characters and plays them in turn, until it finally destroys them. Ancient knowledge is a game whose secret is circular reversibility, such as appears in the unfolding tragedy, but it also governs the highest philosophical knowledge, the knowledge that confronts the enigma shared with tragedy: ushered in by impressive and ferocious but subtle distinctions, Greek knowledge thematizes and lays them bare as powerfully as it first established them. Dominating everything is a game played by many players with their differing levels of skill and bravura though none possess the rules of the game or know the result. We are still moving in the area of Dionysus's toys—indeed, we have never left it.

It is enough just to see Euripides in his real, imperfectly transcendental, position, in his double bond of binder bound, for the tragedy's rotating, reversible structure to unwind, along with the horizontal logic of sacrificial substitution that produced it, toward which it tends irresistibly, changing it, partly at least, into cognitive substitution. On the one hand, Euripides's own views are obviously not those of the characters: not the ambiguous, odious cruelty of Dionysus, the ferocious mysticism of the chorus of bacchantes, the opportunistic piety of Cadmus and Tiresias, or Pentheus's rationalistic blindness. On the other hand, it is the character system, left to itself by the nonapparent mediator who set it up, that reveals its nature as representation that imprisons in itself the representing no less than the represented while the fidelity with which it represents its own functioning redeems it and provides its ultimate cognitive value, identifiable in each element of the representational system no less than in the whole formed by its elements.

All the characters' moves are orchestrated to achieve an end greater than their individual parts, attaining complete expression only within the overall symbolic scheme, where all the countless details scattered throughout the text take on their full significance with revelatory effect. This overall narrative and imaginal scheme, this labyrinth of reticence and signs, speaks to us in an encoded language of something that underlies all representations; and since it is encoded, it moves them gently from within in a process of persistent allusion to a mediatory content that is artistically effective to the extent that it fails to mediate and consequently becomes more manifest the more it is denied, the more it fails to pursue its objectual goal. This foundational but destabilizing content that determines the relationship established by tragic knowledge with the mythical-ritual knowledge from which it originated is the preserve of the wise, *in primis* of the tragic author, but it is only accessible in the disorienting ways of a mediation that fails to mediate, of an objectuality without an object, of a double bind that permits and prevents knowledge.

Knowledge hangs over the characters like a sort of ontological prerequisite: it is only in relation to knowledge that they can define themselves and assert their personal identities. All the characters invoke knowledge in turn; each identifying it with his own self and accusing the others of having a false and perverted image of it.[4] Each bears his own truth, with its consequent language, both fulfilled and refuted within the overall revelation of events, as we have already seen in the quarrel between Minos and Pasiphae. This means that each character in himself has only his own knowledge, his own *logos*, and is unable to arrive at the fuller knowledge that would come from comparing the partial knowledges that claim the field. All the players in this game are exclusively themselves, and each expects his own truth to subsume and cancel all the others: from this comes their tragic nature, their being the tools of a knowledge defining them because it surpasses them, and of a truth fulfilling them because it blinds them. But not even the author, in his presiding position over the system, possesses the whole truth of the system: its paradoxical nature and the reciprocal implications of its elements certainly imply that something of the author's knowledge remains in the individual characters, and vice versa. Impartiality and complicity combine, intertwine, reinforce, and cancel each other out according to circumstances. At a higher level the author shares in his characters' cognitive paradox, while at a lower level, their knowledge is fallacious but partly real. It is because they are partly right that the traditional theories about the characters in the *Bacchae* are wrong. Thus Girard is not entirely wrong to perceive something of the author in the chorus but makes the mistake of taking a fixed perch in the spectrum of the text's vibrations and resonances as orchestrated by Euripides.

We will now look at the principal examples of *sophia* and *logos*, all equally necessary and all equally inadequate, manifested at different levels by the various characters in the tragic *fabula*. A fascinating and sinister gallery of portraits unfolds before our eyes.

2. The Wheel of the Characters

Firstly, there is the knowledge of Pentheus, the character that attracts our attention more than any other on account of his stubbornness and the horrifying fate awaiting him as punishment for it. His knowledge is all one with the vaunted self-sufficiency of the *polis*, of its institutions and mediations, hard-won in a conscious historical process, conscious, too, of its achievements. It might even be said that the Theban king's claim to speak with authority concerning knowledge represents that wholly human rationality determined to see only what is in what is, in line with the clear-sighted realism characteristic of the Athenian elite in the second half of the fifth century.[5] Translating Georg Wilhelm Friedrich Hegel into Greek-Athenian terms: what is rational is real, what is real is rational. That might well be Pentheus's motto; his rationality is the rationality of power, of self-control and control over others, of a planning, organizing force that punishes any deviation. What can be clearly recognized, then, as we look into this character, is the Athenian illusion of self-sufficiency in the time of Pericles, the illusion of a certain sophistical rationalism, in its more practical, public aspect at least. Virtually, this is already an Enlightenment-type pretention to dominate the doubles of violence by means of the *logos* of law and reason.

A further parallel, passing through Christianity's dislocating and dissociating filter, can be drawn with contemporary European history, under the illusion that the violence about to convulse the continent could be contained by reason and science. Europe's fate, with its blend of awareness and blindness, was anticipated by Nietzsche in his prophetic *mania* and contemplated by Thomas Mann with objectivity but also with a sense of involvement. And the *Bacchae* together with its unfortunate protagonist do not fail to interact with Mann's work. There is a visible and intentional parallel between Euripides's Pentheus and the great writer Gustav von Aschenbach, the main character and autobiographical projection in Mann's novel *Death in Venice*. Aschenbach is seduced by the beauty of the young Tadzio, and is finally turned upside down by the unstoppable crisis of his ordered world, a crisis represented by the epidemic of cholera, coming from India like Dionysus,[6] and by the "frightful dream" of "the god stranger" ("*Der fremde Gott!*" as the frightened and excited dreamer calls him)[7] that culminates in an omophagic ritual foreshadowing the imminent destiny of the protagonist and his epoch. The analogies with Pentheus are interiorized in the modern mode, but find another correspondence in a degrading disguise, given that in the attempt to attract Tadzio Aschenbach grotesquely tries to look younger with clothing and makeup, dying in this attire while staring at the unattainable youth transformed into a "pallid and sweet psychagogue."[8] *Death in Venice* anticipates the collective drama developed by *The Magic Mountain* into a more historical and choral arrangement, a further step in the *descensus ad inferos* later resumed in *Doktor Faustus* under the pressure of the new catastrophe of the Second World War.

Mann's modern Pentheus has an unmistakably intrapsychic and desiderative accent, not to mention a guilty conscience of fully Christian descent, although both characters patently belong to a wider historical process to which we belong as well. Pentheus remains a man on the ancient model, living in a world of sacred mediations dominated by precepts and prohibitions, and reacts to them with unconsciously analogous logic, and in this objective, external manner he is swiftly infected and overwhelmed. Within these limits, and thanks to the representational space they make possible, Dionysus's opponent can well represent the human illusion of independence from religion, of enjoying a large degree of freedom in regard to divine mediations that he thinks he does not need. More than anything else, this was an Athenian illusion, the arrogance (*hybris*) of a ruling class for whom whatever would not fit into the defining, mandatory circle of a human totality set on mediating itself, on being its own object, had to be thrown out, crushed. Euripides must have been familiar with this attitude, just as it is evoked by Plato in the characters of Callicles in the *Gorgias* and Thrasymachus in the *Republic*.

Consequently, Pentheus's *logos* is energetic, bold, and imperious. Images of punishment and exemplary retaliation abound: his iron nets to capture the maenads with (ll. 231–32), Dionysus's severed head (l. 241), and the stoning meant to give the Stranger a taste of a bitter bacchic orgy (l. 357). But it is the excessive self-assurance of his speeches that betrays his debilitating one-sidedness and essential madness, as becomes apparent in the erotic ambiguity of the dialogue with his antagonist in chains, which evinces the unrecognized fragility of his social and sexual role. Like the Athenian demagogues, and the sophists attacked by Plato, he is under the illusion of being able to control the violence at the base of political power, which can actually rebound at any time against those that use it. The Theban king proudly asserts himself in images of punishment and the use of force, but they are just so many anticipations of his own imminent fate: the nets are the ones he will be captured in, stoning to death is to be his fate on top of the fir tree-thyrsus, and the severed head will be his own. From the very beginning, Pentheus's words have unsuspected double meanings, their dramatic effect gradually increasing as the end approaches, right up to the last nightmarish scene, the last stichomythia, the final confrontation in alternate lines of verse between the god and himself. His one-sided rationality, only willing to see appearances, is punished with hallucination, the obsessive vision of doubles whose existence he has stubbornly denied up to that point. Besides the striking parallel to Nietzsche's insanity, it also calls to mind the self-destructive frenzy, the objectual collapse, spreading like wildfire through Europe in the summer of 1914 and, if we stay in Euripides's time, the civic conditions familiar to him, the rash of persecutions and trials in Athens and the hardening of social and political relations, leading to a power collapse within the city before spreading abroad. And this fitting parallel to the decline of the most knowledgeable and ambitious Hellenic *polis* provides a glimpse of how things appeared to an onlooker from the distant kingdom of Macedonia, unlikely not to have felt a touch of political vindication at these terribly instructive events.

Both those who refuse the doubles tackled by ritual mediations and those who think that they can use them as they please are condemned to repeat and embody them, becoming the instruments of their triumph. Pentheus sees two suns, two Thebeses, and Dionysus appears to him with the monstrous, revelatory features of a bull.[9] The manifestations of the god, so systematically rejected, now take revenge on their opponent with ruthless symmetry. His desire for domination is now revealed for what it really is, a mad dream of omnipotence: "Do you think I could carry the crags of Cithaeron / on my shoulders [*omois*], together with the bacchantes?" (ll. 945–46). His delirious rationality translates into crazy technical details: "Shall we take levers? Or will I have to raise Cithaeron with my own hands, / putting my shoulders [*omon*] or arms under the peaks [*koryphais*]?" (ll. 949–50). Pentheus has named the parts of the body that his own slaughter will start with: the word ὦμος, shoulder, is used twice. Cithaeron with its Nymphs and maenads will fall on the young, arrogant king of Thebes, in a play of ambivalences and associations that form a prelude to the passage about the doubles and Dionysus in the shape of a bull: Pentheus's arms and shoulders will end up beneath the peaks, that is, beneath the heads of the bacchantes.[10] In the grip of the effects of the objectual destruction that ritual was supposed to canalize but now promotes, Pentheus was never closer to the truth, as Dionysus sarcastically points out. He is a double unaware of his nature as a double. This disastrous, constitutional blindness seals his fate: "You don't know what you are living for or what you are doing, much less who you are," Dionysus tells him at their first encounter.[11] From this blindness comes the fascination with his adversary, now definable in Girard's mimetic terms, an ever-growing fascination that finally leads to his downfall and the restoration of his role as king-victim.

From their first appearance, Cadmus and Tiresias define themselves repeatedly as wise men, as if needing to convince themselves.[12] They defend religious conservatism at all costs, affirming, on Cadmus's cue, that man should not despise the gods (l. 199) or—and this is Tiresias's—should not dare to say a word against "the fatherland traditions, for a long time handed down" (l. 201). They speak the language of reasonableness, common sense, and well-balanced, scrupulous prudence. Tiresias, as we saw in his speech about hierogamy, undoubtedly represents the peak of religious and liturgical knowledge associated with a seemingly authoritative, consolidated mediatory tradition. But this is a complete illusion. The mediations on which he relies are now unable to ensure the promised object, to found the objectual world at one time guaranteed by them. To see this, we need only glance over the mythical-ritual *rhesis* delivered by Tiresias as he endeavors to persuade Pentheus to give up his impious plans.

His skillful explanation of the birth from Zeus's thigh attempts to defend the religious tradition against the rationalistic criticism that the young king of Thebes has adopted as his own. The explanation represents not so much a philosophical rationalization as the rationalization that was made possible by the myth, indeed *was* the myth, and was the origin of philosophy. Tiresias demonstrates great knowledge of the symbolic and imaginal aspects of myth and ritual; on the other hand, he is unwilling to see their ultimate, literal origin, which nevertheless definitely transpires with irrepressible logic from his own words. In this way, he appears as the classic figure of the short-sighted, conservative priest who fails to realize that by willfully insisting on the tradition he shows it to have a different meaning, besides showing its impotence to mediate objectual reality, the community's most urgent need. As a prophet he ought to channel the Dionysian *mania* into ritual, but he knows both too much and too little to do this, and although he clearly sees Pentheus's mistake, he is unable to remedy it through *peitho*, persuasion, pointlessly telling him that power, *kratos*, by itself has no *dynamis*, no real mediatory force among men, and provides no objectual impetus.[13]

Tiresias is right: the word *kratos* indicates strength not in a physical sense but deriving from superiority, prevalence, so that it remains ambiguous and dependent upon fortune,[14] and therefore in need of an external and superior reason that can give it legitimacy and make it *dikaios*, just. It is precisely the situation of Pentheus, and yet Tiresias himself is desperately in search of a superior reason transforming *kratos* in mediation. His own defense is actually inspired by a secret defenselessness, so that it is emptied out and made profoundly contradictory, as we see from his arguing that the *new* divinity should be venerated according to the ancestral cults as handed down intact from time immemorial. What the blind seer is unwilling to see is that the new god has his roots in the tradition precisely because he displays *kratos* (i.e., prevailing force) to a completely unprecedented degree. The tradition transfigured *kratos*, thrusting ahead with it as long as it retained objectual value, but the contradiction between startling innovation and atavistic confirmation effectively means the breakdown of this life-restoring capacity, the failure of this transformative metabolism; the rift appears irreparable, as plain and simple destruction. In this fashion, the ambivalent force of *kratos*, rather than becoming *dike*, justice, degenerates into *bia*, the pure, brutal violence that is the factional *stasis* of civil war described so implacably by Thucydides.

Tiresias and Cadmus who accompanies him no longer accord to the violence associated with the sacred mediations any value as objectual redemption, and so their warnings turn out to be simply threats, absolutely powerless to convince and persuade since they end up confirming the antiobjectual destruction of which the king of Thebes accuses the cult of Dionysus. Their religious conservatism is thus exposed as a flimsy ideological shield, and as complete impotence, a debility mercilessly underlined by their advanced age and Tiresias's infirmity. When they first appear, they are in the grip of a frenzied illusion of youthfulness induced by Dionysian arousal, but in the end they have to hold each other up because "it's not nice for two old men to fall over."[15] They are too deeply conditioned by violence to be aware of it, and yet too aware to get fully involved in the Dionysian frenzy, which amounts to saying that their position lacks the ecstatic mean that would allow the two extremes to come together generatively and make the divine *ekstasis* the prerequisite for consciousness rather than its antithesis. They steer a middle course too lukewarm and calculated to be effective either way. Not by chance, in giving his final advice, part paternal and part pathetic, to his grandson, Cadmus asserts his belief in the new god although it is not true, lying out of convenience (ll. 334–35). The wisdom of Cadmus and Tiresias goes no further than hypocritical devotion; no longer knowing how to channel and justify its own violence, it projects it outside in an unrelated fashion as an end in itself, externalizes it in a scheme of mechanical retribution, blaming it all on the imminent scapegoat. Cadmus's paternally opportunistic advice is followed by Tiresias's openly retaliating answer.

This difference of emphasis also corresponds to the characters' differing functions. Once the function of *memento* assigned to Tiresias by Euripides has been fulfilled, there is no longer any need for him to take an active part in the story. Cadmus, on the contrary, is a more ambiguous and complex figure. Above all, he is afraid, a human state of mind that motivates his words and actions. With masterly irony Euripides underscores the clumsy artfulness of the *pietas* of Cadmus. He has Cadmus ask Tiresias whether they should go to Cithaeron in a chariot, a real parody of his royal attributes and fated to come true at the end of the story when Cadmus is condemned to drive a chariot and command a barbarian army. Then, together with his spouse Harmony, he is transformed into a monstrous serpent, a most fitting punishment for the founder of the dragon breed and for the hierogamy of the labyrinth.[16] Cadmus can be seen as a typical, civilized bourgeois[17] of the sort Euripides might have encountered in contemporary Athenian society, ignorant of his own origins, blissfully convinced that civilization is a calm and peaceful affair where you get along quite nicely by observing certain rules of behavior, the less effort it costs the better. In this respect he also fits the pattern of certain humanists, then and now, who consider violence to be always the result of unreasonable behavior; in the meantime, while they refuse to see its causes, this violence completely conditions and finally overwhelms them. And so, to start with, the god punishes Cadmus by bringing him face-to-face with the horror that, in his superficial way, he thought could be avoided; with this a note of humanity comes to prevail, previously obscured by the grotesque, horrendous aspects of the *fabula*. Immediately following the *sparagmos* on Cithaeron, Pentheus's grandfather gathers up his wretched remains scattered over the mountainside; and while this provides fitting retaliation for the illusory, bankrupt nature of his wisdom, it is also the first evidence of a human *pietas*, no longer ideological, to come out of the collective catastrophe. What brings Agave to her senses and induces her to gaze at the heavens, a symbol of the transfigured victim, is Cadmus's pityingly lucid, horrified look; and that restores greatness and truth to the character, though it coincides with his total defeat, confirmed at the end of the play by his merciless punishment.[18]

The character of Agave merits separate treatment, starting from her dialogue with Cadmus, and this would seem a suitable point to look at it in detail. It is already obvious that her function is to conclude, but she not only closes the story as a whole, at first by gesture and finally by her words, but also her character marks the furthermost point reached in tragedy's reflection on itself, a reflection spurred by the tragic wisdom sustaining the entire system. It is only right therefore that she should close the chapter, thereby opening the extreme perspective offered by Euripides's final period, with his courageous critique of religious mediations, now ineffectual though the objectual need that they once fulfilled still remains, and his search for a different transcendence to redeem and save humanity rather than destroy it like a plaything.

As compared to the human, defeated suffering of the scene between Cadmus and Agave, the tone of the chorus of bacchantes is very different as they boast of sanctifying their life, not unlike the Idaean initiates. In the fourth stasimon, the opposition of the human knowledge— τὸ σοφὸν—with *sophia*, real knowledge (i.e., knowledge of divine things) seems to be complete and resumes the utterance made by Tiresias to Cadmus:

> I don't envy knowledge [*to sophon*];
> I pursue other things, that are great
> and manifest [*phanera*]: we are brought to the best [*ta kala*]
> by holy living day and night,
> keeping ourselves pure, and by worshipping
> the gods, disdaining unjust customs.

The refrain of the stasimon does not leave room for misunderstandings about "the things . . . great / and manifest" in which the chorus takes pleasure:

> That manifest [*phaneros*] justice should come with a sword,
> and pierce right through the throat
> of the ungodly unholy outlaw offspring
> of Echion, born of the Earth.[19]

There is a brutal opposition between what is "manifest," as coming from the god and imposing itself with performative immediacy, and the *sophon* that was that of high Athenian culture with its rational and humanizing demands, which a great gulf divided from the archaic inhumanity of the ongoing war. The Dionysian chorus has arguments much more convincing than Tiresias's to go against the *sophon* of Athenian philosophers and intelligentsia, and applies the opposition, already proclaimed in the first stasimon, between that vain intellectual knowledge and the true *sophia*: "Knowledge [*sophon*] is not wisdom [*sophia*], / the thinking [*phronein*] of things that are not mortal [*me thneta*]" (ll. 395–96). We will not understand the passage if we do not grasp the intensive and realistic meaning of such *phronein*, which by no means counters an already defined and numinous sphere of the immortals over against the sphere of mortals, but focuses on the ceaseless transposition between mortals and immortals, immortals and mortals.

Thinking, for the ritual circle of immortals and mortals, is not a mere intellectual process, it is an experience: the rite has to be lived before being thought of, and it is this precedence that feeds thinking and transforms it into a *sophia* bestowed by the god. The wisdom of the chorus is the numinous wisdom of the god-possessed (*entheoi*), their experience described in exceptionally precise, insightful terms. It is knowledge of a mystical and disturbing kind, ranging from complete passivity—when the maenad is without her god she is painfully "alone, forsaken" (l. 609)—to an ecstatic, all-powerful frenzy after metamorphosis into the god has taken place. The relationship is one of total dependence and total adoration revealing, from within, the full telluric force of the archaic cults and of the still earlier primordial ecstatic event. The worshiper lives only in the presence of his god; truth for him is a living, vibrant, cruel presence, an event that happens, comes to him, and saves him. The chorus, then, is speaking the language of the most savage, most originary mediation, in which the word appears as divine power, hierophany and manifestation of the *sacrum* and of the *sacrosanctum* of the Idaean initiates. Images and metaphors all become terribly real: reality itself is a metaphor for the god, the maenad a metaphor for Dionysus. Pentheus is fated to die simply because his death is evoked and described. His head is already severed, his throat slit from side to side solely because the god-possessed have spoken the word that is power, and sung their chant that is strength. It seems the difference between the maenads' *enthysiasmos* and the abstract, impotent conservatism of Tiresias and Cadmus could not be more pronounced, since the mediation of the divinity is now totally experienced and stated by the former, and all contradiction between startling innovation and ancestral foundation seems to have disappeared, since the sudden appearance of

Dionysus coincides with the manifesting of a primordial truth, radically new because radically old, the final outcome because it was the first. Yet what is missing is the essential, teleological aspect of every sacrificial mediation: the objectual restoration, the rebirth of life and the world. The only object that the *choros* manages to evoke, together with the theophanic vision of the god, is the ferocious destruction of Pentheus and the city that he represents, and that vision clearly coincides with the scene of omophagy, with the "ecstasy of flesh devoured alive" (l. 139), the emotional and ritual heart presented immediately, and traumatically, in the parodos. So the mediation of the chorus does not mediate, and the flesh and blood of the victim-god do not become the medium of anything or act as a bridge toward an object, a human reality restored to itself complete and strengthened, as they did in the primeval experience of physical, magical sharing, as reconstructed from Robertson Smith's scene of the totemic meal. The *choros* does not therefore present the solution to the crisis but instead causes it to penetrate into the experience of the source that was meant to resolve the crisis by ritualizing it. Here we have theophanic mediation imploding and then exploding, like a volcano where the pressure in the incandescent chamber underground builds up catastrophically before the final incandescent eruption. Once we understand this, we also realize that the unanimity displayed by the bacchantes in their claims to fusion with the god is nothing but a fanatical mask covering a fatally double unity, a double nature that seeks to reach the One while its every word and gesture would dismember and irreparably destroy it.

The language of the chorus calls for obedience and at the same time reveals the antiobjectual horror of its mysticism, through which the theophany becomes a kratophany and which in turn becomes a manifestation of naked violence, converging implosively to destroy the very notion of *phainesthai*, the manifesting of the divine that brought the world into being. Once it is noticed, the canker of doubleness is felt to be present in every word spoken by the *choros*, thus eating away and undermining all its declarations of oneness with the divine, all pretense to monolatry. What the chorus is doing is essentially blackmail, and the implicit rationality of blackmail conflicts disastrously with the mystical enthusiasm declared by its orgiastic companions. Radicalized to excess, the Dionysian representation can no longer reconfirm itself and it is this very impotence that becomes the definitive target for the fury of the chorus. The duplicity and multiplicity that should have been transcended in the theophanic unity of the rite reappear in the double of the chorus, the group of maenads, who unintentionally wreak vengeance on Pentheus: Theban women transformed into avenging Erinyes without their realizing it, who discover what they have done afterward, utterly disoriented and emptied out. Ternary symbolism reappears in the three groups of Theban bacchantes and in the three stages of the murder of Pentheus,[20] but the regenerative power is no longer there, nor the transitive circularity with the divine that it should symbolize and promote. In its one-sided justification without an object or a purpose, no *obiectum*, the cult is self-defeating. The unwilling maenads repudiate in horror what they have done, while the real ones confusedly rehearse their motives in a way that carries no authority now and is without *peitho*. There is no final reassembling of the *symbolon*, of the dismembered, re-membered object. And so the violent unity pursued by the chorus turns out to be no less double and unsuccessful than the knowledge defining the other figures in the tragedy. On the one hand, the chorus's essential doubling, mediated and further filtered through the accounts of the maenads' activities, maintains the last representational concealments, but on the other it makes the group violence of the chorus directly visible, the ascetic hypocrisy of the sons of Ida laid bare. The investigation of the collective sacral mediations at the origin of tragedy already seen in the *Cretans* thus comes to its contradictory conclusion, thanks to and within the limits of the system's centrifugal oscillation. This expresses and proclaims the failure of the divine mediation itself, that is—the wavering hub at the center of all power and knowledge—at the very moment of its affirmation and triumph.

3. The Anobjectual Mediation of the God

The question of Dionysus is the most complex of all; he is both the mediatory peak of the *fabula* devoted to him and an abyss destroying all mediation. The twofold character of sacrificial mediation and knowledge about it is made explicit in him and speaks with an insolent voice. He is the divinization of the objectual crisis and of the double bind of tragedy that reveals it to us once it is shown to be uncontrollable, with its oscillatory, destructive nature completely realized. He is a divine mediation that no longer serves its purpose and yet is maintained with all its virulence as a theogonic event, to which it is religiously and mediatorily so close, indeed inseparable. It would be only a slight exaggeration to say that Euripides's Dionysus is the living death of God, unable to completely take the form of a historical event because he lacks Christian historicization, the watershed experience of the death of the son of God and of a resurrection that becomes a divine and human event. Instead, in the Dionysus as portrayed in the *Bacchae* the human is involved and merged with the divine in an inextricable double bond; they call up and cancel each other, completing the theological implosion already brought out by the chorus. The character in Euripides is a god no longer able to die and be born again in his divine form, who humanizes himself in order to dehumanize himself to make humans die and not be reborn, thereby reaffirming himself. But the price is to destroy his world and the conditions of his cult: it is a theogony without a birth and a birth without a god, a theology without a transitive, object-giving *logos*; its *logos* has become an absconding god, in an overturned, distorted manner unable to detach itself from its divine matrix, and so transforms the god himself into a persecutory daemon, into the daemon of persecution.

For this reason, his language is proudly absolute from the very start, when the divinity appears in person (and *persona* since it is a tragic mask) to set the whole tragedy in motion with a sort of sensational *ex machina*. At the same time, it is the deceptive, evasive language of human and divine disguise, of the double nature that becomes god and man without being able to join the two: Dionysus is the divinity who shows himself to mortals but disguises himself as a human being. He comes from afar, by distant exotic ways, and yet he is the god of total presence, of absolute proximity. Through such deceit he exacts full, unconditional surrender: it is impossible to struggle against him (*theomachein*[21]); the least sign of resistance may call down the most terrible punishment. The city of Thebes dares to doubt his divine nature and is made an example of, while Pentheus, the victim-king, man of the city and of suffering, is made its scapegoat. Right from the start, the peremptoriness of the language of Dionysus is the peremptoriness of his double nature, cosmically brutal and, in reality, humanly vulnerable.[22] Fire and Water, Heaven and Earth, Life and Death attended the birth of the *dithyrambos* god: he is the living embodiment of all aspects of the originary hierogamy, and that has its repercussions on imminent events in a way that is even too human. The initial opposition, the motive force behind the whole tragedy, appears in the very first line, in the contrast between Heaven and Earth: "In the Theban *land* I did come. It's me, *Zeus*'s son [i.e., of the Uranic god par excellence]." The cosmic totality represented by his "morphogenetic" birth, and proudly announced in the prologue, is actually fractured and death-bearing, dominated as it is by an unquenchable thirst for revenge.

A Theban and a stranger, a male with female features, a god disguised as a man, Dionysus is an originary, indomitable doubleness; to fight him is doomed from the start merely because of the attempt. The automatic nature of divine punishment, brilliantly explored by Sylvain Lévi in Brahmanic theology, is also found in Dionysus in the *Bacchae*, which technically qualifies him as a *numen* in the archaic Roman sense, as a numinous impersonal force acting for itself according to the ritual treatment received, completely independent of all moral considerations, exactly like the vindictive Aphrodite in the *Hippolytus* or Lyssa in the *Herakles*. The difference between this numinous Dionysus in the *Bacchae* and the archaic *numina* of the Romans and of the *Brahmana*, as well as the punitive *numina* in Euripides's earlier tragedies, is its unprecedented interaction with the human world that it has come to destroy: Dionysus receives a partial humanization that is only apparent and deceptive, bringing to light the human community's "dishuman" foundation and thus detaching it from the mediatory process that alone can give it objectual significance and visibility. It is the religious noumenon going against its phenomena, the missing link between the two dimensions that should be connected because divided and divided because connected. The divine mediator that no longer mediates becomes a mirror for the human interlocutors to see their own violence reflected, their elusive adversary, unbeatable because every time they themselves supply it with the energy to beat them.

This is why the *logos* of Dionysus is mysteriously invincible. Pentheus is powerless against it and forced to admit that the Stranger is well practiced in the use of language (l. 491). His talk is strange and unexpected (l. 650), while there are hidden traps in his incomprehensibly alluring invitations. These divine, intractable words, with their savage, ironic superiority that always has the last word, take on further resonance as soon as we see them in the cultural context of contemporary Athens. It is his complete mastery of the art of using words that makes Dionysus the religious and historical confutation of the sophists' illusion of dominating and determining events through their *techne*. The word, the *logos*, is so powerful because it is founded on something that is not simply words. This is the constant background to the speeches recorded by Thucydides and really why they are so enthrallingly eloquent, continuing tragedy's investigations in the field of historiography. Every word spoken by Dionysus is obliquely oracular, an ambiguous enigma that is insoluble because it involves and describes the interlocutor's preverbal foundation, the source of a more originary *logos* found widely in Greek civilization, pervasively in fact. However, in the fifth century a more practical oratorical *techne* started to develop, still surrounded by the aura of ancient magical performance but, for that very reason, consciously exploiting it to persuade and influence. From here stems the backward movement of the tragedy's verbal, spoken dimension. The *logos* of the god reverts to being a lethal verbal double bind, as in the sacrificial rites that gave rise to the enigma, in the ambiguous pronouncements of the Delphic oracle, and in the archaic enigma contests that ended in the death of the less knowledgeable contestant: the mere attempt to converse or argue with Dionysus proves lethal, transforming the sentences of the dialogue into judicial death sentences, into fatal, definitive pronouncements[23]—a sacrificial *reductio ad unum*—at-one-ment—that is resolved in multiplying doubles since it lacks the leverage of effective objectual mediation, of the organic reconstruction of the world.

The mirror of the Dionysian *logos* shatters into a thousand shards, into the myriad reflections made visible by it. Whoever has anything to do with Dionysus becomes double simply because the sacrificial *numen*, the *daimon* of sacrifice, reveals the double nature previously hidden within him and now leaping into view, an unrelated chaotic multiplicity that this sinister, anobjectual divine mediation can no longer unify. In the next chapter I shall analyze the terminal dynamics of this collapsing revelatory power. Pentheus, the cousin of Dionysus, becomes his double in the end because that is what he always was: his dismemberment repeats the noumenal fate of the *numen*, and at one time *was* the *numen*, a fate now transformed into death inflicted by the god, a death that inverts to become the death of the god, the death of god, the death that *is* god. The Nietzschean announcement, reaching the extremes of modernity, is confirmed to be the oldest Event (*Ereigniss*).

In this transhistorical sense, pertaining to the noumenon revealed in its historical phenomena, the fate of Dionysus's enemy anticipates the fate of Nietzsche, crossing the watershed of the death of the god that was turned,

Christianly, into the death of God, to insanely incarnate the Dionysus that he had invoked, perniciously taking the gain in representational clarity as a chance to dominate, and taking the humanization of the killing of God for the beyond-humanization of killing humankind. In the union of the two Dionysian cousins everything is still inextricably mingled and distinct, resulting in an agnition of violence in which doubleness is disastrously fulfilled. Pentheus comes to be the living enigma of himself, and its solution is the *sparagmos* of its bearer. Ultimate knowledge appears to reunite with initial knowledge, the god's knowledge with the knowledge of his detractor: first and last, above and below, good and evil converge until they coincide, only to diverge irremediably forever: they re-member only to be dismembered once and for all. The double-binding contradiction of representation and rite ought to find its solution in the god, except that his triumph itself certifies its nonsolution. Rather than resolving, the ritual solution undoes, in the sense of the Greek verb *luein*, which also means to destroy.

As we have seen, Tiresias's hierogamy in the Orphic papyrus and the Eleusinian Mysteries, a *coniunctio* to be understood as a *complexio oppositorum*, is repeated at the high point of the tragedy and underscored by a great fire covering Heaven and Earth.[24] But it differs from Orphism and Eleusis in that this union of opposites, this atonement, brings no salvation, no fertile union, no *complexio*. The sacrificial reassemblage, symbolically anticipated by the Messenger-Pentheus-Dionysus triad at the beginning of the account of the *sparagmos*,[25] reaches definitive failure in Dionysus himself and is underlined by the description of Pentheus being torn to pieces at the hands of the three daughters of Cadmus. As the tragedy comes to a head, the *numen* who saves brings no salvation but only punishment and destruction. The dispersed *symbola* of Pentheus are recomposed, but no resurrection of any kind ensues; in its place we find only a collection of butchered remains. For this reason, there is no omophagy, not only because of the horror but because its premise and final outcome, the metamorphic resurrection of the devoured god, is undermined by the representation of the text itself. The duplication of the *mythos* carried out in the tragedy blocks the mediatory and metamorphic process driving it: nobody eats Pentheus and nobody becomes Pentheus. His *disiecta membra* remain just what they are, unrelated bits of a body, a shattered world. Here tragic oscillation reaches its finest, most spectacular result in retroacting cognitively on the contradiction at its origin. And now, since everything is concluded, comes moment for Agave: the one who concludes and closes.

4. Agave's *Mnema*

Among all Euripides's memorable female characters, there is something unique, something peculiarly, specifically memorable about Agave. And yet, as a character, she seems to offer few salient points for comment beyond the merely functional aspect: she appears to be simply a variable dependent on the story's development, a puppet on a string pulled by the *numen*, just as much as the other Theban women, and, at the decisive moment, the blind instrument of the will of Dionysus, the god's executrix, her son's executioner. But here Euripides's art is at its most subtle, giving dramatic life to a mythological being struggling against the myth of its very origin. We have already encountered a similar pattern in Pasiphae, but here there is a virtuosity derived from a vast accumulation of experience, not only theatrical. Agave presents a symbol of unprecedented power when she awakens from her Dionysiac sleep to contemplate what she has unwittingly done.

Let us read the climax of the dialogue with her father which brings her back to consciousness:

Cadmus First turn your gaze to heaven [*aither'*].
Agave Here, but why are you suggesting I look at it?
Cadmus Is it the same or does it appear to you with some change?
Agave It is brighter than before and clearer.
Cadmus Is it still fluctuating with your soul [*psyche*]?
Agave I don't understand what you're saying, but I feel I'm coming back to my senses [*ennous*] and my mind [*phrenon*] is changing.
Cadmus Would you then listen and answer wisely [*saphos*]?
Agave Yes, since I've forgotten what we said before, father.
Cadmus What household did you go to when you married?
Agave You gave me to the Sown-Man [*Sparto*], as they say, to Echion.

Cadmus So, what child did you deliver to his household?
Agave Pentheus, by my union with his father.
Cadmus What head [*prosopon*] do you have in your arms?
Agave A lion's, as the hunting women say.
Cadmus Look at it properly, now: it won't take much time.
Agave Ah! What do I see . . . ? What have I got in my hands . . . ?
Cadmus Examine it and understand wisely [*saphesteron*].
Agave Wretched me, I see the most horrific sorrow.

We are watching the deconstruction of the cosmic-symbolic machinery of Pentheus's massacre, since Cadmus starts from the same Heaven (*aither*, the sky in the intermedial, pneumatic sense) against which Pentheus was outlined at the top of the tree in his attempt to flee from the *sparagmos*. As we behold the fluctuating sky over the Cithaeron and descend from it for the last time, we suddenly reach Agave's fluctuating soul and anticipate the gruesome emotions she is about to feel. The frequent use of verbs of perception and opinion (*verba videndi* and *verba docendi*) expresses an increasing alternation of Dionysian delusion and recovery of correct vision, of true wisdom. But this is the definitive reversal of knowledge and its objectual significance, for true sight is one and the same with pure horror, annihilating the family rules and roles insistently repeated in the dialogue and instrumental in Pentheus's mother recovering her senses (*ennous*, the very opposite of being *entheos*). The final object of knowledge is the radical negation of any object and knowledge. The household of the Sown-Man, the *Spartos* Echion, is the very center of the destruction of both family and *polis*. Particularly remarkable is the use of *prosopon* for describing Pentheus's head, which is actually the mask of the character held in the actor's hand. Since the same actor played Agave and the dismembered king of Thebes, this is an impressive example of metatheatrical reflection on the overall sense of tragic representation. The custom of having one actor perform both roles undoubtedly goes back to Euripides himself,[26] and it introduces an alienation effect pointing toward the deepest meaning of the plot and highlighting the moral and cognitive need for saving a different level of human awareness.

The spectacular scenes of the mother discovering that she is holding the head of her son and then desperately crying on his lifeless body savaged by her own hands are the most moving moments of the drama and perhaps the most vulnerable to modern misunderstandings. To reduce their content in the customary way to the psychological *pathos* inherent in the situation has the effect of diminishing their intended representational and cognitive import, not because *pathos* is absent but because it could in no way be simply a psychological state, neither for spectators nor, on stage, in the epilogue to the story of Pentheus, the man of suffering, of *penthos*. For a fifth-century Greek theater-goer, the spectacle of a mother becoming aware of having between her arms her son's severed head and keening over his body butchered by her own hands, with their correspondence to specific, well-known myths and rituals that the author wants his audience to reflect on, were certainly not just the sensational coups de theatre that a modern playgoer might perceive. The psychological patheticism characteristic in the late- and postclassical period, has reference, within fixed limits, to an ever-present sacred background and constituted an effort to transform certain themes, known or intuited as to their true nature in other ways, into literature, into a reassuring topos. In fact, the religious symbolism of Pentheus's sacrificer-mother, her sacral and metasacral role, is crystal clear as soon as we think of it in its real context.

There is a pattern symmetrical to the god's retaliation: Agave gives concrete form to the labyrinthine hierogamy on her reluctant son, as well as to the gender change that takes place when he is sacrificially disguised before being led away to Mount Cithaeron, a metamorphic meaning further underscored, always with metatheatrical effect, by the one actor playing the two roles. Agave is the living emblem of Dionysus's triumph, the totally befogged instrument of a superior will that strikes her with the archaic sacrifices of the divine child, the extermination of entire families at the heart of prehistoric sacrifices connectable with the labyrinthine hierogamy. In her, the failure of divine justice is manifest more than ever: retaliation here is too symmetrical to prevent its human origin from emerging, and too divine for a different human order to replace it, a *compositio membrorum* unlike the one performed by Pentheus's mother. Agave, who dismembers her son, is the one to re-member him afterwards, in the *disiecta membra* of his poor body and, still more, in the memory of the appalling deed itself, with no redemption either human or divine. Her maternal role is, so to speak, crowned with success and unbearable failure, a female mediation seeing the object that she created destroyed through her own blind actions, her own madness.

This extraordinary function of the character occurs in a scene where Agave, weeping for her dead son, names every single part of his body; unfortunately, the text in turn has been ironically dismembered: the scene is lost, and we are faced with the difficulty of reconstruction. However, a fraction of the scene can be reconstructed from the *Christus patiens*. Thus, after recomposing Pentheus's body, we recompose the text that tells us about it. The question here is more philological in nature and concerns the *compositio membrorum* of the scene which is attributed in its entirety to the mother by many commentators but was probably shared with Cadmus, who picks up the pieces scattered over Cithaeron while his daughter completes this act of compassion by bringing the head and setting it in place. The spectators would be able to read this gesture perfectly well since, presumably, they would be seeing the mask of Pentheus already used on stage and read it as *symbolon* for his horrifically severed extremity. The hypothesis that Cadmus and Agave together carry out the *compositio membrorum* in two stages actually intensifies, with an authentic decomposition of the divine *compositio*, the cognitive and revelatory significance of the procedure, which no sacred or divinizing conviction is capable of transforming into rebirth as before. The *symbola* already seen in the Gurob papyrus reacquire their originary value but lie in pieces like a broken plaything, like a dead body that instead of being reborn, remains the macabre object of an autopsy.

Agave becomes the tragic, living memory of what has happened, and in lines that represent the real close of the tragedy she repudiates the memory of the Dionysian cult:

> I will go where
> neither contaminated Cithaeron may see me,
> nor I see Cithaeron more,
> nor memory [*mnema*] of the thyrsus exists [*anakeitai*]:
> to other bacchantes I leave it.[27]

Reinforced by the thrice-repeated negative at the start of consecutive lines, these words set the seal on the entire tragic *fabula*, skillfully expressed in verbal moods and semantic reechoing not completely translatable into modern European languages since the moods go from the desiderative optative in the first verb (I will go) to the optative of prayer in the second (may see me)—the verbal mood of the invocations to the gods, invocations by now impossible—and finally to the indicative ἀνάκειται ("exists"—literally, "to be consecrated," the very verb Pentheus had applied to himself at l. 934) corresponding to a memory no longer existing in fact, designated by the term μνῆμα which connotes also a tomb.[28] The thyrsus has become the tomb of Pentheus, as his mother in a more subjective way, a personal nuance that makes one think she is alluding to the cancellation of her own memory, of her own tomb, a mournful detail to be compared to the Platonic will to transform his own tomb into a *metrion*, a performative medium able to reconcile death and life. Nothing of the sort happens in the ravaged world of the late Euripides. The woman would like to cancel in herself the execrable "memory of the thyrsus" but she is one and the same with it, so that she will be free only by cancelling any personal memory through her death.

The mother of Pentheus does not deny the continuation of the cult of Bacchus; what she denies is that the cult means anything to her anymore, which amounts to admitting its mediatory ineffectiveness and the disastrous objectual collapse. What might seem a residual distinction reveals itself actually to be the deepest negation possible in a Greek context, refuting the persecutory conclusion attributed by Girard to the *Bacchae*. Both the context, theatrical and civic, for this sort of impotent exorcism and its position as the final word on the matter forestalls any idea of a subjective or personal retreat. This is the final sentence, in every sense, of the Dionysian *fabula* and of the rite that gave it bloody substance.

Can tragic knowledge show us a greater achievement, or a more pertinent failure? At the start Agave is characterized by thorough cognitive ignorance, but suddenly, like an indelible trauma, she is marked by the deepest knowledge possible in the ancient world, and the defeat of this knowledge condenses and consumes all others. Seen in this somber light, she becomes the *symbolon* of tragedy itself, speaking for Euripides as he contemplates all that his art has been forced to reveal, through the immemorial destiny at the origin of that art, the origin, too, of his characters and the public, and of the writer himself, fated to circulate among them. Agave is the double bind of a tragic origin, and of a tragedy that can speak of nothing but the origin: it is human phenomenon discovering it is bound and double bound to a noumenon inevitable and horrible. This double bind chained to itself is the final glaring failure in the chain of tragic knowledge that we have been examining.

A simple review of the leading characters in the drama, placed within their effective system of functioning, shows them to be organized as a hierarchy with a wealth of distinctions and functions. However, this hierarchy becomes destabilized and frustrated in the course of events. The conflict in the text between the various characters' diverse and partial knowledge results in their reciprocal obliteration, symmetrical destruction that we might easily, but distortingly, interpret as an aesthetic end in itself. The cognitive extremes joining and intertwining in Agave's destiny demonstrate the transitive circularity that destructures the whole representation but at the same time makes possible a more consistent and intangible circularity that belongs to another order of knowledge coming into view in outline although not quite fixed. Just as it is coming to be realized, knowledge self-destructs, in a similar way to what happened in the Athens of Pericles and Phidias, with its countless and ineffective wise men. Euripides knew them and was obviously influenced by the prodigious intellectual climate they brought about. It is thus perfectly plausible that he saw the failure of Greek and Athenian knowledge as the failure of tragic knowledge itself. This metasapiential recognition enables the conclusion itself to be overturned, and enables us to recognize his recognition as a success of a different character and order, not measurable by the short-sighted parameter of immediate success but over a time span of millennia, a long eventful history in which the present interpretation has a place.

The next and final step in our analysis of tragic knowledge is to take a closer look at the extremely real and supremely unreal mechanism that could lead to such an epilogue. This will also involve the transition from divine to human mediations, from a religious and collective dimension to a more psychological and personal one, not yet stabilized but recognizable in its developing features.

7.

The Power and Failure of Divine Mediation

1. Theatrical Doubles Ancient and Modern

Further analysis of the *Bacchae* will consist of satisfactorily decoding its system of transformations—that is, its changes of *morphe*. And for that, we must further consider the divine mediator, the pivotal immaterial center around which it all revolves. The problem is that this center of mediation, instead of assigning places and functions, destabilizes and destroys them, the reason being that it no longer fulfills its role as authentic transcendence and consequently lacks an objectual goal to fix and becomes incapable of restoring a sociocosmic order, a life-giving hierarchy.

The contrast with Athena's role in the *Eumenides* by Aeschylus could not be more pronounced. Instead of the sexual and gender ambiguity of the divine protagonist of the *Bacchae* we find a univocal and reassuring feminine virility that, with its parthenogenesis and chastity, guarantees total control of the dangerous sphere of sexuality and its corresponding familial, social, and moral organization:

> No mother, in fact, begot me,

> and wholeheartedly [*hapanti thymo*] I pursue all that pertains to males
> [*to d'arsen*]
> except for nuptial bonds: I completely belong to my father.[1]

The Aeschylean Athena is one and the same with the supreme authority of her father, Zeus, from whose head she was born. If on the one hand this excludes her from sexual generation, on the other it puts her in an ideal position to ensure it. We have already ascertained that her birth from Zeus's head originally had a meaning analogous to Dionysus's birth from Zeus's thigh, and now we see the hierogamic-sacrificial symbolism evolving to become masculinity without male attributes, femininity removed from coupling and therefore from any contention. The transgenerative and univocal nature of the *Parthenos*, the Virgin of the Acropolis, releases the generative force of community from the horrible misdeeds perpetrated in the family of the Atreides, and thus introduces eternal Justice:

> Zeus the assembly-inspirer [*agoraios*] triumphs
> and our strife [*eris*] directed to the good
> forever wins.[2]

The ambiguity of ἔρις is still there but is powerfully "directed to the good," and its victory is the result of an eternal and vital tension, as in Heraclitus.[3] Unfortunately, in the Athens and Greece of Euripides this marvelous balance is lost, as we see in the *Bacchae* where that other child of Zeus shows up to intentionally and systematically foment collective disasters and arouse the most destructive quarreling, being a provocative and promiscuous figure determined to subvert and dissolve all familial and creative/procreative order, all affective and social bonds other than the blind and fanatic devotion of his thiasos. The unfailingly univocal role of Athena, the city's tutelary goddess, with her capacity to transcend the bloody archaic religion from which she descends, is followed by an analogous role-player, though totally plurivocal and equivocal.

A gulf divides the Euripidean Dionysus from the transcendent and transcendental verticality of the Aeschylean Athena: he presents himself to the public as a transcendence affirmed and denied at the same time, as a continuous intermingling of the roles his divine mediation ought to distinguish, as a steady withdrawal of the divine difference ceaselessly reasserted by the offended son of Zeus. The transformative, elusive, disruptive centrality of Dionysus in the *Bacchae* has been recognized by more perceptive commentators though not the mediatory function that his divine figure ought but fails to perform, nor the overall system into which he should fit but is going to destroy.

The obverse of this problem is the difficulty of evaluating the recognizably human motives behind the behavior of this nonfunctional mediator who sets himself on a level with his mortal interlocutors while, with sadistic pleasure, he plots their ruin; on the contrary, the traditional mythological catalog of his enemies aims to emphasize his capacity to integrate a new order—ritual, agrarian, and social—in which he has a necessary, indispensable part, as had occurred with the advent of wine in the Neolithic period. The traditional Dionysus brings tension into city life from outside; the rural realm of nature—wild, alien, and disturbing—presents a threat to the *polis*, something against which it has to defend itself and, at the same time, something that it needs. The Dionysian *numen* absorbs the city's tensions and terrors and projects them into the woods and fields, permitting savage purges to take place from time to time in order to restore common law, and relations dealing not only with the world of women, the lower classes, and outsiders, but also with the dark Dionysian side of every individual in the community, in the same way that drinking to excess on holidays refreshes the orderly routine of the workaday world. Plato himself in the *Laws* allows ritual banquets, where the citizens can drink under the patrol of an elderly fellow-citizen who remains sober: even the highest philosophic rationality pays its debt to Dionysus, and this is not the smallest achievement of Platonic thought.[4]

What marries the objectual sphere to sacrificial destruction is the hierogamy of Wet and Dry: what Nietzsche would call the harmonious tension between Apollinian and Dionysian elements, while for Bataille it is the dynamic counterbalance between work and the *dépense* that renders the results of work useless and again pursuable, between marriage subject to its usefulness and orgiastic *eros* that undermines and confirms it, with the advantage in the ancient hierogamy of a holistic sense of the *kosmos* and society, for modern thinkers only a distant memory. However, to confirm the appositeness of what Tiresias says also confirms that none of it functions in the *Bacchae*, and there is no need for further exegesis to demonstrate this. The real question now is to understand more in depth the viewpoint or perspective adopted by Euripides. Attempts to keep him in a limbo of conventional Greek classicism were never successful, and he was appreciated in the postclassical period as much as he has been misunderstood and belittled in modern times, but equally he cannot be modernized by making inappropriate Freudian or feminist claims for him, nor demystified religiously or sacrificially, which, though not so wide of the mark, is anachronistic and foreign to his religious sensibility. One further observation needs to be made about interpretive paths and pitfalls in the *Bacchae* in order to finalize an overall comment at this point and introduce the theme of the next parts of the book, and it relates to my line of study developed over a score of years devoted to Euripides's masterpiece and its various associated themes.

Girard's interpretation is undoubtedly the point of reference for any serious study of the anthropological and sacrificial content of the *Bacchae* and is the real continuation of research by such classicists as Dodds or Jeanmaire. It has the advantage over them of being based on a more organic theory of the sacred and sacrifice, and so escapes their rationalistic limitations and the narrower horizons of their disciplines. However, his theoretical focus is purchased at the price of leveling down Euripides to fit his opposition of Dionysus to Christ. Euripides has to remain bound, double-bound, to a dependence on sacrifice, the evidence for it detected in the first stasimon of the *Bacchae* by the author of *Violence and the Sacred*, as we have seen. The contrast served to substantiate Girard's claim for the insuppressible truth of the Judeo-Christian tradition that by bringing to light the victim exposes the victimary complicity of all previous cultures or any that remain extraneous to it. This thesis has a heuristic force not to be confused with its literal truth, and it is worth going over the argument again to distinguish the good points from the defects.

In fact, it is not very hard to argue that the Judeo-Christian tradition appears to be far from aware that its genius lies in the defense of victims: abundant evidence can be found in Bible texts hinging on the total extermination of enemies (an ideology more verbal than real but indicative of a certain mentality nonetheless); on the countless forms of revenge adopted by Middle Judaism and Christianity in enjoying eschatological triumph over their adversaries; and on the indifference, evident even in some passages of the Gospels, toward all victims not corresponding to Christ or those who bore witness to him and met all the moral and doctrinal requirements.[5] And there seems to me no need to say anything in particular about what happened later. Without lingering now on the Jewish and Christian history, which does not warrant any romantic illusions, we can easily infer that in Israel, the ancient Christendom, and the ancient world as a whole it is impossible to find "victim" functioning as universal and theoretical category. On the contrary, we observe historical-cultural situations completely submerged in religious, social, and symbolic mediations to be understood in their specific meaning and objectual achievements. Thus we must avoid applying naively modern categories, without giving up the idea and experience of the victim, so long as we take it in its existential contents which unite it to our own experience.

However, that in no way alters the fact—indeed it accentuates it—that certain important texts and passages by the great thinkers of the Old Testament, culminating in the teachings and attitude of Christ, in effect contain something like a concern for victims that is not found in other cultures, the Greek and Roman cultures for a start, but without forming a compact, monolithic block on the side of the weak and defeated *as such*. There is a certain inspiration that way, but it is like a vein of gold ore: it needs to be identified and properly evaluated among many other more predictable and less precious mineral veins. Therefore, to give it the absolute value assigned to it by Girard, it would be necessary to postulate that this, and this alone, is the real Jewish and Christian revelation; in itself this position may simplify or console, but it stands apart from history, which it willfully ignores, and from understanding matters that hold no interest for it.

As to the other side of the question, relating to Greek civilization chosen as a particularly relevant and influential example of a pagan culture founded on the sacrifice of victims, sacrificial mediations as I call them unquestionably prevail, at the expense of innocent victims, which are never considered as human beings and often are actually turned into monsters; and yet it is not impossible a priori to see these as victims and see the processes leading up to them. On the contrary, Euripides's tragedy shows that, at a certain point, the Greek world achieves this retroacting capacity, in a way that differs substantially from the Jewish and biblical manner, that is, by tracing the persecution of victims to human order and disorder as part of a mediatory ambience much more cosmic and ontological than theological and historical, as compared to the Jewish. This capacity for moral and cognitive discovery and acquisition is the fruit of development inherent in every human culture, with its origin in rite and myth, and of a potential for interaction that mythical-ritual knowledge triggers at a certain moment, or rather through a series of gradual acquisitions, leading to new thresholds of knowledge and awareness.

Once we realize the dramatic problem of the human costs of the mediations needed by mankind, we find ourselves with two opposing and complementary requirements. The first is to recognize those costs, and here Girard's chiaroscuro has proved useful. Secondly, we must not be blocked by a contrast that may at any moment become "Manichean,"[6] but pursuing the inquiry, we must show the universal nature of the process, how it answers to the deepest fibers of our human cultural dimension and awareness. This pursuit is compatible with a choice of faith, and in a profound and relevant way it actually invites such a choice but not exclusively the Jewish or the Christian religion since it calls on *every* cult, belief, and religion to rethink its assumptions and aims as a whole. Historically, *some* elements and currents in the Jewish and Christian traditions have seen its presence advance but in no way exclusively or by being exclusive since this presence serves its purpose, fulfills its objectual meaning, once it enters into dialogue with the religions and cultures that it had to exclude along the way in order to develop and assert itself.

That, more or less, is the course I have followed, starting from Girard's contrasting of Dionysus and Christ, then coming to realize the need for a more complete overall vision that could include what led *from* Dionysus *to* Christ, and finally recognizing through my mediatory theory the universality of a process no less universal for having obviously had its outstanding and defining moments, like all phenomena in human history, that are not part of preestablished schemes but a reflection of the countless circumstances of their origin, opposition and interaction, and development. In that way we remove any hint of an apologia on behalf of a particular religious denomination and gain instead an apologia for humankind throughout its history, through all the complex drama of winning a mediatory and objectual dimension as permanent as possible, a drama confirmed by the fragility of its results and, in some cases, even extending down to our own day, showing us all to be part of an infinitely greater human and historical adventure.

In the Intermezzo dealing with Greek and Roman civilization and Christianity, these remarks will be fully developed, but they are also very relevant to our understanding of the epilogue to the *Bacchae*, where Girard's theoretical tools are effective in practice but their perceptions need to be correctly understood and circumscribed. The last outcome of relations between Dionysus and Pentheus turns out to be a dramatically recognizable instance of what Girard calls internal mediation, reciprocal mimetic fascination ending in catastrophe, and that was also my own initial analysis. However, it is remarkable that Girard did not immediately exploit this chance to apply his theory to a terribly eminent text of great antiquity and thereby gain prestigious confirmation for the theory itself. On the contrary, he confines his comments to a few memorable passages, without any overall reconstruction of such an impressive progression. This real reticence is not difficult to explain: to have insisted on the validity of his theory when applied to the ultimate clash/encounter between Dionysus and Pentheus would have meant admitting that certain aspects of the theory were already present to a significant extent in Euripides's tragedy. The chiaroscuro between dependence on sacrifice and total freedom from sacrifice would have come out as altered or disproved just when it appeared to be confirmed. Since, quite clearly, if Euripides possesses essential knowledge about desire and its sacrificial outcome, it is proof of an awareness incompatible with the above confrontational scheme.

With a proper textual instinct, Girard, in *Violence and the Sacred*, concentrates on the tragedy's religious and ritual background; however, he has to remain virtually silent about the close parallels to the phenomena of desire as it emerges in his analysis of great modern writers, and this has a twofold effect: on the one hand, the distance from the mythical-ritual dimension becomes excessive; on the other, he tends to assume a kind of desire too close to its modern manifestations, as if it were a force in itself independent of historical factors, thereby becoming for him the ubiquitous, limiting invariable of the mimetic factor, actually necessary but inadequate for understanding human cultural behavior. This is precisely the gap filled by my idea of mediation, of a collective sacral model shared by all, independent and irreducible as an objectual source for the community: what for us is a more individualized desire develops within this model and becomes recognizable historically.

Within this framework, too, there develops the cognitive retroaction that has gradually thrown light on the cultural and human phenomena made possible through collective mediations and the fact of their origination in them. The conclusion of the *Bacchae* most movingly illustrates this historic cultural moment. We will now, then, begin a correct interpretation, giving Euripides's text all it is due.

At the final stage of the relationship between Dionysus and Pentheus, it is increasingly difficult to distinguish one from the other as their roles become bewilderingly identical, so much so that we could speak of a sort of binary system, the Dionysus-Pentheus system, rather than of two separate individuals.[7] This stage corresponds to what Girard, in *Things Hidden*, calls interdividual psychology,[8] using a term conceptually influenced by the psychiatrist Jean-Michel Oughourlian, whose ideas made a significant contribution to the book. The concept of interdividual psychology refers to preindividual situations, that is, where relationships of mimesis and desire come to predominate causing individuals to merge and thus making that network visible, a network not philosophically intersubjective, since that assumes subjects already exist and interact, but inter-dividual, where the "inter-" unites and divides single individuals to make them momentarily in-dividuals and then makes them disappear again as soon as it comes to dominate the developing mimetic relationships.[9] This is clearly an advance on the untenable philosophical and phenomenological concept of intersubjectivity, but it is achieved by subordinating the collective factor as such, defined in a negative way whereas instead it acts as a positive identifying principle for everyone—in line with Freud's intuition in *Mass Psychology and Analysis of the Ego*—and so is the first collective "subject" and "individual," though still rudimentary and inchoate. The individuality of the individual therefore derives from the collective process and is not opposed to but made possible by it, both historically and culturally; and this tallies with the characteristics and dynamic creative force of my mediation, taking us beyond the psychologism in Freud's identification, and still there in Oughourlian's definition.

We must conclude that there is much to learn from Euripides's drama since it shows a situation deliberately and consciously worked out, being explored within a more originary historical-cultural frame, and so it affords a wealth of firsthand information that a modern theoretical approach, viewed as the repository of awareness, cannot provide. Euripides must guide us in this exploration, as I said before, but this once more poses questions about the retroacting nature of theater that allows it, and we need to clarify further the inner workings of how this happens, as far as they can be reconstructed from the Athenian scenario, and as they would reappear in modern times.

Theater is based on the spectacular vision of the doubles, as Girard recognizes without however realizing that the theatrical doubles go back to a precise form of mediation, semiritual and semiliterary, achieving an objectual significance however unstable in performance, since it makes the doubles visible and causes them to interact. This public and institutional aspect of the Athenian theater is not to be ignored as simply a neutral framework—since it is the reason for the birth of tragedy in Athens, as we shall see in the next chapter—but supplies the motivation and context for a representation of the doubles willed by the powerful and the populace alike, and designed to revive those doubles in controlled, para-ritual ways, the memory of which lives on in the Aristotelian catharsis. In other words, the cognitive content of the tragic genre is anything but accidental and at first with Aeschylus answers political ends that are all one with the religious, sapiential, and even judicial aspects of the onstage drama. However, the inquiry develops exponentially from the start thanks to its symbolic retroaction with the representational doubling, acting like reflections in a series of mirrors, leading us to notice aspects and facets hidden from view at first glance. In other words, concealment itself serves as a means to acquire knowledge, discrediting Girard's view of a one-way mythical concealment that, in the course of time, could only stratify and thicken until it finally became indecipherable.

Theatrical mediation, then, has sapiential implications by definition, institution, and structure, even if this knowledge comes in varying degrees of power and complexity. The principle of authorial impersonality or, if you prefer, of the tragic double bind, is this cognitive vision of the play of doubles developed according to its internal logic, the cognitive equivalent of the ritual division of the *symbola*, of the decomposing and recomposing of the sacrificial *harmonia*. If the author shows ideological bias or the audience is conditioned in favor of one party, as happens not infrequently, then the vision may be flawed and lose at least some part of its cognitive value. But this is not the case in the great fifth-century tragedians, and especially in a daringly original writer like Euripides, and even when they sustain contingent political motives, factional interests, or more personal positions, they never relinquish tragedy's prismatic reflections, constantly throwing flashes of light on events. But this game with mirror images and knowledge is not the end of it; indeed, it goes on repeatedly, multiplying its various proliferating levels, and we delude ourselves if we think the tragic doubles can ever be resolved.

This makes possible a further type of complicity, which consists in maintaining the representation of the doubles and confirming it by considering their mirror reflections, their tragic ambiguity, to be the only true reality—or nonreality, which amounts to the same thing. Such complicity and complacency can fascinate and absorb any literary criticism unaware of it. Girard is not unaware of the danger and links it to the origin and very nature of theater,[10] but he fails to perceive the system's cognitive value, its objectual value as mediation, and he is so concerned about a theatrical or aesthetic 'addiction' that he shows no hesitation in taking the most drastic steps to avert it, in line with his idiosyncratic reductionism. For Girard, undermining the doubles representation by exposing its contradictions, that is to say, by revealing its senselessness, poverty, and—from a more comprehensive viewpoint—tedium, means casting doubt on and denying the validity of theater itself. In his interpretation, this is what we find in Shakespeare's last plays—*The Winter's Tale* and *The Tempest*: metatheatrical masterpieces that by demythologizing the representational play of the doubles reach the extreme limits of the tragic and theatrical genre. As a conclusion, this is consistent but hardly acceptable either theoretically or historically. With his antisacrificial stance, Girard attributes an antiaesthetic impulse to Shakespeare much more appropriate to himself since, for Shakespeare, exploding the vices of the theater is like demystifying love, painful but certainly not meant to put a stop to falling in love, aiming perhaps at making it a little more difficult to go about it in the wrong way, or rather in an anobjectual way. Girard maintains that Shakespeare's ability to overcome the theatrical doubles or, to be more exact, the ideology of the theatrical doubles, is due to the influence of Christianity, a reading with a historical basis, though Shakespeare's success does not come about in the aggressive, competitive manner characteristic of the theorist of imitative rivalry. One can, and must, speak of Christianity's transcending the doubles of human rivalry, even if this is understood as an objectual tendency and not to be claimed as a sure acquisition, but the fact remains that the process does not take place in the terms imagined by its apologist. Typically, his difficulty lies in not recognizing, or not sufficiently at least, that for Christianity transcendence does not mean condemnation but redemption, not iconoclastic destruction but incarnation, recognizing and redeeming art as well, achieving its retroacting, cognitive aim. He sees the danger of making a myth of the literary and theatrical double bind, being the first to fall under its spell, and imagines obviating it by getting rid of the double bind, the source of all his concerns, but fails to realize that in doing so he is eliminating the very reality that needs to be saved, as well as the prime energy for saving it, provided it could be successfully redirected. It is always the problem of man's redemption that, theologically as well, must start from a resource outside himself but also requires him to mobilize and commit all the resources available to himself: otherwise he devolves into a puppet bereft of all that makes him human.

In this sense, it seems to me, Alessandro Manzoni's Christian tragedies are most revealing; they complete the creative cycle of the genre in modern literature and support a thoroughgoing comparison with Shakespeare. Manzoni's heroes grow gradually aware of their total involvement in the tragic event, in what he calls by the telling name—coming from Aristotle's *Poetics* but having a labyrinthine descent—of the "knot" (*nodo*);[11] and if involvement leads the protagonists to defeat, it is this that saves them spiritually by giving them access to Christ's saving mediation. In this way, their misfortune, the misfortune of the Longobard prince Adelchi and his sister Ermengarda, becomes "provident" (*provida*), sanctifying not only their personal history but somehow also the artistic form that gives it expression. But, as so often happens where an uncomfortable truth is at stake, nobody seems to have noticed Manzoni's solution, sometimes explained away as the result of Shakespearian influence (which is undeniable, as for his contemporary Georg Büchner, but is an enhancement not a diminution of their originality). In spite of his theoretical shortcomings, due to his almost Platonic obsession with the criteria of moral decency in literature, it is Manzoni who points the way forward, obeying his objectually human and poetic perception, therefore objectually true, of the knot of the human drama and human love. Leaving aside further textual and theoretical commentary to come later, in particular at the close of my inquiry, it will be interesting now to follow these rather brief remarks about Manzoni with a no less concise excursus regarding the attitude prevailing in modern culture toward the tragic, a necessary prerequisite to analyzing our own position in relation to Euripides and the *Bacchae*.

European culture, only too ready to censor an embarrassing Catholic like Manzoni, was to go on mourning the loss of the tragic genre only to see tragedy brought back onto the stage so fully and obsessively in the historical events of the twentieth century. The tragic became the representational, symbolic place of the lost sacrificial mediation, or of the longing for a neosacrificial revival, an attitude that enables us to understand the anthropologic-religious significance not only of Nietzsche's endeavors but also of Wagner's art that inspired *The Birth of Tragedy*. We cannot understand the sacrificial nostalgia for *Kultur* unless we grasp this intrinsically theatrical aspect: Wagner is the background to Thomas Mann's *Reflections of a Non-Political Man*, just as operatic music accompanies Hans Castorp into the final disaster of the First World War. Despite and because of all these enthusiasms, the Valhalla of the persistently sought-after mediations was doomed to collapse as in the *Ring of the Nibelungen*, undermined by the cognitive retroaction that reveals its real meaning, and the true greatness of the Wagnerian tetralogy. Sacrifice is unconscious theater; theater is sacrifice, both conscious and unconscious, achieving fulfillment if it transcends itself, if it can see itself from outside, from a viewpoint that becomes its own and gives it new life otherwise forestalled from emerging by being closed in on itself.

Theater is too ritualistic to be false and too false to function as ritual, and becomes aberrant semiritual when detached from its objectual matrix: the extremes reached in ancient Rome with slaves and criminals being actually tortured and killed during mimed performances not only proves the postritual character of Roman theater, but also shows the danger presented by the proximity of real violence. The Roman mime's defense against violence was to make spontaneously fall the further stage in the representation, the stage of the spoken word, at the climax of the story,[12] but all such violence goes back to the immense theatrical, para-ritual machinery of the arena games where the controlled growth of violence was intended to testify to the grandeur and power of Roman rule. This extreme performative development was therefore bound up with exceptional circumstances and required the empire to go on expanding victoriously throughout the world so as to be a fully functional success, which only confirms its dangerousness. The twentieth-century avant-garde was not always aware of this danger, even though Antonin Artaud's "theater of cruelty,"[13] which so readily springs to mind whenever we talk of an overreaction to the complacency of middle-class theater, never forgets its nature as a theatrical gesture recalling its own origins symbolically, rather than reproducing them irresponsibly in a way that would obliterate its history and identity.

But today we have the mass and banalized caricature of avant-garde experimentation. The entire hysterically mediatized age in which we live resembles one gigantic semi- or posttheatrical workshop, that is, relating to an apparent anobjectual theatricality, where every credible mediation is brought down with the consequent representational and de facto destruction of all human objectuality. The violence destroying what is human turns spontaneously into a representation that re-confirms it, since both the violence and its representation are drawn into being and nurtured by the mediatory and objectual vacuum. Immersed in violence and thinking that we know it and are exposing it, we transform it into stereotyped, serial images, trifling pastimes reaching the point of senile silliness, and meaningless holograms designed for individuals with no objects. We have betrayed our philosophical legacy from the most original thinkers of the last two centuries—their understanding of the death of mediation, of God, recognizing the very source of mediation there—and we are reluctant to admit what made those thinkers great: their awareness of the need to go back to that first outpouring so as to avoid losing its objectualizing potential, though practically all of them, in their various ways, remained shackled by the historical lack of object that was their starting point. The neotragic explorings of Nietzsche, Wagner, and Gabriele D'Annunzio (whose extraordinary dramas can tell us a great deal about this subject) have thus given rise to the most tragic of ironies, the real twilight of tragedy now bereft of their prophetic and artistic stature. And so we must return now to the first half of the twentieth century and the incredible, disaster-fraught scene described by Thomas Mann.

Contemporary history teaches us that everything becomes tragedy, the worst type of tragedy, unenlightened by knowledge and darkly borne down beneath a huge weight of stupidity and power unless what ancient tragedy shows us is recognized and made the object of historically conscious meditation. The warning coming from the *Bacchae* is invaluable, not so much because its message is essentially the same today as it was 2,500 years ago but because it evidences a process still at an initial stage that is psychogonic, not psychological, a process now at an extremely advanced stage, in danger of proving terminal, progressing from psycho-gony to the ultimate psycho-agony of death. This is proof that the death of God is the death of mankind if its real meaning is not understood. And there could be no better introduction to Dionysus as he finally appears in Euripides than Nietzsche, who proclaimed the death of God; but we must always remember that with Nietzsche, the modern philosopher, we are looking at the outcome of what is still just beginning in the ancient dramatist.

In the following passage we sense the fascination exerted by Dionysus over Nietzsche, soon now to be engulfed by Dionysian *mania*, a fascination bringing us back to the erotic aspects that Euripides subordinated to sacrifice and that emerge in Nietzsche as a means to make sacrifice visible again. The god-obsessed philosopher of the will to power evokes him in terms sinisterly like the description of the honey-man in the Mesopotamian hierogamy:

> I have seen it, his halcyon smile, his honeyed eyes [*Honig-Augen*], now
> deep and veiled, now green and lascivious, a tremulous surface.
> Lascivious, drowsy, tremulous, hesitant,
> the sea wells up in his eyes.[14]

Here, after the "orgiastic soul" (*orgiastische Seele*), speaks "the orgiastic soul of woman," the same female "orgiastic soul" with which Pentheus is to fall in love when, grotesquely, he plays the part. The tragic hierogamy is about to be celebrated, but the woman speaking to us in Nietzsche's text is not simply the archaeological equivalent of a maenad, of an Ariadne waiting for her Dionysus-Theseus at the center of the labyrinth; this now raving, wild female mediation is the expression of an objectual crisis that now prevails and is so far advanced as to coincide openly with the object being sought, with the figure able to mediate it, and with the philosophical postulant seeking it. While Euripides shows us a bloody, ancestral past becoming psychology, Nietzsche offers the symmetrical and contrary spectacle of a psyche about to collapse as it unearths its bloody, ancestral past, immodestly revealed only in the recesses of a mind on the verge of breakdown. The metaphor of the sea welling up in Dionysus's eyes translates an ancient sacrificial image into a clearly erotic one (its most explicit equivalent is found in the Marquis De Sade); at the same time, the psychic, desiderative significance brings the ancient sacrificial stratum to the surface, taking us back once more to the originary situation of a crazed mob throwing itself on its victim. This attraction should not be confused with desire because it steers impulses of animal origin, detached from their biological object during the objectual crisis, toward an Object that unites them and gives them meaning with a transcendent force that is no longer biological. In Nietzsche none of this works but essentially none of it is concealed from us, and so we come to a zone of convergence between divine mediation that becomes madness and madness that becomes divine mediation, both failing tragically.

With the radical subjectivity assumed by the modern author, the old terms of tragic mediation and ritual mediation implode, and we discover in Nietzsche, as in Euripides, that Dionysus is sweet, divinely sweet, and nothing is sweeter than devouring him. In this way, Nietzsche's fatal attraction for Dionysus is not essentially different from Pentheus's. As Dionysus says to Ariadne, according to Nietzsche at a time when he was approaching madness: "O Ariadne, you yourself are the labyrinth: nobody ever gets out of you,"[15] a phrase perfectly expressing with modern words what Pentheus could say to his numinous cousin. Whoever does not get out of the labyrinth comes to incarnate the labyrinth, starting with the god who was the first to be killed there and whose macabre statue, hungry for fresh victims, stands at the center, the bronze statue of the Minotaur conjectured by Frazer, the tangled intestines of tragedy's knot. Girard's defensive, limiting reactions to the ritual and theatrical doubles hardly come as a surprise: when he thinks of Dionysus, he thinks of Nietzsche's terrible fate. The modern Pentheus helps us to understand the fate of the ancient Pentheus is to be the scapegoat for Dionysus and to reveal him. This is our point of arrival, and now it is our turn to go on stage, to tread the boards of a theater of cruelty, both ancient and modern; and it is not the cruelty of the theater but rather the theatricality of a cruel being, the cruelty of man. In the end, after tracing so distant and challenging a history, and in the light of the conclusion to the *Bacchae*, as of Nietzsche's career, we can say: *tua res agitur*—it is a matter (*factum*, πρᾶγμα) that concerns you.

2. A God, Most Terrible and Sweetest for Mortals

Euripides's Dionysus is a symbolic, performative labyrinth that Pentheus enters never to leave. In the course of their encounters, we see Pentheus gradually approach the *arrheton*, the inexpressible of sacrificial mediation that becomes expressible by turning into the attraction of desire. As Pentheus approaches closer to Dionysus, Dionysus's attitude changes, becomes calmer, persuasive, and ominously friendly, the attitude of the predator who feels that his prey is already caught. What is most striking in the *Bacchae* is this ineluctable, hypnotic approach to indistinctness that has remained structurally identical in the collective and ritual crises as well as in the psychic and desiderative crises. We are dismayed, excited, and even full of admiration, without understanding exactly why.

The most evident aspect of the relationship between the two characters is also the easiest aspect to misunderstand, especially as it is frequently found in Greek culture, the first culture to begin to develop a clear perception of individual desire starting from the sacral mediations that defined it and made it recognizable: the aspect of seduction, of fascination, to be linked to the mythical-ritual notion of *charis*, the divine attraction that can easily turn out to be a trap. The whole plot might be defined as a daemoniac device to seduce, daemoniac in the sense of the Greek *daimon* (corresponding to a certain extent to the Latin *numen*), the divine *charis* that must entice the prey into the trap set for it. The aim here is to restore historical likelihood to the analysis while avoiding the further trap of an unrelated tragicism prone to admire drama as a separate dimension whether mythographically (i.e., no longer mythical-ritually), psychically (i.e., psychologistically), or as literature (i.e., aesthetically). If we give way to these easy temptations, all interchangeable because all equally engaged in detaching the representation from its semantic, cognitive object, then we are also seduced to a certain degree and consequently give a sigh of relief when Pentheus is killed instead of us, the victim, a substitute for Dionysus and the audience, and for this reason, too, Dionysus becomes sweeter than honey. The catharsis works, at an ever more impoverished level compared to the originary sacrificial purification. If Euripides's tragedy had furthered these tendencies and limited itself to re-presenting traditional mythical themes or reworking them in a literary fashion, giving the educated public and the critics something to play with, it would not have appeared so original as compared to the preceding Dionysian tragedies of Aeschylus. Undoubtedly, those were moving closer to the mythical-ritual content of the story and remained further away from the literariness that gained ground after Euripides, when the creative period of Greek classical tragedy had come to an end, and that became more pronounced in the Hellenistic period when the mediation of the *polis* was overtaken by the centers of ecumenical power stemming from the kingdom of Macedonia, from the mediation of that *Dionysus redivivus*, Alexander the Great.[16]

By reading a fairly extensive section from the penultimate dialogue between Dionysus and Pentheus, a prelude to the maenad disguise of the latter, we can follow the final unfolding of this seduction, steeped in daemoniac/daemonic *charis* and in desire still embedded in the sacral recesses that gave it substance and succor:

Dionysus I would make a sacrifice [*thyoim'*], rather than getting furious [*thymoumenos*]
and kicking [*laktizoimi*], you mortal, against the prick [*pros kentra*] of the god.
Pentheus And in fact I am going to make a sacrifice [*thyso*], by carrying out
a great massacre of women on Cithaeron, that's what they are worthy of!
Dionysus Flee, all of you: it will be an unworthy sight,
your bronze shields fleeing before the thyrsi of the bacchantes!
Pentheus We are wrestling with this impossible [*aporo*] Stranger:
he is never silent neither when he suffers offense nor when he gives it!
Dionysus My friend, there must be a way to settle matters.
Pentheus What? Make myself slave to my slaves?
Dionysus I shall bring those women to you, without needing arms.
Pentheus Alas! You are already contriving a trap [*mechana*] for me!
Dionysus What trap? Don't I want to save you, with my arts?

Pentheus It is just a pact between yourselves to enjoy the bacchanals forever.

Dionysus I have a pact but—believe me—it is with the god.

Pentheus Bring my arms and, you, stop talking [*pausai legon*]!

Dionysus Ah!
All the women together on the mountain, wouldn't you like to see [*idein*] them . . . ?

Pentheus Yes, indeed! And I'd pay gold for it, lots of gold.

Dionysus Why such a sudden strong desire [*erota*]?

Pentheus Though I should suffer, I would like to see them drunk.

Dionysus Would you willingly see things painful to you?

Pentheus Know this clearly, I would watch them in silence, from behind the fir trees.

Dionysus They will flush you out, even if you steal up on them.

Pentheus Then I shall have to reveal [*emphanos*] myself: you are right about that.

Dionysus Right, I must be your guide. Shall we go?

Pentheus Guide me at once then, let's waste no more time.

Dionysus But first put on a linen peplum.

Pentheus What? Man that I am, must I end up [*telo*] dressed as a woman?

Dionysus So they won't kill you, if they happen to see you are a man.

Pentheus You are right about that, too: you really know it all [*palai sophos*].[17]

The Greek text contains a wealth of puns and sacrificial references, starting with the evident double meanings in the first exchanges. We should note in particular the numerous points where the characters use identical or very similar words, emphasizing the growing identity of their roles. Of significance are the verbal references to wisdom in ll. 816 and 824, and the use in l. 822 of the verb τελέω—the verb of initiation—to indicate dressing up as a woman.[18] We are close to the point when Pentheus, just like Dionysus, will show himself ἐμφανῶς (l. 818), fully manifested, as the king of Thebes will say presenting himself dressed as a female follower of the god.

Nonetheless, merely stylistic and textual analyses, however useful in themselves, would after all add little to our investigation since they are no help in reaching the ultimate level of historical and cultural comparison. It is far more stimulating to start from what we find striking and absorbing in the dialogue, what it seems to be saying about desire and psychology, a content coming down to us through thick enormous historical filters that here appear to grow thinner, transparently thin. The fascinating nature of this content leads us to the mediatory premises that mask it or make it possible according to how they are seen. This is the most interesting interpretive question since it poses the question of the real nature of the text and so determines our relationship to the text.

The dialogue between Dionysus and Pentheus, making visible the potential implications of the relationship between the two characters, might be said to lend itself well to psychological analyses, perhaps only too familiar, and we could recognize a whole range of psychoanalytical impulses and perversions in Pentheus: sadism in l. 809, the anobjectual desire to buy everything with money in l. 812, masochism and voyeurism in ll. 814 and 816, and transvestism in the last lines. This impression is not wholly arbitrary, as we know from our comments on the appearance of erotic desire in Euripides's tragedies, and to some extent it fits with what happens in the scene, but since the character's personality could not conceivably change four or five times in the space of a few lines, clearly what we have here is a single real force and not some disturbing invention of Euripides's. In Girard's perspective, this single force is mimetism, the mimetic attraction between the two opponents who at the end become indistinguishable in the interdividual phase of metaphysical or ontological desire, the polarization that absorbs the rivals in one another and threatens their very existence; and there can be no doubt that the clarity and simplicity of Girard's explanation marks a great advance on previous interpretations. However, the Girardian type of approach is always open to the objection that it overmodernizes archaic situations since mimetic desire makes important aspects clear but fails to completely explain them or provide us with a context, operating as an essentially extracultural invariable. The interdividual analysis realizes part of the truth, but it is only the final, not to say the implicit and even redundant, part of what Euripides makes us perceive as a result of a religious mediation failing to function, not as its prerequisite and cause.

It is enough to insert the religious variable, it does not matter to what extent and intensity, in order to reach the correct interpretive level. The scene's terrible fascination lies in this copresence of two historical processes, coexisting and copenetrating, making it impossible to say where the psychological begins and the religious ends since both share in a single breakdown; while enabling their differentiation, it has still to provide for it because divine mediation is no longer stable and psychic mediation has yet to establish itself. And having recognized that, we can approach the tragedy's mediatory assumptions to observe more accurately their power and crisis, and note the point at which the failure of their controlling power opens the way to psychic phenomena that would become ours, that are already ours in an archaic, alienating *status nascendi*.

The dialogue occurs immediately after the miraculous release of the god and the messenger's account of the first bacchanal, foretelling in its turn the last and decisive bacchanal that brings the story to a close. The initial reference to sacrifice is both technical and allusive, and takes us, from l. 794 onward, into an unmistakably dense semantic area: the equivalence of *thuo* (to sacrifice) and *thymoo* (to become furious) elicit the homonymy of θύω in the sense of sacrifice and θύω meaning to rage and crave through the Homeric notion of θυμός, the life force and the heart as the seat of desire and anger.[19] Pentheus's *thymos* shows us the transition from fury to the sacrifice that ought to placate it; but this time his fury is directed against the fury of the bacchantes, and their fury rebounds on his own through the fury of the *daimon*. All this crisscrossing of competing, converging *thymoi* ends in a destructive *thuein* that, far from bringing peace, is quite unable to transfigure and crystallize a supreme divine mediation. As a result, the initial *thymos* becomes more visible as an endowment of the individual imperfectly mediated by the god, as an unburned residue that returns to us, the audience, in the form of desire. Concealed within the correspondence between the verbs, which overlap like two meanings of a single verb, there is an irremediable difference, evinced by the fact that the fury of the Dionysian women, quite correct from a technical and theological standpoint, is none other than the punishment inflicted by the god on the Theban women—which amounts to saying that there is no difference in principle between Pentheus's intended sacrifice, in l. 796, of his female relatives and fellow citizens transformed into maenads, and the sacrifice that they will make of him. So what we are seeing here is a triumph of sacrifice that attests to its own inefficacy, rendered tangible, and an inefficacy that makes tangible the power of sacrifice, all the more frightening the more inevitable it is, even when its ritual prerequisites begin to crumble and lose their force, exposing something unforeseen by the initial ritual: the story of the *Bacchae*, the tragic genre that made the telling of the story possible, down to the various modern theories that attempt to explain both, collecting together their several *membra*, no less *disiecta* than the remains of Pentheus scattered over Cithaeron.

This powerless power, this triumph both defeating and defeated, is what makes Dionysus *aporos*, that is, with no path for escape, neither actively, in the sense of providing one, nor passively in the sense of having one; the twofold meaning gives rise to the differentiation between the two characters and, at the same time, undermines it to produce a contrary movement: a duplication moving toward identity and an identity that remains duplication. And it is this potentially unlimited principle of duplication and deprivation that makes Dionysus absolute master of the *logos*, never remaining quiet, always having the last word, closing off every dialogue to his own advantage, and always coming out on top whether offended or offending. This *logos* is in no way a word of a modern type: it is a performative power of duplication with its implicit origin in an *unum*, an event generating language because it precedes language, a convergence in which acting and suffering become *unum* (achieve at-one-ment). The decisive transition occurs straight after the reference to the Stranger never being quiet, with his ironic "to settle matters," commented on straightaway by Pentheus's image of being like a "slave to my slaves," a sort of double negation, positional and semantic, anticipating what will shortly happen. Euripides swiftly strips away all the means that had prevailed up until then in the civilized context of the *polis*: in the first place, the weapons that the king had meant to use to ensure obedience to the rules ("I shall bring those women to you, without needing arms"); Pentheus's attempt to reply to this, calling for the arms that represent his power, ends in a fatal command; he orders the Stranger to break off the *legein* and not make use of the *logos*; the *daimon* answers with an interjection that signals the approach of the climax of what was a rite and now becomes a psychological turning-point as well, the point at which a *thymos* breaks in to become yearning, sudden desire, and ἔρως.

A reading in terms of desire and interdividuality might be applied more appropriately at this juncture, not as the last demystification but rather as the outcome of a development shown as it begins in the scene in the *Bacchae*; and the starting point for this development, and its point of arrival, is not a negative entity, a simple *nefas* to be shunned, but a mediatory reality in which individuality originates and is lost should the conditions of its mediation fail, or should it lose objectual significance. That is much more likely to occur at a stage, such as in the ancient world, when individual objectuality has become a fact but is still far from being stabilized, still closely dependent on ritual factors that, having brought it into being, can just as easily annul it with brutal suddenness. This explains the partial dismantling of the relationship between god and mortal, leading to partly defining, rather than openly revealing, their even too human reciprocity.

From this point of view, Dionysus appears to act like a seducer, moving in and trapping his victim with all the most artful ruses of seduction, and heading toward a disaster that becomes inevitable in the end, while the ritual relationship with his followers appears to be one of successful seduction and ought to end with the supreme mediation of the seducer-god but instead begins to look like a seduction desired by the humans, making Dionysus himself an inhuman rather than a superhuman being. As Tiresias tells Pentheus at the beginning of the play, the god is flattered by praise, just like the king of Thebes.[20] Worship in Greek tragedy becomes more and more a *thymos* existing between men and gods, an ambiguous oscillation that reveals and conceals according to the spectrum of indetermination that defines it. This is why Dionysus in the *Bacchae* is in constant need of new worshippers to adore him, just as the seducer must always be making new conquests. The *daimon* charmer is insatiable, with no interest in his worshipers as individuals but only in the act of worship, continually repeated by fresh neophytes, by new submissions. Those who do not worship him must be converted or punished. We might even say that this explains his perpetual wandering: his old followers are never enough for him, never enough to prove his divine nature. He never shows much interest even in his most faithful female followers: one person who refuses to worship him means much more to him than the whole race of maenads. He concentrates on that one, seduced in his turn by what appears completely *other* to him. The ritual relationship of worship, of divine mediation, which the sacrifice should determine definitively, is questioned and begins to shift, becoming unstable and oscillating dizzyingly. The face of the god is not "unmasked" since the mask is the condition of his ontological and/or representational existence, but his face comments on the mask, shows it to be in close, reversible contact with human masks, and transforms it into the Dionysian mirror, reflecting all the characters, a sinister reflection making visible a light of darkness.

In this fleeting anthropological and historical *reductio* of Dionysus, this nonreductionist reduction created in Euripides's masterpiece, the human dynamic leading to the story's epilogue becomes apparent, the μηχανή to trap Pentheus as well as stage machinery for Dionysus to appear deus ex machina in an elaborate, mechanical divinization that no longer divinizes anything. What reasons, human or inhuman, lie behind the disastrous failure of Dionysus's mediation? The closest parallel is with Pandarus in Shakespeare's *Troilus and Cressida* as his figure emerges from Girard's analysis, sinisterly manipulating other people's desires to avenge his failure to fulfill his own, a bitter representation of the playwright himself and his defeated desires. Such a character was fully human by Shakespeare's time and could not have been created without Christian psychological realism, but the function and paradox of Pandarus are anticipated in Euripides's Dionysus. The continuity in the line of inquiry followed by the two dramatists is truly remarkable: Shakespeare takes up and develops Euripides's problems with the representational freedom granted by Christianity. This freedom allows him to show desire openly, freeing the representation from myth and creating a literary and theatrical space to forge a new tragic ambiguity, so much so that we find similar characters in modern theater: the more ironic Ligurio in Niccolò Machiavelli's *La mandragola*, before Shakespeare, and afterward the more benign Don Alfonso in Wolfgang Amadeus Mozart's and Lorenzo Da Ponte's *Così fan tutte*. Girard is unaware of the mediatory self-sufficiency of this ambiguity, held back by a fear of the doubles that gives his analyses a rationalistic and moralistic tinge, not unlike Manzoni's rationalizations in a way but without the benefit of the doubles of literary creation. The freedom of Shakespeare's characters is the despairing yet fruitful ambiguity of men who, while not acknowledging the possibilities or significance of Christian mediation, are nevertheless steeped in it and exploit the tragic freedom of which Nietzsche would be both a leading exponent and victim.

Euripides could not draw on a mental universe of such richness and variety, nor conceive of possibilities that the moderns were to abuse, but this only makes his research the more admirable in the dry essentiality of the action, bringing the proliferation of the doubles so abruptly to an end in the final catastrophe. Dionysus is Pandarus without Christianity, he is Daedalus, the playwright, and the prophet who ought to provide the answers, but this god, too divine not to drive us to despair and too human not to fill us with disgust, submits to and is emptied out by his symbolic functions. He is moved by them just as they move all the other characters, like a puppet on a string. The mirror of Dionysus is blind, and finally breaks. There being no way to undo it, the knot of the tragic double-bind is sliced clean through, with a drastic formula that anticipates the anecdote of the Gordian knot, severed by Alexander the Great with a single sword-stroke.

By applying to tragedy a form of euhemerism—the later theory of Euhemerus according to which the gods were divinized human heroes—we can state that it is Pentheus who makes Dionysus a god through the violence of his fight against him: this hatred ends by clothing its object in a divine, elusive light. The divine goad that he can no longer kick against, from the point of view of its result, is none other than this: the goad *is* the god—tragic euhemerism—and just as true in a collective sense since the community itself triggers the mediation of the god that seduces it. All the Thebans attack Dionysus and become secretly fascinated by him. In denying his divinity, they let themselves be hypnotized by him; but that in itself somehow justifies their initial opposition. This makes Dionysus both omnipotent and unacceptable, giving him back the archaic stratum of the *daimon*, the *numen* that acts as an impersonal principle always ready to strike at human beings, to punish them for wrongdoing that appears increasingly unwarranted and arbitrary, or to abandon them to the vortices of a human condition disdained by the gods, as can be seen respectively with Aphrodite and Artemis in the *Hippolytus*.

Whether hated or worshipped, Dionysus is the mathematical result, as it were, of divine mediations no longer functioning and human mediations that have yet to work; and this is the only type of interpretation to explain the tragedy's contradictory and confusing aspects. Dionysus is the traditional god and, at the same time, the symbol of the *thymoi* of human beings. Among other matters, this explains better the ambiguity of the third person form, in addition to the first plural, sometimes adopted by Dionysus in speaking of himself, an ambiguity that it would be too simplistic to explain solely by the fact of his being disguised as a human being.[21] Pentheus, in his turn, is the real *pars pro toto* of human mediations failing to crystallize into divine mediation, the real alter ego of what Dionysus should be if the rite functioned. As a result, the sacrificial solution finally returns, although in an explosive and exploded form that makes the text more effective but the ritual action less so, in the form of a new mediation that will become literary but is not yet firmly established as such (which occurs in the following Hellenistic period when political mediations are set up and represented by new centers of ecumenical power). With painfully didactic clarity characteristic of much that he says, although it goes stubbornly unrecognized by the person directly involved, Dionysus sums up his role, both ancestral and imminent, in these words: "You are the only one to suffer for this city, the only one" (l. 963). The *reductio ad unum*, atonement, now appears but leaves the *reductio* process visible, the humanity of the *unum* on which the collective and textual movement converges without reunification.

We can now go back to the psychological progression of the dialogue and avoid introducing excessive fractures relative to the divine mediation that sets it going. The king of Thebes's transition from his armed aspect to his disarmed, defenseless aspect, succumbing to the blandishments of the god, is first apparent in the immediately preceding lines when Pentheus summons the army to one of the city gates. The armed mobilization would appear to be complete, except that the focus shifts treacherously from the god himself to an obsession with the god-possessed women. In fact, it all happens in the course of an increasingly close dialogue with the Stranger. Gradually and unconsciously Pentheus excludes his direct opponent from his intended reprisals, creating a neutral zone where, without realizing it, he appears more and more curious about his adversary until he comes to seek his complicity.

This change starts to appear in Pentheus's admiration of the youthful aspect of his enemy and becomes quite obvious once the king, in his palace, has deceived himself into thinking, first, that he has tied up Dionysus in the form of a bull and, secondly, that he has killed him as a ghostly apparition (φάσμα). This parodies the killing of the Minotaur in the labyrinth,[22] and perhaps the Eleusinian visions as well, and can be associated with the omitted sacrifice in the *Cretans*, while it anticipates Pentheus's sacrificial fate, as he is about to fall prey to Dionysus Zagreus. At the same time, to avoid the too modern connotations of an antireligious parody, we must not leave it out that such apparitions, such *phasmata*, are an intermediate, pneumatic reality for Euripides. The mistake of Dionysus's foe does not lie in mistaking mirages for reality, it lies in not recognizing their intermedial and *imaginalis* nature, a clue of the displaced but real presence of the god, ironically watching the whole scene.

These are important nuances, though they do not change the concluding result. The deceptive labyrinth of rationality, with its belief in its own self-sufficiency, like the labyrinth of rituality with its conviction of self-perpetuation in virtue of itself, comes crashing down, like the royal palace of Pentheus, to make way for another labyrinth, the labyrinth of the human being with its need for mediations and with its objectual sphere always exposed to the danger of collapse. The reciprocal polarization of seducer and seduced goes ahead with nothing to stop it. The bacchantes are now no more than a pretext for the culminating rapprochement of the two adversaries, for achieving the fusion of the divine and human; besides, that was part of their traditional role, but now it causes a final, fatal confusion with a uniting that only disunites, a hierogamy that divides forever.

When Pentheus calls for his arms in order to lead the soldiers on to Cithaeron, the opposite, hidden extreme of his opposition emerges; this follows a dynamic that we also find, at the psychic level, in the masochistic submission secretly contained in the caricature of sadistic domination. When considered in context, the psychological modernization makes it possible to admire the mediatory ambiguity that reveals a glimpse of it within the sacral symbolism, glittering like an element within its containing mineral: the scene already cited where Pentheus imagines he is butchering Dionysus's *phasma* while the god looks on in amusement (ll. 629–31) is a perfect example of the illusory, endogenous nature of his fury, his *thymos*, as well as its strictly ritual and magical origin. It is safe to say that the entire theatrical armory of contemporary perversions is potentially present in these lines, including the elementary, direct commerce of prostitution, evoked by the "lots of gold" that the Theban king, in his sudden mad possession, would willingly pay for the favors of the possessed women.

But this should not make us overlook a series of increasing contaminations; indeed it should underline their sacral origin. At one time regulated and made meaningful by the ritual eroticism that Georges Bataille investigated, these are now superimposed on top of each other and develop toward an unstoppable crescendo. Pentheus's eroticism degenerates into a transgression of such enormity—among the bacchantes arousing the young king's *eros* are his mother and sisters—that only the most enormous ritual reprisal can restore some sort of balance, though the system has been sent so heftily off-balance that any real readjustment is impossible. The tensional, dynamic balance in archaic orgiastic rites between rules and transgression, noted by Bataille, ceases to be the para- or preobjectual equivalent of sacrifice, when it revives the destruction of objectuality to restore it again afterward, and leads instead to the destruction of the community's entire objectual sphere, represented here by the royal function of Pentheus, never so much king of his city as when he shows himself unworthy of it.

The investigation of sacred monarchy that began, as we have seen, with Minos in the *Cretans* reaches its furthest point here, passing from a king who was to die *in place of* the community to a king who dies as *representative* of his community, to become its *pars pro toto* since the community as such dies along with him. There are thus two types of ritual and political sacrifice: the effective sacrifice allowing the community to live on, though in any case already in the *Cretans* this is not the case; and the sacrifice anticipating and representing its death as a collective entity to which we may already relate the killing of Pasiphae, and yet the most appalling example is the king of Thebes in the *Bacchae*. The most exterior political level of the work, addressed to the Macedonian king Archelaus, is not troubled by this situation, thanks to the story's Hellenic/barbaric register which concentrates immediate blame on the failure of the Greek political mediator while the divine mediator remains swathed in a cloud of neoarchaic sacral motivations and so never has a really destabilizing effect. In the end the whole *fabula* stands on the undemonstrated but systematically asserted assumption that nothing terrible would befall the city of Thebes, and therefore Greece, as long as it recognized the sovereignty of the god of sacrificial ecstasy and did not surrender to the *hybris* of Athenian rationalism and its will to dominate. A political reading is no substitute for other readings and is limited to providing their background, but this background makes it possible to test the other readings and keeps them safely compatible with a mediatory world that had to recover fully by looking at different mediations, and different worlds.

One last interpretive aspect should attract our attention: our own position as modern readers vis-à-vis the tragic epilogue of the *Bacchae*. Have we the right to draw a teaching from the conclusion of Euripides's drama? And within what limits?

3. The Lesson of a Drama

The first problem to which the modern readers tend to pay attention is what we may call the moral problem, implicating the personal responsibility of the characters. It is obvious that this line of reflection falls outside the ambit of Euripides's cultural universe but not entirely since, here too, our observations continue the ancient reflection, clearly recognizable in a tragedy like Sophocles's *Oedipus Rex*, and take it to their ultimate consequences. And the more specifically moral aspect obliges us, whether we want to or not, to make a judgment, the reasons for which are removed by the plot but not the final hidden object, the sense of human life, the objectual significance of the ethical distinctions that underpin human existence and that the divine mediations are no longer able to guarantee.

The inevitable question then arises about what attitude to adopt toward the ruthless punishment meted out to Pentheus, besides the question of the real extent of his guilt, which consists, more than in his failure to worship Dionysus, as Tiresias maintains, in his not asking questions as to why it was necessary, in his remaining completely unconscious of the human need to have an objectual sphere and the supreme mediations that alone are able to procure it. It is a failure of his collective role as king and thus an individual failure as well, a renunciation of the value of the individual that is the great spiritual discovery of Greek classical culture, though always within the frame of the *polis*. The individual unable to read the collective factors allowing him to exist is headed for the worst defeat because he loses the narrow possibility of choice that would be his only resource. This is the start of an infernal course that leads to the destruction of the individual's objectual worth since it is the individual who remains blind to the slender but decisive resources that would assist in the conquest of self and help to achieve a small but fundamental objectual salvation, the restoration of simple everyday life; in effect, the chorus states as much in the first stasimon but goes no further than to repeat the reasons for a savage mediation devoid of objectual functions. Actually, not even remembering the necessity of collective mediations is enough.

Euripides's silent commentary lies at a deeper level compared to the interpretive schemes intervening in the course of the plot; however, we can reach it if we see it as a continuation of our own and identify the slight link connecting the two. The subject is a theme that pervades Greek culture in its classical period, starting with the dramatic questions assailing it at the end of the fifth century, but one that it does not manage to develop within its historical boundaries: the meaning of individual freedom never acquires independent status in respect to the dominant idea of *eleutheria*, the freedom seen by the Greeks as primarily the freedom of the community itself or such as the community recognizes, as Hannah Arendt understood in her analysis of public action in the ancient classical world.[23] Nevertheless, in the fifth-century crisis, there is a growing perception of the individual's faculty for choice, which does not fit into the overall picture, but arose from the manifest failure of social and political mediations as well as the religious.

In this situation Pentheus serves as a terrible warning. In fact, his mad ignorance of Dionysian madness destroys the only possible bulwark that might save him, an ability to break free from the most destructive of fascinations. Dionysus tells us as much in his ferocious *rhesis* where he remarks on the total success of his diabolical plan of sacrificial seduction:

> 848 Women, the man has cast himself into the net [*es bolon*],
> 847 and will go to the bacchantes, where his punishment [*diken*] will be death.
> Dionysus, the task [*ergon*] is yours now: you are not far away.
> We shall be avenged for him. First, make him mad,
> fill him with vain fury, since in his right mind
> he would never dress up as a woman.
> But he will if he is out of his mind.
> I want him to be a laughingstock for the Thebans,
> to be paraded around the city dressed as a woman,
> after the threats that made him so terrible [*deinos*] at first.
> But I go now to make him beautiful [*kosmon*], to go down into Hades
> slain by a mother's hands,
> Pentheus, and he will know who is the son of Zeus,
> Dionysus, in every way a god,
> most terrible and sweetest for mortals.[24]

Dionysus is going to accomplish the ἔργον of sacrifice, prepared by the disguises and the furious cults of the god, and with a final ignominious walk, the route of the Athenian convicts to death who had to cross the city receiving the mockery and blows of the crowd, evidently modelled on the walk of the *pharmakoi*. The coordinates of the sacrificial *ergon* are symbolically the same of hierogamy: to Pentheus's mother corresponds Dionysus's father Zeus, to Agave's son going toward an awful punishment corresponds the triumphant son of the king of the gods. Being *kosmos* should make the victim capable of giving order and beauty to the entire cosmos but, needless to say, in the Greek historical cosmos there is neither order nor harmony. Dionysus's divine ancestry destroys Pentheus's human ancestry, and therefore destroys any possible relationship between men and gods.

With these words, Euripides's Dionysus reasserts his own ruthless motives and indirectly, by way of negation, the motives for the human rationality pursued by Greek civilization, toward which it also inclined especially when it was seen to be trampled on and violated, a rationality capable of recognizing and safeguarding the objectual value of human life for what it is. In this, Christianity's vision of mankind and its relationship to divine mediation was to be profoundly different, and yet it was to provide a precise answer to the need expressed by Euripides behind the tragic mask of his *fabula*. Girard's code, with its total opposition of the ancient and Judeo-Christian universes, helps us recognize the gap between the two but prevents us from recognizing the continuity that makes the discontinuity significant. From this viewpoint, it might be said that Dionysus the exterminator in the *Bacchae* corresponds to what the Gospels were to call the *skandalon* or Satan, not because his *daimon* coincides antihistorically with the Miltonic *pandemonium*, as Christians came to define the devils and the pagan demons collectively, but because it really fails to respond to the longing felt by the Greeks, as by all human cultures, to achieve what is human and realize its objectual significance.

The idea set before us by Euripides is that once we have put our trust in Dionysus, in *this* Dionysus, falsely mediatory and dishumanly antiobjectual, once a certain threshold has been passed, there is nothing to be done, no going back; but the most terrible idea is that Dionysus's victims choose to put themselves in his hands. In regard to this specific aspect, an interdividual type of analysis with its intransitive demystifications reveals both its usefulness and inadequacy since it tends to nullify any individual whose mediatory and objectual prerequisites it does not recognize. The observations developed up to this point entitle us to underscore what has always been maintained by the best of the Jewish and Christian tradition, namely, that the individual human being, in all its immense frailty, is not merely the result of greater forces, not simply a prefix, "in-," to be deleted in order to coin a new theoretical term, but the last word, the last resort, in the face of the infernal unleashing of objectual destruction. The individual, who appeared to be ridiculed by the predominance of the processes generating him, is not an illusion but a fragile, hard-won end result, the very core of the objectual value, both bodily and imaginal, of every single man and woman, of what we may frankly call their dignity, however narrow may be the margin of their freedom of choice.

This is what makes the seduction experienced and accepted by Pentheus so terrible, and not only for ourselves since in fact it continues a concern running through Euripides's text: as an old-fashioned Christian might have said, Pentheus sells his soul to the devil, where the ancient *daimon* becomes the Christianized demon, that is, a divine mediator degraded to be an anobjectual, murderous principle. Demonology is nothing but a theology of archaic and defeated gods, as we shall see dealing with the passage from pagan polytheism to monotheism in the Middle-Judaic religious thinking. However, the very important as much as unnoticed detail is that this demonological defeat, already visible in the *Bacchae*, expresses a substantial dissatisfaction on the divine mediations of the Greek world, studied by Euripides with a profundity never acknowledged by scholars. This theological/demonological defeat becomes a defeat of the human being, a human objectuality terribly missing his goal.

What makes Pentheus so awesome is that he illustrates this step, central to the destiny of every human being and equally secretive: "You are a terrible [*deinos*], terrible being and terrible trials [*pathe*] await you."[25] The *pathe* in this allusion are the pains of ancestral mediations without which mankind could not have survived or existed, but they include the immeasurable suffering entailed by lack of respect for the deepest purposes of divine and human mediations, including the arrogant ignorance and ignorant arrogance shown in our own day. The *deinos*, the *tremendum* that is the drug that feeds on horror, entails the *pathos* that rouses our sentiments and makes sentimentalists of us in our incomprehension. The reckless king of Thebes unconsciously throws to the winds that single, impalpable resource that we do our utmost to dispel in order to return to the old, insane unconsciousness. A character from ancient Greece makes us know evil, and we perfect the evil by refusing the remedy. The drama of freedom trampled down and ignored *is* a drama within the drama, and Euripides is fully aware of it; his authentically moral impulse makes our moralism and sophisms look pale by comparison.

One last observation concerns free will in the world inhabited by Pentheus; still not knowing what use to make of this tiny yet incalculable resource, it is unable even to see the problem in its entirety. Without adequate cultural and religious mediations, Pentheus is irresistibly brought to coincide with his antagonist, and his very small margin of freedom is resolved and dispelled in deterministic action. The desires of both characters come to coincide as by a fatal flaw: Pentheus relives his rival's sufferings (*pathe*), his Titanic destiny, the dismembering that recalls a now impossible remembrance; with no further transformations, the circle of the labyrinth closes, or rather collapses on whoever has entered it. There is no way out from Ariadne, from Dionysus. There is only one corollary to giving up individual freedom, one unfailing consequence, the triumph of objectual destruction, the predominance of blind violence. Hellenic civilization was not to be without answers in the face of this dilemma, such as the great sapiential mediation concerning the individual and the soul that Socrates introduced. This was developed by Plato, his pupil, in a polemic against the tragic theater that had flaunted the question on the public stage but gave no answers, and actually compounded the problem by presenting an image of divine mediations that was distorted and, in the final analysis, reversed. It will be fascinating to observe how the search for an answer is not satisfied within the historical and cultural boundaries of classical Greece but needs to go beyond, to confront Judaism and Christianity and, at times, to join them in their quest for a higher divine mediation.

Our analysis of Euripides's masterpiece can be said to be essentially concluded as regards what it had to tell us about the profoundest Greek thinking about sacrificial mediation, though perhaps we need a remark or two to introduce the following Intermezzo, so as to enable us to tackle the comparison between ancient civilization and Christianity that forms the keystone of the present work. The epilogue to the *Bacchae* ought to make us appreciate a capacity that is ours if we want it though we normally make no use of it: simply to name the horrors of Dionysus ἐμφανής, manifest, for what they are, to see the bleak human, and inhuman, reality that in one way or another is concealed by the symbols, the *symbola*, of sacrificial mediations.

Girard's ideas undoubtedly played an essential part in the acquisition of this dimension, which is both moral and cognitive, with his reiterated statement that all human culture derives from the victims, the foundation of its greatness and meanness. Nevertheless, the attitude taught us by Girard is not sufficient in itself, since it leads to moral condemnation of the entire history of mankind. Such condemnation makes little sense, as it postulates the presence in human history of an absolute moral greatness that men have violated, without in the least considering the conditions by which men might just become capable of recognizing their own victims. Alongside this ability to call things by their right name, there is another no less important ability noted by Bataille, namely the ability to see the blinding radiance spreading out from sacrificial violence, its inner power to transform a savage act in itself merely natural, into an act of attention that is no longer instinctual, a preparation for the eventual reversal in a still distant future toward shared caring, sympathy, and compassion. It is what Bataille experiences as he looks at photographs of the Chinese death of a thousand cuts; it is an ecstatic feeling, and the basis of what he calls *communication*, the sudden transitivity between human beings who have nothing else in common. Bataille's experience is so powerful that it puts him in *real* contact with another human being who is present only as an image, rather blurred and faded with age. If tragedy and all human sacrificial mediations are to be viewed correctly, then these two requirements, these two directions, have to be brought together, while considering above all their contradiction, the destructive and creative double bind, the infinite source of pain and knowledge, brutal interruption and surprising transitivity, killing and rebirth.

This leads to a further observation. How easy we find it to avoid the copresence of both extremes and their necessity, in a double unwillingness that makes us indignant when we ought to be understanding and understanding when we ought to be indignant. Either way we miss the mark because we fail to understand that the only correct historical perspective is, as it were, binocular and must coordinate both sides defining the field of vision in order to obtain the third *imaginalis* dimension of depth, thus enabling us to gauge space and move in it—that is to say, to know and live it. And so we show how far we fall short, not only of the Jewish and Christian ethics that we profess to follow or oppose, not only of the Socratic and Platonic ethical values that are our common heritage, but also of the truth that speaks to us behind or through the mask of tragic theater. In spite of all our superficial or erudite discussions of Greek tragedy, as soon as we set it in relation to ourselves, it creates an unbearable sense of déjà vu that estranges us from the tragic and perhaps condemns us to suffer some far-fetched comedy. The language of tragedy, having ignored the true greatness of Shakespeare, Manzoni, Büchner, and the other great explorers of tragedy in European culture, has devolved into the commonplaces of journalism and mass literature, not because there are no tragic realities to be written about, seeing that nothing produces or increases tragedies so much as the negation of tragedy, but because we avoid the words and ideas to name them, let alone explain them. Must we conclude that the only theatrical metaphor suitable to define us is tragi-comedy?

Euripides and the Greeks really do have a great deal to teach us about this matter, about what use we should make of a freedom that our alternate, complementary oscillations show we are unwilling to use; and in this regard the true *fabula* of the *Bacchae* can tell us a great deal. However, the moment has arrived to reconstruct in outline the conditions that led to the birth of tragic knowledge and the general context of a civilization that was able to push so far ahead in exploring its sacrificial mediations. In this way the comparison that I intend to reach, and have only mentioned in passing so far, should at last become accessible and begin to take shape.

8.

The Birth of Tragedy, the End of Classical Greece

> He showed him the first sheet of paper. The traveler would have liked to say something complimentary but could see nothing but lines repeatedly crossing each other, like a labyrinth, covering the paper so densely that the blank spaces were barely visible. "Read it" the officer said. "I can't" the traveler answered. "But it's perfectly clear" said the officer. "It's really ingenious" the traveler said evasively, "but I really can't make it out." "Quite so" the officer replied, laughing and putting the paper away, "it's not a school exercise in calligraphy! You need to read it over and over again. Eventually you'd understand it as well. Of course it can't be the usual simple lettering: it doesn't have to kill straight away, but after an interval of about twelve hours on average."
>
> —Franz Kafka, "In the Penal Colony"

1. The Need for Tragedy and Its Superseding

Our inquiry so far implies more specific questions about the nature of Greek wisdom in general and of the Athenian tragedy in particular with its distinctive form of knowledge, amounting to a wider reflection on the civilization that made them possible. There is no simple answer, and once again we shall have to start from a series of clues that remain just so many fragments unless we analyze their overall meaning in context. And, beyond single hypotheses and gaps in the evidence, the context that speaks to us through scattered but consistent traces is a vibrant and at times dramatic one. Analysis of those traces will give us an idea of the religious and cultural mediations in which tragedy took shape and moved, and enable us to probe in a general way the nature and origin of the sapiential environment that gave birth to tragedy, to be connected and compared with the more variegated and intercultural environment of the Ionian colonies that had given birth to philosophy a century before.

The nature of the subject as history should not create the impression that this is a pure essay in historical scholarship. Certainly, the historiographical aspect cannot be ignored, but much more is involved here. Tragedy's paradoxical knowledge is meaningful as a historiographical and historical question in the sense that it touches on the nature of human history and what it can relate and understand about itself. Any approach with the idea of tragedy as a predefined and classified genre would therefore be useless since it would block from the very outset the cognitive transition, the disguised and revealing contamination that is the soul of tragic theater. In the same way, tragic knowledge is not the neutral tool of a knowledge that has already been given, nor can it be made the indifferent object of an inquiry that takes its tools for granted and files away in some archive what ought to be its discoveries, thereby nullifying every real discovery. Tragedy would never have come into existence without investigating its own nature, or without a growing controversy over the means of expression used and its purpose as seen by the public. Tragedy is theater—that is to say, the theatrical animal that is man—investigating itself. It is the theater of the origin that proves to be the origin of theater, the formulation of the originating enigma and of the labyrinth space of human genesis that the public can accept seeing only on the stage, and even then it must be heavily veiled, transformed by its disguises to allow every kind of diversion and ambiguity. Knowledge in Greek theater is therefore indirect and hidden and exists only as long as it obeys the rules defining its fiction, maintaining inviolate the double bind on which it feeds. The outlook that we are allowed to glimpse is potentially so radical that it would eventually compromise any theater, and even the cultural reality itself coming from the theatrical origin. So inevitably, over the centuries, Greek drama also became, at an interpretive level, a place to evade the origin, to institute the literary criticism that determined its concealment, thereby substantially continuing the deception of the characters in tragedy, as we saw in regard to the interpretive history of the *Bacchae*. Few traps are as insidious, since it is set by the same text that helps to undermine it and also supplies the elements to recognize it. A curious, ironic semitragedy—a metatragedy or para-tragedy according to the seriousness or inconsistencies of its implications—looms over a large part of the vast bibliography on the subject and over the bibliographical tombs of our cultural mausoleums in general, awaiting a catharsis that will never come unless it is as breaking-up in indifference, like that fading into irrelevance that awaits anyone who evades the problem that was his own, and should have been his to tackle.

The ironically tragic death wish of our knowledge of tragedy can be gauged by a specific reference, easy to verify if we are prepared to follow its inexorable inner logic. Alone among nineteenth-century scholars and philosophers, Nietzsche recognized Greek tragedy for what it was; however, his motives were so partial and reckless that he was brought to relive, this time in a solipsistic and psychic form, the fate of the tragic ghosts that he obsessively invoked. The failure to perceive this drama *in* the drama and *about* the drama has had disastrous hermeneutic consequences; it has prevented Nietzsche's investigations from being seen as the continuation of Wagner's remarkable intuitions, and prevented recognition of the pertinence of the contributions made by Gabriele D'Annunzio and Thomas Mann who resumed those investigations. And thus a whole piece of European and Western culture has been cancelled, but it is remarkable to note the repercussions of this cancellation on the interpretation of the history of Greek theater. The example of the author of *The Birth of Tragedy* is so terrible that nobody else has really dared to venture down the same path, and even a scholar like Colli, steeped both in the Greek world (studying its archaic and pre-Socratic wisdom) and in the philosophy of Nietzsche (preparing the best edition of his *Sämmtliche Werke*), takes good care not to include tragedy among the essential manifestations of Greek knowledge as a focus deserving special attention and the collection of sources. He carefully avoids any real mise au point with *The Birth of Tragedy* and, above all, with the origin of Nietzsche's personal tragedy.

The counterexample to this strategy of evasion could only be the other obsessive extreme of Nietzsche's oscillations, the tragedy confronted and mysteriously overcome by Christ, an opposite tale to the story of Dionysus, and one that his modern prophet would silence forever and yet to which he always returns. This observation is not to be understood directly at the level of historical and religious content, implicitly taking a stance pro or contra, taking sides ideologically or apologetically in an interminable polemic that makes any philosophical or scientific advance impossible. What interests me first of all is the phenomenological and historical emergence of an event and an experience—Christ's crucifixion and resurrection—in which a tragic history of the same type is faced and objectually overcome with the living, victorious affirmation of the ideals of the person who suffered that tragedy unto death and thereby struck a deadly blow at the root of the symmetrical retaliatory logic that prevented the figures of tragedy from breaking out of the circle imprisoning them.[1]

There can be no doubt that the great Greek tragedians aimed to achieve similar transcendence, but their growing difficulties show how far beyond the horizons of their world that solution still lay. Aeschylus's Athena is certainly evocative and solemn when she intervenes at the end of the *Eumenides*, as we have seen, but she fails to give full effect to the mediatory role of the divine; it remains the expression of an Hellenic world looking to the divine for the answer to its internal convulsions. If we possessed the *Prometheus Unbound*, the companion tragedy completing the *Prometheus Bound*, we would know much more about the theology of Aeschylus; however, we are justified in thinking that not even those two great plays came up with a solution to reconcile the impersonal collectivism of the religion of the *polis* with the longing for salvation found in the mystery cults and Orphism, to which Aeschylus was close. Sophocles shares Aeschylus's assumptions on the one hand but, on the other, he records and ratifies their failure, showing his heroes to be ever in need of a divine mediation that they never tire of seeking, and even the supreme effort of *Oedipus at Colonus*, written and performed after the death of Euripides, fails to settle the questions raised by the hero on stage, and embodied by him in his own mythical origin.[2] Those questions relate to a transcendent mediation not recognizing what is represented and therefore void of an object, its final outcome not differing greatly from the anobjectuality of Euripides's Dionysus.

Once we have the idea of divine mediation, and understand the necessity of its objectual realization for it to be said to have achieved its purpose, we also have the coordinates for comparing Greek tragedy and Christianity without the apologist's bias either way, that is, either attributing predetermined value to Christianity as truth or giving credit to traditional schemes of a *praeparatio evangelica*. In themselves, such schemes might be preferable, recognizing at least that the *praeparatio* has independent cultural value, but they are conditioned by a prior choice from which the interpretation derives and so lack the objectual respect that should be the effective, effectual complement of knowledge. The predominance of one message, one content, over another, after the anobjectual manner of modern ideological debate, should not be our concern, but instead the emergence of historical and cultural phenomena giving different answers to the same basic problems. Their great value to us lies in this diversity, since even the lack of an answer possesses a certain richness in its touching poverty and testifies to a condition that none of us, as human beings, can claim is alien; just as vice versa the possession of an answer, while superficially obviating debate, leads to the unspeakable emptiness of a drama evaded and finally refused, of a human object destroyed in the suffering and inconsolable intransitivity that makes it close to us and alive. And so we have reached a different idea and understanding of *praeparatio evangelica*.

Consequently, omitting quite a few steps that I shall discuss at the end of the book, we can state that Christ's resurrection is the definitive return to life of the tragic hero more fully humanized in Judaism, as narrated earlier in the great antitragic tragedy of the book of Job—written in the Hellenistic age under the detectable influence of Greek tragedy, as is shown by the awareness of human sorrow, the dialogic style, and the philosophical references.[3] On account of this unplanned, noninvasive recognition of human objectuality and its real dramas, we ought to add that Christ's resurrection, understood as a religious and historical phenomenon that unquestionably manifested itself whatever our opinion of it, stands against nothing and nobody, nor certifies a theological truth against other claims dismissed as false by the tribunals of religion and history. Relieved of all denominational or sectarian assumptions, the redemption from death obtained by the mediator of what was to become the Christian religion reveals its potential for solving what the world of Greek tragedy can represent but cannot resolve. What we obtain by this is Nietzsche's entire interpretive and historical sphere of action, around which he moves without ever touching the center, except in the self-destructive form of madness; and we also arrive at a better definition of the center of gravity for Thomas Mann's reflections, our original starting-point. Those reflections are still embroiled in the tragic ambiguity that conveys the problem's complex nature, insurmountable except in the fragmented, unrelated intransitivity of death and catastrophe.

Once again there emerges a quest spanning thousands of years, and ignored by our cultural arrogance, convinced as it is that it is the repository of all consciousness and rationality. The tragic and para-tragic blindness of which we are willing victims is so firmly rooted that it can easily sound bizarre or provocative to state that a credible answer to the tragic contradiction is to be found in Alessandro Manzoni's Christian tragedies (and—I would add—in the biblical inspiration of Georg Büchner's dramas),[4] a credible answer because it is not a denial (not only a denial, but an affirmation of love even through death). And the Byzantine writer who in the *Christus patiens* used lines from the *Bacchae* and other tragedies and gave them a Christian meaning sensed that Christ's story is the indelible paradigm of tragedy, and its solution, not because it solves tragedy in the dissolving sense of the word but because it keeps it safe in itself and becomes its permanent symbol and touchstone, its *figura* recognizable beforehand as *prae-figuratio* (the real *praeparatio*) and afterward as *con-figuratio* (a continual *praeparatio*, fed by its past and so open to the future).

The origin of tragedy is not the only thing that I shall be trying to reconstruct from circumstantial evidence in this chapter. Nor will it merely outline my hypothesis explaining the origin of the expressive means used performatively by tragedy and made to interact, a hypothesis that makes no claim to being definitive. The means utilized by tragedy are the various languages of words, gestures, and the arts, as well as the written texts in which the tragedies were preserved for us, since wordplay in the texts themselves, graphic as well as phonetic, seems to count among these means. The genre can also be traced back especially to the quest for the real *figura* of man, for his recognizable, knowable oneness and objectual redemption, a quest for which the tragic stage becomes the sapiential and visual workshop, and appears to us as a sort of figural thinking, that is, an imaginal and rational thinking that takes shape and develops as representation of itself, reproducing and contemplating itself *in figuris*.

But let us now begin with a general but by no means exhaustive survey of the context of classical Greek drama, and the anthropological and objectual implications to be drawn from that context. The first feature to be examined arose in our analysis of the *Bacchae*, the sapiential connotation of the tragic text, of the strange cognitive spectacle that it intended to be, and was.

2. The Vision of the Enigma

Tragedy was an advanced and distinctively figural phase of thinking about sacrificial mediation permeating the highest level of Greek culture. With tragedy, this thinking made a qualitative leap and became accessible to a wider audience, appearing as mediation in full public view, though that made it no less arduous or complex to decode. The key to interpretation was freely available to the citizens of the *polis* without any ritual or initiatory restrictions, free for all to use within the limits of their own culture and awareness, up to the highest degree of knowledge, which was the prerogative of the wise man, that is, the man who has understood, the man who has *seen*. This allusive, stratified character undoubtedly presupposes a restricted circle of intellectuals who possess a knowledge not accessible to the majority, as Girard maintains about Shakespeare, an observation that can be extended to include all the great figural thinkers of our past, that is, artists who were thinkers and not only artists, bearers of a new human and spiritual objectuality that conflicted with the opinions and interests of the majority who are normally little inclined to recognize in themselves phenomena ranging from mean-minded envy to savage violence. The need to communicate to the public was at the same time a need to survive with the public, a paradoxical situation familiar to everybody active in the field of the arts and entertainment, but if properly understood, obliges us to look more closely at the origin of the expressive means being used. And nobody is more in danger of potential lynching by the public than those who reveal its embarrassing secrets and expose the contagious transitivity whose shifts and disguises form the basis of theater.

The paradox makes clear the enormous difficulty of knowing the factors on which our lives depend and also the necessity of the process since there would be no paradox if it did not exist, positioned at the center of the representational and cognitive operation being considered here, at the nerve center of the human *mythoi* where that operation occurs. The necessity of the process in no way diminishes the risks faced by anyone who wants to intercept and interpret it; indeed it shows it to be no less necessary than the figural object that absorbs all the effort. The double binds of the mediations that we need are present in all we do and think, more or less like the genetic code in our body cells, but there is a difference: errors of transmission are more frequent and interactions more immediate and dramatic in the cultural code of which we are made because its system has more complex ramifications than the natural one. And the difficulties in Euripides's double-binding relationship with his audience have already been sufficiently indicated: at one extreme the audience was unconsciously blind; at the other it showed seer-like awareness—extremes that the character of Agave in the tragedy finally brings together in herself, holding up a mirror to the audience in which, if they were willing, they could see themselves. We would be wrong to imagine any kind of intellectual or aesthetic self-indulgence in Euripides's constant dexterous maneuvering.

The minority addressed by Euripides undoubtedly belonged to the Athenian elite of his day. Their mediatory awareness in the political, religious, and historical field emerges almost superabundantly from Thucydides's *Peloponnesian War*, but there is nothing smug or consolatory about it—in spite of the Athenian historian being understandably tempted in that direction—because what such knowledge brought to light was the violent origin of all human mediations without exception. This acquisition goes hand in hand with the falling away of traditional religious mediations, made evident in Thucydides not only by the repeated violations of sacral prohibitions and abuse of temple asylum during fighting between the Athenian and Spartan blocs, but also by the disaster in Sicily when the religious *pietas* of Nicias, waiting for "three times nine days" after a lunar eclipse according to the soothsayers' prescription, only served to propitiate the trap being set for the Athenian army, losing precious days for the retreat.[5] This elite, it must be assumed, had an aristocratic outlook, such as we find in a work like the pseudo-Xenophontic *Constitution of the Athenians*;[6] besides what supporters of this aristocratic stance intended, there are also objective circumstances linking it to tragedy's particular kind of initiatory knowledge. There is something indirectly and desperately "democratic" in tragedy, using the term in a sense that must mediate between its ancient discriminatory, elitist meaning and its modern, essentially participatory sense which derives from Christian mediation. Tragic knowledge's profoundest message, in all its terrible reality, is accessible to anyone who succeeds in understanding it to some extent in terms of his or her own experience. It is secretly visible for all to see. The *pathos* of visibility, the borderline between visible and invisible, is an indispensable ingredient in gaining access to tragedy's universe of knowledge.

Greek knowledge is an act of seeing, uncovering, revealing the concealment (*a-letheia*), analogous to what occurred in the gradual visions of Eleusis. The perfect tense of *horao*, *oida*—I have seen—is equivalent to the present tense of the verb εἴδω, know, while *eidos* and *idea*, form as perceived by both our physical and mental eye, derive from the same root ιδ- (cf. Lat. *video*). The wise man is the man who knows much because he has seen much, as the name of *Poly-idos* indicates, a character protagonist of a lost Euripidean drama connected to the *Cretans*.[7] He was the soothsayer who successfully resuscitated Glaucus (the Shining One), son of Minos and Pasiphae, after he had drowned in honey, recalling once again the death-in-the-labyrinth theme, and like Daedalus, Polyeidus just manages to escape with his life. Many people attribute this power to the man who has seen and knows much, the man who is *seen* by many. Argus is another figure that can be seen to correspond to Polyeidus in origin: his body is completely covered in eyes, a mythical projection, artistic in a Hellenic way, of all eyes falling on the victim, he was later transformed into the Argus killed by Hermes. The first seeing was when the eyes of the lynchers converged with murderous intent on a single focal point, the victim, literally covered and pierced by the hate-filled eyes surrounding him. This is the "eye of death" of Ereshkigal, the Sumerian goddess of the afterlife, and the wide-eyed stare of the Anunnaki and of the statues of the Mesopotamian worshipers. Presumably it indicated their complete availability for the divine vision, but to a modern eye it looks at once sinister and haunted, by way of an association that is not so arbitrary as its obviousness might suggest. The first *eidos*, the first center of a visual field no longer instinctive at the dawn of man, is the being that bloodily enables man to bring himself into focus, and knowing that blindness—our blind spot—is the condition for its objectual results should not make us blind to the cost. Pentheus's destiny derives from the blind spot in everybody's vision and is bitterly visual, since he expects to see without being seen but in the end *is seen*.[8] This goes back to a background in ritual where seeing double was mediated by sacrifice to prepare for its final *unum*, its atonement; it is reproduced and destabilized by theatrical duplication, leading to duplication of another type. In these several senses, when Pentheus sees nothing but monstrous doubles around him, Dionysus, now in taurine form, tells him in a mocking tone: "now indeed you see what you have to see."[9]

Here, Pentheus is hallucinating on the edge of the objectual crisis, but it is through what he sees that we have our own vision, the tragic vision of the sacrificial doubles. If theater originated as representation of the doubles, then it is best exemplified by tragedy, which develops the representation to the absolute limits possible in the Hellenic world, triggering a retroaction that exceeds those limits potentially at the moment when it confirms them. This does not mean that tragedy is the ultimate in theater and insuperable, as seems to be suggested by a certain tendency to glorify Shakespeare and the tragic authors. Quite the contrary. Another possibility exists *in* and *of* the theater, supported by Manzoni but not understood by the critics, the possibility of reaching a vision of the loser, the one who pays for the others and for the system to which he belongs, transforming and overturning, however, the tragic means that make the vision possible, even if it is a possibility reserved for a Christian universe, the possibility of a tragic resurrection in a spiritual rather than material key, the prospect of a resurrection of tragedy to break the prevalence of the passive *mythos* and the combinatory solutions favored by the public. Such a remark is not to be understood in a strictly religious or edifying sense, as is no less true for a dramatist like Büchner and his desperate affirmation of love, for him the only freedom available to human beings. Far from sounding an alien note in the world of Greek tragedy, these observations allow us to strike other chords otherwise destined to remain silent, or rather inaudible, given the deafness prevailing in modern trends in interpretation.

A transcendent, incarnate mediation appeared historically necessary to enable a way to be opened for objectual redemption in the sphere of tragedy, after the historical Christianity had mounted a long and fierce opposition to the theater and rejected its mediation as too involved with rites and sacrifice. And this reminds us of a human significance that, from being representational, must become ontological (from representative it becomes presentative) in order to realize itself and gain a salvation attainable through accepting its opposite. Greek tragedy has in view a prospect of this sort, one that fulfills mankind's objectual aspirations, but fails to attain them, able only to indicate the solution, doubly bound as it is to the bond that binds it and alone might unbind it. Reasons for salvation turn out to be the causes of perdition; reasons for freedom lead to an iron-bound determinism; and truth becomes the most terrible confutation. As it unfolds the tragic story inexorably follows this sequence, with any minimal variations having no effect on a logic that will always strike down somebody else (as in the apparently "happy endings" of some of Euripides's mature tragedies like *Andromache*, *Ion*, *Helen*, and *Iphigenia in Tauris*); and this silently underscores the fact that the sequence ought to be reversed, casting a completely different complexion on things and leading to the opposite outcome, as explored by Euripides in his first surviving, singular masterpiece, the *Alcestis*. However, even this happy ending, the return of the wife from the realm of the dead, is muffled in the three-day silence that she has to observe, to say nothing of the fact that the play oversteps the strict limits of the tragic genre, contaminated by features of satirical drama.[10] The apparent exceptions thus confirm the established rule.

This postulatory kind of situation, this search for an answer that is expected without ever formulating the question, not only transforms the tragic story into the performative equivalent of the question but reveals its structural relationship to a motif that would otherwise turn out to be what it usually appears to be, to critics and public alike, a clever and imaginative embellishment to make the *fabula* more evocative by spicing it up with the supposed mysteries of the divine everybody pretends to believe in as soon as it becomes unessential. What I am referring to is the oracular background of many stories; translated into terms of knowledge, this is the enigma. Before examining the religious implications, we will begin with a phenomenological analysis of the sapiential enigma and its relationship, as far as it can be reconstructed, to the structure of tragedy. In fact, the enigma is the origin in a logical-sacral formulation, the origin of tragedy and its characters but more mediately the origin tout court. And for the wise man, it has to be said, this origin is both a goal and a trap, a clever and lethal μηχανή.

Greek knowledge is double by birth and calling, and its conceptual, performative *mechane* is the enigma. Its historical and philosophical importance is rightly claimed by Colli though he takes care not to go into its anthropological connections and implications.[11] The Greek enigma, as he brilliantly describes it, is situated at the birth of Western philosophy; as soon as we see it in context it helps us to understand the source of all our logical and mental categories, a specifically religious, cultic, and magic source, and not a generically metaphysical one as Colli maintains displaying his own tendency to abstraction typical also of Greek philosophical thought but divesting it of its mediatory and intermedial thrust. He has more success in noting the competitiveness characteristic of this form of expression, competition between man and divinity, and between one wise man and another, a competitive *pathos* turning into a deadly *pathos* for the loser whether the loser be any man in his unequal contest with a god, or a wise man unable to extricate himself from the trap set by his opponent. And yet these contests are not metaphysical matches or exceptional tussles suspended in a void. They are the regulation by ritual of otherwise dangerous behavior, institutionalized and mediated publicly before the community, starting from sacrifice. This sacrificial mediation of the magically empowered word is to be found in many cultures but in Greece is unmistakably characterized by a horizontal public sharing that determines its distinctive development, turning it into a test of skill in handling the *logos* before the admiring citizenry of the *polis*, its use extolled in public gatherings, tribunals, business, and the social life in the *agora*. The religious and cultural factor is modified and diluted not because it loses importance or actually vanishes as the arrogant cliché supporting a nonreligious Greek culture maintains, but because that factor was felt to be primarily a shared, civic heritage, a force that every active member of the community had a right to use as a means to exercise his intelligence and freedom. The element of violence in the archaic enigma of preclassical and classical Greece recedes and diminishes, though it is always present and ready, from time to time, to strike the bearer of the *logos* who is seen to be not up to the mark as poet, philosopher, politician, or strategist. This is the soil in which the *logos* of tragedy grows and prospers, unraveling in an emblematic story what is implicit in the enigma, its final solution coinciding with the solution of the hero whom it touches.

The Greeks also called the enigma *griphos*, a net or trap, on account of its sacrificial origin, felt less strongly but never completely lost. It is the *problema*, a menacing obstacle appearing before us, that we must overcome: its etymology is from *proballein* (throwing forward, primarily in a hostile sense), belonging to the same sacrificial semantic area as *symbolon*.[12] To propose or put forward an enigma was expressed by *ainigma proballein*: "προβάλλετε" says Gorgias, challenging the Athenians who had come to hear him in the theater,[13] thereby making theater of the competitive *logos*, evincing the very roots of the performances staged there. The *ainigma* is the challenge, the gamble, the aggressive face of the *logos*; in tragedy it becomes the story—αἶνος—that conceals and reveals αἰνός, meaning what is terrible in the sense of *deinos*,[14] itself a term on which Heidegger has made penetrating remarks.

In his *Einführung in die Metaphysik* (*Introduction to Metaphysics*), a course given in 1935 and published in 1953, Heidegger inaugurates the second period of his thought in which he takes leave of the epoch of metaphysics in order to return to the originary thinking of the pre-Socratics. There, in the course of commenting on the first stasimon of Sophocles's *Antigone* devoted to the "tremendous" greatness of man, he translates *deinon* (an impersonal neuter) as "the Disturbing" (*das Unheimliche*), something disquieting whose noumenal and anomalous position—we must add—corresponds to Freud's *das Unheimliche* (the Uncanny). Heidegger's analysis shows that this *Unheimliche* is phenomenologically linked to the essence of man, rejecting any naturalistic approach to human history:

> The fundamental mistake [*Grundirrtum*] . . . lies in the opinion according to which the beginning of history [*der Anfang der Geschichte*] would be something primitive and still backward, awkward and weak. It is the very opposite. The beginning is what is most disturbing [*Unheimlichste*] and most violent.[15]

The *Unheimlichste* is the rendering of the *deinoteron* applied by Sophocles to define man as "thing," that is, entity: "Many things are disturbing [*deina*] but no one / is more disturbing [*deinoteron*] than man."[16] The nearness of the Sophoclean text inspires Heidegger, who intercepts without hesitation the real nature of human origin under the shield of poetry, in his view what is closest to the original dis-veiling through language. Had he given objective contents to this insight by connecting it to Freud's *Unheimlich* and to the wonder (*thaumazein*) that according to Plato and Aristotle is at the root of philosophy, he would have found the ecstatic dimension springing out from "what is most disturbing and most violent." Such a *deinon* that is an *Anfang* converges with the "beginning/principle" (*arche*) of the pre-Socratics, a concept that unites the Titanic event and the cosmic beginning of the origin myth in an ontological process, endowed with a force productive and in itself originating. But not by chance it is a tragic text that locates the originary and originating *deinos* in human being, since tragedy is the sapiential form capable of freely expressing this experiential truth without the heavy task of harmonizing it with the laws of *kosmos* and *physis*.

The tragic wisdom conquered its expressive freedom at a high price, agreeing to obey the *ainigma* of a marvelous story becoming nightmare, of *aînos* becoming *ainós*. The first stasimon of *Antigone* describes man as *pantoporos* and never *aporos*, except at death, a description that contains for Heidegger the essential interpretation of the *deinotaton* that is man[17]—a proper inference, though Heidegger clearly has in mind his "Being-toward-death" (*Sein zum Tode*),[18] the existential condition of the human being (*Dasein*, Being-there) become aware of his own extreme limit and thus capable of thinking about the problem of Being as distinguished from the single entities.[19] But in antiquity the human paradox of being *pantoporos*/*aporos* is first of all a ritual challenge, not an abstract existential riddle, and *aporos* is the almost technical definition of the ritual victim with no escape. For this reason, the enigma is *aporia*, where there is no escaping and whatever you say or do is wrong, as we see brought to life in words and action on the tragic stage: the Stranger is described as impossible, *aporos* (l. 800) by Pentheus, trapped by that time in the outspread net of the Stranger's invincible *logos*. And the term ἀπορία is also applied to Pentheus's hopeless situation at the top of the fir tree (l. 1102). Everything becomes more archaic and dreadful, and the *ainigma* revealed to be the concrete display of the sacrificial *deinos*, the accomplishment of the beginning at the very end, the manifestation of the end as the one and only beginning.

The aporia of the enigma corresponds terminologically and topologically with the aporia of the labyrinth, its translation into expressive and logical-verbal terms in which the way out is the same as the way in, as it is in the dance-labyrinth, cave-labyrinth, and building-labyrinth. To find the way out we must know the way in, now beyond recall, which only the *aletheia* of Mnemosyne will enable us to find again, analogous to Orphism in its aim to retrieve and redeem the Titanic guilt. Depending on our use of it, on how we manage to make our way through, the labyrinth symbolizes perdition or salvation, a reminder of the unsettled reversible nature of all our objectual achievements, attained and retained only by way of a delicate network fraught with conditions and combinations.

This ambiguous, slippery salvation finds a more specific symbol in the thread of Ariadne; originating in mythical-ritual representation it becomes a theme of knowledge and initiation, appearing in the form of a rope when Theseus and his companions dance, and seen again as the thread that Daedalus tries to pass through the spirals of a snail's shell.[20] The labyrinth mythologem proves to be a set of themes and patterns, mythemes as Lévi-Strauss called them, with almost no limit to their possible combinations, branching out and intertwining in a tangled maze that ceases to be simply content and becomes interpretation and methodology. But the process is long and involved and starts from *within* a mythologem that, from this viewpoint, is in continuity with our interpretive effort, even though it may be far-off and rarely encountered; and that fact, to a certain extent, justifies the combinatorial play in my analysis. Putting the accent on this tangled web proves relevant if it reproduces the purpose of the mythical-ritual stratification more consciously, helps to further its most hidden intentions, and also includes strata of a literary and mythographic kind in the reconstruction, since the ancients saw them as essentially a continuation of the more archaic strata. We demonstrate our much-vaunted rationality not by opposing myth unrealistically and intransitively annulling its transitive logic, but by our ability to recover what separates and unites us in regard to what we call myth. Our rationality consists in finding the thread to disentangle this skein, and the further back we go, the more literal it seems as a metaphor, an action creating significant shifts, a vertical labyrinth appearing through time, presenting us with the various labyrinths of which it is composed. If we just follow their thread it will lead us back to Ariadne and her *mythos*, and then we must do our best not to leave her stranded in a hermeneutic void, the victim of a historical and philosophical betrayal.

The interpreting Theseus is immediately rewarded when he takes up Ariadne's thread. The entire labyrinth is equivalent to a fabric patiently woven throughout with the thread of Ariadne, to Persephone's Orphic peplum where the weaving of the world is depicted, to the cloth woven by the Moirae that decides the life and death of mortal men, and to the geometrical trap of Arachne, the spider, where the path followed by predator and prey is one and the same.[21] But Ariadne's thread overlays the maze too neatly as it maps it, too closely to tranquilize by signaling a reassuring objectual success. Ariadne, the ancient goddess that Nietzsche was to transform into the crazy phantom of his desire, dies at the hands of Artemis "in sea-crowned Dia through Dionysus's accusations [*martyriesi*]" as Homer tells us,[22] using a technical term that indicates marital misbehavior and so evokes the most inauspicious outcome of the labyrinth hierogamy. Homer's version of the usual Dionysian rescue in the myth is clearly more archaic and at once ties up, even literally, with another thread of the skein. The thread is the inseparable attribute of the daughter of Minos and Pasiphae (and attribution of inseparability is always a basic sign of identity in myth, and usually a victimary sign as Girard states), and it becomes the grim cause of her death: she is abandoned on an island and, like Arachne, hangs herself, a macabre labyrinthine *symbolon* often reproduced in rites as a hanged doll. This cord corresponds fully to the rope held by the dancers closing in on the victim, and to the rope with which the ties of Ananke, Necessity, are bound.[23] The knot of the labyrinth is not to be untied with impunity, the knot of two intertwining serpents chanced upon by Tiresias, the hierogamy of Heaven and Earth, and the noose that hangs Ariadne-Arachne, just as it would hang her sister, Phaedra. The labyrinth is *aporos* by definition: the traces running through it remain reversible, and the salvation made possible by them can be revoked, shifting its fatal price through space, when paid by someone else, and time, when the blow is held back, in the dilatory, mocking fashion of Apollo the Ambiguous, familiar to us from tragedy.

Inevitably, this has repercussions for knowledge as it develops by following the windings of the labyrinth, with the plan of the labyrinth reproduced in the mental labyrinths of its mythical creator and of the tragedian who duplicates it in terms of theater, developing it as spectacle. Hellenic knowledge, with its insight into the essence of men's lives, illustrates the price to be paid for the mediations that make the world livable and knowable and becomes, within the limits set by these same mediations, the expression of the inexpressible, the violation of the inviolable, a bold and reckless aporia inciting and questioning the enigma by which it is questioned. Thousands of years later, this extreme possibility would be tragically realized in Nietzsche; on the brink of insanity, he uses images of the labyrinth by which he was obsessed to describe his triangular amorous relationship with Wagner and Cosima: "Who apart from myself knows what Ariadne is!"[24]

Unlike the modern and Faust-like Nietzsche, the Greeks knew they could only express the inexpressible, touch on the *tremendum*, and make the *ainós* the object of an *aînos* formulating its *ainigma* as long as they did not violate the mediatory rules that make it objectually tolerable, not looking too closely at the masks of Ariadne and Dionysus, making them appear and speak according to the proper rules. Tragic knowledge, and in general the knowledge of those pursuing paths close to it, such as Heraclitus, lies in the art of taking away on the one hand what has to be kept on the other, a creative ambivalence providing invaluable information about the real historical ways in which human cultures learned to retroact on their own formative states. Greek knowledge begins to resemble at its most daring, though unbeknownst, however, the modern manner of stark demystification and iconoclasm; it proceeds contrariwise with sideways, indirect movements, layered with allusions that are by no means incompatible with the evident plan; indeed they imply it while calling it into question, precisely because they do call it into question. The tragic mask covers and sustains, blocks the representational movement and thus concentrates it, and sets it moving again; it expresses a single state of suffering and from that fixed point all other expressions are imaginable; it cannot tell all and for that very reason it speaks.

We have given particular attention to the enigma and its relation to the language of tragedy, not only for the external reason that written texts are all we have of Greek theater but especially because of the role of the *logos*. Its importance for Greek culture cannot be overrated, nor for philosophical knowledge, in part coeval with it but destined to enjoy a much longer life. Besides, language was also destined to become the great conundrum of twentieth-century philosophy, mysteriously linked to the very essence (or lack of essence) of human being, as Heidegger himself shows and we shall see when we deal with Walter Benjamin and Ludwig Wittgenstein. So we will carry on with our reconstruction of tragic knowledge, and its reflections in modern thinking, by looking at the knot, the double bond of the *logos*, at the enigma of the birth of articulate language or rather, recognizing the enormous scope of a theme that I shall not pretend to tackle here, the birth of the linguistic *function* that became articulate utterance with a potentially unlimited range of symbolic side-effects.

3. Origin of the Linguistic Function

We have seen that in order to understand how the Hellenic wise man came into being and evolved, we need to understand how his labyrinthine "Daedalian" *logos* arose and evolved, an origin and evolution on which Greek philosophy has more than a little to say.

The treatment of language/*logos* in Greek wisdom begins with the archaic sage possessed by the divine *logos* to the point of being killed by it and, some centuries later, finds a rationalized expression in Aristotle's definition of man as "the only animal [*zoon*] possessing [*echei*] the faculty of speech [*logon*]," that is, as an entity taking part in *zoe* inasmuch as it "has" the *logos*.[25] The Aristotelian *logos* is the human being's specific way of being a ζῷον, his *differentia specifica* and also his ontological difference, but quite different from Heidegger's, because it gives the speaking *zoon* the possibility of sharing the life of Being through the communicative experience of entities (*onta*). Aristotle's conception of *logos* is far more flexible and comprehensive, and not by chance he presents it while dealing with the essential characters of man in the *Politics*. When he refers to the *logos* as "the faculty of speech" in the public space of the *polis*, he is specifying the previous and still generic description of man as *politikon zoon*,[26] and the acquired definition based on *logos* includes, and does not exclude as Arendt says,[27] the cognitive and intellectual aspects, as highlighted by the final definition of man as the only animal having "the intuition [*aisthesin*] of good and evil, just and unjust."[28] It is a great ontological communication starting from the animal realm (many animals are social) up to the capacity of distinguishing what is axiologically superior within experience thanks to the communicational and intermedial faculty of *logos*. As it gradually passed through the sophists' discovery of the conventionality of *nomoi*, that is, the human laws, and Socrates's humanizing and objectualizing inquiry, the Greek *logos* cooled down, from a still heated relationship with its sacred springs to Aristotle's ontological-rational setting, destined soon to become the more encyclopedic and specialized mentality of Hellenistic culture.[29] At any rate, along this journey from the possessing divine *logos* to the possessed human *logos*, reversibility is always possible since the divine *logos* though becoming a logical-rhetorical tool but remains as such divine to some degree.

It is interesting to see how Heidegger took the contrary view of the relationship between man and language, later influencing Arendt's interpretation as well. At the beginning of his second period, Heidegger writes that man and language "both *belong* [*zugehören*] to Being [*Seyn*[30]] in the same originary way [*gleichursprünglich*],"[31] one-sidedly simplifying the Aristotelian complex reasoning about human beings and *logos* in favor of the supposed compactness of pre-Socratic thought. Yet, by doing so, he transforms Aristotle's definition of man into the truncated formula of *zoon logon echon* and therefore, by analogy and contrast, into an undetermined ontological sameness devoid of the double relationship with *physis* on the one hand and with the superior axiological levels of reality on the other. Instead of being a dynamic means of communication with the totality of Being, the language inseparable from man becomes a sort of enclosure shutting him off from the rest of the world, losing in objectuality what it gains in a pathos for the origin basically unknown to the ancient world.

A more complete description of the wide field embraced by the present inquiry induces us to face questions more radical and at the same time more complete than the ones faced by the ancient and modern thinkers we are considering, not to cancel their contributions but to recover them at a higher level, in the ceaseless rumination that is thought. For this an inquiry on the origins of the Greek *logos*, that is, the first *logos* presenting itself both as divine and human (a paradoxical copresence we shall find in the prologue of John), has to push still further our reflection into the past, to the formation of the first linguistic utterances, the first human *logos*, which I would mention not so much to explain language as to give an idea of a possible direction for further thinking and research that throws light on the inner features of the Greek *logos*.

From various points of view, articulate language sums up elegantly and immediately the peculiar characteristics of the human species, here intended as a plural considering that the very first species of the genus *Homo* already appears to be capable of articulate language, reaching up to the enormous linguistic and abstractive capacities of *Homo sapiens*. Language expresses in a direct and speaking manner the enigma of human being without needing to go into difficult and controversial definitions or to appeal to the differences between nature and culture that end up by being formalistic and empty, as Bataille objects against Lévi-Strauss, and by assuming what they should corroborate. The result of this formalistic impasse is that often the only effective answer is the crass postpositivism (i.e., positivism devoid of the ontological content of the old facts) into which any questions regarding mankind seem to subside nowadays, and lapse into silence, a silence nevertheless much more eloquent than one might suppose. Questions about mankind can and must be given their voice, and the simplest, most phenomenological way is to start from man as the "talking animal," as the *zoon* possessing *logos* because possessed by *logos*. This means, more precisely, to start from language as a phenomenon having in itself something originary, inasmuch as it manifests itself and speaks through man. The mature Heidegger was not wrong in seeing language as the extreme frontier of openness (*Erschlossenheit*, *Offenheit*) to Being, except that he left aside its communicating and talking intentionality which aims at the fullness of object, not at its emptying. And that was the Hellenic experience of the *logos*; it was never simply a word spoken or thought, but a divine force that entered the speaker, gave or took away power and persuasiveness, *peitho*, with the distinctive logical-cognitive value that was to make Greek philosophy great.

But in contemporary philosophy, a similar reason gives language the role of an absolute, nontranscendable field, a negative way to preserve the intangibility and transcendence of language. The most influential philosopher in this regard has been Wittgenstein, and his thought can be usefully compared to Benjamin's ideas on language. Benjamin considers language as the revelatory irruption of the originary Word and the magical medium giving name to things,[32] and making visible the web underlying the dispersive stream of representations,[33] while Wittgenstein considers language as the nontranscendable field of representation, an unsurpassable limit from which it is impossible to give a sense to what lies beyond. The author of the *Tractatus logico-philosophicus*—a title inspired by Spinoza's *Tractatus theologico-politicus*—rejects Frazer's anthropological inquiry[34] and declares the purpose of preserving the mystery of the ineffable; as the very last proposition of the *Tractatus logico-philosophicus* reads: "What we cannot speak about we must pass over in silence [*muß man schweigen*]."[35] Wittgenstein's conception exasperates Kant's division between phenomenon and noumenon to the point of declaring transcendence—the Kantian noumenon—even unthinkable, so that human beings are left with a limited bunch of scientific sentences and, in Wittgenstein's second period, linguistic games (*Sprachspiele*) that coincide with living experience (*Erlebnis*).[36]

The success of this thinking has been huge because it seemed to settle once and for all any metaphysical question by eliminating linguistically the very possibility to conceive the noumenon. And yet, a revealing misunderstanding lies behind Wittgenstein's success. Actually, the drastic simplification argued for in the *Tractatus* was meant to preserve the import of transcendence, concerning the sense of the world that is not part of the world, whereby, "if there is any value [*es einen Wert gibt*] that does have value,"[37] it "can alter only the limits [*Grenzen*] of the world, not the facts [*Tatsachen*]—not what can be expressed by means of language," and this finally amounts to the following fact and proposition: "The world of the happy man [*Glücklichen*] is a different one from the world of the unhappy man [*Unglücklichen*],"[38] a phrase that seems to be a mere consequence of what precedes but actually represents the very center of the *Tractatus*. This paradox cannot be explained; it can only be contemplated: "There are, indeed, things that cannot be put into words [*Unaussprechliches*]. They *make themselves manifest*. They are what is mystical [*Dies* zeigt *sich, es ist das Mystische*]."[39]

It is a position not so distant from Husserl's phenomenology, where the Kantian noumenon makes itself manifest, but this time with such a powerful short-circuit between scientific logic and ethical awareness of human sorrow such as to transform what for Husserl is a premise into an acute and paralyzing conclusion. The assumption and result of this wonderful sort of positivistic cage ending up in a *zen* philosophy lived with Christian sensitivity is in any case the cancellation of any mediatory and objectual dimension of both language and the linguistic entity that we are. No wonder that Wittgenstein's ascetic abstinence from "what we cannot speak about" (but after having been spoken about) was stripped of its ethical commitment and paradoxical strength, and disastrously simplified by his followers oblivious of the metaphysical anxiety of *Mitteleuropa* and ready to throw out the very idea of a historical origin and an objectual destination for language, culture, and man. And undoubtedly Lévi-Strauss's cultural anthropology marks another critical moment in this trend, leading on to semiotics in the same way that Wittgenstein's ideas were to give rise to analytical philosophy. In spite of that, the modern formalistic interpretation of language, analogous to society in Durkheim, contains in itself the totalizing function characteristic of ancient mediations, and though it is easy for this now overwhelming tendency to surreptitiously destroy the creative tension between ecstatic transcendence and its objectual presence typical of mediations, it does not entirely destroy this hidden tension and its generative central position, perceptible even in the most glacial programs of formal logic or philosophy of language.

It would not be difficult to strike back at these linguistic absolutizations with the blunt instrument of a hypothesis explaining the origin of language, possibly formulated along the lines of Girard's theory, no less antistructuralist in intention than in what it states. Without straying from our field of inquiry, would not the Greek enigma, as a double bind in verbal form, actually suggests its origin? And surely the ambivalent, dangerous *logos* communicated by the enigma derives from the mythic accusations, "the accusations of Dionysus," from which the victim cannot exonerate himself whatever he says or does? And if we go further back toward cultural forms that are to some extent more archaic—that is, developing with a greater stability that *may* have maintained more ancient religious and social institutions almost unaltered or less altered—we arrive at the utterances and cries of the participants in the rite, we come to the crowd, the victim at its center unheard. Through repeating the sacrificial event, the savage uproar first began to be organized and orderly; rhythmic repetition was the birth of music, at its origin indistinguishable from the dancing that went with it and from the language accompanying the rite, language that became gradually more articulate until, at a certain point, it was codified in the form of myth.

Though stimulating and valuable in part, this kind of approach is not enough; it restores to us only the outer skin of the phenomenon under consideration, reducing it to its own categories without analyzing the linguistic, rational factor that causes them to be regarded as the most valid, indeed the only real categories; in other words, it fails to really thematize the fact that it also itself belongs to the same linguistic-cultural process thus revealed. While everything in Lévi-Strauss is language, and cultures are seen as abiding by the same rules of operational and formal transformation as govern human languages, the result of Girard's antistructuralism is that for him nothing is language since it is only a verbal covering for carefully concealed universal violence, with liberation only possible through the *Logos* of Christ, which belongs to a pre- and postlinguistic sphere; in comparison with Christ's *Logos*, the human *logos* can only attest to its own sacrificial dependence, its basic falsity and impotence. This explains why Girard has little to say about the birth of language, with disappointingly generic comments that appear irrelevant when set in relation to his ideas as a whole.[40] These extreme viewpoints oscillate around a center of gravity, avoided by both but clearly outlined by their mutual opposition: the experience of collective mediation, the sole source of language, in its turn transposed, translated bodily, into the linguistic system, transmitting to the system its power to evoke ecstasy and achieve the objectual construction of reality. And so the proper path for us to follow is to take language seriously, not as a self-sufficient, intangible system but as a full manifestation of its own history in the form of language.

The immediately striking feature of human language, verbal or symbolic, is its power to duplicate reality, a power relating to the polar extremes of the double bind and also to Girard's ideas about imitation and doubles. However, these concepts reveal their limits as description when the explanation is pushed beyond them, as in the case of a transforming experience where imitation, mimetic doubles, and human double binds all come together to restart from there with a constructive, organizing force that cannot be reduced to the *status quo ante*. The double always implies a transition or juncture generating it, and my idea of mediation provides this. Thus the origin of language is to be unfolded, rather than explained, applying the phenomenological and radically genetic method to which I subscribe, with the prerequisite task of restoring the object of study from which it starts since the very notion of object is assumed in its entirety in the method from the outset.

If we examine the underlying dynamics of linguistic phenomena, we discover the same discontinuous, transcendent structure reproduced by all human cultural manifestations as their implicit, internal genetic code; except that here it occurs in a manner peculiar to linguistic phenomena, since they speak, communicate, by establishing a proximate field, a common field, that generates meaning, that *is* meaning. Language does not exist because speakers exist, but speakers exist because language exists; they are pronounced, uttered by language in order for them to utter it, and named by language so as to be able to name all things with it. Benjamin's ideas on language went in the right direction without catching the genetic role of human mediation as historical and ontological experience directed to objects starting from a divine Object and interacting with the previous instinctual objects at the biological level. In the prelapsarian state of the first man in the second anthropogonic myth of the Bible (Gn. 2:4–25), the nomothetic faculty of assigning a name to everything in creation is given him by God, that is, by the supreme divine mediation that created and mediated all things and, as a consequence, is language in a source-like, necessary way—the *Logos* as Christianity would say. And every creature receives its name not as a final label for a preexisting entity but as a process of recognition and formation that completes and confirms the creature's purpose, that is to say, its objectual status, so much so that the nomothetic activity of the first man is fulfilled only by the creation of the first woman, without which his very essence, and therefore his very language as well, would remain devoid of object.

That can mean only one thing, that language in origin is a process that brings things into being in the very act of naming them, a ritual procedure, or more precisely, a magical one, as Benjamin acutely perceived,[41] that historically became more and more human. Any view or use of language that ignores its magical power and provenance is not only fated to understand nothing of literary and poetic language but also obliterates the very source of all human linguistic functions, its originary ecstatic-objectual value. That is to say, human language originates as a formula, as a spell and magic word, a sound effective in itself because it is bound, doubly bound up with an experience at source empowering the magic formula and making it identical to the thing evoked.[42] The idea of the performative aspect of language—in which what is said is true not because of an external reason, a predefined criterion of reality, but in virtue of what is pronounced, as with commands and imprecations—is not new, but it turns out to be absolutely right from a phenomenological-genetic point of view and only lacks a broader explanatory picture to justify it. And here, linguistic and expressive phenomena come to our aid by providing a further revealing hint.

If we consider the overall structure of verbal language and music, their close relation, we can see that it refers to a center neither verbal nor musical and, for that very reason, the source of sounds, words, and all possible phonic meanings. This center takes its place, *bestows* itself, as an original reality, a break in continuity alone capable of giving form to the formless and order to chaos; in other words, it asserts itself as an Object that becomes a source of mediation and as a Mediation that becomes an achievable object. In origin, such a mediatorial, objectual center, given and expressing an external, absolute power, had to be transcendent, religious, and divine because its ecstatic structure remains recognizable in all its subsequent evolutions. This inference is so inevitable and so little arbitrary that the only way to avoid it would be to deny religion the right to exist and enjoy scientific status, as in fact is attempted nowadays. But, for the present, enough has been said in a general way, and enough is here all we need, about the antireligious and antiobjectual censures of science when it refuses to recognize any origin for itself, let alone an objective and object, an *obiectum*. The question now is what precisely, in sufficiently explanatory terms, is this mediatory, ecstatic-objectual center to which language, music, and the representational mediation of tragedy all refer? What is the heart of the labyrinth of the *logos*, the core of its magic performative power? Here we come to the keystone, the point of convergence for all my analyses, the point from which they set off again, intended not to impose an ingenuously preprepared explanation inviting criticism for its numerous shortcomings owing to an inevitable lack of knowledge, but to propose a line of thinking, an attitude toward methodology and history capable of placing and organizing knowledge, present and future, in a field in which much remains to be discovered.

The mysteriously objectual center of the meanings of all sounds, of all objects created by communication and sound, can only be something that is not sound but so pregnant with meaning as to confer meaning on any sound or noise made after that instant, and also projecting retrospective meaning onto previous sounds and noises. This center is *silence*, the silence of the slaughtered victim that breaks in on the uproar of the collective crisis and transforms it into *order*, in the two senses of the word seen in Anaximander, as a command issuing from there and, by that very fact, as order imposed from there. The victim speaks with eloquence unknown to the living, and this silence, pregnant with all future words, is the nonlinguistic genesis of language, the void of instinctual objects, holding them in suspense before it makes them meaningful and designates them, transforming them into symbolic and cultural objects, implicitly naming them simply by making them perceptible. Wittgenstein was not wrong in seeing the ineffable as the transcendent limit of language, except that this very limit *is* the origin of language itself.

The ecstatic, meaningful silence, without which no word or sound would exist, is the source of man's words and sounds, of the human expressive, linguistic function: it is the silence following the omophagic slaughter and retrospectively, in the reconstruction of an event graven in everyone's memory, the silence of the victim turned to stone at the instant of death and subsequently, in the objectual developments that will make the body perceptible as *obiectum*, the silence of the sacrificed victim. We can conjecture a similar relationship between the final stillness of the appeased sacrificers that is mediated and signified by the stillness of the murdered victim, and the gesticulation before and during the killing, gesturing that starts from central, repeated immobility and passes through successive sacrificial mediations to become dance.

The human linguistic function took shape from the chaotic clamor of the collective crisis, stilled overall in the deadly silence of its fatal conclusion, a silence mediated by the designation contained in the victimary *obiectum*, in its magical, mystical body—to use more evolved but equally applicable terminology for this inchoate phase. The function consists in a transitive, signifying power that extends to embrace everything closely related to the collective experience of life and makes it speak. From its origin as silent mediation, it spreads out as sounded mediation and makes a linguistic object of everything concerning the central mediatory event in the auditory sphere. It is not sacrificial substitution but significant expansion starting from sacrifice, acknowledged and shared across the board by everyone, to the point that substitution should be seen as the direct consequence of this process, not as its external, mechanical cause. The sacrificeable objects are in some way fixed by the mediatory event, receiving existence through being permeated by the linguistic mediation. To be named is to be sacrificeable, to be sacrificed: for this reason, archaic cultures saw taking a name as equivalent to taking over the magic essence of a being, but then the first safety precaution was to keep it hidden, to adopt substitute names. It is, of course, anachronistic to speak of a name in the grammatical sense, that is, as a noun. We know nothing of the more remote forms of human protolanguage, but it may be fairly assumed that no distinction was made between nouns and verbs; probably, there was a series of linguistic objects dominated by the performative aspect of action and change of state, especially in connection with those absorbed by the meaningful stream of sacrifice. For this reason, we ought to speak of linguistic functions, with neither the possibility nor the need to translate them into valueless reconstructions.

We have sufficient elements to establish that the earliest language of all was a sacred language, a divine utterance attributed to the sacrificial event, and also to the victim as far as it became perceptible as an object in itself.

The divine language, endowed with power to objectualize and coincident with a command causing things to exist the instant that it nominates them, is the same language that speaks to archaic communities in myth, causing their world to exist in narrating and explaining it. Without this aura of magical-sacral power, without the power of the most intense ritually directed mediation, nothing can be understood about the functioning of magic formulas and prayer, or even about the elementary, ancestral capacity of musical and verbal languages to arouse emotions, nor about the arts that use those languages. Ancient Greece provides a perfect example of the magical-ritual significance of the literary and artistic sphere, professionally specialized in Greece but still close to its religious roots, evident in tragedy and poetry and in the close ties with music, an aspect that fascinated the Wagnerian Nietzsche when he wrote *The Birth of Tragedy*.

As we learn from Plato, poetic inspiration was awesome for the Greeks, a force that took possession of the singer-poet with the impersonal pervasiveness and magic automatism of the *daimones*, and made him emit sounds and words independent of his will. Inspiration by the archaic Muses was a frightening experience, something like the trance that overcame the Pythia, as we saw when analyzing the nature of the ancient inhabitants of Parnassus,[43] and really a duplicate of the maenads that inspired Euripides. From this we can deduce that in ancient Greece, as in later periods, every real work of literature, like every real musical composition, reproduces in itself the origin of the language that it uses. This is the nonlinguistic center that it draws on for the power of speech, for expression. With his outstanding mediatory knowledge, Plato reacted against the indiscriminate use of sacrificial mediations and their artistic derivatives; his ideal State banned all uncontrolled use of mythology, poetry, and music as well as dancing, while tragedy was actually subject to a specific ban since it made use of all these arts in a way dangerously detached from the religious and philosophical mediations that could maintain their objectual value. Not an absolute interdiction, as Plato himself stresses in the *Laws* expressing a penchant for tragedy and poetry quite obvious to a reader of his dialogues, but one that is necessary, to the extent that these literary forms prove to be axiologically and ethically irresponsible and ruinous. It is highly meaningful that the progressive plan of Plato's teachings, organized and graded in an authentic philosophical *ratio studiorum*, aimed to reproduce a similar transition from the initial and intermediate rudiments of the *logos* to higher levels intended for the esoteric circle of his best pupils, finally reaching the peak of knowledge with ecstatic contemplation, an ecstatic threshold not meant to conflict with the aesthetic dimension but to mediate it and protect it from any anobjectual degeneration. And Christianity was to show a similar concern—as did the Fathers of the Church, Dante, and modern writers and thinkers like Manzoni and Simone Weil—the only difference being that what becomes incarnate, opening up new horizons for representation and expression, is the supreme *Logos* of the divine mediator.

Needless to say, postclassical antiquity, after Aristotle's *Poetics*, and subsequently postmedieval modernity disregarded the Platonic and Christian prohibitions, and not without good reason though ignorant of their motives for doing so. As a result, within a few centuries there was a growing mediatory and objectual depletion in artistic expression and in philosophy that had thrived through comparison with art. Modernity, especially, unmindful in its superficiality of the warnings coming from Plato and Christianity, increasingly denied that the greatest art, and the art of theater with its particular performativity, had anything to do with the objectual reality of the origin; as a result art was forced to take refuge in the initiatory dimension already known to the ancient world, making a multilevel reading of an enigmatic script, destined to the double bind of having to speak out and survive in public. Music, on account of its close links to dance and ritual, was subject to even stricter religious and moral proscriptions, and took longer to shake off the censures of the Platonic and Christian type. On the other hand, Christianity's criticism, with the objectual motivation behind it, brought the art of sounds to unprecedented thresholds of interiorization and representational cognitive development, and to new interactions with the art of theater.

Musical theater was restored, thanks to the liberating character that Western Christianity derived from the historically committed nature of its mediations, and the relationship of music and drama rose to new splendor, culminating in the exploring of mediation by Giuseppe Verdi and Wagner, in love and politics and in myth and ritual respectively. Wagner's idea of total drama, which came to infect Nietzsche and European culture generally, was without precedent not only in reinforcing the dramatic and musical power of tragedy with its complementary capacity for visual involvement but above all in reviving the idea of the sole origin of all arts in sacrificial mediation, with music performing its unifying, dynamic function as the most ancient medium, preceding all predefined objects and therefore capable of evoking them from nothing. Developments in modern theater show that ancient tragedy was already an indirect exploration of the origin of all art forms,[44] and this retroactive, reflexive character resurfaced with explosive results in the upheavals of modern art. In contemporary Europe the sacrificial exploration of all the arts has become the destruction of all the arts, an anobjectual and antiobjectual destruction, confirming the worst fears of Plato and Christianity and leading to the Babel-like confusion of all contents and forms in the perverse mechanisms of mass exploitation and of a market fixed by the mafias of the art world. And yet, music and dance still offer a phenomenological clue to understanding the aesthetic Babel in which we live: the serial decomposition of the compulsive dance music of our discos and parties takes us back to the tribal rhythms, the sound ecstasies of the origin, along with abundant alcohol and psychotropic substances as in the most archaic Dionysian rites. The sacrificial and mediatory origin of our language, of our languages, is, in short, so little a matter of chance that all our efforts to forget and erase it, in the deceptive self-referentiality of logical formalism and the logic of the marketplace, only serve to confirm it. How can we ignore an enigma that appears in our every word and gesture?

There is no escaping the riddle, and it must be faced with decision if we are not to risk being swallowed up in it. First, then, since the enigma relates above all else to verbal language, we will take a closer look at its origin, the genesis of the vehicle of all rational communication, of this very book that is trying to talk about it. Greek drama becomes even more helpful here since it comes down to us in writing and so contains all the essential elements for our analysis. The text was declaimed and sung, but because it followed a logic delving down toward the mediation at its origin never to be attained fully, running through it there is the silence of ecstasy and horror, the stylized yet terrifying cry that interrupts the *logoi* of tragedy, and a character's lack of words at the moment of catastrophe, the sepulchral silence of Jocasta and Phaedra resolved to hang themselves. Tragic language goes back in its pain to the shouts and sounds of the origin, interrupted by the silence of the originary ecstatic event. In this regard, we have to think of the crucial role played in the tragic texts by interjections such as *ai*, *iou*, *io*, and *oimoi* (helas), often repeated as in a funeral threnody, and expressing a paradoxical copresence of the strongest meaning and the impossibility of describing it in words. It is not a mere negation of the verbal web of the text; it is rather the extreme utterance of its unnamable result, from which all the text derives its real power. It is the end of language, but at the same time its very source.

Sacrificial rite does not leave us without fitting parallels and exhibits in the climactic moment of the victim's death this capacity of reversal keeping the last tracks and remains of the victim, and in particular his last phonetic remnants, so to speak. At this absolute zero of verbal language, the rite accurately reproduced the victim's bodily noises—heart beats, throbbing, breathing, and wheezing—everything had to be there to make certain of the mediation and its objectual meaning. These protolinguistic elements are found in such phenomena as the gift of tongues, ecstatic word-making, and the ritual litany,[45] which is particularly effective when it condenses into the so-called primeval numinous sounds, of which the Indian syllable *om* is a classic example, and could be seen as corresponding to the victim's last breath at the moment of sacrifice. Gradually, more articulate expressions developed from these formidable blocks of significant mediations. The language we use is a buried, forgotten tragedy, but everything we say is secretly steeped in it, showing the most repressed face of its modern exaltations. Just as the sons of Cronus, swallowed whole, sit in their father's stomach, so the most archaic content rests, strictly undigested, in the apparent void of contemporary formalism.

After this long digression on language, actually an ingress disguised as egression, we can come back to the genesis and vicissitudes of the sapiential language in Greece, always following Ariadne's thread of tragic wisdom.

The origin of the Greek *logos* and its constituent ambiguities is easily traced back to the forms that communicated the ambivalence of the sacred language, for example, enigmatic expressions or ritual riddles accompanying sacrifice, repeating or varying the first inexplicable enigma of the bloody mediation from which all our lives rise and rearise, and the enigma of the sacred language that derives from it and expresses it. The linguistic ritualization of sacrifice and the power for sacral mediation of the divine language are then put to further use, with the aim of controlling and directing objectually all conflicts, rivalries, and destructive impulses inside and outside the group. Ritualized conflict based on magic formulas and the swapping of accusations and insults found in the early stages of legal institutions are just two variants that evolve on the way from duels and contests between priests, magicians, and soothsayers to the challenges of wise men and the competitive dimension of the Greek *logos*.[46] It is fascinating, for example, to see how the same structure first noted in a Sumerian duel between a sorcerer and a sorceress to resolve a dispute between two cities,[47] persists in a riddle-solving contest between Mopsus and Chalcas. The two losers, the sorcerer and Chalcas, are both sentenced to death; their fate is expressed in very similar images: the sorcerer's eyes mist over, his mind becomes confused, and then he is thrown into a river, while the dejected Chalcas immediately falls into a sleep of death.[48] If tragedy is knowledge, then the opposite is equally true, that is, knowledge is tragedy, from the very earliest times. While we compare the Sumerian contests with the Greek enigma-dueling, we can also glance at the characteristics of the wise man and his *logos* in the Hellenic world.

The Greek wise man is the evolved, more independent version of the religious mediator—shaman, sorcerer, priest—entrusted, on behalf of the group, to deal with ritual and sapiential matters concerning the *sacrum* and the language of the *sacrum*. From the start, this language carries with it the privileges and risks of a position deriving from the objectual expansion of sacrifice into the culturally most important specializations in the community closely involved in the reversible dynamics of substitution. Daedalus is a transformation of Minos and the sons of Ida, a Minos with the ability to manipulate the language of the sacred, in his case the visual, spatial, and choreographic language of the ritual mediations in his technically expert, manipulative keeping.

In Greece, the wise man gradually comes to detach himself from an exclusive relationship with religion, displaying creative energy and a spirit of initiative unknown to the sacerdotal sage of the civilizations of the Near East. Daedalus is still tied to ritual but, within certain limits, may confidently refashion its forms and symbols. This is due to the unstable polycentric structure peculiar to Hellenic civilization, which allowed unusual freedom and multiplicity, a marked difference from the centralized civilizations of the Near East. At the same time, the importance of the *logos* in civic life and in the decision making of assemblies increasingly oriented the role of the Greek wise man toward the possession and use of verbal language. For the most part, the priests and scribes of the Near East remained tied to a monarchic temple structure and consequently to a caste system while the Greek wise man appears much more nomadic and rootless. Since Greece had no centralized institutions comparable to those of Mesopotamia or Egypt, the wise man tended to move around from *polis* to *polis*, a sort of marginal casteless figure ready at all times to avoid his role as potential victim and take refuge in another city-state. Daedalus escapes from Athens and takes refuge on Crete. And then, to escape from the labyrinth built by himself, he invents flight, an invention somewhere between mythical and metaritual. Even if the sacrificial doubles, Perdix and Icarus, recall the ancient fate of the wise man and the sacrificial sphere from which he could not escape, it is still significant that the attempt to flee the constrictions of now inadequate sacral mediations should become the subject of myth.

These remarks are enough to make clear the originality of the Greek wise man, his potential for development, and also his limitations. Not only the tragic system but the fate of Greek knowledge is played out in a paradoxical oscillation rich in mediations that interact with the conditions of their formation, opening up unexpected cognitive horizons, though without any solution to settle the objectual crisis. This double-binding juncture with ritual and its language, in relation to the *logos* developing the *polis*, enables us to grasp the historical link between knowledge and tragedy. To see this more clearly, we now need to isolate other important elements of the context we are moving in. The most striking and outwardly apparent of these is the mask in Greek theater, a para-ritual apparition that covers and shows, speaks and hides, a mask not only visual but intimately verbal.

4. The Knowledge of the Mask and the Mask of Knowledge

Greek enigmatic knowledge had its most illustrious antecedent in the Delphic oracle of Apollo the Oblique, brother of Dionysus; the sacrifices dedicated to him involved dismemberment, recalling the omophagic sacrifices of the Idaean initiates on Crete.[49] Delphi was the largest center for the development of the mantic (*mantike techne*), that is, the art of prophesying through inspiration, the ability to read the will of the gods by means of an ecstatic condition that produced a verbal babble promptly transcribed by the priests to express the final version of the oracle, in a form as complete as it was mysterious. Mantic derives from *mainomai*, the same verb describing the sacrificial madness of the maenads. As the state of poetic possession also indicates, the form of mantic prevalent in Greece centered on the *logos*, and since it was sacrificial and mediatory the *logos* performed a founding function as well: during the waves of colonization, it was the Delphic oracle that guided the foundation of new cities. The relationship between the enigmatic, oracular *logos* on the one hand and civic life on the other defines the space in which the figure of the wise man evolved, always closely linked to sacrificial knowledge. Again, it was the Delphic oracle, originating in dismemberment, founder of cities, that designated the wisest man among the Greeks; and, explicitly or implicitly, the same oracle hovered over the events of tragedy as their source and concluding resolution. Just as the enigma is potentially a tragedy in miniature, so tragedy is an enigma manifested performatively, to be unlocked with the visible and invisible, revealing and concealing key of a sacrificial resolution that resolves less and less, a sacrificial mediation indicating and removing its own object, and so guaranteeing the objectual crisis that it was supposed to surmount. In that way the enigma shows itself to be an anticipation of tragedy, an archaic form of that linguistic and visual expression of the doubles. Our reading of tragic texts should therefore be double, a cognitive duplication bound not to forget the decrease, the halving, from which its redoubling arises:[50] the visible representation is always accompanied by the sapiential meaning, hidden behind the mask of the text like the actor's face behind the tragic mask. Ostensibly the mask conceals, but secretly reveals, the horror, the *ainós*, and is the most eloquent symbol of the double level of interpretation which tragedy and more generally the knowledge of *logos* involve. The specifically theatrical use of this means—a material means but, by the same token, a symbolic one, whose effectiveness depends on its effective ability to conceal—calls for some extra investigation. The mask is, first and foremost, a tensional function, which arises from precise needs and actions.

In his book on Dionysus, Walter F. Otto writes, almost phenomenologically, that the mask "is the symbol and the manifestation of that which is simultaneously there and not there: that which is excruciatingly near, that which is completely absent—both in one reality."[51] This is an acute observation; nevertheless it sounds more evocative than explanatory if we focus on its paradoxical formulation: the phenomenon of mask is both antithetical and unitary, no doubt, but this is only the beginning of our inquiry, not its conclusion. Otto's description keeps concealing a Kantian noumenon still waiting to be recognized and does not reach a phenomenological-historical level. The question that we really have to decide is whether we want to see the mask as it superficially appears to us—that is, as something terrible and numinous, not human—or as it really is in human, anthropological, and historic terms—that is, as a boundary that divides in order to open a new access and conceals in order to make visible again what is behind. The phenomenological results of the divine, enigmatic appearance of the mask must certainly be considered but need to be brought to interact with a more comprehensive explanation, continuing and extending the selective ritual movement hinted at and denied, started and stopped, by the surface of the mask.

Girard's attitude is opposite and symmetrical to Otto's erudition. In a few brilliant pages in *Violence and the Sacred* devoted to analysis of the mask he puts particular stress on the representational aspect of the monstrous doubles of the crisis, and concludes rather bluntly: "There's no point in wondering about the 'nature' of the mask; it is in its nature not to have any one, since it has them all"—a trenchant assertion that falls like an axe on any possibility of reflecting on knowledge in Greek tragedy. "The use [*port*] of the mask in Greek theater therefore does not require any particular explanation; it is absolutely no different from other practices."[52] In its own way, Girard's stance has a liberating flavor, forcing us to concentrate on the essential, with the mask as the means to an end and not a lovely exterior to be contemplated for its own sake; however, its initial assumption that every cultural detail is only a detail compared to the universal mechanism of the sacrificial foundation—the Girardian noumenon—amounts to the same position as Otto's seen from the other side. Girard completely overlooks the fact that every culture creates a precise mode of access to the objectual phenomenon, and increasingly interacts with its own line of development, transforming it into an object of knowledge. So, understanding what the Greeks thought of the mask and how they utilized it is by no means inessential since it helps us to assess how they saw their own seeing at the theater, their own visual theatrical knowledge.

The right approach is to be found at a point exactly halfway between the phenomenal suggestions of Otto, still under the spell of the subject, and Girard's noumenal urge to simplify and take it apart in order to disengage the proliferating doubles and lay bare the ritual mechanism, resulting yet again in a refusal to acknowledge the cognitive independence of tragedy. At a halfway point, not because it is a compromise but because it is mediating and mediatory, hinging on the central place of the medium is the construction and destruction of cultures. Examining seriously the constituent phenomena of the mask does not mean endorsing its deceptive appearances but, instead, understanding its causes and effects from a point of view imposed by the mask, and on the invisible plane that it implies. If we recover the most elementary, concrete elements of the masked disguise, we can grasp its effective power as well, ridding ourselves of all ambiguous enthusiasm and aestheticizing indulgence before we start. After describing the general character of this symbolic tool, we will move on to its specific features in Greece.

In itself the nature of the mask and ritual disguises has a relatively simple *ratio*: as means of concealment they made it possible for one to kill without being recognized and so without provoking vendettas, an absolutely imperative necessity when the victim was inside the group. If we reconstruct the real scene corresponding to the killing recalled in the Titan myth, we can imagine a child chosen from the tribe that has to be killed without provoking any reaction from his family. The Titanic disguise consisted in covering the body with white chalk, obliterating their individual identities so as to appear a fearsome, anonymous emanation of the sacred mediation. In obedience to this mediation they all gather once more around an objective, a common *obiectum*, that is then brutally destroyed to guarantee the community's objectual sphere and ensure the continuing life of the group. The masking overlaps sacrifice even to the point of coinciding with its execution, but is not a simple sacrificial covering, as it gives effective, performative expression to the sacral mediation needed by the community.

The mediatory transition makes it possible to correct the risk of excessive utilitarianism appearing in the reconstruction: for much of human history, though things cannot be said to have really changed even now, the benefits coming to human groups have been the objectual spin-off of attempts at adaptation to internal and external conditions of life, under the pressure of chronic urgent need that had nothing to do with calculation; besides, there was neither the occasion nor the competence to calculate. The objectual purpose of human beings is a question of general orientation rather than conscious planning, making visible, on a cultural level, an even more complex and interactive analogue of the adaptive processes that govern biological evolution. This objectual finality does not correspond to any intention, but to an *intentionality* directed toward objects as is born from an experience of Object, paving as side effect the way to an intention that is initially collective and later, through a very long process, more individual. The mask expresses this intentionality destined to become intention but still not established as such; and nevertheless it does not limit itself to being an absence referring to a presence, for it is already in itself a force becoming present, though not yet in the terms it will make possible. In other words, the ritual disguise functions not because it misrepresents and renders unrecognizable but because it really and magically transforms, taking us into another reality. The mask is therefore not a phenomenon covering a noumenon, but an exchange between these two dimensions; and for this reason it is not merely a means, an effective agent, or a factor serving to hide a preexisting identity, but an element that acts to produce identity. Hence the first identity was the identity of the mask, and it explains why the Greek and Latin for a mask, πρόσωπον or *persona*, came to indicate a person as we understand the word. The mask, then, corresponds to the face of mediation put on by everyone to derive a personal identity, both *personata* ("impersoned") and im-personating; lasting just as long as the rite lasted, it was nevertheless the only true identity. If, on the one side, the uniformity of masks served to defuse any possible reaction against the single authors of the ritual act, on the other the condition of being all identical was the performative intermediation capable of giving a collective and later individual identity.

Thus the masks of the rite became a means to channel tribal violence, to prevent it being turned against the members of the tribe; where necessary, it had to be watertight and impenetrable because it supplied their collective identity, representing the mediation in which they all identified. Now as in the past, military uniforms have a similar function of mediatory uniformity, expressing a collective personality that is performatively effective; not to mention all the other collective signs that complement and complete identification, such as insignia, flags, nameplates, coats of arms, and badges. A soldier or policeman does not wear a uniform because of the function that he performs but performs that function because he wears the uniform, so much so that the real disguising of a policeman or soldier occurs when he is not in uniform, when he goes about incognito, temporarily stripped of his collective identity; that identity remains guaranteed by a badge or identity card, but he must be prepared to resume it promptly when there is no longer any reason to be disguised in plain clothes. The collective, corporate identity derives its prestige and power, that is, its mediatory ascendency, from its relationship to the violence resolved by public mediation because it is fed by it and characterized by it as a *border* identity: just as soldiers guard state borders and police defend the law from a position on the ill-defined borderline between legality and illegality, so the ritual mask is situated on a knife-edge between a peaceful life and devastating violence, marking the impassable watershed between the two, making visible a narrow zone of communication and division. Thus the mask does not mark a border but is itself the border, the line of de-finite and finite division.

The mask refers to a radical absence, the absence of the death taking place behind it, and to a total presence, the presence of the glorious, victorious mediation; between these two dimensions there is no static division but a dynamic tension that can vanish or fall away, if its energy flags and the borderline between visible and invisible no longer holds. The mask is therefore a danger signal as well, a sign that the ritual is in progress and not yet concluded, its intransitivity none other than transitivity being developed at full pitch; and the mask is always ready to strike if necessary or if its role as a protective surface of exchange goes unperformed. In Greece it could become the Medusa's petrifying stare with its sinister power to make a mask of whoever looked on it. The tragic mask reminds spectators not so much that the tragedy is taking place as that all the community's masks and defining border lines are dynamic facts and have to be kept up, that they are energy sources needing to be fueled or they may vanish dramatically. The mask visualizes a collective life that can change to collective death at any moment, and gives material form to the idea that any sacrifice of a single part is worth the maintenance of its warning, bordering surface, any war is worth the defense of its bastion.

The paradox of Greek tragedy is that it is required to stage and keep up the mask of collective mediations and at the same time stimulate, interrogate, and in the end call them into question. Let us recall the moving scene of Agave holding in her hand the head/*prosopon* of her son, herself impersonated by the same actor who was impersonating him. The collective mediations seek confirmation in their theatrical representations, but this involves a reversal of roles, because the decision somehow rests with the representation as its symbolic tribunal: theater appeared to be a reflection of the acquired mediations, but it now reflects on them, a partly independent cultural mediation that, however, sees its object waver and at the end disappear, destroyed by a stage sacrifice apparently more real than real sacrifices.

Originally an effigy of Dionysus, the tragic mask reveals itself in the end to be the mask of the Gorgon. How to look her in the eye? The tragic actor can no longer wear his mask as a tribal gesture like the child killers with their faces painted white, but neither can he remove it, as the modern actor does, and act like one of us. The border that the mask is must remain, but tragedy oscillates at an increasing rate across the barrier, the watershed, trying out various paths and, in a more radical way, continuing Orphism's recovery of the Titanic mask.

There is a relevant item of news in this regard. Thespis is the traditional founder of tragedy, in the time of Pisistratus, and before he adopted removable masks made of wood and material he is said to have covered the actors' faces with white chalk.[53] This remarkable unsolicited evidence shows the clear link to Orphism's researches. The tragic writer obviously knew just what he was doing when he had his actors wear masks: he was seeking the right mask to tell us something underneath that could not be shown directly. Athenian tragedy is, then, a sort of Orphic initiation open to all-comers, a metareligious meditation in which the mask becomes research about a definitional limit, an enigma put on the stage but whose author lacks the answer, an enigma set before a public by definition lacking any answers at all. The challenge made by Gorgias, "*proballete*," is launched anew between the mask and the public, in a continuous exchange bringing exciting results but finally leaving the answer vacant and in suspense, earning severe criticism from philosophical knowledge and marking the start of tragedy's decline.

The wisdom of the mask—that is, the wisdom of tragedy—can help us to understand the mask of wisdom, provided we follow up the stimulus of tragedy's investigation to a point unattainable in Greece because it involves anthropological and historical research into Dionysus, impossible at that time and in those terms exactly because of the looming presence of the god. To this end, we must do precisely what the tragic avoids because it has to feed on the performative force coming from the rite: we must discover its origin. The birth of knowledge in Greece and its surprising developments cannot be understood without first explaining the birth of tragedy. Ever since Nietzsche's day, this enthralling enigma seems to have epitomized and encapsulated the enigma of Greek civilization, formulating in Hellenic terms the enigma of our own culture. And by explaining the birth of tragedy we also explain European culture since it recognized itself in tragedy, presaging in its own time the approach of unthinkable tragedies, tragedies now completely unmasked save perhaps for a gas mask.

Nietzsche is best equipped to supply the essential elements for a solution here, but it is also in his best interest to prevent us from combining them successfully. Rather than trace tragedy back to its birth, he wanted to bring about the rebirth of an unprecedented tragic mediation, providing a stronger, renewed Dionysian impetus for relaunching the terms of the ancient mediation. Going beyond the initial Wagnerian impulse, too close to a Christian redemptive objectual aim, Nietzsche pursued an objectual destruction without precedent, having in view a definitive cyclical rebirth, a neo-Dionysian mediation with nothing tragic about it since it would burn up all that was tragic in itself, destroying the illusory balance with the Apollinian, which is still the underlying argument in *The Birth of Tragedy*. The ultimate outcome of Nietzsche's interest in Greek drama could only be a celebration of the death of ancient and modern drama in a definitive eschatological *drama* completely unrelated to the Hellenic model.

In order to obtain a more truthful picture, therefore, we need to accept Nietzsche's assumptions but turn them in the opposite direction, reverse his ideological program and peel off the mask or rather the many masks continually worn by the philosopher of Zarathustra. What emerges is an archaeological excavation with many strata, which I will now try to sketch out with the sole aim of illustrating the nature of the subject and the possibilities for further investigation being opened up. And the most important stratum of this excavation in the world of tragedy is its ritual nucleus, which can be perfectly identified if we use the right tools to excavate and the right stratigraphic criteria.

5. The Sacrifice of the *Tragos*

It still must be said, however, that the young Nietzsche's reappraisal of Dionysus is nowhere more to the purpose than in the case of tragedy and, in spite of his already unbalanced and misleading manner, nowhere hits the mark with greater success. Notwithstanding all the erudite, irate objections of Ulrich Von Wilamowitz-Möllendorf, not wrong in themselves but become the standard example for generations of specialists attempting to keep the secrets of Attic drama under lock and key, Nietzsche is essentially right. For that matter, this conclusion is easy to reach: it suffices to cast a glance, even the least contextual, at the problem tackled by Nietzsche in a pioneering spirit.

Presiding over the birth and development of this theatrical form there could only be Dionysus, the divinity of a thousand names and shapes, the god of doubleness, the mask-god par excellence. The archaic image of Dionysus was a masklike face fixed to a stake, whose identity is repeated on the stage, held between Agave's hands and impersonated by the masks of the actors, all variously reflecting a single enigma, the enigma of Dionysus himself. During the Greater Dionysia, every character acting in front of the orchestra, with its altar to the god (the *thymele*, from *thuein*, to sacrifice), reflected, realized, and to a certain extent incarnated the god. One god, Dionysus, speaks to us through a variety of sensible appearances. In Greece he is the only god to fully develop rites of disguise and ecstatic identification, the precedent for sacrificial metamorphosis to become theatrical metamorphosis. There is no reason to doubt Aristotle's word when he says that tragedy originated in the *dithyrambos*, the dithyramb, a hymn to Dionysus in the shape of a bull; this became τραγῳδία in Attica, the song of the *tragos*, the he-goat.[54] When Euripides refers to the "dithyrambic" god (*Bacchae* 526), he is alluding specifically to the sacrificial origin of his art. The unifying factor of sacrificial and Dionysian mediation not only agrees with the evidence, it also supplies an internal solution to an apparent conflict in the data; and here we begin to break through the surface of Nietzsche's deceptive explanation, a real interpretative mask designed to prevent us, and Nietzsche himself, from seeking any further explanation. Besides, in the exegetical history of the origin of tragedy, misunderstandings become more frequent the further we go in examining the evidence, and so the capacity to explain apparent textual contradictions shown by an organic theory of sacrificial mediation should be appreciated here as in few other places. What we have here is consistent language, a fact only confirmed by the critics' partial misunderstanding of the data, demonstrating yet again the semi- or para-tragedy of those who cannot or will not understand tragedy.

The two traditional etymologies of the word *tragodia*—song for the goat sacrifice and song of the goat-men—now appear as perfectly complementary, since the rite presupposes metamorphic identification with the ritual victim, first sacrificed as guilty and then worshipped as divine, as Calasso correctly understands,[55] followed by the central sequence of the ritual cycle as Girard understands it.[56] However, we ought to add, this information is not only relatively late but tells us about the background history, a sort of skeleton still without any living content. On its own the information remains juxtaposed, the central mediatory factor is missing, the unifying experience without which it becomes incomprehensible with the passage of time.

In any case, a competitive factor is present from the start, as the etymology of *protagonistes* suggests; the term denoted both the frontline fighter and the first actor, the sole actor initially, the first agonist; his antagonist evidently was the public in the ritual guise of the chorus, accusing the agonist on stage of being an enemy to Dionysus. The sacrificial goat therefore incarnates both Dionysus, invoked in ancient times by the hides worn by the goat-men, and his dark side, the enemy of the god, the anti-Dionysus torn to pieces by the group.[57] This recalls the similar polar opposition between the Egyptian god of dismemberment, Osiris, and Seth, his brother and killer, a real anti-Osiris representing the god in his monstrous aspect, a projection of his lynchers who see him as an evil being to be neutralized. It is precisely the opposition of the *tragos* eating the vine or the hero fighting the Dionysian cult to show the essential bond with the god. What joins the two is sacrifice, though it goes unmentioned in the sources simply because the stage representation had taken its place, passing through the transformation of a para-theatrical rite. The Pentheus-Dionysus system, with its double structure reproducing the verbal developments as well as the forms of the sacred contest mentioned earlier, brings us, then, to the very origins of tragedy, the victimary mediator in his dual aspect, while the group of goat-men dancing and singing in the *choreia*, the dance of the labyrinth and Curetes, is transformed into the *choros*. Within the originary collective framework, and again in a subdivision implicitly into three parts, the opposite extremes of the sacral mediations are met once more in the figure of Dionysus, who kills and is killed, slaughters and is slaughtered. Subsequently, when the standard number of tragic actors rose to three, the scheme became more complex and varied, transferring the Dionysian contest to the stage and turning it into a tragic vicissitude with the *choros* no longer as the direct antagonist but as its lateral interlocutor. But the semicircular shape of the Greek theater reminds us that the public completes the dramatic interplay by providing the necessary background while the stage completes it by closing it off with the tragic circle of the characters, a group more properly to be seen as a segment of a circle that includes the chorus as well as the spectators and the entire theater. At the same time the circular structure of the *theatron* shows that all of it is put back into circulation in the community, being presented as a warning, instructive performance, in a spectacular mediation that reworks sacrifice, making it an object of representation and knowledge.

The main features of the transition from ritual to tragedy can now be understood but not the specific historical process that led to it, reshaping and organizing those features into something original and innovative. And if that process is not to elude us, our point of reference at this stage has to be Eleusis; this reference, too, was surely and brilliantly intuited by Nietzsche. When seen in relation to the Mysteries, the evidence of the use of Orphic masks by Thespis becomes even more eloquent. A few general comments here, together with what we saw in analyzing the Gurob papyrus, can illustrate how tragedy and Eleusis are closely related without in any way implying their identity. Eleusis can give us the ritual mediation that the thinly scattered, late fragmentary information about goats and goat-men cannot provide.

Drama originated from the *dromenon*, the ritual representation in which the sacred *thing* was performed—that is, the sacrifice (*sacrum* or *sacra facere*), the *dran* in the *Cretans*. It was thus a more or less metaritual development of the rite, using the rite's power of symbolic signification to go beyond it, while nevertheless keeping its representational content intact. To a degree unparalleled in Greece, Orphic-Eleusinian wisdom gave deeper cognitive significance to the *dromenon* as a system of transformations based on the *symbola* and centering on the *symbolon*. Tragedy's metaritual representation seems therefore to imply the rite where mediation of a mystery-initiatory type was most organic and complete, that is, Eleusis.[58] And the connection becomes difficult to deny if we assume at the start that the *arrheton* at Eleusis was, in one form or another, the collective murder of Dionysus.

Our argument is strengthened further when we consider the centrality of the Eleusinian Mysteries to Athenian religious and social life. And even if tragedy did originate in some village in Attica or in the Peloponnesus, as more than one scholar has claimed, the essential point would still need explaining, that is, why tragedy came into its own at Athens, a city that points directly to Eleusis through the connection with Dionysus. The presence of theatrical-type rites at various places in Greece attests the strongly representational character of the Greek *dromenon*. In several instances, this must have given rise to ritual representations that might even be defined as "tragedies manquées." And such a strongly representational character can be distantly linked by way of Crete to the sacred representations of the Osiris rites and of other eastern cults.[59] Against the background of an older Mediterranean substratum, the para-theatrical character of Greek rites, besides indicating the origin of the Athenian *drama*, also reveals its distinctive and innovative nature. It was only in the Orphic-Eleusinian center of Athens that the *dromenon* was to become tragedy, on the basis of a long ritual evolution that can be traced back to Crete and its oriental contacts.

The connections noted by Nietzsche are confirmed rather more than he would have wished or thought possible. As was often the case, he did not take his discoveries seriously enough and refused to understand the whole truth about the Dionysian sacrifice: that it was not comparable to a kind of Wagnerian opera untroubled by Christian infiltration. In this way, his very capacity to divine the sacrificial mediation underlying ancient drama, as well as the modern impossibility of going back there on the same terms, comes together with his failure to give proper weight to either, self-destructively combining, to complete the parallel with the *Bacchae*, the perverted ritual knowledge of Euripides's Dionysus and the symmetrical but opposite recalcitrance of Pentheus.

However reckless as to their motivation and results, and precisely on that score, Nietzsche's historical intuitions reveal his sure instinct, his expert knowledge of the subject. The vital links binding tragedy to Orphism and the Mysteries, and tragedy's cognitive investigation into them, are brought out by a range of evidence that only finds its full justification in the perspective being presented here—to start with, the frequent significant references to terms and texts throughout the tragic corpus,[60] such as the relevant examples from Euripides collected in this study. Other details enrich our scenario: Aristotle records that Aeschylus—who came from Eleusis, by the way—was accused of divulging the *arrheton*, the secret of the Mysteries, in his tragedies.[61] Such a charge could only have arisen from doctrinal agreement evident to initiates, and Clement of Alexandria tells us that Aeschylus defended himself by declaring he had never been initiated to the Mysteries, which leaves room for conjecture that this was because he saw in them an inferior manifestation of his own knowledge.

The traditional objection that it is incorrect to speak of any kind of theatrical representation at Eleusis merely begs the question, imagining that theater should already exist where there was no theater. The problem is rather to explain how Greek theater arose from something that was *not* theater and yet, from a logical and historical point of view, represented its immediate antecedent. Proof that the Eleusinian representations were not directly theatrical comes from the sacral liturgical value of the *legomena*, the "things spoken," words only pronounced at crucial moments in the rite. The real Eleusinian representation, however, was the *arrheton*, the inexpressible source of all representations and all languages, the collective murder. Only the inexpressible is tragic. Undoubtedly, tragedy frees the *dromenon* of Eleusis from its magical-religious bonds: the "things shown" became masks, the "things done" stage action, and the "things said" the text, within the audio-visual setting of music and staging. But the *arrheton* of human origin remains the silent center of the *logos*, of the *tragodia*. The elements of the *drama* are thus inferred from within, and we understand their symbolic interchangeability: each is a *symbolon*, arising from and converging on the source of symbolism itself.

We can now understand the nature of the Aristotelian problem of the so-called unities in tragedy and why it continued for centuries to vex the history of the interpretation and misunderstanding of the genre. The indefinable unity, violated and required by every line of tragic verse, is none other than the unity of the victim, the goat, the murdered Dionysus, his *reductio ad unum*, his atonement. What sacrifice could there be without the fundamental unity, the only unity explicitly named in the *Poetics*, the unity of action?[62] Aristotle's genius was close enough to the rite not to forget it and far enough away from it to render it abstract; typically, he perceived the formal structure of an archaic content that by then was fading into the background. That content was the *symbola* and the *symbolon*, the sacrificial and theatrical parts handed out by the *Moirai*, the unspoken language on which every word is founded. This is the vision (*theama*) that tragedy sets before us in the metaritual space of the *theatron*. But the vision must speak to us, must tell us the enigma that no word can solve, the enigma of the unity of tragedy, of man's hidden unity, the silence in which it consists and from which every plurality, every word is reborn.

This silence is not simply verbal but written, made up of signs that have become and will become writing. I am not just referring to the fact that we can access the tragic corpus in written form, in itself an accidental circumstance though far from marginal historically speaking, but to the part already being played by writing for fifth-century authors. For them it represented a second level of reception and understanding, obviously destined for the better-educated more affluent public in a position to buy and read the expensively produced rolls on which the stage dramas were transcribed.

Some years ago the relationship of the oral tradition to writing was the subject of a lively debate, and as happens in these cases, it became a fashionable topic, distorting the terms of the question, with the help of the celebrated contrast drawn by Plato between written, and therefore dead, books and dialogue among living persons.[63] This, however, neglects the fact that Plato's criticism presupposes a power to evoke and influence in the written text, not the contrary. And more generally, it ought to be said that in antiquity the two were not so starkly opposed as we moderns are ready to imagine. Reading in silence was not the habit in classical times—at most it was confined to personal correspondence—and books were usually read aloud and in company.[64] In other words, writing was not felt to be an independent textual entity but the vehicle for *logoi* charged with expressive and verbal force, a vehicle endowed with its own originary magical-communicative power while having its place in a broader flux of forces linked to *logos*.[65] In regard to writing, therefore, Plato's aim is not to liquidate the written dialogues setting out his position but to place them in the correct perspective of his philosophical *paideia*, his quest after truth through living dialogue and dialectic, for which the written version is no more than an introduction and preliminary.

The silence recognizable in writing is therefore a sort of absolute base point in the classical world, a starting point but also a point of arrival if we think of the more cultivated public watching the tragedy on stage and then going to read the texts appropriately copied onto the rolls. The written aspect of tragedies, for us the only authentic aspect, is not a straitjacket, then, or a mere accident to be deplored; above all, it is the start and resumption of an effective device reaching its climax in the representation on stage. However, it can be reconstructed "archaeologically" if we set it within the intricate web of its background history, connections, and implications. Writing is in fact sonorous, since it is soundless in a way that is generated and generates, it is a symbolic dimension, the source of sound and its end, a graphic-performative power fully attesting to its origin, its ancient magical-religious nature. The extensive unity of tragedy thus appears equivalent to the question of the intensive unity of its writing, and of the unity generally at the origin of writing. In what way can we recognize and read this writing that "speaks" and the alphabet of signs that lie at its core?

6. The Originary Writing

Tragedy, a vision that speaks and language that has to be seen, is led to evade the center, on which it is compelled to converge, and dragged toward a black hole that calls forth its eloquence and sets its masks and scenery in motion but finally engulfs all words, all visions. The mask that expresses the enigma and tries to solve it refers all the time to the silent visibility that shows it and provides a silent commentary on its utterances, leading to the silence of the drama's denouement, not so much the solution to the enigma as the dissolution of its addressee and bearer, who is reduced to silence and withdrawal at the end of the performance, which is its visual conclusion as well. Thus there is a crossing-over of tensional planes: words and silence, vision and the invisible confront each other during the performance and converge in the *katastrophe*, the final words of the *choros* that signal the rapid ending of the *theama*. In order to understand how writing relates to this complex tragic dialectic between words and what is not words we must go back briefly to the ritual origin of the enigma.

If it is true to say that prophecy by oracle, with which the enigma is connected, developed more than any other form of prophecy in Greece, it should be stressed that the basis of this preeminence was the archaic sacrifice evidenced in dismemberment rites and myths at Delphi. The most archaic form of divination was actually from the intestines of the sacrificed victim and reached a high degree of specialization in Mesopotamia. The oldest practice is documented among Celtic peoples, who interpreted the will of the gods by means of human victims as well. Tacitus provides illuminating evidence when he writes of the Druids who "held it a sacred duty to venerate the gods by sacrificing prisoners and to consult them through human intestines."[66] The wise man was the man who read the victim as a sign and set of signs, who guided the ritual response from the things shown in the examined viscera and eventually by the things said, the words concerning destiny in which, technically speaking, the enigma consisted, summing up the preceding phases in a cognitive form. To this sequence corresponds the triad of past, present, and future, the province of the seer and wise man[67] in itself of shamanistic origin,[68] and associated by Plato with poets in the passage in the *Laws* dealing with poetic inspiration. This triad is recalled symbolically in the Delphic tripod, awarded as tradition has it to the wisest man among the Greeks and containing the remains of a dismembered victim who is to be viewed as corresponding to Apollo-Dionysus himself.[69] Ritual triad and temporal triad come to be the same thing, in a circularity aiming to invert its unilineal succession: the past is the action just performed, the dead victim; the present is his things shown as a whole, his bloody, confused, and yet revealing signs; and the future is the things said, the response to the outcome of sacrifice and the acquisition of a new divine awareness. The symbolic interpretation of the Delphic tripod can be taken further. The circular shape of the opening not only recalls the transitive and objectual circularity that was to resolve the sacrificial triad, in the hopes of the postulant addressing the god, but also the cognitive circularity, the prestigious much-coveted attribute of both knowledge itself and whoever possessed it at any particular time. However, the tragic wisdom and the possible tragic destiny of the sage recall to us that the reversibility is never reached once and for all, since it must be renewed each time starting from the dismembering and re-membering content of the tripod.

We now have the elements necessary to conclude that the first enigma is the map of the body of the victim, animal or human, in which everyone looked for signs that the objectual crisis was at an end and the saving mediation successfully achieved. This body map was the nonmetaphorical antecedent of the Cretan labyrinth: the proof comes from the Babylonian "viscera records," tablets used by the haruspices that had the convoluted patterns of victims' intestines traced on them. In Babylonia, the intestine was called the "palace of the viscera" and interpreted as an image of the afterlife.[70] A prehistoric engraving in the Sahara representing the cross-section of the body of a buffalo shows a double spiral like a labyrinth starting from the center of the body, evidently reproducing the animal's guts.[71] We should have no illusions: Ariadne's thread and the rope uniting the dancers are the victim's intestines transformed, respectively, into myth and ritual. There is a scene in Ovid where Pasiphae, in her passion for the bull, kills the heifers and squeezes their intestines in her hands as a mark of triumph.[72] If, as seems likely, this episode derives from Euripides, then we can be certain that the labyrinth of intestines was present as a theme in the *Cretans*. Further links can be made to the rite of hierogamy. In the Gilgamesh epic, Ishtar asks the hero to mate with her but he refuses, telling her how his other lovers met a tragic end. In revenge, Ishtar sends the celestial bull; Enkidu kills the animal and threatens to hang the intestines from Ishtar's arms, in the classical Babylonian version,[73] or to tie her up in the bull's guts in the Sumerian version.[74] It is palpably obvious that these ritual details derive from the earliest hierogamies, with a revealing increase in violence between the Babylonian edition and the Sumerian. The intestines and guts in our texts belong to the male animal but must originally have been those of Ishtar herself, disemboweled after mating. The intestines hanging on the goddess's arms imply an identity that is underscored and set in motion by using the same intestines to tie her up, allowing us to glimpse a single bloody deed centered on a woman's body. Again, a Saharan rock painting depicts a masked man joined to a woman by an enormous phallus:[75] it is not hard to imagine the really bloody outcome if the woman was completely penetrated by such a phallic object as long as a lance.

The labyrinth of viscera is found again in twentieth-century literature. In a remarkable piece by the Italian writer Giorgio Manganelli entitled *A Labyrinth's Awareness of Itself* (*Autocoscienza del labirinto*) a voice introduces and defines itself as a labyrinth: "Enormous, vast viscera, sown with false directions, indecipherable routes and a map, accurate and unknown." The labyrinth appears to itself as a language indecipherable in itself because it coincides with the person who should understand it: "But if the labyrinth reforms before my eyes like a total, inaccessible language, what will my task be? Will I have to learn a language that can only talk to itself of itself, will I in fact have to be that language myself?"[76] The labyrinth is the language, the cultural system of man at grips with the impenetrable problem of imagining and explaining himself, an obvious metaphor for literature as well. The labyrinth makes tormented, metalabyrinthine attempts at description in the mess of organs, ruins, and signs that compose and decompose it, corresponding not only to man's present situation of mediatory disorientation and objectual disintegration but also to an unknown, impending scene of origin. After these attempts, it becomes completely lost in itself. At this point it comes to contemplate a female statue, worn down by time to a fragment: a "woman of stone" (femmina di sasso) with a face that "seems to allude to inveterate blindness."[77] Here, the deep structure of labyrinth symbolism reemerges in its essentials: from its sacrificial origin starting with the body to the female divinity of the hierogamy, and from the unknown origin of human language to the impossibility for anyone still its prisoner to describe it. But in its intransitive closure, this impossibility also signals a fresh start, the definition of a new relationship, and a different path to be followed. Trying at all costs to describe itself, the labyrinth speaks to us and is coming to light, the visceral labyrinth of what we are.

A modern writer can draw on resources of metaphysical irony unknown to ancient Greece, but they refer back, through an archaeological link that is also a contrast, to the cluster-like point of departure for contemporary literary invention, to the "total, inaccessible language" of a sacred origin that loomed over and permeated everything in Greece, translating into physical signs that by themselves imposed a publicly acknowledged interpretation and permitted more fragile, revocable cognitive spaces, the patrimony of narrow circles that had to move within the coordinates of broader mediations of which they were part. The ritual labyrinth was still too close not to suffer its symbols in silence. This is the preamble of and conclusion to the written labyrinth of tragedy.

The *ainigma* becomes vision in tragedy, immersion in the *ainós*, the horror. This horror is the mask, the visual border of the sacred victim, a mask when looked at closely almost overwhelming with the concrete signs of killing, no different from what happened to the initiates of Cybele or from what happens, in a more symbolic theatrical form, to Agave when she appears with the mask-head of her son. These are not simply associated images: parallels are to be found in other cultures. In an African initiation rite, the forehead of the young male initiate was covered with the viscera of a freshly killed goat:[78] this splanchnic, visceral mask shares precise similarities with the Mesopotamian demon Humbaba, Huwawa, or Khubaba, the enemy of Gilgamesh, whose face was intestinal in form, which emerges unquestionably from some sculpted images that have been found.[79] To connect this with Greece and Greek theater would not appear to be too speculative. Masks found in two archaic Greek shrines made in a period predating theater have an intestinal shape, and to all appearances are modeled on Humbaba.[80]

The labyrinth is a map, a congeries of signs in which our origin is incised, written. It is no accident that a writer like Manganelli feels the need to verify his medium by developing a stratigraphic image of writing, reclaiming the indecipherable necessary space of the labyrinth as space that denies space, as symbol that shatters and nullifies all symbols, sign and burial-place of signs, living and ghostly representation of the afterlife. The labyrinth is the bloody prehistory of all our languages, a prehistory of the sign that was *written* before it was spoken as, with a formalistically deconstructionist accent, Jacques Derrida intuited. The labyrinth is all future meaningful traces as a whole; it is the first hieroglyph, in which the symbol converges with the thing symbolized, is itself the thing symbolized, as Manganelli perceived. Derrida would have us believe the contrary, that is, that in writing the thing reveals itself as sign and thereby loses every real connotation in the postmodern consciousness's necrotic empire of signs. But the writing of the origin remains bloodily real, inviolable to any modern or postmodern attempt to erase it or rewrite it to suit its own purposes. The first hieroglyph is the body of the victim, the first ideograms are his organs and limbs, the signs cut into the surface, signs that had to be read; these signs were divine scripture to be received, decoded as for example in the ancient practice of chiromancy, and actually transcribed into artificial signs on the body in the form of tattoos. That, then, is the origin of writing. Many prehistoric finds reveal figures excessively carved with signs: spirals, whorls, and wavy lines. These finds are often images of goddesses, sometimes snakelike to look at, their limbs interlaced like a tangle of serpents, the labyrinth of intestines that *was* Ariadne. This labyrinth of limbs, wounds, intestines became writing. The body signs began to arrange themselves in incised sequences of expressive graphemes, hieroglyphs, cuneiform incisions, and alphabetical symbols. Phaedra, it will be recalled, was able to accuse Hippolytus by means of the letter attached to her hanged body, transforming her very body into incised characters; Euripides's text is itself a surprising example of this metamorphosis. Nothing escapes the enigma, starting with writing that was its instrument.

With the enigma of the body's writing, of sacrifice, tragedy reveals itself as the conscious and blind representation of the process that created it as text, organizing its linguistic expression. The actor putting on the mask, the character trying in vain to unravel the enigma that instead unravels him, is man struggling to spell out the labyrinthine text of himself, until he comes to coincide with it, to incarnate it *in corpore vivo*, on a par with the condemned man in Kafka's "In the Penal Colony." In this extraordinary short story an explorer visits an island where, as the officer in charge of execution explains to him, the condemned man is subjected to a nightmarish machine that writes the sentence by carving its characters on his body again and again until, when he finally understands the reasons for his death sentence, the diabolical device kills him. This barbaric custom has fallen into disrepute; nevertheless the officer hopes to arouse the visitor's comprehension and solidarity by showing him its design, which is as complicated as a labyrinth and no longer understood by anyone, and also by performing an execution. The explorer reacts with horror, so the soldier in despair finally throws out the convict waiting to be tortured and subjects himself to the horrific machinery. Yet even in this last desperate exhibition things go wrong since the machine no longer works properly. The old wisely sadistic process becomes butchery, and the officer is quickly killed while the device falls apart once and for all. In all likelihood, this modern apologue represents Europe face-to-face with the sacrificial traditions of the countries it discovered, but unable to understand their rationale nor its own involvement in the very same needs.

The symbolic strength of Kafka's story, narrated in a frank and matter-of-fact way, documents a distressful and at the same time liberating awareness not open to characters in tragedy. Once again, comparing ancient and contemporary literature stimulates us to perceive differences that are made to stand out by their precise points of resemblance. The catastrophic conclusion to the twentieth century's series of sacrificial representations reminds us of the concluding but not conclusive catastrophe toward which the tragic character gravitates, enchained in the double bond that gives him life since he is ready for death and lets him live since he is a concentrate of nonexistence, because of his double nature as irremovable mask and masked victim.

Any writing, whatever it is, always has reference to an addressee, to a public that wants those signs and reads them because it makes them in the first place. This brings us to another essential aspect, another *symbolon* of the *symbolon* of tragic mediation: the originary collective aspect, represented on the two connected and distinct levels of chorus and spectators.

7. Spectators and Chorus

Among the false accusations made against Euripides in *The Birth of Tragedy*, the sharpest is that he takes "the spectator [*den Zuschauer*] on stage" and gives him the right to judge and evaluate rationally what was happening in the tragic spectacle,[81] with the result of destroying the powerful Dionysiac unity of the Aeschylean drama. The accusation as such is false, since Euripides wanted the public to understand his dramas in their religious and historical contents, and thus not according to the intellectualistic rationality Nietzsche is ready to attribute to him and his most outstanding spectator, Socrates. Nevertheless, the charge reflects in a distorted manner a tendency present in the Athenian tragedy from its very start. We catch the point if we overturn from within the premise of Nietzsche's argument, that is, the Dionysian identity of chorus and audience. Actually, the initial ritual identity was doomed to quickly develop, multiply, and break because of its inner tensions. Are not the acts of remembering and dismembering parts of only one process, more than ever in the symbolic and cognitive tearing apart of theatrical re-presentation?

This proves to be true starting from the very beginning of the Greek tragic theater. The *hypokrites*, who can be described as the actor answering the chorus and so submitting to its judgment,[82] is the hero who tries to solve the triple enigma of man's past, present, and future in his *hypokrisis*, his judgment-performance. The victim's viscera were forbidden to be shown on stage, but by means of the mask, they were made secretly, pervasively present—re-presented, that is. The viscera-mask is the secret mirror of Dionysus in which the *hypokrites*'s destiny of death hides, more or less as Dionysus's death is already contained in the mirror that the Titans give him: the *symbola* of dismemberment become the *symbola* of the written and spoken words, to return them to what they were in origin. The future is revealed as the past in the eternal present of sacrificial updating and transformation. Through words, songs, and music the audience were able to dismember and devour the mask-god symbolically, in a metaphorical omophagy.

Thus the Greek drama was based on a metaperformative and cognitive reproduction of the Dionysiac sacrifice from the start, and this is still recognizable in Aristotle's catharsis, described by him while defining tragedy itself: "Tragedy then is imitation [*mimesis*] of an action [*praxeos*] serious and brought to completion, . . . such that by means of piety and fear [*di'eleou kai phobou*] it achieves a purification [*katharsin*] from such passions [*pathematon*]."[83] The crystal-clear formula sounds logical and psycho-logical but actually conceals a disquieting cultic theorem: the *pathemata* correspond to the *pathema* of Dionysus, and in order to rid oneself of its pitiful and fearsome presence, the bearer of the *pathema* must be purified, expelled. Thus the Aristotelian κάθαρσις corresponds to the purification-expulsion of the *pharmakos* and transforms it in a rational and moral revision intended to bring the irregularities, the broken segments of the tragic circle, back within the circularity of socially accepted mediations. This has been the real rationalizing turning point in the interpretive history of tragedy, needless to say far less appealing to the Dionysian and Wagnerian author of *The Birth of Tragedy*, and as always he was not completely wrong.

No doubt the cathartic mediation of the *Poetics* turns out secretly to be an illusion, or rather it turns out to be empty to the extent that the *polis* is now empty, assuming the incipient decline of the phenomenon that is being described. However, the layers of the Aristotelian rationalization are much richer and more complex than Nietzsche supposed and follow the intimate structure of the phenomena analyzed, exploiting their previous performative rationale and rationality in a more abstract way, as Plato and Socrates had already done in their own way. The information transmitted by Aristotle is real and is made available by the loosening of the para-ritual and ritual bonds that made tragedy in the fifth century such a tremendously intense theatrical experience, a *katharsis* so strong as to be untheorizable. If, then, we are to understand the catharsis of the *Poetics* we must hold two planes together, the originary experience with the plane of rationalization that made it assimilable to the principles of Aristotelian philosophy. Spectators in the fifth century, as they attended to the victim and attended his "execution" and the play about him, felt that they were delivering themselves from evil and felt called on to return each time to expel the *pharmakos*, without any *Poetics* to justify them. And in the second half of the fourth century educated members of the tragic audience also felt the need to explain what was happening to them, and so transformed the para-ritual *theama* into a philosophical *theoria*, turning the thrilling emotional experience of the *theama* into a semipsychological, conceptualized purging of its deepest feelings.[84] Aristotle's *homo rationalis* no longer thinks that his analytical distinctions and nice divisions of rhetoric and style still stink of the sacrificial altar, nor that the compassion, *éleos*, that he feels for the tragic hero, considered by Aristotle to be the distinguishing feature of tragedy, derives from *eleós*, the ritual slab on which the victim was torn to pieces.[85] Yet the very limits of the Aristotelian conceptualization show its concealed strength, more easily forgotten centuries later in the increasingly impalpable process of metapurification of the literary and philosophical myth.

Omophagy, first transformed into theatrical experience and subsequently into philosophical rationalization, follows a process of evolution and involution in modern times to become erudite ritual, a totemic meal of bloodless writings and a silent, empty academic catharsis. But the unintentional necrophagy of erudition for erudition's sake cannot completely destroy the life that it will not see, not even bothering to be an onlooker. Even through badly damaged fragments, the apparently passive object of our dissections still retains its power to disrupt and create difficulties for the false certainties of the rationalism that those fragments classify and put on file. After the antitragic exorcisms of his teacher Plato, Aristotle's line of interpretation begins a process of detached rationalization, interrupted by the reverse trend of Christian censure, that ends by paying its debt, by somehow closing the circle with its objectual disintegration, making once more unconsciously visible what had ceased to be so after having been consciously visible in part. This is the premise of Nietzsche's reaction against the erudite atmosphere of his classicist education. The very one-sidedness of his criticism reproduces in reverse the opposite blindness and points to a completion that needs to be pursued and realized. Along this long and twisted journey we can conclude, then, that we are also part of the public for tragedy and that the evolution and stratagems of the Athenian audience are our own, not less than the following historical stages going from Aristotle to Nietzsche. Without this assumption, any research is bound to prove sterile, to fall short, more or less tragically, of its object of study. One sign of the operation's validity is that a more penetrating reconstruction is easier to make and results in a unified picture that can both distinguish and unite the ancient and modern points of view.

Initially, the audience identified with the chorus of goat-men, the actors of the *dromenon*, but then, unlike what Nietzsche says, it differentiated itself through the social and metaritual developments of the *tragodia*. The chorus developed into the mediatorily ambiguous mirror of the audience, torn between *phobos* and *éleos*, between fear and pity, in a state of cognitive blindness feigning not to know what the audience knew full well, that is, the final outcome of the story, according to the "much refined hypocrisy" (*raffinierter Heuchelei*) that Freud writes about in the last pages of *Totem and Taboo*.[86] The chorus feigns ignorance of what the audience knows, while the audience pretends to have no part in the chorus's involvement. They are both *hypokritai*. But tragedy, with its oscillatory dynamic almost reproduced in mime by the stylized dancing of the *choros*, tends to distinguish the audience with an increasing awareness of its role and then to draw it deeper and deeper into its labyrinth of signs and *logoi*, reaching a partial form of reversal in the *Bacchae*: the chorus continually repeats how matters are going to end, but the audience is so traumatized that it would prefer not to know the outcome.

The *Bacchae* makes more visible a destabilizing circularity typical of the mature Athenian drama, according to the principle of tragic impersonality. Through its duplication in the Theban women (corresponding to the two horns that sprout from the head of Dionysus), the chorus reverts indirectly but incisively to its distant origin as a group of lynchers and we, the audience, cannot avoid identifying with the chorus because the killing is carried out by the Theban women and they, no different from ourselves, would not want to believe in Dionysus. Through the interchangeability of audience and chorus, the god turns into the reversal of his cult's aim of salvation, into the antiobjectual depletion of his divine mediation. Hidden by the further mask of the text, the author is aware of it all. He, too, is torn between fear and pity and is the first not to possess the key to the enigma he has made himself interpreter of, the key to the text he is the apparent author of but really restricts himself to just reading. Like an archaeologist faced by an inscription of which only a tiny part is decipherable, he can make out enough to read his own defeat there, his own cognitive sentence (condemned to know but not to know enough) in a sense that can become Kafkaesque for us but at any rate refers to a constitutive double bind, to writing that is theatrical, liturgical, and corporeal, in itself a condemnation because a condemnation brought it to light. The author is the *hypokrites* of the spectators, of the characters, and in the final analysis of himself.

This is not to say that the tragic author moved in a kind of vacuum, which the parallels with twentieth-century writers might lead one to think if they are detached from the common ground where I have situated them. As I have already said, modern parallels are useful to create a better picture of the ancient context and the true extent and depth of a single thematic span, joining both in the complementary asymmetry of their different positions. In ancient Greece there is an explicit recognized tradition corresponding to the implicit disconnected modern traditions, and it is this explicit recognition that makes possible a fresh return to the revealing modern disconnectedness. Far from being the rationalizing destroyer of tragic knowledge described by Nietzsche, Euripides had an illustrious precedent, already mentioned in our discussion of Tiresias, the blind seer in the *Bacchae* who no longer wants to see anything but before that was blind because he had seen a great deal, too much in fact.

8. Homer

With the paradoxical results of tragic knowledge, distributed on various levels, we have come a long way from Orphism and Eleusis, as Euripides's critical attitude has already shown us, and as Aeschylus's refusing to be initiated suggests. Orphism and the Mysteries are not only far from exhausting the content of tragedy, they cannot even completely explain its origin. For fuller understanding we need to examine to the more specifically literary ingredients of the tragic genre: literature's origin from sacral mediations in the form of poetry as a musical and rhythmical expression of the divine sphere, a linguistic and symbolic space where it was possible to relive the myth thanks to possession by numinous forces visiting the group by means of the verbal mask of storytelling, and passing through the filter of the mental mask of memory that reveals and conceals. Tragedy was a specific new phenomenon that contained within itself another element answering to a definite name, though almost as mythical as Orpheus: Homer, whose importance in the Greek world cannot be exaggerated. The greatest Greek poet is the next step in our exploration of the origin of tragedy.

For the ancient Greeks, Homer was the supreme example of sacred poetic inspiration and, for this reason, the first among tragic poets and the undisputed model for writers of tragedy properly speaking.[87] This was stated by Aeschylus in person, according to a late but reliable testimony: he "declared that his tragedies were helpings [*temache*] taken from Homer's table,"[88] and we should not miss the connotations of *temachos*, literally a slice of fish or meat carved at a meal, in the style—one is tempted to add—of the dish imagined by Shakespeare's Brutus, albeit with the clear conscience of someone who believed sacrificial meals were a cruel necessity reserved for gods and heroes. For all the Greeks, except for a handful of exacting philosophers such as Plato, Homer was the greatest wise man, the supreme *auctoritas*, the source of life-giving lymph for their history and culture. At this point, we naturally ask ourselves why this should have been. Was it for sublimely stylistic reasons, as our literary idealism would have it, or rather for reasons of content, a dramatic content closely linked to the sacred character of his epic poems? Did the Greeks have any definite reasons for regarding blind Homer as a seer?

It is difficult to talk about Homer. Legions of impassioned scholars have gone before and produced a whole series of acute analyses evidencing the Homeric world as extremely primitive, almost to a point beyond belief; and yet this very primitiveness is redeemed by some category *ex machina*, such as the clarity or limpidity of the Greek spirit. Rohde, Nilsson, Snell, and Dodds have added much to our understanding of the Homeric world. Nonetheless, there is almost constant embarrassment over the behavior of the characters, variously dissected and dismembered to such a point that it seems anachronistic to talk of explanations that are psychologically credible and decipherable in our terms. The accepted diagnosis is given by Nilsson, *psychische Labilität*, echoed by Dodds in a milder form: "Homeric man has no unified concept of what we call 'soul' or 'personality.'"[89] Undoubtedly psychological beliefs in Homeric times differed greatly from our own, but it has to be remembered that it is not a question of psychology but of systematically tracing human behavior and feelings to divine mediations and their dynamics which are uncontrollable although active in a whole series of spiritual, mental, and somatic entities—in a word, intermedial, those entities concerned with an intermediate dimension that is both human and cosmic—of which even the memory is lost, either because we are blind to the evidence or find it incomprehensible. But unexpectedly, by measuring the gulf separating us from Homer, a bridge can be thrown across enabling us to understand what we have in common with him and his world. The explanation for the great diversity of behavior and sentiment described in his epics is the full possession of, or rather by, those mediatory factors that are instead completely lacking in our lives though the need for them is still urgent, and are now experienced in psychological forms and in the evasive anobjectual forms of our media. Our mentality and psychology bear absolutely no direct relation to those of Homer's heroes, but precisely this points to what we share with them: our common dependence on collective mediations, constantly under the threat of objectual crises that jeopardize them and so allow uncontrollable mimetic behavior to break out and proliferate.

This explains why the reader today is just as involved in and fascinated by the Homeric epics as his audience was almost three thousand years ago. More striking than the huge gulf separating us from Homer, to be fathomed only by philology, is the similarity, so embarrassingly simple as to remain unexpressed and misunderstood. This embarrassing similarity is our absolute need for mediations and the fragility of the human world and human objects as soon as those mediations start wavering, their transcendence no longer in a position to guarantee them. The shadowless simplicity with which all this is narrated is almost bewildering for its unapologetic directness, and gives us the shockingly elementary content that is the authentic muse of all great writers, especially those who become eponymous, which is like saying mediators, of an entire culture, of a nation's history and language. For this reason, the Greeks admired Homer and we admire Dante, Shakespeare, Cervantes, Racine, Goethe, Dostoevsky, and Melville, poorly protected as we are by the myth of their sublime style.

We will briefly examine the beginning of the *Iliad*, the most basic and certainly the earliest Homeric text. From the opening verses there emerges a radical crisis blocking access to the object and spreading death and destruction in the form of a massacre among the Achaeans caused by Apollo, and a transparent image of plague. A Girard-type interpretation can tell us a great deal about such a devastating opening, taken up again by Sophocles when he sets a pestilence at the start of *Oedipus Rex*.[90] And it seems confirmed by the explanation, the *aitia*, of the disaster: the quarrel between Achilles and Agamemnon for possession of the fair Briseis as the substitute for the daughter of a priest of Apollo they had to release (almost a double in her very name Chryseis). But the girl is a mere pretext; they are really fighting for top place in the Greek army, another Homeric archetype reworked by Euripides in *Iphigenia in Aulis*. We need only reread the episode and at once we find rivalry for possession erupting invincibly, roused by the object possessed by the rival, who is also the envied model, the unreal object. "You expect me to give up my gift, when you already have yours?" Agamemnon asks Achilles.[91] The consequences are devastating; the amount of violence in the *Iliad* is only comparable to the *Mahabharata* in world literature. Blood flows everywhere with the blindest, most gratuitous ease, and always triggered by the same motive, a rivalry to possess something that gets completely forgotten in the course of the struggle. This is already a good explanation, and yet it has the weakness of its strength, limited by being applicable indiscriminately and independently of the content and by ways always used by men in their attempt to overcome these painful situations, which suggests there is something else to both problem and solution: and as always the "pretragic" Homer shows us the way.

The plague brought on by the arrows of Apollo, spreading death and grief through the Achaean army, is not the sign of a generic mimetic crisis but more specifically indicates the collapse of the divine mediation caused by a *miasma*, a ritual impurity infecting the body of the Greek expedition. For Girard this is the mythic disguising of internal conflict among the Greeks that threatens the survival of the community, and that is a perfectly plausible explanation. However, it overlooks the detail that the essential point in Homer, as in all ancient cultures, is the unattainable nature of an object that goes far beyond the object disputed by the two illustrious rivals, namely, collective life and identity. In other words, the crisis could well be triggered by a real plague or by any other natural catastrophe and the effect would be the same, making conflict between members of the community the consequence and not the immediate cause, but the underlying problem always remains the failure of the group's protective mediations and of the objectual sphere that represents its life, not so much individually as collectively. Having recognized the real point of departure presented in the *Iliad*, we can understand something else, namely a still earlier cause: in itself, the clash between Greeks and Trojans is for the possession of another woman, Helen, but underlying that, both display an essentially wrong attitude of *hybris*, the arrogance that stops at nothing to obtain what it wants, a basic mediatory and objectual instability involving both men and gods. The divine sphere mirrors the human sphere, according to a principle of reversibility presiding in a world where all is connected and all can blow up if one link does not hold.

Potentially this is already the situation of mediatory crisis created in the tragedies, although the viewpoint that I think I discern in the *Iliad* is less sharply defined, adumbrated in the way each episode is presented, a compositional principle that indeed permeates the whole work, confined almost always to reproducing and reworking much older epic material in which divine and human intervention occurs without any censure, as automatically as in the *Brahmana*. What we have here is a textual process not far from the textual and hermeneutic stratifications of the books of the Bible. The complex development of the Homeric text with layer after layer superimposed through time and interacting one with another—a reason for which Giambattista Vico rightly solved the Homeric question in the sense of a collective identity of the author—makes us see, once we approach closely and regain their mediatory and objectual significance, how close, almost shockingly so, Homer comes to our own reasons for living or not living, and our need for a human world constantly under threat and beset by the countless factors on which it depends.

The conclusion is that Homer's poetic knowledge, especially the *Iliad*, analyzed so poetically by Simone Weil, is an indispensable prerequisite of tragedy and its double aspect as history that reveals and at the same time distances the content of the *mythos* in the fabulous stylized dimension of the tragic narrative. We now possess some important elements that bring us closer to the context in which Greek tragedy was born. To complete the reconstruction of this genesis in greater detail, we need to take a closer look at the possible influence of Orphism on tragedy and tragedy's use of Homer. A singular scenario now opens out for our inquiry, returning us once more, and it could not be otherwise, to Athens.

9. Orphism and Pisistratus

In its mystery mediation, Orphism in Greece developed remarkably deep sapiential insight into violence. For Orphism, the only way for man to rid himself of violence was through the cathartic, purifying liturgy of the *symbolon*, of which Eleusis is the most notable and complex example. This ritual expressed symbolically, in every sense of the word, the *dromenon*, the sacrifice that had to be performed, manifested, and expressed in language. In the competitive, verbal dimension of the *polis*, this clearly tended toward the representational development of *drama*. However, the overall framework of Orphism's saving mediation remained largely magical-ritual, preventing the representational content from freeing itself and attaining more complete cognitive independence. That emancipation must have begun, with a certain difficulty, when considerations about the holding power of human and divine mediations were introduced into the still ritualistic representation of the *dromenon*, considerations such as we find in Homer. And it must have taken place in a sociocultural context where it was not only acceptable but clearly advisable. That context can be fully recovered once we have the clues needed to recognize it, and the part played by Orphism here is by no means secondary.

This mediatory and sapiential recovery took place, as far as the Athenian culture and the birth of tragedy are involved, against the background of Pisistratus's Athens, where historical changes linked to the emergence of classical Athens led to the strengthening of cults open to the lower classes, as at Eleusis, and to the introduction of semicultual activities accessible to all citizens, such as the tragedy contests.[92] From now on, the new Greater Dionysia festivities included a three-day tragic trilogy competition, following the sacrifice of the bull and the declaiming of the dithyrambs, to which was added the complementary and compensatory double of the satyr-play, not counting comedy which had an altogether different origin and came to rival tragedy in the savage clownish comedies of Aristophanes.[93] Homer's epics, by way of Orphic knowledge, are an integral part of this grandiose mediatory project. Amid all this feverish cultural and religious activity, the Homeric epics were written down at about the same time. To the name of Onomacritus, who is attributed with the work, we can add those of Orpheus of Croton and Zopyrus of Heraclea, both exponents of Orphism in southern Italy.[94] These wise men evidently considered Homer's epics, belonging to the same sapiential tradition as the epics of Hesiod and the Orphics, to have much the same importance as the *hieroi logoi*, which were expanded at this time: Homer's *logoi* were sacred because they were concerned with the true nature of divine mediations and the human madness that departs from them, which actually contaminates and as a result makes them destructive.

We can safely assume that the Orphic wise men were aware of the shared basis of Homer's divine inspiration and the Titanic myth and noted how one set of texts threw light on the other. The connection was made still easier by the fact that Orpheus was the traditionally miraculous representative of the same poetic wisdom having a numinous origin. As an attempt to redeem man from his violence through writings that recount the violence, Orphism's *hieroi logoi* inevitably interacted with Homer, turning his works into other sacred writings, even though the Homeric tradition, already strong and rooted in traditional poetic mediation, kept its independence. The cultural milieu that we glimpse through the birth of tragedy is imprecise as to detail but quite clear in its overall meaning, with Orphism performing the essential role of cultural and ritual mediation. In this perspective, certain scattered clues take on new life and meaning. Pisistratus himself may well have been close to the spirituality of Orphism: his behavior was singularly mild and nonviolent for his time, as both Aristotle and Herodotus testify.[95] The strengthening of the Eleusinian Mysteries and the introduction of the Greater Dionysia, with the new intense representational power of tragedy, clearly suggest an ambitious scheme, of genius I would say, for deeply remolding all the public mediations of Athens. It is impossible to imagine such a scheme coming about except in close consultation with daringly innovative wise men who had profound knowledge of the rite, its signs and symbolism: only the Orphic wise men fit this description.

An anecdote recorded by Herodotus is sufficient to show how far Pisistratus and his entourage were fascinated by the new symbolic and metaritual possibilities of the theater. When he seized power for a second time, the tyrant was preceded into the city by a cart carrying an imposing woman dressed as Athena. The Athenians were so amazed that they fell down and worshiped her.[96] This politically motivated para-sacral staging alludes to the future relations between the tyrant and the city as a kind of hierogamy and has exact parallels with an important civic ceremony in which the *hieros gamos* with Dionysus was repeated symbolically or in reality.[97] It appears to have been a definite attempt at politico-ritual renewal of the city, in view of the inadequacy of traditional institutions to cope with the rise of the newly democratic Athens. The development of tragedy fits easily into a general picture of this type. It also helps to explain the connections between Aeschylus's later *Eumenides* and the evolution of the judicial machinery, intended by the Athenian *polis* to realize a new transcendent ideal of Justice.

Herodotus's later comment on the Pisistratus episode is skeptical, just as the portrait he draws of his character is ambiguous: a wise man but one dangerously inclined to pretense and theatricality. Solon's comment on the episode, in Diogenes Laertius, is still more explicit, making direct reference to Thespis's tragedies: "That's where such things come from."[98] In Plutarch, Solon reprimands Thespis because tragedy's lies would turn up again "in the contracts" (*en tois symbolaiois*).[99] Fictitious or not, these episodes may be evidence of a polemic against tragedy much earlier than Plato, as the enigmatic form seems to show. The words are spoken by one wise man against other wise men, against the tragic writers and, behind them, the Orphics. This all helps us to understand Herodotus's depiction of Onomacritus as craftily deceptive,[100] as well as the crisis experienced by the Orphic movement in the fifth century.

The grandiose attempt to create a new civic and political mediation based on Orphism failed, but the outcome was very different from what the conservatives had hoped. The turbulent development of the Athenian *polis* led to *logos* and the new wisdom being explored more courageously and developed with ever-increasing independence, as we see in the art of Euripides. At the same time, by a sort of *damnatio memoriae*, the relations between Orphism, tragedy, and politics were erased from the collective memory.[101] This was not the only Orphic-sapiential experiment in politics. In these same years the Pythagoreans in southern Italy, presumably in contact with Athens, attempted to gain direct control of Croton and other Greek colonies through a group of wise men, and once again failed, leading to riots and much bloodshed.[102] Plato played this card for the last time when he tried to use Orphism to bring about a grandiose politico-sapiential mediation with a mystic-religious basis and was equally unsuccessful.

These attempts show how political knowledge of sacrifice existed alongside initiatory knowledge of it as did political thinking as well, fully aware of the necessity of sacrificial mediations and the need for their renewal, a form of knowledge no less fascinating than better-known forms and recognizably brought together with an effort at synthesis in the philosophic knowledge of Plato. However, the question that springs to mind as we conclude this survey of the birth of tragedy and my analysis of the power and significance of sacrificial mediations in ancient Greece, has to do with the actual tenor of the cultural scene that I have tried to reconstruct and the real significance of the conceptual and intellectual elements discernible in it. How is it possible to pass from myths and rites lost in the mists of time to figures deemed to be recognizable and familiar, such as Plato and Aristotle? What can have occurred to lead from myths and rites apparently irrational in character (a nineteenth-century cliché that still conditions historiography today) to the rational philosophers of the fourth century, a rationality that we think we understand and do not cease to admire, though at times in inverse proportion to our real grasp of the matter? The answer to these questions will round off this examination of the more sensitive and critical aspects of Hellenic sacrificial mediations.

10. An Intermediate Form of Rationality

In analyzing the features and origin of tragedy, we have come face-to-face with a close, crucial intertwining of the various forms of knowledge, in an unfamiliar, dramatic, and animated context. In place of the conventional image of Greek culture we now have a lively, composite cultural scene, which would be impossible to understand without Orphism, the mythical-ritual prerequisite of both tragedy and philosophy. Tragedy is the outcome, literally spectacular but also spectacular in content, of a sacrificial wisdom still to be more satisfactorily profiled by modern historians. Philosophy is the other great sapiential mediation that transformed sacrifice, passing through mythology, into a specific manifestation of the universal laws of the *onta* and the *physis* to be studied on their own. The archaic and classical *polis* was the cradle and the frame of such developments, both in Athens with its rich religious heritage and much earlier in the variegated world of colonies, open to cultural influences coming above all from the Near East, but the *polis* was also the center of gravity for the other main forms of knowledge, intertwined with or influenced by Orphism as well: poetry, the most ancient and prestigious wisdom, and historiography, in itself a variety halfway between the narrative élan of myths and epic poems and the search for rational causes of philosophy. All these branches stem from only one root, the Greek city, absorbing all the attention and creativity of the wise men, who were no longer priests or religious professionals like shamans or seers, but learned citizens who, though retaining traits of those traditional figures, pursued an autonomous knowledge of the *physis* and shared it with their fellow citizens.

Politics, literally understood as the life and self-awareness of the *polis*, is an integral part of this scene and often implies a precise stance and participation on behalf of the citizen-sage, ranging from full-blooded conservatism to an extremely daring utopianism. At that time, of course, these political features were not as we understand them nowadays. Instead, as we saw with the establishment of the principle of tragic impersonality and Plato's reactions to it, they constitute the antecedents and highly instructive terms of comparison for our own attitudes, increasingly uncertain and perilous in the circular reversibility of our para-tragedies. This does not mean that all the archaic and preclassical philosophers were lawgivers and political reformers as Dicaearchus held, the ingenious follower of Aristotle who sought with his theory to criticize the specialized and abstract tendency of philosophy in his time.[103] Nevertheless, though tendentious and fruit of a gap between theoretical and practical knowledge that was unknown in the archaic and classical *polis*, Dicaearchus's reconstruction was not arbitrary. The main difference lies in the totalizing nature of Greek thinking in the sixth and fifth centuries, to which Plato tried to give new life. What we find in the classical wise men until Plato is a deep awareness of the need for ritual mediations. Starting from the cosmic-sacral framework in which he moves, the wise man comes to be conscious of the social and political significance of his wisdom, but almost from the very start (to the extent we can ascertain it) his totalizing awareness had to face the problem of an incongruity between the order of the *kosmos* and the order of the city that should reproduce it in its microcosm, because of the human unwillingness to meekly follow natural, cosmic, divine laws that should have been absolute and necessary. A gap, a break, is at the base of Greek wisdom since the beginning. While the mature tragedy directly displays this problem on the stage of myth and history, it is for philosophy to live and suffer the contradiction in its full cognitive extent.

In this regard, an eloquent witness is Heraclitus, who never stops denouncing the foolishness and corruption of his fellow citizens, using words worthy of a Jewish prophet: "May you never fall short of your riches,

Ephesians, so that your wretchedness shine!"[104] These words express an unlimited contempt and trace back not to abstract principles but to certain actual conflicts, of which luckily some vivid moments survive in other fragments like the following, absolutely the most dramatic:

> The Ephesians would deserve [*axion*]
> to hang themselves all
> and leave the city
> to young boys,
> for they banished [*exebalon*] Hermodorus,
> the strongest [*oneiston*] among them,
> saying:
> "Let no one among us be the strongest [*oneistos*]!
> If there is one, let him go elsewhere
> and among others!"[105]

The Ephesians who en mass expel "the strongest [*oneiston*] among them"—literally the cleverest one and the most capable of being useful to their community—are responsible for an axiological overturn and commit a real sociopolitical lynching subverting the universal order. The ruthless verbal retaliation of the indignant philosopher is inevitable and consists of a reversal of the collective violence provoked by this catastrophic lack of knowledge. Heraclitus's style is wonderful, but its prophetic tone raises an unanswered question: from where did the wicked and envious Ephesians take the power to reject the best one among them? In other words, why this singular exception from the universal law of the "ever-reversing" (*palintropos*) harmony woven by the divine Fire?[106]

To Heraclitus's eyes the question already contains its answer, since his divine Fire "supervening will judge and seize all things,"[107] but in his attitude there remains something unsolved, a failed explanation of the reason why the large majority of men behave in such a way, satisfying themselves "like beasts, with their belly and genitals, and what's most shameful in us."[108] The extraordinary fragment on Hermodorus's ban, a complete tragedy in a nutshell, already shows us, in ancient terms, the scenario of collective incomprehension of Nietzsche's aphorism 125. The Ephesian wise man expresses all this with the freshness and density of the first time, and with a sharp spontaneity still unacquainted with the huge complications that will take millennia to unfold themselves.

The great awareness reached by philosophers also emphasizes the specific difference of their solutions, which make a substantial inversion compared to tragedy moving from the very same problems. While tragedians exhibit on stage the *phainomenon* of human violence leaving the final answer to their public, philosophers want to explain all by means of a cosmic-ontological principle, knowing that the destiny of human community depends on an axiological control of violence. The same consciousness that emerges in tragedy as a final and paralyzing result remains subordinate in philosophy to the sapiential solution proposed. This philosophical awareness was boldly developed by the sophists, found a marvelous moment of unstable balance in Socrates, and then came to be rearranged and synthesized with Plato, who tried to resist the sophists' overfree use of the cultural tradition by carrying out a mediatory recovery of the old wisdom of *physis* reconciling it with the new awareness of human objectuality.

The subject would be huge, of course, but for our purposes it is enough to realize its constitutive terms and historical/theoretical tendency, capable of shedding light also on many features of the modern loss of divine mediations and human objectuality. We obtain a fascinating ancient/modern diptych where in the ancient panel political lucidity remains hidden under the cloak of religious, ontological, cosmic mediations, while the modern West would have produced an analogous lucidity with Niccolò Machiavelli and Thomas Hobbes, who nevertheless displayed it openly because of the increasing collapse of traditional reference points, to which an extreme awareness appeared to be the only remedy.

The reciprocal intertwining of differences and resemblances, gained thanks to the opposing and complementary views of tragedy and philosophy, is perhaps the sign that the spectrum of the comparison between the Greek culture and ours is rich enough to allow us to conclude this first part. But this also historically implies the ascertainment of an interpretive failure. With all their convenient ambiguities our interpretations of Hellenic civilization have wasted themselves on the similarities and differences from ourselves. We have used the figure of the Greek wise man as a mask for expressing an intellectual freedom due to Christianity that we are unwilling to admit, as a philosophical covering for violence that we are unwilling to see in ourselves, and as an erudite puppet in whom we can project and conceal what really belongs to us. Entirely absorbed in its surreptitious rituality, modern rationalism shuts its eyes to the obvious fact that the religious is not marginal to Greek wisdom but quite simply central, and takes refuge in a myth of rationality having sprung miraculously from nothing. A consistent strategy, for that matter: after a story like that has been accepted, any fairy tale could be told. And so we have managed not to see that Greek reason, even in what might seem its more "enlightened" aspects, is not self-interestedly opposed to the religious manner of the revolutionary arguments of modern times; on the contrary, it defines itself in relation to the religious since the object of its investigations are mediations and it knows to a considerable degree that they go back to the sacred and that without sacral mediations not even rationality could take shape and exist.

Once we get free of the learned disquisitions of centuries of projective history, the real terms of Hellenic knowledge emerge practically on their own, thanks as well to better contributions worthily recognized amid so much subtle or patent falsehood. One wonders, besides, how much ancient Greece would have been studied if it had not become the object of deification by brilliant minds and sentimentalists, proving the historically sound assertion that the prejudicial is often a prelude to the judicial, that is, that our prejudices, if we can only break free of them, prepare the way for our judgments. What would turn out to be unacceptable to many scholars is the hybrid, and yet scandalously consistent, character of the archaic wise man, a little like Euripides's Minotaur; and it is well known that whatever upsets our perceptive and mental schemes is instinctively removed from the field of perception, whether that perception is cultivated or more down-to-earth. But the hybrid, and oddly unitary, character of this historical and conceptual chimera derives from the fact that his knowledge is situated at a transitional stage between the magical-performative rationality of mythical-ritual knowledge and the instrumental rationality of a form of knowledge no longer aware of the rite. This gives the Greek wise man of the archaic and classical periods certain characteristics, which appear to be incompatible, conflicting, such as shamanistic ecstasy alongside refined rational analysis, and a secular open-mindedness as well as an obsession with ritual. These curious features are not folklore or colorful description, or even the latest example of the historical conditioning of our anobjectual perspectivism. They are the expression of

Greek wisdom at its most original and profound finally brought to light by a mediatory and sacrificial approach that avoids all reductionism and throws an indirect but penetrating light on those investigating it, on ourselves. And so we are better placed to evaluate Orphism's position, undeniably documented but not much help until we include it in an organic interpretive movement taking us to the next comparison with Christian mediation.

Orphism played a distinctive and fundamental role in cultural transmission, fostering the development of more complex and advanced forms of knowledge from the Mysteries initiation that was still markedly magical-ritual in nature. Orpheus is the archetype of the divine wise man, a lover of beauty and *eidos*, and nevertheless secretly bound to Dionysus's fate of dismemberment, the origin of the capacity of the Muses and art to "remember." No less a wanderer than Orpheus, Orphism itself, whose severed head sailed the seas singing his oracles, performed a vital function as symbolic and cultural metabolizer in Greek civilization with a capacity to penetrate and cross-fertilize evidently aided by its secret organization. It should not be confused with religious movements as we know them, but its diffusion was certainly helped by great mobility and an undoubted tendency to proselytize. This cross-cultural, chameleonlike character also makes it elusive unless we are prepared to view its direct and indirect manifestations as a whole. Greek wisdom certainly does not correspond to Orphism but, as Anaximander shows and Plato confirms, it passed through Orphism since it passed through the reflections about myth and rite, about the religious, first brought together in Orphism. This prompts a more general reflection regarding the whole evolution of mankind's cultural systems. Many forms of magical, mythical, and ritual knowledge have marked mankind's long laborious progress from a biological stage narrowly dependent on immediate needs and instinct to the cultural, mediated stage in which men gained access to the object and to a world needing to be confirmed, strengthened, and expanded every time. And all those forms of knowledge passed through so that operative and rationally advanced models might be developed. Greek Orphism provides a splendid example of how it may have happened in antiquity, in a civilization close to us and yet remote historically and mentally, but actually both farther away and closer than we are accustomed to admit.

Despite gaps in the information and its partiality we can reconstruct an outline of the cognitive and mental transition associated with Orphism that had a formative influence on Greek philosophy. *Aitia*, the accusation against someone, is much more than a legal concept as Werner Jaeger holds in his rationalistic blindness to the real power of religious mediations:[109] actually, it was the blame imputed to the victim, such as the accusations of Dionysus against Ariadne or the "accusing words" of Ereshkigal to Inanna. Starting from this premise, the mythic *aitia* became the concept of cause in Orphism as in all cultures, but it took on the further genealogical meaning of "guilt of the fathers," of Titanic guilt.[110] Up to this point it is hard to see anything particularly innovative since there is no idea of a cause of a historical or theoretical type. If we must speak of genealogy, what we have in the Orphic religious explanation is the mythical genealogy of the sacral and divine forebears, an acquisition that made it possible to reconstruct, down through the generations, a sacral or legendary history of mediatory value as concerns the past, making it knowable and organizable. This process had gained ground with the dynastic genealogies of the great sacred monarchies and, through steps to be now examined in the Intermezzo, will pass from the Mesopotamian kingdoms into the Jewish conception of history. However, this passage happened via the genealogies of Ionian thought in the sixth century[111] closely connected to the beginning of the wisdom of *physis*, and here we can appreciate the specific value of the Orphic contribution, invisibly responsible for this triangular influence along which historiography was born. In Orphism the Titanic guilt is absolutized as a generative mythic event to be relived and overcome through the rite. That brings us to the key issue: an extremely powerful mythical-ritual complex causing the whole history of mankind to be experienced in an eschatological perspective, now definitively objectual, suggesting similar mastery of other more evolved variants of knowledge; that mastery, however, was to be developed in the more widely operative field of cognition. In that way the origin in Greece, through the power of *logos* to transform and expand, becomes a device that can also be possessed intellectually.

Through this reconstruction we gain greater insight into the formative and performative dynamics of archaic rationality. Greek reasoning develops in close dialogue with the preceding magical-sacral type of rationality, whose strength lay in creating a stable image of the world through a set of formulas and means effective in bringing reliable order out of the chaos of natural forces, ever ready to strike, an order that could be steered, assisted, and corrected. We ought not to miss the highly pragmatic concern for its real effectiveness evinced by this type of magical-sacral rationality. There is nothing dazed or mysticizing about it, after the style of Lucien Lévy-Bruhl's prelogical knowledge; on the contrary there is an all-out battle with nature to attain an operational knowledge ascribable to laws: the performative rite, the magical formula, and the spell are the first forms of scientific law, enabling nature to be dominated by discovering its rules. Ernesto De Martino's earlier researches made a fundamental contribution to our understanding of the role of magism in colonizing and stabilizing the world,[112] though the central place of sacrificial mediations in providing the shaping energy for these processes is not covered by his work. The ecstatic-sacrificial aspect forms an integral part of the transforming power of archaic religions but takes on a strictly objectual direction oriented toward conquering and maintaining the real world.

This is the first immense phase of codifying and developing archaic rationality in which we really need to distinguish several prehistoric stages connected to the cultural and physical development of the various human species involved, and the extremely important stages linked to the Neolithic revolution and the creation of the first settled civilizations, by now with a hierarchic theological view of the world. At this point we need to realize that it is not through some miraculous materialization that Greek rationality differentiates itself from this very lengthy process (even to suggest such an idea today as a scientific proposal would appear grotesque), nor is it brought about by social and political phenomena within the *polis*, as in the Marxist structuralist argument of a Vernant, but by profound creative interaction with the various forms of religious knowledge that had developed in or had influenced Greece. Orphism acts as a catalyst in this process of cultural transformation, concentrating in itself the objectualizing intermedial power acquired by *logos* in the *polis*. Greek rationality is intermediate between archaic rationality and our own rationality because it could not be more intermedial, that is, magical-rational. Thanks to this unrecognized position, it transmitted to the other ancient cultures and then to the whole West the subtle and irresistible magic of human rationality, master of itself and the world.

Tragic, philosophical, and historical knowledge develop in relation to a common substratum of the esoteric, mystery, and Orphic traditions, and in creative interaction with Homer's poetic wisdom, in which all three traditions share a common goal in seeking a deeper meaning concealed beneath the appearances of myth, reality, and past tradition. The enigma of man's temporal triad becomes, with a revealing oxymoron, the *prophecy about the past* with which, by making an explicative-causal reconstruction of past events, the Cretan Epimenides succeeded to define Athene's guilt and free it from its ills.[113] The historian Santo Mazzarino traces the origin of Greek historical thought back to this formulation of Orphic wisdom, though without making an internal comparative analysis of the Orphic conception.[114] By this means, however, the whole of Greek knowledge becomes a kind of prophecy about the past, a passionate, dramatic investigation of Greek and human history and its determining factors. An origin open to investigation exists and the wise man looks for it, following one route or another, utilizing the *logos* and investigating its features, its primitive writing. This explains the deeply organic nature of archaic Greek knowledge at its source, an expression of a world in which knowledge is one thing because it is about unity: the unity that had to inhere in the mediation to make it operative and the unity of the sacrifice conferring unity onto the mediation. Here, too, is the explanation of the unitary, all-embracing figure of the wise man: whether tragedian, poet, philosopher, or historian, he is primarily and essentially one who knows, who *has seen*. "Knowledge is one," *hen to sophon*, Heraclitus declares,[115] pursuing the same tensional unity also in the theological field, in the wake of Anaximander and Xenophanes, and paving the way for the Judaic heno- and monotheism.

Nevertheless, this unity is destined to break up as soon as it is conceived, undermined by the twofold nature of the enigma, by the powerful constructive and destructive dynamics that benefit the Greek *sophia* and yet hold it hostage. Knowledge's path is marked by the structural duality, the double-binding ambivalence enabling it to develop its exceptionally creative but never really stable mediations, as evidenced by the rapid evolution of the principle of tragic impersonality. The problem of the unity of tragedy is revealed to be the problem of the unity of wisdom, a unity required for its functioning and at the same time denied by it. There was no agreement among wise men as to how to resolve its ambivalence in practice and in theory. What kind of interpretation, what complexion was to be given to this knowledge? Religious (with the dilemma between Olympic and Mystery religion), political (with the dilemma between democratic and oligarchic tendencies), or philosophic (with the implicit conflict between different schools of thought)? And in all these cases, and in others besides, how was it to be used? Publicly, open to the *polis*, or restricted to a minority? The dilemmas and differences grew to be irreconcilable, involving the very status of a knowledge that succeeded in being too human to be completely divine and too divine to be completely human. What could knowledge really mediate or show? A religious truth, an ideal principle, or a harshly concrete reality? An event to be retold after the fashion of poetry and tragedy, or a cosmic law to be theorized in the manner of philosophy?

We are still far from having done with Greek culture, and at this point we would need to look specifically at its more successful form of knowledge, philosophy. From the final decades of the fifth century until the middle of the fourth it vied with tragedy, eventually prevailing to become the cultural mediation capable of future conquest, at the price, however, of an incapacity to tackle contemporary problems. I have already examined this subject in previous studies and propose to develop it further in the future, but my present aim is otherwise, not to reconstruct the civilization as a whole but to outline some of its strong and critical points, which appear as weak points when viewed from other perspectives such as historical, institutional, and political success. The failure of the Hellenic classical culture thereby becomes clear, and the reasons for it are the same as those that brought about its major achievements. Thanks to its polycentric structure and the relative freedom it allowed, Greek civilization experienced a cultural explosion unequaled in the ancient world but it suffered from permanent political instability as a result of that same polycentrism, with the Peloponnesian War as its most sensational consequence as well as the failure of the Athenian policy of expansion that offered the only possible way to unite Greece and make it a great Mediterranean power. Athenian tragedy follows the course of the conflict and provides the most pertinent commentary, reflecting its various stages and vicissitudes. In Sophocles and partly in Euripides we are shown the attempt to assert a democratic, civic ideology and finally, in Euripides's mature tragedies but also in the vein of doubt running through Sophocles's later works, we sense an awareness of failure both of the *polis* and of the divine world that should have been its mediatory axis, its supreme objectual guarantee.

Now that we have investigated the factors surrounding its origin, we must admit that tragedy provides the most magnificent commentary on the decline of the world that gave it birth and a reason to exist, the most moving epicedium to the end of classical Greece that will make modern European intellectuals dream. However, this very end is also a new beginning. The Greek civilization does not lose its vitality during the political collapse begun at the close of the fifth century, and gives us an example that ought to make us reflect—namely, the possibility of fostering culture and philosophy by meditating on the underlying reasons for its own decline and the means available to respond to it. Following the deaths of Euripides and Sophocles, these efforts can be seen to mark the end of the tragic genre's period of greatest splendor; at the same time, in Socrates and Plato, they produced a grand project for new spiritual and sapiential mediation, followed by Aristotle's rational exploration of reality as it is, a systematic and more worldly approach that traced the rational coordinates of Hellenistic civilization. The destiny of Hellas remained nonetheless unchanged, but their efforts left a legacy whose consequences still affect our lives, or ought to do so unless we want to obliterate our roots, the most vital, hidden part of our heritage, with a single limitation, not really recorded in thousands of years of interpretations: the Socratic and post-Socratic thought cast aside the testimony of tragedy, Plato by censuring it, and Aristotle by rationalizing it, and neither recognizes the cognitive and poetic greatness of authors who had successfully represented defeat, violence, and death without lying, without answers to stifle the questionings of mankind before they could be heard, let alone resolved.[116] Nietzsche was the only one to note this defect in Socrates and Plato, and for the wrong reasons since he asserted the logic of violent reprisal, the logic of Dionysus in Euripides, which was in fact the sign of the god's failed mediation. Greek tragedy more than any other form of ancient culture raised questions that could only be answered by Christianity. And it is symptomatic of the phenomenon's complexity that Christianity gained ground in the ancient world by rejecting theater as such, and yet prepared a different more human theatrical sense that was to be the sense of modern theater, our modern consciousness when it is inclined to be itself.

This brings us back to the thorny and therefore stubbornly evaded question of the difference between ourselves and the ancients, between their enigmas lacking in possibilities and our enigmas not wanting any answers.

So far we have been largely concerned to find out who the ancients were in relation to ourselves, but it is time we began to understand who we are in relation to them. This means that the Christian element, peripheral to our reflections up to this point, must be thematized and understood from the privileged critical viewpoint of sacrificial mediations. The moment has come, then, to make the comparison between Dionysus and Christ that is the medium of this inquiry into mediations ancient and modern, and forms the subject of the second volume of this work. It is only by way of this crucial interconnection that the transition can be made from one to the other, from them to us and from us to them.

To prepare the way for this comparison and transition, it will be useful to take another look, in the Intermezzo, at the major premise of our inquiry, the Orphic and mystery salvation symbolized at the start by Dionysus's toys. This will provide material and starting points for us to tackle at once the anthropological, religious, and historical implications of the similarities and differences between Dionysus and Christ, between salvation through Orpheus and salvation through Christ. The polarization Dionysus/Christ must not deceive us, nor appear as too partial, because it is the result and the symbolic expression of a hidden and larger history, the meeting and clash of the most important cultural mediations of the ancient world in the melting-pot of the Mediterranean. This is the overall subject of the following Intermezzo.

Intermezzo

The Toys of Dionysus

Comparison of Civilizations in the Hellenistic and Roman Periods

The god: day night,
winter summer,
war peace,
repletion hunger.
And he changes (but remains one) like fire
when mixed with an aroma
gets named as each one pleases.

—Heraclitus of Ephesus

9.

Judaism and Christianity in the Greco-Roman World

1. Approaching the Question

To return now to the *Protrepticus* where Clement of Alexandria discusses the Titanic myth and the toys encountered in the Gurob papyrus will provide an approach to comparing historically the mediations of Dionysus and Christ, and enable us to make the transition from one to the other through this Intermezzo. What Clement says there will be a useful starting point for describing a wider and unexpected picture, involving not only the classical Greek culture with which we began, and which was overcome by the universalistic version of Hellenistic civilization, but also the Roman civilization that led the Hellenistic universalism to full realization and experienced the spread of Christianity while hosting the Judaism from which it sprang. With this in view I want to go back to the distinctive features of Orphism, taken to be a cult representing the more advanced soteriological expectations of the classical world, bearing however in mind that cults of oriental origin with similar initiatory features proliferated in the Roman Empire. And I shall extend the analysis to embrace early Christian apologetics, by this time in a position to contend openly with contemporary pagan culture.[1] If what I am attempting to do in this intermission is successful, we shall have the means to get to the root of Christian mediation, besides considering the formation of Judaic monotheism, and reconstruct an outline history of the events leading from ancient Greece to the situation in Europe that we have already considered through Thomas Mann's depiction in *The Magic Mountain*.

Early Christian apologetics in the specific case of the *Protrepticus* of Clement of Alexandria yield essential information about the Dionysian and Eleusinian cults and take us back to our initial investigation of Dionysus and Orphism. The following passage gives a detailed description of the toys used by the Titans to entice the child Dionysus so that they may tear him to pieces:

> The mysteries of Dionysus are indeed absolutely inhuman. While he was still a child [*paida*], the Curetes leapt around him in an armed dance, but the Titans came up stealthily: after they had beguiled him with childish toys [*athyrmasin*], these Titans tore him limb from limb, even though he was just a child, as the Thracian Orpheus, the poet of initiation [*teletes*], says: "the top [*konos*], the revolving, rumbling toy [*rhombos*], and the pliant dolls, and the beautiful golden apples of the clear-voiced Hesperides." And it will not be useless to mention as deserving blame the useless symbols [*symbola*] of this initiation: the knucklebone [*astragalos*], the ball [*sphaira*], the top, the apples, the revolving, rumbling toy [*rhombos*], the mirror [*esoptron*], and the fleece.[2]

In this significant piece of evidence, the Curetes again appear on the scene performing their protective dance around Dionysus, only this time the Titans "stealthily" slip in to take their place, and ensnare the child with their toys. This draws on the already mentioned version of the myth recorded by Firmicus Maternus, where Zeus entrusts Dionysus to the Curetes and Hera sends her aides, the Titans, to kill him.[3] In Clement's account, there immediately follow references to Pallas Athena and to Zeus who intervenes when he smells his son's roasted flesh.

The passage completes the list of toys in the papyrus, though we might perhaps add the narthex, a stalk of giant fennel much like a thyrsus used in initiations.[4] The tenor and exact detail of Clement's account give us a good idea of the strategy adopted by early Christian thinkers to deal with the religious—and one might say epistemological—problems posed by paganism. The serious nature of these problems is exemplified by a second-century pagan critic, Celsus,[5] a Greek-speaking thinker adhering to Middle Platonism, the philosophical movement that in Roman times reacted against the skeptical setting of the New Academy and wanted to go back to the metaphysical thought of Plato, to clarify its typical reticence and interpret it in a systematically spiritualistic sense already monotheistic in a Greek fashion compatible with the traditional polytheism. The Middle-Platonic theology starts from a first transcendent God (ὁ πρῶτος θεός), distinguishing a series of intermediate divine levels (Intellect and World Soul, or second and third God),[6] and is of primary importance for better understanding the conceptual frame of Christian theology and metaphysics. Nevertheless, the very first anti-Christian work known to us was written by a Middle-Platonist like Celsus, with the polemical title *Alethes logos*, to be interpreted either as *On the True Doctrine* or *A True Account*,[7] with an ambiguity possibly intentional. This has been largely preserved thanks to Origen's extensive criticism of it in *Contra Celsum*, one of his few surviving works, and the longest, written in Greek. Meaningfully, *Contra Celsum* was composed on request of Ambrose, the friend and disciple of Origen who sent him Celsus's book long after its appearance, evidently because it was still felt to be dangerous in its arguments. We shall consider Origen's work in the next chapter, but it must be noticed here that even his answer, though much deeper from a spiritual and religious viewpoint, had to be quite long and repetitious in its reasoning, and so not only because dictated, as usual in antiquity, a practice naturally resulting prolixity since texts were often not reread and revised. A real problem was lurking behind the old and apparently outdated polemic of *Alethes logos*.

Celsus comes out swinging, motivated by political fears that Christian pacifism presented a threat to the empire's integrity. This Middle-Platonist, who as such held a semi-monotheistic or henotheistic and providential reading of Plato's thought, denies any originality in the new religion and accuses it of having fundamental similarities to previous cults: "The ceremonies of the Christian religion are similar to Egyptian rites."[8] He notes that Christians worship a man put to death and deified, just like the cults of many other peoples; in his eyes, this made Christianity's claim to uniqueness appear really grotesque, a caricature of all other religions that, unlike Christianity, could count on an age-old tradition. That, for this pagan polemicist, was a sign of their total conformity with the laws of the *kosmos* as well as with those governing every human community. Why worship Christ—he asks himself—"rather than Asclepius and Dionysus and Heracles?"[9] The cultural obstacles that Clement had to overcome in the *Protrepticus* several decades before Origen thus take us to the heart of the question of the similarities and differences between Dionysus and Christianity and show us that it goes back to the beginnings of the Christian religion and its initial expansion in the provinces of the Roman Empire.

We can ignore the traditionalist objection as less worrying for Christians who appealed to a different tradition and, above all, to its decisive innovation offering salvation; what proved embarrassing was the comparative objection raised by Celsus. In fact, several apologists in antiquity attempted to show that these similarities resulted from copying their religion, the so-called *furta Graecorum*,[10] a remarkably tenacious argument even among modern scholars and apologists, as we have seen. Celsus was probably writing in reply to Justin Martyr, the first Christian writer whose works survived, who tried to take the best from pagan culture and use it in defense of his religion.[11] Justin states quite adamantly that the pagan myths were invented by evil demons after hearing the Jewish prophecies about Jesus Christ, in order "to deceive and mislead mankind" and "make men think that the things said about Christ are a fabulous story [*teratologian*] as the things said by the poets."[12] And it is interesting that Justin is particularly interested in using the following argument, with its mythical and intermedial tenor, to deny any analogy at all between the *sparagmos* of Dionysus and Bible prophecies foretelling the sufferings of a future Messiah through the metaphors of the vineyard and wine:

> On hearing these prophetic words, the demons said that Dionysus was a son of Zeus, they claimed he invented the vineyard and had wine used in his mysteries, and they taught that he ascended to heaven after being dismembered [*diasparechthenta*].[13]

Justin's argument continues Judaism's claim that the knowledge of Moses was of greater antiquity than pagan knowledge,[14] and shows us a new Christian tradition, as yet inchoate, that refers back to the "foundation of the world" mentioned in Matthew. Revealingly, however, he tries to use this argument to counter a comparative criticism that evidently predated Celsus.

Justin's reasoning derives its persuasive force from what was obvious to a reader in ancient times but is incomprehensible and unreal to the modern reader, namely the existence of a host of spirits and intermedial bodies that influence human beings for their good or harm. So it is a question of identifying the only real and right mediation of Christ's revelation, having availed ourselves beforehand of the benign intermediation of the universal *logos* that Justin derives from stoicism and Middle Platonism,[15] and avoiding the false, lying intermediations of the wicked *daimones*, ever ready to spin their fairy stories and deceive anyone not so well-equipped with *logos*.[16]

We no longer possess the mediatory structure supporting the apologist's reflections, but we have also lost sight of the comparative motivation for them, with the result that some Christian scholars still resort to the *furta* argument to support the earlier date and uniqueness of the story of Christ. This argument is in fact even less well-founded than the Jewish claims of predating Hellenic wisdom, which will be considered later, and it tells us not a little about the influence of denominational motives on what ought to be the subject of dispassionate scientific study. While it is true that Christianity has sometimes influenced pagan cults and myths,[17] those cases are exceptional and, besides, lead to conclusions almost the opposite of what they were intended to support: in fact, it was by starting from precise points of resemblance that Christianity was able to influence certain pagan cults, and it ought to be unnecessary to add that the evidence from pre-Christian times leaves no room for doubt as to the existence in classical culture of events involving death and resurrection, which are also fully attested in cultures worldwide, although they remain more fragmentary and much less clear than the Gospel narratives of Christ's Passion.[18] When we come to analyze Euripides's *Alcestis*, we shall see just how subtle and complex the notion of rebirth in the flesh after death could be in the ancient world; and the *Alcestis* is by no means an isolated example since it belongs to a religious context in which the idea of some kind of objectual re-formation postmortem was far from foreign. Taken as a whole, the *furta Graecorum* argument must have sounded circular to its pagan opponents, while to modern ears it sounds like a dogmatic ruse with no sense of history. Neither case provides a real answer to Celsus's objection. Justin's idea of showing how the best parts of classical culture anticipated Christianity was to prove more fertile eventually, but an answer to the pagan arguments that was stronger and more detailed theologically began to appear in early patristic writings in Greek, in writers such as Clement and above all Origen. However, before we examine the extract from Clement and come to grips with the difficulties faced by early Christian apologetics, we must take an overall look at the difficult context in which the new creed had to operate.

The Christian claim to uniqueness, expressed in real terms by a refusal to sacrifice or recognize the divine (i.e., sacred and mediatory) nature of the emperor was, for pagans like Celsus, unacceptable and provocative since it cast doubt on the political and sacral mediations of their entire society. For the first time ancient society as a whole was rebuked de facto for its dependence on traditional sacrificial rites. The Christian position lacks the subtlety of the religious critique developed in tragedy five centuries before, which in any case remained within the world of Greek sacrifice. Instead, motivated by an alternative message and consequent lifestyle, it rejected en masse the mediatory and theological assumptions of the Roman world. This was so provocative that common gossip, twisting the Christians' rejection around and throwing it back at them, turned their liturgical meetings, which centered on the celebration of the Eucharist, into sexual orgies and horrifying sacrificial banquets, Thyestean feasts where children were devoured (the so-called *flagitia*, shameful actions). These slanders might perhaps have found an initial impulse from the excesses of some deviant Christian groups and some Gnostic sects that were confused with the standard Christian communities,[19] but probably they were maintained and fostered by the secrecy surrounding the Eucharist,[20] in which only those who had completed the *cursus* of Christian initiation might partake, with the result that a caricature of Holy Communion was superimposed on the bloody event recalled in Orphism. The apologetic dialogue *Octavius* by Minutius Felix (second century) records the charges made by the pagan Caecilius, who presents us with a distorted, more detailed version of the Titanic myth and rite in which the Christians initiate new converts by making them wound a child covered in flour, then lick its blood and finally share out the flesh.[21]

We might seem to be in the middle of the mythogenesis theorized by Girard except that this time the mythical type of accusation is made against a religious foe whose ritual conduct is deemed to be criminal and savage. Christianity appears as a sort of anti-Orphism; instead of leading mankind from Titanic violence to Dionysian salvation, it moves in exactly the opposite direction: mankind civilized by Rome is taken back to Titanic, barbaric violence with the objectual destruction of all that Roman civilization guaranteed. The attack therefore consists in projecting onto the opponents a sacrifice sensed as archaic and so far removed from the current mentality that it makes the Christians appear to be the enemies of mankind as, in fact, they were considered to be by orthodox minds in the empire. Tacitus, for example, with typical graphic severity, practically justifies Nero's completely unwarranted persecution of the followers of this *exitialis superstitio* "because of their hatred of mankind,"[22] a blame previously reserved above all to the Jews.[23] Hundreds of years later, Christians in their turn made similar charges against the Jews,[24] in what Girard calls persecution texts where the enemy is successfully demonized but not divinized because of the influence of Christian demystification. However, this scheme assumes a mechanical distinction between the two transfers, and besides, in its strictest form, it breaks down when the historical documents are examined. In the Roman period we find an analogous type of demonizing and nondivinizing accusation, with no possibility of attributing them to any Bible or Christian influence; that similar behavior was not uncommon in the pre-Christian period is evinced by the accusations made against witches in both Greece and Rome, or by the propaganda attacks on opponents during the Roman civil wars.[25]

Girard's scheme, then, needs to be replaced with a different historical phenomenon, which is the endeavor to confirm one's own identity-making mediations by saddling one's enemies with earlier and more archaic stages now regarded as ignominious in the mediatory economy being asserted: those who oppose this identity are behind the times, a scandalous testimony to a stage in civilization's past, and perceived as destructive of a hard-won objectual sphere that is to be defended *unguibus et rostris*, tooth and claw. However, this shows in more realistic and detailed terms that the Christian position not only brought sacrifice into the light but also raised the question of what was the most just and, in every sense, most civil interpretation of it. The aim of the accusation of Titanic infanticide appears twofold, first to persuade that the Christians also resorted to sacrifice and second that it took the form of a *crimen*, a regression to bloody primitive ritual conduct, condemned by both the law and the power of Rome. In short, with the followers of the new sect sacrifice becomes a problem, a principle to be defended against an alien and unsettling religious mediation.

But how did sacrificial mediation work in ancient Rome? We need to answer this question if we are to have a more credible context for the spread of the Christian mediation within the vast structure of the Roman Empire.

2. The Roman Mediatory Context

The early Christians lived in a world dominated by the grandiose politico-religious mediation of the Roman Empire, a human and political universe apparently self-sustaining and secure in the promise that it would last forever. The divine world itself was one of its functions, according to its distinctive magical-ritual pragmatism, enabling Rome to assimilate every and all cult in the rite of *evocatio*, and this must be considered one of the secrets of its military expansion and enduring hold on world power.[26] Roman sacrificial mediation differs fundamentally from Greek mediation, doomed through its extreme diversity and fragmentation, both internal and external, to collapse on itself and consequently fail to create any centralized control. Rome, nevertheless, from its earliest days right to the end, remains the undisputed center, not because it is a single unit but because it is a multiplicity triumphantly united around a mediation that represents its various parts, as is shown by the legends and historical events concerning the city's formation and the struggles between patricians and plebeians.[27] In the founding myth of Romulus and Remus, the Eternal City has its origin in a quarrel between two brothers, resolved through unification at the hands of the victorious party, achieved through fratricide but without ignoring the contribution made by the defeated party. From its very foundation, then, Rome is a place where internal conflict is resolved by a reconciling mediatory synthesis, dragging behind it, however, the unresolved residue of a crime that remains hanging over Rome's *caput*, that is, over its head, its chief who must, at a certain moment, fall in order to guarantee the *pax deorum*, to ensure the undisturbed furtherance of the reconciliation. According to a secondary tradition, highly revealing as such traditions often are, Romulus was torn to pieces by his senators,[28] a memory of ancient dismemberment rituals that fits in with Rome's foundation myth as a form of compensation and power renewal.[29] This ritual scheme for interpreting the mediatory foundation reappears sensationally in Caesar's assassination,[30] the fratricide of Pompey who presents himself as the great peacemaker. By being killed Caesar pays off his remaining blood debt and begins the long period of the principate and empire.

This brief analysis brings out some essential elements. Roman mediation takes the form of surmounting internal conflict through a conciliation that unites, giving a spur to expansion, and stabilizes by the supplementary sacrifice of the chief architect of reconciliation. Thus the Roman sacrifice does not function immediately but in a two-phase action, made necessary by the dramatic manner of its institution and its centrifugal, expansionistic consequences. Rome's dominion is guaranteed by repeating this formula, with the assassination of Caesar bringing institutional stability and ushering in the period of empire.[31] Roman domination was thus made possible, not hindered, by the chronic recurrence of civil war that actually provided renewed mediatory energy every time, fueling expansion in proportion to how far it overcame ever-increasing internal conflict. Behind this expansion lay the idea of universal sovereignty, being founded on reconciling the *res publica* and *civitas* in their entirety, and finally ratifying the principle of an empire to embrace all mankind. The enemies of Rome thus become the enemies of mankind, and every war tends to assume the features either of a big-game hunt, where the prey are inhuman aliens to be killed or tamed as wild beasts, or of a fight against civilized human beings who should then, logically, be included in the empire as their due. Wars, in short, are either to be classed as *venationes* or as civil wars. The end of Rome was not so much due to continual barbarian onslaught as to the fact that the attacks began to be seen as *external*, as a foreign war: after hundreds of years of assimilation and cross-border contact, not to mention the widening influence of Christian anthropology, it was impossible to simply regard these peoples as savage beasts and put up defenses against them. At this point the empire found itself without the necessary mediatorial resources to draw a decisive advantage from its own internal clashes and could only collapse, though the eastern part was to prove a brilliant survivor, which is not so strange given the very long Roman experience and resilience in dealing with internal divisions and conflicts that finally became to some extent civil wars. In its later stages, the empire vigorously and successfully resisted huge external pressures and internal imbalances; broken up by Diocletian, it was reunited after other civil wars under Constantine, who founded a new capital at Constantinople, before being definitively split in half to form a Western and an Eastern empire. In the meantime, however, with Constantine, it had absorbed Christianity, which shows a much more interesting and complex interaction than the conventional picture in the Christian religion undermines the immense imperial fabric and causes its collapse.

But the most surprising aspects of this civilization regard the internal functioning of its sacrificial mediations. Roman sacrifice retains the archaic character of its magical-performative power, substantially independent of the desires or representations of the sacrifice, or to put it better preexistent and foundational vis-à-vis them, and there is nothing inward-looking about the religion of the *res publica*, nothing intimate in our sense of the word, since its cults are a question of doing, of *sacra facere*:[32] it is an orthopraxis rather than a religious faith, no doubt involving emotional reactions and personal beliefs[33] but always on the basis of the objective meaning and effects of the religious praxis itself. It resembles the Greek *polis* cults in this respect but differs utterly from them as a system and in its capacity for extroflexion. Consequently, visibility is everything in the Roman cults, and the shared, displayed aspect present in every sacrifice takes on a kind of qualifying precedence, a central importance validating the sacrifice; at the same time the ritual character of sacrifice changes to become legal and political, taking concrete form in figures and institutions that embody *in toto*, and with the same unifying, performative rationale, the *medium* around which the *res publica* gathers. Indeed, it *is* the *res publica* itself, its own mediator since it is a fully realized, reconciled whole containing both worlds, the supernal and the infernal worlds, Heaven and the Underworld. Such a concrete, flexible and self-centered solution justifies us in stating that the gods and ancestors of the Romans are conceived as existing, as operative, only in relation to the city and its cults, and are otherwise destined to remain in the state of *umbrae* or *larvae* to be neutralized with appropriate rites. The Roman *sacrificium* is not a *spectaculum* performed before the *civitas* but is the *civitas* become *spectaculum* of itself in its various ramifications and extensions, a *sacra facere* publicly displayed and shared, performed and witnessed by all. These various facets are brought together and coordinated in the public ceremonial of the triumph accorded to victorious generals.[34] In the magically effective presence of the authorities and priesthoods, the victor makes a theatrical kind of parade of his living trophies, offering the *res publica* a symbolic and de facto illustration of its real extent, its true scale as a completed whole. And then the human trophies, if they were accorded existence, acquired the status of subjects or citizens of Rome, but if on the other hand they were regarded as naturally inferior and thus no part of *humanitas*, they were *eo ipso* executed or destined for the arena spectacles.

All this had a sensational effect on the theater, revealing by itself how far Roman civilization differed from the Greek, and it is apparent precisely in the powerful cultural influence exerted by the latter, though a superficial glance might suggest the opposite.[35] A specialized theater bound by specific prohibitions such as that conceived and created in fifth-century Athens was actually impossible in Rome where every sacrifice was a spectacle and every spectacle was a sacrifice. And so, even after the Hellenic influence introduces Greek theatrical forms in Rome, they remain narrowly elitist and become part of an erudite combinatorial game among literati, mythographers, and encyclopedic authors, whereas the really crucial spectacular mediations are decided elsewhere and do not *represent* sacrifice, they simply *do* it. There are limits and prohibitions in Roman theater as well, but they fall within an immensely vaster combinatorial whole where they are moved about and changed at will, ultimately coinciding with the entire social and public life of Rome. Thus there is a continual whirligig of variants and compensations, ranging from *mimus*, mimed performances in which condemned prisoners and slaves were often actually killed as part of the show, a sacrificial hyperrealism—inconceivable in Greece—counterbalanced by a lack of the spoken word in the salient scenes, to the cultivated Senecan tragedies with their proliferation of sacrificial imagery, and probably intended for public recitation at court as well as private reading.[36] All together this is an amazingly rich and varied literary, para-theatrical, and theatrical scene, though there can be no doubt that the arena games represent the high point and synthesis of this proliferation of spectacles, a real compendium of the Romans' worldview and sacrificial mediations in performative form.

The *ludi circenses* took place in the amphitheater, that is, in a doubled theater that gives material expression to the *civitas* as a whole, with its priesthoods and authorities right up to the supreme authority of the emperor. The arena shows are the triumph in an expanded and emphatic form, sometimes on an exaggerated scale as proof of Rome's exaggerated power. The community in the form of a series of concentric circles surrounds and encloses all the inferior beings whose status is outside *humanitas*; slaves, gladiators, prisoners of war, and wild animals are all strictly interchangeable in being forced to fight and/or be killed; with the realism of the mime and of Roman law, they re-present the alien world subdued by Rome and attest to its perennial dominion, *imperium sine fine*.[37] And in this, it should be noted, the status of the actors involved is not defined ontologically once and for all but is positional and functional and depends on their relative strength, on condition that the formula of the magic, mediatory power works and ensures the success of the *spectaculum*. Victory for the inferiors condemned to shed blood in the arena could mean their lives would be spared, a sacrificial reversibility that remained unchanged when the gladiators became professional para-sportsmen; similarly the emperor, supreme guarantor of the entire system, could send whoever he wanted into the arena, but this was because he always bore the aura of himself becoming a victim of the system, as he was the main mandatary of the *civitas* in the form of *imperium*, a power originally military.[38]

The life of Gaius Caesar, known as Caligula, provides a good example of this reversibility. At the games one day, according to Suetonius, he ordered a particularly tall and good-looking spectator to go down into the arena and join in the combat, and when the young man won two matches the emperor bound him, made him dress in rags, and cut his throat after a reviling tour in the city;[39] even more chilling is another episode, reported by Dio Cassius, in which a *damnatio ad bestias* (execution by wild animals in the arena) was short of prisoners and Caligula ordered some spectators to be taken at random to serve this purpose first cutting their tongues out so they could not protest.[40] Suetonius's account of Caligula's death visits retribution on him in a sarcastic form and, though based on authentic historical details,[41] was probably deliberately constructed by the writer who was Hadrian's archivist and sought to please that emperor by contrasting his benevolent rule with the brutal inhumanity of his predecessors: in fact, Caligula in his turn does meet a violent death, but his assassination, plotted to take place immediately after the Palatine games, actually occurs shortly before. This is subtle, savage irony to underline the fact that the emperor Gaius, described as a bloodthirsty *monstrum* and a great enthusiast for theatrical and arena games himself becomes the object of the *ludus* and makes a truly bloody *spectaculum* of himself.

The *ludi circenses* are striking proof of how everything at Rome was actually or potentially sacrifice, setting in motion, destabilizing, or even obliterating the distinction between fact and fiction, between representation and real presence. And not for nothing Rome in particular codifies juridically and psychologically the subjective notion of the concept of *persona*; the theatrical mask becomes a juridical person and eventually a person in the individual, ontological sense (hence the difficulty in translating the term into Greek during the Christian Trinitarian disputes, since *prosopon* still carried connotations of the theater and fiction, while its sense as "face" was too shallow).

At this point I think that we are in a position to understand why Christians rejected theater almost totally. For the Fathers of the Church *theatrum* meant primarily the Roman *spectaculum* without any subtler distinction in regard to the classical genre that had, in any case, been moribund for centuries. In this perspective Clement is in part an exception: though his condemnation of all the theatrical spectacles was unreserved, he not only had greater knowledge of classical theater, having been born in Athens, but he also sought to recover anything that might serve his apologetic ends.[42] We should not overlook the fact that he utilizes the tragedies of Euripides, above all the *Bacchae*, as written texts rather than stage dramas—as we shall see—and in some slight measure anticipates our own use of them. In short, Christians either saw the theatrical dimension as dead and harmless, or more usually felt that it was a living, aggressive, performative reality and consequently judged it to be totally *damnanda*. For Christian writers there is practically complete transitivity and reciprocity between theatrical representation and its real presence, but it is an equivalence that they derived from the prevailing Roman view.

This should make it easier to understand the radically serious nature of the Christian rejection of *sacrificium*, by which is meant the rejection not only of sacrifice but of all the accompanying sacred acts, such as the burning of incense and swearing of oaths, that attested to its performative effectiveness. It would make no sense to reduce the matter to a formal or legal dispute over a particular act linked to the imperial cult. Some modern historians have a bad habit of giving little credit to the interpretations and representations of the actors involved, whereas they ought to be the very first to be heard and carefully listened to. And in this case there can be no doubt that both the Christians put on trial and their Roman judges regarded the question as decisive and central: the former because the cult of the emperor compromised and undermined their faith in Christ; the latter because the *auctoritas* of the empire was compromised and undermined by the recalcitrance of the Christians. And both were right from their differing viewpoints. As men of the ancient world they understood perfectly well that there was no renouncing sacrifice; it was pivotal to the mediations that provided their points of reference, the ultimate, unique sacrifice of Christ or the huge daily *sacrificium* that conferred everlasting prestige and divine power on the *imperium Romanum*. Although we have yet to deal with the question of the relationship between the newly born religion and sacrifice, it is safe to say that sacrifice could not be ignored or taken lightly by Christian theology, then at the height of its formative stage, either for the confrontation with pagan cults and their associated ideologies or from a more internal viewpoint. We need to understand that merely opposing sacrifice would not have sufficed to make the new religion credible, and without a specific, positive answer to sacrifice it would have been put completely out of the running.

However, there is not only conflict between Christians and pagans. We need to remember that persecution is far from systematic and continual, and occurs in cases where the Christian position could not be ignored, usually when the authorities acted on hostile reports or a popular uprising made the Christians ideal scapegoats for whatever was causing social unrest.[43] This circumstance is by no means irrelevant when we consider that Christianity could hardly have survived if the imperial machinery had set about systematic repression—the fate of Manichaeism some centuries later showed that a religion could not last when it was totally opposed by the political regime. The intermittent, fitful concern is however no accident; for the Romans, Christianity remained an anomaly, a trivial matter in itself, the illogical behavior of fanatics that a few examples by way of warning would serve to discourage. And with that the Roman mentality fell back into its pragmatic syncretism, channeling all cults into the mainstream of the imperial mediation. The authorities cared very little about the religious content of this Judaic sect, and it was only after the fall of Jerusalem that it began to be perceived as a new phenomenon in respect to the many tendencies of Middle Judaism (the more self-identifying Judaism that formed between the third century BC and the two Jewish wars).[44]

But the more advanced Roman thinking about sacrifice and the sacrificial mediation of Rome can also be seen to correspond to the Christian message, at least potentially or implicitly. What I have in mind are such figures as Cicero or Virgil. Cicero had personal experience of the persecutory implications of the Roman legal and political system, and to a certain extent theorized them in his rhetorical precepts and legal praxis, while Virgil examined the sacrificial genesis of the Roman people and power, and retold the story in the *Aeneid*.[45] At the end of the epic Aeneas kills Turnus and so brings the war against the Latin coalition to an end, but it is a cruel, violent act, asymmetrical and unredeemed, and hangs sinisterly over the destiny of Rome on a par with Dido's curse. Lucan's *Pharsalia*, written when Nero was emperor, is more striking still; it presents an epic reappraisal of the civil war between Caesar and Pompey and sets out to show the inexpiable nature of Romulus's "original sin" in killing his brother.[46] Thus, for the greatest Roman writers, Rome appeared to be marked by sacrificial excess, a dark, ever-impending side to its glory from which no good could come. However, such insight was unknown to the majority of people, submerged by force, the Roman cult of force that becomes law, right, and the rationale of dominion.

It could even be said that Rome fulfills the idea of the independence of the *polis* that Pentheus supported, now on a global scale and with very different resources: the Thebes of the Roman *res publica* has the capacity to switch, in the single figure of the emperor and as needs dictate, from an all-conquering Dionysus like Alexander the Great to an unwilling Pentheus to be slaughtered like a savage beast. In spite of a genius for flexibility reflected in the pragmatism and social mobility that are a further secret of its power, this imperial Thebes is also pervaded by growing anxiety about internal and external stability, or rather about the stability of the *limes*, the imperial, symbolic borderline between the exterior and the interior, barbarism and civilization, an anxiety affecting not only the more advanced intellectuals, as already mentioned, but in time the politicians holding power as well. And obviously, for the prevailing mentality, these fears could only be overcome by reaffirming the majestic Roman mediation, the tremendous military, political, and administrative organization whose ruins were to inspire nostalgic admiration in Edward Gibbon, the Enlightenment historian of the decline and fall of the Roman Empire, the same *imperium Romanum* whose supposed destruction by Christianity was to provoke fits of rage in Nietzsche as he wrote *The Antichrist*.[47] And so we return to the context of Celsus's attack against Christianity in an age of growing uncertainty about the future of empire.

What I have just said on the Roman capacity to deal with internal divisions and fights could be applied to some extent to Judaism and Christianity. Celsus's text reminds us not only that the field of religion contained numerous competing positions in the Roman Empire but also that the Christian position was not monolithic or unified, the proof being the difficult, contested break with the Judaism in which it originated and the various claims coming from different positions within Christianity itself or in contiguous cultural areas to have the exclusive right to interpret the teachings attributed to Christ. The hard struggle to arrive at a shared and historically effective version of Christ's mediation was not proof of the relative or propagandistic value of the version that came to prevail in the Great Church, though that is something always to be reckoned with in cases like this; rather, it proves its absolute significance as a complex, stratified process of theological comprehension following the traumatic separation from the Middle-Judaic matrix, a conflict-torn rupture that touched vital, fundamental nerve-centers in Judaism and in what was to become a separate but oddly sisterlike religion, making it also necessary to examine the vexed development of Judaic henotheism and of what modern scholars were to call monotheism, a category apparently simple enough but calling for clarification on several points.

While the concept of henotheism, also obviously modern, presents no particular problems, being applicable with various gradations and nuances to a whole range of ancient theological trends from henolatry (as with Akhenaton's Aton) to exclusive, expansive claims regarding other divinities (as with the Assyrian Assur and the Babylonian Marduk), the same cannot be said for the idea of monotheism confused, in different ways, with henotheistic-type positions, as in the annoying modernizations of the cult of Aton endorsed by the authority of Freud, and worse still with the archaic notion of the uranic deities, as in the old anachronistic idea of the *Urmonotheismus*; and the question has only been further confounded by applying abstract interpretive criteria that take no account of the mediatory context in which monotheism evolved. However, far from negating the historical centrality of the concept, this Babel of misunderstandings only serves to confirm it and shows the need, if we are to reach a correct understanding, to place it within the lengthy cultural sequence that has brought it down to our own day. Actually, the Greek root of the word itself appears by no means unrelated to the evolution of Judaism in its maturity and suggests the Hellenic origin of the very idea of a μόνος consistently applied to the divine according to the rules of the *logos*, of the θεολογία.

Further clarification will follow but already, in these introductory remarks, the relevance of Judaic monotheism is self-evident, confirming it to be one of the ancient world's most enduring legacies. But it needs to be understood in terms of its real genesis, which differs considerably from the accounts as in the Bible, though they are our principal source of information. The hand we have been dealt from the comparative deck of cards appears far richer and more intriguing than the usual oppositional schemes; its unexpected combinations and disorienting contaminations will help us understand the rules of the game that we must follow.

3. Characteristics of the Jewish and Christian Mediation

In the first place, for a better contextualized view of what we are talking about, we need to bear in mind the unsettled state of early Christianity, as reflected in Celsus's polemical tract, and that several centuries were to pass before it emerged as a religion organized according to certain inalienable, highly formalized principles, the so-called dogmas. This was also the result of a strong counteroffensive.

The second century witnessed a fuller discovery of the spiritual and soteriological meaning of Christ's figure and message brought about by a metaphysical and ahistorical method of interpretation that set Christ's life within a complex mythical drama, with the Jewish God playing the part of a deceiving demon who makes creation take the form of matter but leaves open a possible mission of spiritual salvation guaranteed by Christ, while the Crucifixion was only apparent and phantasmal (Docetism), such a death being deemed unworthy of his position as supreme divine mediator. This religious tendency goes by the name of Gnosis or Gnosticism, and it provoked a sharply realistic reaction from the Christian churches, stressing the historical nature of Christ's life, death, and resurrection. This triggered a process to define what may be regarded as the orthodox Christian position, and also led to Christ's significance as Christological mediator being better articulated in theological and metaphysical terms. Celsus mixes Christian ideas of a pre-Gnostic and Gnostic character with Christian positions that were or were destined to become more orthodox in nature, which shows him to be only partly aware of the tenor of the ongoing debate but at the same time highlights difficulties that threatened to undermine and destroy the stability of a religion still lacking certain features that it was to acquire later.

It should be noted that the Gnostic version of Christianity takes away all historically sacrificial implications from Christ's death, while the realistic reading of the Great Church, the work of Irenaeus of Lyons and successive Church Fathers in answer to Gnosis, maintained a certain sacrificial realism, albeit expressed theologically, in interpreting Christ's death. A paradoxical situation results with Christianity denying sacrifice to the Romans but forced to defend it against the Gnostic dismissal of its significance, a difficult balancing act that pits *one* sacrifice against all *other* sacrifices and takes us straight to the conflict with Judaism. And Celsus unhesitatingly seizes on this to hurl further gibes at what he saw as the religious monstrosity of Christianity. To traditionalistic Jews, the idea of a Son of God offering himself as a sacrifice for mankind seems a destabilizing, scandalous pagan *contaminatio*, creating doubt based on the difference of the God of Israel and all too ready, besides, in the Christian variant preached and disseminated by Paul, to mix shamelessly with pagan peoples, rejecting circumcision and purification practices.

Before we consider the intricate process of differentiation and opposition between Christians and Jews, the contending ritual positions in regard to sacrifice can be simplified and roughly summed up as follows. The Romans want to put sacrifice to practical use as and when it suits them, the more grandiose and spectacular the sacrifice, the greater the glory accruing to the empire being celebrated and the greater the terror instilled in its vanquished enemies. The Christians reject all forms of sacrifice in the name of a single, unique, and unrepeatable sacrifice, although its precise nature has still to be ascertained in this study. The Jews accept any sacrifice to God that does not compromise his mediatory uniqueness (another idea not yet ascertained in our study), and so they allow sacrifice provided it is restricted and subordinated to the empty transcendent center of every sacrificial and ritual cult. The peculiar and critical character of the Christian position comes into view if we recall the clever solution to the problem of coexistence reached by the

Jews and Romans: a daily sacrifice in the Temple in the name of the emperor, exempting the Jews from all further forms of religious homage to the Roman authorities.[48] The Christians, on the other hand, once they began to perceive themselves as distinct from the Judaic *ethnos*, could not accept any compromise because for them there was only one permissible sacrifice, the unique, abiding Eucharist. This is a religious issue, and its terms of exclusion and reciprocal involvement have inevitably eluded modern scholars, influenced as they are by the collapse of all mediation, and free to study its remnants at will and reconstruct single pieces but never coming to see them as an organic whole. Those who are more perceptive and more deeply involved in the study merely revive the old diatribe unilaterally and identify with one side in the struggle, thinking to unearth the long-forgotten reasons behind it and bring it back to life, though it is apparently dead.

This is the case with Girard who brackets together the Jewish and Christian positions in view of their total opposition to sacrifice, in Judaism by pursuing a strategy of purist differentiation, and then in Christianity through an authentic example of theological deception in which sacrifice is put on a level with Satan and is fooled by being given free rein and being allowed to prevail.[49] Starting from his mimetic, satanic definition of sacrifice, Girard argues for a drastic differentiation of Judaism from surrounding pagan religions, achieved through two complementary criteria: devictimization of God and dedivinization of the victim. The two ritual transfers are thus deconstructed and demolished, clearing the way for Christianity's antisacrificial position, where God reverts to being the victim, but this is in order to unmask the entirely human mechanism governing all religions and cultures.[50] In this perspective, traditionalist Judaism opposes Christianity because it wants to hold fast to the difference of the God of Israel in respect to the forms of pagan sacrifice, a difference definable at this point as revealed—or at least as having been attained if we are to keep our inquiry on more historically verifiable ground.[51] This intransitive interpretation may help us to grasp the inevitability of sacrifice, but it prevents us from seeing the terrain shared by the competing parties, while its schematic nature falls short of effective historical and documentary control criteria. And yet Girard teaches us that total opposition in the human world is the sign of secret influence and not of unrelated difference, unless we fall in with a revelationist scheme adopted a priori. Certainly, that influence is to be interpreted in mediatory terms appropriate to human cultures and not in Girard's bluntly mimetic terms; the only alternative to them is a no less conflictual revelation of mimetic rivalry that is, in his view, the inevitable outcome of human relationships. If we are to understand more we must follow a historical method closer to the mediatory dynamism that shaped Judaic henotheism/monotheism and made possible the development of Christianity. A more detailed explanation will take us to the embryonic stage of the greatest religious mediation in the classical world to be put alongside the speculative and philosophical mediation of Greece. We obtain a kind of quadtych where Rome and Christianity produced in their turn a central and dual panel, connecting and joining the Jewish and Greek external valves. This complex and contrasting process actually fulfilled relationships that had existed for centuries but were rarely made explicit, or rather were almost always concealed by the final religious organizations. Anyway, let us consider the possible origin of the Jewish religion within the frame of the Mediterranean and Near-Eastern civilizations.

At the same time we must clear the ground of antisacrificial misunderstanding. Even a cursory glance at the texts and evidence makes it quite clear that what was to become monotheism, and was initially only a national polytheistic cult developing increasingly toward henotheism, had its origins in sacrifice, indeed in human sacrifice. Early Judaism was wholly dependent on the sacrificial mediations that were the rule among all peoples in the ancient East. But in time a small prophetic group came to reject human sacrifice and exterior ritualism, declaring the need to replace them with a cult based on justice in which legitimate sacrificial rites were an integral part, a position never repudiated even by Jesus. Thus there exists a whole series of degrees and nuances to prevent us from interpreting the theological and ethical spiritualization characteristic of the mature Jewish religion as a sudden inexplicable development, as a miraculous counterrevelation. Our guiding idea of mediation together with the more significant findings in the historical-critical field can suggest an explanation, helping us to understand how the Judaic religion took shape, with its henotheistic, and only finally monotheistic, theology that was to mark it out from the other religions of the ancient world. At this point I draw on the results of the most recent and reliable reconstructions regarding the origin and development of the Yahwistic cult, in particular on the work of the Italian Semitist Giovanni Garbini. Although some of his conclusions are questionable, he appears relatively free of denominational bias and mindful of the strictly sacrificial background to a surprising and little known history.[52]

Originally Yahweh was a typical Semitic god similar to the Phoenician Baal, endowed with power to control lightning and storms,[53] and associated particularly with the underworld into which he regularly descended and then returned, accompanied by his consort goddess, Asherah,[54] in a hierogamic enactment of death and resurrection recalling the Dumuzi-Tammuz and Inanna-Ishtar cycle, transposed into Greek mythology in the story of Adonis and Aphrodite.[55] One quite sensational detail regarding the Yahwistic cult is that, even in the Temple in Jerusalem, it had Dionysian features including orgiastic rituals and prostitution, both male and female.[56] It is worth remembering in this connection that Dushara or Dusares, the god of the neighboring Nabatheans, was very similar to the Greek Dionysus,[57] an underlying resemblance that only grew stronger in the Hellenistic period though was already a shared underlying basis.[58] At the heart of the archaic cult of Yahweh is the figure of the sacred monarch, fated to repeat sacrificially the god's destiny of death when his powers of fertility declined, which takes us back to the hierogamy scenario already seen in Minoan Greece while, through the influence of Philistine peoples from the area of Crete and Anatolia, the Jerusalem Temple itself shares definite similarities, even linguistic (*dabir = labir-*), with the Cretan labyrinth as a symbol of the afterlife.[59] In historical times, however, the monarch (designated in the Western Semitic languages with the root *mlk*, from where the Hebraic *melek*[60]) managed to impose the use of a sacrificial substitute, the *molk*, the sacrifice of the firstborn male, associated with a sacred mating, its fertility supposedly guaranteed by the ritual offering.[61] Hierogamy itself probably ceased to be practiced in its crudest form around the end of the third millennium BC,[62] but sacrifice of the firstborn can be considered as its continuation since the son dies in place of the father, thus allowing him to renew his creative power in the sacred coupling.

Traces of this obscure ritual history can be clearly seen, albeit distorted and displaced, in the biblical texts. With a linguistic shift from a common noun in ritual to a proper noun, the Bible records the *molk* ceremony as performed in honor of Moloch, and it is easy to see that this fictitious theonym, a further modification of the vocalization of *mlk*,[63] conceals the identity of the archaic Yahweh.[64] Besides this data, Hebrew Scripture contains many traces of human sacrifice, apparent and not so apparent but all perfectly recognizable when my comparative method for myth and ritual is applied, and we shall certainly have occasion to come back to them.[65] The ancient Jewish Passover was a festivity centering on the *molk*, and the account in Exodus has preserved it in the shape of the supreme divine punishment meted out to Egypt, thus providing an etiology of much more recent date for this ancient feast, a date as far forward to the late Hellenistic period to be exact.[66] The road leading to monotheism was clearly neither straight nor smooth, and if we are to reconstruct it we must approach the biblical material in the appropriate historical-critical spirit since the picture hinted at above has little to do with the idealized, ideologically oriented reconstruction presented in the Bible. Events as described in the stories of the patriarchs, the exodus from Egypt, the conquest of Palestine, the kingdom of David, and the building of Solomon's Temple are the fruits of legendary sagas designed to provide a prestigious past for the Yahwistic cult and are without historical parallels.[67] King David himself corresponds to the ancient figure of the *dawid*, the beloved of the king, a favorite fated to die in place of the king in emergencies that endanger the monarch's mediatory power.[68]

The first theological developments of Yahwistic mediation that can be reconstructed are indissolubly linked to the history of the two Jewish kingdoms. The Northern Kingdom called Ephraim or Israel had its capital at Samaria and was the more powerful; Yahweh became its principal god in the ninth century BC, cohabited with other gods, and was also worshipped in bovine form.[69] The smaller Southern Kingdom or Judah arose later with Jerusalem as its capital. A crucial change occurs in 722 BC when the Northern Kingdom collapses under attack from the Assyrian Empire; as a result, the kingdom of Judah inherits the name of Israel and its religious legacy, as well as part of the population including members of the ruling class and prophets. Reconstruction of events becomes highly problematic not only because of the extreme bias of biblical sources but also because the religious reform attributed to Josiah, the last great king of Judah, and accepted by many scholars as providing the background to the future monotheism,[70] betrays the perfunctory features of an artificially contrived legend.[71] In all likelihood, human sacrifice and above all the *molk* continued to be performed up to the end of the preexilic period;[72] but between the eighth and seventh centuries the prophetic movement in both states pursued an ethical development of the Yahwistic cult that was fiercely critical of human sacrifice, though most of the political class must have turned a deaf ear to it judging by the persistent, sorrowing tones of the prophets. However, it constitutes the most important antecedent for what was to become the spirituality of the Bible,[73] and it increased its influence when the political power passed from the Northern Kingdom to Judah with Israel's religious remnant and memory.

The events of the kingdom of Judah are still more difficult to reconstruct because of the heavy reinterpretations of the postexilic period. In any case, the small state clearly tried to defend its independence among its powerful neighbors but finally had to succumb. Following the defeat and death of Josiah at the hands of the Egyptians in 609 BC, a dramatic sequence of events culminates in the conquest of Jerusalem by Nebuchadnezzar, king of Babylon, in 587/586 BC,[74] after the last king, Zedekiah, settled in Jerusalem by the Babylonian king as representative of his dominion, attempted to form an alliance with Egypt.[75] Zedekiah was harshly punished, the political and social structures within the city and kingdom were dismantled though not completely destroyed, and the governing class, together with the most qualified artisans, were deported in waves.[76] Nevertheless, the conventional image of the Babylonian exile as a time of hard humiliating servitude is, at least partially, a misrepresentation: the data coming from the Bible are few and unreliable, while the archaeological finds show a prosperous economic situation in the Jewish colony, and all the historical hints point to a benevolent treatment of the Jewish chiefs by the Babylonians.[77] The exile became a period of fundamental incubation for the future development of the Yahwistic religion thanks to a vigorous interaction with the Babylonian environment and its highly developed culture, as shown in the biblical texts, though this does not mean that the exilic experience was not a problem. Quite the contrary, on solving the problem depended the survival of the Jewish religious and cultural identity.

My thesis is that the emotional and cognitive germ of what was to become monotheism can be traced back to theological reflection about the long series of politico-military defeats leading to the collapse of the two kingdoms, reflection that was the prerogative of the prophetic movement and found a pivotal moment in the Babylonian exile. The dynamic core of this thinking consisted in inverting the relationship of protection/obedience typical of the covenant-based theologies of Near-Eastern religions. While politico-military victories are seen everywhere else as confirming the power of the national god and the bond of obedience, the frequent debacles in the ancient Jewish kingdoms, instead of loosening that bond, actually strengthen it because the prophetic interpretation ascribing defeat to religious unfaithfulness tends to prevail, tinged by moral motivations and involving the monarch in the first instance, as author and guarantor of the covenant, closely followed by the governing class and the people, though it is not easy to separate the more ancient parts of the texts from later revisions that are systematically antimonarchical for reasons soon to be made clear.[78] Indeed the prophets at their most audacious and visionary consider politico-military disaster as confirmation of the Yahwistic mediation that is not direct and factual but based on the reversal of the visible, human logics of power, and bears witness to a different power of God, an authority supertranscendent and invisible yet present in history that remains the place to confront and finally reveal the authentic power of the national god. An innovative religious mediation begins to take shape, further developed and enriched during the Babylonian exile through close contact with the ideology and culture of the imperial capital, the marks of their influence unmistakably present in the future Bible.

The way forward to a clearly monotheistic form was, however, unpredictable, and the path actually taken is now unrecognizable as a consequence of theological and textual revision systematically projecting the origin back in time in a supreme effort to differentiate the form achieved from pagan cults in the first place and then from the Christian heresy. It is still not possible to talk of real monotheism in the exilic and postexilic periods but rather of henotheism spiritualized and transformed into a theology of history that breaks with human sacrifice, accepting the prophets' criticisms, and may possibly be swayed as well by the ineffectiveness shown by the *molk* during the unsettled preexilic times. Indeed, the national god coexists with other divine powers that have proved successful in this world. This is the case when the Persian overlords to whom the Jews must submit allow some of the exiles to return to Jerusalem, and so inject a fresh religious influence from Zoroastrian Mazdaism that was also moving in a definably premonotheistic direction.[79] However, the essential point is that both Judaism and Mazdaism lack precisely the category of *monos* understood theologically and conceptually in an exclusive sense, quite simply because their worlds are full of sacral presences and forces, inevitably resulting in plurality: a "one and only" God is nonexistent; instead there is a preeminent God who asserts his power by defeating opposing forces and surrounding himself with forces subordinate and well-disposed to himself. It should be noted that plurality and opposition coexist, in an axiological, hierarchical organization reaching down to a lower, opposing level that passes over into a sort of qualitative unreality, into an evil equivalent to the objectual negation from which the divine mediation must provide salvation.

In order to start reasoning exclusively in terms of a divine *monos*, of a sole omnipotent divine mediation, a category of the kind had to become capable of representation and argument. This was made possible by the Hellenistic influence, whose philosophy overcame the intermedial and imaginal crowds of spirits thronging the religions of the East and Hellenic religion itself through the ontological conceptualization of the problem of the One and the Many that took place in Platonic and Aristotelian circles. The sophisticated Platonic solution to hierarchize Parmenides's Being so as to make it compatible with the plurality of the Ideas reaches full expression in the Aristotelian doctrine of the Unmoved Mover,[80] the One perfectly realized and, as such, not susceptible to change or movement and therefore moving unmoved the whole universe. For its part, the universe is finally intended to assimilate to the One through an ontological and cosmic *mimesis*, with nothing mimetic in the modern sense about it since it is none other than the divine mediation in its ontologically hierarchicized realization.[81] This splendid solution, however, could not escape the conceptual assumptions from which it sprang and resulted in an icy, impersonal image of God, though Plato tried in vain to make it more accessible by introducing elements of Orphism and soterial mythology. To transform this exclusive legacy of a restricted cultural elite into a living and credible religious experience it had to encounter and be contaminated by Judaic henotheism in its long, tormented history. The idea that Plato was influenced by Judaism, an old Jewish and Christian argument polemically revived by Nietzsche, needs to be reversed, simply because in Plato's time there was as yet no real monotheism in Judah. Its development, on the contrary, precisely followed the indirect but powerful influence of Greek philosophy. At the end of the book XII of *Metaphysics* devoted to the Unmoved Mover, Aristotle unequivocally states, quoting Homer: "entities [*onta*] do not want to be governed [*politeuesthai*] badly. 'A command by the many [*polykoiranie*] is not good: let the commander [*koiranos*] be one!'"[82]

At the same time, we realize the great originality of the future Judaic monotheism when we remember that neither Plato or Aristotle nor the Hellenistic schools conceived God as one and personal: their divinity remains cosmic and impersonal and coexists with a plurality of divine submediations, unifying reality thanks to an axiological and ontological preeminence coincident with its own law and *logos*. It was only by way of Israel's dramatic quest that the Greek conceptualizations were able to metamorphose and become a claim for a single, personal God, lord of heaven and earth, of the cosmos and mankind. The principal text showing this synthesis is Genesis; in a position to draw freely on Canaanite, Phoenician, and Mesopotamian myths while taking account of the theological rationalizations begun by Hellenic philosophy, it was in all likelihood first written down in the second century BC.[83] Indeed the greater part of the biblical corpus in all likelihood took on its shape in this same period,[84] a mighty undertaking to bring together and organize the Judaic traditions, taking advantage of the achievements of Greek rationalism while reasserting the peculiar, unique nature of the religion of Judah.

An eloquent double check on this gradual attainment of the divine *monos* is to be seen in Zoroastrian Mazdaism. While unifying theological tendencies of a premonotheistic kind are present, it would be pointless to look for any explicit theology regarding the oneness of God, not so much because of its dualism, ascribable at this point in time to a hierarchic mentality and not to a contrastive binary one, but because the problem is not yet apparent in terms of the logical and conceptual criteria familiar to us through the influence of Greek philosophy, modernized moreover and detached from its ontological and cosmic frame, thereby losing its capacity to reconcile opposites in an axiological hierarchization. Nor is that all. The Hellenic influence acts on Judaic thinking not as a sudden experience but over several centuries starting with the conquest of Alexander the Great, and most likely preceded by other contact when we remember that the Persian Empire was the womb of Ionic philosophy.

Jesus's ideas, and Christian thinking after him, must be seen as part of a complex debate as yet not carried on in the abstract terms of the Greek *monos*, and so rightfully belonging to the developmental stage of monotheistic belief along with the other positions and tendencies in Middle Judaism. The Christian Trinity is not at all a scandalous variation of a closed, completed Jewish monotheism, but rather the Christian answer to the problem of the oneness of God and of God's relationship to a plurality of spiritual and worldly entities, taking its inspiration from the Middle-Judaic idea of the divine triad of Wisdom that acts as a spiritual consort to Yahweh and to the Spirit (*ruah*, feminine in Hebrew) that continues Yahweh's creative activity.[85] Rabbinical Judaism closes the debate for its part by asserting the transcendent oneness of God, with a definition not eliminating the mediatory and intermedial problems of the old Judaic henotheism but merely putting them to rest, as is proved by the developments of the Qabbala in medieval times. Similar comments could be made regarding the radical development of Islamic monotheism which restates in a different way the problem of how to relate intermedially with the transcendent and absolute mediation of God.

In conclusion, just as a monotheism born all of a piece from some otherworldly revelation has never existed, so the mediatory enigma faced by monotheism can never be said to have been defined and solved once and for all, as is clearly evidenced by the formation of different tendencies in Judaism and, at a later date, of different monotheisms fighting bitterly among themselves. And the only grounds for the total opposition raised by the various monotheisms against the polytheism from which they came are self-assertion and self-confirmation. This is interestingly reflected in Middle Judaism itself when, reworking both Judaic myths and Persian demonology, it starts to represent the alternation of polytheism/monotheism in the *mythos* of the rebellion against Yahweh by part of the angelic host,[86] doomed to form a swarm of devils corresponding to the gods of neighboring peoples. This belief was shared by Jesus, passed on to the religion that he inspired, and taken up again by Gnosticism, which includes Yahweh among the devils, not without a certain remote justification. The more advanced Judaic theology, in such texts as the Genesis account of the Fall and the prologue to the book of Job, presents believers with the same enigma since it turns out God allows evil to exist and, to a certain degree, it appears to be a part of his powers.

Likewise, the profound nature of this debate shows that a purely historical and documentary reconstruction will not suffice to do justice to the origin of the phenomenon of monotheism. As with other scholars in their reconstructions, Garbini is unable to explain the originality of the monotheistic mediation, and actually introduces a mechanical, external explanation: the interruption of the *molk* imposed by the Persians, thus sowing a suspicion that the prophets' criticisms of human sacrifice were really an attack on the institution of monarchy motivated by self-interest, namely the priesthood's desire to gain control of the offerings made at the Temple in Jerusalem.[87] The true picture, on the other hand, reveals a seeking and striving toward a single theological mediation marking a new frontier of objectual and ethical achievement. Begun by the prophetic movement, it took the concrete form of henotheism with a national background, matched itself against the great neighboring cultures, and absorbed the unifying, clarifying influence of Greek philosophy. And yet, this is not the whole story, since a very important event has still to complete it, though little known and highly controversial. In spite of its conjectural status, and by reason of the very secrecy by which it was surrounded, this event provides us with the crucial missing link in our picture and displays before our eyes the real and dramatic meaning of the greatest religious creativity during Middle Judaism.

Sacrifice remains the mainstay of this henotheistic and premonotheistic mediation and is the key both to its functioning and to understanding it, but there had been a sinister revival of the ancient *molk* just at the beginning of the postexilic period. The return from exile is marked by a traumatic event fraught with future developments that seriously affects its outcome. This was the double assassination toward 515 BC of the Davidic king, Zerubbabel, and his prophet and high priest Zechariah during a Temple ceremony, probably during his coronation, at the hands of the priest Joshua with the support of a substantial part of the exilic priesthood and of the population that had remained *in loco* and opposed the restoration of monarchy. Joshua thus takes command as high priest and also becomes governor on behalf of the Persian king.[88] The Bible histories, though they provide strong circumstantial evidence, say nothing about this event, and yet it is the final detail we need to complete the picture, at least in part, since its effects on the postexilic religious and Middle-Judaic tradition were to be felt for a long time, causing splits in the priestly caste whenever one of its members might object to such a savage act as motivated by greed for power. Certain members of the priesthood in Jerusalem keep alive the aspiration for a royal mediator, a Messiah (from the Hebrew *Mašiah* = Anointed, by way of the Aramaic *Mešiah*) of Davidic descent to restore the relationship to Yahweh according to justice, even if assisted or guided by a priestly mediator expressing the compromise with other elements of the priesthood unwilling to relinquish their supremacy.[89] For their part, those elements develop the antimonarchical ideology prevalent in the historical books of the Bible, which only makes the divisions within the priestly caste more acute.

The most theologically advanced and critical part manages to discern original sin not only in the Temple cult but in human history as a whole, tracing it back to an act of rebellion by man against a God not exempt from mythological ambiguities, and to the subsequent killing of Abel by Cain. The first murder, fratricide, alludes to the innocent Zerubbabel, his name preserved in an abbreviated form by the biblical character, and to the Qenites or Cainites from whom Joshua descended. And this bloody act quickens Christ's harsh criticisms of those running the Temple when he blames them for "all the righteous bloodshed on the earth, from the blood of righteous Abel to the blood of Zechariah son of Barachiah, whom you killed [*ephoneusate*] between the temple and the altar [*thysiasteriou*]" (Mt 23:35).[90] This searing documented accusation has a subtlety and pertinence that is to be attributed to the historical Christ, since in one brief passage it evokes the first homicide in human history and the shameful murder of Zerubbabel and his prophet carried out in the Temple: an original sin to be wiped away only through the cleansing of the Temple, the new message proclaimed by the rabbi of Nazareth that makes the mediation of the true God finally accessible. We shall see more of this when we come to consider the establishing and stratification of the Christian message, which is to be strictly interpreted, as to its origin, as the adoption of a position in regard to unresolved problems that had bedeviled postexilic Judaism for centuries.

The bloody end of monarchy as an institution carries enormous consequences for the postexilic evolution of Judaism, interacting with previous thinking about sacrifice and the historical conditions for access to the Yahwistic mediation, and leaving the sacrifice of the *molk* prominent in the very heart of Israel's reconstituted identity when, theologically speaking, prophets and priests had tried to put it behind them. This not only intensifies and makes far more concrete the previous hopes for a restoration of the monarchy by a descendent of David, hopes that now start to become messianic, but also distributes title to the covenant horizontally since, in the absence of a royal mediation that title must fall to the priestly class; eventually, however, it is extended to the people as a whole and, in its most audacious formulation, to the entire human race.[91] This gives rise to a mythical-ritual hermeneutics applied to men and history, aiming to interpret what had happened in a way acceptable to all involved and to make it possible with considerable effort to make out the signs of the presence and will of Yahweh. The most profound theological statement relating to this is contained in the Songs of the Suffering Servant (*Ebed Yahweh*) in Isaiah 49–55 which came to be part of the oracles composed in exile and afterward, attributed by modern scholars to the so-called Deutero-Isaiah. These Songs appear different from the sequence of Isaiah 40–48,[92] and refer to a dramatic event that perfectly fits with the killing of Zerubbabel.[93] In their powerful and original message, they must be due to a single author who probably wanted to insert them in the Isaiahan tradition and its reference to the Immanuel, the regal descendant destined to save Israel.[94] Their pivotal theological point is that the Davidic king maintains his mediatory role through suffering unjust treatment himself and by offering the people as a whole the possibility of acknowledging their faults and repenting, to become the chosen people and so continue to perform his function of divine mediation, a fundamental prerequisite for the future Christological and Christian mediation.

In principle, it becomes possible to make an overall reconstruction though the details elude us because of the weight of censorship, while the various stages, systematically refashioned in later theological syntheses, are very hard to distinguish clearly. Israel and some of its minority groups repeatedly experienced being on the losing side, encouraging the idea that divine omnipotence invisibly defends the weak and oppressed such as the Suffering Servant and other figures in the Bible characterized by innocence, literally *in-nocentes*, incapable of doing harm. From the punitive Yahweh demanding human sacrifice, we have arrived at a God transcending the typically human logic of reprisal and violence and willing to renew his promise to keep faith with and protect the very people guilty of violating the covenant.[95] In this way the sufferings of the oppressed become an effective means of ensuring that the divine mediation prevails: thus we have a resemanticization of sacrifice that historicizes it to make it humanly visible, and individualizes its significance so far as to make sacrifice the offering of one's own life to God. Meanwhile God is increasingly spiritualized as the criteria by which the divine will is recognized undergo a complete reversal, which could be used to justify an atheistic skepticism just as soon as the most sublime theology. Intellectual freedom, nurtured by Greek rationalism, becomes possible for a minority of thinkers, mainly linked to the sapiential tradition, and is exemplified most splendidly by Ecclesiastes. Unlike Greece, however, philosophical skepticism in Israel is not opposed to religious mediation but deepens it, intensifying the efforts to demythologize (always to be understood as the development of an advanced form of *mythos*) that are a vital ingredient of monotheistic theology.

The religious philosophy of Middle Judaism is bewilderingly rich in content and develops in innumerable directions; besides those already mentioned, other notable groupings share a common reaction, though with different theological ideas, to the "founding" sin of the murder of Zerubbabel: the Essenes, with their spiritually radical quest for ritual purity, developed from a breakaway group of priests of the Temple cult; the Qumran monastic sect, originating in an apocalyptic extremist group of Essenes,[96] broke off all its normal religious relations with the Temple and considered itself to be already part of the heavenly realm, with the aforementioned eschatological interruption of the Temple sacrifices; the Enochic sect, named after its mythical founder Enoch, also held apocalyptic ideas but was much more influential because of its historical and social commitment and sought, as an alternative to the Jerusalem priesthood and as a remedy for the post-Creation rebellion of the angels, a mediator or mediators capable of guaranteeing the definitive dominion of Yahweh over Israel and all creation.[97] Christ's teaching fits squarely into this animated debate, and in its highly original answer we can recognize not only apocalyptic themes, coming from Enochic Judaism through the theology of the book of Daniel,[98] and a theological development of the Songs of the Suffering Servant but also the spiritual and intellectual freedom of the more open-minded strains in Judaism. Greek influence is an indispensable element in all this religious ferment, in a twofold sense as assimilation and as cause of an identifying reaction; and that translates into an outstanding confrontation both practical and theoretical having to do with the paradox of the One and the Many from the theological viewpoint. The outcome is monotheism in its twofold guise: Jewish, ensconced behind the transcendent *monos* of the Mosaic God, and Christian, organized around a God incarnate and ultimately trine.

The clash between Judaism and the Christian movement provides the background to the broader religious and ideological conflict between pagans and Christians, to which we must now return. Starting from the historical Jesus, Christianity develops the figure of the Christic and Christological mediator through a process continually torn by controversy into the fourth century and beyond. And it should be observed at once that the peculiar character of this mediator only serves to assist and intensify the process leading to monotheism as we know it, having reached what we might define as a point of no return. From the first, immediately after Christ's execution, his followers attribute complete, definitive mediatory and sacrificial powers to the Galilean rabbi, which very soon proves incompatible with previous religious and theological mediations: in the first instance with Jewish mediations and secondly, but not secondarily, with pagan mediations. In Middle Judaism we come across the idea of God coming down among mankind to assert his mediation once and for all:[99] taking its cue perhaps from this idea and in any case developing the prophetic and messianic call for a divine mediation concretely present at a historical and existential level, Christianity now implements a theological concentration in the incarnate mediator that crystallizes the tension between the One and the Many characteristic of Middle-Judaic philosophy where there is a single God with a numerous train of mediators able to ensure his present and future sovereignty. It is the mediatory uniqueness attributed to Christ, and claimed by himself as we shall see, that scandalizes the multifarious strains of Judaism, while Rabbinical Judaism would itself claim to be unique and blame Christianity for its intolerable theological duplicity.

The Christian solution of a single, definitive mediation incarnate in Christ was destined in its turn to come into conflict with the ideology of Rome, strong in its determination to dominate any and every mediation within its own *imperium*, that is, within the living totality of human and divine mediations, and by so doing qualifying the *imperium* as real and objectual. From this we also understand, by one of those historical ironies that often ease the way to lasting change, that Rome shows Christianity the way ahead by transmitting its own potentially unlimited capacity for cultural and cultual metabolization to the new religion. Just as Judaic henotheism could not have arisen or developed into monotheism without the stimulus and model of Near-Eastern regal and imperial mediations as well as Hellenism's decisive contribution, so Christianity would not have become what it did become, bringing the seeds of universalism derived from Judaism to complete fruition, had it not found itself surrounded by the universal mediation of Rome with its power to bring the One and the Many to coexist pragmatically. It is true that for three centuries the conflict appeared insoluble, but very often conflict in history is a symptom or prerequisite of influence and assimilation, or even their consequence, as in the case of Judaism.

Here we are in the very midst of a dense tangle of convergences and divergences between Greco-Roman civilization, Judaism, and Christianity, made all the more inextricable by layers of mutual conditioning, no less reciprocal than the disagreements and accusations that divide the contending parties; and what shall come out of all these various aims is unforeseeable and incalculable, which is typical of human history where conflict and destruction in themselves draw new boundaries of definition and identity. So we must reject every partisan approach if we are to reach a contextual historical understanding in line with the available phenomenological findings; and the idea of mediation, in my opinion, makes it easier to recognize the common threads and shared elements, the tangencies and intersections.

With the information gathered in this survey of the various mediations competing with the religious paradigm inspired by Christ, we will now return to the mystery and Orphic experience of the Greeks that Clement compared to Christianity to see if we can find a shared context, at least in part or initially, that can further our investigations and at the same time confirm their underlying unity. We need to understand how far we can establish analogies and differences, not so much and not only in respect to Greek philosophy, a task that would call for a separate inquiry, but primarily in regard to the mythical-ritual knowledge that was our starting point and that can give us the most direct and widely found comparative parameters, namely the religious parameters that could be shared by a large part of the population as well as men of culture. So let us take another look at the Orphic toys first encountered in analyzing the Gurob papyrus and brought up again by Clement. Our aim is not to close the circle but to set it in motion again, to open up new historical and interpretive pathways, new thresholds of cognitive retroaction.

4. Toys for Slaughter

Though apparently far removed from the strongly theological and historical atmosphere of Judaism and Christianity, the Dionysian play and mystery symbols allow us to regain the magical-ritual dimension that forms their necessary background. The historical relevance is perfectly clear since, as we have seen, the most ancient Yahwistic cult contains Dionysian elements found widely in the ancient East and reinforced by the syncretism of the Hellenistic and Roman period. This is not to say that the Judaic and Christian mediation has no unmistakable features of its own, but they are the outcome of a far more involved history than their final forms might suggest. This material will serve to bring together and give substance to our comparative investigation, but to do so we must go back to the very beginning, to the bloody source of all human and divine mediations, visualized and made accessible through the mythical-ritual language of Orphism's Titanic drama.

The Orphic toys can be said to express the motives and purpose of the Dionysian *sparagmos*, a reminder of its cause and final result that becomes a summary of the experience and knowledge of initiation. In many rites of initiation, after the killing and rebirth of the youthful initiate has been ritually represented, such toys are put aside to symbolize the end of childhood.[100] In our case the initiation represented is the Orphic ritual of the *symbola* in which the *disiecta membra* of Dionysus are reassembled to bring about the resurrection of the god with whom the believer identifies. The list of toys in the Gurob papyrus underlines their function as a symbol of salvation. Until now the ritual element in human play has been often misunderstood, preventing these symbols from being correctly interpreted either wholly or in part. Kerényi, for example, saw them as mere toys, albeit qualified by the fact they belong to a child: "These are not mystic symbols [*keine mystischen Symbole*] but real toys worthy of a Divine Child."[101] The divine qualification is not out of place, only it fails to explain how it is possible, what is its real origin. Evidently Kerényi's humanistic idealization of Dionysianism led him to instinctively avoid an inquiry hardly consonant with his aims: for if such harmless playthings as these really do possess sacrificial meaning, whatever are we to say about all the other Dionysian symbols? This brings to mind the irrepressible sarcasm of Nietzsche on the brink of madness but, for that very reason, more than ever aware of the real nature of the toys of Dionysus, when he was confronted by the caricatural rationalizations of the extremely erudite Lobeck;[102] Kerényi apparently has not reflected on this.

Besides, a ritual origin in no way conflicts with the use of these objects in play, since all human play derives its substance from sacrificial symbols. The origin of the Orphic toys and human toys in general could not be less playful and is concerned not so much with childish amusements as with the games that adults play, serious games, Titanic games that are dangerous in a very different way. And that is why such sacrificial playthings are to be found in initiation rites everywhere.

The relevant explanations offered by the Orphics fail to meet either modern rational criteria or Judaism's theologically more developed criteria. In Greece, philosophy developed these criteria from an ontological-cosmic viewpoint, with a freedom and independence favored by the political organization of the *polis* and by the absence of a priestly caste holding centralized power. Orphic knowledge, on the contrary, was completely absorbed with the magical-ritual effectiveness of the toys; nevertheless it was known without a shadow of a doubt that their origin was in Dionysian sacrifice, for which they expressed the reality and the goal of salvation. By way of exposition, I shall here trace the outline of the ritual cycle of sacrifice as far as it can be reconstructed on the basis of the available data and using the principal ethnological theories that have incorporated that data into a consistent whole. By superimposing the modern interpretive context on the ancient ritual context, it should be possible to produce a common ground, an objective and objectual medium conveying knowledge and enabling comparison. The basic sequence derives from the ritual cycle described by Frazer, Durkheim, Roger Caillois, and Bataille, until the description made by Girard in his mimetic terms; the scientific and theoretical references are, however, secondary to the anthropological, historical, and cultural reality transmitted by these ritual symbols, a reality that we can recover through an analysis following their phenomenological and genetic structure.

We will start with Orphism's most important ritual object, the mirror (εἴσοπτρον or ἔσοπτρον) we have found at the end of the Gurob papyrus. In the ancient world the mirror was used for divination (catoptromancy), especially a concave mirror providing a distorted image (*speculum monstrificum*), and most probably the type usually prescribed for Orphic initiations.[103] Colli, in referring to the use of these symbols in Neoplatonism, gives an abstract metaphysical interpretation of the Orphic mirror that hinges on the contrast between appearance and original reality, between phenomenal appearances and noumenal foundation: a contrast not in itself out of place but needing to be translated into historically adequate terms on a par with the mask, which resembles the mirror in several ways and is also used in catoptromancy.

In Girard's terms, the mirror could be said to symbolize mimetic reproduction, the repeated and apparently innocuous imitation that leads as if by magic to the monstrous game of the rival model, and to the proliferation of the doubles. However, far from obviating the problem of the attainment and purpose of mediation, this only emphasizes it. Indeed, the mirror, a valuable object in antiquity sometimes made of precious metal, carries connotations of brightness and attractiveness, but because of the deceptive nature of its reflecting surface these may be either genuine or specious. Because it is for these convergent reasons magical, the mirror is attributed with re-productive powers: its doubling image can ensure double possession, although doubling can in its turn halve and reduce to nothing what appears in the mirror, and even visualize the image of what we do not want to see, like the child Dionysus who sees his own image made monstrous, anticipating his imminent fate, and then immediately afterward the Titans. The magical-transmissive aspect predominates because it relates to the power of the mirror to multiply or distort the image that was conceived in antiquity as a shadowy likeness emanating from objects and intercepted by human receptive organs. The Orphic *esoptron* symbolizes the power to duplicate and manipulate the reality of this world that Orphism wants to make permanent in the life after death; thus it begins the process of salvation leading from the Titanic event—an evil duplication—to Dionysian salvation: the final, benign duplication. The mirror is a mask of light with the implication, for initiation, of leading beyond the mirror surface and appearances, as in *Alice through the Looking Glass* where the reflection reveals another, more real dimension.

The modern world can no longer count on collectively shared transcendent mediations. Consequently, it no longer believes in an intermedial reality guaranteeing transition to a divine object, to another life on the other side of the mirror. Lacking the capacity to run the gamut of variations between reality and appearance, it has moved in the opposite direction, toward the destruction of all appearances through demystifying explanation. Alternatively—as at present—it hides behind mere appearances that are considered better than ordinary reality, in itself disappointing and empty. And so, instead of mirrors, we have a whole series of reflecting electronic surfaces that become the only "real" reality, the one medium mediating on nothing because it assumes an objectual void. Nevertheless, we should retain the power of modern demystification to produce an effective explanation, not in order to rush into a history-denying objectual negation but to demystify demystification itself and recover the whole historical process from which it arises.

Behind Dionysus-Phanes, the god of appearance, behind Dionysus contemplating his own distorted image, we discover the chalk-coated faces of the Titans, understood as the lynchers, the ritual murderers of the god. However, this discovery should not obliterate the sense of mediatory reversibility, of objectual redemption whose threshold and price are shown by the Titanic mirror. This myth of Dionysus and the Titans also helps us determine the anthropological meaning of the more literary Narcissus myth,[104] and of what psychoanalysts call narcissism, fairly enough as long as its appearances are not taken literally, which is what Freud does though in the end through the libido of the ego he recognizes it as the phenomenon giving rise to collective identification. Behind Narcissus's mirror of water (the oldest form of mirror) there is indeed always *someone*, under the traditional disguise of the divine wrath, and, like Narcissus remaining mortally fascinated by his unrecognized face, Dionysus sees his face reduced to a mask with the mask-faces of his lynchers behind him. In both cases, the victim dies because of the bright pernicious surface that drew him to it so hypnotically. While these awful apparitions really existed in the eyes of the ancients, they also stood at the start of a path leading to salvation when the "fine appearances" of the divine world were finally revealed as true. The other toys show the consequences of these assumptions, both what was feared and what was hoped and longed for.

The golden apples of the Hesperides are linked to the mirror by their lustrous surface and derive from the same Phoenician and Canaanite mythology as the *mythos* of Eden in the book of Genesis with its desirable but forbidden fruit.[105] The apples refer to a common object on which everyone converges, either because they dispute its possession or because it is a mediatory object that can guarantee salvation. They are a recurrent symbol in Greek mythology: Eris, Strife, throws a golden apple among the three rival goddesses in the Judgment (*krisis*) of Paris. The garden of the gods where the golden apples grow lies far to the west, a symbol of death and salvation from death, while a hundred-headed dragon guards them against theft. This same *polykranos* dragon represents Dionysus in the *Bacchae*, incarnating the god as destroyer or savior depending on the outcome of his mediation.[106] It is over the possession of the apples that the "clear voice" of the Hesperides is heard to be raised, a synonym for the fascinating and deadly din of the fighting, or vice versa for the salvation attained in the farthest reaches of objectual negation.

The term *konos* indicates the spinning top here, but its primary significance in Greek is vegetal, meaning a "pinecone," a further reference to the ritual alternation of life and death. As a funerary symbol, indeed, the pinecone figures on many tombs in classical antiquity to evoke the rebirth of life from its dry, woody substance. But it is also the arboreal symbol at the top of the bacchantes' thyrsus, which appears to be originally the branch of a conifer used to strike the victim or hang him. The "revolving, rumbling toy" (*rhombos*), also called a bull-roarer or rattle, is a cult instrument found among many primitive peoples; it makes a deafening noise when whirled round and round and is the same ritual instrument used in the *Cretans* to produce the "thunder [*brontas*] of Zagreus the night wanderer."[107] Top and *rhombos* both represent the frenzied circling movement of the collective rite and the hallucinatory effects of rhythmic shouting and orgiastic music, the same delirious music of the maenads and the Curetes/Corybantes. These toys, characterized by dizzying movement and loud noise, reproduce the ritual crisis preliminary to sacrifice in which the community's mediations and objectual sphere are put in jeopardy, only to be victoriously reaffirmed after the experience of their destruction, exactly like the Orphic believer who trusted in being reborn after the fearful crossing-over through death.

The ball, with its characteristic unsteady rotary motion that transmits to anyone playing with it, is another reference to the convulsive stages preceding sacrifice. On the one hand, the circular form develops the persecutory form of the circle; on the other, however, it suggests the objectual circularity that sacrifice is intended to restore, and also therefore the circularity that links all aspects of the rite and is the visible and implicit sign of its success, an observation equally valid for all the other toys. The ball brings to mind many aspects: the competitive symbolism of the golden apple that everyone wants to reach, the unpredictable fall of the dice and the resulting choice of the victim, the reversibility of death and destruction given material form by its spherical surface, and, finally, the entire globe of heaven and earth indicated by the word σφαῖρα. Besides, in a sacrificial context like the ancient world, the ball's wealth of macabre symbolism could not fail to impress: it is the head of the victim, *pars pro toto* par excellence, and like the severed head of Orpheus that goes on singing (another motif of Phoenician origin[108]), it contains the power of the victim, an audible and visual symbol, linked to the further *pars* of the mask, which becomes the mediatory form through which to conceive and interpret the world. The same form, though with modern symbolic inversion, is recalled in Bataille's *Acéphale*. In the case of Greek Orphism, the singing head of Orpheus represents the *logos* of salvation that has prevailed over death, and confirms the power of his poetic *hieroi logoi* over the forces of the afterlife. The journey into the underworld made by the divine singer while still alive, in his unsuccessful bid to rescue Eurydice, is a dramatic anticipation of a longer journey that must pass through the Dionysian violence of dismemberment to reach its goal.

The Orphic toy of the *sphaira* also provides the occasion for a brief comparative digression confirming its ritual significance. Our modern ball games descend distantly from rites of decapitation; the capital act of scoring is a distant but still structurally recognizable transformation of the act of beheading and is a good omen, a benediction, like killing a victim or enemy. The Maya and Aztec ball game was spectacular in character, halfway between sacrificial rites and modern ball games, and it was extremely difficult to make a score, but when one did, one or more players of the losing team were offered in sacrifice to the divinity, usually by decapitation.[109] This beheading ensured the regular evolution of the solar cycle and the stability of the cosmos in its circling movement, while any player facing death in fearless fashion was commemorated as an example of heroic devotion worthy to be identified with and confirming the mediatory pillars of the community and universe. In the *Bacchae*, the ludic-sacrificial sense of the Greek *sphaira* is evoked in the scene of the maenads "whose bloody / hands played ball [*diesphairize*] with the shreds [*sarka*] of Pentheus."[110] Quite clearly the ritual cultic behavior underlying this scene is no literary invention of Euripides.

The dice and astragali refer to divination rites, the origin of our games of chance, and ritually correspond to the random, fatal choice of the sacrificial victim on which Girard insists. However, we must on no account overlook the creative force, the magic dynamism of concentration and transformation, and their being present together here. In Orphism the motif of chance is closely bound up with the motif of necessity and relates to the double bond of contingency and cogency, to chance that determines destiny and so becomes the law of the world.[111] Tyche, Fortune, implies Ananke, Necessity, to which the running knot of the labyrinth corresponds, the Moira that distributes the parts of the victim and before anything else assigns the first part, the part of the victim himself, in itself endowed with mediatory and distributive power to make it possible to distinguish and recognize the various parts of the world and provide the community with coordinates to give it direction and reassurance. These aspects are condensed in the Orphic image of the divine child at play, a metaphor in which innocence coincides with violence, the fortuitousness of the premises with the compelling necessity of the results. The helpless victim becomes the executioner, his childlike unconsciousness becomes inscrutable will, and the presence together of these opposites confirms the victim's power of divine mediation, as appears clearly in one of Heraclitus's most evocative and controversial fragments, the fragment about the rule of Αἰών (literally age or eon), a matter of casting dice:

> The age [*aion*] is a child [*pais*] at play [*paizon*] casting dice on a checkerboard [*pesseuon*]: of a child [*paidos*] is the realm.[112]

In the Greek of the period *aion* referred to a human life-span,[113] and so the immediate meaning here appears to be that individual existence is puerile. However, such a reading by itself is still partial and subjectivist since it takes no account of the religious and symbolic context of this saying. The Orphic source of the image helps us understand that for Heraclitus the life of the individual obeyed a more profound law that comes to be embodied in the fascinating, elusive figure of the divine child.[114] *Pesseuein* has a deliberate expressive nuance following *paizein*—to play in the simplest sense—and means to play at *pessoi*, often mistranslated as "chess" or "draughts" but in fact a game similar to backgammon where dice or astragali are thrown and the player then makes his move, perfectly blending chance and skill, luck and calculation. Men in respect to the gods are like children in respect to adults, absorbed as they are in their childish games, but this piece of knowledge allows us to stand the initial metaphor on its head since, on a higher plane, men are themselves the playthings of the divine child who combines accident and necessity in their lives, and thereby displays the dynamic structure of the whole universe in the causal organization typical of destiny and sacrifice. The sacrificial background of the Orphic symbol emerges from many other Heraclitean fragments where the inexorable laws of Fire, including lightning and Polemos (War), replace ritual sacrifices, now partly surpassed and integrated into Heraclitus's new conception, which can explain the paradox of the One and the Many without bloodshed, while the interpretation offered by the Dionysian rituals of dismembering/re-membering was still savagely bloody.[115]

Besides being indebted to Anaximander and Xenophanes, Heraclitus's theological ideas show evident signs of Zoroastrian influences,[116] and in the vision of the divine One, they present us with an excellent early example of the effectiveness of Greek philosophy in achieving unity in the theological field. The divine One reconciles opposites in itself and maintains them in the tensional unity of the universal *Logos*, its *complexio oppositorum*, which is also exemplified by the fragment set as the epigraph to this Intermezzo. Orphic knowledge never reaches these levels of theological-cosmic conceptualization, but it prepares them and then interacts strongly with them, as we can see in the fourth-century Derveni papyrus where Heraclitus and Parmenides are both utilized in its own magical-soteriological vision.[117] The reference in the Gurob papyrus to "ONLY ONE DIONYSUS" (εἷς Διόνυσος) is to be attributed to a tendency analogous to that of Heraclitus: though this *heis* (one) is not the *monos* of monotheism and reveals a different evolution, holding together the plurality of the divine and its overall, composite unity by ritual means.

The flexible dolls, also mentioned by Herodotus,[118] show us the result of the divine child's throw of the dice: they are counterparts to the dolls representing Artemis that are hanged with Ananke's knot or, in more refined rites, simply swung to and fro. The use of these ritual dolls is most intriguing because it ties in with their continuing use in puppet theater today; this theatrical use already existed in ancient Greece, but we know little about the exact form it took. Theater originates as a representational development of the representation of sacrifice, a development only possible if a sequence or segment, no matter which, of the act of sacrifice remains subject to a ban, thereby permitting the other sequences to be represented. In Greek tragedy, neither violent action nor its immediate result, dead bodies, can be shown, nor the faces of the victims and perpetrators of violence. In puppet theater, on the other hand, the actors are not physically present on stage, but a puppeteer remains behind the scenes playing and pulling the strings, and so it becomes possible to represent violence because its real substratum has been removed; a different resonance of meaning is produced because the puppet on its string comes to represent human existence that is made possible and moved by mediatory and sacrificial forces in a similar way to an automaton. Plato develops this metaphor quite extraordinarily: he imagines a man-puppet open to being pulled by divine mediations consubstantial with it or, contrariwise, by ineffectual human mediations, human in the other-directed, degrading sense of uncontrolled passions.[119]

And lastly the fleece, representing the skin of the victim, refers to the final part of the rite, the sacrificial metamorphosis that is the rebirth of the sacrificed animal, corresponding to the rebirth of the human victim in more archaic rites. The ritual victim was normally flayed, and his skin was one of the divine parts assigned to the priest.[120] Since the skin covers the whole body, it evokes the totality of the victim in a real way, and to don the victim's skin was to change one's nature by magic mimetism: to get inside the god's skin, as the Aztec priests did, was to *be* the god, to resurrect him. This significance of the skin, its power to metamorphose and transform, is at the origin of the aegis, the mythical shield of Zeus and Athena, of Dionysus's *nebris* of doeskin and of all the half-animal, half-human figures in which Greek mythology abounds.

Sacrificial metamorphosis by means of the skin shows us humankind's most primitive form of objective and objectual possession as total *physical* possession of one's *obiectum*; this principle is at the root of cannibalism, ritual disguise, and later theatrical disguise. Here we can discern the archaic evolution of the mask as a physical object related to the skin and the head.[121] Uniting both aspects, the skull was adopted in religious and ritual contexts for how it appears to us, that is, as a mask: the bones within the head are, as it were, turned inside out to become a facial skin, monstrous and revealing. The evidence of prehistoric finds proves the cult of the skull to be one of the most ancient, with the skull frequently sucked clean in anthropophagic rites; while in classical religious art and architecture the representation of an ox skull, the bucrania, is a frequently found motif. The use of a skin held on sticks or a head stuck on a pole are to be linked to this set of symbols; the head becomes the Dionysian mask hanging from a pole, or from Agave's thyrsus. Just as the skin is the *outer* mask, so the flayed and scoured skull is the *inner* mask revealing the hidden but nonetheless real stratum of what we are when alive, an argument extendable to the skeleton as a whole but without sending out the macabre message we think of. The secret of skulls and skeletons lies in the sacral almost theatrical reversibility that they document: the living man changes into his bones, but just as the performer's ritual, theatrical disguise is the precondition for a return to normality, so do the bones of the dead promise the symmetrical countertransformation of a return to life. The Mazdaist resurrection was linked magically to the conservation of the bones of the dead, free from the uncleanness of putrefied flesh and ready to be reborn in a definitive intermedial body;[122] and the Middle-Judaic idea of resurrection gave a similar value to the bones, a belief suggesting once again a direct or indirect influence from Iranian religion.[123] A further trace of this value for resurrection is to be seen in the importance given by the Gospels to a detail in the Crucifixion: the fact that Christ died before it became absolutely essential for the Roman soldiers to hasten death by breaking his legs in order to avoid desecrating the Passover by the exposure of a corpse. However, it ought to be added that the manner and significance of Christ's resurrection, involving the full objectual circularity of a person elevated to a definitive relational life, also sets it apart from these magical-intermedial assumptions.

In the ancient world the corporeal symbolism of the mask, linked to the head and the anatomical skin/skeleton complex, cannot be separated from the sacrificial actions that give it magical and apotropaic powers. All these aspects are brought together in the most spectacular way in the Greek symbol of the head of the Medusa, the mask-monster killed by Perseus with the aid of a mirror or by using Athena's shield as a mirror. After cutting off the Gorgon's head, Athena fixes this head-mask to her shield, while in another version of the myth she flays the Gorgon and makes the aegis from its skin.[124] The Medusa's victims are turned to stone because they are transformed like her into the skull-mask of the sacrificial rite, petrified into skeletons and skulls. This, however, is the prerequisite for the victorious mediation of Athena, the daughter of Zeus, and for the objectual triumph of Perseus, the hero who saves men from the petrifying stare of Thanatos.

The masks of his toys help us to understand the mask-god Dionysus in his various appearances. Dionysus is Proteus, the god of metamorphosis, of the incessant, universal, sacrificial transfiguration. One of the many versions of his Titanic death tells how Dionysus tries to escape from the Titans through a series of transformations but is eventually torn to pieces in a final Cretan manifestation as a bull.[125] His mask is a symbol of limitless multiplicity, horizontally in the thousand assumed forms and vertically in the continual superimposing of one mask on another.[126] At each throw of the dice, Dionysus, mirror-god of the Manifold that becomes One, shows us a new face. This is because he always obeys the same law, the law of sacrificial plasticity, coming to its highest pitch in him and producing kaleidoscopic bloodshed, very similar to the Hindu gods, Prajapati in particular. By the same token, this law attests to the saving principle of divine reversibility, of life and death as interchangeable, the guarantee of their reversal in mankind's favor. There is no difference in the archaic nature of Yahweh, god of the dead, of hierogamy and the *molk*; these vestiges recede into cultual prehistory only after lengthy vicissitudes, and when Yahweh is finally transformed into a relational god of love; he is, however, himself the medium of sacrifice, only he gives it completely objectual value. This unifying, redeeming outcome can only be understood if we grasp the preceding ritual and metamorphic plurality, and what makes clear that reciprocal relationship and its ruling purpose is the Greek vision, ritual rather than conceptual, of the One and the Many.

The thousand masks of Dionysus conceal the masks of the Curetes/Titans, and they in their turn, like all other group-divinity disguises, are masks of the collective origin and bring up to date a drama annulling objectual significance because its business is to restore it. Orphism teaches that humankind arose from the ashes of the Titans/Curetes and can only find salvation through remembering and reliving their drama, in a cognitive impulse to which the present inquiry cannot be said to be, nor would wish to be, extraneous. The function of these collective *daimones* is the same as that of the original men, the autochthons, those born from the Earth, often associated with metalworking and found in many places in Greece. In *The Scapegoat* Girard describes their indiscriminate violence as characteristic, a symmetrical multiplication of the doubles that leads to their self-destruction. They are the Spartoi (the "Sown"), the warriors that sprang from the dragon's teeth sown by Cadmus at Thebes just after he had slain the beast, symbolizing for Girard the mimetic violence that is immediately regenerated as the *draco redivivus* of the warriors who set about killing each other.[127] And in fact, one of the five surviving Spartoi, Echion, is the father of Pentheus, the man of dragon stock killed by the bacchantes, by the fawns that play on the green meadows of Cithaeron (ll. 866 ff.).

All this throws light on an area usually cast in shadow but does so at the price of plunging the brightest area, the essential area for the Greeks, into darkness: the light of divine salvation that, even when the outcome of the divine *drama* is unfavorable, is the light of representational, conscious, and axiological redemption as in the Athenian *drama*. This cognitive, moral, and artistic salvation, though incomplete and tragically defeated, and indeed precisely *because* it is incomplete and defeated, stands in a necessary relationship to total saving redemption; without the previous experience of its absence it would have remained unattainable, just as monotheism would have remained inconceivable without the historical proof of the inadequacy of the plurality of divinities in the face of the human drama of suffering and defeat.

At this point, if we are to progress beyond generic historical and philosophical considerations and avoid falling into the ever-present trap of anachronism, the question inevitably arises as to the precise nature of the knowledge that these symbols represented for Orphism. It goes without saying that Orphic thinking in itself did not conform to philosophy's highly differentiated speculative criteria, so it could not reason in the anthropological and historical terms made evident throughout this analysis. The order in which the toys are listed does not reflect the sequence of the ritual cycle as it might be set out in a modern descriptive approach; instead, the various stages are interlaced into a single vision that must have been effective above all as liturgy and magic, while the reciprocal linking together of all elements in the vision, their circular reversibility, is the determining factor, the condition, for the success of the rite. Here, in a word, is a ritual procedure showing us the performative equivalent of the philosophical procedure of the One and the Many and its religious background, without our needing even to consider the phenomenon of philosophy's actual interaction with Orphism, which surely would have been less effective than it was without more profound, antecedent affinities.

This observation is most general (which is not to say generic) and does not enter into the question of content, which has often been lost, and would, in any case, require a separate inquiry; nonetheless it helps us to understand the performative and cognitive ambit of such cults. The theurgic power they display, far from excluding the cognitive aspect, actually contained it within itself, since all knowledge came from it, the knowledge that described its mythological causes and salvation-working effects. This type of knowledge was a distant ancestor of our own; in the case of Orphism, it fitted into the context of a great civilization, interacted with it, contributing its Titanic knowledge of which the toys of Dionysus were the initiatory *symbolon*. The items listed and their order may vary, but what remains unchanged is their significance as an intuitive, experiential representation of sacrificial mediation and what it makes possible to achieve in a living experience of how the paradox of the One and the Many functions and becomes a means of salvation. In their magical-ritual way the Orphics comprehend (Latin *com-prehendere*, to grasp altogether) that only by recapitulating the various aspects and moments of the passion of Dionysus can they relive it and so be saved through it. Dionysus's toys therefore come to sum up and fulfill the spiritual quest and yearning for salvation already seen in the Gurob papyrus. At the beginning of the Homeric *Hymn to Demeter* composed under an unmistakable Eleusinian influence, the narcissus plucked by Persephone when Hades abducts her is described as "the lovely toy [*athyrma*]" (l. 16),[128] a toy, then, that concentrates in itself not only the sacrificial meaning of the funeral hierogamy but also the initial act of the Mystery drama that transforms it into individual salvation. And of a similar nature must have been the long-awaited salvation connected with the ancient Yahwistic cult.

These remarks confirm that the quest for objectual salvation is a need immanent in Dionysian and Orphic mediation even if it takes the form of a mediation that never achieves complete humanization, never becomes a human object revealed in all its historicity as happens in mature Judaism and in Christianity. In any case, sacrifice is no obstacle to this objectual quest but is its source and intermediary. The real question, then, is something else: the completeness or not of the objectual conquests permitted by a sacrificial mediation, the extent and depth of the objectual world—which is to say the human world—that it opens up; and here there are significant differences between one religion and another, one culture and another, one epoch and another, differences that become more significant the more they belong to a common background, to combined and stratified influences. Every collective mediation is instrumental in defining the world, causing a community's experiences and history to interact with its environment and with the critical situations that it has to face. The results of such complex interaction can be highly diverse and represent very different degrees of objectual realization.

The example of the Mesoamerican civilizations with their sacrificial hypertrophy is highly significant. Their overriding concern to ensure the daily course of the sun and the regular functioning of the universe compelled these cultures to make human sacrifices on a daily basis; this reached its apex in the carnage of the Aztec Empire, continually driven to fight wars of conquest mainly for this purpose. Dependence on human sacrifice caused the Mayan civilization to implode when a severe crisis in agriculture brought the economy to its knees and the cities proved unable to respond; as a consequence, they were simply abandoned, their inhabitants reverting to the old subsistence way of life in the forest. The collapse of the Aztec civilization occurred with extreme rapidity not only because of technological shortcomings but also, if not primarily, because the subjected peoples rebelled against the constant demand for human lives to feed their rulers' huge sacrificial machinery. On the other side of the sacrificial spectrum, Manichaeism provides another particularly interesting example. It was conceived by its founder Mani as a real universal religion, with teachings drawn from Judaism, Christianity, and even Buddhism, as well as from Mazdaism.[129] Such an ambitious theology, superior even to Christianity in certain universalistic aspects, came to grief, however, on account of its extreme dualism between the forces of good and evil, albeit always understood in a hierarchically axiological sense, and its blanket condemnation of violence against all living creatures including even those used as food. The resulting sacramental organization was highly complicated: the perfect adherents, the elect, could only eat food prepared by auditors or catechumens, the still imperfect followers, to whom they had to grant absolution.[130] The repercussions on social and political life of such a drastic religious mediation were extremely serious and led to Manichaeism being banned wherever it spread—from the Sassanid and Roman empires as far as China—and it died out completely in the space of some centuries.[131]

In this perspective, Christianity, building on Israel's turbulent history and theological development, extended the boundaries and horizon of the objectual sphere in the ancient world thanks to the emancipation from sacrifice that it assured, its relative freedom from ritualistic and legalistic excesses, its emancipation from ties of an ethnic or national order, and its very different concern for the weak and the downtrodden which had no parallel in Greco-Roman society. There was therefore an advance in objectuality that we shall have to evaluate, but its progress can already be traced within Greek culture, including its critical thresholds and creative responses: the *polis* religion and its collectivism are inadequate, indifferent to the fate of the individual and society's outcasts, while Orphism develops its soteriological mediation, open to individuals and those excluded from participating in the *polis*. And then, following the discoveries of poetic knowledge, we have the critical response of tragedy, especially from Euripides who objects to the ritual limitations of Orphism, its bigotry bereft of an autonomous moral dimension, and its lack of a real answer to the problems of disorder and violence. Euripides thus gained a sapiential perspective giving him freedom and independence from which he derived a highly original religious and spiritual position, but it was aimed at a small intellectual minority, like the philosophy of Socrates and Plato, and never found its way for becoming a historical reality. Hellenic civilization presents a variety of conflicting religious and sapiential mediations, evincing the fact that the problem of their objectual fulfillment remained unsolved in spite of extraordinary achievements in the cognitive field. And our conclusion, unusual but no less consequential for all that, must be that the most thorough and searching development of this debate occurs when Greek culture is absorbed by Judaic culture, giving rise to the Christian response, fraught with fresh difficulties but also with pertinent solutions that Christianity carried in itself over and above any historical perceptions of its individual exponents. This is the background, no less powerful for being hidden, against which the civilization of Rome, strong in its universal super-mediation capable of absorbing all mediations, runs up against the Christian alternative in a critical confrontation pregnant with developments for the future.

We have now gained a wealth of historic-cultural data about the struggle between Christianity and paganism, including a comparison of the nascent religion with its formative matrix in Middle Judaism, and enhanced moreover by the eventful history of the formation of Judaic henotheism and its monotheistic developments. It is time now to approach the theme from another viewpoint deeper within Christianity in order to complete our exploration of the main religious and sapiential mediations of the Roman and Hellenistic worlds, before we come to the second volume, which is primarily devoted to the Christian mediation. To this end, Clement, with his Hellenic culture and his markedly comparative spirit, will once again prove invaluable, but it is Origen who provides us with the appropriate framework. By updating Christian thinking by bringing it in line with the criteria of the more sophisticated Middle Platonism, his theological genius laid the foundations for the future, while his impressive exegetical commentary on the Bible gives the initial impulse to an independently Christian vision of human history understood as the history of salvation. Such a survey of the earliest patristic writings in Greek will be the subject of the next chapter, which will conclude our analysis of the toys of Dionysus, and so bring this historical Intermezzo to a close.

10.

The Comparative Question between Judaism and Christianity

1. Comparison with Paganism in Origen and Clement

To proceed with our examination of the dense web of interconnections among Greece, Rome, Judaism, and Christianity, we shall almost have to undo our work so far since we must now regain the protagonists' perception of the religious questions that they themselves at the time considered to be most urgent and vital; this is a perspective that we need to have quite clear if we are to obtain an adequate vision of events. What we have learned in reconstructing the genesis of Jewish monotheism along with its contributory influences forms part of an implicit background that was only partially understood by the actors involved, which—in the passage from Middle Judaism to the birth and development of Christianity—at once makes it necessary to distinguish between the first Christian generations, belonging for the most part to the Judaic environment and in a position to learn of circumstances that subsequently fell into oblivion, such as the murder of Zerubbabel, and later generations that came increasingly from the pagan population and knew nothing of those distant events. The distinction can be broken down into three essential phases: first, Jesus and his followers, fully participating in Middle Judaism; then those Christians who dissociated from it but were still aware of the specific reasons for the rift; and thirdly, patristic and conciliar Christianity now beginning to define its dogma. This historical and chronological division makes it possible to set out the comparative aspects according to three connected and yet distinct points of view; at the same time, it raises the correlated question as to the validity and grounds of Christianity's claim to see continuity between the three phases, a claim that it has always made. With these points in mind we will return now to Origen and *Contra Celsum*, placed at the crucial moment in time when the foundations of Christian thinking are being laid in dialogue with Greek culture and the future theological and conceptual language of the Great Church is taking shape.[1]

The Middle-Platonic writer Celsus had been completely forgotten when, in a much more advanced phase of Christian elaboration of the Platonic influence, Origen took up cudgels against him,[2] in a retrospective contest in which their different historical traditions played a crucial role,[3] and even more so, their respective philosophies of history, related to the important debate in middle antiquity on the presence and meaning of divine providence. This shared aspect emphasizes the profound difference in the mediatory contexts of the two authors and their almost opposite understanding of history. For Celsus it is a cyclical, universal process taking place in the kosmos according to the eternal laws of tradition and an impersonal divinity. For Origen it is a unique and linear drama of salvation that starts with the creation according to the plan of a personal God, a drama that embraces all humankind and the entire world as composed of single creatures and consists in the actions of individuals precisely situated in space and time. For the Middle-Platonic pagan philosopher the vicissitudes of human life are subject to natural and divine laws and simply result from them; for the Church Father human history reveals the true meaning of God and subordinates to itself the entire cosmic-natural sphere, which functions as a symbol and test course for man's relationship to God. A *kosmos* exists for Origen as well, replete with various entities—intermedial, astral, angelic, and demonic—and with influences that must be directed toward salvation or perdition; the determining factor, however, is the relationship with a personal God that is realized within the history of creation and through the individual process of free moral acceptance of God's mediation. The total duration of the *kosmos*—corresponding to the concept of *aion* that, in Origen, often indicates the time span of a creature or a cycle of creatures[4]—has its beginning and end decreed by God and so is rightfully part of the history of salvation, though it cannot be said that Origen's sense of history is like our own: it is theologically oriented and includes all spiritual, pneumatic (with the transitive ambiguity of *pneuma*) beings capable of obeying or rebelling against God; even the very stars are endowed with superior intelligence, as they were for most ancient philosophers, and are an object of Christ's redemptive action as well,[5] while the cosmic *aion* itself is subdivided into an unspecified number of eons. Nevertheless, the direction is indicated, and can be clearly traced from the start of the apologia, though the differences from our modern mentality are considerable: they situate Origen firmly in the ancient world, and it would be a serious anachronism to ignore them.

Following the same order as Celsus, Origen begins his attack by contrasting the new "barbaric doctrine" with the Roman idea of law, and then at once extends it to the contrast with the Greek model of philosophical rationality. The basis of his argument is the miraculous power of this "barbaric doctrine" that first manifested itself in Jesus and then spread far and wide, overcoming countless obstacles on the way:

> As regards the Christians, on the other hand, both the Senate and, at certain moments, the emperors, and the army, and the people, and even the relations of those embracing the faith, fought openly against the Word [*logo*], and with an attack by such powerful forces they would certainly have stopped it spreading further had not its divine power [*theia dynamei*] enabled it to grow and so widely prevail as to conquer the whole world [*holon kosmon*] that had conspired against it.[6]

This "divine power" is not the result of some external thaumaturgy but corresponds to a new, overwhelming mediation now making its appearance in history,[7] and subordinating all the opposing forces of the previous *oikonomia*, the old mediatory regime. On this premise Origen bases a series of comparisons—moral, religious, philosophical, and even magical—in which the touchstone provided by Christianity is so complete and sure that there is no difficulty in admitting the partial anticipations that paved the way for it in other cultures. Revealing in this respect are the frequent references to the power of Jesus's name, a name endowed with theurgic power in itself, presaged by the power of Abraham's name and faintly foreshadowed in the divine names adopted by pagan cults.[8] Christianity is the decisive divine mediation that surpasses and subsumes in itself all the other ritual and magical mediations, emptying out from within, as it were, even the politico-sacral mediations of Roman power. This manifestation, which originates outside history but is realized within it, provides a different criterion for its interpretation and makes it possible to recognize the human mechanisms of force and power for what they are; it lays them bare in the sense that it deprives them of the mediatory efficacy that was the source of their previous ascendancy and authority. The advent of Christ's doctrine is both a metaphysical irruption and a revolutionary, spiritually subversive, historical dynamic:

> From the beginning, indeed, everything conspired against the spread of his doctrine [*logon*] throughout the world: emperors in different periods, their generals and army commanders—in a word anybody with any authority, as well as all the city governors, the soldiers and populations.[9]

Origen's perspective shows us the right approach for interpreting the other Christian texts that we shall be concerned with: there is no anthropological process to be brought to light since for Origen—as for all Christians in the early centuries, though the situation was to remain unchanged in the following centuries—no anthropological and immanent plan exists distinct from and independent of God's creational plan and the evil, subordinate plan of the supernatural agents that rebelled against him. The one factor that counts is the true revelation of God, which leads to exposing the demonic forces opposing it and at last opens up a space for humankind to exercise free choice, consequently designating those who refuse the evidence of the truth to be historical agents of the antiobjectual forces of evil. This also results in a clear sense of superiority over the great wisdom of the Greeks, much admired by Origen nonetheless:

> A carefully considered examination of the conduct of Jesus's apostles shows that their success in teaching Christianity [*ton christianismon*] and making men submit to the word [*logo*] of God could only have come from a divine power [*dynamei theia*] because there was no power of eloquence in

> themselves, no ability to set out an argument applying the skills of dialectic or Greek rhetoric to win over the listeners.[10]

This attitude is very different from the approach of Clement who, in order to persuade men of the truth of the Christian religion, adopted the philosophical precepts, rhetoric, and forms of argument that appealed to a cultivated pagan public. But Origen's aim is not to justify the uncultivated style of Hebrew and Christian scripture; instead, he gives it a contrary significance: not a mark of cultural inferiority but a sign of spiritual superiority, of divine election, for the same reasons that social and political inferiority becomes a sign of the omnipotence of God in the scriptural revelation through the weak and gentle person of Christ who proclaims it. His mediation subverts the previous systems of mediation from the center, setting in their place the authentic divine providence (*pronoia*, as both foresight and foreknowledge, and *oikonomia* as skillful management[11]) capable of transforming human impediments into driving forces and exploiting the world power of Rome as an unconscious means to spread the Word. Indeed, the propagation of the Christian religion could never have taken place in a divided world like that of classical Greece:

> The existence of many kingdoms would have seriously hindered the spread of Jesus's teachings throughout the inhabited world [*oikoumenen*]; . . . besides, men would have had to wage war and fight for their homelands, which was the case before Augustus's time and even earlier when need arose, as with the war between the Peloponnesians and Athenians, and other conflicts of the sort involving one nation against the others [*heteron pros heterous*].[12]

In contrast to the general disesteem of the material world and its history, characteristic of much of the age's spirituality and, more dangerous for Christianity, of Gnosticism too, this passage reflects a basic theme in Origen's idea of providence. For him, it is an axiom that God does not just act "upon" the world, to make it function according to his rational laws (general providence) but intervenes within the world to foster the characteristics and constitution proper to his creatures, and so gives them the possibility of freedom of choice (individual providence).[13] Christian *pronoia* does not consist in simply surmounting material reality but rather in its full objectual realization; and what guarantees and fulfils this is Christ's resurrection, conceived by Origen as access to an intermedial, pneumatic reality besides, definitively in harmony with the spiritual, incorporeal sphere. His inspiration here comes from Paul, but according to a metaphysical-cosmic register that reinterprets Middle-Platonic themes by applying them to the revelation contained in the scriptures in order to express and define it better. This is something that he could not have done—as we are now in a position to say—if interaction with the Greek philosophical tradition, above all the Platonic school, had not played a decisive part in composing many books in the Old Testament.

This cultural revision, carried out in several stages, leads to a new synthesis, the prelude to future developments in doctrine and religion. Origen sets Christianity on an equal footing with the great pagan culture, to confront and challenge its capacity to respond to the spiritual crisis in the ancient world that had increased massively in the wake of the politico-military upheavals suffered by the empire in the third century. In earlier times the Roman civil wars confirmed and gave fresh impetus to the might of the *res publica*, but now the internal power struggles add weight to the continual pressure on the frontiers, so that there is a real danger of division or defection by large parts of the Roman dominions. Particularism threatens to get the upper hand of the previous universalism that was not so much the deliberate result of something specific as a driving force that nothing and nobody could stop; and the secret of Roman mediation lay precisely in its capacity to represent and achieve a whole, in its unfailing control of the dialectic between interior and exterior, between civilization and barbarism. In the third century this security begins to crumble and the Christian mediation emerges as an alternative, having already given pagan culture cause for concern in the preceding century, as the writing of Celsus shows. As the Christian alternative becomes an authentic cultural challenge, the pagan Middle-Platonic philosophy sees a period of renewal by way of response with the Neoplatonism of Plotinus and his pupil Porphyry whose line of attack follows Celsus but with better-informed and better-founded subtlety where Celsus had been still partly misinformed and imprecise,[14] and obviously unaware of the profound interaction between the Greek philosophy he upheld and the Bible vision he despised. The climate now is one of all-out ideological and political conflict, with Christianity eventually emerging as triumphant in the fourth century, an epoch-making reversal, the Christians coming to occupy the place and functions of Roman power and renewing its glories, on the theological level, with the clashes over definition of Christological and Trinitarian dogmas, and with the subsequent proclamations of theological truths, increasingly solemn and consolidated, up to the *imperium sine fine* as implied by their transcendent, inviolable definitions.

Christianity's replacing of the *imperium Romanum* is still very little understood; for one thing, there is misunderstanding of the Roman mediation with the originality of its revision and expansion astonishingly underrated, and a leveling-down of the Christian mediation to its simple religious specificity, thereby underrating its overall impact on ancient civilization. The transition associated with Constantine and his acceptance of legal status for the Christian cult in the Edict of Milan in 313 plants the seeds of things to come in the pervasiveness with which Christianity inherits and resemanticizes Roman universalism,[15] even so far as to repeat its history to a certain degree. In the fourth and fifth centuries the civil wars that had produced the principate and the empire, cyclically marking their history, are transformed into metaphysical wars since metaphysics is now the battlefield to decide the mediations of the future, and the cultural potential springing from the victorious religious mediation is fully displayed in the Christological disputes, though the price paid is to detach that potential from the decadence of the real historical context and concentrate instead, by way of reaction, on the transcendent. The mark of this imprinting on Christianity is particularly strong in the East, where the continuance of the Roman Empire reinforces the metaphysical, ascensional impulse that takes the Greek genius for philosophy into the vertical dimension of theology and mysticism and leaves the governing of the earthly *physis* to an empire at any rate willed by God. In the West, on the other hand, because of the collapse of the imperial institutions, the church has to concern itself with worldly affairs; there develops a Christian mentality having a different awareness of history and society, and an unprecedented fusion takes place between the spiritual universalism of the gospel message, in which the highest aspirations of Judaism influenced by its experience of Persian and Hellenistic culture find expression, and the earthy, earthly universalism of Roman power with its rational approach to law and organization and its ruling sense of preciseness. In this mingling of civilizations, the Hellenic element is latent, an undercurrent but nonetheless incisive, and it is no accident that it finds its most mature, Christianly classical, expression in the thirteenth century when the West rediscovers Greece with Aristotle, making possible the spiritual universalism of Thomas Aquinas and Dante. Eric Voegelin, a philosopher with much knowledge of civilizations, has fully grasped the classic-Christian character of the thought of Aquinas and its miraculous but equally delicate equilibrium between tradition and modernity (*modernus* is after all a medieval concept!), which was to be destroyed by the modern age,[16] while Voegelin missed seeing that same equilibrium in Dante since he did not grasp the core of the religious vision of the *Divine Comedy*.[17]

Obviously this all refers to later times when Christianity had emerged as the clear winner. If we are to learn more about its initial development when the final outcome was by no means a foregone conclusion, we must go back beyond Origen, back to Clement, to a stage when the terms of comparison are still fluid and undergoing definition, so as to leave open various possibilities and remain close to the great pagan culture, though this proximity was not to last, seeing that more diversified and selective attitudes came to predominate in early Christianity. We thus retrace certain underlying themes of Christian mediation that can be summed up in the paradoxical nature of the Eucharist, difficult to classify. Our greater knowledge of the facts can then be brought to bear on the main points of Origen's apologetic to check its essential consistency with the original gospel message, a verification of no little importance in view of the claim always made by orthodox Christianity, that is, by self-defining institutions of the church, against any deviation classed as "heretical," the claim to represent an innovative and alternative tradition, faithfully handed-down, in which continuity predominates, at least qualitatively, over discontinuity. Our present inquiry will also be able to show up "shadowy areas" in the tradition, neglected or unclear aspects that represent so many margins for potential doctrinal development as well as for possible dialogue with other traditions.

One of the reasons for interest in Clement of Alexandria is his knowledge of the prestigious pagan culture, especially the Greek in which he was deeply read as is evident from his use of Greek literary and rhetorical forms. Traditionally exhortative works with the title of *Protrepticus* had educational and philosophical purposes: the best-known example is Aristotle's,[18] and this was the eloquent model for all these early Christian treatises, more so for Clement who appears to be well acquainted with Aristotelian philosophy.[19] Thanks to his knowledge, Clement develops and differentiates Justin's aim to exhort to Christianity by annexing the best parts of Hellenic culture and utilizing them against paganism with the argument that they anticipated Christianity though remaining insufficient compared to Christ's revelation.[20] This is an eloquent sign that the writer is still thinking within the cultural parameters of antiquity, Christ's message being the means to achieve its salvation and final fulfillment. Looked at another way, from the aspect of Christian opposition to the classical heritage, there is a contrary wavering hostility that rejects everything because it lacks criteria of selection and accepts no compromise in its need to assert itself, finding refuge in eschatological expectations that express a yearning for the final advent of the Christic mediation to which nothing actually appeared to respond in the real world. In this work Clement displays mastery of a different kind, even if a certain urge toward *captatio benevolentiae* results from the influence of the literary genres used. However, this does not mean that his achievement results from syncretism or forced annexations: what emerges here is an alternative way of reading that alters the parameters of the classical mentality from within.

In other words, this is no improvisation; Clement's sureness in identifying the two figures closest to Christ's message is quite striking: Plato, whose philosophy is the main source of inspiration for the new religion in organizing its theology conceptually and is fully justified as such from a historical viewpoint; and Euripides, "who had eyes for the truth alone and despised the audience,"[21] a penetrating definition of the cognitive research carried out by this Athenian playwright in his hard-hitting provocative tragedies. These two intellectuals possessed the greatest mediatory and spiritual awareness in pre-Christian antiquity, and it is remarkable how Clement's findings converge to some extent with the present inquiry, conducted according to modern interpretive criteria. His reflections could be neither so fully articulated nor so detached, just as his conclusion is disarmingly simple and patently infringes on the methodology that a modern scholar is bound to follow in writing history: if Euripides and Plato had known Christ, he concludes, they would undoubtedly have become Christians! And as if that were not enough, these retrospective conversions include what are for us imaginary figures but for Clement evidently still contained an element of truth, not only symbolic but also intermedial, and able to be taken for the real world as represented both ontologically and morally. Even Pentheus would have been saved if only he had had the chance to listen to the words of Christ! Particularly striking after our analyses of the *Bacchae* is his quotation of the passage where the king of Thebes is finally in the throes of doubles hallucinations:

> "Truly I seem to see two suns and two Thebeses" someone said, seeing ghosts [*eidolois*] in his bacchic frenzy, drunk with complete ignorance: I feel pity for him because he is drunk and I would call on him, while he is in this foolish state, to wise salvation, for the Lord welcomes a sinner's repentance and not his death.[22]

This has nothing to do with what we understand by dramatic and literary criticism; in the final analysis Clement agrees with all the Church Fathers in their constant, irrevocable rejection of the theater, considering that the *Protrepticus* only transposes the same intermedial realism in a parenetic key. However, besides giving us a more contextual view of the real tenor of theater in antiquity, the ontological inversion in the Christian attitude induces a stimulating reversal of the critical unrealism on which we pride ourselves; it poses a question that our formalism chooses to ignore and sends us back to the painful convergence transmitted through Euripides's text, providing an answer that eluded the religious and cultural mediations of several centuries before. Set Clement's words beside the hellish agnition of Dionysus as a bull in the *Bacchae* and we at once recognize the changed atmosphere and tone, the objectual acquisition of humanity that has occurred. Contrasting the Christian God's love of conversion and forgiveness with the doubles of which Pentheus is the willing victim causes a theological/theatrical short-circuit that makes us almost relive the sense of audience participation in a performance of the tragedy, but deriving now from a divine mediation of a different nature, transcending the bounds of the tragic universe, an intermedial reality, as Clement sees it, in which there are *eidola* to be debunked and surpassed. For him, Euripides is great because he demystified the bacchic and theatrical *eidola* from within and showed negatively what Christianity achieves positively thanks to the wise, compassionate mediation of God that completely overturns the factors of perdition and death, all the tragedies of humanity, and makes them instrumental in salvation. The passage goes on to contrast Mount Cithaeron, "theater of tragedies," with the mount of another *logos*, no longer labyrinthine and made up of sharing in sacrifices, a *logos* that can finally provide an answer to the doubles of the tragedy, not through its ignorance of them but because it knows them. This mount, now standing in place of the bloody mountain in the *Bacchae*, is Golgotha, the place of the Crucifixion. And even Tiresias, the priest figure who in the *Protrepticus* represents the Greek wise man and his inability to give spiritually objectual answers ensuring salvation, will now be able to regain his sight without any sacrificial hierogamy. What we lose by way of distinctions, since they still lie in the future, we gain in terms of the unifying power of this synoptic vision.

Clement's intermedial and mediatory realism always keeps firmly to the religious meaning of the symbols and themes touched on, and moves in the direction of a pedagogic gradualism that is already present in Paul and reappears in Origen. The *symbola* of Dionysus and the Mysteries are not senseless, they simply no longer serve a purpose; as Clement puts it, using the image of initiation rites for adolescents that is also to be found in Paul's epistles: "you yourself will pass beyond the emptiness of custom quite spontaneously like boys who throw away their toys [*athyrmata*] once they become men."[23] Dionysus's toys must certainly be cast aside, but only after a spiritual growth that has been nurtured by them. Immediately following the passage quoted Clement refers to Eleusinian Mysteries in which the Christian God will act as hierophant for man and the bacchanals of the real Mysteries will be celebrated;[24] we can appreciate the pertinence of this image if we think of the Dionysian elements in the Yahwistic cult, though in all likelihood Clement had no knowledge of them. His thinking here is already moving toward what Origen develops as a divine mediation that manifests itself in history and helps to bring out the most deeply hidden potential of its inner characteristics.

Clement's idea, along with other Christian apologists such as Justin, is to extract what was spiritually valid from paganism and exploit its mediatory energy, releasing it from the violent elements and implications holding it back. At the same time, there is no independent cognitive and historical approach available to Clement; he lacks the information that results from modern historiography's attempt to keep clear of denominational concerns, and reaches no evaluation in itself as to the functioning of mediations; for him, they remain active forces to be either followed or overcome in a pitched battle, at the height of a phase of great cultural change. In other words, Christian apologetics in the early centuries, in the passages and themes that we have looked into, appears to have no answer yet to Celsus and his comparative objection. The force of his argument derives not from the speculative powers of its author but from its historical and anthropological relevance, which escapes both parties since both assume it rather than thematize it and suffer its effects in one sense or another rather than consider it with scientific detachment. We, in our turn, by assuming such detachment, are guilty of a much more insidious bias since it is detached in a very different way from the real phenomena that once provided it with content and a reason.

So far we have introduced and situated the comparative question. It is now time to look more closely at its implications, premises, and ramifications, utilizing what has emerged so far on the level of historical inquiry into classical antiquity, including not only Christianity but also the earlier Judaic component. Before we go back to Origen and the historical significance of his position, we need to deal with the assumptions and scope of the objections raised by the pagan critics, and these can be concentrated in a ritual parallel that takes us, yet again, straight to the central theme of sacrifice.

What I am referring to is the highly controversial question of the Eucharist, which we already examined in its ability to influence the Western reading of myth in connection with ritual. A discovery that relates to all this, and that will be examined in the second volume, is that there are certain lines of reflection in the Christian texts brought together in the New Testament that go beyond the more limited terms disputed by Christians and pagans when they began to clash in the second century. We are going back closer and closer to the comparison between paganism and Christianity from which we started drawing in the modern thought of the nineteenth and twentieth centuries. The difference is that we have now to approach the representative subject of the Eucharist understanding what was its strongest point in antiquity, its cultic reality and power.

2. The Crux of the Eucharist

Our wide-ranging and detailed theoretical and historical survey has almost brought us to the fine dividing-line, the point of juncture and disjuncture in comparing Dionysus and Christ, a comparison that is Nietzsche's legacy to contemporary culture. While his intention in comparing the two was to demonstrate the irrelevance of the exception represented by Christianity, Girard polemically returned to the subject to prove the contrary, the central relevance of Christianity, the truth of Christ crucified as against the falsehood of Dionysus. Just as Nietzsche's contrast served to restore unknown or neglected aspects of Greek civilization, so Girard's reply to Nietzsche undoubtedly catches something of the early Christian position with its innovative radicalism that translates as a final, radical, spiritual *renovatio*. The problem is that Girard achieves this at the expense of the real context in which Christianity took shape and spread, and he ignores, besides, the background events of Middle Judaism that differed considerably from any description that those involved at the time could, or would, have given of them. Instead, the historical facts show an absolutely intermedial and performative mentality on both sides, according to which proclaimed truths had perforce to translate into decisive experiences, to produce self-evident undeniable results and a victoriously objectual world that would prevail over all the evil forces threatening it.

This last remark about the intermedial mentality in ancient times, usually ignored by present-day commentators, has its obvious repercussions on our argument and brings us back to the Christian ritual revolution in the ancient world. The comparison between Dionysus and Christ could not have been restricted to their respective histories, their respective *mythoi*, which is what Girard does, in the final analysis, under the influence of Lévi-Strauss's structuralist textualism and his emphasis on myths. Nietzsche, it must be said, does in fact refer explicitly to the "martyrdom" (*Martyriums*) of the two divine figures,[25] and therefore to the ritual and ontological content of the two *mythoi*, but he fails to register their mediatory, fulfilling tenor, their will and capacity for objectual reconstitution albeit on analogous, opposing planes. As long as we limit ourselves to this typically modern refractoriness, the essence of the argument going on in the early Christian centuries is bound to elude us since what was at stake, for those engaged in the contest at the time, was the performative effectiveness of the religious mediations that they appealed to, their ontological reality to bring about change and salvation: in a word, their ritual and objectual force, the magic, theurgic, and sacramental power of their name. And from these comments alone it is possible to infer how far sacrifice was, in any case, an integral constitutive part of all religious debate and represented an essential element requiring to be steered in one direction or the other and not affirmed or denied abstractly on the basis of theoretical principles.

To avoid any terminological or conceptual misunderstandings that might arise from the associations of "magic," it would be well to point out that, in Christianity, the category should not be leveled down to its generic, syncretistic meaning in middle and late antiquity. Instead, it must be referred to the experience of a new performative and sacramental approach that drew its objectual force from a corresponding mediation and rejected the previous magical-ritual forms, considered regressive and antiobjectual. However, this process of differentiation was possible precisely because the contending parties still shared common ground in the transformative power of religious mediations, realized in rites, especially sacrificial rites. So we can, and should, speak of an antimagic polemic present in Christianity from the very start, continuing throughout its history, and finally influencing the antimagic rationalism of modern science;[26] but Christianity's antimagic stance originates in the one objectually effective mediation, the mediation of Christ that draws all magic power into itself and transforms it into a humanly objectual experience and a relationship of salvation with God, or rather into a sacrament. Within this framework the miracles attributed to Jesus by all four Gospels, and certainly a qualifying feature of his historical mission,[27] reveal their central position, continuing in the sacramental and liturgical acts accepted or instigated by Christ within the multifaceted ideological and religious world of Middle Judaism, which in turn must be located in the Hellenistic-Roman melting-pot whose shaping influence had been profoundly felt through both borrowings and rejections. These poorly signposted paths bring us to the watershed, to the most sensational liturgical gesture that brings us face to face with the paradoxical place of sacrifice in Christian mediation, as loathsome to the Jews as to the Romans.

The synoptic Gospels show baptism as accepted by Jesus for himself, and the fourth Gospel as actually performed by him and his disciples—so strange and untoward a detail must be regarded as historical,[28] considering besides the presence of baptism as the sacrament of admission in all Christian churches. Apart from baptism, the Gospels attribute a determining liturgical gesture to Jesus: the institution of the Eucharist or Holy Communion, which occurred during the Last Supper according to Paul (who provides the earliest *testimonium*) and the synoptics, and was announced in Christ's preaching according to John. The Eucharist is a thanksgiving in which Christ's transformed and transforming body and blood is offered to the faithful. Immediately adopted as the basic rite in all Christian communities (confirming its antiquity and historicity), this liturgical act bears an embarrassing resemblance to certain pagan ceremonies, so much so that Justin devotes a particular confutation to the resemblance, applying his theory of imitation by devils to the bread and water ritual used in initiation to Mithras[29] (a directly cultual *furtum daemonum* this time, more than a mythological *furtum Graecorum*).

However, these efforts could be inverted and applied equally to the universal *traditio* of gods and peoples that Celsus appealed to and so only underscored the pagan criticisms, and actually ended by adding fuel to the accusations of practicing a regressive and wicked ritual, seeing how very differently the Greco-Roman rituals had developed to become capable of spiritualization and symbolic interpretations judged to be incomparably more worthy and more appropriate to divinity. At the end of the third century Porphyry considered the Eucharist to be an abominable act of cannibalism, and "not just bestial and absurd [*atopon*], but more absurd than any absurdity [*atopematos pantos atopoteron*] and more beastly than the nature of any beast."[30] The principal Christian sacrament turns out to be the scandalous touchstone for all comparative assessments of other sacrificial cults, whether they are reasserted in ways considered better-founded and civil or grouped together under one general condemnation as was the case, through the influence of Greek logic, of the monotheisms competing directly with Christianity and eventually, the same logic developed more abstractly and rationalistically, of modern culture as well. The Eucharist, in a word, has always been the key argument put forward to demonstrate the sacrificial and barbarous character of Christianity. In spite of these concentric attacks, more traditional Christianity, notably the Catholic Church (together with the Greek Orthodox churches), has remained steadfast in defining the nature of the Eucharist, by stressing the real presence of Christ's flesh and blood in the species of the bread and wine, while only the Catholic Church came to uphold the medieval doctrine of transubstantiation, that the bread and wine undergo substantial change but remain the same in appearance (species). Even Martin Luther, while rejecting transubstantiation, admits consubstantiation (change but maintenance of the sensible/real substances); Ulrich Zwingli, on the other hand, already follows a symbolic interpretation based on parallelism rather than transformation that eventually comes to prevail among Protestants.[31] Protestantism's opposition to any residual magic in Christianity exercised a fundamental influence on modern rationalism, but it failed to see that the problem posed historically by magism has not vanished but shifted, since it corresponds to the problem of the objectual effectiveness of the mediations needed by mankind. Nor can theological rationalizations dodge the comparative question since it concerns the very origin of the symbolism that they use.

If the sacramental, ontological reality of transubstantiation lays itself open to the objections raised by comparatists, its similarities to many other rites become more numerous as soon as we widen the criteria, becoming even more universal than the first detractors and apologists respectively hoped and feared. Indeed, the Eucharistic species of bread and wine are found in Tiresias's hierogamy of Wet and Dry, in the mystic union of Demeter's cereals with the wine of Dionysus. Analogous rites are documented in the civilizations of the Near East, often making use of beer, a much more ancient alcoholic beverage than wine in many cultures, while fully part of this same substratum is the well-attested use and symbolism of bread and wine in Middle Judaism in a ritual and even eschatological key.[32] We can realize the size of the problem if we note an additional fact, destined to be forgotten with the passage of time though the first Christians were very probably aware of it, which is that the Dionysian-type elements formed part of the cult of Yahweh from the very start, proving its crudely sacrificial nature, and only subsequently combined with Hellenistic syncretisms that nonetheless had solid links with the liturgy of the Temple. And that is why the Bible's censures on the orgiastic and sacrificial elements in the Yahwistic religion involve *in primis* the Temple rituals, about which we know almost nothing since they proved to be in disaccord with the theological line that it was intended to make prevail. And in fact the little information filtering through mostly refers to generically deprecated pagan rites, serving as a dumping ground for what the Jews were unwilling to admit about their own religious history. This led to a purist attitude, stimulating a new line of reflection about the real nature of God and the spiritual cult appropriate to him, though we should not omit the propagandistic and manipulative ends unless we are to be satisfied with a conventional image of Judaism, as well as of Christianity, that has no place in historical inquiry although it recurs in a vast number of studies conditioned by denominational concerns.

It is easy to understand the religious repercussions of an uncritical attitude here if we recall that, in all probability, these anti-Dionysian and antiorgiastic censures inspired the hostility toward human sexuality that characterizes many books and passages in the Bible and was later taken over by the more official, institutional line in Christian doctrine. Here, too, it should be noted, this reaction brought in themes for an objectual reflection absolutely essential for our part, considering the close relationship that has always obtained between sexuality and the sacrificial sphere, confirmed by the *molk* ritual itself since the sacrifice of the firstborn, at least in early times, was accompanied by a ritual of copulation, continuing a variant of the ancient hierogamies in which the male offspring was killed.[33] The historically conditioned nature of Jewish and Christian antisexualism becomes evident, in any case, once we reflect that human sexuality's origin in sacrifice by no means signifies identity with it and, more generally, that sacrificial destruction was the very means of mediation that made possible all human achievements differing from that destruction. Jesus himself to a certain extent accepts Middle Judaism's strict rules about sex, as we shall see, but he does so on the basis of a divine mediation through which the entire objectual dimension of human love in all its various aspects can be restored, freed from the prurient, morbid trap of ritual or para-ritual eroticism. The wealth of Middle-Judaic thinking on this subject emerges clearly from such a scandalous and magnificently erotic book as the Song of Songs, written in the first century BC, influenced by Hellenistic models and yet completely original in its unprejudiced vision of sexual love as an experience capable of bringing men and women to live and understand the meaning of God's love.[34] This vision is by no means foreign to Jesus's thinking on the subject and was accepted by the most advanced Jewish and Christian thinkers, such as Aqiba and Origen,[35] in the guise of the love between God and Israel or between Jesus and his church; this is not at all a bigoted, allegorical travesty, as Garbini mistakenly believes,[36] but a transposition of the very same vision into theological and ecclesiastical terms, as confirmed by Origen's further reading of the bride of the Song of Songs as a symbol of the believer's soul.

But staying with the Eucharist, and drawing closer to the viewpoint of the earliest Christian texts, we can already say that Jesus's practice, as far as it can be traced back to him or at least to the first communities of his followers that ascribed to him the institution of the sacrament, is very different from the strictures to be found in the final form of many Bible texts. Instead, with daring simplicity, he seems to take up the Suffering Servant's sacrificial logic of expiation, with its repossession and inversion of the murder of Zerubbabel comparable to the sacrifice of the *molk*, a subject that the Epistle to the Hebrews will tell us more about. In the Eucharist, as related by Paul, the synoptics, and John, Christ identifies the bread and wine with his own body and blood, a gesture that takes over and resemanticizes the sense of the most archaic rite underlying the Passover,[37] and finds a symbolic correspondence in the religious calendric time attributed by the Gospels to the Crucifixion. The scholarly debate is not about the week days of Passion, which for all four Gospels are from Thursday to Sunday, but about the discrepancies over the precise day of Passover, Friday for the synoptics and a much more reliable Saturday for John,[38] but it is a matter of fact that the theological reading of all four evangelists see Christ's violent death as a sign of a new Passover. This strange, unprecedented Passover of blood belies every purist interpretation of the Jewish Passover and steers us toward a choice made by Jesus personally, as we shall be able to verify in the second volume.

For a critical comparatist, however, the sacramental power of Christ's choice and gesture would clearly recall the sacrificial images and practices that had greatest power in the ancient world, that is, the Dionysian or those of analogous divinities that were part and parcel of the prehistory and history of the Yahwistic cult; the resemblances are such that it is actually possible to see the Eucharist as an attempt to condense and reconcile the ancient Judaic rite with the rites of the Gentiles. The sacramental process of transubstantiation, as it was to be called in medieval theology, conserves in itself all the transfiguring intensity of the Dionysian metamorphoses in a strictly controlled but quite recognizable form. This can be verified not only in the sacrament as a whole but in both species of the Eucharist that go back to a twofold complementary symbolism of ancient origin—actually the most ancient of all if we subscribe, as I do, to Freud's hypothesis that omophagy is the sacrificial form at the scene of origin—and that in Christian communion refer to each other reciprocally as in a double, quantitative and qualitative, synecdoche that is strictly unitary in each of its parts. In its present form the symbolism of the Eucharist presupposes the discovery of agriculture and goes back to the Neolithic period, but it actually perpetuates more ancient symbolism in which the flesh and blood represented and *were* the victim as a whole in every single part and transmitted the victim's power of regeneration.

To start with, we will take the species of bread that appears first in the texts, probably because the immediate mention of wine might too easily arouse more literal associations with sacrifice. The sacrificial symbol of corn or bread, a metaphor for the god who dies and is reborn offering himself as food for his followers, shows a certain continuity with the salvation symbolized in the ear of corn reaped in silence at Eleusis, another sacrificial toy that builds on and completes the narcissus plucked by Persephone. And the convergence between the Orphic-Eleusinian rituals and the Christian is not so much a matter of direct borrowing but results from the presence of the same mythical-ritual substratum in the archaic rite of Yahweh as originally practiced in the Temple, which left clear traces down to the time of Jesus. A very similar theme appears in John in the image of Christ and his followers who must die and rise again like a grain of wheat so as not to "remain alone" and to give themselves as food to anyone whose hunger can be thus satisfied.[39] The same metaphor reappears with Paul in 1 Corinthians and is commented on in several places by Origen.[40] The implications of the passage are highly complex and typical of the fourth Gospel, but that in no way alters the fact that the evangelist resorts to typically sacrificial imagery to visualize the destiny of the Son of God, deeming such imagery to be symbolically appropriate and having in mind, besides, an audience of "Greeks," certainly of Greek-speaking gentiles.[41]

By pursuing this line of inquiry we will be able to give the right emphasis to the points of contact between the Christian mass and the Eleusinian rite, without forcing or superimposing from outside. These points are not so extemporary or accidental considering that the experience of both rituals consists in participation in events surrounding a god who dies and is reborn, with a similar liturgy centering around things "said," "done," and "shown." One significant difference, though, is that Dionysus is devoured in the middle of the rite and born again at a later stage while Jesus is eaten by his followers *ante eventum* at the Last Supper, a commemoration in advance, and *post eventum* in the ritual commemoration that becomes possible after his final resurrection. But it must be added that the sacrament's specific differences, on which the Christian mass hinges, remain a dead letter unless seen against a common background, which is the factor that can bring them into relief and give them depth at the same time.

The associations with Dionysus and sacrifice become still more direct with the second species, the wine, strictly understood to be red wine, according to Jewish and ancient usage, on account of the obvious symbolic associations.[42] In the Orphic tradition wine figures as the last gift of Dionysus to men,[43] for the reasons eloquently illustrated by Tiresias in his *rhesis* to Pentheus, and the structural analogy to the Eucharist is strikingly clear once we note the appearance of the same liturgical and symbolic dynamics. Just as Dionysus is poured out as a libation to the other gods, in *Bacchae* 284, so Christ's blood is poured from the chalice for all humankind; the aim is salvation in both cases, and we witness the complete identification of the divinity with the cult medium that makes it effectual and present, although at different levels of participation and transitive circularity. Euripides's image is so powerfully pertinent that the imprisoned Paul in the epistles uses the same verb (*spendomai*) in reference to his possible martyrdom.[44] This example is by no means isolated in the New Testament; the Epistle to the Hebrews shows an impressive development of the theme of Christ's blood, poured out for our sins with an entirely different significance for salvation in respect to the blood of animals sacrificed in the Temple.

The blood motif is so densely present in this epistle,[45] in relation to the themes of sacrificial substitution and the Jerusalem cult, against a background I regard as secretly Eucharistic, that it seems best to devote a separate parenthesis to it as a start to help us get to the heart of what the New Testament texts have to tell us. The most fascinating discovery is that the early Christian texts contain clearly thought-out and conscious answers to the comparative questions, answers that became a dead letter, at least in part, when the Christian movement broke away from the Middle-Judaic sphere.

The sophisticated Judeo-Christian thinker who wrote the Epistle to the Hebrews, anonymous unfortunately like so many authors of the New Testament, shows us Christian thought at an initial formative stage, still involved with the internal contradictions in Middle Judaism and fully informed as to the doctrinal and sacramental solution brought to them by Christ's teachings and witness. The text is an audacious historical and theological exploration of the experiential, performative, and transformative nature of the Crucifixion, and I believe it contains a hidden Eucharistic doctrine, whose premises we will examine in the second volume when we come to deal with the founding pericopes of the sacrament. What invites a crypto-Eucharistic reading of the Epistle to the Hebrews is noting how it uses the interpretive means then available, namely theology and allegorical exegesis, against a background of Jewish cult and Greek philosophy that undergoes developments of complete originality in the Judaic context. So this will be a first verification of what we have begun seeing about the Jewish and Christian awareness of sacrifice, and the sacrificial implications of the postexilic history, with the related comparative problems.

3. A Crypto-Eucharistic Reading of the Epistle to the Hebrews

In view of the references to the Temple cult and the heavenly liturgy celebrated by Christ, what Hebrews has to say about blood is intensely liturgical and metaphysical. The writer appears to come from the Alexandrian Judaism profoundly influenced by Plato's philosophy, whose leading figure was Philo, the main representative of the Judaic Middle Platonism,[46] but for the Platonism of the author of Hebrews, evident in his constantly distinguishing heavenly archetypes and earthly derivations according to a method of typological and allegorical interpretation later associated above all with Origen, has its center of gravity and meeting point in the historical and existential experience of which Christ is the model and absolute mediator.[47] This crucial role of history, unknown to Plato's philosophy, is brought out fully in the grave-toned chapter dedicated to faith (πίστις) that starts with the definition of *pistis* as "the real substance [*hypostasis*] of things hoped for, the inconfutable evidence [*elenchos*] of things [*pragmaton*] not seen" (11:1).[48] The meaning of ὑπόστασις as the real, substantial foundation takes us into a sphere that is practically the opposite of the modern subjective understanding of "faith,"[49] and refers to a historically tested and therefore probative experience. And the term ἔλεγχος seems to take on once more its Aristotelian sense of proof by confutation, the elenctic proof, so precisely as to suggest a firsthand knowledge of Aristotle's works that were fully accessible in the library of Alexandria:[50] elenctic proof is the demonstration of the supreme principles of the real such as the Unmoved Mover and the principle of noncontradiction that, being situated at the summit of Being and *logos*, are demonstrable not from other premises but by confuting their negation since knowledge of them coincides with clearing the field of all obstacles to it and having intellective experience of it.[51] However, the Judaicizing and Christianizing of these premises take us to a radically altered plane of reflection and action.

What the author of Hebrews has in mind is proof through experience, the way in which "the ancients obtained a good report" (*emartyrethesan hoi presbyteroi*—11:2), where the verb indicates a token objectively received by the will of God but one that interacts closely with the lives of those prepared to welcome it, thereby deserving to be called *presbyteroi*, "elders," and so worthy of veneration. The name is not a mere matter of chronology but refers to their founding, typological precedence, since through their "good report" they have opened up new transitivity between heaven and earth. Indeed, their witness of faith completes the creation and brings about an essential reversal from the invisible to the visible that is the very substance (*hypostasis*) of the *elenchos*, of the inconfutable divine evidence set out just before in the definition of *pistis*: "Through faith we understand that the ages [*aionas*] were framed [*katertisthai*] by the word [*rhemati*] of God, so that things that are seen were not made from things that do appear [*phainomenon*]" (11:3). The "inconfutable evidence of things not seen" thus becomes visible not because it is simply manifested with a sacral or naturalistic transition but because there is someone who historically and by way of witness shows the transition from what is not seen to what is seen. What this means is revealed by a key passage in the preceding chapter of the epistle when Christ, who comes "into the world" (*eis ton kosmon*) is made to utter words adapted from Psalm 40: "You have wanted neither sacrifices nor offerings [*thysias kai prosphoras*], but you have prepared [*katertiso*] a body [*soma*] for me."[52] Here for the first time we encounter the creational verb *katartiso* signifying providential preparation, firstly of the various "ages," a term that in my opinion can indicate here, as in Origen, an entire series of cosmic-historical cycles willed by God,[53] and secondly of the body of Christ, providentially prearranged before the *kosmos* to complete the plan of creation. Sacrifices and offerings are not rejected as religious acts in themselves but because they are still inadequate in the face of this central act that Christ's acceptance transforms into a decisive moral and ontological reversal: "Then I said: 'Behold, I am here' [*idou heko*]" (10:7). The real nature of Christ's action/crucifixion emerges in the transition from the plural of the sacrifices and offerings that preceded him (*thysias kai prosphoras*) to the singular of the single offering of his body (*tes prosphoras tou somatos*—10:10) and the "one sacrifice" (*mian . . . thysian*—10:12) consciously suffered by him in order to expiate the sins of all humankind. The blood of Christ crucified, understood in this sense of a single, deliberate sacrifice, is the theological thread that runs all through the epistle, and it is also inevitably sacramental, although the Eucharist is not explicitly mentioned.[54]

I shall come back shortly to the connection of the epistle with the Eucharist, recognized by a long tradition but denied by most contemporary commentators. Meanwhile we should note how this leading theme of the sacrificial translates into a performative theology of history. The author carries on following the chronological order of Genesis but takes a slight but significant skip forward: after referring to the creation of the "ages" and the nonapparent manifestation of "what is seen," he tells the story of Cain's murder of Abel, the emblematic beginning to human history and the history of salvation:

> By faith Abel offered a more excellent [*pleiona*] sacrifice to God than Cain, and thereby it was witnessed [*emartyrethe*] that he was righteous, God testifying [*martyrountos*] that his gifts were pleasing, and although dead, he yet speaks thereby. (11:4)

The first thing to note is that Abel's sacrifice is "more excellent" not simply because his animal sacrifices are more pleasing to God but because he puts himself in place of them, anticipating the sacrificial substitution of Christ. This makes room to hypothesize that more is intended by this allusion to the first murder/fratricide in history as a sacrifice anticipating Christ's, that there may be a more specific allusion to the original sin of postexilic Judaism and the Temple cult, the murder of Zerubbabel, an ancestor of Christ in the line of David, at the hands of Joshua-Cain.[55] This is suggested by the genealogical, founding role attributed to the episode and by the repetition of the verb *martyreo* in a context concerned with moving beyond the Temple cult, aiming to persuade its audience to break with a religious and ritual organization inadequate in itself and quite invalid as mediation. The fact that this criticism occurs after the destruction of the Temple, as suggested by the penetrating but not detailed reference to its cult, qualifies it as a grandiose posthumous reflection designed to spur its interlocutors to make a critical reappraisal of their past, both recent and more distant, and to acknowledge Christ as Israel's only authentic heir.

The attack on the Temple cult, under its knowledgeably theological tones, is extremely fierce and apparently intends to settle for the last time the old *querelle* that had split the priesthood in Jerusalem from the Judaic community in Alexandria.[56] The infratext that I hypothesize gains support from a particular expression used in 9:25, where Christ's single sacrifice is contrasted to the repetition of sacrifice in the Temple and the high priest's entering the Holy of Holies once a year "with the blood of others" (*en haimati allotrio*). In itself, the term *allotrios* (another person, a stranger) should apply to the blood of the animals poured out in the Temple to expiate the sins of the priest and people (9:7), but in this limited sense it appears odd and disproportionate since the blood's stated value as expiation and substitution suggests the idea that it is the blood of *another* human being, poured out, moreover, *in place of* the blood of the high priest, indeed actually making the ritual function of his office possible. The murder of Zerubbabel, the Davidic legitimate descendant, together with his high priest Zechariah, by the priest Joshua successfully explains the oddness of the expression and its implications, and it provides the antecedent to fully justify the emphasis given at the beginning of chapter 11 of the epistle to the "greater sacrifice" offered in his own person by Abel-Zerubbabel in place of the animals that he had sacrificed, an offering only interpretable in the theological reworking of the event reached by the Songs of the Suffering Servant. The counterproof for this reading is that ignoring it, as has been the case so far, prevents us from completely understanding the epistle's impressive sacrificial structure and results in an interpretation wavering between taking its content too literally or a rejection that only perpetuates that literalism by failing to access the theological and sacramental significance of the guiding theme of blood, and presenting once more, at the exegetical level, the difficulty of understanding the paradoxically ontological symbolism of the Eucharist.

Further confirmation is forthcoming if we take to its conclusion the ritual and performative logic that the epistle reappraises in a spiritual and

Christological key. The text states that "it is not possible that the blood of bulls and of goats should take away sins" (10:4), and this impossibility in principle is much better understood if we bear in mind that those sins consisted not in generic, indefinite wrongdoing but took concrete form as a bloody deed: the politico-religious assassination of Israel's lawful mediator in the holy place appointed to legitimize his mediation. At that juncture any saving mediation was no longer possible and, for hundreds of years, countless animal sacrifices were repeatedly made in vain, completely powerless to wash away the blood of Abel, the mark of the sin of humankind and of Israel. With this the author implicitly passes judgment on the ancient Yahwistic cult and its ties with the world of the dead, a somber funereal connotation apparently alluded to by the "works of death" (*nekron ergon*) from which Christ has purged humanity in order to induce "worship of the living God" (9:14). Christ has made the last remaining reparation by offering in sacrifice the body prepared for him, transforming his gesture into a voluntary and supremely moral choice, "not by the blood of goats and calves, but by his own blood entering once into the Holy of Holies, he obtained our eternal redemption" (9:12). In that way the dead works are overturned to become a definitive manifestation of the living God, and to refuse this supreme offer means to submit to his final judgment (10:31), to preclude oneself from the resolving choice that had transformed a place devoted to the slavery of death and sin into a gateway to freedom opened up by the blood of Christ (10:19).

What the epistle sets before us with this extraordinary allegorical and typological apparatus is the symbolic and figural representation of the *symbolon* in its original, transfigured acceptation. Exegesis and sacrament come together again and restore the importance of Judeo-Christian Platonism in Hebrews; its various aspects are concentrated in the definition of *pistis* applied to Abraham's sacrifice of Isaac, an event that takes on momentous implications if the interpretative key that I support is used, since it comes to represent concretely and *in figuris* the alternation between the different ages, that is, between a Judaism still slave to the *molk* and a Judaism that was able to be rid of it through the heroic choice made by the descendent of Zerubbabel:

> By faith, Abraham, when he was put to the test, offered up [*prosenenoken*] Isaac, his only begotten son [*monogene*] in sacrifice [*prosepheren*]—although

> it had been said to him: "In Isaac shall your descendency be glorified," reckoning that God had the power to raise up even from the dead, thus he had him back from God, at the moment of greatest danger, and it was as a symbol [*en parabole*]. (11:17–19).

It is a solemn passage, and the final expression puts a stylistic and theological seal on it; ἐν παραβολῇ is usually correctly translated with its symbolic-figural meaning of a narrated event but also conveys the meaning of a testing time of very great danger.[57] In my opinion both meanings should be retained in an inclusive and not exclusive reading, since only both together can provide the density of thought characteristic of Hebrews.[58] And the nuance of an absolutely real danger well suits the tragic situation being described, the more tragic when we remember what the author has in mind: the bloodily performed human sacrifices from which the episode in Genesis derives, with the further resonance of the allusion to Zerubbabel, to an original sin of postexilic Judaism that becomes the sin of all mankind. For its part, the Jewish tradition in Christ's time certainly preserved the memory of Isaac as really sacrificed,[59] and so confirms the reality of the ritual background to the Bible story. The dreadful significance of such scriptural memories is too often forgotten, and in the case in point, the prefiguring of Christ's sacrifice as it comes down to us in Genesis appears incomplete when we reflect that Christ on the cross was really killed. The essential point of the *parabole* of Abraham and Isaac is certainly the fact that the son is restored to the father alive, and this fact, so unexpected and touching, assumes the total reality of what was about to occur, and normally occurred, as the author of Hebrews knows full well. The *parabole* of Abraham and Isaac therefore corresponds to the typological sign, both *imaginalis* and historically real, of what was to be Christ's resurrection and to the moment of supreme danger, to what Bataille would call *chance*, and only to be reversed from complete destruction to unimaginable objectual resurrection by total acceptance. The overthrow of ancient human sacrifice is accomplished with Christ and becomes the key to interpret the whole of Jewish history, the whole history of mankind.

There is never any explicit mention of the Eucharist in the epistle, for the very good reason that the overall theological structure of the epistle comments and expands on it; and we shall come back to the ex silentio motives for the fourth Gospel's omission of any account of the instituting of the

Eucharist at the Last Supper, one of not a few points of contact between the Gospel's theology and Hebrews.[60] The Epistle to the Hebrews sees Christ's sacrifice as having been made once and for all and at the same time perennially present, in perfect solidarity between heavenly liturgy and earthly commemoration; and it requires a certain effort not to see in this the silent presence of the Eucharistic sacrament. If correct, the exegetic and theological inference authorizes us to conclude that the epistle holds the Eucharist to be the permanent and definitive link between human history and the eternal liturgy in heaven, thanks to the mediation and commemoration of Christ that has turned the violence of the Temple cult into a perpetual sacrifice of love.

The comparative argument to be deduced from the text as a whole is incisive and crystal clear. The Epistle to the Hebrews consciously reflects and transmits the idea that the power of Christ's sacrifice to save is due precisely to its perfect isomorphism in regarding the sacrifices made by men; of these the Temple cult is the ambiguous liturgical synthesis, covertly including the human sacrifice that marked the outset of its postexilic phase, just as it has marked human history from its very beginning as well as the history of Israel. And from the philosophical and theological point of view, it is notable that the author of Hebrews regards the Eucharist as an event both in time and beyond time, joining together the hyperuranian world described by Plato and the terrestrial world, this theater of endless violence and house of death to which Christ offers the only alternative.

As we see, the theological-philosophical meditation on Christ's sacrifice contained in the Epistle to the Hebrews presents us with one of the peaks of Christian thinking in the course of its formation and begins removing our doubts that the comparative question might have slight relevance or substance in the more advanced theological developments of Christianity. At the same time, the nuanced and allusive argumentative procedure followed in the epistle shows how much the comparative aspects were delicate and easily misleading.

We find the same procedure both cautious and bold in other passages of the New Testament. It is the fourth Gospel that has Christ pronounce the words "I am the true vine" (15:1), the vine whose grapes, "crushed in the winepress of the Passion," as Origen writes using another Dionysian metaphor, produced the Eucharistic blood.[61] This declaration throws more light on the image used by Jesus in the synoptics to indicate the wine that he has just consecrated: "the fruit of the vine," a usual liturgical periphrasis in Judaism.[62] However, we have to note that the metaphoric and metamorphic identification of Christ as the true vine in the Gospel of John, with its underlying symbolic dynamism, recalls the vegetable metamorphoses of Dionysus *dendrites* and many divinities linked to tree sacrifices. In fact, Dionysus's most typical vegetable transformation, highlighted in Orphism, was as a vine, obviously related to sacrifice through the wine that aided its performance. When Christ says that he is the one *true* vine, whether or not he is Christ as developed by the evangelist and/or the historical Christ, he is implicitly seeking to differentiate his message of salvation from the spurious salvation of the *other* vines of the Dionysian type cults widespread in the eastern part of the Roman Empire. There was one example on the borders of Palestine: Dusares, the wine divinity worshipped by the Nabatheans; this god was not so remote from the more archaic Yahweh, very similar to the Greek Dionysus, and also associated with the vine.[63] But Christ's allusion must be more incisive and warranted. According to Flavius Josephus and Tacitus, there was a gold reproduction of a Dionysian-type vine in the Temple itself.[64] This fact suggests that Christ in John is contrasting his salvation, offered through the blood-wine of the Eucharist, to the spurious salvation of the Temple cult, and it accords with the fourth Gospel's emphatic positioning, at the start of his mission, of Christ's driving the "moneylenders" from the Temple and of the prophecy regarding the Temple of his body, destined to be destroyed and rebuilt in three days. As in Hebrews, the Jerusalem cult is assimilated to the other cults: not to accept Christ, for these authors, is to refuse the only valid religious strain in Judaism and, to all intents, to relapse into some sort of pagan religion, made worse by rejecting the fulfillment of all Israel's expectations and prophecies.

From the phenomenological viewpoint, in respect to the Dionysian rites, a decisive change undoubtedly occurs in the Christian communion, but if we fail to grasp the substance of the historical and ritual context concerned, we remain stalled at a descriptive level, our way barred to access the authentic phenomenology concerning genesis and history, and we are easily led to defend the specificity of the Eucharist, toning down its ritual content and so willy-nilly emphasizing the symbolic, as it were syntactic, aspect. There is an indispensable symbolic dimension to the Eucharist, but if we attenuate its realism even slightly the result is to attenuate or actually lose its symbolic substance as well. The Christian communion therefore is not symbolic in the usual meaning of the word; it is symbolic in the more fundamental sense that recalls the *parabole* of Hebrews, and so it can fairly be said that the Eucharistic sacrament is a new version of the mediatory event that gave rise to symbolism, the "re-presentation" (that is, the repetition of a single, really present act) of the sacrificial *symbolon*, the most archaic scene of origin in fact that our analysis can reach back to. However, leaving aside the superficial comparative assessments usually accompanying this subject, the semantic value assigned to the Eucharist and Christ's sacrificial death again brings up the question of its being a substantial evolution of the Mystery *symbolon*, finally canceling its historical value.[65]

Celsus observes that if the Christians had a wish to put any other pagan figure in place of Christ, a spurious and inconsistent figure in his opinion, they might always choose Orpheus, "as everyone admits, a man endowed with a holy spirit [*hosio pneumati*] and who also died a violent death."[66] The pagan polemicist intuits that Orphism anticipates the basic structure of the Christian religion and, with his double standard noted by Origen, praises the Orphics for a spirituality he despises in the Christians. However, if we take his arguments seriously, we discover analogies between the Orphic-Mystery religion and Christianity that appear significant taken as a whole rather than as separate details:[67] (1) Collective violence, mankind's origin from the Titanic lynching, lies at the root of Orphism's mythical-historical vision; this convergence is even more significant when we think of the most recent dating for Genesis and its etiological account of how evil came into human history. (2) The Orphic follower can save himself from the Titanic violence by divinizing himself in the divine child Dionysus, in a similar way to what happened with the Egyptian followers of Osiris and to what must happen to the Christian who follows Christ; the result is salvation in the form of rebirth (resurrection), and the correspondence grows when we consider that the archaic Yahwistic cult presented an equivalent drama, though it occurred within a hierogamy that has disappeared from Christian belief. (3) This makes necessary repetition of Dionysus's sacrifice, his passion (*pathema*), and here, too, there is a parallel in the Judaic world, the *molk*, the sacrifice of the first-born male child, acting as a hidden antecedent of Christ's Passion. (4) The message of salvation is increasingly addressed to the individual, according to a logic that starts to be independent of social condition. (5) This individual is endowed with an immortal soul that is conceived in a form tending toward the spiritual, though the Orphic soul, subject to metensomatosis, is still without the individual features that start to appear within the collective mediation of Middle Judaism and assume a more stable form in Christianity. (6) Three possibilities are envisaged in the Orphic vision of the afterlife, which was taken up again by Plato within a far more complex spiritual vision: divinization in heaven, expiation through reincarnations, and eternal punishment for noninitiates; this three-part division shows a certain correspondence to the future Christian paradise, purgatory, and hell, even if Christianity's eschatology appears to come from Judaism, which, in turn, was probably influenced by Zoroastrianism.[68] (7) There is a henotheistic-type tendency, although it is not possible to talk of monotheism in Orphism, or even of monolatry, but rather of henolatry; however, one of Orphic theology's most advanced points is the idea that there is only one Dionysus, under the many names of polytheism, though this assertion is made in a Hellenistic text, the Gurob papyrus, and therefore reflects the influence of Greek philosophy that was—as I have said already, but it is worth repeating—the first to apply, in theo-logical terms, the dialectic of the One and the Many to reach a better definition of God.

How, then, are we to assess these convergences or common background features without generic overlay, blind (at least partially) to the differences? How to avoid the dilemma of a forced identificationism and an equally forced differentialism? Once again, Origen provides us with important pointers, from his position as a strategic figure in the Christian thinking that evolved in a Hellenistic and multicultural city such as Alexandria. The unknown author of the Epistle to the Hebrews may well have belonged to the same intellectual environment that was extremely rich, testifying to the interchange between Judaic, Greek, and Christian culture that we must delve into if we are to pursue our inquiry.

4. An Argument both Simple and Complex

Faced with Celsus's comparatist argument, Origen, in the first instance, relies on a counterargument that might be called phenomenological-moral since it refers to moral changes observable in Christians independently of any prior assumptions about the truth or otherwise of their beliefs. Following on what Clement had already argued, Origen observes that an objective comparison of pagan myths and rites with the Christian message shows the objectual superiority of the latter: Christ's capacity to regenerate men and women, giving them words of hope and life and providing his example enabling them to do good, is contrasted to the cruelty, ambivalence, and moral indifference of pagan religion:

> Christianity's accusers [*kategoroi*] take no account of the many people in whom passions and the vortex of sin are stamped out, and all those whose savage customs are mitigated, thanks to our doctrine [*tou logou*]. And yet, proud as they are of their spirit of community [*to koinonikon*],[69] they ought to have expressed their gratitude to that doctrine and testified to the fact that, even admitting there is no truth in it, it has nevertheless done mankind a great service.[70]

The sally about "spirit of community" is not directed only at Celsus but at all of patriotic Roman culture that reproached Christianity for failing to share community values. And yet, Origen retorts, even if we look no further than the social and historical effects of Christianity, with impartiality, its moral and civilizing value has to be admitted, not to mention how those effects accord with the causes adduced by Christians themselves. The theme of the power of Jesus's name reappears, a power capable of taming and defeating the evil intermedial forces and introducing a more charitable, gentler lifestyle:

> The name of Jesus wards off anxieties from the minds of men, besides demons, and still today, diseases; it engenders a wonderfully meek and modest spirit [*ethous*], love of one's neighbor [*philanthropian*], goodness and kindness in all those who do not pretend to be Christians for the sake of an easy life or other human needs but sincerely accept the doctrine [*logon*] of God and Christ and future judgment.[71]

The reference to those who pretend to be Christian out of self-interest for their own advantage shows us that Origen has no illusions about Christianity in his day as it started to show signs of worldliness and careerism,[72] signs that would obviously become more marked in the following century when the church was granted official recognition by the Roman Empire.[73] At any rate, Origen has complete faith in the power of Jesus's name to bring about such moral and even physical change in those who sincerely believe that it makes the Christian condition in this world already rewarding, essentially rewarding in itself with the ultimate reward of the "future judgment" no more than its consequence. Jesus's name is all one with his *logos* and nothing but its historical and personal epitome, while its performative effectiveness is the transforming, transfiguring consequence of its authentically divine origin. Salvation, then, is already won in this life and coincides with the experience of the life and love of Christ's *logos*, according to the intentions of the achieved eschatology found in John, which also was to be the most characteristic mark of Eastern Greek Christianity. But let us now consider the credibility of Origen's argument in modern rationalistic terms, that is, quite apart from the experience of faith: indeed, as a rule, such terms are not concerned with what the personal experience of faith might mean in times remote from our own.

For us the exact opposite is true: it is a more loving and human attitude that alters men's lives and wards off the specters and demons of violence and persecution, which, however, only highlights unmercifully the huge problem of how to foster or actually revive such an attitude. Modern rationalism has in fact proved quite powerless to solve the problem and has turned instead to the sorry surrogates of ideologies. Let us come to grips with the hidden core of Origen's thinking: our more rational mentality should not indeed forget that an ideal of life, which we can only define as more human and more completely objectual, has been arrived at through the *pistis* in a theological, metaphysical, and sacramental mediation directed to that end. And the task of a maturely historical vision is to collate both sides of the process in question, the objectual, whose presence and effects we can verify, and the mediatory that corresponds to the experience of faith. Starting from these premises, we are in a position to verify the comparative importance of Origen's thinking.

It is remarkable that, thanks to the moral argument, Origen is finally capable of making a direct comparison with the core of Dionysian mythology:

> Is not the narrative of these events, especially when interpreted correctly, more worthy of respect [*semnotera*] than the story of Dionysus, killed by

> the Titans, cast down from the throne of Zeus and dismembered by them [*sparassomenou*], then reassembled again afterward, as though brought back to life and lifted up to heaven?[74]

The purport of these words is substantially objectual. The dignity of Christ's death is not a magical and exterior attribute: the adjective *semnos* keeps its meaning of holy, venerable, and expresses the writer's religious sentiments, but is actually emancipated from the old schemes of sacredness and sanctity, from their toll in human life and bloodshed. In Origen's mind that meaning is not separable from the connotation of a human dignity that has suffered outrage but is reaffirmed by virtue of Christ's spiritual awareness in facing death, keeping himself uncontaminated by the brutal violence all around him, transforming it into a power for revelation, an opportunity for salvation.

If we compare the Christian mediation with the ethics of antiquity, even at their most exalted, we must realize that it really does bring in a new accent, a new language, and a new attitude to life, easier almost to deny than diminish. Augustine points it out polemically in the *De civitate Dei*, with the confidence of someone who knows that the world has definitely changed and moved on in respect to all previous ages. Nevertheless, it would be a mistake to take the Christian position literally and reproduce all that it affirms, hardly less of a mistake, historically speaking, than its relativization as mere cultural and ideological rotation. Christian ethical principles, so sensational as compared to the mentality and customs of antiquity, are not the expression of an unrelated difference, but rather they express an intensification and turnaround that holds the future within it for the simple reason that it brings to fulfillment what was best in the ancient world. The undeniable resemblances and the shared intermedial background end by underlining the distinctive nature of the Christian mediation, but that in its turn confirms the inevitability of the background that it defines itself against and stands out from.

In this connection Hellenism provides a precedent of more general, wider relevance, but no less pertinent for that when we consider the dense web of a thousand threads that bind it to the developments and more advanced achievements of Judaic thinking. And Orphism provides the pilot example: where it differs from the salvation offered by Christianity it shows up the real value and the inadequacy of the Socratic-Platonic response, both at the same time, accentuating the historic conditioning and authentic significance of the Christian solution. The two connected but distinct levels of popular religion and philosophical formulation, often juxtaposed and contrasted to one another in Greece, find a single vision in Christianity, at once cultural and speculative, sacramental and cognitive, whereas in Orphism there is a decided imbalance toward the cult.

While there is a tendency toward spiritual motivation in Orphic-Eleusinian salvation, the ideal remains magical-ritualistic: salvation is only attainable on condition of completing the prescribed rites of initiation and purification. Those not ritually purified, the noninitiated, are doomed to eternal punishment, a doctrine not unlike Christianity's traditional attitude to baptism where everlasting torment is reserved for the unbaptized. In the theology of Augustine, this same attitude was to raise again the specter of collective responsibility,[75] never by the way completely exorcized from any of history's great religions. There exists no preferred position on these matters since all religious mediations have used axiological and legal exclusion as a means to define their identity; and yet this field of irreconcilable ideological conflict provides the most eloquent proof of how eschatology has been thoroughly vetted and refined as a result of a combination of cultural factors, none of which was sufficient in itself to produce the change, but combined together brought notable margins for development into Christian and Judaic eschatology, as well, for that matter, as into Zoroastrian and Islamic eschatology.[76]

In this respect, the most profound, enduring spiritual achievement of ancient Greece comes down to us not so much from Orphism in a narrow sense as from the philosophical ideas sparked off by Orphic eschatology, particularly in Plato, which apply a criterion of equality and justice that tended to hold good for all men, in accordance with the requirement of the conceptual universality of the *logos*. However, the need of Greek philosophers to find an identity-defining, axiological *logos* that could be applied universally, quite separate from magical-ritual intermediations, such as is expressed toward the end of the introductory discussion on the nature of Justice in the first two books of Plato's *Republic*, remains within an elitist sapiential domain, with the religious and ontological-cosmic planes inseparable in principle.[77] And if we turn our attention to the great civilization that united the whole Mediterranean world, a similar observation applies to Rome's finest objectual achievements in ethics, with Seneca, and in law, symbolized by extending the title of *civis romanus* universally under the *Constitutio Antoniniana* of Caracallus in 212 AD.[78] These achievements in turn center on what can be defined as a politico-cosmic complex, and so are never disjoined from the axiological recognition of a balance of powers adopted as a sacral and objective sanction, either to be obeyed through submission, which is the ultimate meaning of the universal extension of Roman citizenship, or evaded through death, as Seneca theorized and finally put into practice. In order for all this to reach new frontiers of objectualization and humanization, it was necessary for the Greek and Roman objectivizations, the philosophical and the juridical-political, to encounter the tiny Jewish nation with its troubled sense of history and transcendence, and with its theology marked by the disorienting Christian developments. The peculiar nature of this encounter, both assimilation and conflict, ensured objectual supremacy to Judaic and Christian salvation, but in the fields of abstract thought and action, on the contrary, it had to yield that supremacy to the other two great cultures of the ancient world. However, that suggests the potential developments contained in the Christian assimilation, both of Greek philosophy and of Roman law, an assimilation that was only pursuing the effects of previous influences left incomplete.

If we set all these various elements in motion, what emerges is a hard-fought and extremely diversified process, in which the divisions helped to promote identification and to call into question principles considered as established. The heterogony of ends that results is not only valuable as historical reconstruction, it also becomes a motive for an overall reappraisal of traditions that claim to be defined once and for all, whereas their real origins tell us a different and more surprising story, with more unexpected developments that are not solely concerned with the past. Let us see then how we can recognize the more unmistakable features of the Judaic mediation and especially of the Christian mediation in this critical context that will need to show greater flexibility and credibility than the usual interpretive schemes.

5. Mediatory Heterogony of Ends

Far from warranting any purist theory in relation to the surrounding pagan environment, the peculiar nature of Judaism and Christianity turns out to be the result of a whole series of indirect influences and propitious contaminations—in the same way that Greek civilization emerged from the creative reworking of numerous cultural influences, especially from Mesopotamia, Egypt, and Persia; and that Roman civilization was shaped by actively absorbing the Etruscan and Italic civilizations, over and above the Greek influence. Thus Judaism, in the peak phase of establishing its identity, that is, during Middle Judaism, interacts with massive foreign influence, which itself suggests the length of time involved in intermedial and mediatory progression. This is fully confirmed by the puritanical criteria of ritual and sacral conformity that set the Jewish people apart from all others in antiquity, and the reason is twofold: negatively, because Judaic Puritanism is the response to a desire to be different that implies the close vicinity, without but even more within, of what it so strenuously desires to be distinct from; and positively, in that this Puritanism contains and in turn nurtures a level of theological reflection that far from diminishing or denying the Hellenic influence, makes it still more decisive and enhanced. The outcome in its originality is the fruit of interaction over many centuries transformed to become the living substance of another organism. This last observation on the authentic tenor of relations between the Judaic and Hellenistic-Roman cultures induces some further remarks about methodology and history that have wider significance and are not irrelevant to the anthropological and ethical vision developed by Judaism and Christianity.

Where history and culture are concerned, too often we forget that opposition and rejection can be the sign of the dramatic progress of some transforming assimilation. As with the evolution of living creatures, and in an even larger measure on account of the exponential complexity of the processes involved, the new form arises as a successful adaptation of what it repudiated, as what it destroyed reborn and refashioned. Sacrifice shows itself to be a law of human and historical existence since it is a cultural development of a universal law of creative destruction that dominates the natural world with growing or lessening degrees of organization and complexity. And the fact that religious knowledge in all cultures centers entirely on interpreting and implementing the meaning and repercussions of sacrifice provides a glimpse of the huge legacy of knowledge contained there. Mediation is nothing but a supreme intensification of this dynamic structure of reality as a whole, and the perfect ambivalence that entitles us to interpret it in two ways, either as a law immanent to a natural world in itself inexplicable or as an opening toward a transcendence manifested there, confirms that freedom is mediation's most fragile and important result, since it is freedom that sanctions the retroacting openness that ventures on the incalculable and boosts the finite to such a point that it takes a leading role of qualitatively infinite worth. Thus we are now in a position to understand why, in general and specifically, thinking about sacrifice proved the high point of Greek and Roman philosophy, as it was also of the religious ideas that Judaism and Christianity evolved in constant dialogue, both interactive and frictional, with their antagonists and among themselves. The example of Orphism enables us to consider the distinctive nature of the Judaic and Christian mediations starting from a theme with little appeal to the modern reader: the ancient obsession with criteria and rules of purity.

As a start we might note that the Middle-Judaic ideal of religious purity consists ultimately in sharpening and ritualizing Israel's sense of weakness and unworthiness before the true Yahweh, which had been the driving, leavening force in preexilic prophetism and in the consequent henotheism during and after exile, and would gradually develop into monotheism. However, we miss the decisive aspect of this phenomenon if we fail to see that it depends on interaction with the great Greek culture, and what clearly prevails there is not so much the defensive answer provided by rules of ritual conformity and purity, which would assume contact has already penetrated deeply, but rather the remarkable reworking of the Greek contribution by Judaism's more audacious leading thinkers. Greek historiography taught Jewish writers and thinkers the full import of historical necessity, and the tragic genre showed them the devastating power of misfortune. These are implicitly recognizable as assumptions behind those two great masterpieces of Bible literature, the book of Job and Ecclesiastes, with their general thesis of the senselessness of man's life in this world. Simone Weil's idea that the most exalted parts of the Old and New Testaments are essentially Greek-inspired is too one-sided but reflects a real connection by which the more passionate Semitic, oriental nature brought out the more human content that lay hidden behind the Greek masks of the community and the *kosmos*.

We can grasp how strongly opposed and subterranean were the various paths that eventually led to the development of Christianity and Rabbinical Judaism if we reconstruct the Middle-Judaic debate in a way that is neither apologetic nor tendentious; and as a debate in which Jesus of Nazareth also has his rightful place. Much of the debate can be traced back to the nature of the Judaic reaction to universalism, first to the Greek form and then to the Roman; on the one hand, it counters with Jewish particularism while, on the other, it develops innovative and creative forms of universalism. The notions of purity and ritual conformity, with their avowed, uncompromising antipagan differentiation, function as a focal point to concentrate Judaic identity in the face of powerful influences, and this in turn spurs minorities within Judaism to react with the aim of unlocking the objectual potential of this achieved identity. The ideological opposition to Hellenism that developed under the Maccabees, and drew with it the question of why so many were reluctant to follow the cult of the one true God, fostered the myth of original sin, both human and angelic, and ultimately, among many Middle-Judaic tendencies, the theology of the one possibility offered to Israel of salvation by justification, and therefore by faith, understood as obedience to the divine commandments, above all collective obedience, but in any case an obedience due to them. The rules of purity, with the legalistic exaggerations recorded in Essenism and at Qumran, where it would appear even bodily functions were in some cases forbidden on the Sabbath,[79] arose from the need to purify man to make him less unworthy of God's justification, not to procure it for him of course, since he could never deserve it. This obsessive emphasis, stretching the two terms of Judaic mediation almost to the breaking point, prepares the way for unforeseeable breakthroughs and makes it possible to imagine the most unexpected reversals. All of this was to come about with Jesus of Nazareth.

Through John the Baptist's teaching, Christ's own teaching starts with a theological framework similar to the Essenian, but he transforms the Baptist's monothematic emphasis on divine grace into its positive absolutization, revealing itself as a dynamic for salvation attracted and almost activated by the sinful condition of human existence. What might have become a sign of impossibility and despair is reversed and becomes a hope that can become a certainty, since what fosters that hope is its own negation: it is enough for a man to recognize his own unworthiness, and he opens up toward his fellow men, starting a reversibility of mercy to which the divine mercy cannot fail to respond for the simple circumstance that such mercy is the very definition of the infinitely relational nature of God, of his creative and loving omnipotence. Through completing a process of this kind, which can be reconstructed, conjecturally of course, on the basis of the religious issues being debated at that time, Jesus was able to announce the new and spiritually revolutionary idea that God's love is made infinitely available thanks to the willingness of mankind, of every individual man and woman, to forgive the wrongs done to them by their fellows. At this point a religious mediation without precedent in these terms begins to crystallize, and though it takes shape within Middle Judaism, it contains the seeds of a future differentiation. This is apparent from the polemical element in Gospel accounts, which was certainly accentuated in later Christian positions but is so incisive and relevant that its core must go back to Jesus; and it provides, besides, the only valid explanation for the fierce hostility shown by the Jewish ruling class.

The aim of the attacks on the Pharisees that feature prominently in all four Gospels is, in the first instance, to undermine the Pharisaic idea that a believer might justify himself, at least in part, by fulfilling the ritual and legal forms.[80] This would appear to confirm the Essenian and Qumran type of theological extremism except that the rabbi of Nazareth transforms their theological absolutization into a brand-new revelation of God's love now finally accessible to Israel and all mankind. Consequently, leaving aside for the moment the crucial point of the murder of Zerubbabel, Christ's criticisms could not fail to strike, as he fully intended, at the heart of the Temple priesthood and its self-interested, outward show of legality. At the same time, he struck an indirect blow at those sects and tendencies in Middle Judaism that, like the Qumran community, absolutized ritual conformity as a sign of the justice accorded by God and went so far as to uphold divine determinism to preserve God's omnipotence, unable to see the potential for renewal and salvation in a divine omnipotence fully fathomed in its real spiritual and liberating nature. (Such theological difficulties and potentialities were to return at the Reformation, though with a crisis in sacral mediations of a very different order.) The transitivity of the divine mediation, the secret goal of Middle-Judaic theology, was blocked by all these solutions until it unexpectedly came to full flower in the preaching of the rabbi of Nazareth.

The inspiration for Judaic and Christian rigor, and its significance, can be seen in asceticism, the purified attitude par excellence. The Orphics regarded asceticism as a prerequisite for salvation, and as the consequence of an alternation at the opposite extreme to the ritual violence through which initiates had to pass, as we saw in the omophagy/vegetarianism sequence followed by the Idaean saints in the *Cretans*. Greek thinking at its most advanced repeatedly stressed the inadequacy of such a totally sacral approach; to name but a few of the outstanding examples, there was the pre-Socratic criticism of bloody sacrifices, the demystification, no less implacable for being indirect, performed by the tragedians especially Euripides, and the spiritual rationalization introduced by Socrates and systematized by Plato. To these could be added the rationalism of sophists and historians, respectively pragmatic and analytic-narrative. All these huge efforts to move ahead, however, came up against the impossibility, through intellectual activity alone, of passing from an inherited fund of reasoning and knowledge possessed by a privileged minority to collectively and publicly shared mediations.

Here it is possible to recognize the role of Judaic developments in unhitching divine mediation from the ritual work dependent on sacrifice, which made an objectual transcendence by God conceivable and cleared the way for a theo-logical explanation of his nature and uniqueness under the two-pronged thrust of Greek metaphysics and an extremely lively, confrontational internal debate. It was not a question of separating from sacrifice a God already defined ipso facto in monotheistic terms, but rather of sacrifice acquiring new meaning as a result of a different way of relating to the God of Israel, eventually perceived as the one God of all mankind. In essence, the process establishing monotheism corresponds to the problematization and resignification of the bond, which is a double bond, between sacrifice and the divine, according to which their relationship intensifies and tends to invert. In the religions of antiquity it is sacrifice that guarantees the divine, in the power and variety of its cults—in fact, *is* the divine, as in Dionysianism and in the theological background to the *Bacchae*; in mature Judaic theology, on the contrary, the divine transcends sacrifice and gives it its value, subordinating it to itself in a kind of double excess: an excess of evil, if human or demonic violence makes it the principal reason behind the cult, and an excess of good, when God turns it into an emergency means to restore his sovereignty over history and mankind through a mediator who, in his infinite willingness to sacrifice himself, directs mankind once more toward the infinite objectual excess of God, who is thus set on the path to asserting his uniqueness. This is the path first pursued by the theological developments of the Songs of the Suffering Servant, and it is the path Christ will follow resolutely, and thereby assert the significance of the God of Israel's mediation as the definitive objectual achievement, passing beyond all alternations of opposite extremes and dependence on blood because it takes on itself the price to be paid for them. Returning now to the objectual implications Origen focused upon, these can be taken at a purely phenomenological level, independently of any more personal option of ours, and will provide a primary criterion for us to understand what makes the Christian religious mediation, following in the wake of the Judaic, different from Greek and Roman religiosity, a difference that was to enable it in time to make use of the best of those cultures thanks to a dynamism whose central pivotal point of comparison and revitalization lay in sacrifice.

The salvation of the Gospels responds to a primary prerequisite for receiving the grace that saves, one not found at all, in its full formulation, in Orphism and Greek civilization, nor in the civilization of Rome: unconditional love for one's neighbor—that is, love ever ready to forgive, to sacrifice its own object at any time so as to become the manifest vehicle of God's unconditional love. This forgiving love between human beings, mediated by the love of God and in turn mediating it and making it accessible, is the core of Christ's preaching, and this message is certainly historical considering its character as a theological *unicum* with the potential to overcome every barrier of a social and cultural type, and even ethnic and religious barriers as well.[81] This observation is important for setting out the argument correctly, but not enough in itself to be satisfactory: if we want to deepen our understanding of the historical genesis and the meaning itself of the forgiving and supremely transitive love that Jesus talks about, we need to realize, in the first place, that it is an answer to Middle Judaism's toughest attitudes regarding identity, and that without those attitudes it would hardly have come to clear expression; secondly, that such a revolutionary definition of love had a decisive impact on preceding pagan ideals that remained far removed from it until short-circuited by the genius of Christ's preaching. Thus all the universalistic hints that Jesus could find in Judaism's more audacious lines of thought are fulfilled; these had, besides, been blocked by the more nationalistic reactions so that it was only by forcefully restarting the pagan/Judaic pendulum that the potential latent in their confrontation could be released. And it is no accident that an ideal of such importance was conceived in the age of Augustus and Tiberius, that is, during the first great political and ideological affirmation of the Roman Empire: its horizontal universalism is answered by

Jesus with another, vertical, transcendent, and yet fully incarnate universalism, the universalism of the *basileia* of God.

The message of the Kingdom contains an appeal to an ideal of universal peace and of a free and generous amnesty. This came into Judaism from the royal and imperial ideologies of the ancient East and Hellenism, where it applied especially at the start of a new reign.[82] The Roman Empire rejuvenated and extended this ideology to the furthest confines of the known world.[83] The preaching of the Kingdom of God would not have been possible or comprehensible without this preceding history and without the presence of the Roman imperial ecumene in the background, but it is precisely these analogies and influences that make us appreciate the originality of the gospel reworking, the spiritual strength that through exalting weakness and meekness as the real manifestation of God's omnipotence, had the power to overthrow the supreme show of force that Roman *magnanimitas* always was, in effect. The historical circumstances, in the light of the immeasurable consequences that they opened up, are seen to be an antecedent that does not exhaust the significance of what followed from it but, on the contrary, underlines its mediatory value, the vertical capacity to reveal an unforeseen, infinite meaning, in a similar manner to what happened at the beginnings of culture, but it is now enhanced by an unprecedented cognitive and objectual retroaction.

Beyond reconstructing the various phases in the development of the Christian message and making any connected theoretical observations, what is already striking on the phenomenological and historical level is the objectual outcome of the *pistis* in the divine mediation incarnate in Christ: the boundless love-forgiveness toward one's fellow men regarded in their unique individuality, and the principle of the human being's divine origin and destiny in his integral historical reality. Thus the awareness of the need for logical and distributive consistency in sacral and divine mediations gained by the Greeks, the universal political and legal order developed and implemented by the Romans, and Judaism's discovery of the human objectuality of the divine mediation are all humanized and brought to completion. It is not important how directly or indirectly all these influences are received; what counts is the final outcome of their protracted subterranean interaction, condensing into a perception that is subtly but decisively altered by historical human existence. In the Christian message Christ's incarnation is a unique historical fact; for that very reason it proves to be divine, and human life becomes a unique, unrepeatable event manifesting the will of God and deciding man's eternal destiny. Each moment in human life can be a *parabole* in the same way as the scene of Abraham and Isaac in the Epistle to the Hebrews.

Once we recognize the important part played by the great pagan culture in the development of Christ's Judaic theology we can appreciate its specific difference, which can only be defined by starting from the historical *genus* to which it belongs. We have already glimpsed the riches contained in the early Christian texts, still engaged in the Middle-Judaic debate and full of information subsequently lost. And it was logical that such an intricate web of hybrids and interferences should elude commentators writing immediately afterward, which is not to say that the positions being put forward were all equal, since some, Celsus for example, saw only the incompatibility of the resulting historical consequences, while others, such as Origen, by drawing on Judaic and Christian sources, derived a position more compatible with the potential fertility of the premises; and those Christian polemicists who held Christian and pagan mediations to be quite incompatible might be said to have performed an intermediate role in helping to clarify the identity of this religion still *in statu nascendi*, similar to the role played by the more antipagan positions in Middle Judaism.

As a consequence, the new, explosive element in Christ's teaching and in the choices that he made completely eludes Celsus, who blatantly despises Christ's crucifixion and compares it to the ferocious revenge of Dionysus in the *Bacchae*.[84] In spite of all his belief in the spiritualization of Middle Platonism, for Celsus only a god capable of punitive retaliation was worthy of the name. And that observation makes us more aware than anything else of the distance that separates us, or ought to separate us, from the violence of the world of pagan Rome that was remorseless because it was thought necessary for mediation and regarded as a source of prestige.

Celsus views the events of the Passion only from the perspective of power and force, making him particularly scornful of the disciples for their mass abandonment of Jesus at the time of his arrest. For this pagan polemicist, it all went to prove the disastrous impotence of a religious conception that was not only worldless but perniciously capable of destabilizing a world the writer clearly sensed to be no longer so very secure, faced by a growing void within and a threat of attack from outside. The gestaltic reversal being brought about by Christianity in the perception and evaluation of these same events reveals the fine dividing line between one mentality and the other. This axiological, perceptual revolution, more than any other factor, is a measure of how near the Roman mediation was to its end and of a future belonging to the Christian mediation. The change is not only historical and cultural but substantial and cognitive since there can be no doubt that the Christian position marked an increase in objectual awareness, compared to the insensitivity displayed by Celsus, so to speak, in blissful innocence.

The author of the *Alethes logos* fails to see that Christ's death is not an act of violence he submits to blindly as in the case of Dionysus and Orpheus, even if for them there is some final salvation in view that however remains shrouded in the unreachable necessity of the ritual; instead, Christ's death is, as Origen notes, an act consciously performed for the salvation of mankind,[85] an individual experience and *so* an infinite one that speaks to other individuals, arousing the same infinite force in them, a personal witness and *so* a divine one, addressed to other people and kindling the same divine presence in them. In disengaging itself from the impersonalizing or prepersonal dimension of Orphic metensomatosis and Dionysian divinization, the resurrection of Christ is all the more striking in that it must be considered as experiential and not calculated; Christ's resurrection affirms the uniqueness of the body and its being all one with the soul in the incarnate infinitude of the divine mediation, even if this idea of oneness is developed by way of the ancient vision of intermedial and pneumatic states that transform the body and make it incorruptible. In Orphism, on the contrary, as generally in Greek and Roman culture, there is no escape from the eternal return of mythical-ritual and cosmic repetition. In modern times Nietzsche was to attempt to update and revitalize this same eternal return by infusing it with the unprecedented mediatory meaning of the death of God, obtaining as a result the affirmation, in negative terms, of the infinite value of human, historical experience that is the legacy of Judaic and Christian mediation. Comparison of the Orphic myth of origin and the parallel myth of origin in the Bible evinces the finely drawn but deep divide between the two worlds and helps us understand more in detail how they intermingled and differentiated, providing new hints about the formation of biblical tradition.

Mankind's Titanic origin appears to us as a mythical-numinous event, preceded in time by the Golden Age when men were not violent, and it can be defined, more by way of analogy, as original sin. Orphism has no notion of sin with moral connotations; rather there is objective culpability, a wicked state with nothing intentional or spiritual about it, which is not to say it bears no relationship to the Genesis account of the Fall of mankind's ancestors. Quite the contrary in fact. As mentioned in the previous chapter, the first book in the Bible dates from the second century BC. This is implied by the narrative's psychological, colorful vividness, as in the story of Joseph and his brothers, patently deriving from Hellenistic novels[86] and taken up again in modern times by Thomas Mann in his Tetralogy, and is made still more apparent by the highly organized and advanced theological thinking, a skillful combination of Mesopotamian, Judaic, and even Enochian myths,[87] perhaps utilizing the Orphic myth of mankind's Titanic origin as well. The violence of the Titanic *mythos* is still symbolically present within the gesture of eating the forbidden fruit from the tree of knowledge, equivalent to Dionysian omophagy if we think of Dionysus *dendrites*, that is, of the tree as an anthropomorphic symbol corresponding to the victim,[88] but it becomes bloodily flagrant in the homicidal act of Cain, the firstborn. What must attract our attention at this point, if the comparisons proposed are correct, is the extraordinary complexity of the theological-narrative operation carried out in Genesis.

Indeed, the account of mankind's original sin is accompanied by subtly critical comments about the traditional Yahwistic mediation. This transpires from the twofold account of the creation of man; one is more theological and spiritual and contains an explicit eulogy of love between man and woman that is very different from the moralistic vision of sex found in many other Judaic books, while the other is more openly mythical and ambiguous, having the death of Abel at the hands of Cain, his jealous brother, as its direct consequence. The allusion here to the assassination of Zerubbabel enables us to identify the author as an anonymous dissident priest, assisted by his school, who is expressing his dissent but avoids any open polemic such as would have excluded his work from the writings deemed canonical. He puts forward the idea of mankind undergoing a lengthier, subtler, religious and moral pedagogy in order to make its own discovery of the real face of God through the imperfect images created by itself. The story of the killing of Abel refers to the need to detach the Yahwistic cult from the rituals of human sacrifice once and for all and expresses the opaqueness of the divine mediation before it comes to be quite distinct from human wickedness in a laborious historical process corresponding to the history of Israel taken as representative of the whole of human history. Human freedom, once it has accepted the authentic mediation of the one true God, the God who is on the side of Zerubbabel but rejects all revenge on his killer, is called on to pursue that arduous course against much opposition. The sense of the mythic motif of God's resting on the seventh day is not confined to establishing a holy-day/holiday, invented to differentiate the Jews from other peoples, but also alludes intriguingly to a God who, having completed the creation, deliberately retires and becomes inactive in order to leave human beings free to make their choices and even their mistakes, considered to be inevitable so that they may learn at their own expense which mediation is the right one to be looking toward.

Through this dense network of borrowings and references we come to appreciate the objectual progress achieved by the priestly editorial board of Genesis, who must be seen as responsible for editing the Pentateuch as a whole together with the historical books and the oracles of the old prophets (the Law and the Prophets), the result of a compromise among the different currents of Judaism in the second century (probably between 159 and 152 BC according to Garbini).[89] It is a cyclopean undertaking that puts preexisting myths and sagas to fresh use, transmitting to us their sacrality and ambiguity which require constant theological, historical, and moral revision. The sin committed by our first forebears still has the inexplicit, indeterminate nature of the myths of origin but is no longer committed by equally indeterminate mythical beings. These are human actors, in a story no longer simply divine, whose actions obey psychologically understandable motivations; these combine with the initial material to form a whole made up of great figural and theological knowledge. It requires a mature reader to interpret this correctly and, if its real message is to be grasped, one who wants to push ahead in understanding the real God of mankind and Israel.

Taking our cue from the huge theological and editorial scheme of the Pentateuch and part of the historical books, the reference to the figural level allows us to take a more thorough look at the analogies and differences between Greek and Judaic historiography and to approach a theme already touched on in the Epistle to the Hebrews, the figural interpretation of history, a theme we shall have to return to in the second volume in order to understand the biblical and Christian vision of history and its relationship to myth.

6. The Figural Interpretation of History

In the Epistle to the Hebrews we saw the creative way in which Platonic idealism was translated into a historically transcendent and incarnate theology of history. In doing this, in masterly fashion, the author also marked the fulfillment of a long interaction between Judaic thinking and Greek philosophical influence. And where these two coordinates intersect we find the notion of τύπος, the suprasensible model that is nonetheless fully present in history and is expressed by the biblical, exegetical, and historically *imaginalis* idea of *figura* (figure in Latin).

The *figura* represents an interpretive key within history, and within the *mythoi* at the origin of history, but cannot be reduced to either of them since it is a real archetype (a *typos* deriving from the *arche*) realized in time: as a theme it derives historically and conceptually from Plato's concept of ideas as universal, that is to say, collective models of the sensible world that, to a certain extent, has a part in those ideas. This is the origin of the typological method applied so successfully by Philo and Origen and present within the ambit of the New Testament in Paul and the Johannine school as well as in Hebrews. But what brings out the specific character of the Judaic religious tradition is its distilled, long-term interaction with the highest philosophical-spiritual vision of Greek culture, or rather that interaction enables it to be defined thanks to the heterogony of ends that presided over the multifaceted formation of monotheism. As archetype or *typos* the Judaic tendency is to be considered neither superordinate in respect to its sensible *antitypos* nor detachable from its historic reality, in a process culminating in the idea of the incarnation of divine Wisdom in the figure of Christ. In principle, the *mundus imaginalis* of the supernatural world, evoked by the intermedial means of the ritual/myth apparatus, finds its point of full realization. As a result of this mediatory/intermedial convergence Christianity can recognize all those who anticipate or realize the Christian message as *figurae Christi*. In the stratified account of the Fall given in Genesis, this perception of the significance and historical origin of the divine mediation and of the consequent human history, is to be seen at the moment of its first germination, and we gather its full sense if we unravel the various stages in the fast-paced mythical narrative. In the following story of Cain and Abel, on which the author of Hebrews concentrates, what was not explicit in the myth of Adam and Eve is immediately made clear in a parabolic *consecutio* in which we can catch the difference in tone of the Bible story, observable in process of evolution in the magnificent metamorphosis of sin: from being a mythical demon crouching at Cain's door it turns to grief at having murdered his brother. And no less incisive are the changes in the framework and overall sequence in which these originary events are set.

The Bible *mythos* of origin is presented as a detailed historical event whose distance from us in time can be calculated exactly using the genealogies and toting up the ages of the patriarchs, extended beyond belief but always precisely specified in the text.[90] Modeled initially on the genealogies of the early Greek historiography,[91] themselves borrowed from the genealogies of Greek mythology and the equally mythical royal genealogies of the Near East, the really striking aspect is their overall transformation: from superhuman ancestries, where the royal figures had a blend of divine or monstrous features, we come in Genesis to entirely human lineages made up of recognizable individuals, wishing to have many children and a long life, and dying in the fullness of years at peace with the world, thanks to the mediation of a personal God always close to them.[92] Here, according to Garbini's suggestion, the influence of Epicurean philosophy on biblical materialism should be recognized in the indifference of God to human affairs and the appreciation of worldly pleasures once they are moderated by the wisdom of the true philosopher.[93] In itself such influence is quite plausible, but it must be traced to the brilliant sabbatical theology of the author(s) of Genesis, where the divine mediation is not at all the mediation of a *deus otiosus* but of a loving and provident God who wants his creatures to be free and desires their freely given love, free from all theological and soteriological blackmail. The close tie that exists between this theology and the ideas of Jesus of Nazareth is self-evident, but this clarification now gives us a better understanding of the relationship to the Greek historiographic models, and if on the one hand, it highlights the contribution made by the logical clarity of Hellenic culture, on the other it brings out the distinctive nature of the Judaic position.

Greek historiography is the factual register of happenings chosen as exemplary within the cyclical laws of the *kosmos*, and what matters is that they should conform to the reasoning and criteria of *logos*. When used correctly, this reproduces in itself the *logos* of the human and cosmic world whose author is a vibrant, intellectually curious narrator like Herodotus or an implacable, superbly objective analyst such as Thucydides. The exemplum (that is the *polis*, the event, or the individual who is part of both) illustrates the law and is the more illustrious (in the etymological and intermedial sense of *illustris*, shedding light) the more faithfully and courageously it succeeds in doing this, passing beyond its individual character to reach a higher principle. This process of realization is perfectly expressed by public speaking, by the *rhesis* in which the historical figure explains the reasons guiding his actions in the best words that the historian can put into his mouth, since only this kind of operation can restore to events the universal truth manifested in them without finishing there. Eloquence, at least in part, fills the ever-open margin of exemplarity that is seldom equaled by experience. The historian's task is to carve out memorable anecdotes, to record, perfect, and polish them like a sculptor who smooths the surface of a statue until it becomes sublimely beautiful and the cause for endless meditation.

Judaic historiography takes in the conceptual coherence and broad range of Greek historiography but uses it to move in an opposite direction, albeit with all the fluctuation and rearrangement involved in the lengthy process leading from the Yahwistic national mediation to the monotheistic mediation. It is a case of theological integration that finally ends in a complete reversal. The individual is not an exemplum illustrating a cosmic law: there is a universal law, but it is supracosmic because it is the will of a personal creator God, and the individual is not an exemplification of the law, to be chosen as representative, because he or she is an active interlocutor in whom the law is manifested and realized as a human relationship and as a choice. This *principium individuationis* is one of the greatest achievements of the Bible tradition, and hints of it are present *ab antiquo* in the Judaic tradition. These are strengthened during the dramatic events of the exile and postexilic period, and further defined in comparison with Greek ideas, where the thorny dilemma between collective and individual responsibility is keenly perceived and stressed in philosophy and in tragedy. Already in what we can reconstruct of preexilic theology this individual was initially the chosen people, the collective interlocutor of the national god, but very soon it became the single individual, since the people was felt to be and was experienced as a moral subject responsible for its covenant with God, and so was increasingly sensed as made up of single individuals responsible for better or worse, with a representative case of one or a few individuals excerpted from the frequent cases of collective unfaithfulness. Yahweh finally appears as the supreme individual, individualizing all those who receive his message and find a place in their hearts for his inscrutable law; and this process is already spectacularly visible in the prophetic books, especially in the vocational texts where the prophet discovers his raison d'être in listening to the word of God and can no longer erase it or distance himself from it, since that would mean destroying his ontological and historical constitution, his personal and moral objectuality. One of the Bible's most humanly touching texts, the prophet's lament in Jeremiah 20:7–18, exemplifies this situation very clearly.

The creative, tensional circularity thus set up between collective factors and individual consciousness runs right through Judaism and then passes on to Christianity, however much institutional ideologies in all ages have sought to blunt its unpredictable dynamism in the name of some collective and impersonal theology. The people of Israel achieve their status as a collective personality through the exceptional individual who receives and transmits the word of God, but that individual stands out from all others because he places himself at the service of his divine Mediator, becomes his faithful servant, even so far as to accept the fate of being the Suffering Servant of the people. Judaism in the Hellenistic period takes these ideas to a breaking point in its thinking about unhappiness and wrongdoing, as we see in Job and in Ecclesiastes, but always restores the circularity of the divine mediation because the mediation itself feeds on them, makes man's drama its own, and wants to provide an answer. It is not hard to understand how Jesus shaped his own figure and mission on these precedents, and also how, in Judaism, there comes to be no difference in principle between theology and the writing of history, since history is the sphere in which God's sublime and individualizing power is manifested, his will as creator of man and the world.

We now have enough information to look more closely at the Christian mediation, and its specific significance, in its historical and comparative context. However, before we enter into the merits of Christianity and what distinguishes it from the rest of the ancient world's legacy of religions and forms of knowledge, it is worth assessing the legitimacy of the claims for continuity made by Christian apologists in respect to the original message, that is to say, the transition from the initial phase of Jesus in a Middle-Judaic context to the phase when Christianity has separated from Judaism, with a view to the later phase of Christianity with which we shall need to establish a relationship hermeneutically speaking. The question to be answered in this Intermezzo is whether or not there is a continuity of transmission verifiable with modern historical and cognitive means. And for the answer we go back to Origen.

7. Origen's Answer

For precise reasons Origen in the first instance answers Celsus's criticisms in a double register, historical and moral, that actually corresponds to a single criterion, and one that could not be more biblical, identifying history with implementing the Good, and salvation with the history of salvation. All the same, Celsus's comparative argument is side-stepped rather than confronted and destined to reemerge in modern times in more systematic forms. Origen fails to make clear the structural equivalence existing between events in pagan myths and rites and the story of Christ, and it remains obscure for much of the history of Christianity; in the same way, third-century Christianity had put well behind it the old, unresolved *querelle* between the priestly class in power, heir to the murderer of Zerubbabel, and dissident priests promoting an alternative opposing form of Yahwism. Once Christianity had separated officially from Judaism in the first and second centuries, it left behind the vexed religious and moral problems that had tormented Middle-Judaic thinking, constituted its secret greatness, and animated Christ's challenge to the priestly and Temple establishment. And a similar observation holds good for rabbinical Judaism, sheltering behind its exclusive definition of monotheism and its systematic anti-Christian polarization.

What we see here, in short, is amnesia on three counts: the real tenor of the Middle-Judaic debate, the real intentions of the historical Jesus, and the real significance of the comparison with paganism are all forgotten. This means that historical awareness in the West did indeed develop from Judaism and Christianity, and from the sensibility that led to rediscovering classical historiography, but it was also fostered by cancellations and simplifications no less significant, which can induce intransitive reasoning à la Foucault about the impossibility of achieving any organic view of history, since every age reinvents history to suit itself, or vice versa can lead to recognizing that history never proceeds in a linear sequence or in Hegelian cycles but rather by alternations, influences, interminglings, and breaks that also, and especially in their negation, open the way to unexpected combinations and unthought-of thresholds of perception from which there may come a retroaction of rediscovery and awakening to awareness. This, I believe, is what happened in the West with the particular developments of the Christian mediation, and secondly, but not secondarily, with the Judaic mediation, from which we must conclude that the historical vision developed in the West is not yet fully self-aware. In the Christian sphere this vision remains within the theological mediation that developed it, while in later nonreligious historiography, it fails to attain an objectual recognition of the religious and cultural mediations that allowed it to take shape. For two thousand years the debate has been at a standstill, or rather it has never shifted from the level of partisan polemics or overcome the specialist divisions that debate nothing because they see nothing outside their own particular field.

If we concentrate on the comparative theme we started with, which proves to be the main thread running through this inquiry, we note how it allows us not only to supply a content to and motivate the clash between supporters of paganism and the Judeo-Christian tradition but also to reconstruct the history of early and Middle Judaism as well as the differentiation within Middle Judaism of Christic Judaism, of what was to become Christianity. Thinking about this subject got underway again as a result of the attempts, supported on opposing fronts by the arguments of Girard and Nietzsche, to answer the comparative question by taking a fresh look at an ancient truth through a modern conceptual scheme; however, these efforts have not really changed things since the contrasting positions are upheld and defended without coming to recognize a more comprehensive history. Instead, the way forward must be to fully recover this history in terms of its phenomenology and hermeneutics, since there would be little sense in noting signs of historical awareness on one side alone, our awareness being the result of both, with differences in distribution and emphasis that are not to be evened out. And if from the ancient world we derive a fact-based knowledge at the origin of our scientific objectivity that tends to render everything uniform within its ontological and cosmic parameters, from Judaism and Christianity there comes a historical and existential knowledge of the *hic et nunc* of human lives that could hardly have missed the enigma of the resemblances between the stories of Dionysus and Christ.

On this question of religious comparison, what matters is not only the declared intentions, the conscious representations, such as those I have attributed to the author of Hebrews, but still more the interactions and combinations between historical and cultural processes that we need to perceive as a whole for their objective and objectual significance. And so it becomes important to verify whether Origen in the *Contra Celsum*, that is, in the most important apologia surviving from early Christian times, succeeds in at least reflecting phenomenologically, into things themselves so to speak, on the twofold, convergent theme of the similarity in the difference and the difference in the similarity between Christianity and paganism, between Christ's Passion and sacrifice.

The answer uncovered by such an inquiry is positive. At a certain point Origen approaches the anthropological and religious mystery of the sacrificial origin of the objectual mediations that men need, and notes the inexplicable capacity whereby a single individual takes on himself the ills of an entire community:

> In fact it appears, on the basis of certain mysterious reasons [*logous*] unfathomable for the majority of mankind, that there is this natural disposition [*physin*] in the nature of things [*en te physei ton pragmaton*] by which one just man, prepared to die of his own free will for the good of the community, succeeds in exorcizing [*apotropiasmous*] the wicked demons responsible for plague, sterility, shipwrecks, and similar woes.
>
> Let them speak, then, those who refuse to believe that Christ died on the cross for mankind, and let them say if they also intend to reject the many stories [*historias*], widespread among Greeks and barbarians alike, about those who died for the common good in order to save cities and populations from the misfortunes that beset them! Or will they maintain that those events are true but that it is instead quite incredible that this man, as they consider him to be, offered to die to defeat the great demon, prince [*archontos*] of demons, who had subjected all the souls of men that ever appeared on earth?[94]

This highly remarkable passage contains not only the essential facts of the problem, still all intertwined in a single mediatory and intermedial vision, but at the same time the objectual solution, expressed with vigor though not yet perceived in all its implications. His words are not far in themselves from comparable passages where a refined Middle-Platonist such as Plutarch explains human sacrifice as an extreme means to appease evil demons,[95] but Origen assumes this mysterious necessity in order to overturn it from within by selecting the Christlike example of "one just man, prepared to die of his own free will for the good of the community." In this way much remains not said, but the mediation of Christ becomes a lens for reading these circumstances in a thoroughly new fashion. In this way Origen intuits the victimary scheme, where the victim takes the ills of the community on himself, in spite of failing to isolate the element of human responsibility in that scheme, the historical, active presence of a collective process. According to his view, the occurrence of mass violence and its necessity if social groups are to survive obey "mysterious reasons unfathomable for the majority" and appear as phenomena inherent "in the nature of things"—ἐν τῇ φύσει τῶν πραγμάτων—that is, in the inner characteristics of what happens and is done. Origen traces these events back to the mediatory and intermedial factors on which his vision depends, as does the vision of his contemporaries, of the first generations of Christians, and of Jesus himself. The distinction between appearance and substance, which in antiquity remains ritually reversible and was to become in modern gnosiology the sharp division between phenomenon and noumenon, begins to become a historical process where all is potentially revealed, though that will be possible only at the end of time. The "nature" Origen is speaking about is not a cosmic-metaphysical datum as it was in Greek philosophy, nor cosmic-scientific as in modern philosophy, but a battlefield where the domain of "the great demon, prince of demons, who had subjected all the souls of men that ever appeared on earth" is active, and where Christ has brought the definitive answer, offered as salvation to the whole created world. Origen takes up the gospel doctrine of Satan, of the idolatrous and violent mediation dominating men's lives before the coming of Christ, prepared for by Judaic monotheism.

This would seem to confirm Girard's interpretation of Satan as the symbol of the sacrificial foundation at the origin of mankind, but this is only partly the case. In the first place, and not unlike Plutarch, Origen is not condemning sacrifice as such, since in itself it expresses a law "in the nature of things," but in Christ's death as sacrifice he identifies the key to correctly interpret all similar events and to give them the power to save starting from its own exclusive mediation. Sacrifice is not set in opposition to nonsacrifice but rather the one true sacrifice is contrasted to the others to the extent that they are not yet mediated by Christ. Besides, a second and just as important feature is that Origen is talking about the demons as intermedial forces absolutely objective in his eyes, again like in Plutarch, with the difference that all this is translated into personal and moral terms because these demons are spiritual beings that rebelled against their creator; and it requires the right mediation to be saved from them, which is the mediation of God, able to preserve us thanks to the sacramental power of his word and name.[96] Here Origen adheres to the Judaic *mythos*, shared by all Christians and followed by Jesus, as well as by the synoptic Gospels (John is a partial exception that I shall need to discuss in the second volume), in presenting the exorcisms as Christ's greatest miracles and as the unquestionable sign of his divine descent. The Gospel of Mark goes so far as to put its first Christological declaration into the mouth of an "unclean spirit" (*pneumati akatharto*): "I know who you are: the Holy One of God" (1:24). In the same way the term *skandalon*—which indicates mimetic desire for Girard, the desire that becomes rivalry and so trips up against its own model-obstacle—in the Gospels and in Christian authors indicates the human response to the constant threats and temptations of objectively demoniac forces, resulting in behavior for which human beings are responsible since it is their own free choice, but it goes back to the mediatory and sacral causes of a creatural level rebelling against God, about which human beings are called on to take a position.

Girard's interpretation of Satan and the *skandalon* has stirred up exegetical waters that had become somewhat stagnant, with commentators usually constrained either to a literalism basically unacceptable to modern readers and devoid of all historical considerations, or to rationalizations that exclude whatever lies outside the modern mental picture as being irrational. But in doing this Girard has reduced a vast hermeneutic span down to suppositions about demythologizing knowledge of the origin that find no textual support, thus ignoring the history he wants to explain and consigning the huge weight of evidence for a literal belief in the devil, coming from hundreds and hundreds of years of Christianity, to the ad hoc category of persecution texts. The historical evidence, on the contrary, reveals a far more internal, gradual process of knowledge forming *within* the mythical representations of a religious tradition and due to them; this process develops the idea of evil supernatural forces, inferior nonetheless to the divine Mediator, that involve the human creature's faculties of understanding and choice, since it is called upon to choose between the mediations of salvation and perdition. And without doubt this is the interpretation worked out and announced by Jesus, which takes data typical of Middle Judaism and often utilized in an apocalyptic key, and turns it into a factor calling for urgent attention from man, face to face with the Son of man, to adopt the flexible formula used by Jesus to refer to himself: that is to say, in the presence of an extraordinary prophetic mediator who brings the word of God and proclaims the Kingdom in the everyday lives of men, at the very heart of their historical, existential reality. The figure of Satan thus becomes a means for interpreting this human and historical reality, a tool for knowledge, as in Origen. The expression he uses, *archon*, echoes similar expressions in the Gospels, in particular "the prince of this world" (*ho archon tou kosmou toutou*) in John 16:11, that far from any loss in effectiveness when translated from the language of the time, reveals a core of meaning no less valid today than it was then. And these arguments can be used to support the idea that the tradition consists in this work of translation, transmitting the message received, in the face of the constant danger of misrepresentation involved in the action of *tradere* (handing over), though the risk must be run if the tradition is to keep to history and not in its turn to misrepresent it.

The translation lives up to expectations, even if the historical contextualization circumscribes it and brings it down to a healthy state of realism. "Prince" is a title of royal power, and as such cannot be ignored by anyone having anything to do with it, while it also expresses the personal nature of the power. And so we find ourselves with a system that acts as a person, and yet has no ontological basis of its own; this was made clear by later theological reflection, still within a metaphysical framework that took away none of the realism from its demonological beliefs, traced back to the spiritual level of the objectively existing intermedial world. Where the fully ontological status is also and above all valid—it should be noted—as axiological status, it is synonymous with what is a just and fitting existence because it is sanctioned by and in harmony with God, synonymous in other words with the only objectual condition worthy of the name. In this way Christian theological and metaphysical thinking, in symbolic and mythical terms, successfully explains how it comes about that Satan needs this world in order to hold dominion and exist, why he needs subjects to obey him, ratify his existence, and provide the solidity that he cannot have on his own, according to what all early Christians believed about the pagan gods, unanimously identified as demons. This is why Origen writes that the "prince of demons" subjects "all the souls of men that ever appeared on earth": the chief of demons is a principle of inner domination, of perverse mediation, only to be opposed by a stronger mediation, the mediation of the Christian Word providentially and secretly intervening in history and in the lives of men, with conceptual complications that are worth mentioning.

The ontological distinction of Evil as nonbeing is still missing in Origen; it was to be developed particularly by Augustine, albeit with the difficulties bound up with the fact that this nonbeing keeps its axiological and performative status as privation of the only authentically objectual existence, existence in God, and that is why Evil in Augustine is destined to persist in the form of the *massa damnata*. Origen, for his part, as a result of inadequately distinguishing Evil as a principle of negation from the creatures who share in it, is reluctant to admit that some creatures can be doomed a priori to damnation with no chance to repent; in an attempt to resolve this aporia he hypothesizes a universal apocatastasis, the final redemption of all creatures, devils included,[97] an idea already present in Mazdaist eschatology.[98] As an idea of objectual redemption it certainly seems more in harmony with the inspiration of the gospel message and could be harmonized with later developments in metaphysics and theology by distinguishing absolute nonbeing from moral and axiological nonbeing, as such open to possible redemption. Origen's attempted solution was not at all well received or taken to be in keeping with the spirit of the Gospels as he intended; on the contrary, it provoked reactions that can now, many centuries later, be recognized for what they were. This and other doctrines attributed to Origen were condemned by the church as heretical and led to the destruction of many of his writings—the greatest loss suffered by early Christian literature. Instead of being appreciated for the precious historical significance of his writings he became a theological scapegoat for orthodox Christianity: the condemned writings could not have been heretical since no dogmas as yet existed for them to contravene.[99] If this statement of fact is a lesson to us in avoiding all undue mythicizing about what has been called orthodoxy, it also highlights the truth that such unfair treatment has been the price of progress in thinking, and to reach this point of understanding that the devil of the tradition is not an ontologically real figure but a principle.

In the passage from *Contra Celsum*, then, Origen does not have complete mastery of the argument since its exact outlines elude him, but he follows its constitutive factors and meaning, and thus ensures a precision and balance to his words that could be defined as scientific. And that leads to another observation of no little weight. In order to demonstrate the historical reality of the story of Christ, Origen implicitly relies on arguing for its similarity to pagan histories, not for how it differs from them. His line of reasoning is as subtle as it is penetrating: the figure of Christ has such force that his detractors need only admit its being *on a par* with their histories and the decisive difference of his sacrifice of love will assert itself, precisely on the basis of a need for salvation already present in those histories, a need running right through human culture and waiting to be recognized and redeemed. This similarity shows the reversal brought about by Jesus, whose choice transforms violence into a sacramental offering and the greatest of disasters into an act of redemption. In short, the passage allows us to recognize that the ideas of Origen, decisive for the future history of Christian thinking, possess real awareness of the objective and potentially objectual significance of Christ's mediation and are basically in continuity with the gospel message.

Having ascertained so much, we can also note how the latent force in Origen's argument is not exploited to the full, his remarks being confined to stories about "those who died for the common good." He lacks any perception of the story that lies hidden behind many pagan myths and rites, the story of the victim of collective violence; he does not comprehend that the "wicked demons responsible for plague, sterility, shipwreck, and similar woes" coincide, in the resulting *reductio ad unum*, with the "one just man" whose death has the mysterious power of warding them off; and he is still unable to see, behind those "wicked demons," the community in the grip of a harrowing mediatory and objectual crisis. The anthropological and philosophical noumenon remains such, but contains the future possibility of being read historically, a possibility that was not only future, given that we find its main point at the very beginning of *Contra Celsum*:

> When false witness was borne against our Savior and Lord Jesus Christ, he "was silent" and "did not reply" to the charges laid against him

> [*kategoroumenos*] because he was convinced such false testimony could be demolished much better by his life as a whole and by the work he had done among the Jews; and so the wrongdoing they accused him of [*kategorias*] could also be better confuted that way than by making some kind of speech in his own defense.[100]

This is the mark of the dignity of Jesus, regal and divine, and so human as well; and the subject returns again toward the end of the work. After mentioning Orpheus, Origen contrasts Christ's silence with celebrated sayings of Greeks as they faced torture and death, extolled by Celsus for showing a far more admirable attitude than Christ's.[101] By simply stating the bare fact of Christ's silence, Origen has already said what is essential. There is nothing judicial, polemical, or categorial about it, since its strength lies in the fact itself (*factum*, πρᾶγμα), that is, in weakness transformed into witness that speaks for itself by virtue of what is done to it. As Origen stresses, making reference to the Suffering Servant in one of the finest passages in *Contra Celsum*:

> In fact, he neither said nor did anything out of place [*ouden . . . atopon*] but truly "as a sheep led to the slaughter [*epi sphagen*], and as a lamb before the shearer, he was dumb [*aphonos*]"; and the Gospel also says that "he did not open his mouth."[102]

Jesus neither said nor did anything *atopon*, "out of place" in the sense of incorrect and unlawful, which is a direct quotation from the Passion in Luke, where the so-called good thief reminds his fellow that the man being crucified between them has done nothing *atopon* (23:41). The adjective appears all the more revealing if seen beside Porphyry's invective against the Eucharist, "of all absurdities the most absurd" (*atopematos pantos atopoteron*), meaning completely inappropriate in every sense of the word for sensible people, civilized in philosophical and political terms. The spatial connotation of the Lucan phrase is extremely dense and underlines the fact that Jesus, having been found guilty, becomes literally *atopos*, outside the *topoi*, the "places" of respectable people and outside their topics of conversation, their accepted common places; and so his position shifts, from the places of the living to the nonplace of the Crucifixion. And it is from this nonplace that the dying

Jesus tells the good thief he will be in paradise that very day, that is, in the transcendent place where the spiritual conditions of the Kingdom of God will be fulfilled. The details are figural, but they tell us of an experience to be found within all human mediations, the experience of those who are *aphonoi* because others do the talking, and of those who are *atopoi* because all the *topoi* have been taken by others.

To conclude this comparative review, acting as an interlude between classical Greek culture and Christianity, we now possess the elements to say that Origen's investigations show us an identity beginning to form historically and culturally. Those investigations manage to catch the implications of a tradition and successfully transmit it, though some part remains elusive; and the identity in the making is ours, a first person plural demanding to be explained and determined, seeing that it can include the Western identity and, to a certain extent, an identity that has become worldwide.

So we reach an intermediate goal in our dialogue, whose position midway has provided us with significant means for historical and interpretive intermediation; it now remains to historically examine Christianity in the next book, hopefully enabling us to return with a clearer picture to the problematic situation we started from, that is, theoretical thinking about man elaborated in the last centuries. What can the New Testament tell us in its own words, especially in the Gospels, about the questions dealt with so far? As the arguments we shall be touching on are largely unexplored, it becomes inevitable that we offer a series of hypothetical readings, but the knowledge to be gained from them is not hypothetical, nor are the historical processes that can give life and meaning to all the themes and connections I shall be attempting to interpret. We shall reencounter the symbolism of the sacred marriage, the divine mother and divine child, the triad of the ritual cycle, the labyrinth, and the afterlife; but all these symbols and *mythoi* will appear profoundly transformed in a way to make them reveal another, increasingly objectual and human meaning.

However, the first step must be a preliminary explanation of the method to follow in approaching the Christian sources. A thorny issue, as in one way or another it is not separable from the very person inspiring them, the Son of man, the rabbi of Nazareth, the most mysterious character of Western history, and even more mysterious if we consider that he was born, lived, and died in the ancient Near East. But behind this question, *his* question, we shall discover one of the most exciting and least appreciated intellectual adventures of European culture: the discovery of the historical Jesus.

Notes

Preface: The Black Sun of Europe

1. German edition T. Mann, *Der Zauberberg,* ed. M. Neumann (Frankfurt a.M.: Fischer, 2002). My previous analyses of the episode are presented in G. Fornari, *Fra Dioniso e Cristo: La sapienza sacrificale greca e la civiltà occidentale* (Bologna: Pitagora, 2001), 1–9; and *Da Dioniso a Cristo: Conoscenza e sacrificio nel mondo greco e nella civiltà occidentale* (Genova-Milano: Marietti, 2006), 5–13.
2. Quote from L. Crescenzi, introduction to T. Mann, *La montagna magica,* ed. L. Crescenzi, It. trans. R. Colorni (Milano: A. Mondadori, 2011), lxxv.
3. On Nietzsche and Freud, see the following Introduction. Mann's claim that he had not read the works of Freud before finishing *Der Zauberberg* might reveal a concern to preempt psychologistic misunderstandings of the novel. In any case he did know Freud's ideas, as is shown by T. Mann, *Tagebücher 1918–1921,* ed. P. De Mendelssohn (Frankfurt a.M.: Fischer, 1979), 521 (and 806n), where he expresses interest in a review of *Jenseits des Lustenprinzip.*
4. Mann, *Der Zauberberg,* 1:742. Henceforth, for reasons of interpretative consistency, quotations are generally made from the original texts, and translations are vetted or made by the author, except for a few cases checked against the original text when they are primary sources.
5. On the novel, see following, vol. 1, chapter 6, § 2.
6. I will use the adjective "mediatory" in reference to mediation as a supreme cultural and symbolic source, and the adjectives "intermedial," "intermediate," and the like to refer to mediation as medium.

7. Mann, *Der Zauberberg,* 1:743.
8. Mann, *Der Zauberberg,* 1:744–45.
9. Mann, *Der Zauberberg,* 1:745–46.
10. On the sources used by Mann, see the notes in Mann, *Der Zauberberg,* 2:315–17, that anyway do not realize their pertinence.
11. Mann, *Der Zauberberg,* 1:746.
12. Mann, *Der Zauberberg,* 1:746.
13. Mann, *Der Zauberberg,* 1:747.
14. Mann, *Der Zauberberg,* 1:748.
15. G. Fornari, *A God Torn to Pieces: The Nietzsche Case,* Engl. trans. K. Buck in collaboration with the author (East Lansing: Michigan State University Press, 2013).
16. On the religious meaning of *Faust*'s conclusion, see vol. 2, chapter 5, § 7.
17. I will present Girard's interpretation in the Introduction, § 4.
18. F. Nietzsche, *Sämtliche Werke: Kritischen Studienausgabe,* ed. G. Colli and M. Montinari (Berlin-New York: De Gruyter, 1980), 13:265–67, 14[89]; R. Girard, "Dionysus versus the Crucified," *Modern Language Notes* 99, no. 4 (1984): 816–35.
19. Quote from the neoclassical Italian poet Ugo Foscolo (*Dei sepolcri* 158), with reference to the secrets of political power unmasked by Niccolò Machiavelli.
20. Mann, *Der Zauberberg,* 1:1085.
21. T. Mann, *Betrachtungen eines Unpolitisch* (Frankfurt a.M.: Fischer, 1956), 162.
22. T. Mann, *Joseph und seine Brüder* (Frankfurt a.M.: Fischer, 1966), 1:662.
23. On D'Annunzio, see Fornari, *A God Torn to Pieces,* 43–47 and 64–66.
24. Mann, *Der Zauberberg,* 1:748–49.
25. Mann, *Der Zauberberg,* 1:1083.
26. Mann, *Der Zauberberg,* 1:1084.

Gnosiological Introduction: A Disregarded Philosophical Tradition

1. German text in F. Nietzsche, *Sämtliche Werke: Kritischen Studienausgabe,* ed. G. Colli and M. Montinari (Berlin-New York: De Gruyter, 1980) (henceforth NSW), 3:480.
2. Cf. G. Fornari, *A God Torn to Pieces: The Nietzsche Case,* Engl. trans. K. Buck in collaboration with the author (East Lansing: Michigan State University Press, 2013), 60–61.
3. NSW, 3:481: "Diess ungeheure Ereigniss ist noch unterwegs und wandert."
4. NSW, 3:480–81.
5. NSW, 3:481.
6. Cf. Fornari, *A God Torn to Pieces,* 72–74.
7. NSW, 1:26.
8. NSW, 1:28.

9. É. Durkheim, *Les règles de la méthode sociologique* (Paris: Flammarion, 1995), 120.
10. Durkheim, *Les règles de la méthode sociologique,* 120–22.
11. G. Fornari, *Storicità radicale: Filosofia e morte di Dio* (Massa: Transeuropa, 2013), 289–358; Fornari, *Mito, tragedia, filosofia: Dall'antica Grecia al Moderno* (Roma: Studium, 2017), 46–49, 53–54, 219–38, and 245–62.
12. E. Husserl, *Logische Untersuchungen,* ed. U. Panzer, vol. 19, part 1 (The Hague: Nijhoff, 1984), 10.
13. W. Robertson Smith, *Lectures on the Religion of the Semites* (London: Black, 1894), 338 ff.
14. *S. Nili narrationes de caede monachorum,* in *Patrologia Cursus Completus, Series Graeca,* ed. J.-P. Migne (Paris, 1860), 79:589–694.
15. As rightly noted by R. Girard, *La violence et le sacré* (Paris: Grasset, 1994), 286.
16. J.J. Atkinson, "Primal Law," in *Social Origins,* by A. Lang (London: Longmans, Green and Co., 1903), 209 ff.
17. Also deducing similar behavior among African elephants (Atkinson, "Primal Law," 222).
18. Girard, *La violence et le sacré,* 284, is inexact in denying this discovery to Atkinson; Freud's discovery consisted in being first to see the *significance* of the hypothesis.
19. S. Freud, *Totem und Tabu: Einige Übereinstimmungen im Seelenleben der Wilden und der Neurotiker* (Frankfurt a.M.: Fischer, 2007), 196.
20. Freud, *Totem und Tabu,* 196. The long note quoting Atkinson follows at this point.
21. *Massenpsychologie* is to be translated *Mass Psychology* and not *Group Psychology* as Freud's focus is on human mass as such, not on a simple group meant as a psychosocial phenomenon (see below, § 6).
22. S. Freud, *Massenpsychologie und Ich-Analyse: Die Zukunft einer Illusion* (Frankfurt a.M.: Fischer, 2007), 96.
23. Freud, *Totem und Tabu,* 217 (J.W. Goethe, *Faust,* I, 1237).
24. P. Gay, *Freud: A Life for Our Time* (New York: Doubleday, 1988), 328–34.
25. É. Durkheim, *Les formes élémentaires de la vie religieuse* (Paris: Le Livre de Poche, 1991), 52; Durkheim, *The Elementary Forms of Religious Life,* Engl. trans. K.E. Fields (New York: The Free Press, 1995), 8–9 (with some interventions).
26. Durkheim, *Les formes élémentaires,* 52; Durkheim, *The Elementary Forms,* 9.
27. Durkheim, *Les formes élémentaires,* 52; Durkheim, *The Elementary Forms,* 9.
28. Durkheim, *Les formes élémentaires,* 730–31; Durkheim, *The Elementary Forms,* 442.
29. This possibility clearly emerges, though just hinted at, from the speech given by Durkheim at a meeting held in Paris at the beginning of 1914, on which see the report in S. Lukes, *Émile Durkheim: His Life and Work. A Historical and Critical Study* (New York: Harper & Row, 1972), 514–20.
30. See the synthesis of their positions just after the publication of the book in Lukes, *Émile Durkheim,* 506–29.

31. A freedom that must be exerted both for good and evil, so that criminals are no less necessary than great reformers or revolutionaries: Durkheim, *Les règles de la méthode sociologique,* 158–68; on Durkheim's projects of a "science" of morality, see Lukes, *Émile Durkheim,* 420–23.
32. Durkheim, *Les formes élémentaires,* 49–50.
33. The pivotal meaning of this work, not developed by the author himself, is stressed by L. Scubla, *Lire Lévi-Strauss: Le déploiement d'une intuition* (Paris: O. Jacob, 1998), 288–93, with attention not to Durkheim but to the problem of myth.
34. C. Lévi-Strauss, *Les structures élémentaires de la parenté* (Paris-La Haye: Mouton, 1981), 562–64.
35. Lévi-Strauss, *Les structures élémentaires,* 560.
36. Lévi-Strauss, *Les structures élémentaires,* 566. The author quotes from the French edition of the essay "Die Sprache und der Aufbau der Gegenstandswelt" (1932), in E. Cassirer, *Gesammelte Werke,* ed. B. Recki (Hamburg: Meiner, 2004), 18:116: "Die Sprache . . . ist selbst ein Mittel der Gegenstandsbildung."
37. G. Bataille, *Œuvres complètes* (Paris: Gallimard, 1973–), 8:43.
38. Bataille, *Œuvres complètes,* 8:29.
39. Bataille, *Œuvres complètes,* 8:40.
40. Bataille, *Œuvres complètes,* 8:62.
41. Bataille, *Œuvres complètes,* 9:72.
42. Bataille, *Œuvres complètes,* 8:66.
43. As emerges clearly from his *Théorie de la Religion* in Bataille, *Œuvres complètes,* 7:281–361.
44. For a wide exposition of the Girardian mimetic theory, see W. Palaver, *René Girard's Mimetic Theory,* Engl. trans. G. Borrud (East Lansing: Michigan State University Press, 2013).
45. R. Girard, *Dostoïevski du double à l'unité* (Paris: Plon, 1963).
46. R. Girard, *A Theater of Envy: William Shakespeare* (Oxford: Oxford University Press, 1991); the French translation, with some variants, appeared beforehand in 1990 at the wish of the publishers.
47. An original mimetic approach to Cervantes and the birth of the modern novel is in C. Bandera, *Mimesis Conflictiva: Ficción literaria y violencia en Cervantes y Calderón* (Madrid: Editorial Gredos, 1975); Bandera, *"Monda y desnuda": la humilde historia de Don Quijote. Reflexiones sobre el origen de la novela moderna* (Madrid: Iberoamericana, 2005).
48. Girard, *La violence et le sacré,* 286.
49. Girard, *La violence et le sacré,* 354.
50. Girard, *La violence et le sacré,* 360.
51. Girard, *La violence et le sacré,* 353.
52. Girard, *La violence et le sacré,* 325.

53. Girard, *La violence et le sacré,* 314.
54. Girard, *La violence et le sacré,* 289; Lévi-Strauss, *Les structures élémentaires,* 562.
55. I refer in particular to the conclusion of C. Lévi-Strauss, *L'homme nu* (Paris: Plon, 1971), 559–621.
56. Girard, *La violence et le sacré,* 351.
57. Girard, *La violence et le sacré,* 362. The emphasis in the English translation is mine.
58. W. Benjamin, *Ursprung des deutschen Trauerspiels,* in Benjamin, *Gesammelte Schriften,* ed. R. Tiedemann and H. Schweppenhäuser (Frankfurt a.M.: Suhrkamp, 1991), 1, pt. 1:211.
59. On Benjamin, see also below, vol. 1, chapter 8, § 3.
60. Girard however takes no account of animal behavior as recorded by Darwin, and noticed again by Atkinson and Freud.
61. Girard, *La violence et le sacré,* 18; cf. G. Lienhardt, *Divinity and Experience: The Religion of the Dinka* (Oxford: Clarendon Press, 1976), 23–25.
62. R. Girard, *Des choses cachées depuis la foundation du monde: Recherches avec Jean-Michel Oughourlian et Guy Lefort* (Paris: Grasset, 1991), 55 ff.
63. J.G. Frazer, *The Golden Bough: A Study in Magic and Religion* (New York: Macmillan Co., 1951), 308–41; A.M. Hocart, *Kings and Councillors: An Essay in the Comparative Anatomy of Human Society* (1936; repr. Chicago: University of Chicago Press, 1970); Bataille, *La souveraineté,* in *Œuvres complètes,* 8:262–95.
64. Girard, *La violence et le sacré,* 157 ff., 448–58; Girard, *Des choses cachées,* 73–82.
65. Girard, *Des choses cachées,* 146–50.
66. Fundamental essays regarding persecution texts are collected in R. Girard, *"To Double Business Bound": Essays on Literature, Mimesis, and Anthropology* (London: Athlon Press, 1988), 155–98.
67. R. Girard, "Les malédictions contre les Pharisiens et la révélation évangélique," *Bulletin du Centre Protestant d'Études de Genève* 27, no. 3 (1975): 5–29.
68. The episode of Peter's denial is widely examined in R. Girard, *Le bouc émissaire* (Paris: Grasset, 1982), 221–42.
69. The most significant book in this regard, essentially rounding off his career, is R. Girard, *Achever Clausewitz: Entretiens avec Benoît Chantre* (Paris: Carnets Nord, 2007).
70. R. Girard, P. Antonello, and J.C. De Castro Rocha, *Evolution and Conversion: Dialogues on the Origin of Culture* (London-New York: Continuum, 2007), 39–40.
71. C. Lévi-Strauss, *La pensée sauvage* (Paris: Plon, 1962), 295–99; the inconsistency of such a view just starting from the dynamic meaning of the Lévi-Straussian thought is argued in Scubla, *Lire Lévi-Strauss,* 87–90 (and elsewhere), in relation to a neglected process of mediation made possible by the unity of ritual and myth.
72. Girard, *La violence et le sacré,* 310.
73. Girard, *La violence et le sacré,* 310–11.

74. Girard, *La violence et le sacré,* 320.
75. Girard, *La violence et le sacré,* 321.
76. As already observed by B. Latour, *Nous n'avons jamais* été *modernes: Essay d'anthropologie symétrique* (Paris: La Découverte, 1994), 66–67.
77. Girard, *Des choses cachées,* 107.
78. Girard, *Des choses cachées,* 108.
79. Girard, *Des choses cachées,* 139.
80. Girard, *Des choses cachées,* 114–15.
81. Interestingly Eric Gans attempts to clarify Girard's scene of origin by stressing the aborted gesture by which the prehuman animals tabooed a disputed object, making it meaningful (E. Gans, *The End of Culture: Toward a Generative Anthropology* [Berkeley: University of California Press, 1985], 19–38); however, in that way Gans does not recognize at all the role of the initial object, which could be anything at all for him, and so exposes the contractualist premise latent in Girard's scheme.
82. Girard, *Des choses cachées,* 117.
83. Girard, *Des choses cachées,* 139 ff.
84. For my interpretation of the cultural significance of burial, see G. Fornari, *Da Dioniso a Cristo: Conoscenza e sacrificio nel mondo greco e nella civiltà occidentale* (Genova-Milano: Marietti, 2006), 33–34.
85. B. Vandermeersch, "Le più antiche sepolture," in F. Facchini et al., *La religiosità nella preistoria,* Ital. trans. L. Comoglio and A. De Lorenzi (Milano: Jaca Book, 1991), 21–53; B. Vandermeersch, "Ce que nous apprennent les premières sépultures," *Comptes Rendus Palevol* 5 (2006): 161–67.
86. See below, § 7.
87. I shall say more about the most important of these finds in § 8; it must be added that the use of "aesthetic" decorations by *H. sapiens* dates back roughly to the same period and that new finds might modify again the present state of knowledge.
88. See the clear explanation in S. Condemi and F. Savatier, *Neandertal, mon frère: 300.000 ans d'histoire de l'homme* (Paris: Flammarion, 2016).
89. G. Manzi, *L'evoluzione umana: Ominidi e uomini prima di Homo sapiens* (Bologna: Il Mulino, 2007), 116–33.
90. C. Bandera, *A Refuge of Lies: Reflections on Faith and Fiction* (East Lansing: Michigan State University Press, 2013), 9–10.
91. Bandera, *A Refuge of Lies,* 10.
92. Durkheim, *Les règles de la méthode sociologique,* 104–5. I have examined this passage in Fornari, *Storicità radicale,* 41–46.
93. Lukes, *Émile Durkheim,* 302–13.
94. E. Canetti, *Masse und Macht* (München-Wien: Hanser, 1960), 13–105.
95. Durkheim, *Les règles de la méthode sociologique,* 99.
96. Cf. Gay, *Freud,* 395 ff.

97. Freud, *Massenpsychologie,* 39.
98. Freud, *Massenpsychologie,* 53.
99. Freud, *Massenpsychologie,* 55.
100. Freud, *Massenpsychologie,* 68.
101. Freud, *Massenpsychologie,* 81.
102. Freud, *Massenpsychologie,* 82.
103. Freud, *Massenpsychologie,* 83.
104. Freud, *Massenpsychologie,* 85.
105. Freud, *Massenpsychologie,* 86.
106. Girard, *La violence et le sacré,* 316.
107. Freud, *Massenpsychologie,* 62.
108. Freud, *Massenpsychologie,* 63.
109. G. Bateson, *Steps to an Ecology of Mind* (Chicago: University of Chicago Press, 1999), 201–337.
110. Girard, *La violence et le sacré,* 261, 273–79; Girard, *Des choses cachées,* 360–64.
111. As in the original development given to Girard's theory by Jean-Pierre Dupuy. On the possible relationship with the thinking of complexity, see the dialogue in M. Ceruti and G. Fornari, *Le due paci: Cristianesimo e morte di Dio nel mondo globalizzato* (Milano: Cortina, 2005).
112. É. Durkheim, "Représentations individuelles et représentations collectives," in *Sociologie et philosophie* (Paris: Presses Universitaires de France, 2014), 39.
113. Very much in the spirit of Darwin is T.W. Deacon, *The Symbolic Species: The Co-evolution of Language and the Brain* (New York: Norton & Co., 1997).
114. For the chimpanzees, see F. De Waal, *Peacemaking among the Primates* (Cambridge, MA: Harvard University Press, 1989), 57 ff. (the observation is noted in Girard, Antonello, and De Castro Rocha, *Evolution and Conversion,* 127). However, the observations on these animal behaviors are much richer, as already Darwin and Atkinson have shown, and deserve to be the object of specific inquiries.
115. All this does not imply the existence of a "self" but the movement of going "outside" the previous biological level.
116. I use here the "j" instead of the "i" (same pronunciation in Latin) in order to emphasize the etymological formation of the word.
117. It is significant that Girard mentions theories that describe sacrifice as mediation, referring to Henri Hubert and Marcel Mauss's definition (*La violence et le sacré,* 17–18), but only to stress their inability to express its real meaning.
118. It is not a question of terms, of course, and we might well use the term "transference" in order to express a shift of meaning from one level to another, but without the reductionist implications of the Girardian or Freudian usage.
119. The expression *mundus imaginalis* has been used by the French orientalist Henry Corbin, in his *Temple et contemplation,* ed. C. Jambet (Paris: Flammarion, 1980), to

designate the spiritual world studied in the wake of the Platonic tradition by Islamic philosophy, but my use of the concept has little to do with Corbin's metaphysical and archetypal acceptation.

120. C. Stringer and P. Andrews, *The Complete World of Human Evolution* (London: Thames & Hudson, 2005), 132–35.

121. A jawbone belonging to the genus *Homo* and dated to 2.8 million years ago has recently been found in Ethiopia.

122. R. Barba and M. Domínguez-Rodrigo, "FLK North North 1: 'Living Floor' or Natural Accumulation," in M. Domínguez-Rodrigo, R. Barba, and C.P. Egeland, *Deconstructing Olduvai: A Taphonomic Study of the Bed I Sites* (Dordrecht: Springer, 2007), 217.

123. Taphonomy is the scientific discipline that studies how organisms decay and become fossilized.

124. It is of course very difficult to determine whether pigments found in very old sites are intentional and explainable in a symbolic way, as stressed in E. Hovers, S. Ilani, O. Bar-Yosef, and B. Vandermeersch, "An Early Case of Color Symbolism: Ochre Use by Modern Humans in Qafzeh Cave," *Current Anthropology* 44 (2003): 491–522.

125. C.P. Egeland, "Zooarchaeology and Taphonomy of the DK Site," in Domínguez-Rodrigo, Barba, and Egeland, *Deconstructing Olduvai,* 253 and 277.

126. Egeland, "Zooarchaeology and Taphonomy," 276–78.

127. Hesiod, *Theogony* 566. Greek text in Esiodo, *Opere,* ed. G. Arrighetti (Milano: A. Mondadori, 2007); English version from Hesiod, *"Theogony" and "Works and Days,"* ed. M.L. West (Oxford-New York: Oxford University Press, 2008), 20.

128. Useful information in J.A.J. Gowlett, "The Discovery of Fire by Humans: A Long and Convoluted Process," *Philosophical Transactions of the Royal Society B* 371 (2016): 1–12. The difficulty of evaluating the remains of hearths or anthropogenic fires at such early periods must be emphasized.

129. The quote is from the final short discussion of Gowlett, "The Discovery of Fire by Humans," 7.

130. These evolutionary changes are at the basis of the so-called "cooking hypothesis": see R. Wrangham and R. Carmody, "Human Adaptation to the Control of Fire," *Evolutionary Anthropology* 19 (2010): 187–99.

131. The first reliable signs of an increased control of fire date back to roughly four hundred thousand years ago: Gowlett, "The Discovery of Fire by Humans," 5.

132. Gowlett, "The Discovery of Fire by Humans," 5, rightly remarks that techniques of ignition do not require a particular cognitive advancement but again without explaining such a remarkable delay.

133. Vandermeersch, "Ce que nous apprennent les premières sépultures," 166–67.

134. See Vandermeersch, "Ce que nous apprennent les premières sépultures," 164, where the author excludes a religious interpretation of the first known burials as such ("la sépulture ne témoigne pas par elle-même du fait religieux") without giving any definition of religion.

135. Cf. M. Eliade, *Shamanism: Archaic Techniques of Ecstasy,* Engl. trans. W.R. Trask (Princeton: Princeton University Press, 1974), 34, 36–38, 56–58, 108, 429 (typically, the author does not mention the clear relationship of such experiences with sacrifice).

136. D. Lewis-Williams, *The Mind in the Cave: Consciousness and the Origins of Art* (London: Thames & Hudson, 2004); see also J. Clottes and D. Lewis-Williams, *Les chamanes de la préhistoire: Transe et magie dans les grottes ornées* (Paris: La Maison des Roches, 2001).

137. D.L. Hoffmann et al., "U-th Dating of Carbonate Crusts Reveals Neanderthal Origin of Iberian Art," *Science* 359, no. 6378 (February 23, 2018): 912–15, available at http://science.sciencemag.org.

138. In Hoffman et al., "U-th Dating of Carbonate Crusts."

139. The ladder or ladder-like motif as symbol of ascent to heaven is universal and widespread in shamanistic rituals and myths (Eliade, *Shamanism,* 487–90), and the same is true for the shaman's ornithomorphic flight (ibid., 156–58); highly interesting are the analogies between the La Pasiega "dancing" figure and some drawings made by an Eskimo shaman in K. Rasmussen, *Fra Grønland til Stillehavet, Rejser og Mennesker fra 5. Thule Ekspedition 1921–1924* (København: Gyldendalske Boghandel-Nordisk Forlag, 1925–26), 1:330–79.

140. Thus drastically correcting the statement expressed in Lewis-Williams, *The Mind in the Cave,* 285: "Neanderthals could not therefore conceive of a spirit world; nor could they construct social and political relations founded on different degrees of access to that world."

1. The Labyrinth of Mythology

1. For a definition of Middle Judaism, see below, vol. 1, chapter 9, § 2 (and note 44).
2. I prefer to use the traditional dating system not to promulgate denominational bias, but in order to stress the historical origin of a system that became worldwide through a process that is the very burden of the present volumes to elucidate.
3. H. Stegemann, *The Library of Qumran: On the Essenes, Qumran, John the Baptist, and Jesus* (Grand Rapids, MI: Eerdmans, 1998), 175–76. On the Qumran community cf. below, vol. 1, chapters 9, § 3 and 10, § 6.
4. Stegemann, *The Library of Qumran,* 174 ff. and 245.
5. On the historical value of the Eucharistic accounts of the New Testament, see below, vol. 2, chapter 4, § 1.
6. G. Vico, *Opere,* ed. A. Battistini (Milano: A. Mondadori, 2007), 570.
7. S. Moravia, *La scienza dell'uomo nel Settecento* (Roma-Bari: Laterza, 1978).
8. U. Von Wilamowitz-Möllendorf, *Zukunftsphilologie! Eine Erwidrung auf Friedrich Nietzsches "Geburt der Tragödie"* (Berlin: Borntraeger, 1872).
9. On classicists like Jane Harrison and Francis Cornford (S. Lukes, *Émile Durkheim: His Life and Work. A Historical and Critical Study* [New York: Harper & Row, 1972], 399n29).

10. Cf. G. Fornari, *Mito, tragedia, filosofia: Dall'antica Grecia al Moderno* (Roma: Studium, 2017), 193.
11. On this point positions wavered and changed over time, with the most realistic view centered upon ritual finally prevailing: cf. the short history sketched in B. Mack, "Introduction: Religion and Ritual," in W. Burkert, R. Girard, and J.Z. Smith, *Violent Origins: Ritual Killing and Cultural Formation,* ed. R.G. Hamerton-Kelly (Stanford: Stanford University Press, 1987), 1–6.
12. J.G. Frazer, *Myths of the Origin of Fire* (London: Macmillan, 1930).
13. On a reconstruction of this sacrificial ritual, see A. Fraschetti, "La sepoltura delle Vestali e la città," in *Du châtiment dans la cité: Supplices corporels et peine de mort dans le monde antique* (Roma: École Française de Rome, 1984), 97–129.
14. Cf. the shamanistic motif of the origin of fire from the vagina (M. Eliade, *Shamanism: Archaic Techniques of Ecstasy,* Engl. trans. W.R. Trask [Princeton: Princeton University Press, 1974], 363n78). The man condemned as lover of the guilty Vestal was scourged to death in public, and this shows the hidden identity between the punishment for the extinguished fire and the capital punishment for the *incestum,* the worst of crimes since it was something like a definitive extinction of the sacred fire, whereby the female victim was deemed too powerful and impure to be touched and had to die without any physical contact by starvation.
15. Frazer, *Myths of the Origin of Fire,* 21; other myths are related both to women and to violent behaviors with the goal of taking control of fire.
16. R. Girard, *Le bouc émissaire* (Paris: Grasset, 1982), 105 ff.
17. E. Husserl, *Logische Untersuchungen,* ed. U. Panzer, vol. 19, part 1 (The Hague: Nijhoff, 1984), 10.
18. Strabo, X, 3, 11; Strabon, *Géographie (livre X),* ed. F. Lasserre (Paris: Les Belles Lettres, 1971), 70–71: the entire third chapter of book X is a mine of mythological and ethnological information on this subject.
19. On the moderate influence of the Aristotelian tradition on Strabo, see A. Falcon, *Aristotelismo* (Torino: Einaudi, 2017), 26 and 74.
20. F.M. Cornford, *Principium Sapientiae: A Study of the Origins of Greek Philosophical Thought* (New York: Harper, 1965), 214–17 (with reference to M.P. Nilsson).
21. Hesiod, *Theogony* 453 (adapted version from Hesiod, *"Theogony" and "Works and Days,"* Engl. trans. M.L. West [Oxford–New York: Oxford University Press, 2008], 16).
22. Hesiod, *Theogony* 459–72 (Hesiod, *"Theogony" and "Works and Days,"* 17). On the role of *metis* in Hesiod, cf. M. Detienne and J.-P. Vernant, *Cunning Intelligence in Greek Culture and Society,* Engl. trans. J. Lloyd (Chicago: University of Chicago Press, 1991), 57 ff.
23. Hesiod, *Theogony* 485–88 (Hesiod, *"Theogony" and "Works and Days,"* 17).
24. According to Nilsson, "to be connected with the ideas of death and rebirth" (Cornford, *Principium Sapientiae,* 216).
25. W. Burkert, *Structure and History in Greek Mythology and Ritual* (Berkeley: University of California Press, 1982), 18–22.

26. I am following the more detailed and precise reconstruction in *La mitologia ittita,* ed. by F. Pecchioli Daddi and A.M. Polvani (Brescia: Paideia, 1990), 116–27.
27. See below, vol. 1, chapter 2, § 4.
28. Though in a very different context, as rightly emphasized by Pecchioli Daddi and Polvani, *La mitologia ittita,* 127.
29. Thucydides, I, 2–11; see Fornari, *Mito, tragedia, filosofia,* 125–26.
30. P. Grimal, *Dictionnaire de la mythologie grecque et romaine* (Paris: Presses Universitaires de France, 1969), *s.v.* "Épaphos," 141. The italics are mine.
31. Apollodorus, *The Library,* ed. J.G. Frazer, Loeb Classical Library (Cambridge, MA: Harvard University Press, 1921), 1:134–35nn2–4.
32. Strabo, X, 3, 22; K. Kerényi, *Die Mythologie der Griechen,* vol. 1, *Die Götter- und Menschheitgeschichten* (Stuttgart: Klett-Cotta, 1997), 67 ff.; cf. P. Faure, *La vie quotidienne au temps de Minos (1500 av. J.-C.)* (Paris: Hachette, 1973), 163 ff.
33. Faure, *La vie quotidienne,* 309.
34. K. Kerényi, *Labyrinth-Studien: Labyrinthos als Linienreflex einer mythologischen Idee* (Zürich: Rhein, 1950), esp. 34 ff., and cf. Faure, *La vie quotidienne,* 170–72.
35. Plutarch, *Theseus* 21. On the labyrinth, see also the comment in Plutarco, *Le vite di Teseo e di Romolo,* ed. C. Ampolo and M. Manfredini, Fondazione L. Valla (Milano: A. Mondadori, 1988), 223–24n39; for Ariadne, see *Theseus* 20, 1, and also chapter 8 in this book.
36. K. Schmidt, *Sie bauten die ersten Tempel: Das rätselhafte Heiligtum am Göbleki Tepe* (München: Beck, 2016), 216–20; the author makes reference to the theses of D. Lewis-Williams, *The Mind in the Cave: Consciousness and the Origins of Art* (London: Thames & Hudson, 2004).
37. Schmidt, *Sie bauten die ersten Tempel,* 193. Cf. I. Hodder, *The Leopard's Tale: Revealing the Mysteries of* Çatalhöyük (London: Thames & Hudson, 2006), 196–98.
38. M. Gimbutas, *The Goddesses and Gods of Old Europe: Myths and Cult Images* (London: Thames & Hudson, 1982), 125 ff.
39. Kerényi, *Labyrinth-Studien,* 44–45.
40. Kerényi, *Labyrinth-Studien,* 45.
41. Kerényi, *Labyrinth-Studien,* 38–40.
42. Vandermeersch, "Le più antiche sepolture," 21 ff.
43. A.-M. Tillier, B. Arensburg, H. Duday, and B. Vandermeersch, "Brief Communication: An Early Case of Hydrocephalus: The Middle Paleolithic Qafzeh 12 Child (Israel)," *American Journal of Physical Anthropology* 114 (2001): 166–70.
44. J.K. Kozlowski, "Il sentimento religioso nel corso della preistoria: il paleolitico superiore," in Facchini et al., *La religiosità nella preistoria,* 74–75.
45. Strabo, X, 3, 7–10; E. Rohde, *Psyche: Seelencult und Unsterblichkeitsglaube der Griechen* (Darmstadt: Wissenschaftliche Buchgesellschaft, 1980), 2:47–48n3 and 48–49n1; H. Jeanmaire, *Dionysos: Histoire de culte de Bacchus* (Paris: Payot, 1951), 132 ff.

46. For an example of the use of the divine double concept, see M. Untersteiner, *La fisiologia del mito* (Torino: Bollati Boringhieri, 1991), 70.
47. Cf. *The Literature of Ancient Sumer,* ed. J. Black *et al.* (Oxford: Oxford University Press, 2006), 81–83; see below vol. 1, chapter 1, § 4–5.
48. J.E. Harrison, *Themis: A Study of the Social Origins of Greek Religion* (London: Merlin Press, 1989), 195.
49. Girard, *Le bouc émissaire,* 108; cf. M. Eliade, *Histoire des croyances et des idées religieuses* (Paris: Payot, 1978), 1:382–87 (with a wider analysis).
50. On which see § 3 of the next chapter.
51. Girard, *Le bouc émissaire,* 110.
52. G. De Santillana and H. Von Dechend, *Hamlet's Mill: An Essay Investigating the Origins of Human Knowledge and Its Transmission through Myth* (Boston: Gambit, 1969).
53. For a larger treatment, see Fornari, *Mito, tragedia, filosofia,* 155–61.
54. *Coyote Was Going There: Indian Literature of the Oregon Country,* ed. J. Ramsey (Seattle: University of Washington Press, 1999), 254–55 and 285.
55. See Pindaro, *Le Pitiche,* ed. B. Gentili et al., Fondazione L. Valla (Milano: A. Mondadori, 2012), 10–15.
56. *Pythians,* I, 20–21.
57. J. Le Goff, *La naissance du Purgatoire* (Paris: Gallimard, 1981), 273–77.
58. P. Kingsley, *Ancient Philosophy, Mystery, and Magic: Empedocles and Pythagorean Tradition* (Oxford: Clarendon Press, 2009), 217–316 (without any reference to sacrifice). For a different sacrificial analysis of these materials, see Fornari, *Mito, tragedia, filosofia,* 167–84.
59. *Die Fragmente der Vorsokratiker,* ed. H. Diels and W. Kranz (Berlin: Weidmann, 1972–74) (henceforth DK), 31-A69.
60. See Fornari, *Mito, tragedia, filosofia,* 190–99.
61. Kingsley, *Ancient Philosophy, Mystery, and Magic,* 279 ff.
62. Presented by Mauro Ceruti in M. Ceruti and G. Fornari, *Le due paci: Cristianesimo e morte di Dio nel mondo globalizzato* (Milano: Cortina, 2005), 109–10.
63. This is the thesis held by G. Colli, *La sapienza greca,* vol. 1, *Dioniso, Apollo, Eleusi, Orfeo, Museo, Iperborei, Enigma* (Milano: Adelphi, 1990) (henceforth *SG* 1), 34.
64. R. Girard, "Dionysus versus the Crucified," *Modern Language Notes* 99, no. 4 (1984): 822.
65. *SG* 1:17.
66. H. Kern, *Through the Labyrinth: Designs and Meanings over 5,000 Years* (Munich-London-New York: Prestel, 2000), 41 ff., holds that dance is the oldest form of labyrinth, and this confirmation is even more interesting because the author excludes a genetic and unitary explanation of its various forms, given his rejection of the antiquity of the available evidence on the labyrinth as cave (ibid., 43–44).

67. On the honey theme, see K. Kerényi, *Dionysos: Archetypal Image of Indestructible Life*, Engl. trans. R. Manheim (Princeton: Princeton University Press, 1976), 29 ff.

68. Pindar, *Olympians,* VI, 46–47; interestingly the metaphor is characterized as "harsh" (*dura*) in Pindaro, *Le Olimpiche,* ed. B. Gentili et al., Fondazione L. Valla (Milano: A. Mondadori, 2013), 457–58.

69. For this reason, ambrosia is connected also with fat , as shown in R.B. Onians, *The Origins of European Thought about the Body, the Mind, the Soul, the World, Time, and Fate: New Interpretations of Greek, Roman and Kindred Evidence also of Some Basic Jewish and Christian Beliefs* (Cambridge: Cambridge University Press, 2000), 292–94. The author wrongly excludes honey from his explanation, but fat was one of the sacrificial parts devoted to the gods and blood furnishes the missing link.

70. Kerényi, *Die Götter- und Menschheitgeschichten,* 74.

71. J.G. Frazer, *The Golden Bough: A Study in Magic and Religion,* abridged edition (New York: Macmillan Co., 1951), 326–27.

72. Kerényi, *Dionysos: Archetypal Image of Indestructible Life*, 104.

73. Harrison, *Themis,* 7–9; cf. R. Calasso, *Le nozze di Cadmo e Armonia* (Milano: Adelphi, 1993), 357.

74. Harrison, *Themis,* 7–12.

75. J.G. Frazer, *The Golden Bough,* vol. 4, *The Dying God* (New York: Macmillan Co., 1935), 69–75.

76. Strabo, X, 3, 19; cf. Diodorus Siculus, V, 66. Modern commentaries in J.E. Harrison, *Prolegomena to the Study of Greek Religion* (London: Merlin Press, 1980), 499; Kerényi, *Die Götter- und Menschheitgeschichten,* 185–86; and Faure, *La vie quotidienne,* 100–101.

77. Harrison, *Prolegomena,* 484.

78. Kerényi, *Dionysos: Archetypal Image of Indestructible Life*, 265–67.

79. Dante, *Inferno,* XII, 12; the quotation is from an excellent critical edition: D. Alighieri, *La commedìa,* ed. A. Lanza (Anzio: De Rubeis, 1996), 99.

80. Dante, *Inferno,* XIV, 97–102; Alighieri, *La commedìa,* 123–24.

81. No doubt Virgil (*Aeneidos,* III, 104–6), but also Ovid (see A. Martina, *s.v.* "Rea," in *Enciclopedia Dantesca* [Milano: A. Mondadori, 2005], 13:499).

82. Dante, *Inferno,* I, 72 (Alighieri, *La commedìa,* 10): it is the translation of Augustine, *De civitate Dei,* II, 29: "deos falsos fallacesque."

83. On the sources and the interpretive debate, see G. Reggio, *s.v.* "Veglio," in *Enciclopedia Dantesca,* 16:220–23.

84. The incompleteness and instability of Augustine's theory are rightly stressed in A. Dempf, *Sacrum Imperium: Geschichts- und Staatsphilosophie des Mittelalters und der politischen Renaissance* (Darmstadt: Wissenschaftliche Buchgemeinschaft, 1954), 116–32.

85. Dante, *Purgatorio,* XXVI, 43–48 (cf. *Inferno,* V, 46–47). This interpretation is in G. Gorni, "'Gru' di Dante: Lettura di Purgatorio XXVI," *Rassegna Europea di Letteratura*

Italiana 3 (1994): 11–34. On the dance of labyrinth in the Middle Ages, see Kern, *Through the Labyrinth*, 146–48.

86. Dante, *Purgatorio,* VI, 118–19 (Alighieri, *La commedìa,* 327; cf. XXXII, 112).

87. Kozlowski, "Il sentimento religioso nel corso della preistoria," 74–75. Further details on the finding are given in T. Taylor, *The Prehistory of Sex: Four Million Years of Human Sexual Culture* (New York: Bantam Books, 1997), 112–14: the author does not really take into account the sacrificial meaning of the burial but reports the important detail that the woman had a hip deformation making her limp.

2. Orphism and the Eleusinian Mysteries

1. K. Kerényi, *Dionysos: Archetypal Image of Indestructible Life,* Engl. trans. R. Manheim (Princeton: Princeton University Press, 1976), xxxvi; K. Kerényi, *Dionysos: Urbild des unzerstörbaren Lebens* (München-Wien: Langen Müller, 1976), 18.
2. The classical text arguing this position is M. Detienne and J.-P. Vernant, *La cuisine du sacrifice en pays grec* (Paris: Gallimard, 1979).
3. M. Detienne, "Culinary Practices and the Spirit of Sacrifice," in M. Detienne and J.-P. Vernant, *The Cuisine of Sacrifice among the Greeks,* Engl. trans. P. Wissig (Chicago: Chicago University Press, 1989), 20 (M. Detienne, "Pratiques culinaires et esprit de sacrifice," in Detienne and Vernant, *La cuisine du sacrifice,* 34–35).
4. Detienne, "Culinary Practices," 224n85 (it is the final footnote in Detienne, "Pratiques culinaires," 35).
5. See below, vol. 1, chapter 9, § 1.
6. W. Burkert, "The Problem of Ritual Killing," in W. Burkert, R. Girard, and J.Z. Smith, *Violent Origins: Ritual Killing and Cultural Formation,* ed. R.G. Hamerton-Kelly (Stanford: Stanford University Press, 1987), 173. Burkert admits that his hypothesis cannot explain the scapegoat phenomenon and refers to an intermediate hypothesis of a "scene of the origin," where the group, encircled by its predators, lets one member be devoured in order to save the rest. This hypothesis only makes the inadequacy of its predecessor more evident.
7. Burkert, "The Problem of Ritual Killing," 172; W. Burkert, *Ancient Mystery Cults* (Cambridge, MA: Harvard University Press, 1987), 86 ff.
8. M. Foucault, *Les mots et les choses: Une archéologie des sciences humaines* (Paris: Gallimard, 1966); G. Agamben, *L'aperto: L'uomo e l'animale* (Torino: Bollati Boringhieri, 2002).
9. W. Burkert, *Structure and History in Greek Mythology and Ritual* (Berkeley: University of California Press, 1982), 27.
10. W. Burkert, *Homo Necans: The Anthropology of Ancient Greek Sacrificial Ritual and Myth,* Engl. trans. P. Bing (Berkeley: University of California Press, 1983), 82, and Burkert, *Ancient Mystery Cults,* 76.
11. My text is based on J.G. Smyly, *Greek Papyri from Gurob* (Dublin: Hodges, 1921), 1–10 (and plate 1 at the end of the volume); G. Colli, *La sapienza greca,* vol. 1, *Dioniso, Apollo, Eleusi, Orfeo, Museo, Iperborei, Enigma* (Milano: Adelphi, 1990)

(henceforth *SG* 1), 188 and 190, 4[A 69]; M.L. West, *The Orphic Poems* (Oxford: Oxford University Press, 1998), 170–71; P. Scarpi, *Le religioni dei misteri,* vol. 1, *Eleusi, dionisismo, orfismo,* Fondazione L. Valla (Milano: A. Mondadori, 2002), 404; the papyrus was published also in *Die Fragmente der Vorsokratiker,* ed. H. Diels and W. Kranz (Berlin: Weidmann, 1972–74) (henceforth DK), 1-B23. Chevrons indicate only the main reconstructions. For the objects listed at the end of the text, see below, vol. 1, chapter 9. I have also referred to Otto Kern's text and commentary in *Orphicorum fragmenta,* ed. O. Kern (Berlin: Weidmann, 1922), fr. 31, pp. 101–4. Burkert's statement that the papyrus recalls Mesopotamian magic texts rather than Greek models (*Ancient Mystery Cults,* 70–71) is unjustified, and clearly is a result of his flawed interpretation of Orphism and Eleusis.

12. Smyly, *Greek Papyri,* 2.
13. The idea of a compromise both preserving the standard edition of the text and giving an idea of its real structure came to me from Scarpi's edition.
14. West's reconstruction.
15. This is Colli's reconstruction mainly based on Clement of Alexandria, *Protrepticus,* II, 14 (*SG* 1:404).
16. It must be remembered as background that ἱερὰ is also a *terminus technicus* for designating the sacrificial victims. (Scarpi seems to ignore this important detail in his commentary.)
17. West's reading followed by Scarpi, *Eleusi,* 656, *ad v.*
18. This reconstruction is deemed probable by Smyly, *Greek Papyri,* 5, and followed by Colli (cf. A.J. Festugière, Études des religion grecque et *hellenistique* [Paris: Vrin, 1972], 41, in spite of his incomprehension of the Orphic aspects of the papyrus).
19. I follow West's reconstruction, which makes it advisable to insert a verse division.
20. I follow West's idea to emphasize the initiatory formulas to be uttered during the rite.
21. A more detailed study of methodological aspects will be found at the end of the following chapter.
22. *Orphicorum fragmenta,* ed. Kern, commentary: "Vs. 20 et 27 sacerdos mystam alloquitur" (l. 20 corresponds to 19 in my text).
23. H. Jeanmaire, *Dionysos: Histoire de culte de Bacchus* (Paris: Payot, 1951), 473.
24. Text in *SG* 1:176, 4[A 64]. Orphic tablets, almost all with very similar text, have been discovered in Magna Graecia (where finds are the earliest and most numerous) in Thessaly, and on Crete (see J.E. Harrison, *Prolegomena to the Study of Greek Religion* [London: Merlin Press, 1980], 572 ff.).
25. As already said, the critical literature on Orphism is as wide as it is controversial, and a satisfying synthesis is not easy to find: still a good piece of scholarship is A. Loisy, *Les mystères païens et le mystère chrétien* (Paris: Nourry, 1930), 25–50; an important study but partially misleading in its irrationalistic interpretation of the religious phenomena is V. Macchioro, *Zagreus: Studi intorno all'orfismo,* 2nd ed. (Firenze: Vallecchi, 1930); the reconstruction in *SG* 1:31–43, is more satisfactory but influenced by a too philosophical-mystical idea of the movement.

26. Herodotus, II, 81 and Plato, *Letter VII* 335a (*SG* 1:128 and 160, 4[A 12] and [47]). See E. Rohde, *Psyche: Seelencult und Unsterblichkeitsglaube der Griechen* (Darmstadt: Wissenschaftliche Buchgesellschaft, 1980), 2:112–13nn 1 and 3, and more generally 103–36. For the importance of Onomacritus, see W.K.C. Guthrie, *Orpheus and Greek Religion* (Princeton: Princeton University Press, 1993), 115, and Kerényi, *Dionysos: Archetypal Image of Indestructible Life,* 238–43, where, however, the case is overstated; there is a danger of attributing earlier material as well to Onomacritus: *SG* 1:33–35 and note, strikes a better balance.
27. Cf. Burkert, *Ancient Mystery Cults,* 69–73.
28. On Pythagoreanism, cf. Guthrie, *Orpheus and Greek Religion,* 216–18.
29. All the evidence, the fact that finds are spread over a wide area, and the strongly ritual character of Orphism clearly indicate that it predates Pythagoreanism, contrary to the view of G. Pugliese Carratelli, "Orphikòs bios," in *Tra Cadmo e Orfeo: Contributi alla storia civile e religiosa dei Greci d'Occidente* (Bologna: Il Mulino, 1990), 415–16 (cf. the comments in *SG* 1:400–401, note to 4[A 62]): it was philosophy that arose out of religion, not the contrary.
30. For the wandering wise men, see Rohde, *Psyche,* 2:63–69. The *Orpheotelestai* are described critically by Plato, *Republic* 364b–365a, and referred to by this same name by Theophrastus in an ironic context (*SG* 1:204, 4[B 8]); cf. Guthrie, *Orpheus and Greek Religion,* 202.
31. Cf. Guthrie, *Orpheus and Greek Religion,* 116 ff.; E.R. Dodds, *The Greeks and the Irrational* (Berkeley: California University Press, 1951), is wrong to see northern influence as incompatible with Cretan religion.
32. Harrison, *Prolegomena,* 469 ff.
33. For the Apollo-Dionysus identification, see *SG* 1:23–27, and, in relation to Orpheus, 37–39, and more particularly the fragments of Aeschylus and Euripides in 2[A 6] and 2[A 8], 78; see also Rohde, *Psyche,* 2:53–54.
34. Guthrie, *Orpheus and Greek Religion,* 107.
35. Dodds, *The Greeks,* 155. See also Rohde, *Psyche,* 2:17–121, where the treatment is still valid, though limited as to certain points. Guthrie, *Orpheus and Greek Religion,* 120, holds that the Orphics added the Titans to a Cretan originary myth (see below); cf. Kerényi, *Dionysos: Archetypal Image of Indestructible Life,* 241–44. Dodds presents excellent arguments to prove the antiquity of the myth (*The Greeks,* 155–56): see esp. Plato, *Laws* 701c (*SG* 1:160 and 162, 4[A 49]). Cf. *Inni Omerici,* ed. by F. Cássola, Fondazione L. Valla (Milano: A. Mondadori, 1986) (henceforth Cássola ed.), 13.
36. See Harrison, *Prolegomena,* 588–92, and Guthrie, *Orpheus and Greek Religion,* 208.
37. The fathers are the Titans: cf. DK, commentary to 1-B23.
38. See Olympiodorus in *SG* 1:286 and 288, 4[B 77]-[78]-[79].
39. Plato, *Cratylus* 400c: σῶμα like σῆμά (tomb) and like σῆμα (sign); and *Gorgias* 493a–d (*SG* 1:146 and 148, 4[A 34] and [36]). Comparison of the two passages shows that Plato must have been referring to the Orphics in the *Cratylus,* albeit disguisedly. On the presence of Orphism in Plato, see P. Kingsley, *Ancient Philosophy, Mystery, and*

Magic: Empedocles and Pythagorean Tradition (Oxford: Clarendon Press, 2009), 79–132. The subject is usually approached from a rationalistic viewpoint, such as by Guthrie, *Orpheus and Greek Religion,* 242.

40. Tablet found at Turi in *SG* 1:182 and 184, 4[A 67]; facsimile in Harrison, *Prolegomena,* 662.

41. See esp. Nonnus, *Dionysiaca,* XXVII, 205; XXIX, 274; XXXIV, 144; XLVII, 733; and Eustathius, *ad Il.,* II, 735. Cf. Harrison, *Prolegomena,* 491–94, where the correct ethnological value is given to this evidence, and Kerényi, *Dionysos: Archetypal Image of Indestructible Life,* 267–68. The Orphics regarded Τιτάνες and τίτανος, chalk, as having an etymological link.

42. Semele corresponds to the Phrygian goddess Zemelo, the Earth: Cássola ed., 16 and 6.

43. On this burial see B. Vandermeersch, "Le più antiche sepolture," in F. Facchini et al., *La religiosità nella preistoria* (Milano: Jaca Book, 1991), 28.

44. M. Gimbutas, *The Goddesses and Gods of Old Europe: Myths and Cult Images* (London: Thames & Hudson, 1982), 174 ff.

45. Harrison, *Prolegomena,* 575–76.

46. Dante, *Purgatorio,* XXIII, 145 (D. Alighieri, *La commedìa,* ed. A. Lanza [Anzio: De Rubeis, 1996], 535). The parallel is drawn by Harrison, *Prolegomena,* 582–83, who surmises that the name Eunoè also derives indirectly from Orphism (in any case, εὔνοια is found associated with memory in funerary inscriptions).

47. M. Heidegger, "Vom Wesen des Grundes," in *Gesamtausgabe* (Frankfurt: a.M. Klostermann, 1975), 9:123–76.

48. My argument goes against the commonplaces of the neo-Kantian interpretations: for a sharp critique of neo-Kantianism; see L. Goldmann, *Mensch, Gemeinschaft und Welt in der Philosophie Immanuel Kants* (Frankfurt-New York: Campus 1989), 95–128.

49. Guthrie, *Orpheus and Greek Religion,* 161 ff.

50. K. Kerényi, *Labyrinth-Studien: Labyrinthos als Linienreflex einer mythologischen Idee* (Zürich: Rhein, 1950), 56.

51. See, for instance, Aristophanes, *The Frogs,* 341–42, and Athenagoras in *SG* 1:238, 4[B 33], where it is said that the Titans "punished the great starry Heaven." Cf., for following parts as well, Kerényi, *Dionysos: Archetypal Image of Indestructible Life,* 106 ff.

52. Cf. in *Orphicorum fragmenta,* ed. Kern, the commentary to ll. 5 and 27 (*symbolum Eleusinium*).

53. A detailed reconstruction on the ground of the available data, though misled by a partial acceptance of the agricultural and naturalistic explanation, is in Loisy, *Les mystères païens,* 51–82.

54. This unquestionably results from the archaeological findings: G.E. Mylonas, *Eleusis and the Eleusinian Mysteries* (Princeton: Princeton University Press, 1961), 77–105. For further reflections on the general underestimation of Pisistratus's religious and cultural policy, see below, vol. 1, chapter 8, § 9.

55. W. Burkert, *Greek Religion,* Engl. trans. J. Raffan (Cambridge, MA: Harvard University Press, 1994), 285 and 287–88.

56. See *SG* 1:29–31. According to one tradition, Orpheus founded the Eleusinian Mysteries (Burkert, *Greek Religion,* 296); moreover, the *Hymn to Demeter* occurs in a dual version, Homeric and Orphic, both referring to Eleusis (see *SG* 1:410–11, note to 4[B 21]). The evidence of Pausanias is particularly important: see Pausania, *Guida della Grecia: Libro I, L'Attica,* ed. D. Musti and L. Beschi, Fondazione L. Valla (Milano: A. Mondadori, 1982), 14n, 21–26, 308–9.

57. The Lesser Mysteries, coordinated with the Eleusinian rite after the Athenian conquest, were linked to the Anthesteria and must have anticipated a small part of what was later revealed at Eleusis.

58. Burkert, *Homo Necans,* 275, and Burkert, *Greek Religion,* 287.

59. I am using Rudolf Otto's categories in a purely descriptive and phenomenological fashion.

60. Esp. Pindar, *Isthmians* 7: 3–5, Sophocles, *Antigone* 1115–21, and Philodemus (*SG* 1:110, 3[B 1]); see below for Clement of Alexander's significant testimony. As the procession moved toward Eleusis, the followers shouted the name Iakchos and waved branches called *bakchoi;* the figure of the divine child named at Eleusis, Ploutos, is totally insignificant if denied its true Dionysiac identity.

61. C. Penglase, *Greek Myths and Mesopotamia: Parallels and Influence in the Homeric Hymns and Hesiod* (New York: Routledge, 1994), 124 ff. (useful material on Mesopotamia, but the parallels with Egypt leave much to be desired).

62. For the text I adapted the version in *Lorsque les dieux faisaient l'homme: Mythologie mésopotamienne,* ed. by J. Bottéro and S.N. Kramer (Paris: Gallimard, 1993), 283, taking in account also the previous and less complete version of *Ancient Near Eastern Texts Relating to the Old Testament,* ed. J.B. Pritchard (Princeton: Princeton University Press, 1969), 55. For the myth, see T. Jacobsen, *The Treasures of Darkness: A History of Mesopotamian Religion* (New Haven: Yale University Press, 1976), 55 ff.

63. *Ancient Near Eastern Texts,* ed. Pritchard, 54; cf. *Lorsque les dieux,* ed. Bottéro and Kramer, 279.

64. *Ancient Near Eastern Texts,* ed. Pritchard, 56; cf. *Lorsque les dieux,* ed. Bottéro and Kramer, 286.

65. *Lorsque les dieux,* ed. Bottéro and Kramer, 287–89; the conclusion of the myth was not yet published at the time of *Ancient Near Eastern Texts,* ed. Pritchard, and there is a summary on 52n6.

66. See below, vol. 1, chapter 9, § 3, and elsewhere.

67. The most interesting parallel is with the first of the three days of the Thesmophoria in Athens, called the *kathodos* and *anodos,* when the women threw swine into the chasms of Demeter and Core, and then descended into them to recover the remains of previous sacrifices made to ensure fertility of the land; see Harrison, *Prolegomena,* 124–27. For the identification of Eubuleus with Dionysus, cf. Guthrie, *Orpheus and Greek Religion,*

179–80; for swine as symbol of Persephone and for the sacrificial meaning of Hades's abduction, see Burkert, *Homo Necans,* 256 ff.

68. Euripides, *Iphigenia in Aulis* 461 (cf. also, for example, *Hecuba,* 612).

69. See l. 33 of the *Hymn to Demeter:* γαῖάν τε καὶ οὐρανὸν ἀστερόεντα—"Earth and starry Heaven" (Cássola ed., 40). For a reconstruction of what happened at Eleusis, see esp. *SG* 1:382–83 and 387–88, note to 3[A 6] and 3[B 8]. The hierogamy can be linked to other couplings tying in with Cretan mythology: the coupling of Dionysus with Ariadne on the second day of the Antesterie in Athens, and of Iasion with Demeter in a field on Crete (Homer, *Odyssey,* V, 125–28), after which he is killed by a thunderbolt from Zeus: Ploutos is born of this union.

70. Cf. Athenagoras in *SG* 1:240, 4[B 34].

71. Burkert, *Homo Necans,* 282.

72. Gimbutas, *The Goddesses and Gods of Old Europe,* 148.

73. For the identification of the ram with the victim, see Burkert, *Homo Necans,* 113. The rite contains various references to the death of the cult follower (ibid., 283) and there is testimony to his suffering (see Plato in *SG* 1:98 and 100, 3[A 10] and [12], and below).

74. There is thus a triple animal sacrifice, corresponding to what the Romans called *su/ove/taurilia* (Burkert, *Homo Necans,* 282, 282n40, and 293).

75. See the testimony of Plato in *SG* 1:102 and 104, 3[A 15] and [17], and of Aristotle in 3[A 22], 108, and the fragment by Plutarch in 3[B 4], 112 ("a wonderful light").

76. We cannot rule out the use of certain substances to enhance the performance, an idea suggested by the drinking of *kykeon* and the recurrent symbolism of the poppy pod: cf. K. Kerényi, *Eleusis: Archetypal Image of Mother and Daughter,* Engl. trans. R. Manheim (Princeton: Princeton University Press, 1967), 177–180, and Kerényi, *Dionysos: Archetypal Image of Indestructible Life,* 23–27; cf. also Rohde, *Psyche,* 2:16–17. This certainly occurred in the more ancient rites that the Mysteries derive from; the poppy pod image is plentifully evident on Crete: see, for example, J.E. Harrison, *Themis: A Study of the Social Origins of Greek Religion* (London: Merlin Press, 1989), 168, fig. 36. The poppy pod was called ἀστερίσκος and can thus be linked to Ἀστέριος.

77. For the concept of δρώμενον, see Harrison, *Themis,* 42–43. See also F. Vian, "La religione greca in epoca arcaica e classica," in *Le religioni del mondo classico,* ed. H.-C. Puech (Roma-Bari: Laterza, 1993), 97.

78. See the fragment, mentioned above in note 74, in *SG* 1, 3[B 4] ("all those terrible things").

79. Clement, *Protrepticus,* II, 12, 1–2.

80. Clement, *Protrepticus,* II, 20. For the Greek text I use Clement of Alexandria, *Exhortation to the Greeks,* ed. G.W. Butterworth, Loeb Classical Library (Cambridge, MA: Harvard University Press, 1932). The translation tries to render the density of the passage, full of allusions to rituals and myths that the author appears to know very well (see also below, vol. 1, chapter 9, § 1).

81. Cf. K. Kerényi, *The Religions of the Greeks and Romans,* Engl. trans. C. Holme (London: Thames and Hudson, 1962), 113. Loisy, *Les mystères païens,* 68, does not

realize the decisive mention of Dionysus's dismemberment, in spite of his sound assumption that Christian witnesses are very important (ibid., 52).

82. D. Sabbatucci, "Il misticismo eleusino," in *Il mito: Guida storica e critica,* ed. M. Detienne (Roma-Bari: Laterza, 1976), 134–38.

83. On the sexual meanings of this ritual symbol, dating back to the Neolithic, see R.B. Onians, *The Origins of European Thought about the Body, the Mind, the Soul, the World, Time, and Fate: New Interpretations of Greek, Roman and Kindred Evidence also of Some Basic Jewish and Christian Beliefs* (Cambridge: Cambridge University Press, 2000), 113–15.

84. Hippolytus in *SG* 1:114, 3[B 8]. Scholars now tend to accept this evidence as valid (Burkert, *Greek Religion,* 285); for the reaped ear as symbol of castration, see Burkert, *Homo Necans,* 290–91.

85. And at the same time reminiscent of Brimos, the divine child who must be identified as Dionysus: see *SG* 1:115 and 387–88n, 3[B 8] (cf. Loisy, *Les mystères païens,* 71–72).

86. Cf. the Pindar fragments in *SG* 1:124 and 126, 4[A 7], and the fragment from Plutarch mentioned above.

87. Burkert, *Homo Necans,* 68.

88. Burkert, *Homo Necans,* 283 and 285; for this reason, beans were subject to ritual veto in Greece and elsewhere.

89. Cf. R. Girard, *La violence et le sacré* (Paris: Grasset, 1994), 148 and 291 ff.

90. F. De Waal, *Peacemaking among the Primates* (Cambridge, MA: Harvard University Press, 1989), 57 ff.

91. See below, vol. 1, chapter 5, § 2.

92. See below, vol. 1, chapter 5, §§ 2–3.

93. *Ancient Near Eastern Texts,* ed. Pritchard, 645.

94. Kerényi, *Dionysos: Archetypal Image of Indestructible Life,* 35–51.

95. Clement, *Protrepticus,* II, 15, 2; Kerényi, *Dionysos: Archetypal Image of Indestructible Life,* 275–76.

96. Strabo, X, 3, 12.

97. Burkert, *Structure and History,* 130.

98. Kerényi, *Dionysos: Archetypal Image of Indestructible Life,* 195.

99. There are several creation myths based on the masturbation of a primeval god, like Atum in Egypt (cf. T. Taylor, *The Prehistory of Sex: Four Million Years of Human Sexual Culture* [New York: Bantam Books, 1997], 182–83), and similar materials are detectable in the Orphic theogonies: see West, *The Orphic Poems,* 91–92 and 202–6 (with reference also to the Gurob papyrus).

100. I have advanced this interpretation in G. Fornari, *Mito, tragedia, filosofia: Dall'antica Grecia al Moderno* (Roma: Studium, 2017), 140–41 and 332–33; the correct reading of the position of the two ritual victims is presented in E. Villa, *L'arte dell'uomo primordiale,* ed. A. Tagliaferri (Milano: Abscondita, 2005), 13–14.

101. See below, vol. 1, chapter 4, § 3.

102. See the myths of Dumuzi's wedding and premature death in Jacobsen, *The Treasures of Darkness,* 25–73.

103. J.G. Frazer, *The Golden Bough,* vol. 4, *The Dying God* (New York: Macmillan Co., 1935), 113–16 (the author rightly intuits the importance of the sexual aspect but without connecting it to hierogamy).

104. For a detailed reconstruction of the Assyrian ceremony on the basis of the available documents, see J. Bottéro, *Mesopotamia: Writing, Reasoning, and the Gods,* Engl. trans. Z. Bahrani and M. Van De Mieroop (Chicago: University of Chicago Press, 1995), 138–55 (the author is not sure about the connection with the Sacaea festival, but he does not take into account the hidden relationship with hierogamy). It is impressive that the ritual of the substitute king was still performed when Alexander was in Babylonia (as results from Plutarch, *Alexander* 73–74).

105. G. Bataille, *La souveraineté,* in *Œuvres complètes* (Paris: Gallimard, 1973–), 8:270.

106. See H.G. Liddell and R. Scott, *A Greek-English Lexicon,* rev. ed. (Oxford: Oxford University Press, 1996) (henceforth Liddell-Scott), first meaning of the verb συμβάλλω. The sacrificial explanation of the term given here was first presented more briefly in G. Fornari, "From the Labyrinth to the Tragic Mask," *COV&R: The Bulletin of the Colloquium on Violence and Religion* 2 (1996): 6–8, and is endorsed by L. Scubla, "Fonction symbolique et fondaments sacrificiels des sociétés humaines," *La Revue du Mauss semestrielle* 12 (1998): 41–65.

107. Cf. Hippolytus on hemlock-induced impotence (*SG* 1:114, 3[B 8]) applying to ritual chastity, which might then give way to the sexual infringements of the *sacrum.*

108. J.-L. Durand, "Greek Animals: Toward a Topology of Edible Bodies," in Detienne and Vernant, *The Cuisine of Sacrifice,* 104–5.

109. A good comparative analysis of these mythical figures is presented in West, *The Orphic Poems,* 103–7, 203–12.

110. See Damascius in *SG* 1, 4[B 72]; Guthrie, *Orpheus and Greek Religion,* 95–97; *SG* 1:393, note to 4[A 20]. The hermaphroditic figure of Phanes undoubtedly inspired the myth of Aristophanes in Plato's *Symposium* (cf. *SG* 1:417–18, note to 4[B 45]).

111. For the reconstruction of Orphic cosmology, see Guthrie, *Orpheus and Greek Religion,* 78 ff.; on the philological aspects, see West, *The Orphic Poems,* 68 ff. The summary in *Inni orfici,* ed. G. Ricciardelli, Fondazione L. Valla (Milano: A. Mondadori, 2000), xvi–xviii, is useful. See also *SG* 1:22, 4[B 39] ff., and 413, note to 4[B 28]; Damascius's account is in 4[B 72], 278 and 280. Cf. M. Detienne and J.-P. Vernant, *Cunning Intelligence in Greek Culture and Society,* Engl. trans. J. Lloyd (Chicago: University of Chicago Press, 1991), 133 ff.

112. Sophocles, fr. 837 (Pearson) in *SG* 1:94, 3[A 4].

113. DK 22-B15 (see also vol. 2, chapter 5, § 6). On the identity between Dionysus and Hades, see Rohde, *Psyche,* 1:207, 207n2; and *The Hymn to Demeter* where Aidoneus, who is given the Dionysian epithet of god of the many names and abducts Persephone on the plain of Nisa, is clearly Dionysus (see Kerényi, *Eleusis,* 33 and 40).

114. Clement, *Protrepticus,* II, 18 (*SG* 1:246, 4[B 38]), where *Pallas* is derived from πάλλειν, to tremble.

115. Burkert, *Greek Religion,* 57.

116. See Kerényi, *Dionysos: Archetypal Image of Indestructible Life,* 259–61; the heart-phallus identification is also clearly made, with grotesque effect, in Aristophanes, *The Frogs,* 481–86.

117. Cf. Kerényi, *Dionysos: Archetypal Image of Indestructible Life,* 267.

118. Diodorus Siculus, III, 62, 7–8. Generally, Demeter or a similar goddess is assimilated to Isis. In other versions Athena gives the heart to Zeus, who eats it and so resurrects Dionysus, or else it is Apollo who reassembles the body parts at Delphi to resurrect the god, etc.

119. Kerényi, *Dionysos: Archetypal Image of Indestructible Life,* 243 ff.; Clement, *Protrepticus,* II, 18, 2.

120. Kerényi, *Dionysos: Archetypal Image of Indestructible Life,* 294–96.

121. Cf. Kerényi, *Eleusis,* 40 and 65. According to Colli, the expression refers to a golden snake inserted beneath the clothing to recall Zeus's matings (*SG* 1:404, note to 4[A 69]).

122. Cf. Euripides, *Bacchae* 1022–23. For the symbolism of the ass, see M. Untersteiner, *La fisiologia del mito* (Torino: Bollati Boringhieri, 1991), 294 ff., where the ass is presented as a phallic symbol connected esoterically with Dionysus and Apollo (cf. *SG* 1:76, 2[A 4], and the allusion to the Mysteries in Aristophanes's *The Frogs,* 158–59); the ass is also linked to Typhon (Set), the murderer of Osiris (Plutarch, *De Iside et Osiride* 30 ff.). For the papyrus formulae, see also Jeanmaire, *Dionysos,* 473, where the expression "I have drunk" is associated with a ritual drink, in a way perfectly compatible with my interpretation.

123. Cf. G. Fornari, "Immortali/mortali: Il sacrificio in Eraclito," in *Eraclito: la luce dell'Oscuro,* ed. G. Fornari (Firenze: Olschki, 2017), 173, 173nn70–71.

124. Euripides, *Bacchae* 349, 602, 741, and 753 (see also, for example, *Heracles,* 953 and 1307): these passages in the *Bacchae* are considered in chapter 5. Cf. the testimony of Proclus and Olympiodorus in *SG* 1:266 and 286, 4[B 57b] and 4[B 78].

125. Through *reversal,* this member can also be the last, as in the Osiris myth.

126. Liddell-Scott, *s.v.* σύμβολον; Smyly, *Greek Papyri,* 7–8. Cf. Burkert, *Homo Necans,* 41, 41n29.

127. Cf. Homer, *Iliad,* XV, 363, where Apollo destroys a Greek fortification as a child destroys "its childish toys," and *The Hymn to Demeter,* 16, where Persephone reaches out toward the narcissus, a flower linked to the cult of the dead through its narcotic properties, and described as "the lovely toy" (see below vol. 1, chapter 9, §§ 1 and 4).

3. In the Heart of the Labyrinth: Euripides's *Cretans* and Its Philosophical Meaning

1. Editions used: Euripide, *I cretesi,* ed. R. Cantarella (Milano: Istituto Editoriale Italiano, 1964) (henceforth Cantarella ed.); Euripide, *Cretesi,* ed. A.-T. Cozzoli (Pisa-Roma:

Istituti Editoriali e Poligrafici Internazionali, 2001) (henceforth Cozzoli ed.); V. Di Benedetto, "Recensione a Euripide, Cretesi, a cura di Adele-Teresa Cozzoli," *Rivista di Filologia e di Istruzione Classica* 129 (2001): 210–30 (henceforth Di Benedetto ed.).

2. For its richness of religious and anthropological connections, I have analyzed the tragedy in several writings: G. Fornari, "Labyrinthine Strategies of Sacrifice: The Cretans by Euripides," *Contagion: Journal of Violence, Mimesis, and Culture* 4 (1997): 163–88; Fornari, *Da Dioniso a Cristo: Conoscenza e sacrificio nel mondo greco e nella civiltà occidentale* (Genova-Milano: Marietti, 2006), 92–116; Fornari, *La conoscenza tragica in Euripide e in Sofocle* (Massa: Transeuropa, 2013), 25–127; Fornari, *Mito, tragedia, filosofia: Dall'antica Grecia al Moderno* (Roma: Studium, 2017), 281–351. The most reliable date of the *Cretans* is around 433 BC.
3. A detailed interpretation of the *Hippolytus* is in Fornari, *La conoscenza tragica,* 189–279.
4. The fragment comes from Porphyry, *De abstinentia,* IV, 19, 1 (Porphyre, *De l'abstinence,* vol. 3, ed. M. Patillon and A.P. Segonds [Paris: Les Belles Lettres, 1995], 32). On the text, see Cantarella ed., F 3, 23–25 (also 116); Cozzoli ed., fr. 1, 57–58. Cf. J.E. Harrison, *Prolegomena to the Study of Greek Religion* (London: Merlin Press, 1980), 478 ff.
5. Already in my previous studies I was following the reading of *Tragicorum Graecorum fragmenta,* ed. by A. Nauck (Lipsiae: Teubner, 1926), fr. 472, v. 7, p. 505, and my choice now finds confirmation in Cozzoli ed.
6. It is the reading of the manuscripts (Æliani *Porphyrii Philosophi Philonis Byzantii Opera* [Paris: Didot, 1858], 83), defended by J.E. Harrison, *Themis: A Study of the Social Origins of Greek Religion* (London: Merlin Press, 1989), 52, and preferred both in Cozzoli ed. and Porphyre, *De l'abstinence,* 93n293.
7. Harrison, *Prolegomena,* 481; the whole commentary on the fragment from p. 478 is of general interest, as addition to the commentary in G. Colli, *La sapienza greca,* vol. 1, *Dioniso, Apollo, Eleusi, Orfeo, Museo, Iperborei, Enigma* (Milano: Adelphi, 1990) (henceforth *SG* 1), 391–92. H.G. Liddell and R. Scott, *A Greek-English Lexicon,* rev. ed. (Oxford: Oxford University Press, 1996) translates ταυρόδετος with a less probable *made from bull's hide,* which, in any case, gives it sacrificial significance.
8. Cf. P. Chantraine, *Dictionnaire* étymologique *de la langue grecque: Histoire des mots* (Paris: Klincksieck, 1968–74), see *s.vv.* ἅζομαι and ἅγος.
9. É. Benveniste, *Le vocabulaire des institutions indo-européennes,* vol. 2, *Pouvoir, droit, religion* (Paris: Les Éditions de Minuit, 1969), 202–7.
10. Cf. Benveniste, *Le vocabulaire des institutions indo-européennes,* 198–202.
11. Euripides, *Hippolytus* 952–57; Greek text and commentary in Euripides, *Hippolytos,* ed. by W.S. Barrett (Oxford: Clarendon Press, 2001) (henceforth Barrett ed.).
12. On the symbolic connotations of writing, see below, note 23.
13. G. Betegh, *The Derveni Papyrus: Cosmology, Theology, and Interpretation* (Cambridge: Cambridge University Press, 2006), 67–68.
14. K. Kerényi, *Dionysos: Archetypal Image of Indestructible Life,* Engl. trans. R. Manheim

(Princeton: Princeton University Press, 1976), 80–89. More one-sided and questionable but rich with historical and religious evidence is V. Macchioro, *Zagreus: Studi intorno all'orfismo,* ed. C. Pugliese (Milano: Mimesis, 2014), 178–80.

15. Euripides, *Bacchae* 485–86; ὄργια comes from ἔργον (deed, work) and "indicates the bloody deed of sacrifice" when used with such emphasis: K. Kerényi, *Miti e misteri,* ed. by A. Brelich (Torino: Einaudi, 1984), 166 (edition existing only in Italian). See also below, vol. 1, chapter 4.
16. The various Greek terms for ritual possession are substantially equivalent (cf. W. Burkert, *Greek Religion,* Engl. trans. J. Raffan [Cambridge, MA: Harvard University Press, 1994], 109–10), and indicate different complementary aspects of a phenomenon still close to its spontaneous form.
17. On the Orphic influence on tragedy, see below, vol. 1, chapter 8.
18. S. Lévi, *La doctrine du sacrifice dans les Brâhmanas* (Paris: Leroux, 1898).
19. Cf. Chantraine, *Dictionnaire* étymologique *de la langue grecque, s.vv.* δαίομαι and δαίω etc.: from *daio-daiomai* are derived *daimon,* demon, god (readable as the *victim* who is *torn to pieces*) and perhaps *demos,* the people, i.e., the community sharing the sacrifice. A similar etymology is in μείρομαι, I divide into parts, from which comes *Moira,* the mythical personification of Fate (see vol. 1, chapter 5).
20. See also fr. F-2e in Cantarella ed., 22.
21. On the sacrificial self-mutilation referred to as becoming white, cf. E. Canetti, *Masse und Macht* (München-Wien: Hanser, 1960), 376–79.
22. *Die Fragmente der Vorsokratiker,* ed. H. Diels and W. Kranz (Berlin: Weidmann, 1972–74) (henceforth DK), 22-B125.
23. Euripides, *Hippolytus* 386–87 (cf. Theseus's words in *Hippolytus,* 928–31). The term γράμματα indicates the letters of a word and conveys the idea of writing, a precise allusion to the written tablet (δέλτος) with which the hanged Phaedra will accuse her stepson of an attempted rape, then recalled by Theseus 1. 954.
24. From the Oxyrhynchus papyruses: Cantarella ed., F 2-a, 19–20; Cozzoli ed., fr. 2, 59–60; Di Benedetto ed., 222–24 (without the numbers of verses as some indecipherable lines have been omitted).
25. In the first six lines I accept the hypothetical reconstruction of Di Benedetto ed., 224.
26. I follow the reconstructions of Cantarella and Di Benedetto.
27. I follow the reading of Cozzoli ed. <στέρ>νοις, accepted by Di Benedetto ed. as well. In my first studies I had accepted Cantarella's ingenious reading ἁρμοῖς, which deserves to be mentioned.
28. The old reading by Cantarella ed., 20, is good, while Cozzoli ed., 60, is wrongly skeptical. Di Benedetto ed. defends the old conjecture δίπους, but the lambda of <διπ>λοῦς is perfectly recognizable.
29. I prefer the solution of Cantarella ed., that finds parallels also in the ceramic iconography: it is more natural to suppose that the tail of the baby-monster is not visible, and a desire to make anatomical inspections is rather unlikely in a horrified onlooker.

30. The plausible reconstruction of Cantarella ed.
31. I accept <ὀρ>γιλωμάτων of Cantarella ed., while Cozzoli ed. has the wrong reading δωμάτων: in the photographic reproduction of the papyrus the lambda is clearly visible.
32. I preserve Cantarella's reconstruction, with the semantic enrichment of the verb δρᾶν.
33. J.G. Frazer, *The Golden Bough: A Study in Magic and Religion* (New York: Macmillan Co., 1951), 326.
34. J.G. Frazer, *The Golden Bough,* vol. 4, *The Dying God* (New York: Macmillan Co., 1935), 70 ff.
35. DK 22-B54.
36. DK 22-B64. See G. Fornari, "Immortali/mortali: Il sacrificio in Eraclito," in *Eraclito: la luce dell'Oscuro,* ed. G. Fornari (Firenze: Olschki, 2017), 170–82.
37. See F. Frontisi-Ducroux, *Dédale: Mythologie de l'artisan en Grèce ancienne* (Paris: La Découverte, 2000), 45–82; A. Brelich, *Gli eroi greci: Un problema storico-religioso* (Milano: Adelphi, 2010), 140–41.
38. DK 31-B96, l. 4.
39. Homer, *Iliad,* XVIII, 590 ff.; K. Kerényi, *Labyrinth-Studien: Labyrinthos als Linienreflex einer mythologischen Idee* (Zürich: Rhein, 1950), 37–38.
40. L. Mumford, *The City in History: Its Origins, Its Transformations, and Its Prospects* (1961; repr. San Diego: Harcourt Brace & Co., 1989), 3–28.
41. Cantarella ed., F 7, 33.
42. Kerényi, *Labyrinth-Studien,* 44–45.
43. Cantarella ed., 26–28 (F 4; publ. Wilamowitz); Cozzoli ed., fr. 7, 64–65 (the other sequences of the fragment are quoted below).
44. Kerényi, *Dionysos: Archetypal Image of Indestructible Life,* 116 (Kerényi, *Dionysos: Urbild des unzerstörbaren Lebens* [München-Wien: Langen Müller, 1976], 105: "die allen Leuchtende"); cf. Kerényi, *Töchter der Sonne: Betrachtungen* über *Griechische Gottheiten* (Zürich: Rascher, 1944), 177 ff.
45. The classic treatment of this passage is in B. Snell, *The Discovery of the Mind: The Greek Origins of European Thought,* Engl. trans. T.G. Rosenmeyer (New York-Evanston: Harper & Row, 1960), 43–70.
46. Dante, *Purgatorio,* XXVI, 86–87 (D. Alighieri, *La commedìa,* ed. A. Lanza [Anzio: De Rubeis, 1996], 476).
47. Dante, *Inferno,* XII, 12–13 (Alighieri, *La commedìa*, 100).
48. Herodotus, II, 46.
49. See below, vol. 1, chapter 5, § 3.
50. Euripides, *Hippolytus* 193–97.
51. Shakespeare, *Macbeth,* 5, 5, 25–27 (W. Shakespeare, *The Complete Works,* ed. S. Wells et al. [Oxford: Clarendon Press, 1994], 998).
52. Cantarella ed., 28; Cozzoli ed., 65–66.

53. Cantarella ed., 28–29; Cozzoli ed., 66.

54. Harrison, *Prolegomena,* 506.

55. Cantarella ed., 56.

56. Cantarella ed., 31 (F 5).

57. Euripides, *Hippolytus* 782–85.

58. Barrett ed., 275.

59. DK 12-B1: the doxographic source is Theophrastus quoted by Simplicius. My previous readings in Fornari, *Da Dioniso a Cristo,* 409–11; Fornari, *Storicità radicale: Filosofia e morte di Dio* (Massa: Transeuropa, 2013), 374–76.

60. On the Orphic reading of Anaximander: F. Nietzsche, *Die Philosophie im tragischen Zeitalter der Griechen,* in *Sämtliche Werke: Kritischen Studienausgabe,* ed. G. Colli and M. Montinari (Berlin-New York: De Gruyter, 1980), 1:813–17; H. Diels, "Anaximandros von Milet," *Neue Jahrbücher für das klassische Altertum* 51 (1923): 65–75; W.K.C. Guthrie, *Orpheus and Greek Religion* (Princeton: Princeton University Press, 1993), 221–24; G. Colli, *La sapienza greca,* vol. 2, *Epimenide, Ferecide, Talete, Anassimandro, Anassimene, Onomacrito* (Milano: Adelphi, 1992) (henceforth *SG* 2). The rejection of the Orphic influence in W. Jaeger, *The Theology of the Early Greek Philosophers* (Oxford: Clarendon Press, 1948), 57–62, can be explained as a reaction against the theses of Macchioro (defined as "an extreme partisan of the theory of Orphic influence," 58).

61. According to Aristotle, *Physics* 203b, probably containing several remnants of Anaximander's book (DK 12-A15). F.M. Cornford, *Principium Sapientiae: A Study of the Origins of Greek Philosophical Thought* (New York: Harper, 1965), 178 ff., comments on the passage but without considering the Orphic influence; W.K. Guthrie, *A History of Greek Philosophy,* vol. 1, *The Earlier Presocratics and the Pythagoreans* (1962; repr. Cambridge: Cambridge University Press, 2003), 87–89, does not retain his previous view of the Orphic influence on Anaximander but keeps to the theological and philosophical importance of *Physics,* 203b.

62. The influence of the political model on Anaximander is stressed by J.-P. Vernant, *The Origins of Greek Thought* (1962; repr. Ithaca: Cornell University Press, 1982), 60–68, 105–8, 120–28, but without paying attention to its religious background.

63. On Aeschylus see below, vol. 1, chapter 7, § 1.

64. DK 82-B23 (*SG* 1:28); Greek text in G. Lanata, *Poetiche pre-platoniche: Testimonianze e frammenti* (Firenze: La Nuova Italia, 1963), 204–7; cf. M. Untersteiner, *I sofisti* (Milano: B. Mondadori, 1996), 172–73.

65. Plato, *Laws* 719c–d (for the Greek text I follow *Platonis Opera,* ed. J. Burnet [Oxford: Clarendon Press, 1905–]).

66. Plato, *Laws* 719d–e. For a wider treatment, see Fornari, *Mito, tragedia, filosofia,* 352–62.

67. R. Girard, *La violence et le sacré* (Paris: Grasset, 1994), 204, and also Girard, *A Theater of Envy: William Shakespeare* (Oxford: Oxford University Press, 1991), 197. This lack of historical context perhaps explains why, among scholars interested in Girard, there is

also the contrary tendency to modernize too much the Greek tragedians: S. Goodhart, *Sacrificing Commentary: Reading the End of Literature* (Baltimore: Johns Hopkins University Press, 1996), 13–41, on Sophocles; and E. Gans, *The End of Culture: Toward a Generative Anthropology* (Berkeley: University of California Press, 1985), esp. on Euripides, 295–300. A more contextual analysis is in G. Van Coillie, "Antigone: Mimetic Violence, Tragedy, and Ethics," *Ethical Perspective: Journal of the European Ethics Network* 15, no. 1 (2008), 81–102.

68. Girard, *A Theater of Envy,* 248.
69. See below, vol. 1, chapters 8, § 1 and note 3; 9, § 3; and 10, § 6.
70. G. Fornari, *Fra Dioniso e Cristo: La sapienza sacrificale greca e la civiltà occidentale* (Bologna: Pitagora, 2001), 99–104.
71. For a larger treatment of this topic, see Fornari, *Mito, tragedia, filosofia,* 416–24.

4. Sacrificial and Erotic Metamorphoses in the *Bacchae*

1. On these changes, see below, vol. 1, chapter 8, § 9.
2. Euripide, *Les Bacchantes,* ed. H. Grégoire and J. Meunier (Paris: Les Belles Lettres, 1972) (henceforth Grégoire-Meunier ed.), 221. As to reliability of attribution to Thespis, cf. A.W. Pickard-Cambridge, *Dithyramb, Tragedy, and Comedy,* 2nd ed. (Oxford: Clarendon Press, 1962), 116, which raises some doubts; more favorable is R.C. Flickinger, *The Greek Theater and Its Drama* (1918; repr. Chicago: University of Chicago Press, 1973), 20–21; C. Sourvinou-Inwood, *Tragedy and Athenian Religion* (Lanham, MD: Lexington Books, 2003), 168–69, has doubts on the historical existence of Thespis, though the author's reconstructions are invalidated by the lack of an organic theory of sacrifice.
3. Grégoire-Meunier ed., 219 ff.; Euripides, *Bacchae,* ed. E. R. Dodds (Oxford: Clarendon Press, 1986) (henceforth Dodds ed.), xxviii ff. See also S. Mills, *Euripides: Bacchae* (London: Duckworth, 2006), 34–36.
4. On the style of the play, see Dodds ed., xxxvi–xxxviii.
5. He won only five times (out of twenty-two) the first prize at the tragic festival in Athens, and the last was posthumous (a balanced evaluation is presented in Mills, *Euripides,* 8–9).
6. The role of the Macedonian environment is partially underestimated in Dodds ed., xxxix–xl.
7. Cf. A. Beltrametti, "La visita del giovane dio: Dalla drammaturgia di Dürrenmat alla politica di Archelao," in *Studi e Materiali per le Baccanti di Euripide: Storia Memorie Spettacoli,* ed. A. Beltrametti (Como-Pavia: IBIS, 2007), 46–51.
8. Giulio Guidorizzi rightly defines the parodos of the *Bacchae* as a "sort of Dionysian catechism." Euripide, *Le baccanti,* ed. G. Guidorizzi (Venezia: Marsilio, 1989), 18.
9. Here and in other passages from the *Bacchae,* I follow the edition of G. Murray, *Euripidis fabulae* (1909; repr. Oxford: Clarendon Press, 1990), vol. 3, taking into account the edition of J. Diggle, *Euripidis fabulae* (Oxford: Clarendon Press, 1994), though I share the partial reservations expressed by Giorgio Ieranò in Euripide,

Baccanti, ed. G. Ieranò (Milano: A. Mondadori, 1999), xli, and rely on Dodds's fundamental edition for further aid.

10. Strabo, X, 3, 13.
11. See Dodds ed., on l. 123, 84–85; for the triple-crested helm, see J.E. Harrison, *Themis: A Study of the Social Origins of Greek Religion* (London: Merlin Press, 1989), fig. 49 on 194, and 195.
12. On the power of Phrygian flutes, see E. Rohde, *Psyche: Seelencult und Unsterblichkeitsglaube der Griechen* (Darmstadt: Wissenschaftliche Buchgesellschaft, 1980), 2:16 and 16n1.
13. Euripides, *Bacchae* 864–65, 150 and 695, 1122–23. Cf. Rohde, *Psyche,* 2:12n1.
14. Cf. Rohde, *Psyche,* 2:9, 9n4, and 10.
15. A point normally misunderstood by commentators (e.g., Mills, *Euripides,* 21–22).
16. For line division, I follow the Grégoire-Meunier ed. My translation tries to render the text's violent content. 135: It is necessary to understand, for ἡδὺς, *dulcis est ille,* with Murray, Dodds, and Colli; the adj. "wild" expresses opposition to the space of the community. 137: This is the climax of the trance, so simply "fall" is not enough. 139: I feel that "ecstasy" renders well the theophanic state described by the text (for the equivalence raw = alive, cf. W. Robertson Smith's comment quoted in J.E. Harrison, *Prolegomena to the Study of Greek Religion* [London: Merlin Press, 1980], 486). 141: Βρόμιος, literally the "Noisy," but the noise made by human beings gone wild is typically a shout or roar: cf. Dionysus Ἐριβόας, "the one who shouts loudly."
17. Euripides, *Bacchae* 861.
18. On the concept of δεινός in modern philosophy, see below, vol. 1, chapter 8, § 2.
19. Cf. C. Segal, *Dionysiac Poetics and Euripides "Bacchae,"* expanded ed. (Princeton: Princeton University Press, 1997), 23–24. Not catching this decisive ritual climax, Richard Seaford comments that perhaps Dionysus falls to the ground as being "on the goat in the hunt": Euripides, *Bacchae,* ed. R. Seaford (Warminster: Aris & Phillips, 2001) (henceforth Seaford ed.), 164, but in this way we shift from the most archaic Dionysiac rituals to a Renaissance *Baccanale.*
20. For Dionysus Ἀνθρωπορραίστης, see Dodds ed., xix; K. Kerényi, *Dionysos: Archetypal Image of Indestructible Life,* Engl. trans. R. Manheim (Princeton: Princeton University Press, 1976), 190n4, excludes the interpretation as "render of men" and prefers the translation "crusher of men" with reference to funeral rites, but without giving support to his reading.
21. W.F. Otto, *Dionysus: Myth and Cult,* ed. R.B. Palmer (Bloomington: Indiana University Press 1965), 106–7.
22. Plutarch, *Themistocles* 13.
23. Herodotus, VII, 180.
24. A discussion in detail of the episode is presented in G. Fornari, "Immortali/mortali: Il sacrificio in Eraclito," in *Eraclito: la luce dell'Oscuro,* ed. G. Fornari (Firenze: Olschki, 2017), 162–65.

25. The religious identity of these roles as doubles is stressed in R. Girard, *La violence et le sacré* (Paris: Grasset, 1994), 374, with the author's typical one-sidedness.

26. On the origin of the figure of Pentheus, see Kerényi, *Dionysos: Archetypal Image of Indestructible Life,* 69–71.

27. For the Dionysian *sparagmos,* cf. Girard, *La violence et le sacré,* 196–97. For the bacchantes, see the important study by E.R. Dodds, "Maenadism," in *The Greeks and the Irrational* (Berkeley: California University Press, 1951), 270–82.

28. Euripides, *Bacchae* 877–81 and 897–901 (Diggle has l. 877 as corrupt). For the meaning of knowledge and wisdom in the tragedy, see vol. 1, chapter 6, below.

29. On the cannibalistic nature of the rite in the *Bacchae,* cf. Dodds ed., on l. 1184, and Segal, *Dionysiac Poetics,* 39 and 188n46. For the meaning of ἔνθεος, see Rohde, *Psyche,* 2:19–20 and 20n1, and Dodds, *The Greeks,* 87n 41.

30. Cf. Harrison, *Prolegomena,* 484–85; W.K.C. Guthrie, *Orpheus and Greek Religion* (Princeton: Princeton University Press, 1993), 108–9; Kerényi, *Dionysos: Archetypal Image of Indestructible Life,* 97–98. See also Euripides, *Bacchae* 734 ff.

31. For the sacrificial meaning of words deriving from βάλλω, see for example the perceptive analysis of the expression ὠμοφάγιον ἐμβαλεῖν in Dodds, "Maenadism," 276. These expressions are also found in the Gospels, e.g. καταβολή (foundation) in Mt 13:35, providing, as already mentioned, the title for Girard's *Things Hidden;* see also vol. 1, chapter 9, below.

32. See also Euripides, *Bacchae* 1021–23 and *Rhesus* 730 (no longer attributed to Euripides).

33. "But I shall cause blood to flow in giving battle [συμβαλὼν] to the Bacchae," where the blood in question is Pentheus's (cf. Segal, *Dionysiac Poetics,* 24).

34. Cf. the theme of the devoured shoulder in the myth of Pelops, stewed and served up to the gods by his father, Tantalus. For ὦμος, see also comments in vol. 1, chapter 6, below.

35. M. Heidegger, "Platos Lehre von der Wahrheit," in *Gesamtausgabe,* vol. 9, *Wegmarken* (Frankfurt: a.M. Klostermann, 1975), 203–38.

36. Cf. Dodds ed., on l. 513, 141–42.

37. Euripides, *Bacchae* 508 and 367; cf. Dodds ed., 141 and 116–17.

38. Euripides, *Bacchae* 124 and 1106; cf. for example also 463.

39. The analysis of the problem is stereotyped in Mills, *Euripides,* 11–13, where the relationship male/female is explained with reference to the Pythagorean table of opposites (ibid., 123n20).

40. To analogous rites is to be referred the strange myth of Prosymnos or Polymnos, who had taught Dionysus how to go to the netherworld and asking in return to be sodomized once he was back; when the god comes back, he finds out that his friend is dead and sodomizes himself by sitting on a phallus (Kerényi, *Dionysos: Archetypal Image of Indestructible Life,* 311). This myth appears to be the remainder of ritual homosexual couplings connected with sacrifice and turned into initiating ceremonies; on the Dionysian feasts in Attica and Athens based on phallic symbols and sex reversals, see Kerényi, *Dionysos: Archetypal Image of Indestructible Life,* 144–46 and

162–64; cf. W. Burkert, *Greek Religion,* Engl. trans. J. Raffan (Cambridge, MA: Harvard University Press, 1994), 263 and 292.

41. *Die Fragmente der Vorsokratiker,* ed. H. Diels and W. Kranz (Berlin: Weidmann, 1972–74) (henceforth DK) 22-B79.
42. DK 22-B62. See below, vol. 1, chapter 5, § 2.
43. See below, vol. 1, chapters 6 and 7.
44. See below, vol. 1, chapter 6, § 4.
45. Cf. H. Arendt, *The Human Condition* (Chicago: University of Chicago Press, 1998), 30–31, 72, and elsewhere.
46. Plato, *Laws* 739a.
47. Homer, *Odyssey,* XXIV, 212–13.
48. For the meaning and etymology of θυιάς (Thyad, from θύειν, to "rage" and "sacrifice"), see H. Jeanmaire, *Dionysos: Histoire de culte de Bacchus* (Paris: Payot, 1951), 158; cf. Girard, *La violence et le sacré,* 395–96.
49. Euripides, *Bacchae* 306–9. For Dionysus at Delphi, see Kerényi, *Dionysos: Archetypal Image of Indestructible Life,* 204 ff. The composition of the name Δᾳδαφόριος is the same as δᾳδοῦχος, the second priest who held the torches at Eleusis.
50. G. Colli, *La sapienza greca,* vol. 1, *Dioniso, Apollo, Eleusi, Orfeo, Museo, Iperborei, Enigma* (Milano: Adelphi, 1990), 426, note on 5[A 7].
51. Cf. Dodds, *The Greeks,* 80–82, and Jeanmaire, *Dionysos,* 134–35. The Muses punish those who dare to compete with them, such as Thamyris, a musician-bard similar to Orpheus, blinded by them. Sophocles wrote a tragedy about him, playing the part himself. See also Sophocles, *Antigone* 963–65 and 1128–29.
52. Euripides, *Bacchae* 951–52; Jeanmaire, *Dionysos,* 132. The sacrifice made by Aegisthus in Euripides's *Electra* is dedicated to the Nymphs and ends with *his* sacrifice. The myth of Molos might also be cited: he is found decapitated for having raped a Nymph (Plutarch, *De defectu oraculorum* 14: the entire chapter offers important sacrificial evidence). For the Nymphs, see M. Eliade, *Traité d'histoire des religions* (Paris: Payot, 1949), § 69, pp. 180–85. We should not forget that Thyads is one of the names given to the Nymphs.
53. Aeschylus, *Eumenides* 179 ff., 328 etc. For the sacrificial role of the Charites, see also for example Euripides, *Hippolytus* 1148–50.
54. Euripides, *Bacchae* 731, and 977 where they are linked with Λύσσα, Anger (cf. also 851).
55. This good insight is from Harrison, *Prolegomena,* 286–300.
56. Euripides, *Bacchae* 665 and 453 ff.
57. Euripides, *Bacchae* 236 and 402–15.

5. The *Hieros Gamos* of Wet and Dry

1. Euripides, *Bacchae,* ed. E. R. Dodds (Oxford: Clarendon Press, 1986) (henceforth Dodds ed.), 104; Euripides, *Bacchae,* ed. R. Seaford (Warminster: Aris & Phillips,

2001) (henceforth Seaford ed.), 174–75 (both interpreters intuit that something more than a rationalization is involved here but do not go further).

2. Euripides, *Bacchae* 200–203. The lines present some textual difficulties, for which the Seaford ed., 169–70, even suggests shifting them to the long speech to Pentheus after l. 285, but the main objection of Seaford that Tiresias *is* actually sophisticating about the gods misses the deep meaning of his words; therefore, the lines are after all in their proper place and play the function of anticipating the imminent *rhesis* to the enemy of Dionysus (see also note 3, below).

3. Euripide, *Les Bacchantes,* ed. H. Grégoire and J. Meunier (Paris: Les Belles Lettres, 1972) accepts the formerly advanced reading ἐνσοφιζόμεσθα, while the Dodds ed., 94, maintains the verb of the manuscript tradition but would prefer to attribute the line to Cadmus.

4. G. Betegh, *The Derveni Papyrus: Cosmology, Theology, and Interpretation* (Cambridge: Cambridge University Press, 2006), 183–84.

5. Euripides, *Bacchae* 1–5. Some good remarks on this passage are in C. Segal, *Dionysiac Poetics and Euripides "Bacchae,"* expanded ed. (Princeton: Princeton University Press, 1997), 82–83, but to my knowledge no commentator noticed its theological density, particularly in l. 4.

6. See vol. 1, chapter 2, note 42.

7. On his mythology, see Apollodorus, *The Library,* ed. J.G. Frazer, Loeb Classical Library (Cambridge, MA: Harvard University Press, 1921), 362–67, with the notes. Cf. P. Grimal, *Dictionnaire de la mythologie grecque et romaine* (Paris: Presses Universitaires de France, 1969), *s.v.* "Tirésias," 459.

8. Apollodorus, *The Library,* 364n1 (versions of Eustathius and Tzetze).

9. S. Freud, *Totem und Tabu: Einige Übereinstimmungen im Seelenleben der Wilden und der Neurotiker* (Frankfurt a.M.: Fischer, 2007), 184 and 184n1.

10. On Actaeon, see below, § 3.

11. For the fig tree, see comments below. Ivy is variously associated with the vine as a complementary plant: W.F. Otto, *Dionysus: Myth and Cult,* ed. R.B. Palmer (Bloomington: Indiana University Press, 1965), 152–57; K. Kerényi, *Dionysos: Archetypal Image of Indestructible Life,* Engl. trans. by R. Manheim (Princeton: Princeton University Press, 1976), 62–64. See also below, note 13.

12. Cf. K. Kerényi, *Eleusis: Archetypal Image of Mother and Daughter,* Engl. trans. R. Manheim (Princeton: Princeton University Press, 1967), 134.

13. Otto, *Dionysus,* 164. There might be another symbolic link with ivy in the sperm-like odor of its flowers.

14. *Die Fragmente der Vorsokratiker,* ed. H. Diels and W. Kranz (Berlin: Weidmann, 1972–74) (henceforth DK) 22-B5.

15. DK 22-B24.

16. W. Burkert, *Ancient Mystery Cults* (Cambridge, MA: Harvard University Press, 1987), 98.

17. M. Ceruti and G. Fornari, *Le due paci: Cristianesimo e morte di Dio nel mondo globalizzato* (Milano: Cortina, 2005), 120–22; R. Girard, P. Antonello, and J.C. De Castro Rocha, *Evolution and Conversion: Dialogues on the Origin of Culture* (London-New York: Continuum, 2007), 119–22.
18. T. Taylor, *The Prehistory of Sex: Four Million Years of Human Sexual Culture* (New York: Bantam Books, 1997), 184–89.
19. C. Pavese, *Dialoghi con Leucò* (Torino: Einaudi, 1999), 87–98.
20. Otto, *Dionysus,* 157–59.
21. Kerényi, *Dionysos: Archetypal Image of Indestructible Life,* 66–67; cf. W. Burkert, *Homo Necans: The Anthropology of Ancient Greek Sacrificial Ritual and Myth,* Engl. trans. P. Bing (Berkeley: University of California Press, 1983), 224–25 (comparison with the Vedic *soma* on which see below).
22. Cf. J.-P. Vernant, "The Masked Dionysus of Euripides' '*Bacchae,*'" in J.-P. Vernant and P. Vidal-Naquet, *Myth and Tragedy in Ancient Greece,* Engl. trans. J. Lloyd (New York: Zone Books, 1990), 399–400.
23. J. G. Frazer, *The Golden Bough: A Study in Magic and Religion* (New York: Macmillan Co., 1951), 670–75; there is a summary of the rite in J.-P. Vernant, "Ambiguity and Reversal: On the Enigmatic Structure of *Oedipus Rex,*" in Vernant and Vidal-Naquet, *Myth and Tragedy,* 128–29. The rite may have several variants, all deriving from a common structure. Obviously the significance of the rite is not affected where the killing becomes symbolic in later versions.
24. Cf. Plutarch, *Questiones conviviales,* VI, 10.
25. Frazer, *The Golden Bough,* 672–73 (the author mentions a hypothesis of W.R. Paton); cf. 439.
26. Dodds ed., 106, remarks on the correspondence, without admitting that the detail is enough to subvert the cliché of the sophistic rationalization. See below, § 3 and notes 39–41.
27. Shakespeare, *Julius Caesar,* 2, 1, 173 (W. Shakespeare, *The Complete Works,* ed. S. Wells et al. [Oxford: Clarendon Press, 1994], 608).
28. Shakespeare, *Julius Caesar,* 2, 1, 166 (Shakespeare, *The Complete Works,* 607).
29. G. Büchner, *Dantons Tod,* 1, 6, in Büchner, *Werke und Briefe,* ed. K. Pörnbacher et al. (München: Deutscher Taschenbuch, 1988), 88.
30. G. Fornari, "Immortali/mortali: Il sacrificio in Eraclito," in *Eraclito: la luce dell'Oscuro,* ed. G. Fornari (Firenze: Olschki, 2017), 153–62 and 178–81.
31. This is true also of the most advanced physician in the classical world, Galenus (M. Vegetti, "In difesa della razionalità antica: il progetto di Galeno," in Galeno, *Nuovi scritti autobiografici,* ed. M. Vegetti [Roma: Carocci, 2013], 21–26).
32. There are repeated allusions in the text characterizing Dionysus as νόσος: in l. 311 (νοσῇ) and l. 353 (νόσον), given prominence in both cases by the end-line position. The ancients enjoyed playing on the etymology of the gods' compound names: see, for example, A. Cornutus, *Theologiae Graecae compendium,* 30.

33. Euripides, *Bacchae* 378–85 and 421–26.
34. Euripides, *Bacchae* 534–36. I have tried to translate the image literally; cf. also the Thracian *Dionysos Botrys* (Dodds ed., 106).
35. Euripides, *Bacchae* 651. Here and in many other places Dionysus refers to himself in the third person (see vol. 1, chapter 7, below).
36. On l. 289, I maintain the traditional reading θεόν (cf. Seaford ed., 177): the old conjecture νέον (accepted by Diggle) appears redundant with βρέφος and misses the theogonic content of the text; on l. 292, the term αἰθήρ does not indicate simply the air (as in Dodds ed., 107) but the intermedial substance encompassing all the Earth; on ll. 293–94 the reading by Diggle is satisfactory and to be accepted.
37. The reading followed by Diggle, ἐκτιθείς Διόνυσον, can mean both "abandoning (the hostage) like Dionysus" and more directly "abandoning Dionysus."
38. Aristotle, *De generatione animalium* 736b.
39. Kerényi, *Dionysos: Archetypal Image of Indestructible Life*, 273–78; W. Burkert, *Greek Religion*, Engl. trans. J. Raffan (Cambridge, MA: Harvard University Press, 1994), 165–66.
40. R. B. Onians, *The Origins of European Thought about the Body, the Mind, the Soul, the World, Time, and Fate: New Interpretations of Greek, Roman and Kindred Evidence also of Some Basic Jewish and Christian Beliefs* (Cambridge: Cambridge University Press, 2000), 111 and 182–86.
41. On the Vedic horse sacrifice, cf. J. Campbell, *The Masks of God: Oriental Mythology* (New York: Penguin Books, 1976), 194–96. Also to be remembered is the comparable Roman sacrifice of the *October equus* where the animal was directly beheaded, while the hierogamous aspect had disappeared but survived in the severed tail probably substituting the genital organ (cf. Burkert, *Homo Necans*, 69).
42. W. Doniger O'Flaherty, *The Origins of Evil in Hindu Mythology* (Berkeley: University of California Press, 1980), 334.
43. See A.M. Hocart, *Kings and Councillors: An Essay in the Comparative Anatomy of Human Society* (1936; repr. Chicago: University of Chicago Press, 1970), 65–67; cf. Hocart, *Imagination and Proof: Selected Essays* (Tucson: University of Arizona Press, 1987), 52–53.
44. Cf. W. Burkert, *Structure and History in Greek Mythology and Ritual* (Berkeley: University of California Press, 1982), 113.
45. Cf. Burkert, *Structure and History*, 21–22, where the author does not take into account the intertwining of the common Indo-European heritage.
46. Euripides, *Bacchae* 302–4 and 298–301 where the derivatives of μαίνομαι are stressed.
47. Euripides, *Bacchae* 337–40: Actaeon has been previously named in l. 230 and is referred to again in l. 1291. There is an interesting detail in l. 340: the fact that the incident occurred ἐν ὀργάσιν, i.e., in sacred places on the mountains (Dodds ed., 114), where orgies, ὄργια, took place and the destructive fury, ὀργή (*Bacchae* 997–98), was let loose.
48. Frazer, *The Golden Bough*, 404 ff.

6. Sapiential Reflections in the *Bacchae*

1. The interpretive history until the middle of the twentieth century is surveyed and already criticized in Euripides, *Bacchae,* ed. E. R. Dodds (Oxford: Clarendon Press, 1986) (henceforth Dodds ed.), xl–xlvi, but Dodds's conclusive alternative is a kind of naturalistic interpretation of the whole plot; see also Euripide, *Les Bacchantes,* ed. H. Grégoire and J. Meunier (Paris: Les Belles Lettres, 1972) (henceforth Grégoire-Meunier ed.), 230 ff., which finally falls into psychologistic misinterpretations. The antireligious readings of the tragedy, which prevail today in the shallow way just described, overlook that the failure of traditional readings demonstrates not the inadequacy of a religious interpretation of the tragedy, but rather the inadequacy of traditional interpretations of religion.
2. R. Girard, *La violence et le sacré* (Paris: Grasset, 1994), 194–95.
3. See B. Mack, "Introduction: Religion and Ritual," in W. Burkert, R. Girard, and J.Z. Smith, *Violent Origins: Ritual Killing and Cultural Formation,* ed. by R.G. Hamerton-Kelly (Stanford: Stanford University Press, 1987), 16: "I strongly suspect that the *Bacchae* provided the bridge for Girard's move from literature to the myths and rituals of religion."
4. Segal rightly remarks: "For all the emphasis on learning, knowledge is singularly ineffective in the play" (*Dionysiac Poetics and Euripides "Bacchae,"* expanded ed. [Princeton: Princeton University Press, 1997], 317).
5. See, for example, *Bacchae* 501 where Pentheus refuses to see the *god* in Dionysus. For the part played by reason in the character, see cf. H. Jeanmaire, *Dionysos: Histoire de culte de Bacchus* (Paris: Payot, 1951), 142–43.
6. T. Mann, *Der Tod in Venedig,* in *Die Erzählungen, Fiorenza, Gesang vom Kindchen, Gedichte* (Frankfurt a.M.: Fischer, 1966), 512.
7. Mann, *Der Tod in Venedig,* 515–16.
8. Mann, *Der Tod in Venedig,* 525.
9. Anticipated in ll. 618–21 when Pentheus mistakes a bull for Dionysus.
10. Note the use of a compound of βάλλω in this line, where terms with a double sacrificial sense are densely clustered: κορυφαῖς ὑποβαλὼν ὦμον. For κορυφή as "head" cf. ll. 879 and 899.
11. Euripides, *Bacchae* 506: the expression ὅ τι ζῇς ("what you are living for"; *Euripidis fabulae,* ed. G. Murray [1909; repr. Oxford: Clarendon Press, 1990]: *quid sit tua vita;* cf. Dodds ed., *ad.v.,* 140–41), referring to the ongoing objectual destruction of his life, seems definitely preferable to me as *lectio difficilior* to the more banal ὅ τι σὺ φῄς ("what you are saying"), accepted by the Grégoire-Meunier ed., 263 While the Diggle edition limits itself to designating the passage as corrupt, Murray's reading is also accepted by Segal, *Dionysiac Poetics,* 229, and maintained by Euripides, *Bacchae,* ed. R. Seaford (Warminster: Aris & Phillips, 2001) (henceforth Seaford ed.).
12. Euripides, *Bacchae* 179 and 196: but, generally speaking, all the speeches of these two characters oppose the Thebans and Pentheus for their madness.

13. Euripides, *Bacchae* 310. Dodds ed., 111, speaks of "stubborn reliance upon an unproved δόξα," but Tiresias's reasoning is subtler and more objective.
14. É. Benveniste, *Le vocabulaire des institutions indo-européennes,* vol. 2, *Pouvoir, droit, religion* (Paris: Les Éditions de Minuit, 1969), 71–83. The critical remarks in Girard, *La violence et le sacré,* 392–95, are sound but ignore the problem of finding an objectual mediation for *kratos.*
15. Euripides, *Bacchae* 365; cf. Dodds ed., 116.
16. Euripides, *Bacchae* 191; Segal, *Dionysiac Poetics,* 304 (cf. Dodds ed., 90): J. Roux (Euripides, *Les Bacchantes. Commentaire,* ed. by J. Roux [Paris: Les Belles Lettres, 1972], *ad v.* 191) rightly stresses the regal symbolism of the chariot but decontextualizes the line, making it an affirmation.
17. Cf. Segal, *Dionysiac Poetics,* 138.
18. Nietzsche, in chap. 12 of *The Birth of Tragedy,* has grasped the characters of Cadmus and Tiresias, in the sense, however, of the false 'palinode' theory (F. Nietzsche, *Sämtliche Werke: Kritischen Studienausgabe,* ed. G. Colli and M. Montinari [Berlin-New York: De Gruyter, 1980], 1:620–21).
19. Euripides, *Bacchae* 991–96, 1011–16. On lines 995 and 1015 particularly powerful is the anaphora of the three proparoxytone adjectives with the alpha privative ἄθεον ἄνομον ἄδικον (this type of anaphora is found elsewhere in Euripides and Sophocles: cf. G. Fornari, *La conoscenza tragica in Euripide e in Sofocle* [Massa: Transeuropa, 2013], 292).
20. Euripides, *Bacchae* 680–82, 1095 ff.
21. Euripides, *Bacchae* 45, 325, 1255.
22. Cf. Segal, *Dionysiac Poetics,* 81 ff.
23. Cf. what Girard says about *Logos Phobos* in *La violence et le sacré,* 220–21.
24. Euripides, *Bacchae* 1082–83.
25. Euripides, *Bacchae* 1043–47: the three characters go off to conduct a viewing, θεωρίας (1047), a term indicating originally, in its verb θεωρεῖν, a visit of inspection to some sacred place (K. Kerényi, *The Religions of the Greeks and Romans,* Engl. trans. C. Holme [London: Thames and Hudson, 1962], 151–52); here the term conveys the connotation of accompanying a sacrificial victim, besides probably alluding to the Eleusinian Mysteries (cf. Seaford ed., 233), and finally contains a clear reference to the spectators of the tragedy.
26. V. Di Benedetto and E. Medda, *La tragedia sulla scena: La tragedia greca in quanto spettacolo teatrale* (Torino: Einaudi, 2002), 229.
27. Euripides, *Bacchae* 1383–87: it is actually the concluding lines of the tragedy if we consider that the last five lines, though meaningful, are more conventional and common to other Euripidean tragedies as well.
28. The connection of μνῆμα with death is partially acknowledged by Seaford ed., 257.

7. The Power and Failure of Divine Mediation

1. Aeschylus, *Eumenides* 736–38; Greek text in *Aeschyli septem quae supersunt tragoedias,* ed. D. Page (Oxford: Clarendon Press, 1989).
2. Aeschylus, *Eumenides* 973–75.
3. The tensional character of Aeschylus's Athena is rightly emphasized by J.-P. Vernant, "Tensions and Ambiguities in Greek Tragedy," in J.-P. Vernant and P. Vidal-Naquet, *Myth and Tragedy,* Engl. trans. J. Lloyd (New York: Zone Books, 1990), 418–20n4, but he wrongly denies the originality of his theatrical-religious-juridical solution.
4. Cf. G. Fornari, *Da Dioniso a Cristo: Conoscenza e sacrificio nel mondo greco e nella civiltà occidentale* (Genova-Milano: Marietti, 2006), 183–85 and 190–91.
5. Cf. G. Fornari, *Storicità radicale: Filosofia e morte di Dio* (Massa: Transeuropa, 2013), 188–91.
6. I add the quotation marks to stress that the Manichaean religion, far from being the paradigm of dualistic superstition as usually claimed, is a perfect example of a religion persecuted in all the countries and finally destroyed.
7. I used this formula, still in a Girardian conceptual frame, in G. Fornari, *Fra Dioniso e Cristo: La sapienza sacrificale greca e la civiltà occidentale* (Bologna: Pitagora, 2001), 141 ff.
8. See R. Girard, *Des choses cachées depuis la foundation du monde: Recherches avec Jean-Michel Oughourlian et Guy Lefort* (Paris: Grasset, 1991), 399 ff.
9. This psychological view is developed in J.-M. Oughourlian, *Un mime nommé désir: Hystérie, transe, possession, adorcism* (Paris: Grasset & Fasquelle, 1982).
10. Cf. R. Girard, *A Theater of Envy: William Shakespeare* (Oxford: Oxford University Press, 1991), 270–71.
11. A. Manzoni, "Lettre à M. Chauvet sur l'unité de temps et de lieu dans la tragédie," in Manzoni, *Tutte le opere,* ed. by M. Martelli (Firenze: Sansoni, 1973), 2:1671–1711; Aristotle, *Poetics* 1455b, 24 (δέσις).
12. For more detailed information on the Roman theatre, see *Teatri romani: Gli spettacoli nell'antica Roma,* ed. N. Savarese (Bologna: Cuepress, 2015).
13. A. Artaud, "Le théatre de la cruauté," in *Œuvres complètes,* vol. 4 (Paris: Gallimard, 1964), 106–19 and 146–53.
14. F. Nietzsche, *Sämtliche Werke: Kritischen Studienausgabe,* ed. G. Colli and M. Montinari (Berlin-New York: De Gruyter, 1980) (henceforth NSW), 12:47, 1[162].
15. NSW, 12:510, 10[95].
16. See G. Fornari, *Mito, tragedia, filosofia: Dall'antica Grecia al Moderno* (Roma: Studium, 2017), 431–32 and 573–80. Cf. above vol. 1, chapter 4, note 6.
17. Euripides, *Bacchae* 794–824. I have tried to render the text's sapiential reference in the last line.
18. One might evidence, for example, the cross-references in ll. 805 and 291, and in ll. 800 and 1102; and in l. 815 the conjunction ὅμως recalling ὦμος, shoulder, and ὠμός, the uncooked flesh of omophagy, etc.

19. B. Snell, *The Discovery of the Mind: The Greek Origins of European Thought,* Engl. trans. T.G. Rosenmeyer (New York-Evanston: Harper & Row, 1960), 9–22.
20. Euripides, *Bacchae* 319–21; cf. J.-P. Vernant, "The Masked Dionysus of Euripides' *Bacchae,*" in Vernant and Vidal-Naquet, *Myth and Tragedy,* 391.
21. This ambiguity lies at the root of the thesis whereby Dionysus is only a human being: Dodds rightly shows it as untenable, but in turn fails to realize that the ambiguity is real and profound (Euripides, *Bacchae,* ed. E. R. Dodds [Oxford: Clarendon Press, 1986], xlviii–l).
22. Euripides, *Bacchae* 616 ff.; C. Segal, *Dionysiac Poetics and Euripides "Bacchae,"* expanded ed. (Princeton: Princeton University Press, 1997), 30–31.
23. H. Arendt, *The Human Condition* (Chicago: University of Chicago Press), 175–247.
24. Euripides, *Bacchae* 847–61 (ll. 847 and 848 are reversed by an old correction universally accepted by scholars).
25. Euripides, *Bacchae* 971. There is a kind of reversal of the destiny of Dionysus *trigonos* in the triple repetition of *deinos* leading to Pentheus's *pathe* at the end of line as well as at the end of his life.

8. The Birth of Tragedy, the End of Classical Greece

1. See on this the conclusion of the book.
2. G. Fornari, *La conoscenza tragica in Euripide e in Sofocle* (Massa: Transeuropa, 2013), 144–88.
3. An influence of Epicurean physical theory is clearly recognizable in the book of Job: G. Garbini, *Letteratura e politica nell'Israele antico* (Brescia: Paideia, 2010), 144–52. Besides, clear allusions to the Egyptian mythology that are typical of the Judaic Diaspora further confirm a Hellenistic dating.
4. It clearly results from his political manifesto *Der Hessische Landbote;* see the texts and evidence collected in G. Büchner and F.L. Weidig, *Der Hessische Landbote: Studienausgabe,* ed. G. Schaub (Stuttgart: Reclam, 2006).
5. Thucydides, VII, 50, 4 (the temporal formula mentioned by the historian was evidently traditional).
6. See G. Serra, *La forza e il valore: Capitoli sulla Costituzione degli Ateniesi dello pseudo-Senofonte,* Bollettino dell'Istituto di Filologia Greca (Roma: "L'Erma" di Bretschneider, 1979).
7. Its extant fragments are edited and discussed in L. Carrara, *L'indovino Poliido: Eschilo, Le cretesi. Sofocle, Manteis. Euripide, Poliido* (Roma: Edizioni di Storia e Letteratura, 2014), 215–390.
8. On these aspects, cf. J.-P. Vernant, "The Masked Dionysus of Euripides' *Bacchae,*" in J.-P. Vernant and P. Vidal-Naquet, *Myth and Tragedy in Ancient Greece,* Engl. trans. J. Lloyd (New York: Zone Books, 1990), 392.
9. Euripides, *Bacchae* 924. Cf. R. Girard, *La violence et le sacré* (Paris: Grasset, 1994), 239–40.

10. Euripides, *Alcestis,* ed. by A.M. Dale (London: Bristol Classical Press, 2003), xviii–xxii.
11. G. Colli, *Filosofia dell'espressione* (Milano: Adelphi, 1969); Colli, *Dopo Nietzsche* (Milano: Bompiani, 1974); Colli, *La nascita della filosofia* (Milano: Adelphi, 1975).
12. Colli, *La nascita della filosofia,* 78–79; see also J. Huizinga, *Homo Ludens: A Study of the Play-Element in Culture* (Mansfield Centre, CT: Martino Publisher, 2014), 115–18 and 148.
13. Philostratus, *Vitae Sophistarum,* I, 1 in G. Colli, *La sapienza greca,* vol. 1, *Dioniso, Apollo, Eleusi, Orfeo, Museo, Iperborei, Enigma* (Milano: Adelphi, 1990) (henceforth *SG* 1), 364, 7[B 1–cI].
14. For the αἶνος/αἰνός connection, see the definition of the objects of the research of the enigma as *deina* (terrible) in *SG* 1:360, 7[B 1a–VI] (scholia to Dionysius the Thracian): δεινός is the perfect synonym of αἰνός.
15. M. Heidegger, *Einführung in die Metaphysik* (Tübingen: Niemeyer, 1987), 119 (vol. 40 of Heidegger, *Gesamtausgabe* [Frankfurt: a.M. Klostermann, 1983], 164).
16. Sophocles, *Antigone* 332–33; Heidegger, *Einführung in die Metaphysik,* 112 ff. (Heidegger, *Gesamtausgabe,* 40:155 ff.).
17. Sophocles, *Antigone* 360–62; Heidegger, *Einführung in die Metaphysik,* 116 (Heidegger, *Gesamtausgabe,* 40:160–61).
18. M. Heidegger, *Sein und Zeit* (Tübingen: Niemeyer, 2006), §§ 46–48, pp. 235–46 (vol. 2 of Heidegger, *Gesamtausgabe,* 314–27).
19. See also vol. 2, chapter 1, § 8.
20. K. Kerényi, *Labyrinth-Studien: Labyrinthos als Linienreflex einer mythologischen Idee* (Zürich: Rhein, 1950), 47.
21. The figure of Arachne, the weaver, appears to be a late but proper development from Ariadne, and my hypothesis is that it derives from the variant of Ariadne's name *Arihagne;* K. Kerényi, *Dionysos: Archetypal Image of Indestructible Life.* Engl. trans. R. Manheim (Princeton: Princeton University Press, 1976), 99, comments on the divine epithet *Arihagne* as the "utterly pure," from ἁγνός; and W.F. Otto, *Dionysus: Myth and Cult,* ed. R.B. Palmer (Bloomington: Indiana University Press, 1965), 183, observes that the epithet appears on Attic vase paintings and suggests translating it as "untouchable."
22. Homer, *Odyssey,* XI, 324–25: On the Cretan island of Dia and its meaning, see Kerényi, *Dionysos: Archetypal Image of Indestructible Life*, 101, 108–10, 121–22.
23. In several collective female figures there is a hanging motif, or one deriving from swinging. Interesting, though unverified, is the etymology reported in H.G. Liddell and R. Scott, *An Intermediate Greek-English Lexicon* (Oxford: Clarendon Press, 1889), *s.v.,* where the name *Ἀνάγκη* is derived from ἄγχω, I strangle.
24. F. Nietzsche, *Ecce homo,* in *Sämtliche Werke: Kritischen Studienausgabe,* ed. G. Colli and M. Montinari (Berlin-New York: De Gruyter, 1980) (henceforth NSW), 6:348.
25. Aristotle, *Politics* 1253a, 10; Greek text from *Aristotelis Politica,* ed. W.D. Ross (Oxford: Clarendon Press, 1957).
26. Aristotle, *Politics* 1253a, 7–8.

27. H. Arendt, *The Human Condition* (Chicago: University of Chicago Press, 1998), 27.
28. Aristotle, *Politics* 1253a, 16–18.
29. As well shown by W. Jaeger, *Aristotle: Fundamentals of the History of His Development,* Engl. trans. with the author's corrections and additions by R. Robinson (Oxford: Oxford University Press, 1962), 368 ff.
30. An archaic form of the word aiming to indicate its more originary meaning.
31. M. Heidegger, *Beiträge zur Philosophie (Vom Ereignis),* vol. 65 of *Gesamtausgabe,* 497.
32. W. Benjamin, "Über Sprache überhaupt und über die Sprache des Menschen," in Benjamin, *Gesammelte Schriften,* ed. R. Tiedemann and H. Schweppenhäuser, vol. 2, pt. 1 (Frankfurt a.M.: Suhrkamp, 1991), 140–57.
33. W. Benjamin, *Ursprung des deutschen Trauerspiels*, in *Gesammelte Schriften,* 1, pt. 1:215–18.
34. L. Wittgenstein, "Bemerküngen über Frazers *The Golden Bough,*" *Synthèse* 17, no. 1 (1967): 233–53.
35. L. Wittgenstein, *Tractatus logico-philosophicus,* Engl. trans. D.F. Pears and B.F. McGuinness (London: Routledge, 1977), 74; Wittgenstein, *Werkausgabe,* vol. 1 (Frankfurt a.M.: Suhrkamp, 1984), 85.
36. Cf. L. Wittgenstein, *Philosophische Untersuchungen,* §§ 7, 23, etc. (*Sprachspiel*); §§ 35, 155, 157, 165, 171–77 etc. (*Erlebnis*); Wittgenstein, *Werkausgabe,* 1, 241, 250, etc.
37. Wittgenstein, *Tractatus,* prop. 6.41, p. 71; Wittgenstein, *Werkausgabe,* 1:82–83.
38. Wittgenstein, *Tractatus,* prop. 6.43, p. 72; Wittgenstein, *Werkausgabe,* 1:83.
39. Wittgenstein, *Tractatus,* prop. 6.522, p. 73; Wittgenstein, *Werkausgabe,* 1:85.
40. R. Girard, *Des choses cachées depuis la foundation du monde: Recherches avec Jean-Michel Oughourlian et Guy Lefort* (Paris: Grasset, 1991), 145.
41. Benjamin, "Über Sprache überhaupt," 142–43: "ist das Urproblem der Sprache ihre Magie."
42. G. Van Der Leeuw, *Religion in Essence and Manifestation,* Eng. trans. J. E. Turner and H.H. Penner (Princeton: Princeton University Press, 1986), 403–07; cf. Van Der Leeuw, *La religion dans son essence et ses manifestations: Phénoménologie de la religion,* Fr. edition ed. by the author in collaboration with J. Marty (Paris: Payot, 1955) (this is the most up-to-date version of this work which was originally published in German).
43. See above, vol. 1, chapter 4, § 4.
44. It is perhaps interesting to note that sources describe Euripides as a skillful painter.
45. Cf. Van Der Leeuw, *Religion in Essence and Manifestation,* 432–34 (cf. Van Der Leeuw, *La religion dans son essence et ses manifestations,* 423–25).
46. See Huizinga, *Homo Ludens,* 146–53.
47. G. Pettinato, *I Sumeri* (Milano: Rusconi, 1994), 153.
48. *SG* 1:341, 7[A 1]; cf. Huizinga, *Homo Ludens,* 109.
49. An "unspeakable" sacrifice, probably dismemberment, was made by the *Hosioi,* the holy men who assisted the Pythia (see W. Burkert, *Homo Necans: The Anthropology of*

Ancient Greek Sacrificial Ritual and Myth, Engl. trans. P. Bing [Berkeley: University of California Press, 1983], 124–25). They were purified by means of an initiatory sacrifice and have close parallels with the sons of Ida.

50. Cf. J.-P. Vernant, "Tensions and Ambiguities in Greek Tragedy," in Vernant and Vidal-Naquet, *Myth and Tragedy,* 29–48.
51. Otto, *Dionysus,* 91.
52. Girard, *La violence et le sacré,* 248.
53. *Suida,* see *s.v.* "Thespis"; Kerényi, *Dionysos: Archetypal Image of Indestructible Life,* 326–27.
54. Aristotle, *Poetics* 1449a, 9–11 (cf. Aristotele, *Dell'arte poetica,* ed. C. Gallavotti, Fondazione L. Valla [Milano: A. Mondadori, 1990], commentary on 133). For διθύραμβος, see J.E. Harrison, *Themis: A Study of the Social Origins of Greek Religion* (London: Merlin Press, 1989), 129–30.
55. R. Calasso, *Le nozze di Cadmo e Armonia* (Milano: Adelphi, 1993), 54–55.
56. The point has been often misunderstood by commentators. On this question, see W. Burkert, "Greek Tragedy and Sacrificial Ritual," *Greek, Roman and Byzantine Studies* 7 (1966): 87–121: according to Burkert, the song of the τραγῳδòι is linked to a real sacrifice of a *tragos,* but he fails to see that his own interpretation is corroborated by the tradition of the goat-men, even if τραγῳδός means simply "the one who sings the goat" or something similar.
57. The expression "nothing to do with Dionysus" might have originated as an enigma referring to the anti-Dionysus.
58. For the links between tragedy and Eleusis, see J.E. Harrison, *Prolegomena to the Study of Greek Religion* (London: Merlin Press, 1980), 567–70.
59. Starting from Athens and passing by Eleusis, the connection to Crete established by P. Faure, *La vie quotidienne au temps de Minos (1500 av. J.-C.)* (Paris: Hachette, 1973), 320–21, is to be accepted.
60. For example, the lost tragedy Aeschylus, *The Bassarides,* concerning the death of Orpheus, or the analogies between the final scene of *Oedipus at Colonus* and the Eleusinian rite.
61. Aristotle, *Nicomachean Ethics* 1111a, 8–10, in *SG* 1:108, 3[A 22].
62. This is the only clearly detectable unity in Aristotle's text (*Poetics,* 1451a, 17 ff.), while the unity of time goes back to the advice to make the action last one day (1449b, 13–15) and the unity of space can be explained by the static setting of stage in Greek theater. Cf. Fornari, *La conoscenza tragica,* 332.
63. See E.A. Havelock, *Preface to Plato* (Cambridge, MA: Harvard University Press, 1963).
64. On the different possibilities in classical Greece, cf. G. Fornari, "Immortali/mortali: Il sacrificio in Eraclito," in *Eraclito: la luce dell'Oscuro,* ed. G. Fornari (Firenze: Olschki, 2017), 151 and 151n27.
65. Cf. Van Der Leeuw, *Religion in Essence and Manifestation,* 435–37 (cf. Van Der Leeuw, *La religion dans son essence et ses manifestations,* 426–29).

66. Tacitus, *Annales,* XIV, 30; cf. J.A. MacCulloch, *The Religion of the Ancient Celts* (Edinburgh: Clark, 1911), 235 (with the whole chapter) and 247: several sources in antiquity and the Middle Ages testify to these practices.
67. See for example the characterization of Chalcas's wisdom in the *Iliad,* I, 70; *SG* 1:74, 2[A 1].
68. F.M. Cornford, *Principium Sapientiae: A Study of the Origins of Greek Philosophical Thought* (New York: Harper, 1965), 102.
69. Cf. Burkert, *Homo Necans,* 123–24 and 126.
70. Kerényi, *Labyrinth-Studien,* 14: "Palast der Eingeweide."
71. Reproduced in U. Sansoni, *Le più antiche pitture del Sahara: L'arte delle teste rotonde* (Milano: Jaca Books, 1994), fig. 16 on p. 62.
72. Ovid, *Ars amatoria,* I, 317–22; Raffaele Cantarella considers the entire passage 289–326 to be derived from Euripides (Euripide, *I cretesi,* ed. R. Cantarella [Milano: Istituto Editoriale Italiano, 1964], 48–50), an attribution further confirmed by the present analyses.
73. See *L'Épopée de Gilgameš: L'homme qui ne voulait pas mourir,* ed. by J. Bottéro (Paris: Gallimard, 1992), 132.
74. *La saga di Gilgamesh,* ed. by G. Pettinato, S.M. Chiodi, and G. Del Monte (Milano: Rusconi, 1992), 327.
75. Sansoni, *Le più antiche pitture del Sahara,* fig. 192 on p. 247.
76. G. Manganelli, *Tutti gli errori* (Milano: Rizzoli, 1986), 115.
77. Manganelli, *Tutti gli errori,* 125.
78. Initiation rite of the Akikúyu in Harrison, *Themis,* 21.
79. Kerényi, *Labyrinth-Studien,* 14–15.
80. The finds come from an eighth-century sanctuary in Gortyne (Crete) and a sixth-century sanctuary in Sparta, with a typical passage from Crete to Greece: W. Burkert, *The Orientalizing Revolution: Near Eastern Influence on Greek Culture in the Early Archaic Period,* Engl. trans. M.E. Pinder and W. Burkert (Cambridge, MA: Harvard University Press, 1995), 49; A.W. Pickard-Cambridge, *Dithyramb, Tragedy, and Comedy* (1927; repr. Oxford: Clarendon Press, 1997), 254 ff. and figs. 19–25.
81. NSW, 1:78.
82. The word is from ὑποκρίνω, "I submit to judgment." See M. Untersteiner, *Le origini della tragedia e del tragico: Dalla preistoria ad Eschilo* (Torino: Einaudi, 1955), 268–69. The sense of *hypokrites* is the same, even if translated as "interpreter" (F. Ferrari, *Introduzione al teatro Greco* [Firenze: Sansoni, 1996], 17): the person who interprets is, in fact, the one who sets himself in relation to the chorus and reflects its judgment.
83. Aristotle, *Poetics* 1449b, 24 and 27–28; Greek text in *Aristotelis De arte poetica liber,* ed. R. Kassel (Oxford: Clarendon Press, 1965).
84. Cf. C. Bandera, *The Sacred Game: The Role of the Sacred in the Genesis of Modern Literary Fiction* (University Park: Pennsylvania State University Press, 1994), 112–13.
85. Kerényi, *Dionysos: Archetypal Image of Indestructible Life,* 319 and n149.

86. S. Freud, *Totem und Tabu: Einige Übereinstimmungen im Seelenleben der Wilden und der Neurotiker* (Frankfurt a.M.: Fischer, 2007), 211.
87. On this point, see W. Kaufmann, *Tragedy and Philosophy* (Princeton: Princeton University Press, 1979), 159 ff.
88. G. Lanata, *Poetiche pre-platoniche: Testimonianze e frammenti* (Firenze: La Nuova Italia, 1963), 140–41.
89. E.R. Dodds, *The Greeks and the Irrational* (Berkeley: California University Press, 1951), 15; Nilsson quotation on 13.
90. L. Edmunds, *Oedipus: The Ancient Legend and Its Later Analogues* (Baltimore: Johns Hopkins University Press, 1985), 36; cf. Fornari, *La conoscenza tragica,* 48 and 339.
91. Homer, *Iliad,* I, 133–34.
92. Historians admit the existence of such measures without giving them a particular meaning: cf. *The Cambridge Ancient History,* vol. 3, part 3, ed. by J. Boardman and N.G.L. Hammond (Cambridge: Cambridge University Press, 1982), 412–13 (see also below notes 100–101).
93. Cf. L. Canfora, *La crisi dell'utopia: Aristofane contro Platone* (Roma-Bari: Laterza, 2014). On the origin of comedy, cf. G. Cerri, "Tragedia e commedia nel finale del Simposio di Platone (una nuova proposta ermeneutica)," in ΦΙΛΙΑ: *Dieci contributi per Gabriele Burzacchini,* ed. M. Tulli (Bologna: Patron, 2014), 33–41; G. Fornari, *Mito, tragedia, filosofia: Dall'antica Grecia al Moderno* (Roma: Studium, 2017), 211–12.
94. Scholia to Aristophanes in G. Colli, *La sapienza greca,* vol. 2, *Epimenide, Ferecide, Talete, Anassimandro, Anassimene, Onomacrito* (Milano: Adelphi, 1992) (henceforth *SG* 2), 13[B 10]; E. Rohde, *Psyche: Seelencult und Unsterblichkeitsglaube der Griechen* (Darmstadt: Wissenschaftliche Buchgesellschaft, 1980), 2:109 and 109n2; P. Kingsley, *Ancient Philosophy, Mystery, and Magic: Empedocles and Pythagorean Tradition* (Oxford: Clarendon Press, 2009), 143–60.
95. The most interesting testimony in Aristotle is to be found in the *Constitution of the Athenians* 16. For evidence from Herodotus, see the following note.
96. Herodotus, I, 60; the episode is taken from Aristotle, *Constitution of the Athenians* 14.
97. A likely parallel is with the *hieros gamos* of the Anthesteria, where the wife of the *archon basileus,* in the guise of bride to Dionysus, was presumably drawn in a chariot together with an image of Dionysus or with a man impersonating the god. The coupling took place in the *Boukoleion,* the stable where the bull was kept near the residence of the *archon basileus,* associated with Dionysus and the labyrinth hierogamies.
98. Diogenes Laertius, I, 60.
99. Plutarch, *Solon* 29, 6 (Greek text in Plutarco, *La vita di Solone,* ed. by M. Manfredini and L. Piccirilli, Fondazione L. Valla [Milano: A. Mondadori, 1990], 88 and 90). Thespis argued on his side that tragedy was "in play" (μετὰ παιδιᾶς) but, as we have seen already and will see again in the following chapters, play and children, *paides,* have sacrificial significance. This explains Solon's angry reaction, which possibly contains a sapiential reference to the *symbolon.*
100. Herodotus, VII, 6: Onomacritus is caught tampering with the oracles of Museus and

then continues to rig oracles with the Persians. It seems clear to me that Onomacritus was driven away from Athens by the supporters of Pisistratids solely for reasons of political opportunism. This is evidenced by the fact that the charges against him did not originate with them and that there was a reconciliation later in Persia, according to Herodotus, where they supported his false oracles. Plutarch seems to dismiss the charges as slander (*De Pythiae oraculis* 25: *SG* 2, 13[B 1]).

101. Censorship of the sources is also the likely explanation of the silence on Pisistratus even among scholars highly interested in Orphism like Colli. Another study like G. Pugliese Carratelli, *Storia greca* (Milano: Istituto Editoriale Cisalpino-La Goliardica, 1978), 58, mentions the establishment of the Greater Dionysia but ignores the strengthening of the Eleusinian cult.

102. The evidence is not easy to evaluate (cf. *Die Fragmente der Vorsokratiker,* ed. H. Diels and W. Kranz [Berlin: Weidmann, 1972–74] [henceforth DK] 14-A16) but must have a historical basis: see W.K.C. Guthrie, *A History of Greek Philosophy,* vol. 1, *The Earlier Presocratics and the Pythagoreans* (1962; repr. Cambridge: Cambridge University Press, 2003), 174–80.

103. Jaeger, *Aristotle,* 451–60.

104. DK 22-B125A.

105. DK 22-B121.

106. DK 22-B51.

107. DK 22-B66.

108. DK 22-B29.

109. W. Jaeger, *Paideia: Die Formung des griechischen Menschen,* vol. 1 (Berlin-Leipzig: De Gruyter, 1934), 217–20; cf. Huizinga, *Homo Ludens,* 117.

110. Mine is a simple deduction uniting the juridical meaning of the term alleged by Jaeger and the mythical explanation of the Titanic guilt that he does not take into account: the result is a much more convincing picture.

111. See below, vol. 1, chapter 10, § 7.

112. E. De Martino, *Il mondo magico: Prolegomeni a una storia del magismo* (1948; repr. Torino: Bollati Boringhieri, 2007).

113. Cf. Cornford, *Principium Sapientiae,* 75–76.

114. S. Mazzarino, *Il pensiero storico classico* (Roma-Bari: Laterza, 1983), 1:23–37.

115. DK 22-B41. The unitary figure of the archaic wise man is stressed in Cornford, *Principium Sapientiae,* 90.

116. In this sense, it is both appropriate and disappointing that Jaeger finishes his great inquiry on classical Greece only by speaking about Demosthenes (W. Jaeger, *Paideia: Die Formung des griechischen Menschen,* vol. 3 [Berlin: De Gruyter, 1955], 345–74): was not Demosthenes the last tragic character of classical Greece? This shows by itself that Greek independence comes to its end under the opposing influences of tragedy and philosophy, much more than politics.

9. Judaism and Christianity in the Greco-Roman World

1. I shall use the adjective "pagan" and the substantive "paganism" only as a practical indication for the religious and cultural world perceived by Jews and Christians as contrary to their beliefs; the "pagans" themselves will claim their own difference from Judaism and Christianity as the conflict with these religions develops and takes hold.
2. Text in G. Colli, *La sapienza greca,* vol. 1, *Dioniso, Apollo, Eleusi, Orfeo, Museo, Iperborei, Enigma* (Milano: Adelphi, 1990) (henceforth *SG* 1), 244, 4[B 37]: Clement, *Protrepticus,* II, 17, 2–18, 1. According to J.G. Smyly, *Greek Papyri from Gurob* (Dublin: Hodges, 1921), 10, the word σφαῖρα was written in the lacuna of the Gurob papyrus, together with the word πλαταγή, rattle, with the same function as the ῥόμβος in Clement.
3. M.L. West, *The Orphic Poems* (Oxford: Oxford University Press, 1998), 172–73 (cf. J.G. Frazer, *The Golden Bough: A Study in Magic and Religion* [New York: Macmillan Co., 1951], 451).
4. West, *The Orphic Poems,* 156.
5. For evidence on Celsus in the second century, see A.C. Jacobsen, "Apologetics in Origen," in *Three Greek Apologists: Origen, Eusebius, and Athanasius / Drei griechische Apologeten: Origenes, Eusebius und Athanasius,* ed. A.C. Jacobsen and J. Ulrich (Frankfurt a.M.: Lang, 2007), 16–17 (see also below, vol. 1, chapter 10, note 2).
6. See E. Vimercati, *Medioplatonici: Opere, frammenti, testimonianze* (Milano: Bompiani, 2015), 626 and 38–41.
7. The former is the translation followed in Celsus, *On the True Doctrine: A Discourse against the Christians,* ed. J. Hoffmann (New York–Oxford: Oxford University Press, 1987), the latter in P. Siniscalco, *Il cammino di Cristo nell'Impero romano* (Roma-Bari: Laterza, 1990), 64–65.
8. Celsus, *Alethes logos,* III, 17 (for the Greek text I follow the edition of R. Bader, *Der Alethes Logos des Kelsos* [Stuttgart-Berlin: Kohlhammer, 1940]—the numbers of books and paragraphs refer to Origen's work).
9. Celsus, *Alethes logos,* III, 42b.
10. M. Simonetti, *Cristianesimo antico e cultura greca* (Roma: Borla, 1990), 38–39.
11. M. Borret, "Introduction générale" to Origène, *Contre Celse,* ed. M. Borret (Paris: Les Éditions du Cerf, 2008), 5:185–92 (I will make reference to this edition for the Greek text as well); Simonetti, *Cristianesimo antico,* 46–47.
12. Justin, *First Apology,* 54, 1–2. I translate from the Greek text in Saint Justin, *Apologies,* ed. A. Wartelle (Paris: Études Augustiniennes, 1987). On the argument of the demoniac imitation, see also vol. 2, chapter 6, § 1 and note 10.
13. Justin, *First Apology,* 54, 6.
14. Borret, "Introduction générale," 187. This argument dates back at least to the end of the third century BC with the Jewish-Alexandrinian writer Artapanus: G. Boccaccini, *I giudaismi del Secondo Tempio da Ezechiele a Daniele,* It. trans. A. Bardi, revised and augmented ed. (Brescia: Morcelliana, 2008), 141 (equation Moses = Musaeus); on the identitarian definition of Moses's figure in the Hellenistic Judaic culture, see C. Moro,

"Miti di fondazione e priorità etnico-culturale giudaica: l'esempio di Mosè," in *Israele fra le genti in epoca ellenistica: un popolo primogenito cittadino del mondo,* ed. G.L. Prato, Ricerche storico-bibliche (Bologna: EDB, 2015), 177–92.

15. For the influence of Middle Platonism on Christian thought, see J. Daniélou, *Origène* (Paris: Le Table Ronde, 1948), 98–108; and C.H. Dodd, *The Interpretation of the Fourth Gospel* (Cambridge: Cambridge University Press, 1965), 10–73.
16. An excellent exposition of Justin's view is in J. Daniélou, *Message évangélique et culture hellénistique aux II et III siècles* (Tournai: Desclée, 1961), 42–49 and 392–93.
17. Cf. W. Burkert, *Ancient Mystery Cults* (Cambridge, MA: Harvard University Press, 1987), 76.
18. On this question, see G. Fornari, "Resurrezione pagana e cristiana: Il problema comparativo nella resurrezione di Cristo," in *Il corpo glorioso, Il riscatto dell'uomo nelle teologie e nelle rappresentazioni della resurrezione,* ed. C. Bernardi, C. Bino, and M. Gragnolati (Pisa: Giardini, 2006), 28–33.
19. A thesis upheld, perhaps with excessive emphasis, in J. Hoffmann, "General Introduction" to Celsus, *On the True Doctrine,* 11–16.
20. Cf. M. Sordi, *Impero romano e cristianesimo: Scritti scelti* (Roma: Institutum Patristicum Augustinianum, 2006), 254–55.
21. Minutius Felix, *Octavius,* IX. For further evidence, see Hoffmann, "General Introduction," 16–18.
22. Tacitus, *Annales,* XV, 44.
23. Sordi, *Impero romano e cristianesimo,* 109–10 and 243.
24. A. Toaff, *Pasque di sangue: Ebrei d'Europa e omicidi rituali* (Bologna: Il Mulino, 2008).
25. Interestingly, we find both aspects in the most sophisticated Roman literature: Horace, *Epodon liber,* V (an episode of sorcery), and *Carminum liber I,* XXXVII (celebration of Augustus's victory against Cleopatra).
26. See C.B. Champion, *The Peace of the Gods: Elite Religious Practices in the Middle Roman Republic* (Princeton: Princeton University Press, 2017), 125–27, where the emphasis is on the ups and downs of military events; on the oldest textual witness of *evocationes,* see ibid., 142–43.
27. See the evidence collected and discussed in *La leggenda di Roma,* vol. 1, *Dalla nascita dei gemelli alla fondazione della città,* ed. A. Carandini, Fondazione L. Valla (Milano: A. Mondadori, 2006).
28. The crudest version of Romulus's death must be considered the most ancient, as is clearly demonstrated in A. Carandini, *Remo e Romolo: Dai rioni dei Quiriti alla città dei Romani (775/750—700/675 a.C.)* (Torino: Einaudi, 2006), 304–50.
29. On the foundational meaning of ancient Roman history, cf. M. Serres, *Rome: The Book of Foundations,* Engl. trans. F. McCarren (Stanford: Stanford University Press, 1991).
30. On the Roman interpretation of this event starting from the model of Romulus's dismemberment, see Carandini, *Remo e Romolo,* 306.
31. In his *Julius Caesar* Shakespeare founds his analysis of the Roman "double sacrifice"

on the pairing Julius Caesar/Brutus, as highlighted by R. Girard, *A Theater of Envy: William Shakespeare* (Oxford: Oxford University Press, 1991), 200–204 and 223–26; at any rate, at the center of his tragedy there is the mediatory import of the Roman double sacrificial murder (G. Fornari, *Da Dioniso a Cristo: Conoscenza e sacrificio nel mondo greco e nella civiltà occidentale* [Genova-Milano: Marietti, 2006], 307–11).

32. Cf. K. Kerényi, *The Religions of the Greeks and the Romans,* Engl. trans. C. Holme (London: Thames and Hudson, 1962), 219–24, with some warnings useful for avoiding excessive simplifications.
33. See Champion, *The Peace of the Gods,* 3–22, though with a too irrationalistic view of the Roman religious experience.
34. Cf. the detailed reconstruction in Champion, *The Peace of the Gods,* 128–42.
35. This is the serious limitation of the brilliant analyses of P. Veyne, *L'Empire gréco-romain* (Paris: Seuil, 2005). A relevant part of the specialized literature on the Roman *spectacula* is conditioned by a typically modern moralistic approach that is an obstacle in understanding the mediatory and religious framework of the *ludi.*
36. On all these aspects, see *Teatri romani: Gli spettacoli nell'antica Roma,* ed. N. Savarese (Bologna: Cuepress, 2015).
37. On this idea, see L. Storoni Mazzolani, *L'impero senza fine: Lo sfondo secolare dei problemi attuali* (Pavia: Editoriale Viscontea, 1987).
38. Veyne, *L'Empire gréco-romain,* 32–53.
39. Suetonius, *Caligulae vita,* 35. (I do not deal with the historical truth of this specific episode, in any case meaningful for the narrative strategy of the author, but it must be stressed that such events were perfectly likely.)
40. On these and other similar episodes, see L. Lugaresi, *Il teatro di Dio: Il problema degli spettacoli nel cristianesimo antico (II–IV secolo)* (Brescia: Morcelliana, 2008), 146–50.
41. Suetonius, *Caligulae vita,* 56 and 58. Cf. the detailed reconstruction in R.M. Sheldon, *Kill Caesar! Assassination in the Early Roman Empire* (Lanham, MD: Rowman & Littlefield, 2018), 99–107.
42. Cf. Lugaresi, *Il teatro di Dio,* 489–509 (the author wrongly belittles Clement's cognitive use of the Greek theater and does not explain it).
43. Sordi, *Impero romano e cristianesimo,* 103–39; cf. M. Simonetti, *Il Vangelo e la storia: Il cristianesimo antico (secc. I–IV)* (Roma: Carocci, 2010), 60 and 113–15.
44. On the definition of Middle Judaism, see Boccaccini, *I giudaismi del Secondo Tempio* (original edition: Boccaccini, *Roots of Rabbinic Judaism: An Intellectual History, from Ezekiel to Daniel* [Grand Rapids, MI: Eerdmans, 2002]); see also Boccaccini, *Middle Judaism: Jewish Thought, 300 B.C.E. to 200 C.E.* (Minneapolis: Fortress Press, 1991). I shall speak of "Judaism" mainly making reference to the phases antecedent to the destruction of the Second Temple in 70 AD, whereas I shall speak of Hebraic religion or culture with reference to the Jewish religion either posterior or taken as a whole.
45. C. Bandera, *The Sacred Game: The Role of the Sacred in the Genesis of Modern Literary Fiction* (University Park: Pennsylvania State University Press, 1994), 131–74.
46. Storoni Mazzolani, *L'impero senza fine,* 66–69; Carandini, *Remo e Romolo,* 263–98.

47. F. Nietzsche, *Sämtliche Werke: Kritischen Studienausgabe,* ed. G. Colli and M. Montinari (Berlin-New York: De Gruyter, 1980) (henceforth NSW), 6:245–46.
48. Cf. *Storia del cristianesimo: Religione-Politica-Cultura,* ed. J.-M. Mayeur et al., vol. 1, *Il nuovo popolo (dalle origini al 250),* ed. L. Pietri, It. ed. P. Grech and A. Di Bernardino, It. trans. M. Zappella (Roma: Borla-Città Nuova, 2003), 232–33.
49. R. Girard, *Je vois Satan tomber comme l'éclaire* (Paris: Grasset, 2009), 165 ff.
50. Girard, *Je vois Satan,* 170–71, 187–88, 191.
51. This is the inadequate viewpoint I was still maintaining in Fornari, *Da Dioniso a Cristo,* 221, 253, 266, 274, and 315.
52. The literature on the origin and history of the Judaic religion is obviously huge, but the texts and authors useful for a reconstruction that are free from apologetic or merely academic interests are few. The stimulating conclusion is that a study on the real genesis of monotheism and the biblical corpus is at its very beginning.
53. T. Römer, *L'invention de Dieu* (Paris: Seuil, 2014), 263–65; P. Merlo, *La religione dell'antico Israele* (Roma: Carocci, 2009), 38–41.
54. G. Garbini, *Dio della terra, dio del cielo: Dalle religioni semitiche al giudaismo e al cristianesimo* (Brescia: Paideia, 2011), 52–64; Römer, *L'invention de Dieu,* 213–28.
55. Garbini, *Dio della terra, dio del cielo,* 171 ff.
56. Garbini, *Dio della terra, dio del cielo,* 200; Römer, *L'invention de Dieu,* 263–65 (the author makes the sacred prostitution in the Temple come to an end with Josiah's reformation, on which see below, note 71).
57. Cf. Römer, *L'invention de Dieu,* 62–63.
58. G. Deiana, *Il giorno dell'espiazione: Il "kippur" nella tradizione biblica* (Bologna: EDB, 1995), 147–67, gives good evidence for the association of Yahweh with Dionysus and holds that it, together with the goat sacrifice, dates back to the Hellenistic syncretism, but on that basis it becomes impossible to explain the introduction of Dionysian-like cults in the Temple and the preexilic practice of the goat sacrifice (cf. ibid., 159).
59. Garbini, *Dio della terra, dio del cielo,* p. 187.
60. Garbini, *Dio della terra, dio del cielo,* 38.
61. Garbini, *Dio della terra, dio del cielo,* 163–70 and 203–14.
62. G. Garbini, *Letteratura e politica nell'Israele antico* (Brescia: Paideia, 2010), 156.
63. I deem still valid the explanation given by W. Robertson Smith, *Lectures on the Religion of the Semites* (London: Black, 1894), 372n1.
64. Garbini, *Dio della terra, dio del cielo,* 204–5n6; cf. Römer, *L'invention de Dieu,* 181–83.
65. G. Fornari, "Teologie della catastrofe: La nascita del monoteismo," in *Catastrofi generative: Mito, storia, letteratura,* ed. M.S. Barberi (Massa: Transeuropa, 2009), 174–78.
66. Garbini, *Dio della terra, dio del cielo,* 230–31.
67. M. Liverani, *Oltre la Bibbia: Storia antica d'Israele* (Roma-Bari: Laterza, 2004), 275–398; G. Garbini, *Myth and History in the Bible,* Engl. trans. C. Peri (London: Sheffield

Academic Press, 2003); Garbini, *Scrivere la storia d'Israele: Vicende e memorie ebraiche* (Brescia: Paideia, 2008), 198–265; on Moses see also Moro, "Miti di fondazione e priorità etnico-culturale giudaica." All these topics are objects of confessional biases and political identity claims, and also to be mentioned is the phenomenon of archaeological forgeries in order to "prove" the truth (at least partial) of biblical narratives: e.g. the Tel Dan stele was found in 1993 and deemed authentic in many publications (as I. Finkelstein and A. Mazar, *The Quest for the Historical Israel: Debating Archaeology and the History of Early Israel,* ed. B.B. Schmidt [Leiden-Boston: Brill, 2007]), but there are serious philological reasons for questioning its authenticity (G. Garbini, *Il vangelo aramaico di Matteo e altri saggi* [Brescia: Paideia, 2017], 176–89).

68. Garbini, *Scrivere la storia d'Israele,* 17–18; Garbini, *I Filistei: Gli antagonisti di Israele* (Brescia: Paideia, 2012), 297–98; Garbini, *Dio della terra, dio del cielo,* 76–81.

69. Römer, *L'invention de Dieu,* 154–55 and 161. See vol. 2, chapter 4, § 4 and note 63.

70. Cf. N. Finkelstein and N.A. Silberman, *David and Solomon: In Search of the Bible's Sacred Kings and the Roots of the Western Tradition* (New York: Free Press, 2006), 20, 135–37 and ff.

71. Garbini, *Scrivere la storia d'Israele,* 156–64; Merlo, *La religione dell'antico Israele,* 26–27. Römer, *L'invention de Dieu,* 253–76, considers plausible the biblical information on Josiah but incurs a circular argument because, after admitting the legendary character of 2 Kings 22–23, he uses it as proof in the absence of archaeological evidence, apart from an iconographic change in the seals at the beginning of the fifth century and a stele of very dubious date. The nonhistorical character of Josiah's reformation is recognized even by such a prudent historian such as J.A. Soggin, *Storia d'Israele: Introduzione alla storia d'Israele e Giuda dalla fondazione alla rivolta di Bar Kochbà* (Brescia: Paideia, 2002), 312–16.

72. Garbini, *Scrivere la storia d'Israele,* 163–64, 263–64.

73. Fornari, "Teologie della catastrofe," 158–65.

74. Scholars oscillate between 587 and 586 (Soggin, *Storia d'Israele,* 324).

75. Soggin, *Storia d'Israele,* 322–25; Garbini, *Scrivere la storia d'Israele,* 167 (on the possibility of a more complex reconstruction, see ibid., 175–77).

76. P. Sacchi, *Storia del Secondo Tempio: Israele tra VI secolo a.C. e I secolo d.C.* (Torino: SEI, 2002), 23–26; Soggin, *Storia d'Israele,* 325.

77. Garbini, *Scrivere la storia d'Israele,* 179–86; Soggin, *Storia d'Israele,* 326–27.

78. Fornari, "Teologie della catastrofe," 152–58.

79. Cf. G. Gnoli, "La religione zoroastriana," in *Storia delle religioni,* ed. G. Filoramo, vol. 1, *Le religioni antiche* (Roma-Bari: Laterza, 1994), 536–37.

80. The Unmoved Mover is the result of Aristotle's deep reworking of an idea of Plato: W. Jaeger, *Aristotle: Fundamentals of the History of His Development,* Engl. trans. with the author's corrections and additions by R. Robinson (Oxford: Oxford University Press, 1962), 139, 141, and 342–67.

81. G. Fornari, *Storicità radicale: Filosofia e morte di Dio* (Massa: Transeuropa, 2013), 27–28 (Plato) and 301 (Aristotle).

82. Aristotle, *Metaphysics* 1076a (Homer, *Iliad,* II, 204); cf. Jaeger, *Aristotle,* 356.
83. Garbini, *Myth and History in the Bible,* 109–10 and 129–39 (see note below).
84. Garbini, *Myth and History in the Bible,* 77–78; Garbini, *Scrivere la storia d'Israele,* 247–48. See also below, vol. 1, chapter 10, § 6 and note 89.
85. Garbini, *Dio della terra, dio del cielo,* 254–58.
86. Boccaccini, *I giudaismi del Secondo Tempio,* 115–16.
87. Garbini, *Scrivere la storia d'Israele,* 122–23.
88. Sacchi, *Storia del Secondo Tempio,* 42–43 and 73–75; Garbini, *Myth and History in the Bible,* 21, 66, and 77n8; Garbini, *Il ritorno dall'esilio babilonese* (Brescia: Paideia, 2001); Garbini, *Scrivere la storia d'Israele,* 188–97. The Jewish tradition kept the memory of Zechariah's assassination, though with several confusions and later accretions: S.H. Blank, "The Death of Zechariah in Rabbinic Literature," *Hebrew Union College Annual* 12/13 (1937–38): 327–46.
89. Sacchi, *Storia del Secondo Tempio,* 38; Garbini, *Myth and History in the Bible,* 80–82; Boccaccini, *I giudaismi del Secondo Tempio,* 59–60.
90. The verb φονεύω indicates a blood killing, so that the final sacrificial connotation of the altar has to be maintained. Cf. Garbini, *Il ritorno dall'esilio babilonese,* 164–66; see vol. 2, chapter 2, § 5.
91. Garbini, *Dio della terra, dio del cielo,* 236–46.
92. See J. Blenkinsopp, *Isaiah 40–55,* The Anchor Bible (New York: Doubleday, 2002), 76–81.
93. Garbini, *Dio della terra, dio del cielo,* 242–43.
94. On the Immanuel passage (Is 7:14) see vol. 2, chapter 2, § 2 and note 25.
95. Garbini equivocates on this passage attributing Cain's impunity only to a concession made to Joshua (G. Garbini, *Mito e storia,* 23–39; Garbini, *Dio della terra, dio del cielo,* 264).
96. On the history of the Essenes, see H. Stegemann, *The Library of Qumran: On the Essenes, Qumran, John the Baptist, and Jesus* (Grand Rapids, MI: Eerdmans, 1998), 142–62.
97. Boccaccini, *I giudaismi del Secondo Tempio,* 107–25.
98. See vol. 2, chapter 2, § 2.
99. Sacchi, *Storia del Secondo Tempio,* 352–53.
100. J.E. Harrison, *Themis: A Study of the Social Origins of Greek Religion* (London: Merlin Press, 1989), 18–19.
101. K. Kerényi, *Dionysos: Archetypal Image of Indestructible Life,* Engl. trans. R. Manheim (Princeton: Princeton University Press, 1976), 269; Kerényi, *Dionysos: Urbild des unzerstörbaren Lebens* (München-Wien: Langen Müller, 1976), 216. Misunderstanding is rife among commentators, starting with C.A. Lobeck, *Aglaophamus sive de Theologiae mysticae Graecorum causis, libri tres* (Regimontii, 1829). Better, but still insufficient, are the intuitions in W.K.C. Guthrie, *Orpheus and Greek Religion* (Princeton: Princeton

University Press, 1993), 121–23, while the sources are more adequately discussed in West, *The Orphic Poems,* 154–59.

102. F. Nietzsche, *Götzen-Dämmerung,* in NSW, 6:158–59.

103. V. Macchioro, *Zagreus,* 76 ff.

104. The detectable story dates back to Hellenistic, Roman, and late classical sources: the best known version comes from Ovid's *Metamorphoses* (III, 402–510) where Narcissus dies by starvation for being hypnotized by his own image reflected on the water; the hero dies by drowning in Plotinus, *Enneads,* I, 6, 8. As already observed by Pausanias (X, 31, 7–8), the more ancient kernel of the myth is the flower of narcissus, on which see note 128 following.

105. Garbini, *Dio della terra, dio del cielo,* 138 and 245.

106. Euripides, *Bacchae* 1018–19.

107. The ῥόμβος corresponds to the bull-roarer and to the Australian churinga: see É. Durkheim, *Les formes élémentaires de la vie religieuse* (Paris: Le Livre de Poche, 1991), 223–24, also K. Kerényi, *Miti e misteri,* ed. A. Brelich (Torino: Einaudi, 1984), 167, and Harrison, *Themis,* 61, 61n3.

108. Garbini, *Dio della terra, dio del cielo,* 67.

109. L. Schele and D. Freidel, *A Forest of Kings: The Untold Story of the Ancient Maya* (New York: Morrow, 1990), 76–77, 373 and 429n29.

110. Euripides, *Bacchae* 1135–36; Euripides, *Bacchae,* ed. E. R. Dodds (Oxford: Clarendon Press, 1986), ad vv. 1133–36, p. 218, finds the scene "grotesque," but the grotesque was originally part of ritual.

111. Cf. *SG* 1:34n4 and 41 (not by chance the author Giorgio Colli undervalues the theme of chance).

112. *Die Fragmente der Vorsokratiker,* ed. H. Diels and W. Kranz (Berlin: Weidmann, 1972–74), 22-B52.

113. Cf. Eraclito, *I frammenti e le testimonianze,* ed. C. Diano and G. Serra, Fondazione L. Valla (Milano: A. Mondadori, 1980), note to fr. 48, 152–53.

114. Cf. the aforementioned passage in the *Iliad,* XV, 363.

115. G. Fornari, "Immortali/mortali: Il sacrificio in Eraclito," in *Eraclito: la luce dell'Oscuro,* ed. G. Fornari (Firenze: Olschki, 2017), 170–78.

116. M.L. West, *Early Greek Philosophy and the Orient* (Oxford: Clarendon Press, 2002), 165–202.

117. G. Betegh, *The Derveni Papyrus: Cosmology, Theology, and Interpretation* (Cambridge: Cambridge University Press, 2006), 225, 325–48, and elsewhere.

118. Herodotus, II, 48.

119. Plato, *Laws* 902b, 906a.

120. J.-L. Durand, "Greek Animals: Toward a Topology of Edible Bodies," in M. Detienne and J.-P. Vernant, *La cuisine du sacrifice en pays grec* (Paris: Gallimard, 1979), 104.

121. Cf. M. Eliade, *Traité d'histoire des religions* (Paris: Payot, 1949), § 131 and esp. 295 where this transition is made very clear.

122. Gnoli, "La religione zoroastriana," 529–31.

123. Cf. C.D. Elledge, *Resurrection of the Dead in Early Judaism (200 BCE–CE 200)* (Oxford: Oxford University Press, 2017), 51–52; the author stresses the scholarly controversy on this influence (ibid., 52–58), which does not at all exclude other influences and previous hints: at any rate, the long Persian dominion of Israel remains a frame hard to ignore.

124. Euripides, *Ion* 995 ff. and 1421–23.

125. E. Rohde, *Psyche: Seelencult und Unsterblichkeitsglaube der Griechen* (Darmstadt: Wissenschaftliche Buchgesellschaft, 1980), 2:116–19; Frazer, *The Golden Bough,* 450–51 (from Nonnus, *Dionysiaca,* VI). (Cf. above note 41 in ch. 2).

126. For the double mask, see E. Canetti, *Masse und Macht* (München-Wien: Hanser, 1960), 444–45.

127. Cf. R. Girard, *Le bouc émissaire* (Paris: Grasset, 1982), 126–29. At Thebes itself, there exists a link between collective divinities and Dionysian toys in the Cabiri cult, probably Orphic and going back to the sixth century BC (Guthrie, *Orpheus and Greek Religion,* 123–26).

128. This flower is always present in the myth of Persephone's abduction, and its very name could be explained by the slight narcotic effect of its scent (*Inni Omerici,* ed. F. Cássola, Fondazione L. Valla [Milano: A. Mondadori, 1986], *ad v.* 8, p. 468). See also vol. 2, conclusion, § 3.

129. G. Gnoli, "Introduzione generale," in *Il manicheismo,* vol. 1, *Mani e il manicheismo,* ed. G. Gnoli, Fondazione L. Valla (Milano: A. Mondadori, 2003), xxxvii–xl.

130. See the masterly reconstructions in H.C. Puech, *Sur le manichéisme et autres essais* (Paris: Flammarion, 1979).

131. Gnoli, "Introduzione generale," xxxiii–xxxiv and lviii–lxvii.

10. The Comparative Question between Judaism and Christianity

1. M. Simonetti, *Cristianesimo antico e cultura greca* (Roma: Borla, 1990), 47–49.

2. Initially Origen thinks he is a follower of Epicurus, but then he becomes aware of his Platonic interests, without apparently taking a definite position (M. Borret, "Introduction générale" to Origène, *Contre Celse,* ed. M. Borret (Paris: Les Éditions du Cerf, 2008), 129–36); for Origen's position on both philosophies in relation to Celsus, see H. Crouzel, *Origène et la philosophie* (Toulouse: Aubier, 1962), 27–31 (Epicurus) and 49–65 (Plato). For the modern debate on Celsus's identity, see A.C. Jacobsen, "Apologetics in Origen," in *Three Greek Apologists: Origen, Eusebius, and Athanasius / Drei griechische Apologeten: Origenes, Eusebius und Athanasius,* ed. A.C. Jacobsen and J. Ulrich (Frankfurt a.M.: Lang, 2007), 16–19. There is little doubt that Celsus must be inserted in Middle Platonism, as already understood by J. Daniélou, *Origène* (Paris: Le Table Ronde, 1948), 109–21.

3. Borret, "Introduction générale," 32–33 and 208–14.

4. A. Monaci Castagno, ed., *Origene. Dizionario. La cultura, il pensiero, le opere* (Roma: Città Nuova, 2000), *s.v.* "Tempo," 457–58.
5. Daniélou, *Origène,* 207–17; Monaci Castagno, *Origene. Dizionario, s.v.* "Astri."
6. Origen, *Contra Celsum,* I, 3 (Origène, *Contre Celse,* 1:84).
7. Cf. Daniélou, *Origène,* 112–13.
8. Monaci Castagno, *Origene. Dizionario, s.v.* "Magia," 255–56; cf. Daniélou, *Origène,* 53 (see also below). We must not forget that pronouncing Jesus's name meant risking one's own life in times of persecution.
9. Origen, *Contra Celsum,* I, 27 (Origène, *Contre Celse,* 1:148).
10. Origen, *Contra Celsum,* I, 62 (Origène, *Contre Celse,* 1:246).
11. Monaci Castagno, *Origene. Dizionario, s.v.* "Provvidenza," 393.
12. Origen, *Contra Celsum,* II, 30 (Origène, *Contre Celse,* 1:360).
13. Origen, *Contra Celsum,* IV, 99. Cf. Monaci Castagno, *Origene. Dizionario, s.v.* "Provvidenza," 394.
14. An evident circumstance blatantly ignored by many scholars.
15. There was not a formal Edict of Milan according to P. Siniscalco, *Il cammino di Cristo nell'Impero romano* (Roma-Bari: Laterza, 1990), 164–66, but its existence is confirmed by M. Simonetti, *Il Vangelo e la storia: Il cristianesimo antico (secc. I–IV)* (Roma: Carocci, 2010), 192–93. At any rate, this was the beginning of a new religious policy in the empire.
16. E. Voegelin, *History of Political Ideas,* vol. 2, *The Middle Ages to Aquinas,* ed. P. Von Sivers (Columbia: Missouri University Press, 1997), 231–32.
17. E. Voegelin, *History of Political Ideas,* vol. 3, *The Later Middle Ages,* ed. D. Walsh (Columbia: Missouri University Press, 1998), 66–82.
18. W. Jaeger, *Aristotle: Fundamentals of the History of His Development,* Engl. trans. with the author's corrections and additions by R. Robinson (Oxford: Oxford University Press, 1962), 54–60.
19. J. Daniélou, *Message évangélique et culture hellénistique aux II et III siècles* (Tournai: Desclée, 1961), 14–15 and 124–27; cf. W. Jaeger, *Early Christianity and Greek Paideia* (Cambridge, MA: Harvard University Press, 1961), 58–59.
20. On Clement and the pre-Christian philosophy, see Daniélou, *Message évangélique et culture hellénistique,* 50–72.
21. Clement, *Protrepticus,* VII, 76, 3.
22. Clement, *Protrepticus,* XII, 118, 5.
23. Clement, *Protrepticus,* X, 109, 3.
24. Clement, *Protrepticus,* XII, 118–20.
25. F. Nietzsche, *Sämtliche Werke: Kritischen Studienausgabe,* ed. G. Colli and M. Montinari (Berlin-New York: De Gruyter, 1980), 13:266.
26. This is the main thesis of I.P. Culianu, *Éros et magie à la Renaissance (1484)* (Paris: Flammarion, 1984).

27. J.P. Meier, *A Marginal Jew: Rethinking the Historical Jesus,* vol. 2, *Mentor, Message, and Miracles* (New York: Doubleday, 1994) (henceforth Meier 2), 509 ff.
28. Jn 3:22; on the question of baptism in John, see Meier 2:116 ff.
29. Justin, *First Apology,* 66, 4 (cf. *Dialogus with Triphon,* 70, 1 ff. and 78, 6).
30. For the Greek text, see the updated edition Porfirio, *Contro i cristiani,* ed. G. Muscolino (Milano: Bompiani, 2009), 336. Cf. Simonetti, *Cristianesimo antico,* 61.
31. On the early diffusion of the criticism to the traditional doctrine of the Eucharist in the Reformation, see D. Cantimori, *Eretici italiani del Cinquecento* (Firenze: Sansoni, 1939), 80–83, 95–96, 111, 125, 142, and elsewhere.
32. Cf. the witnesses in J. Jeremias, *The Eucharistic Words of Jesus,* Engl. trans. N. Perrin (London-Philadelphia: SCM-Trinity Press, 1990) (henceforth Jeremias 1990), 15–88, where the author reflects the excessive tendency of those years to use later Jewish sources as a valid historical source for Jesus's epoch as well.
33. G. Garbini, *Dio della terra, dio del cielo: Dalle religioni semitiche al giudaismo e al cristianesimo* (Brescia: Paideia, 2011), 150.
34. The critical edition of this work is G. Garbini, *Cantico dei cantici* (Brescia: Paideia, 1992); see also Garbini, *Letteratura e politica nell'Israele antico* (Brescia: Paideia, 2010), 153–72; Garbini, *Dio della terra, dio del cielo,* 275. Interestingly, a profane reading of the Song of Songs as erotic poem is present among the Italian followers of the Reformation (Cantimori, *Eretici italiani,* 116).
35. Cf. Garbini, *Cantico dei cantici,* 350–52.
36. In this way Garbini cancels centuries of Jewish and Christian spirituality. On the disruptive and incomprehensive religious attitude of this great Semitist, see vol. 2, chapter 1, § 5.
37. This is the main point of Jeremias's interpretation, going beyond its details.
38. On this complicated topic, see R.E. Brown, *The Death of the Messiah: From Gethsemane to the Grave. A Commentary on the Passion Narratives in the Four Gospels,* The Anchor Bible (New York: Doubleday, 1994), 2:1350–73.
39. Jn 12:24; cf. W. Burkert, *Greek Religion,* Engl. trans. J. Raffan (Cambridge, MA: Harvard University Press, 1994), 289–90.
40. 1 Cor 15:35–38; Origen, *Contra Celsum,* V, 18–19 and 23; Origen, *De principiis,* II, 10, 3.
41. See vol. 2, chapter 2, § 6.
42. Jeremias 1990, 53 and 223–24.
43. K. Kerényi, *Dionysos: Archetypal Image of Indestructible Life,* Engl. trans. R. Manheim (Princeton: Princeton University Press, 1976), 270.
44. Phil 2:17; the verb is echoed in the deuteron-Pauline 2 Tm 4:6.
45. As far as the New Testament texts are concerned, I do not make any sharp distinction between letter (with a private destination) and epistle (with a public destination), for the Christian texts usually blend these two features together.
46. The Alexandrian traits, though not conclusive because of their diffusion among

Christians of Hellenistic culture, are widely recognized in scholarship and justify the recurrent attribution, suggested by Luther, to the Apollo presented in Acts 18:24–28; cf. C. Spicq, *L'Épitre aux Hebreux* (Paris: Gabalda, 1977), 24–28: C. Marcheselli-Casale, *Lettera agli Ebrei: Nuova versione, introduzione e commento* (Milano: Paoline, 2005), 24–27.

47. The interpreters who minimize the Platonic component (as C.R. Koester, *Hebrews: A New Translation with Introduction and Commentary,* The Anchor Bible [New York: Doubleday, 2001], 97–100) do not consider the innovations introduced by Middle Platonism and the creative reelaboration of the author.

48. Hereafter translations of the New Testament writings are made from *Novum Testamentum Graece,* ed. E. Nestle et al. (Stuttgart: Deutsche Bibelgesellschaft, 2012).

49. Futile is the attempt at finding a concordance between objective and subjective acceptations in Marcheselli-Casale, *Lettera agli Ebrei,* 478–83, without previously clarifying their historical import. On the objective meaning of *hypostasis,* cf. H. Köster, *s.v.* ὑπόστασις in *Theologisches Wörterbuch zum Neuen Testament,* ed. G. Kittel (Stuttgart: W. Kohlhammer, 1933–) (henceforth *TWNT*), 8:573–88.

50. The Aristotelian acceptation of the term is ignored by all the interpreters, simply because its strongest philosophical sense is not taken into account, though its objective and demonstrative value is acknowledged: cf. F. Büchsel, *s.v.* ἔλεγχος, in *TWNT,* 2:473–74.

51. G. Fornari, *Storicità radicale: Filosofia e morte di Dio* (Massa: Transeuropa, 2013), 627–39.

52. Heb. 10:5. The main textual choice of the author is the reading σῶμα, which fits his theological purposes and is taken from the best manuscripts of the Septuagint: probably it is the original Hebrew reading, then changed in the Masoretic text for excluding the Christian interpretation (cf. Koester, *Hebrews,* 432–33).

53. H. Sasse, *s.v.* αἰών in *TWNT,* 1:197–209, interprets ἀιῶνας as worlds in a spatial sense but ignores the theological context referring to a temporal and epochal acceptation.

54. This is the reason why many interpreters exclude a reference to the Eucharist in the Epistle: Koester, *Hebrews,* 127–29; Marcheselli-Casale, *Lettera agli Ebrei,* 680–83.

55. Cf. G. Garbini, *Myth and History in the Bible,* Engl. trans. C. Peri (London: Sheffield Academic Press, 2003), 10–21; on this, see vol. 2, chapter 2, § 5.

56. Garbini, *Myth and History in the Bible,* 6–7.

57. This idea was advanced by L. Costantini, *Le Lettere di S. Paolo, le Lettere cattoliche e l'Apocalisse* (Roma: Libreria Editrice Religiosa F. Ferrari, 1928), 433 and 460–61n81; and accepted by F. Zorell, *Lexicon Graecum Novi Testamenti* (1960; repr. Roma: Editrice Pontificio Istituto Biblico, 1990), *s.v.* παραβολή. The interpretation was rejected by T. Da Castel S. Pietro, *L'Epistola agli Ebrei* (Torino-Roma: Marietti, 1952), 196, but the argument that the syntagma is without article or other specifications is pointless, as the term in other comparable cases is all the same without article.

58. I already argued this reading in G. Fornari, *La bellezza e il nulla: L'antropologia cristiana di Leonardo da Vinci* (Genova-Milano: Marietti, 2005), 373–80.

59. As noticed by Da Castel S. Pietro, *L'Epistola agli Ebrei,* 197, but this very sacrificial realism suggests by itself not to exclude the most dramatic acceptation of ἐν παραβολῇ.
60. Spicq, *L'Épitre aux Hebreux,* 17–19; Marcheselli-Casale, *Lettera agli Ebrei,* 69–71. For the parallel regarding the silence on the Eucharist, cf. Jeremias 1990, 134.
61. H. De Lubac, *Histoire et Esprit: L'intelligence de l'Écriture d'après Origène* (Paris: Les Éditions du Cerf, 2002), 358–59. Dionysus *Lenaios* is connected to ληνός, the wine press (see vol. 2, chapter 2, § 1).
62. Jeremias 1990, 183 (see also vol. 2, chapter 2, § 3).
63. On the widespread existence of Dionysian-like cults in the area and a possible connection to Jesus, see Kerényi, *Dionysos: Archetypal Image of Indestructible Life,* 256–59; cf. V. Macchioro, *Zagreus: Studi intorno all'orfismo,* ed. by C. Pugliese (Milano: Mimesis, 2014), 436–37 and 441–42.
64. Josephus Flavius, *De bello Judaico,* V, 210; Tacitus, *Historiae,* V, 5. See also vol. 2, chapter 2, § 6.
65. As in A. Loisy, *Les mystères païens et le mystère chrétien* (Paris: Nourry, 1930), 199–349.
66. Celsus, *Alethes logos,* VII, 53.
67. The necessity of a comparison between Orphism and Christianity was already asserted by L. Scubla, "The Christianity of René Girard and the Nature of Religion," in *Violence and Truth: On the Work of René Girard,* ed. P. Dumouchel (Stanford: Stanford University Press, 1988), 161 and 270–73n.
68. See also vol. 2, chapter 5, § 5, note 45.
69. The passage is debated but the solution of Borret's edition gives a satisfactory sense.
70. Origen, *Contra Celsum,* I, 64 (Origène, *Contre Celse,* 1:256): the last phrase is also debated, but its overall sense is clear.
71. Origen, *Contra Celsum,* I, 67 (Origène, *Contre Celse,* 1:266).
72. Daniélou, *Origène,* 52–58.
73. Simonetti, *Il Vangelo e la storia,* 219–20, 233–36, and 242–46.
74. Origen, *Contra Celsum,* IV, 17 (Origène, *Contre Celse,* 2:222).
75. L. Cova, *Peccato originale: Agostino e il Medioevo* (Bologna: Il Mulino, 2014), 101–13.
76. Cf. N. Söderblom, *La vie future d'après le Mazdéisme à la lumière des croyances parallèles dans les autres religions* (Angers: Burdin, 1901).
77. Cf. G. Fornari, "Discese agli inferi: La Giustizia nella *Repubblica* di Platone," in *La giustizia dei greci tra riflessione filosofica e prassi giudiziaria,* ed. C. Bearzot and E. Vimercati (Milano: Vita e Pensiero, 2013), 37–41.
78. For the real symbolic and juridical value of the *Constitutio Antoniniana,* see the essay on the papyrus containing its most important evidence: G. Purpura, "Il P. Giss 40, 1," *Iuris Antiqui Historia: An International Journal of Ancient Law* 5 (2013): 73–85.
79. P. Sacchi, *Storia del Secondo Tempio: Israele tra VI secolo a.C. e I secolo d.C.* (Torino: SEI, 2002), 435.
80. Sacchi, *Storia del Secondo Tempio,* 466–67.

81. These are at this point phenomenological remarks to be further confirmed and explained in the second volume.
82. Cf. the social explanation of Christ's teaching on forgiveness as an extension of an ideal usually reserved to the upper class in G. Theissen and A. Merz, *Der historische Jesus: Ein Lehrbuch* (Göttingen: Vandenhoeck & Ruprecht, 1996), 348–49.
83. G.N. Stanton, *Jesus and Gospel* (Cambridge: Cambridge University Press, 2004).
84. On Celsus's evaluation of the Crucifixion, see vol. 2, chapter 6, § 1.
85. Borret, "Introduction générale," 220.
86. A. Catastini, *Storia di Giuseppe (Genesi 37–50)* (Venezia: Marsilio, 1994), 52–58; cf. M. Liverani, *Oltre la Bibbia: Storia antica d'Israele* (Roma-Bari: Laterza, 2004), 112.
87. On the use of myths taken from 1 Enoch in Genesis, see G. Boccaccini, *I giudaismi del Secondo Tempio da Ezechiele a Daniele,* It. trans. A. Bardi, revised and augmented ed. (Brescia: Morcelliana, 2008), 114–21; the author dates the beginning of the Enochian literature to the Persian period, but the cultural influences and the fight among the different theological-political parties point to the Hellenistic period.
88. For this reading, see G. Fornari, "L'albero della colpa e della salvezza: La rivelazione biblica della violenza," in *Politiche di Caino: Il paradigma conflittuale del potere,* ed. D. Mazzù (Ancona-Massa: Transeuropa, 2006), 159–97.
89. G. Garbini, *Scrivere la storia d'Israele: Vicende e memorie ebraiche* (Brescia: Paideia, 2008), 245 ff.; Garbini, *Dio della terra, dio del cielo,* 270–72. On a Hellenistic date for biblical books, see also T.L. Thompson, *Mythic Past: Biblical Archeology and the Myth of Israel* (New York: MJF Books, 1999).
90. On the meaning of genealogies in Genesis, see F. Giuntoli, "Il Pentateuco," in *L'Antico Testamento,* ed. by P. Merlo (Roma: Carocci, 2008), 116–18; Thompson, *Mythic Past,* 89–91.
91. Garbini, *Scrivere la storia d'Israele,* 215 (hence the Hebrew name *toledot,* genealogies, to indicate historiography).
92. Garbini, *Scrivere la storia d'Israele,* 215–20, emphasizes the manipulative and censoring character of the biblical *toledot,* but this is not in contradiction with the general view I attribute to them.
93. Garbini, *Myth and History in the Bible,* 139; Garbini, *Scrivere la storia d'Israele,* 253–55.
94. Origen, *Contra Celsum,* I, 31 (Origène, *Contre Celse,* 1:160).
95. Plutarch, *De defectu oraculorum* 416e–417b and elsewhere; see G. Fornari, "Il sacrificio in Plutarco: un medio-platonico alla ricerca della mediazione divina," in *Plutarco, entre dioses y astros: Homenaje al Profesor Aurelio Pérez Jiménez de sus discípulos, colegas y amigos,* ed. J.F. Martos Montiel, C. Macías Villalobos, and R. Caballero Sanchez (Zaragoza: Libros Portico, 2019), 1:265–83.
96. Origen, *Contra Celsum,* VIII, 31; cf. Monaci Castagno, *Origene, s.v.* "Diavolo," 114–18.
97. My hypothesis is that the missing awareness of the "systemic" character of Christian demonology has increased some difficulties in Origen's thought, connected to

apocatastasis and the destiny of souls (see on this H. Crouzel, *Origène* [Paris: Éditions Lethielleux, 1985], 337 ff.): cf. M. Ceruti and G. Fornari, *Le due paci: Cristianesimo e morte di Dio nel mondo globalizzato* (Milano: Cortina, 2005), 178–79.

98. Söderblom, *La vie future d'après le Mazdéisme,* 292, who questionably refers to this view "à une conception assez superficielle de la gravité du péché et du mal de la vie."

99. Fornari, *Storicità radicale,* 653–54.

100. Origen, *Contra Celsum,* I, 1 (Origène, *Contre Celse,* 1:64).

101. Origen, *Contra Celsum,* VII, 53–57.

102. Origen, *Contra Celsum,* II, 59 (Origène, *Contre Celse,* 1:422 and 424). The first quotation is from Is 53:7; the second from Mt 26:62–63 and 27:12–14.

Bibliography

Æliani *Porphyrii Philosophi Philonis Byzantii Opera*. Paris: Didot, 1858.

Aeschyli septem quae supersunt tragoedias. Edited by D. Page. Oxford: Clarendon Press, 1989.

Agamben, G. *L'aperto: L'uomo e l'animale*. Torino: Bollati Boringhieri, 2002.

Alighieri, D. *La commedìa*. Edited by A. Lanza. Anzio: De Rubeis, 1996.

———. *Vita nuova*. In D. Alighieri, *Tutte le opere*, edited by L. Blasucci. Firenze: Sansoni, 1981.

Apollodorus. *The Library*. Edited by J.G. Frazer. Loeb Classical Library. Cambridge, MA: Harvard University Press, 1921.

Arasse, D. *L'annonciation italienne: Une histoire de perspective*. Paris: Hazan, 1999.

———. *La guillottine et l'imaginaire de la Terreur*. Paris: Flammarion, 1987.

Arendt, H. *The Human Condition*. Chicago: University of Chicago Press, 1998.

———. *On Revolution*. London: Penguin Books, 1990.

———. *The Origins of Totalitarianism*. San Diego: Harcourt, 1994.

Aristotele. *Dell'arte poetica*. Edited C. Gallavotti. Fondazione L. Valla. Milano: A. Mondadori, 1990.

Aristotelis De arte poetica liber. Edited by R. Kassel. Oxford: Clarendon Press, 1965.

Aristotelis Politica. Edited by W.D. Ross. Oxford: Clarendon Press, 1957.

Artaud, A. "Le théatre de la cruauté." In *Œuvres complètes*, vol. 4. Paris: Gallimard, 1964.

Atkinson, J.J. "Primal Law." In *Social Origins*, by A. Lang. London: Longmans, Green and Co., 1903.

Bader, R. *Der Alethes Logos des Kelsos*. Stuttgart-Berlin: Kohlhammer, 1940.

Bandera, C. *Mimesis Conflictiva: Ficción literaria y violencia en Cervantes y Calderón*. Madrid: Editorial Gredos, 1975.

———. *"Monda y desnuda": la humilde historia de Don Quijote. Reflexiones sobre el origen de la novela moderna*. Madrid: Iberoamericana, 2005.

———. *A Refuge of Lies: Reflections on Faith and Fiction*. East Lansing: Michigan State University Press, 2013.

———. *The Sacred Game: The Role of the Sacred in the Genesis of Modern Literary Fiction*. University Park: Pennsylvania State University Press, 1994.

Barba, R., and M. Domínguez-Rodrigo. "FLK North North 1: 'Living Floor' or Natural Accumulation." In M. Domínguez-Rodrigo, R. Barba, and C.P. Egeland, *Deconstructing Olduvai: A Taphonomic Study of the Bed I Sites*. Dordrecht: Springer, 2007.

Barbera, S. "Un biglietto smarrito di Friedrich Nietzsche a Jean Bourdeau, gennaio 1889." *Belfagor* 54 (January 1999): 74–78.

Bataille, G. *Œuvres complètes*. Paris: Gallimard, 1973–.

Bateson, G. *Steps to an Ecology of Mind*. Chicago: University of Chicago Press, 1999.

Bedard, S.J. "A Nation of Heroes: From Apotheosis to Resurrection." In *Resurrection of the Dead: Biblical Traditions in Dialogue*, edited by G. Van Oyen and T. Shepherd. Leuven: Uitgeverij Peters, 2012.

Beltrametti, A. "La visita del giovane dio: Dalla drammaturgia di Dürrenmat alla politica di Archelao." In *Studi e Materiali per le Baccanti di Euripide: Storia Memorie Spettacoli*, edited by A. Beltrametti. Como-Pavia: IBIS, 2007.

Benjamin, W. *Über Sprache überhaupt und über die Sprache des Menschen*. In W. Benjamin, *Gesammelte Schriften*, edited by R. Tiedemann and H. Schweppenhäuser. Frankfurt a.M.: Suhrkamp, 1991.

———. *Ursprung des deutschen Trauerspiels*. In W. Benjamin, *Gesammelte Schriften*, edited by R. Tiedemann and H. Schweppenhäuser. Frankfurt a.M.: Suhrkamp, 1991.

Benveniste, É. *Le vocabulaire des institutions indo-européennes*, vol. 2, *Pouvoir, droit, religion*. Paris: Les Éditions de Minuit, 1969.

Betegh, G. *The Derveni Papyrus: Cosmology, Theology, and Interpretation*. Cambridge: Cambridge University Press, 2006.

Black, J., et al., eds. *The Literature of Ancient Sumer*. Oxford: Oxford University Press, 2006.

Blank, S.H. "The Death of Zechariah in Rabbinic Literature." *Hebrew Union College Annual* 12/13 (1937–38): 327–46.

Blenkinsopp, J. *Isaiah 1–39*. The Anchor Bible. New York: Doubleday, 2000.

———. *Isaiah 40–55*. The Anchor Bible. New York: Doubleday, 2002.

Blinzler, J. *Die Brüder und Schwestern Jesu*. Stuttgart: Katholische Bibelwerk, 1967.

Boardman, J., and N.G.L. Hammond, eds. *The Cambridge Ancient History*, vol. 3, part 3. Cambridge: Cambridge University Press, 1982.

Boccaccini, G. *I giudaismi del Secondo Tempio da Ezechiele a Daniele*. It. trans. by A. Bardi, revised and augmented edition. Brescia: Morcelliana, 2008.

———. *Middle Judaism: Jewish Thought, 300 B.C.E. to 200 C.E.* Minneapolis: Fortress Press, 1991.

———. *Roots of Rabbinic Judaism: An Intellectual History, from Ezekiel to Daniel*. Grand Rapids, MI: Eerdmans, 2002.

Borret, M. "Introduction générale" to Origène, *Contre Celse*. Edited by M. Borret. Paris: Les Éditions du Cerf, 2008.

Bottéro, J., ed. *L'Épopée de Gilgameš: L'homme qui ne voulait pas mourir*. Paris: Gallimard, 1992.

———. *Mesopotamia: Writing, Reasoning, and the Gods*. Engl. trans. by Z. Bahrani and M. Van De Mieroop. Chicago: University of Chicago Press, 1995.

Bottéro, J., and S.N. Kramer, eds. *Lorsque les dieux faisaient l'homme: Mythologie mésopotamienne*. Paris: Gallimard, 1993.

Bovon, F. *L'Évangile selon Saint Luc 1–9*. Genève: Labor et Fides, 1991.

Bracciolini, P. "Poggius Leonardo Arretino." In *Prosatori latini del Quattrocento*, edited by E. Garin. Milano-Napoli: Ricciardi, 1952.

Brandon, S.G.F. *Jesus and the Zealots: A Study of the Political Factor in Primitive Christianity*. New York: C. Scribner's Sons, 1967.

Brelich, A. *Gli eroi greci: Un problema storico-religioso*. Milano: Adelphi, 2010.

Brown, R.E. *The Community of the Beloved Disciple: The Life, Loves, and Hates of an Individual Church in New Testament Times*. New York: Paulist Press, 1979.

———. *The Death of the Messiah: From Gethsemane to the Grave. A Commentary on the Passion Narratives in the Four Gospels*. The Anchor Bible. New York: Doubleday, 1994.

———. *The Gospel According to John*. The Anchor Bible. New York: Doubleday, 1966.

———. *An Introduction to the New Testament*. New York: Doubleday, 1997.

———. *An Introduction to New Testament Christology*. New York-Mahwah: Paulist Press, 1994.

———. *The Virginal Conception and Bodily Resurrection of Jesus*. New York: Paulist Press, 1973.

Büchner, G. *Werke und Briefe*. Edited by K. Pörnbacher et al. München: Deutscher Taschenbuch, 1988.

Büchner, G., and F.L. Weidig. *Der Hessische Landbote: Studienausgabe*. Edited by G. Schaub. Stuttgart: Reclam, 2006.

Bultmann, R. *Das Evangelium des Johannes*. Göttingen: Vandenhoeck & Ruprecht, 1953.

———. *Die Geschichte der synoptischen Tradition*. Göttingen: Vandenhoeck & Ruprecht, 1921.

———. *Die Geschichte der synoptichen Tradition. Ergänzungsheft*. Göttingen: Vandenhoeck & Ruprecht, 1966.

———. *Jesus*. 1926; repr. Tübingen: Mohr, 1977.

———. *Jesus Christ and Mythology*. London: SCM Press, 1966.

———. "Neues Testament und Mythologie: Das Problem der Entmythologisierung der neutestamentlichen Verkündigung." *Gesellschaft für evangelischen Theologie* 21, no. 4 (1941): 15–48.

———. *New Testament and Mythology, and Other Basic Writings*. Edited by S.M. Ogden. Philadelphia: Fortress Press, 1984.

———. *Primitive Christianity in Its Contemporary Setting*. Engl. trans. by R.H. Fuller. Cleveland-New York: The World Publishing Co., 1965.

———. *Theology of the New Testament*. Engl. trans. by K. Grobel. London: SCM Press, 1968.

Burkert, W. *Ancient Mystery Cults*. Cambridge, MA: Harvard University Press, 1987.

———. *Greek Religion*. Engl. trans. by J. Raffan. Cambridge, MA: Harvard University Press, 1994.

———. "Greek Tragedy and Sacrificial Ritual." *Greek, Roman and Byzantine Studies* 7 (1966): 87–121.

———. *Homo Necans: The Anthropology of Ancient Greek Sacrificial Ritual and Myth*. Engl. trans. by P. Bing. Berkeley: University of California Press, 1983.

———. *The Orientalizing Revolution: Near Eastern Influence on Greek Culture in the Early Archaic Period*. Engl. trans. by M.E. Pinder and W. Burkert. Cambridge, MA: Harvard University Press, 1995.

———. "Das Proömium des Parmenides und die Katabasis des Pythagoras." *Phronesis* 14 (1969): 1–30.

———. *Structure and History in Greek Mythology and Ritual*. Berkeley: University of California Press, 1982.

Burkert, W., R. Girard, and J.Z. Smith. *Violent Origins: Ritual Killing and Cultural Formation*. Edited by R.G. Hamerton-Kelly. Stanford: Stanford University Press, 1987.

Calasso, R. *Le nozze di Cadmo e Armonia*. Milano: Adelphi, 1993.

Campbell, J. *The Masks of God: Oriental Mythology*. New York: Penguin Books, 1976.

Canetti, E. *Masse und Macht*. München-Wien: Hanser, 1960.

Canfora, L. *La crisi dell'utopia: Aristofane contro Platone*. Roma-Bari: Laterza, 2014.

Cantarella, E. *I supplizi capitali in Grecia e a Roma*. Milano: Rizzoli, 1991.

Cantimori, D. *Eretici italiani del Cinquecento*. Firenze: Sansoni, 1939.

Carandini, A., ed. *La leggenda di Roma*, vol. 1, *Dalla nascita dei gemelli alla fondazione della città*. Fondazione L. Valla. Milano: A. Mondadori, 2006.

———. *Remo e Romolo: Dai rioni dei Quiriti alla città dei Romani (775/750 –700/675 a.C.)*. Torino: Einaudi, 2006.

———. *Su questa pietra: Gesù, Pietro e la nascita della Chiesa*. Roma-Bari: Laterza, 2013.

Carrara, L. *L'indovino Poliido: Eschilo, Le cretesi. Sofocle, Manteis. Euripide, Poliido*. Roma: Edizioni di Storia e Letteratura, 2014.

Cassirer, E. *Gesammelte Werke*, vol. 18. Edited by B. Recki. Hamburg: Meiner, 2004.

Cássola, F., ed. *Inni Omerici*. Fondazione L. Valla. Milano: A. Mondadori, 1986.

Da Castel S. Pietro, T. *L'Epistola agli Ebrei*. Torino-Roma: Marietti, 1952.

Catastini, A. *Storia di Giuseppe (Genesi 37–50)*. Venezia: Marsilio, 1994.

Celsus, *On the True Doctrine: A Discourse against the Christians*. Edited by J. Hoffmann. New York–Oxford: Oxford University Press, 1987.

Cerri, G. "La riscoperta del vero Parmenide." Introduction to Parmenide, *Poema sulla natura*, edited by G. Cerri. 1999; repr. Milano: Rizzoli, 2006.

———. "Tragedia e commedia nel finale del Simposio di Platone (una nuova proposta ermeneutica)." In ΦΙΛΙΑ: *Dieci contributi per Gabriele Burzacchini*, edited by M. Tulli. Bologna: Patron, 2014.

Ceruti, M., and G. Fornari. *Le due paci: Cristianesimo e morte di Dio nel mondo globalizzato*. Milano: Cortina, 2005.

Champion, C.B. *The Peace of the Gods: Elite Religious Practices in the Middle Roman Republic*. Princeton: Princeton University Press, 2017.

Chantraine, P. *Dictionnaire étymologique de la langue grecque: Histoire des mots*. Paris: Klincksieck, 1968–74.

Clement of Alexandria. *Exhortation to the Greeks*. Edited by G.W. Butterworth. Loeb Classical Library. Cambridge, MA: Harvard University Press, 1932.

Clottes, J., and D. Lewis-Williams. *Les chamanes de la préhistoire: Transe et magie dans les grottes ornées*. Paris: La Maison des Roches, 2001.

Colli, G. *Dopo Nietzsche*. Milano: Bompiani, 1974.

———. *Filosofia dell'espressione*. Milano: Adelphi, 1969.

———. *La nascita della filosofia*. Milano: Adelphi, 1975.

———. *La sapienza greca*, vol. 1, *Dioniso, Apollo, Eleusi, Orfeo, Museo, Iperborei, Enigma*. Milano: Adelphi, 1990.

———. *La sapienza greca*, vol. 2, *Epimenide, Ferecide, Talete, Anassimandro, Anassimene, Onomacrito*. Milano: Adelphi, 1992.

Condemi, S., and F. Savatier. *Neandertal, mon frère: 300.000 ans d'histoire de l'homme*. Paris: Flammarion, 2016.

Corbin, H. *Temple et contemplation*. Edited by C. Jambet. Paris: Flammarion, 1980.

Cornford, F.M. *Principium Sapientiae: A Study of the Origins of Greek Philosophical Thought*. New York: Harper, 1965.

Costa, F. *Tra mito e filosofia: Bultmann e la teologia contemporanea*. Messina-Firenze: D'Anna, 1978.

Costantini, L. *Le Lettere di S. Paolo, le Lettere cattoliche e l'Apocalisse*. Roma: Libreria Editrice Religiosa F. Ferrari, 1928.

Cova, L. *Peccato originale: Agostino e il Medioevo*. Bologna: Il Mulino, 2014.

Crescenzi, L. Introduction to T. Mann, *La montagna magica*, edited by L. Crescenzi, It. trans. by R. Colorni. Milano: A. Mondadori, 2011.

Crossan, J.D. *The Historical Jesus: The Life of a Mediterranean Jewish Peasant*. San Francisco: Harper, 1991.

———. "Mark and the Relatives of Jesus." *Novum Testamentum* 15 (1973): 81–113.

Crouzel, H. *Origène*. Paris: Éditions Lethielleux, 1985.

———. *Origène et la philosophie*. Toulouse: Aubier, 1962.

Culianu, I.P. Éros *et magie à la Renaissance (1484)*. Paris: Flammarion, 1984.

Cullmann, O. *Christologie du Nouveau Testament*. 1955; repr. Neuchatel-Paris: Delachaux & Niestlé, 1958.

———. *The Christology of the New Testament*. Engl. trans. by S.C. Guthrie and C.A.M. Hall. London: SCM Press, 1980.

———. *Les Sacrements dans l'Évangile johannique: La vie de Jesus et le culte de l'Église primitive*. Paris: Les Presses Universitaires de France, 1951.

Daniélou, J. *Message évangélique et culture hellénistique aux II et III siècles*. Tournai: Desclée, 1961.

———. *Origène*. Paris: Le Table Ronde, 1948.

———. *Théologie du Judéo-christianisme: Histoire des doctrines chrétiennes avant Nicée*. Tournai: Desclée, 1958.

De Lubac, H. *Histoire et Esprit: L'intelligence de l'Écriture d'après Origène*. Paris: Les Éditions du Cerf, 2002.

De Luise, F., and G. Farinetti. "L'infelicità del giusto e la crisi del socratismo platonico." In Platone, *La repubblica*, edited by M. Vegetti. Napoli: Bibliopolis, 1998.

De Santillana, G., and H. Von Dechend. *Hamlet's Mill: An Essay Investigating the Origins of Human Knowledge and Its Transmission through Myth*. Boston: Gambit, 1969.

Deacon, T.W. *The Symbolic Species: The Co-evolution of Language and the Brain*. New York: Norton & Co., 1997.

Deiana, G. *Il giorno dell'espiazione: Il "kippur" nella tradizione biblica*. Bologna: EDB, 1995.

Deleuze, G. *Nietzsche et la philosophie*. Paris: Presses Universitaires de France, 1973.

Della Casa, C. *Il giainismo*. 1962; repr. Torino: Bollati Boringhieri, 1993.

Dempf, A. *Sacrum Imperium: Geschichts- und Staatsphilosophie des Mittelalters und der politischen Renaissance*. Darmstadt: Wissenschaftliche Buchgemeinschaft, 1954.

Dennert, B.C. "Mark 11:16: A Status Quaestionis." *Studies in Jewish–Christian Relations* 5 (2010): 1–7.

Detienne, M. "Culinary Practices and the Spirit of Sacrifice." In M. Detienne and J.-P. Vernant, *The Cuisine of Sacrifice among the Greeks*. Engl. trans. by P. Wissig. Chicago: Chicago University Press, 1989.

Detienne, M., and J.-P. Vernant. *La cuisine du sacrifice en pays grec*. Paris: Gallimard, 1979.

———. *Cunning Intelligence in Greek Culture and Society*. Engl. trans. by J. Lloyd. Chicago: University of Chicago Press, 1991.

Dewar-Watson, S. "The *Alcestis* and the Statue Scene in *The Winter's Tale*." *Shakespeare Quarterly* 1 (2009): 73–80.

Di Benedetto, V. "Recensione a Euripide, Cretesi, a cura di Adele-Teresa Cozzoli." *Rivista di Filologia e di Istruzione Classica* 129 (2001): 210–30.

Di Benedetto, V., and E. Medda. *La tragedia sulla scena: La tragedia greca in quanto spettacolo teatrale*. Torino: Einaudi, 2002.

Di Giuseppe, R. "Nascita della filosofia dallo spirito del sacrificio." In *Eraclito: la luce dell'Oscuro*, edited by G. Fornari. Firenze: Olschki, 2017.

———. *Le voyage de Parménide*. Paris: Orizons, 2011.

Diano, C. "Senso dell'Alcesti." Introduction to Euripide, *Alcesti*, edited by C. Diano. Vicenza: Neri Pozza, 1968.

Diels, H. "Anaximandros von Milet." *Neue Jahrbücher für das klassische Altertum* 51 (1923): 65–75.

Diels, H., and W. Kranz, eds. *Die Fragmente der Vorsokratiker*. Berlin: Weidmann, 1972–74.

Diggle, J., ed. *Euripidis fabulae*. Oxford: Clarendon Press, 1994.

Diodore de Sicile. *Bibliothèque historique. Livre III*. Edited by B. Bommelaer. Paris: Les Belles Lettres, 1989.

Dodd, C.H. *Historical Tradition in the Fourth Gospel*. Cambridge: Cambridge University Press, 1963.

———. "Les Sacrements dans l'Évangile johannique: La vie de Jesus et le culte de l'Église primitive. By Oscar Cullmann." Études d'Histoire et de Philosophie Religieuses par la Faculté de Théologie Protestante de l'Université de Strasbourg 42 (1952): 218.

———. *The Interpretation of the Fourth Gospel*. Cambridge: Cambridge University Press, 1965.

Dodds, E.R. *The Greeks and the Irrational*. Berkeley: California University Press, 1951.

Doniger O'Flaherty, W. *The Origins of Evil in Hindu Mythology*. Berkeley: University of California Press, 1980.

Dupont, J. *Études sur les Actes des Apôtres*. Paris: Les Éditions du Cerf, 1967.

Dupuy, J.-P. *Economy and the Future: A Crisis of Faith*. Engl. trans. by M.B. DeBevoise. East Lansing: Michigan State University Press, 2014.

Durkheim, É. *The Elementary Forms of Religious Life*. Engl. trans. by K.E. Fields. New York: The Free Press, 1995.

———. *Les formes élémentaires de la vie religieuse*. Paris: Le Livre de Poche, 1991.

———. *Les règles de la méthode sociologique*. Paris: Flammarion, 1995.

———. "Représentations individuelles et représentations collectives." In *Sociologie et philosophie*. Paris: Presses Universitaires de France, 2014.

Edmunds, L. *Oedipus: The Ancient Legend and Its Later Analogues*. Baltimore: Johns Hopkins University Press, 1985.

Egeland, C.P. "Zooarchaeology and Taphonomy of the DK Site." In M. Domínguez-Rodrigo, R. Barba, and C.P. Egeland, *Deconstructing Olduvai: A Taphonomic Study of the Bed I Sites*. Dordrecht: Springer, 2007.

Eisler, R. *Orphisch-Dionysische Mysteriengedanken in der christlichen Antike*. 1925; repr. Hildesheim: Olms, 1966.

Eliade, M. *Histoire des croyances et des idées religieuses*. Paris: Payot, 1978.

———. *Shamanism: Archaic Techniques of Ecstasy*. Engl. trans. by W.R. Trask. Princeton: Princeton University Press, 1974.

———. *Traité d'histoire des religions*. Paris: Payot, 1949.

Elledge, C.D. *Resurrection of the Dead in Early Judaism (200 BCE–CE 200)*. Oxford: Oxford University Press, 2017.

Eraclito. *I frammenti e le testimonianze*. Edited by C. Diano and G. Serra. Fondazione L. Valla. Milano: A. Mondadori, 1980.

Esiodo. *Opere*. Edited by G. Arrighetti. Milano: A. Mondadori, 2007.

Euripide. *Le baccanti*. Edited by G. Guidorizzi. Venezia: Marsilio, 1989.

———. *Baccanti*. Edited by G. Ieranò. Milano: A. Mondadori, 1999.

———. *Cretesi*. Edited by A.-T. Cozzoli. Pisa-Roma: Istituti Editoriali e Poligrafici Internazionali, 2001.

———. *I cretesi*. Edited by R. Cantarella. Milano: Istituto Editoriale Italiano, 1964.

———. *Le Cyclope, Alceste, Médée, Les Héraclides*. Edited by L. Méridier. Paris: Les Belles Lettres, 1970.

Euripides. *Alcestis*. Edited by A.M. Dale. London: Bristol Classical Press, 2003.

———. *Bacchae*. Edited by E. R. Dodds. Oxford: Clarendon Press, 1986.

———. *Bacchae*. Edited by R. Seaford. Warminster: Aris & Phillips, 2001.

———. *Les Bacchantes*. Edited by H. Grégoire and J. Meunier. Paris: Les Belles Lettres, 1972.

———. *Les Bacchantes. Commentaire*. Edited by J. Roux. Paris: Les Belles Lettres, 1972.

———. *Hyppolitos*. Edited by W.S. Barrett. Oxford: Clarendon Press, 2001.

Euripidis fabulae. Edited by G. Murray. 1909; repr. Oxford: Clarendon Press, 1990.

Fabris, F. *Gesù il "Nazareno."* Assisi: Cittadella, 2011.

Falcon, A. *Aristotelismo*. Torino: Einaudi, 2017.

Faure, P. *La vie quotidienne au temps de Minos (1500 av. J.-C.)*. Paris: Hachette, 1973.

Ferrari, F. *Introduzione al teatro Greco*. Firenze: Sansoni, 1996.

Festugière, A.J. Études des religion grecque et *hellenistique*. Paris: Vrin, 1972.

Finkelstein, I., and A. Mazar. *The Quest for the Historical Israel: Debating Archaeology and the History of Early Israel*. Edited by B.B. Schmidt. Leiden-Boston: Brill, 2007.

Finkelstein, I., and N.A. Silberman. *David and Solomon: In Search of the Bible's Sacred Kings and the Roots of the Western Tradition*. New York: Free Press, 2006.

Fitzmyer, J.A. *The Gospel according to Luke*. The Anchor Bible. New York: Doubleday, 1983.

Flickinger, R.C. *The Greek Theater and Its Drama*. 1918; repr. Chicago: University of Chicago Press, 1973.

Fornari, G. "L'albero della colpa e della salvezza: La rivelazione biblica della violenza." In *Politiche di Caino: Il paradigma conflittuale del potere*, edited by D. Mazzù. Ancona-Massa: Transeuropa, 2006.

———. *La bellezza e il nulla: L'antropologia cristiana di Leonardo da Vinci*. Genova-Milano: Marietti, 2005.

———. "I ciottoli di Don Abbondio: Lettura figurale dei 'Promessi sposi.'" In *Identità e desiderio: La teoria mimetica e la letteratura italiana*, edited by P. Antonello and G. Fornari. Massa: Transeuropa, 2009.

———. *La conoscenza tragica in Euripide e in Sofocle*. Massa: Transeuropa, 2013.

———. *Da Dioniso a Cristo: Conoscenza e sacrificio nel mondo greco e nella civiltà occidentale*. Genova-Milano: Marietti, 2006.

———. "Discese agli inferi: La Giustizia nella *Repubblica* di Platone." In *La giustizia dei greci tra riflessione filosofica e prassi giudiziaria*, edited by C. Bearzot and E. Vimercati. Milano: Vita e Pensiero, 2013.

———. "Figures of the Antichrist: The Apocalypse and Its Restraints in Contemporary Political Thought." *Contagion: Journal of Violence, Mimesis, and Culture* 17 (2010): 53–62.

———. *Fra Dioniso e Cristo: La sapienza sacrificale greca e la civiltà occidentale*. Bologna: Pitagora, 2001.

———. "From the Labyrinth to the Tragic Mask." *COV&R: The Bulletin of the Colloquium on Violence and Religion* 2 (1996): 6–8

———. *A God Torn to Pieces: The Nietzsche Case*. Engl. trans. by K. Buck in collaboration with the author. East Lansing: Michigan State University Press, 2013.

———. "Immortali/mortali: Il sacrificio in Eraclito." In *Eraclito: la luce dell'Oscuro*, edited by G. Fornari. Firenze: Olschki, 2017.

———. "Labyrinthine Strategies of Sacrifice: The Cretans by Euripides." *Contagion: Journal of Violence, Mimesis, and Culture* 4 (1997): 163–88.

———. *Leonardo e la crisi del Rinascimento*. Milano-Udine: Mimesis, 2019.

———. "Mediazione trinitaria: Oggetto salvifico e dimensione estetica in Dante." In *Disordine e ordine: Il fattore mimetico in politica e nella storia*, Proceedings of the COVER Meeting, Salina, June 14–18, 2011, edited by F. Mercadante et al. Milano: Giuffrè, 2012.

———. *Mito, tragedia, filosofia: Dall'antica Grecia al Moderno*. Roma: Studium, 2017.

———. "Resurrezione pagana e cristiana: Il problema comparativo nella resurrezione di Cristo." In *Il corpo glorioso, Il riscatto dell'uomo nelle teologie e nelle rappresentazioni della resurrezione*, edited by C. Bernardi, C. Bino, and M. Gragnolati. Pisa: Giardini, 2006.

———. "Il sacrificio in Plutarco: un medio-platonico alla ricerca della mediazione divina." In *Homenaje al Profesor Aurelio Pérez Jiménez*, edited by J.F. Martos Montiel, C. Macías Villalobos, and R. Caballero Sanchez (Zaragoza: Libros Portico, 2019).

———. *Storicità radicale: Filosofia e morte di Dio*. Massa: Transeuropa, 2013.

———. "Teologie della catastrofe: La nascita del monoteismo." In *Catastrofi generative: Mito, storia, letteratura*, edited by M.S. Barberi. Massa: Transeuropa, 2009.

Foucault, M. *Les mots et les choses: Une archéologie des sciences humaines*. Paris: Gallimard, 1966.

———. *Surveiller et punir: Naissance de la prison*. Paris: Gallimard, 1975.

Fraschetti, A. "La sepoltura delle Vestali e la città." In *Du châtiment dans la cité: Supplices corporels et peine de mort dans le monde antique*. Roma: École Française de Rome, 1984.

Frazer, J.G. *The Golden Bough: A Study in Magic and Religion*. New York: Macmillan Co., 1951.

———. *The Golden Bough*, vol. 4, *The Dying God*. New York: Macmillan Co., 1935.

———. *Myths of the Origin of Fire*. London: Macmillan, 1930.

Freud, S. *Massenpsychologie und Ich-Analyse: Die Zukunft einer Illusion*. Frankfurt a.M.: Fischer, 2007.

———. *Totem und Tabu: Einige Übereinstimmungen im Seelenleben der Wilden und der Neurotiker*. Frankfurt a.M.: Fischer, 2007.

Frontisi-Ducroux, F. *Dédale: Mythologie de l'artisan en Grèce ancienne*. Paris: La Découverte, 2000.

Gaeta, G. *Il Gesù moderno*. Torino: Einaudi, 2009.

Gans, E. *The End of Culture: Toward a Generative Anthropology*. Berkeley: University of California Press, 1985.

Garbini, G. *Cantico dei cantici*. Brescia: Paideia, 1992.

———. *Dio della terra, dio del cielo: Dalle religioni semitiche al giudaismo e al cristianesimo*. Brescia: Paideia, 2011.

———. *I Filistei: Gli antagonisti di Israele*. Brescia: Paideia, 2012.

———. *Letteratura e politica nell'Israele antico*. Brescia: Paideia, 2010.

———. *Myth and History in the Bible*. Engl. trans. by C. Peri. London: Sheffield Academic Press, 2003.

———. *Il ritorno dall'esilio babilonese*. Brescia: Paideia, 2001.

———. *Scrivere la storia d'Israele: Vicende e memorie ebraiche*. Brescia: Paideia, 2008.

———. *Il vangelo aramaico di Matteo e altri saggi*. Brescia: Paideia, 2017.

———. *Vita e mito di Gesù*. Brescia: Paideia, 2015.

Gay, P. *Freud: A Life for Our Time*. New York: Doubleday, 1988.

Gianotto, C. *Giacomo, fratello di Gesù*. Bologna: Il Mulino, 2013.

Gimbutas, M. *The Goddesses and Gods of Old Europe: Myths and Cult Images*. London: Thames & Hudson, 1982.

Girard, R. *Achever Clausewitz: Entretiens avec Benoît Chantre*. Paris: Carnets Nord, 2007.

———. *Le bouc émissaire*. Paris: Grasset, 1982.

———. *Des choses cachées depuis la fondation du monde: Recherches avec Jean-Michel Oughourlian et Guy Lefort*. Paris: Grasset, 1991.

———. "Dionysus versus the Crucified." *Modern Language Notes* 99, no. 4 (1984): 816–35.

———. *Dostoïevski du double à l'unité*. Paris: Plon, 1963.

———. *Je vois Satan tomber comme l'éclaire*. Paris: Grasset, 2009.

———. "Les malédictions contre les Pharisiens et la révélation évangélique." *Bulletin du Centre Protestant d'Études de Genève* 27, no. 3 (1975): 5–29.

———. *A Theater of Envy: William Shakespeare*. Oxford: Oxford University Press, 1991.

———. *"To Double Business Bound": Essays on Literature, Mimesis, and Anthropology*. London: Athlon Press, 1988.

———. *La violence et le sacré*. Paris: Grasset, 1994.

Girard, R., P. Antonello, and J.C. De Castro Rocha. *Evolution and Conversion: Dialogues on the Origin of Culture*. London-New York: Continuum, 2007.

Giuntoli, F. "Il Pentateuco." In *L'Antico Testamento*, edited by P. Merlo. Roma: Carocci, 2008.

Gnilka, J. *Das Evangelium nach Markus*. Mannheim: Patmos Verlag, 2010.

Gnoli, G. "Introduzione generale." In *Il manicheismo*, vol. 1, *Mani e il manicheismo*, edited by G. Gnoli. Fondazione L. Valla. Milano: A. Mondadori, 2003.

———. "La religione zoroastriana." In *Storia delle religioni*, edited by G. Filoramo, vol. 1, *Le religioni antiche*. Roma-Bari: Laterza, 1994.

———. "Le religioni dell'Iran antico e Zoroastro." In *Storia delle religioni*, edited by G. Filoramo, vol. 1, *Le religioni antiche*. Roma-Bari: Laterza, 1994.

Goethe, J.W. *Italienische Reise*. In *Werke*, vol. 11, edited by E. Trunz and H. von Einem. München: Beck, 1989.

———. *Werke*, vol. 3. Edited by E. Trunz. München: Beck, 1989.

Goldmann, L. *Mensch, Gemeinschaft und Welt in der Philosophie Immanuel Kants*. Frankfurt a.M.: Campus Verlag, 1989.

Goodhart, S. *Sacrificing Commentary: Reading the End of Literature*. Baltimore: Johns Hopkins University Press, 1996.

Gorni, G. "'Gru' di Dante: Lettura di Purgatorio XXVI." *Rassegna Europea di Letteratura Italiana* 3 (1994): 11–34.

Gowlett, J.A.J. "The Discovery of Fire by Humans: A Long and Convoluted Process." *Philosophical Transactions of the Royal Society B* 371 (2016): 1–12.

Grasso, S. *Il Vangelo di Giovanni: Commento esegetico e teologico*. Roma: Città Nuova, 2008.

Gray, T.C. *The Temple in the Gospel of Mark: A Study in Its Narrative Role*. Grand Rapids, MI: Baker Academic, 2010.

Grimal, P. *Dictionnaire de la mythologie grecque et romaine*. Paris: Presses Universitaires de France, 1969.

Grosso, M. *Vangelo secondo Tommaso*. Roma: Carocci, 2011.

Guthrie, W.K.C. *A History of Greek Philosophy*, vol. 1, *The Earlier Presocratics and the Pythagoreans*. 1962; repr. Cambridge: Cambridge University Press, 2003.

———. *Orpheus and Greek Religion*. Princeton: Princeton University Press, 1993.

Harrison, J.E. *Prolegomena to the Study of Greek Religion*. London: Merlin Press, 1980.

———. *Themis: A Study of the Social Origins of Greek Religion*. London: Merlin Press, 1989.

Havelock, E.A. *Preface to Plato*. Cambridge, MA: Harvard University Press, 1963.

Hegel, G.W.F. *Gesammelte Werke*, vol. 1, *Frühe Schriften I*. Edited by F. Nicolin and G. Schüler. Hamburg: Meiner, 1989.

Heidegger, M. *Beiträge zur Philosophie (Vom Ereignis)*. Vol. 65 of *Gesamtausgabe*. Frankfurt a.M.: Klostermann, 1989.

———. *Einführung in die Metaphysik*. Tübingen: Niemeyer, 1987.

———. *Die Grundprobleme der Phänomenologie.* Vol. 24 of *Gesamtausgabe.* Frankfurt a.M.: Klostermann, 1997.

———. "Platos Lehre von der Wahrheit." In *Gesamtausgabe,* vol. 9, *Wegmarken.* Frankfurt a.M.: Klostermann, 1975.

———. *Sein und Zeit.* Tübingen: Niemeyer, 2006.

———. "Vom Wesen des Grundes." In *Gesamtausgabe,* vol. 9, *Wegmarken.* Frankfurt a.M.: Klostermann, 1975.

Heiler, F. "The Madonna as Religious Symbol." In *The Mystic Vision: Papers from the Eranos Yearbooks,* edited by J. Campbell, Engl. trans. by R. Manheim. Princeton: Princeton University Press, 1968.

Hengel, M. *The Cross of the Son of God.* Engl. trans. by J. Bowden. London: SCM, 1986.

———. *The Four Gospels and the One Gospel of Jesus Christ: An Investigation of the Collection and Origin of the Canonical Gospels.* Engl. trans. by J. Bowden. London: SCM Press, 2000.

———. *Judaism and Hellenism: Studies in Their Encounter in Palestine during the Early Hellenistic Period.* Engl. trans. by J. Bowden. Philadelphia: Fortress Press, 1974.

———. "Der stellvertretende Sühnetod Jesu: Ein Beitrag zur Entstehung des urchristlichen Kerygmas." *Internationale Katholische Zeitschrift* 2 (1980): 1–25 and 135–47.

Hesiod. *"Theogony" and "Works and Days."* Engl. trans. by M.L. West. Oxford–New York: Oxford University Press, 2008.

Hocart, A.M. *Imagination and Proof: Selected Essays.* Tucson: University of Arizona Press, 1987.

———. *Kings and Councillors: An Essay in the Comparative Anatomy of Human Society.* 1936; repr. Chicago: University of Chicago Press, 1970.

Hodder, I. *The Leopard's Tale: Revealing the Mysteries of* Çatalhöyük. London: Thames & Hudson, 2006.

Hoffmann, D.L., et al. "U-th Dating of Carbonate Crusts Reveals Neanderthal Origin of Iberian Art," *Science* 359, no. 6378 (February 23, 2018): 912–15.

Hovers, E., S. Ilani, O. Bar-Yosef, and B. Vandermeersch. "An Early Case of Color Symbolism: Ochre Use by Modern Humans in Qafzeh Cave." *Current Anthropology* 44 (2003): 491–522.

Huizinga, J. *Homo Ludens: A Study of the Play-Element in Culture.* Mansfield Centre, CT: Martino Publisher, 2014.

Hultgren, A.J. *The Parables of Jesus: A Commentary.* Grand Rapids, MI: Eerdmans, 2000.

Husserl, E. *Logische Untersuchungen.* Edited by U. Panzer, vol. 19, part 1. The Hague: Nijhoff, 1984.

Jacobsen, A.C. "Apologetics in Origen." In *Three Greek Apologists: Origen, Eusebius, and Athanasius / Drei griechische Apologeten: Origenes, Eusebius und Athanasius.* Edited by A.C. Jacobsen and J. Ulrich. Frankfurt a.M.: Lang, 2007.

Jacobsen, T. *The Treasures of Darkness: A History of Mesopotamian Religion.* New Haven: Yale University Press, 1976.

Jaeger, W. *Aristotle: Fundamentals of the History of His Development*. Engl. trans. with the author's corrections and additions by R. Robinson. Oxford: Oxford University Press, 1962.

———. *Early Christianity and Greek Paideia*. Cambridge, MA: Harvard University Press, 1961.

———. *Paideia: Die Formung des griechischen Menschen*, vol. 1. Berlin-Leipzig: De Gruyter, 1934.

———. *Paideia: Die Formung des griechischen Menschen*, vol. 3. Berlin: De Gruyter, 1955.

———. *The Theology of the Early Greek Philosophers*. Oxford: Clarendon Press, 1948.

Jeanmaire, H. *Dionysos: Histoire de culte de Bacchus*. Paris: Payot, 1951.

Jeremias, J. *The Eucharistic Words of Jesus*. Engl. trans. by A. Ehrhardt. Oxford: Blackwell, 1955.

———. *The Eucharistic Words of Jesus*. Engl. trans. by N. Perrin. London-Philadelphia: SCM-Trinity Press, 1990.

———. *Die Gleichnisse Jesu*. Göttingen: Vandenhoeck & Ruprecht, 1965.

———. *Neutestamentliche Theologie*, vol. 1, *Die Verkündigung Jesu*. Gütersloh: Gerd Mohn, 1971.

———. *Unbekannte Jesusworte*. Gütersloh: Mohn, 1963.

Jossa, G. *Gesù e i movimenti di liberazione della Palestina*. Brescia: Paideia, 1980.

Saint Justin. *Apologies*. Edited by A. Wartelle. Paris: Études Augustiniennes, 1987.

Kant, I. *Kritik der Urtheilskraft*. In *Werke*, vol. 5. Berlin: Reimer, 1913.

———. "Die Religion innerhalb der Grenzen der blossen Vernunft." In *Werke*, vol. 6. Berlin: Reimer, 1914.

Kantorowicz, E.H. *The King's Two Bodies: A Study in Medieval Political Theology*. 1957; repr. Princeton: Princeton University Press, 2016.

Käsemann, E. "Aufbau und Anliegen des johanneischen Prologs," in *Libertas Christiana: Delekat Festschrift*. München: Kaiser, 1957.

———. "Das Problem des historischen Jesu." *Zeitschrift für Theologie und Kirche* 51, no. 2 (1954): 125–53.

Kaufmann, W. *Tragedy and Philosophy*. Princeton: Princeton University Press, 1979.

Kerényi, K. *Dionysos: Archetypal Image of Indestructible Life*. Engl. trans. by R. Manheim. Princeton: Princeton University Press, 1976.

———. *Dionysos: Urbild des unzerstörbaren Lebens*. München-Wien: Langen Müller, 1976.

———. *Eleusis: Archetypal Image of Mother and Daughter*. Engl. trans. by R. Manheim. Princeton: Princeton University Press, 1967.

———. *Labyrinth-Studien: Labyrinthos als Linienreflex einer mythologischen Idee*. Zürich: Rhein, 1950.

———. *Miti e misteri*. Edited by A. Brelich. Torino: Einaudi, 1984.

———. *Die Mythologie der Griechen*, vol. 1, *Die Götter- und Menschheitgeschichten*. Stuttgart: Klett-Cotta, 1997.

———. *The Religions of the Greeks and Romans*. Engl. trans. by C. Holme. London: Thames and Hudson, 1962.

———. *Töchter der Sonne: Betrachtungen* über *Griechische Gottheiten*. Zürich: Rascher, 1944.

Kern, H. *Through the Labyrinth: Designs and Meanings over 5,000 Years*. Munich-London-New York: Prestel, 2000.

Kern, O., ed. *Orphicorum fragmenta*. Berlin: Weidmann, 1922.

Kessler, H. *Sucht den Lebenden nicht bei den Toten: Die Auferstehung Jesu Christi in biblischer, fundamentaltheologischer und systematischer Sicht*. Würzburg: Echter, 1995.

Kingsley, P. *Ancient Philosophy, Mystery, and Magic: Empedocles and Pythagorean Tradition*. Oxford: Clarendon Press, 2009.

———. *In the Dark Places of Wisdom*. London: Duckworth, 1999.

Kittel, G., ed. *Theologisches Wörterbuch zum Neuen Testament*. Stuttgart: W. Kohlhammer, 1933–.

Koester, C.R. *Hebrews: A New Translation with Introduction and Commentary*. The Anchor Bible. New York: Doubleday, 2001.

Kozlowski, J.K. "Il sentimento religioso nel corso della preistoria: il paleolitico superiore." In F. Facchini et al., *La religiosità nella preistoria*. Milano: Jaca Book, 1991.

Lanata, G. *Poetiche pre-platoniche: Testimonianze e frammenti*. Firenze: La Nuova Italia, 1963.

Lanier, G.R. "The Rejected Stone in the Parable of the Wicked Tenants: Defending the Authenticity of Jesus' Quotation of Ps 118:22." *Journal of the Evangelical Theological Society* 56, no. 4 (2013): 733–51.

Latour, B. *Nous n'avons jamais été modernes: Essai d'anthropologie symétrique*. Paris: La Découverte, 1994.

Le Goff, J. *La naissance du Purgatoire*. Paris: Gallimard, 1981.

Van Der Leeuw, G. *Religion in Essence and Manifestation*. English trans. by J.E. Turner and H.H. Penner. Princeton: Princeton University Press, 1986.

———. *La religion dans son essence et ses manifestations: Phénoménologie de la religion*. Fr. edition edited by the author in collaboration with J. Marty. Paris: Payot, 1955.

Lévi, S. *La doctrine du sacrifice dans les Brâhmanas*. Paris: Leroux, 1898.

Lévi-Strauss, C. *L'homme nu*. Paris: Plon, 1971.

———. *La pensée sauvage*. Paris: Plon, 1962.

———. *Les structures élémentaires de la parenté*. Paris-La Haye: Mouton, 1981.

Lewis-Williams, D. *The Mind in the Cave: Consciousness and the Origins of Art*. London: Thames & Hudson, 2004.

Liddell, H.G., and R. Scott. *A Greek-English Lexicon*, rev. ed. Oxford: Oxford University Press, 1996.

———. *An Intermediate Greek-English Lexicon*. Oxford: Clarendon Press, 1889.

Lienhardt, G. *Divinity and Experience: The Religion of the Dinka*. Oxford: Clarendon Press, 1976.

Liverani, M. *Oltre la Bibbia: Storia antica d'Israele*. Roma-Bari: Laterza, 2004.

Lobeck, C.A. *Aglaophamus sive de Theologiae mysticae Graecorum causis, libri tres*. Regimontii, 1829.

Loisy, A. *Les mystères païens et le mystère chrétien*. Paris, 1930.

Löwith, K. *Nietzsches Philosophie der ewigen Wiederkehr des Gleichen*. Hamburg: Meiner, 1986.

———. *Von Hegel zu Nietzsche: Der revolutionäre Bruch im Denken des neunzehnten Jahrhunderts*. Stuttgart: Fischer, 1969.

Lugaresi, L. *Il teatro di Dio: Il problema degli spettacoli nel cristianesimo antico (II–IV secolo)*. Brescia: Morcelliana, 2008.

Lukes, S. *Émile Durkheim: His Life and Work. A Historical and Critical Study*. New York: Harper & Row, 1972.

Lundbom, J.R. *Jeremiah 1–20*. The Anchor Bible. New York: Doubleday, 1999.

Lupieri, E. *A Commentary on the Apocalypse of John*. Engl. trans. by M. Poggi Johnson and A. Kamesar. Grand Rapids, MI: Eerdmans, 2006.

McKnight, S. *Jesus and His Death: Historiography, the Historical Jesus, and Atonement Theory*. Waco, TX: Baylor University Press, 2005.

Macchioro, V. *Zagreus: Studi intorno all'orfismo*, 2nd ed. Firenze: Vallecchi, 1930.

———. *Zagreus: Studi intorno all'orfismo*. Edited by C. Pugliese. Milano: Mimesis, 2014.

MacCulloch, J.A. *The Religion of the Ancient Celts*. Edinburgh: Clark, 1911.

Mainville, O. "Le rôle des récits résurrectionelles en Matthieu 28: Une relecture rédactionelle." In *Resurrection of the Dead: Biblical Traditions in Dialogue*, edited by G. Van Oyen and T. Shepherd. Leuven: Uitgeverij Peters, 2012.

De Maistre, J. *Les soirées de Saint-Petersbourg*. In J. De Maistre, *Œuvres*, edited by P. Glaudes. Paris: Laffont, 2007.

Malamoud, C., and J.-P. Vernant, eds. *Corps des dieux*. Paris: Gallimard, 1986.

Manganelli, G. *Tutti gli errori*. Milano: Rizzoli, 1986.

Mann, C.S. *Mark*. The Anchor Bible, New York: Doubleday, 1986.

Mann, T. *Betrachtungen eines Unpolitisch*. Frankfurt a.M.: Fischer, 1956.

———. *Die Erzählungen, Fiorenza, Gesang vom Kindchen, Gedichte*. Frankfurt a.M.: Fischer, 1966.

———. *Joseph und seine Brüder*. Frankfurt a.M.: Fischer, 1966.

———. *Tagebücher 1918–1921*. Edited by P. de Mendelssohn. Frankfurt a.M.: Fischer, 1979.

———. *Der Zauberberg*. Edited by M. Neumann. Frankfurt a.M.: Fischer, 2002.

Manzi, G. *L'evoluzione umana: Ominidi e uomini prima di Homo sapiens*. Bologna: Il Mulino, 2007.

Manzoni, A. "Lettre à M. Chauvet sur l'unité de temps et de lieu dans la tragédie." In A. Manzoni, *Tutte le opere*, edited by M. Martelli. Firenze: Sansoni, 1973.

———. *Tutte le opere*. Edited by M. Martelli. Firenze: Sansoni, 1973.

———. *Tutte le opere*. Edited by A. Chiari e F. Ghisalberti, vol. 2, part 1, *I promessi sposi*. Milano: A. Mondadori, 1977.

Marcheselli-Casale, C. *Lettera agli Ebrei: Nuova versione, introduzione e comment*. Milano: Paoline, 2005.

Martina, A. *s.v.* "Rea." In *Enciclopedia Dantesca*. Milano: A. Mondadori, 2005.

Martínez Maza, C. "La cristianización de los démones mistéricos." In *Estudios sobre Plutarco: misticismo y religiones mistéricas en la obra de Plutarco*, edited by A. Pèrez Jiménez and F. Casadesús Bordoy. Madrid-Málaga: Ediciones Clásicas, 2001.

De Martino, E. *Il mondo magico: Prolegomeni a una storia del magismo*. 1948; repr. Torino: Bollati Boringhieri, 2007.

Marucci, C. *Parole di Gesù sul divorzio: Ricerche scritturistiche previe ad un ripensamento teologico, canonistico e pastorale della dottrina cattolica dell'indissolubilità del matrimonio*. Brescia: Morcelliana, 1982.

Mateos, J., and J. Barreto. *El evangelio de Juan: Analisis lingüistico y comentario exegetico*. Madrid: Ediciones Cristiandad, 1982.

Mayeur, J.-M., et al., eds. *Storia del cristianesimo: Religione-Politica-Cultura*. Vol. 1, *Il nuovo popolo (dalle origini al 250)*, edited by L. Pietri, It. ed. by P. Grech and A. Di Bernardino, It. trans. by M. Zappella. Roma: Borla-Città Nuova, 2003.

Mazzarino, S. *Il pensiero storico classico*. Roma-Bari: Laterza, 1983.

Meier, J.P. *A Marginal Jew: Rethinking the Historical Jesus*, vol. 1, *The Roots of the Problem and the Person*. New York: Doubleday, 1991.

———. *A Marginal Jew: Rethinking the Historical Jesus*, vol. 2, *Mentor, Message, and Miracles*. New York: Doubleday, 1994.

———. *A Marginal Jew: Rethinking the Historical Jesus*, vol. 3, *Companions and Competitors*. New York: Doubleday, 2001.

———. *A Marginal Jew: Rethinking the Historical Jesus*, vol. 4, *Law and Love*. New Haven: Yale University Press, 2009.

———. *A Marginal Jew: Rethinking the Historical Jesus*, vol. 5, *Probing the Authenticity of the Parables*. New Haven: Yale University Press, 2016.

Menken, M.J.J. "Striking the Shepherd: Early Christian Versions and Interpretations of Zechariah 13,7." *Biblica* 92, no. 1 (2011): 39–59.

Merlo, P. *La religione dell'antico Israele*. Roma: Carocci, 2009.

Mills, S. *Euripides: Bacchae*. London: Duckworth, 2006.

Moloney, F.J. "Constructing Jesus and the Son of Man." *Catholic Biblical Quarterly* 75, no. 4 (2013): 719–38.

———. *The Gospel of John*. Collegeville, MN: The Liturgical Press, 1998.

———. *The Johannine Son of Man*. Roma: LAS, 1978.

Monaci Castagno, A., ed. *Origene. Dizionario. La cultura, il pensiero, le opera*. Roma: Città Nuova, 2000.

Moraldi, L. *L'Aldilà dell'Uomo*. Milano: A. Mondadori, 2000.

Moravia, S. *La scienza dell'uomo nel Settecento*. Roma-Bari: Laterza, 1978.

Moro, C. "Miti di fondazione e priorità etnico-culturale giudaica: l'esempio di Mosè." In *Israele fra le genti in epoca ellenistica: un popolo primogenito cittadino del mondo*, edited by G.L. Prato. Ricerche storico-bibliche. Bologna: EDB, 2015.

Mumford, L. *The City in History: Its Origins, Its Transformations, and Its Prospects*. 1961; repr. San Diego: Harcourt Brace & Co., 1989.

Mylonas, G.E. *Eleusis and the Eleusinian Mysteries*. Princeton: Princeton University Press, 1961.

Nadler, S. *A Book Forged in Hell: Spinoza's Scandalous Treatise and the Birth of the Secular Age*. Princeton: Princeton University Press, 2014.

Nauck, A., ed. *Tragicorum Graecorum fragmenta*. Lipsiae: Teubner, 1926.

Nestle, E., et al., eds. *Novum Testamentum Graece*. Stuttgart: Deutsche Bibelgesellschaft, 2012.

Nietzsche, F. *Sämtliche Briefe: Kritische Studienausgabe*. Edited by G. Colli and M. Montinari. Berlin: De Gruyter, 1986.

———. *Sämtliche Werke: Kritischen Studienausgabe*. Edited by G. Colli and M. Montinari. Berlin-New York: De Gruyter, 1980.

———. *Werke: Kritische Gesamtausgabe*. Edited by G. Colli and M. Montinari et al. Berlin-New York: De Gruyter, 1999.

Nolte, E. *Der europäische Bürgerkrieg 1917–1945: Nationalsozialismus und Bolschewismus*. München: Herbig, 1997.

Nussbaum, M.C. *The Fragility of Goodness: Luck and Ethics in Greek Tragedy and Philosophy*. Cambridge: Cambridge University Press, 2001.

Nygren, A. *Eros and Agape*. Engl. trans. by P.S. Watson. London: SPCK, 1982.

O'Collins, G. *Jesus Risen: An Historical, Fundamental, and Systematic Examination of Christ's Resurrection*. New York: Paulist Press, 1987.

Omero. *Iliade*. Edited by R. Calzecchi Onesti. Torino: Einaudi, 1974.

Onians, R.B. *The Origins of European Thought about the Body, the Mind, the Soul, the World, Time, and Fate: New Interpretations of Greek, Roman and Kindred Evidence also of Some Basic Jewish and Christian Beliefs*. Cambridge: Cambridge University Press, 2000.

Origène, *Contre Celse*. Edited by M. Borret. Paris: Les Éditions du Cerf, 2008.

Osculati, R. *Schleiermacher: L'uomo, il pensatore, il Cristiano*. Brescia: Queriniana, 1980.

Otto, W.F. *Dionysus: Myth and Cult*. Edited by R.B. Palmer. Bloomington: Indiana University Press, 1965.

Oughourlian, J.-M. *Un mime nommé désir: Hystérie, transe, possession, adorcism*. Paris: Grasset & Fasquelle, 1982.

Palaver, W. *René Girard's Mimetic Theory*. Engl. trans. by G. Borrud. East Lansing: Michigan State University Press, 2013.

Pausania. *Guida della Grecia: Libro I, L'Attica*. Edited by D. Musti and L. Beschi. Fondazione L. Valla. Milano: A. Mondadori, 1982.

Pavese, C. *Dialoghi con Leucò*. Torino: Einaudi, 1999.

Pecchioli Daddi, F., and A.M. Polvani, eds. *La mitologia ittita*. Brescia: Paideia, 1990.

Penglase, C. *Greek Myths and Mesopotamia: Parallels and Influence in the Homeric Hymns and Hesiod.* New York: Routledge, 1994.

Perrin, N. "Die Christologie des Markus-Evangeliums: Eine metodologische Studie." In *Das Markus-Evangelium*, edited by R. Pesch. Darmstadt: Wissenschaftliche Buchgesellschaft, 1979.

Pesce, M. *Da Gesù al cristianesimo*. Brescia: Morcelliana, 2011.

Pettinato, G. *I Sumeri*. Milano: Rusconi, 1994.

Pettinato, G., S.M. Chiodi, and G. Del Monte, eds. *La saga di Gilgamesh*. Milano: Rusconi, 1992.

Pevarello, D. *Il discorso eucaristico in Giovanni 6: unità e messaggio. Complessità e ricchezza di un caso di ipertestualità*. Bologna: EDB, 2012.

Pincherle, A. *s.v.* "Agostino." In *Enciclopedia Dantesca*. Milano: A. Mondadori, 2005.

Pickard-Cambridge, A.W. *Dithyramb, Tragedy, and Comedy*. 1927; repr. Oxford: Clarendon Press, 1997.

———. *Dithyramb, Tragedy, and Comedy*. 2nd ed. Oxford: Clarendon Press, 1962.

Pindaro. *Le Olimpiche*. Edited by B. Gentili et al. Fondazione L. Valla. Milano: A. Mondadori, 2013.

———. *Le Pitiche*. Edited by B. Gentili et al. Fondazione L. Valla. Milano: A. Mondadori, 2012.

Pippin Burnett, A. "The Virtues of Admetus." In *Greek Tragedy: Modern Essays in Criticism*, edited by E. Segal. New York: Harper & Row, 1983.

Platonis Opera. Edited by J. Burnet. Oxford: Clarendon Press, 1905–.

Plutarco. *La vita di Solone*. Edited by M. Manfredini and L. Piccirilli. Fondazione L. Valla. Milano: A. Mondadori, 1990.

———. *Le vite di Teseo e di Romolo*. Edited by C. Ampolo and M. Manfredini. Milano: Fondazione L. Valla; A. Mondadori, 1988.

Porfirio. *Contro i cristiani*. Edited by G. Muscolino. Milano: Bompiani, 2009.

Porphyre. *De l'abstinence*, vol. 3. Edited by M. Patillon and A.P. Segonds. Paris: Les Belles Lettres, 1995.

Prinzivalli, E., and M. Simonetti. *Seguendo Gesù: Testi cristiani delle origini*, vol. 1. Fondazione L. Valla. Milano: A. Mondadori, 2010.

Priotto, M. *Esodo: Nuova versione, introduzione e commento*. Milano: Edizioni Paoline, 2014.

Pritchard, J.B., ed. *Ancient Near Eastern Texts Relating to the Old Testament*. Princeton: Princeton University Press, 1969.

Prosperi, A. "Morire volentieri: condannati a morte e sacramenti." In *Misericordie: Conversioni sotto il patibolo tra Medioevo ed età moderna*, edited by A. Prosperi. Pisa: Edizioni della Normale, 2007.

Puech, H.C. *Sur le manichéisme et autres essais*. Paris: Flammarion, 1979.

Pugliese Carratelli, G. "Orphikòs bios." In *Tra Cadmo e Orfeo: Contributi alla storia civile e religiosa dei Greci d'Occidente*. Bologna: Il Mulino, 1990.

———. *Storia greca*. Milano: Istituto Editoriale Cisalpino-La Goliardica, 1978.

Purpura, G. "Il P. Giss 40, 1." *Iuris Antiqui Historia: An International Journal of Ancient Law* 5 (2013): 73–85.

Rahlfs, A., ed. *Septuaginta id est Vetus Testamentum graece iuxta LXX interpretes*. Stuttgart: Bibelgesellschaft, 1979.

Ramsey, J., ed. *Coyote Was Going There: Indian Literature of the Oregon Country*. Seattle: University of Washington Press, 1999.

Rasmussen, K. *Fra Grønland til Stillehavet, Rejser og Mennesker fra 5. Thule Ekspedition 1921–1924*. København: Gyldendalske Boghandel-Nordisk Forlag, 1925–26.

Reale, G. *Autotestimonianze e rimandi dei Dialoghi di Platone alle "Dottrine non scritte."* Milano: Bompiani, 2008.

Reggio, G. *s.v.* "Veglio." In *Enciclopedia Dantesca*. Milano: A Mondadori, 2005.

Rescio, M. *La famiglia alternativa di Gesù: Discepolato e strategie di formazione sociale nel Vangelo di Marco*. Brescia: Morcelliana, 2012.

Reynolds, B.E. *The Apocalyptic Son of Man in the Gospel of John*. Tübingen: Mohr Siebeck, 2008.

Ricciardelli, G., ed. *Inni orfici*. Fondazione L. Valla. Milano: A. Mondadori, 2000.

Robertson Smith, W. *Lectures on the Religion of the Semites*. London: Black, 1894.

Rohde, E. *Psyche: Seelencult und Unsterblichkeitsglaube der Griechen*. Darmstadt: Wissenschaftliche Buchgesellschaft, 1980.

Römer, T. *L'invention de Dieu*. Paris: Seuil, 2014.

Rossé, G. *Il Vangelo di Luca: Commento esegetico e teologico*. Roma: Città Nuova, 1992.

S. Nili narrationes de caede monachorum. In *Patrologia Cursus Completus, Series Graeca*, edited by J.P. Migne. Paris, 1860.

Sabbatucci, M.D. *Il misticismo eleusino*. In *Il mito: Guida storica e critica*, edited by Detienne. Roma-Bari: Laterza, 1976.

Sacchi, P. *Storia del Secondo Tempio: Israele tra VI secolo a.C. e I secolo d.C.* Torino: SEI, 2002.

Sanders, E.P. *Jesus and Judaism*. Philadelphia: Fortress Press, 1987.

Sansoni, U. *Le più antiche pitture del Sahara: L'arte delle teste rotonde*. Milano: Jaca Books, 1994.

Savarese, N., ed. *Teatri romani: Gli spettacoli nell'antica Roma*. Bologna: Cuepress, 2015.

Scarpi, P. *Eleusi, dionisismo, orfismo*. Vol. 1 of *Le religioni dei misteri*. Fondazione L. Valla. Milano: A. Mondadori, 2002.

Schäfer, P. *Die Geburt des Judentums aus dem Geist der Christentums: Fünf Vorlesungen zur Entstehung des rabbinischem Judentums*. Tübingen: Mohr Siebeck, 2010.

Schele, L., and D. Freidel. *A Forest of Kings: The Untold Story of the Ancient Maya*. New York: Morrow, 1990.

Schmidt, K. *Sie bauten die ersten Tempel: Das rätselhafte Heiligtum am Göbleki Tepe*. München: Beck, 2016.

Schmitt, C. *Antworten in Nürnberg.* Edited by H. Quaritsch. Berlin: Dunker & Humblot, 2000.

———. *Ex Captivitate Salus: Erfahrungen der Zeit 1945/47*. Berlin: Duncker & Humblot, 2010.

Schnackenburg, R. *Das Johannesevangelium*. Freiburg: Herder, 1967–83.

Scholem, G. *Jewish Gnosticism, Merkabah Mysticism, and Talmudic Tradition*. New York: Jewish Theological Seminar of America, 1965.

Schweitzer, A. *Geschichte der Leben-Jesu Forschung: Von Reimarus zu Wrede*. Tübingen: Mohr, 1906.

———. *The Quest of the Historical Jesus: A Critical Study of Its Progress from Reimarus to Wrede*. Engl. trans. by W. Montgomery. New York: Macmillan, 1968.

Scipioni, L.I. *Nestorio e il concilio di Efeso: Storia dogma critica*. Milano: Vita e Pensiero, 1974.

Scubla, L. "The Christianity of René Girard and the Nature of Religion." In *Violence and Truth: On the Work of René Girard*, edited by P. Dumouchel. Stanford: Stanford University Press, 1988.

———. "Fonction symbolique et fondaments sacrificiels des sociétés humaines." *La Revue du Mauss semestrielle* 12 (1998): 41–65.

———. *Lire Lévi-Strauss: Le déploiement d'une intuition*. Paris: O. Jacob, 1998.

Segal, C. *Dionysiac Poetics and Euripides "Bacchae."* Expanded ed. Princeton: Princeton University Press, 1997.

Segalla, G. *Sulle tracce di Gesù: La "Terza ricerca."* Assisi: Cittadella, 2006.

Seidensticker, P. *Die Auferstehung Jesu in der Botschaft der Evangelisten: Ein traditiongeschichtlicher Versuch zum Problem der Sicherung der Osterbotschaft in der apostolischen Zeit*. Stuttgart: Verlag Katholisches Bibelwerk, 1967.

———. *Zeitgenössische Texte zur Osterbotschaft der Evangelien*. Stuttgart: Verlag Kath. Bibelwerk, 1967.

Serra, G. *La forza e il valore: Capitoli sulla Costituzione degli Ateniesi dello pseudo-Senofonte*. Bollettino dell'Istituto di Filologia Greca. Roma: "L'Erma" di Bretschneider, 1979.

Serres, M. *Rome: The Book of Foundations*. Engl. trans. by F. McCarren. Stanford: Stanford University Press, 1991.

Shakespeare, W. *The Complete Works*. Edited by S. Wells et al. Oxford: Clarendon Press, 1994.

Sheldon, R.M. *Kill Caesar! Assassination in the Early Roman Empire*. Lanham, MD: Rowman & Littlefield, 2018.

Simonetti, M. *Cristianesimo antico e cultura greca*. Roma: Borla, 1990.

———. *Studi sulla cristologia del II e III secolo*. Roma: Institutum Patristicum Augustinianum, 1993.

———. *Il Vangelo e la storia: Il cristianesimo antico (secc. I–IV)*. Roma: Carocci, 2010.

Siniscalco, P. *Il cammino di Cristo nell'Impero romano*. Roma-Bari: Laterza, 1990.

Smyly, J.G. *Greek Papyri from Gurob*. Dublin: Hodges, 1921.

Snell, B. *The Discovery of the Mind: The Greek Origins of European Thought*. Engl. trans. by T.G. Rosenmeyer. New York-Evanston: Harper & Row, 1960.

Söderblom, N. *La vie future d'après le Mazdéisme à la lumière des croyances parallèles dans les autres religions*. Angers: Burdin, 1901.

Soggin, J.A. *Storia d'Israele: Introduzione alla storia d'Israele e Giuda dalla fondazione alla rivolta di Bar Kochbà*. Brescia: Paideia, 2002.

Sordi, M. *Impero romano e cristianesimo: Scritti scelti*. Roma: Institutum Patristicum Augustinianum, 2006.

Sourvinou-Inwood, C. *Tragedy and Athenian Religion*. Lanham, MD: Lexington Books, 2003.

Spicq, C. *Agapè dans le Nouveau Testament: Analyse des textes*, vol. 3. Paris: Gabalda, 1959.

———. *L'Épitre aux Hebreux*. Paris: Gabalda, 1977.

Spinoza, B. *Werke*, vol. 1, *Tractatus theologico-politicus*. Edited by G. Gawlick and F. Niewöhner. Darmstadt: Wissenschaftliche Buchgesellschaft, 1989.

———. *Ethica Ordine Geometrico demonstrata*. In *Werke*, vol. 2, *Tractatus de intellectus emendatione—Ethica*, edited by K. Blumenstock. Darmstadt: Wissenschaftliche Buchgesellschaft, 1989.

Stanton, G.N. *Jesus and Gospel*. Cambridge: Cambridge University Press, 2004.

Starcky, J. "Pétra et la Nabaténe." In *Supplément au Dictionnaire de la Bible*, vol. 7. Paris: Librairie Letouzey et Ané, 1961.

Stegemann, H. *The Library of Qumran: On the Essenes, Qumran, John the Baptist, and Jesus*. Grand Rapids, MI: Eerdmans, 1998.

Stegemann, W. *Jesus und seine Zeit*. Stuttgart: Kohlhammer, 2010.

Storoni Mazzolani, L. *L'impero senza fine: Lo sfondo secolare dei problemi attuali*. Pavia: Editoriale Viscontea, 1987.

Strabon, *Géographie (livre X)*. Edited by F. Lasserre. Paris: Les Belles Lettres, 1971.

Strauss, D.F. *Das Leben Jesu für das deutsche Volk bearbeitet*. Leipzig: Brodhaus, 1864.

———. *Das Leben Jesu kritisch bearbeitet*. Tübingen: Osiander, 1840.

———. *The Life of Jesus Critically Examined*. Edited by P.C. Hodgson. London: SCM, 1973.

Strauss, L. *On Maimonides: The Complete Writings*. Edited by K. Hart Green. Chicago: University of Chicago Press, 2013.

———. *Persecution and the Art of Writing*. 1952; repr. Chicago: University of Chicago Press, 1988.

———. *Spinoza's Critique of Religion*. Engl. trans. by E. Sinclair. Chicago: University of Chicago Press, 1997.

Stringer, C., and P. Andrews. *The Complete World of Human Evolution*. London: Thames & Hudson, 2005.

Surya, M. *Georges Bataille, la mort à l'œuvre*. Paris: Gallimard, 1992.

Taylor, T. *The Prehistory of Sex: Four Million Years of Human Sexual Culture*. New York: Bantam Books, 1997.

Theissen, G., and A. Merz, *Der historische Jesus: Ein Lehrbuch*. Göttingen: Vandenhoeck & Ruprecht, 1996.

Thompson, T.L. *Mythic Past: Biblical Archeology and the Myth of Israel*. New York: MJF Books, 1999.

Tillier, A.-M., B. Arensburg, H. Duday, and B. Vandermeersch, "Brief Communication: An Early Case of Hydrocephalus: The Middle Paleolithic Qafzeh 12 Child (Israel)." *American Journal of Physical Anthropology* 114 (2001): 166–70.

Toaff, A. *Pasque di sangue: Ebrei d'Europa e omicidi rituali*. Bologna: Il Mulino, 2008.

De Tocqueville, A. *De la démocratie en Amérique*. Paris: Gallimard, 1997.

Untersteiner, M. *La fisiologia del mito*. Torino: Bollati Boringhieri, 1991.

———. *Le origini della tragedia e del tragico: Dalla preistoria ad Eschilo*. Torino: Einaudi, 1955.

———. *I sofisti*. Milano: B. Mondadori, 1996.

Van Coillie, G. "Antigone: Mimetic Violence, Tragedy, and Ethics." *Ethical Perspective* 15, no. 1 (2008), 81–102.

Van Oyen, G. "The Empty Tomb Story in the Gospel of Mark and Michel Foucault's Concept of 'Heterotopia.'" In *Resurrection of the Dead: Biblical Traditions in Dialogue*, edited by G. Van Oyen and T. Shepherd. Leuven: Uitgeverij Peters, 2012.

Vandermeersch, B. "Ce que nous apprennent les premières sépultures." *Comptes Rendus Palevol* 5 (2006): 161–67.

———. "Le più antiche sepolture." In F. Facchini et al., *La religiosità nella preistoria*. Milano: Jaca Book, 1991.

Vegetti, M. "In difesa della razionalità antica: il progetto di Galeno." In Galeno, *Nuovi scritti autobiografici*, edited by M. Vegetti. Roma: Carocci, 2013.

Vernant, J.-P. "Ambiguity and Reversal: On the Enigmatic Structure of *Oedipus Rex*." In J.-P. Vernant and P. Vidal-Naquet, *Myth and Tragedy in Ancient Greece*, Engl. trans. by J. Lloyd. New York: Zone Books, 1990.

———. "The Masked Dionysus of Euripides' *Bacchae*." In J.-P. Vernant and P. Vidal-Naquet, *Myth and Tragedy in Ancient Greece*, Engl. trans. by J. Lloyd. New York: Zone Books, 1990.

———. *The Origins of Greek Thought*. Ithaca: Cornell University Press, 1982.

———. "Tensions and Ambiguities in Greek Tragedy." In J.-P. Vernant and P. Vidal-Naquet, *Myth and Tragedy in Ancient Greece*, Engl. trans. by J. Lloyd. New York: Zone Books, 1990.

Verrecchia, A. *La catastrofe di Nietzsche a Torino*. Torino: Einaudi, 1978.

Veyne, P. *L'Empire gréco-romain*. Paris: Seuil, 2005.

Vian, F. "La religione greca in epoca arcaica e classica." In *Le religioni del mondo classico*, edited by H.-C. Puech. Roma-Bari: Laterza, 1993.

Vico, G. *Opere*. Edited by A. Battistini. Milano: A. Mondadori, 2007.

Villa, E. *L'arte dell'uomo primordiale*. Edited by A. Tagliaferri. Milano: Abscondita, 2005.

Villari, L. *Settecento adieu: Dall'illuminismo alla rivoluzione*. Milano: Bompiani, 1989.

Vimercati, E. *Medioplatonici: Opere, frammenti, testimonianze*. Milano: Bompiani, 2015.

Voegelin, E. *History of Political Ideas*, vol. 2, *The Middle Ages to Aquinas*. Edited by P. von Sivers. Columbia: Missouri University Press, 1997.

———. *History of Political Ideas*, vol. 3, *The Later Middle Ages*. Edited by D. Walsh. Columbia: Missouri University Press, 1998.

———. *Die Rassenidee in der Geistegeschichte von Ray bis Carus*. Berlin: Junger & Dünnhaupt, 1933.

Volpi, F. *Il nichilismo*. Roma-Bari: Laterza, 1996.

Voltaire, "Précis du siècle de Louis XV." In Voltaire, *Œuvres historiques*, edited by R. Pomeau. Paris: Pléiade, Gallimard, 1957.

Waal, F. De. *Peacemaking among the Primates*. Cambridge, MA: Harvard University Press, 1989.

Walt, L. *Paolo e le parole di Gesù: Frammenti di un insegnamento orale*. Brescia: Morcelliana, 2013.

Weil, S. *Attente de Dieu*. Paris: La Colombe, 1950.

———. *Intuitions pré-chrétiennes*. Paris: La Colombe, 1951.

———. *Œuvres complètes*, vol. 6, *Cahiers*, part 3. Paris: Gallimard, 2002.

Weiss, J. *Die Predigt Jesu vom Reiche Gottes*. Göttingen: Vandenhoeck & Ruprecht, 1892.

West, M.L. *Early Greek Philosophy and the Orient*. Oxford: Clarendon Press, 2002.

———. *The Orphic Poems*. Oxford: Oxford University Press, 1998.

Von Wilamowitz-Möllendorf, U. *Zukunftsphilologie! Eine Erwidrung auf Friedrich Nietzsches "Geburt der Tragödie."* Berlin: Borntraeger, 1872.

Wittgenstein, L. "Bemerküngen über Frazers *The Golden Bough*." *Synthèse* 17, no. 1 (1967): 233–53.

———. *Tractatus logico-philosophicus*. Engl. trans. by D.F. Pears and B.F. McGuinness. London: Routledge, 1977.

———. *Werkausgabe*, vol. 1. Frankfurt a.M.: Suhrkamp, 1984.

Wrangham, R., and R. Carmody. "Human Adaptation to the Control of Fire." *Evolutionary Anthropology* 19 (2010): 187–99.

Wright, N.T. *The Resurrection of the Son of God*. London: SPCK, 2003.

Zévaès, A.-L. *Damiens le regicide*. Paris: Editions de la Nouvelle Revue Critique, 1933.

Zorell, F. *Lexicon Graecum Novi Testamenti*. 1960; repr. Roma: Editrice Pontificio Istituto Biblico, 1990.

Index

N

O